THE GREAT DIVERGENCE

THE PRINCETON ECONOMIC HISTORY

OF THE WESTERN WORLD

Joel Mokyr, Editor

THE GREAT DIVERGENCE

CHINA, EUROPE, AND
THE MAKING OF
THE MODERN WORLD ECONOMY

Kenneth Pomeranz

With a new preface by the author

PRINCETON UNIVERSITY PRESS

PRINCETON AND OXFORD

FIRST PAPERBACK PRINTING, 2001
FIRST PRINCETON CLASSICS PAPERBACK EDITION,
WITH A NEW PREFACE BY THE AUTHOR, 2021
NEW PAPERBACK ISBN 9780691217185
LIBRARY OF CONGRESS CONTROL NUMBER: 2020949716

THIS BOOK HAS BEEN COMPOSED IN TIMES ROMAN

PRESS.PRINCETON.EDU

PRINTED IN THE UNITED STATES OF AMERICA

CONTENTS

PREFACE

The Great Divergence began as an introductory chapter for a different book, intended to synthesize the literature on the advantages that western Europe already enjoyed in the emerging world economy of the seventeenth and eighteenth centuries. Like most other people in the field, I believed that these were advantages that had emerged over centuries of gradual growth across much of the region and were manifested in slightly higher productivity, slightly more efficient markets, and other homegrown benefits. Taken together, they made it logical both that industrialization had begun in Europe and that Europe had been able to project its political power around the globe, reinforcing these economic rewards.

But as I reviewed the literature—both recent works and ones I had read over a decade earlier, as a graduate student who had not yet shifted my focus toward Chinese history—I found myself becoming less and less convinced of this summary. Instead, Europe as a whole seemed no more prosperous than east Asia before 1800 and its richest regions no more so than the richest parts of east and perhaps south Asia. Equally important, there was no clear evidence of improvement in the living standards of ordinary Europeans over the long haul.

There were also signs—rarely emphasized in older works, but clearly present—that in the more densely populated parts of Europe (including some of its richest areas), early modern growth was hobbled by environmental problems and resource constraints; while those regions achieved some relief by trading handicraft manufactures for land-intensive goods from elsewhere, that trade was not growing fast enough to offer a permanent solution, especially since population growth was accelerating. All of this made even England and Holland look more like China's Yangzi Delta, and a few other wealthy places in Asia, than had been previously recognized. Those similarities called out for replacing, or at least complementing, the old historical chestnut—"Why didn't China (the Yangzi Delta) wind up like Europe (England)?"—with the rarely asked question of why England hadn't wound up like the Yangzi Delta: a relatively wealthy, heavily marketized agro-commercial economy with lots of handicraft industry but no breakthrough to rapid, energy-intensive, sustained growth, and, in the absence of such a breakthrough, a system that was facing increasingly serious population and environmental pressures. That question also suggested that the answers would need to explain a fairly late and sudden divergence, rather than one that had been developing inexorably for hundreds of years. Finally, it pointed toward explanations that highlighted Europe's access to vastly expanded amounts of land-intensive products from the Americas, and to a partly fortuitous set of circumstances that led to a massive expansion of coal mining (which, among other things, greatly eased pressure on western Europe's dwindling forests). By arguing that divergence was late and contingent, that it was not wholly produced within Europe, and that it was best understood by noting not only the ways in which European regions held advantages but also the manner in which they had resembled other places (or underperformed them, as in agricultural yields), the book challenged received wisdom in several ways and attracted far more attention than I had expected.

Twenty years of debate and new research have now piled up, which go far beyond what I can discuss here.[1] Some of it, of course, would have happened without *The Great Divergence*. The spectacular growth of China's economy stimulated interest in its earlier history and in possible links to the early modern dynamics I discussed. Meanwhile, our mounting environmental problems— linked to our gargantuan energy consumption—helped attract attention to an argument in which both environmental constraints on growth and the significance of new energy sources loomed large. Though the book itself was not the only catalyst of the "great divergence debate," it seems appropriate for this Princeton Classics edition preface to reflect on some of this still-burgeoning literature.

I would divide this literature into three clusters. A heavily quantitative cluster has focused on the "what" and "when" of divergence: trying to specify and compare trends and levels in per capita income and real wages across numerous early modern locales. The second cluster, larger and mostly qualitative, has focused on the "how" and "why" of divergence. Sometimes these works have

---

[1] Ten years after its publication, a useful forum on *The Great Divergence* appeared in *Historically Speaking* 12:4 (September 2011): 10–25, with contributions by Peter Coclanis, Jan DeVries, Philip Hoffmann, R. Bin Wong, and myself. A more recent retrospective is Prasannan Parthasarathi and Kenneth Pomeranz, "The Great Divergence Debate," in Giorgio Riello and Tirthankar Roy, eds., *Global Economic History* (London: Bloomsbury Academic, 2019), 19–37. Here, as in those essays, I have limited myself to reflections on discussions in English. For my reaction to the debate as it has played out in east Asia, see my introduction to the Japanese translation of *The Great Divergence*: *Daibunki: Chugoku, Yoroppa, soshite Kindai Sekai Keizai no Keisei* (Nagoya: Nagoya University Press, 2015), 1–16. The lengthiest criticism of *The Great Divergence* was probably Philip Huang's "Development of Involution in Eighteenth Century Britain and China? A Review of Kenneth Pomeranz's *The Great Divergence: China, Europe, and the Making of the Modern World Economy*," *Journal of Asian Studies* 61:2 (May 2002): 501–38; followed by my response, "Beyond the East-West Binary: Resituating Development Paths in the Eighteenth-Century World," *Journal of Asian Studies* 61:2 (May 2002): 539–90; and Philip Huang, "Further Thoughts on Eighteenth-Century Britain and China: Rejoinder to Pomeranz's Response to My Critique," *Journal of Asian Studies* 62:1 (February 2003): 157–67; and Kenneth Pomeranz, "Facts Are Stubborn Things: A Response to Philip Huang," 167–81. Huang did identify one genuine error, which concerns how I allocated labor time (and thus imputed earnings) between weavers and spinners of cotton cloth. The error—which makes no difference to the book's argument but could mislead somebody wanting to use this data for other purposes—is corrected in this edition, affecting the last full paragraph on p. 102 and the section of appendix E running from the bottom of p. 320 to the top of p. 323.

centered on issues that I emphasize in this book—particularly matters of resources, energy supplies, and environmental conditions, taking varying stances on their importance. My third grouping covers ways in which *The Great Divergence* has been brought to bear on issues beyond its own scope, and could itself be divided into three groups. There are works that deal with other early modern divergences, looking at both comparisons and interregional connections to reframe "the rise of the West" and acknowledge that it was probably more contingent than most scholars once thought; given the diversity of those works, I can do no more than note a few of them here.[2] There are works that deal with more contemporary issues directly related to the main topics of my book, including problems of economic development, environmental sustainability, and legacies of empire today. Finally, there are works that have been influenced by the methodology of *The Great Divergence*, particularly its strategies of comparison.

The quantitative, "when and what" literature is the easiest to address. Works published in the past decade have changed our estimates of the historical GDP figures for various European countries from roughly 1300 to 1850; others have tried (based on much slimmer evidence) to do the same for China, India, Japan, and elsewhere.[3] Crucially, much of the literature about China

[2] On other regional divergences, see, e.g., Prasannan Parthasarathi, *Why Europe Grew Rich and Asia Did Not: Global Economic Divergence 1600–1850* (Cambridge: Cambridge University Press, 2011); and Timur Kuran, *The Long Divergence: How Islamic Law Held Back the Middle East* (Princeton, NJ: Princeton University Press, 2011). For analyses of military power that draw on *The Great Divergence*, see Philip Hoffman, *Why Did Europe Conquer the World?* (Princeton, NJ: Princeton University Press, 2015); and Tonio Andrade, *The Gunpowder Age: China, Military Innovation, and the Rise of the West in World History* (Princeton, NJ: Princeton University Press, 2016).

[3] On GDP, see particularly Stephen Broadberry, Hanhui Guan, and David Daokui Li, "China, Europe, and the Great Divergence: A Study in Historical National Accounting, 980–1850," *Journal of Economic History* 78:4 (December 2018): 955–1000; Jan Luiten Van Zanden and Bas van Leeuwen, "Persistent but Not Consistent: The Growth of National Income in Holland, 1347–1807," *Explorations in Economic History* 49 (2012): 119–30; Stephen Broadberry, Johann Custodis, and Bishnupriya Gupta, "India and the Great Divergence: An Anglo-Indian Comparison of GDP per Capita, 1600–1871," *Explorations in Economic History* 55 (January 2015): 58–75; Paolo Malanima, "The Long Decline of a Leading Economy: GDP in Central and Northern Italy, 1300–1913," *European Review of Economic History* 15 (2010): 169–219; Erik Buyst, "Towards Estimates of Long-Term Growth in the Southern Low Countries, ca. 1500–1846," slide presentation, https://warwick.ac.uk/fac/soc/economics/seminars/seminars/conferences/venice3/programme/buyst.pdf; Bozhong Li and Jan Luiten Van Zanden, "Before the Great Divergence? Comparing the Yangzi Delta and the Netherlands at the Beginning of the Nineteenth Century," *Journal of Economic History* 72:4 (December 2012): 956–89; Mikolaj Malinowski and Jan Luiten van Zanden, "Income and Its Distribution in Pre-Industrial Poland," *Cliometrica* 11 (2017): 375–404; and Debin Ma, "Modern Economic Growth in the Lower Yangzi Region of China: A Quantitative and Historical Perspective," Foundation for Advanced Studies on International Development (FASID) Discussion Series Paper, 2004-06-002. The literature on real wages is also voluminous and important but bears less directly on the divergence debate, so I

treats the Yangzi Delta as a distinctive region, estimating its per capita GDP at 50–75% above that of the entire empire—and facilitating the kind of comparisons that I argue were often more revealing than comparisons between China and European states a fraction of its size.

Here it is important to differentiate two meanings of "great divergence." The first one concerns comparative living standards: when did per capita incomes in Europe, or its richest parts, surpass those in China, or its richest parts? The second, which is probably more important, asks when *any* part of the world shifted from the generally slow and episodic per capita growth that had characterized many economies over many centuries to the (thus far) rapid and sustained growth in both population and per capita income that has characterized increasingly large parts of the world over the past two centuries. These two questions need not have the same answer: economic booms in Antonine Rome, the early Caliphate, Song China, and at other moments may have been world-leading, but they did not usher in modern economic development. And even significant differences in per capita GDP today (when we have less reason to doubt the underlying data) often do not indicate qualitative differences of the kind that separate the preindustrial world from ours: US per capita income is about one-third higher than Britain's or France's, but nobody doubts that they are fundamentally the same kinds of economies.

If we provisionally accept the GDP estimates, they suggest that as late as 1700, China's GDP per capita was probably roughly comparable to the European average, though below much of western Europe; the Yangzi Delta was perhaps roughly even with the Netherlands (the richest place in Europe) and slightly ahead of Britain. Moreover, non-Dutch, non-British Europe was no better off in 1800 than in 1500. However, Britain and the Netherlands soon pulled significantly ahead of the Yangzi Delta in the 1700s—not because they grew much but because China's great eighteenth-century population boom seems to have eventually pushed down per capita income in all regions.[4]

This represents an earlier divergence than I had suggested but not dramatically earlier. It is still much later than those proposed in many previous works,

omit most of it here. For one particularly important example, see Robert Allen, Jean-Pascal Bassino, Debin Ma, Christine Moll-Murata, and Jan Luiten Van Zanden, "Wages, Prices and Living Standards in China 1738–1925: In Comparison with Europe, Japan, and India," *Economic History Review* 64:1 (February 2011): 8–38. A fairly detailed version of my doubts about what wage comparisons between China and Europe tell us is "Standards of Living in Rural and Urban China: Preliminary Estimates for the Mid-18th and Early 20th Centuries," paper for panel 77, World Economic History Congress, Helsinki, 2006. For a different critique of wage comparisons, see Kent Deng and Patrick O'Brien, "Establishing Statistical Foundations of a Chronology for the Great Divergence: A Survey and Critique of the Primary Sources for the Construction of Relative Wage Levels for Ming–Qing China," *Economic History Review* 69 (November 2016): 1057–82.

[4] Broadberry et al., "China, Europe, and the Great Divergence," especially 989–90.

which generally argue that Europe had permanently surpassed Chinese income levels by the Renaissance at the latest.[5] The date itself, however, matters less than its implications for possible explanations. Even an early 1700s divergence is far too late to be consistent with some old historiographical warhorses (which also have other serious weaknesses). If this separation occurred because only Europe had sufficient freedom and property rights to incentivize growth, or because Confucianism was much more hostile to improving material welfare than Christianity, or because geography and climate determined very different futures for the two ends of Eurasia,[6] these differences would have manifested themselves sooner. Instead we are pointed toward narrower differences and specifically early modern conjunctures.

Meanwhile, these same studies suggest that the second, more fundamental, kind of divergence came later—because when Dutch and British per capita incomes surpassed the Yangzi Delta's sometime in the 1700s, they did so despite stagnating. As Jack Goldstone has noted in a recent essay, Dutch GDP per capita in 1800–1807 was only 5 percent above previous peaks in the 1590s and 1640s, and almost all of Britain's per capita growth between 1270 and 1800 came in two concentrated spurts accompanied by population decline: one in the late 1300s and one in the late 1600s.[7] Apparently, then, even the most dynamic parts of Europe still were not experiencing sustained per capita growth prior to 1800, while other parts of Europe had stagnant or falling per capita GDP;[8] they "pulled ahead" only because China's per capita GDP was falling. (This decline probably began in poorer, less commercialized regions, affecting the Yangzi Delta mostly toward the end of this period—essentially

---

[5] See, for instance, Angus Maddison's very influential *The World Economy: 1–2001 AD* (N.p.: OECD Publishing, 2004), vol. 1, p. 11, https://read.oecd-ilibrary.org/development/the-world -economy/the-world-economy-1-2001-ad_9789264022621-21-en#page11.

[6] David Landes, *The Wealth and Poverty of Nations: Why Some Are So Rich and Some Are So Poor* (New York: W. W. Norton, 1999); Jared Diamond, *Guns, Germs, and Steel: The Fates of Human Societies* (London: Jonathan Cape, 1997); Deepak Lal, *Unintended Consequences: The Impact of Factor Endowments, Culture, and Politics on Long-Run Economic Performance* (Cambridge, MA: MIT Press, 1998). There are also, it should be noted, books that insist on the importance of early divergences but do not rule out the possibility of subsequent convergences and thus rough parity at some later date. See, for instance, Walter Scheidel, *Escape from Rome: The Failure of Empire and the Road to Prosperity* (Princeton, NJ: Princeton University Press, 2019); and Ian Morris, *Why the West Rules—For Now: The Patterns of History and What They Reveal about the Future* (New York: Farrar, Strauss and Giroux, 2010).

[7] Jack Goldstone, "Dating the Great Divergence," forthcoming in *Journal of Global History* (2021), with comments by Stephen Broadberry, Paolo Malanima, Jan Luiten Van Zanden, and Jutta Bolt, and a response by Goldstone.

[8] See sources in note 3, plus Leonardo Ridolfi, "The French Economy in the Longue Durée: A Study on Real Wages, Working Days, and Economic Performance from Louis IX to the Revolution (1250–1789)," *European Review of Economic History* 21 (2017): 437–38; and Ulrich Pfister, "The Timing and Pattern of Real Wage Divergence in Pre-Industrial Europe: Evidence from Germany, c. 1500–1850," *Economic History Review* 70 (2017): 701–29.

the pattern I described, though beginning in the early rather than the late eighteenth century.)[9] It is probably significant, as Stephen Broadberry writes in reply to Goldstone, that early modern Britain and the Netherlands seem to have alternated between growth and stagnation, rather than growth and regression; but that is still not sustained growth, especially because the stagnant periods lasted far longer than the growth spurts. Moreover, it still leaves open the possibility that eighteenth-century stagnation could have been regression—and/or nineteenth-century growth more halting—if the era's accelerating population growth had not been accompanied by the relief of land constraints through coal and American imports, much as I had suggested.[10]

Possibility, not certainty. Tracking the timing and magnitude of divergence has been hard enough; weighing the many possible causal factors—the "hows" and "whys"—is much harder.

Some notable recent attempts to trace the long-term roots of European growth have focused on science, technology, and increasing "human capital" (that is, education and skills)—topics I discuss only briefly.[11] This is not the place to review these works, except to note that they conflict with my arguments only if they assert both that these trends gave northwestern Europe a capacity to innovate that would have overcome any conceivable resource bottlenecks, and that distinctively European scientific practices were indispensable for developing the technologies of the first Industrial Revolution—particularly steam engines. The former claim would be empirically untestable; the latter seems dubious, especially since some crude steam engines were created prior to Newcomen and Watt.[12] Other important works shared my interest in connections between European—particularly British—growth and overseas activities but highlighted different fruits of those often-violent interactions, such as imported industrial techniques and expanded

---

[9] For an argument suggesting declining market integration in China, beginning in the north, see Daniel M. Bernhofen, Markus Eberhardt, Jianan Li, and Stephen L. Morgan, "Assessing Market (Dis)integration in Early Modern China and Europe," Center for Economic Policy Research discussion paper 11288, May 2016.

[10] For a very different analysis that also highlights the importance of land-saving imports to Britain's escape from a world with important Malthusian features, see Kevin O'Rourke and Jeffrey Williamson, "From Malthus to Ohlin: Trade, Industrialisation, and Distribution since 1500," *Journal of Economic Growth* 10:1 (March 2005): 5–34.

[11] See particularly Joel Mokyr, *A Culture of Growth: The Origins of the Modern Economy* (Princeton, NJ: Princeton University Press, 2016). For papers on various aspects of knowledge, technology, and the great divergence debate, see the discussion papers of the Project on Useful and Reliable Knowledge in Global Histories of Material Progress in the East and West (URKEW) of the London School of Economics.

[12] See, for instance, Neville Morley, "Trajan's Engines," *Greece and Rome* 47:2 (October 2000): 197–210; Joseph Needham (with assistance from Wang Ling), *Physics and Physical Technologies*, vol. 4, pt. 2 of Needham et al., *Science and Civilization in China* (Cambridge: Cambridge University Press, 1965), 135–36, 225–26, 255, 369–70, 387.

markets;[13] however, our arguments seem more complementary than necessarily conflicting.

Other discussions have focused less on the creation of new technologies than on their diffusion, and more on how the problems that innovators addressed varied across time and space. While it is easy for modern people to assume that important technological innovations will be labor-saving, and generally capital and resource-absorbing, this was not always the case. As late as 1720, English patent applications were penalized if the invention would reduce labor demand—even though England had more expensive labor than most of the world. [14] Jean-Laurent Rosenthal and R. Bin Wong have hypothesized that Europe's political fragmentation and frequent wars—surely disadvantageous in the short run—may have made its premodern industry particularly likely to locate within city walls; and since cities had cheaper capital than rural settings (concentration making it cheaper for lenders and borrowers to find partners), and more expensive labor (given higher rents and food costs), Europeans may have been more prone than others to seek labor-saving, capital-using (and often, I would add, energy-using) production techniques. This did not immediately make European industries superior, but it may have pushed them along paths that ultimately led toward modern industry. [15]

In a more empirical vein, Robert Allen's work on "why the Industrial Revolution was British" emphasizes a combination of high nominal wages and easily accessible coal. This made early steam engines, which were extraordinarily wasteful of fuel, economical for pumping water out of British mines, and virtually nothing else; but once a market existed for steam engines, it was worth tinkering to improve them along any possible axis, eventually making them sufficiently fuel-efficient (and safe) to be adopted in many, many set-

[13] Parthasarathi, *Why Europe Grew Rich and Asia Did Not*; Joseph Inikori, *Africans and the Industrial Revolution in England: A Study in International Trade and Economic Development* (Cambridge: Cambridge University Press, 2002). It is worth noting, as Inikori has, that pre-1945 historiography often emphasized external factors in British industrialization. It is also worth noting that emphasizing foreign links does not have to go along with emphasizing violence. Kevin O'Rourke and Jeffrey Williamson, for instance, have consistently highlighted the centrality of trade and globalization in both starting and sustaining British/European growth but have not emphasized the role of coercion.

[14] Margaret Jacob, *The Cultural Meaning of the Scientific Revolution* (New York: Alfred A. Knopf, 1988), 92–93. See also Christine McLeod, *Inventing the Industrial Revolution: The English Patent System, 1660–1800* (Cambridge: Cambridge University Press, 1988), 158–81, noting that only 3.7 percent of patent applications during the Industrial Revolution cited labor-saving as a goal.

[15] Jean Laurent Rosenthal and R. Bin Wong, *Before and beyond Divergence: The Politics of Economic Change in China and Europe* (Cambridge, MA: Harvard University Press, 2011), 99–128.

tings.[16] This story requires very little knowledge of abstract science (awareness that air has weight, which existed beyond Europe). Instead, economics and geography decisively differentiate England from both France and Jiangnan. Moreover, agriculture plays only a secondary role in this story. Growing demand for labor, largely driven by booming overseas trade, drew people out of the English countryside, forcing farmers to adopt capital-intensive, labor-saving innovations; this reverses many historical arguments that begin with an agricultural transformation "releasing" labor and generating capital for commercial and industrial expansion.[17] This de-centering of agriculture is confirmed by evidence that agricultural labor productivity in the Yangzi Delta was still within 10 percent of English levels even near 1820, while its land productivity was several times higher—so that its total factor productivity in agriculture far exceeded that of any European locale.[18] Thus, explanations for divergence that rely on the supposed backwardness of "peasant agriculture" or the necessity of "agrarian capitalism" will not fly, and eliminating explanations that emphasize the sector employing over half of all workers until about 1985 is no small step forward.

In some sense, the potential compatibility of sustained economic growth and small-scale, family-based agriculture should have been clear already from various real-world examples, particularly in societies growing irrigated rice (which can generate extremely high per acre yields and has few economies of scale). Kaoru Sugihara, in particular, has outlined an "east Asian path" to modern prosperity that fits well with my basic picture of leading early modern regions.[19] Both of us describe a "resource-intensive" Western development path and a more labor-intensive pattern of east Asian growth while insisting that the latter need not be a dead end. Sugihara further argues that—despite significant convergence over the past several decades—the east Asian path remains distinctive and sufficiently less resource-intensive and more labor-absorbing to be a preferable model for poor countries today.[20]

---

[16] Robert Allen, *The British Industrial Revolution in Global Perspective* (Cambridge: Cambridge University Press 2009), 2–3, 135–81.

[17] Allen, *The British Industrial Revolution*, 25–79.

[18] Robert Allen, "Agricultural Productivity and Rural Incomes in England and the Yangtze Delta, c. 1620–c. 1820," *Economic History Review* 62:3 (August 2009): 541; and Li and Van Zanden, "Before the Great Divergence?," 975.

[19] Sugihara and I developed these ideas independently until we met at a conference in 1998, when I had already submitted the manuscript for *The Great Divergence* and he had already drafted what became his seminal article "The East Asian Path of Economic Development: A Long-Term Perspective," in Giovanni Arrighi, Hamashita Takeshi, and Mark Selden, eds., *The Resurgence of East Asia: 500, 150, and 50 Years Perspectives* (London: Routledge, 2003), 78–123.

[20] For doubts about the environmental sustainability of worldwide industrialization, even along the east Asian path, and questions about how well recent Chinese growth fits that model, see Kenneth Pomeranz, "Is There an East Asian Development Path? Long-Term Comparisons,

This takes us beyond "the great divergence debate" to major questions concerning the future of economic growth, particularly in connection with the environment. With the growth of comparative, global, and east Asian environmental history there have been valuable attempts to explore this book's hypotheses about early modern environmental problems and the importance of extra-European resources to Europe, to track changes in energy use and their relationship to growth in different places and periods, and to look at adaptations to resource pressure in east Asia specifically.[21] Among other things, taking economic dynamism outside the North Atlantic seriously seems important for understanding, rather than assuming, the environmental implications of capitalism and the implications of twentieth- and twenty-first-century "developmental states" (whether "capitalist" or not) for contemporary dangers and possibilities.[22] I am skeptical of arguments that suggest that modern east Asian developmentalism is much more sustainable than Western-style growth has been, or less exploitative;[23] understanding non-Western "developmentalisms" includes recognizing that they have many of the same implications as Western varieties. But it is important to continue historically informed conversations about this. It is also worth noting that the more we see the onset of sustained per capita growth in *any* place as a contingent outcome, dependent on multiple transregional processes, the more doubt is cast on various still-popular tales in which prosperity, science, and democracy have all unfolded as expressions of a single, European, essence. That the fruits of conquest, mass death, and slavery in the Americas may have been crucial to the early stages of this transition further undermines any simple story of progress. Moving beyond the academic social sciences, while keeping in mind these

Constraints, and Continuities," *Journal of the Economic and Social History of the Orient* 44:3 (2001): 322–62; and Pomeranz, "Water, Energy, and Politics: Chinese Industrial Revolutions in Global Environmental Perspective," in Gareth Austin, ed., *Economic Development and Environmental History in the Anthropocene* (London: Bloomsbury Academic, 2017), 271–90.

[21] Klas Rönnbäck, "New and Old Peripheries: Britain, the Baltic, and the Americas in the Great Divergence," *Journal of Global History* 5:3 (November 2010): 373–94; Saito Osamu, "Forest History and the Great Divergence: China, Japan, and the West Compared," *Journal of Global History* 4:3 (November 2009): 379–404; and John Richards, *The Unending Frontier: An Environmental History of the Early Modern World* (Berkeley: University of California Press, 2003).

[22] Kenneth Pomeranz, "World History and Environmental History: Introducing an Agenda," in Edmund Burke III and Kenneth Pomeranz, eds., *Environmental History and World History* (Berkeley: University of California Press, 2009), 3–32. For one milestone in the huge literature on modern developmental states, see Meredith Woo-Cumings, ed., *The Developmental State* (Ithaca, NY: Cornell University Press, 1999). For a stimulating account of how energy intensification in Asia (and the environmental impact thereof) does and does not differ from North Atlantic experiences, see Elizabeth Chatterjee, "The Asian Anthropocene: Electricity and Fossil Developmentalism," *Journal of Asian Studies* 79:1 (2020): 3–24.

[23] See, for instance, Giovanni Arrighi, *Adam Smith in Beijing: Lineages of the Twenty-First Century* (London: Verso, 2009).

questions about both origins and sustainability, I have been very gratified to see this book's arguments reflected in Amitav Ghosh's *The Great Derangement*, a work that makes deeply unsettling arguments about what coping with today's environmental emergencies requires, as well as what histories of empire and economic development do and do not imply about environmental justice.

Rather than offer brief and inadequate reflections on these enormous problems, I close with some words about theory and method. The methodological points that *The Great Divergence* emphasizes were hardly unprecedented, but apparently they had been sufficiently overlooked so that their reassertion struck a chord. That comparisons should involve areas of at least roughly comparable scale—the Yangzi Delta and Britain and/or the Netherlands, or Europe and China, rather than Britain and China—seems obvious once stated, but it has often been obscured by our tendency to take modern nation-states for granted as the units of history (and data collection). That there was enough transregional contact in early modern times (if not before) to prevent our ability to make classical comparisons of fully independent entities was also a straightforward claim with which others were also grappling in different ways, including Charles Tilly's "encompassing comparisons" (published before my book) and Michael Werner and Bénédicte Zimmermann's somewhat later "histoire croisée."[24] Perhaps most influential was this book's insistence on "reciprocal comparisons" (also stressed by my then-colleague R. Bin Wong[25]): that, in contrast to the many social science comparisons that normalized some version of a European trajectory and asked why other places did not follow it, we should treat each term of a comparison as equally "deviant," so that it was more fruitful to ask (for instance) why the Yangzi Delta was not Britain if one simultaneously asked why Britain had not become the Yangzi Delta. This seemed, then and now, a productive way to acknowledge critiques of Eurocentric social science without abandoning the immensely valuable project of comparison or the possibility of large-scale narratives.[26]

The *combination* of these strategies was perhaps unusual, and it has been taken up by people working on other world regions. Gareth Austen's sweeping essay on the potential value of reciprocal comparisons using African

---

[24] Charles Tilly, *Big Structures, Large Processes, Huge Comparisons* (New York: Russell Sage Foundation, 1984); Michael Werner and Bénédicte Zimmermann, "Beyond Comparison: Histoire Croisée and the Challenge of Reflexivity," *History and Theory* 45 (February 2006): 30–50.

[25] R. Bin Wong, *China Transformed: Historical Change and the Limits of European Experience* (Ithaca, NY: Cornell University Press, 1997).

[26] For one version of this critique that has been particularly influential among historians, see Dipesh Chakrabarty's *Provincializing Europe* (Princeton, NJ: Princeton University Press, 2000).

examples is particularly noteworthy;[27] the argument of another Africanist, Morten Jerven, that thinking with reciprocal comparisons should make us leery of global comparisons that rely heavily on GDP figures,[28] returns us to where this essay began (though historical GDP is likely less skewed for China/Europe comparisons than Africa/Europe ones). This approach has also been taken up far from this book's thematic foci: it figures, for instance, in several of the essays in *Comparative Early Modernities*, dealing with art, literature, political ideas, and other areas, and figures indirectly in Martin Powers' eye-opening recent book on how Chinese political ideas influenced debates in early modern England.[29] With luck, readers will continue finding varied uses for this this book, even as they question some of its arguments.

[27] Gareth Austin, "Reciprocal Comparisons and African History: Tackling Conceptual Eurocentrism in the Study of Africa's Economic Past," *African Studies Review* 50:3 (December 2007): 1–28.

[28] Morten Jerven, "An Unlevel Playing Field: National Income Estimates and Reciprocal Comparison in Global Economic History," *Journal of Global History* 7:1 (2012): 107–28.

[29] David Porter, ed., *Comparative Early Modernities: 1100–1800* (London: Palgrave MacMillan, 2012); Martin Powers, *China and England: The Preindustrial Struggle for Justice in Word and Image* (London: Routledge, 2018).

ACKNOWLEDGMENTS

LARGE PROJECTS create many debts. The complicated path of this project, which originally began as a chapter for a very different book, made the comments and counsel of many people even more important than usual.

Many people have read and provided helpful comments on some version of this manuscript: Steven Topik, Timothy Guinnane, R. Bin Wong, Daniel Segal, Joel Mokyr, Andre Gunder Frank, Edmund Burke III, Randolph Head and the students in his world history seminar, James Given, Jack Goldstone, Robert Marks, Dennis Flynn, Richard Von Glahn, and Jason Hecht. Along the way, pieces of the project were also presented at many conferences and workshops, where colleagues too numerous to list provided incisive and useful suggestions. The thoughtful comments that always emerge at meetings of the All-UC Group in Economic History are particularly noteworthy. This being the age of cyber-collegiality, I also owe thanks to Joshua Rosenbloom, Alan Taylor, and Samuel Williamson, who organized an exceptionally helpful electronic discussion after I presented a short version of the book's argument on EH.NET. The provocative ideas and helpful suggestions that arose from that discussion (and a later one on H-World, moderated by Patrick Manning) were immensely helpful.

Since this book took me far beyond the area of my training, I also relied on many colleagues who helped steer me to what I needed to read in fields they knew far better than I did; along with many of the people listed above, Robert Moeller, Anne Walthall, and James Lee were particularly helpful. Other colleagues helped move the project along in other ways: Peter Lindert, John Wills, Jonathan Spence, Deirdre McCloskey, Ken Sokoloff, and Hamashita Takeshi stand out from a long list.

A list of debts this long risks diluting the acknowledgment to any one colleague; that is not, of course, my intent. Bin Wong deserves special mention for reading through two versions of the manuscript, talking through problems with the argument, and brainstorming about bibliography; though I have come to take his high level of collegiality for granted, it is anything but ordinary. It is also a special pleasure to have a belated opportunity to give thanks in print to Dan Segal. It is hard for me to imagine learning more from anyone than I have from Dan these twenty-plus years, either about the subjects that interest both of us or about what it means to have good friends. Since I believe every person on this list has raised at least some objections to the argument, the usual statement that none of them is responsible for the errors I persist in is worth reiterating.

I have also benefited from considerable material support while writing this book. It began to take shape (though in a very different form) while I was on a leave to work on another project, generously supported by the University of California President's Research Fellowship and an ACLS/SSRC/Ford Foundation Joint Fellowship in Chinese Studies. Much of the writing was done during a subsequent leave made possible by the largesse of the John Simon Guggenheim Memorial Foundation and the University of California, Irvine. This book has been considerably improved by the help and encouragement offered by Peter Dougherty of Princeton University Press and his assistant Linda Chang, and by the deft and careful copy-editing of Jennifer Backer.

My personal debts are no smaller than my professional ones. Much of this book was written under difficult circumstances, which would have been far more difficult without the help of many people. When trouble hit, old and new friends, colleagues, and a remarkable set of neighbors all rallied around in truly extraordinary ways. I cannot list them all, and I would be very sorry to leave any of them out, so a collective thank-you will have to do; it is no less heartfelt for being general.

Last but never least, my family has shown remarkable strength during these years, without which I could not possibly have found any time or calm in which to write. David, Jesse, and Benjy needed and showed courage and determination far beyond what one expects from young children; they met their challenges again and again, while always remaining warm, sweet, and loving children. I owe a great deal to all of them.

As for my wife, Maureen Graves, what is there to say? An analogy we have heard often these past few years seems apt. Having planned a trip to Paris, we found ourselves in New Zealand instead—and Maureen has never lost sight of either the goal of getting back to Paris or the possibility of enjoying New Zealand, if you just stop looking for the Louvre. This balancing act has taken patience, perseverance, vision, and love, far more of each than I can ever explain or give adequate thanks for. But as one small gesture of appreciation, this is her book.

Irvine, California
September 1998

THE GREAT DIVERGENCE

INTRODUCTION

COMPARISONS, CONNECTIONS, AND
NARRATIVES OF EUROPEAN ECONOMIC DEVELOPMENT

MUCH OF modern social science originated in efforts by late nine-
teenth- and twentieth-century Europeans to understand what made
the economic development path of western Europe[1] unique; yet
those efforts have yielded no consensus. Most of the literature has focused on
Europe, seeking to explain its early development of large-scale mechanized
industry. *Comparisons* with other parts of the world have been used to show
that "Europe"—or in some formulations, western Europe, Protestant Europe,
or even just England—had within its borders some unique homegrown ingre-
dient of industrial success or was uniquely free of some impediment.

Other explanations have highlighted relations between Europe and other
parts of the world—particularly various forms of colonial extraction—but they
have found less favor with the majority of Western scholars.[2] It has not helped
matters that these arguments have emphasized what Marx called the "primitive
accumulation" of capital through the forcible dispossession of Amerindians
and enslaved Africans (and many members of Europe's own lower classes).
While that phrase accurately highlights the brutality of these processes, it also
implies that this accumulation was "primitive" in the sense of being the *beginning* step in large-scale capital accumulation. This position has become un-
tenable as scholarship has shown the slow but definite growth of an investible
surplus above subsistence through the retained earnings of Europe's own
farms, workshops, and countinghouses.

This book will also emphasize the exploitation of non-Europeans—and
access to overseas resources more generally—but not as the sole motor of
European development. Instead it acknowledges the vital role of internally
driven European growth but emphasizes how similar those processes were to

---

[1] It should be noted here that "western Europe," for most authors, is a social, economic, and
political construct, not an actual geographic entity: Ireland, southern Italy, and most of Iberia, for
instance, did not have much of the economic development usually held to be characteristically
European or western European. I will generally use the term in a geographical sense, while pointing out that the areas often taken to stand for "Europe" in these comparisons (e.g., the southern
Netherlands, or northern England), might be better compared, in both size and economic characteristics, with such units as China's Jiangsu province, rather than with entire subcontinents such as
China or India.

[2] Note, for instance, the generally negative current mainstream verdicts on the arguments of
Eric Williams (1944), Andre Gunder Frank (1969), Samir Amin (1974), etc. A good general
critique of the overseas extraction thesis is DeVries 1976: 139–46, 213–14.

processes at work elsewhere, especially in east Asia, until almost 1800. Some differences that mattered did exist, but I will argue that they could only create the great transformation of the nineteenth century in a context also shaped by Europe's privileged access to overseas resources. For instance, western Europe may well have had more effective institutions for mobilizing large sums of capital willing to wait a relatively long time for returns—but until the nineteenth century, the corporate form found few uses other than for armed long-distance trade and colonization, and long-term syndicated debt was primarily used within Europe to finance wars. More important, western Europe had by the eighteenth century moved ahead of the rest of the world in the use of various labor-saving technologies. However, because it continued to lag behind in various land-saving technologies, rapid population growth and resource demands might, in the absence of overseas resources, have forced it back onto a path of much more labor-intensive growth. In that case it would have diverged far less from China and Japan. The book thus calls upon the fruits of overseas coercion to help explain the *difference* between European development and what we see in certain other parts of Eurasia (primarily China and Japan)—not the whole of that development or the differences between Europe and *all* other parts of the Old World. A few other factors that do not fit firmly into either category, such as the location of coal supplies, also play a role. Thus the book combines comparative analysis, some purely local contingency, and an integrative or global approach.

Moreover, the comparative and integrative approaches modify each other. If the same factors that differentiate western Europe from, say, India or eastern Europe (e.g., certain kinds of labor markets) are shared with China, then comparisons cannot simply be the search for a European difference; nor can patterns shared at both ends of Eurasia be explained as unique products of European culture or history. (Nor, of course, can they be explained as outgrowths of universal tendencies, since they distinguish some societies from others.) The resemblances between western Europe and other areas that force us to turn from a purely comparative approach—one that assumes essentially separate worlds as units of comparison—to one that also looks at global conjunctures[3] have another significance as well. They imply that we cannot understand pre-1800 global conjunctures in terms of a Europe-centered world system; we have, instead, a polycentric world with no dominant center. Global conjunctures often worked to western Europe's advantage, but not necessarily because Europeans created or imposed them. For instance, the remonetization of China with silver from the fifteenth century on—a process that predated the European arrival in the Americas and the export of its silver—played a crucial part in making Spain's far-flung New World empire financially sustainable; and hor-

---

[3] For a discussion of comparisons between entities that are assumed to be systemically interrelated rather than truly separate (which he calls the "encompassing comparison"), see Tilly 1984.

rific, unanticipated epidemics were crucial to creating that empire in the first place. Only after nineteenth-century industrialization was well advanced does it make sense to see a single, hegemonic European "core."

Most of the existing literature, however, has remained set in an either/or framework—with either a Europe-centered world system carrying out essential primitive accumulation overseas[4] or endogenous European growth called upon to explain almost everything. Given those choices, most scholars have leaned toward the latter. Indeed, recent scholarship in European economic history has generally reinforced this exclusively internal focus in at least three ways.

First, recent research has found well-developed markets and other "capitalist" institutions further and further back in time, even during the "feudal" period often thought to be the antithesis of capitalism.[5] (A similar sort of revision has occurred in analyses of medieval science and technology, where what was once disparaged as the "Dark Ages" has now come to be seen as quite creative.) This has tended to reinforce the notion that western Europe was launched on a uniquely promising path well before it began overseas expansion. In some recent treatments, industrialization itself disappears as a turning point, subsumed into centuries of undifferentiated "growth."

To put matters slightly differently, older literatures—from the late nineteenth-century classics of social theory to the modernization theory of the 1950s and 1960s—stressed a fundamental opposition between the modern West and its past, and between the modern West and the non-West. As more recent literature has tended to narrow the first gap, it suggests that the second gap—European exceptionalism—goes back even further than we thought. But it is a central contention of this book that one can just as easily find grounds to narrow the gap between the eighteenth-century West and at least some other parts of Eurasia.

Second, the more market dynamics appear even amid supposedly hostile medieval culture and institutions, the more tempting it has been to make market-driven growth the *entire* story of European development, ignoring the messy details and mixed effects of numerous government policies and local customs.[6] And if legislative fiat at home added only small detours or

---

[4] E.g., Blaut 1993: 186–206.

[5] For a good recent example, see Britnell 1993.

[6] For a good example of the tendency to minimize the importance of both legislative changes and popular custom, see the large literature reinterpreting the decline of English open fields. These fields were once thought to represent a collective ethic hostile to nascent capitalism and to have been destroyed by legislation as more individualist, less paternalist ideas became dominant in Parliament. It is now common to argue that open fields in fact represented a rational strategy for individuals in a world of fluctuating harvests and no insurance and disappeared largely because gradually declining interest rates made another form of harvest insurance—namely grain storage—cheaper and more effective than keeping one's land in many scattered plots likely to have slightly different soils and micro-climates (e.g., McCloskey 1975a, 1975b, 1989). A further

occasional slight shortcuts to European development paths, why should coercion overseas—in places far from the main action of the story—be worth much attention? Meanwhile, an increasingly exclusive focus on private initiatives has not only provided an enviably clear story line, but a story line compatible with currently predominant neoliberal ideas.

Third, since this ongoing process of commercialization touched much of preindustrial western Europe, much recent literature treats whatever is left of the Industrial Revolution as a *European* phenomenon, rather than, as used to be common, as a British phenomenon spreading later to the rest of Europe.[7] Such a move is challenged, not only by a mass of older scholarship, but also by more recent work suggesting that England had already diverged from the continent in crucial respects centuries before the Industrial Revolution.[8] But the shift from a British to a European focus has been facilitated by the aforementioned tendencies to deemphasize politics and to minimize the conflict between "traditional" practices and rationally self-interested individuals, making it easier to minimize variation within western Europe.

Positing a "European miracle" rather than a British one has important consequences. For one thing, it again makes extra-European connections seem less important. Most of western Europe was far less involved in extracontinental trade than Britain was: so if it was "Europe" rather than "Britain" whose commercial growth led smoothly to industrial growth, then domestic markets, resources, and so forth must have been adequate for that transition. Moreover, if growth was largely achieved through the gradual perfection of competitive markets, then it seems implausible that colonies beset by mercantilist restrictions and unfree labor, to name just two problems, could possibly have been dynamic enough to significantly effect their mother countries. Thus Patrick O'Brien, a leading exponent of a "European" view, concedes that *British* industrialization, in which cotton played such a crucial role, is hard to envision without colonies and slavery, but then continues:[9]

Only a simplistic growth model with cotton as a leading sector and with British innovation as the engine of Western European growth could support an argument that the Lancashire cotton industry was vital for the industrialization of the core. That process proceeded on too broad a front to be checked by the defeat of an advanced column whose supply lines stretched across the oceans to Asia and the Americas.

consequence of this view, discussed (and disputed) on pp. 76–80 below, is the claim that the absence of any comparably successful government assault on traditional open fields in France was not as important an impediment to French development as earlier historians had generally held.

[7] For two classic, though very different, statements of the British-centered view, see Landes (1969) and Hobsbawm (1975). One of the most explicit and trenchant critiques of this view is O'Brien and Keydar 1978.

[8] See, e.g., Snookes 1994a, Wrigley 1990: 101–2.

[9] O'Brien 1982: 12.

He then concludes that "for the economic growth of the core, the periphery was peripheral."[10]

Such arguments make Europe's overseas expansion a minor matter in a story dominated by emerging economic superiority. Empire might be explained *by* that superiority or might be independent of it, but had little to do with creating it. The resulting narratives are largely self-contained in two crucial senses: they rarely require going either beyond Europe or beyond the model of free, competing buyers and sellers at the heart of mainstream economics. For those scholars who also explain the increased speed of technological change largely in terms of a patent system granting more secure property in creativity, this closure becomes almost complete.

The emphasis on "European" industrialization has also tended to shape the units used in our comparisons, often in unhelpful ways. In some cases, we get comparative units based simply on contemporary nation-states, so that Britain is compared to India or China. But India and China are each more comparable in size, population, and internal diversity to Europe as a whole than to individual European countries; and a region within either subcontinent that by itself might be comparable to Britain or the Netherlands is lost in averages including Asian equivalents of the Balkans, southern Italy, Poland, and so on. Unless state policy is the center of the story being told, the nation is not a unit that travels very well.

A second durable approach has been to first search for things that made "Europe" as a whole distinct (though the particulars chosen often really describe only part of the continent) and then, once the rest of the world has been dropped from the picture, to look within Europe for something that made Britain distinct. These continental or "civilizational" units have so powerfully shaped our thinking that it is hard to shake them; they will appear here, too. But for many purposes, it seems more useful to try a different approach, anticipated in important ways by my colleague R. Bin Wong.[11]

Let us grant the following: few essential characteristics unite, say, Holland and the Ukraine, or Gansu and the Yangzi Delta; a region like the Yangzi Delta (population 31,000,000–37,000,000 circa 1750, depending on the precise definition) is certainly big enough to be compared to eighteenth-century European countries; and various core regions scattered around the Old World—the Yangzi Delta, the Kantō plain, Britain and the Netherlands, Gujarat—shared

[10] Ibid. In his work with Keydar on Britain and France, O'Brien makes the much more convincing but rather different point that European industrialization was not *simply* the diffusion of British innovations to the rest of the continent. France, for instance, concentrated on different industries, which often involved finishing British semi-finished goods. But the very complementarity between Britain and France that shows the possibility of different routes to industrialization also suggests that we cannot simply remove British industrialization from the story and say that had that not happened, the continent would have industrialized anyway. And the British story, as we shall see, is unimaginable without two crucial discontinuities—one created by coal and one by colonies.

[11] Wong 1997.

some crucial features with each other, which they did not share with the rest of the continent or subcontinent around them (e.g., relatively free markets, extensive handicraft industries, highly commercialized agriculture). In that case, why not compare these areas directly, before introducing largely arbitrary continental units that had little relevance to either daily life or the grand patterns of trade, technological diffusion, and so on?[12] Moreover, if these scattered cores really had much in common—and if we are willing to allow some role for contingencies and conjunctures—it makes sense to make our comparisons between them truly reciprocal: that is, to look for absences, accidents, and obstacles that diverted England from a path that might have made it more like the Yangzi Delta or Gujarat, along with the more usual exercise of looking for blockages that kept non-European areas from reproducing implicitly normalized European paths.

Here, too, I am following a procedure outlined in Wong's recent *China Transformed*. As Wong points out, much of classic nineteenth-century social theory has been rightly faulted for its Eurocentrism. But the alternative favored by some current "postmodern" scholars—abandoning cross-cultural comparison altogether and focusing almost exclusively on exposing the contingency, particularity, and perhaps unknowability of historical moments—makes it impossible even to approach many of the most important questions in history (and in contemporary life). It seems much preferable instead to confront biased comparisons by trying to produce better ones. This can be done in part by viewing both sides of the comparison as "deviations" when seen through the expectations of the other, rather than leaving one as always the norm. It will be my procedure in much of this book, though my concrete application of this reciprocal comparative method has some significant differences from Wong's, and I carry the approach onto rather different terrain.[13]

This relatively untried approach at least generates some new questions that put various parts of the world in a different light. For instance—and here again I largely agree with Wong—I will argue that a series of balanced comparisons show several surprising similarities in agricultural, commercial, and proto-industrial (i.e., handicraft manufacturing for the market rather than home use) development among various parts of Eurasia as late as 1750. Thus the explosion of further growth in western Europe alone during the nineteenth century again becomes a rupture to be explained. By contrast, some recent literature, by limiting itself to intertemporal European comparisons and finding similarities there (which are real enough), tends to obscure this rupture. Thus, such

[12] On the limited utility of "civilizations" as a unit, see Fletcher (1995: 3–7); Hodgson (1993: 17). On continents, see Wigen and Lewis (1997).

[13] For example, I place greater stress than Wong does on global conjunctures and reciprocal influences and bring more places besides Europe and China into the discussion; I also say little about some of his topics, such as state formation, and much more about some he does not treat extensively, such as environmental change.

literature also often barely passes over important contributions to industrialization—especially conjunctural ones—which may appear as taken-for-granted "background" in a comparison limited to different periods in Europe.

A strategy of two-way comparisons also justifies linking what may at first seem two separate issues. The point at which western Europe became the richest economy need not be the same as the point at which it broke out of a Malthusian world into one of sustained per capita growth. Indeed, most of what I have called the "Europe-centered" approaches argue that western Europe had become uniquely rich long before its industrial breakthrough. And if our only question were whether China (or India, or Japan) could have made its own breakthrough to such a world—i.e., if we normalize the European experience and make it the pattern one would expect in the absence of "blockages" or "failures"—it would no longer be very important to ask when Europe actually escaped a Malthusian world: it would matter far more that it had been for a long time on a path bound to lead to that breakthrough eventually. Meanwhile, the dates by which it had definitively surpassed other places would tell us little about other possibilities for Europe and only about when those other places had taken their detours into stagnation.

But if we make reciprocal comparisons and entertain the possibility that Europe could have been a China—that no place was bound to achieve dramatic and sustained per capita growth—the link between the two becomes closer. If we further argue—as I will in subsequent chapters—that some other parts of the eighteenth-century world were roughly as close as Europe was to maximizing the economic possibilities available to them without a dramatic easing of their resource constraints (like that made possible for Europe by fossil fuels and the New World), then the link between the two issues becomes closer still.

The two questions are still separable: differences in climate, soil, etc., might have given different areas different preindustrial possibilities. But it seems unlikely that Europe enjoyed a substantial edge in those possibilities over all other densely settled regions, particularly since the evidence presented later in this book suggests that it did not in fact become much better-off than east Asia until industrialization was well under way. Or it might turn out that although Europe did not pull ahead of east Asia until the eve of industrialization, certain institutions were in place by a much earlier date that did make industrialization bound to happen after all; that even without the Americas and favorably located fossil fuels, technological inventiveness was already sufficient to sustain growth in the face of any particular local resource shortages, and without resorting to the extremely labor intensive solutions which sustained aggregate, but not per capita, growth elsewhere. But the strong assumptions that such an assertion of inevitability would require begin to look shaky once we actually hold Europe up against the standard of some other preindustrial economies—especially since the last few centuries of European economic history before industrialization do not show consistent and robust per capita growth. Thus, two-way comparisons both raise new questions and reconfigure the relationships among old ones.

Thus, this book will emphasize reciprocal comparisons between *parts* of Europe and parts of China, India, and so on that seem to me to have been similarly positioned within their continental worlds. We will return to continental units and to still larger units, such as the Atlantic world, when our questions—such as those about the relationships of cores to their hinterlands—require it. And in some cases we will need to take the entire world as our unit, requiring a somewhat different kind of comparison—what Charles Tilly calls the "encompassing comparison," in which rather than comparing two separate things (as classical social theory did) we look at two parts of a larger whole and see how the position and function of each part in the system shape their nature.[14] At this level, which I emphasize more than Wong does, comparison and the analysis of connections become indistinguishable. The importance of keeping the analysis reciprocal, however, remains. Our perception of an interacting system from which one part benefited more than others does not in itself justify calling that part the "center" and assuming that it is the unshaped shaper of everything else. We will see, instead, vectors of influence moving in various directions.

Variations on the Europe-Centered Story: Demography, Ecology, and Accumulation

The arguments positing that western Europe's economy was uniquely capable of generating an industrial transformation generally fall into two clusters. The first, typified by the work of E. L. Jones, argues that beneath a surface of "preindustrial" similarity, sixteenth- through eighteenth-century Europe had already moved far ahead of the rest of its world in the accumulation of both physical and human capital.[15] A central tenet of this view is that various customary checks on fertility (late marriage, a celibate clergy, etc.) allowed Europe to escape from the otherwise universal condition of a "pre-modern fertility regime" and thus from a similarly universal condition in which population growth absorbed almost all of any increase in production. Consequently, Europe was uniquely able to adjust its fertility to hard times and to increase its per capita (not just total) capital stock over the long haul.

Thus, in this view, differences in the demographic and economic behavior of ordinary farmers, artisans, and traders created a Europe that could support more non-farmers; equip its people with better tools (including more livestock); make them better nourished, healthier, and more productive; and create a larger market for goods above and beyond the bare necessities. The central

[14] Tilly 1984.   [15] Jones 1981, 1988.

arguments underlying this position were laid out over thirty years ago by John Hajnal:[16] they have been elaborated since then, but not radically altered. However, as we shall see in chapter 1, recent work on birthrates, life expectancy, and other demographic variables in China, Japan, and (more speculatively) Southeast Asia has made what Hajnal thought were unique European achievements look more and more ordinary.

The significance of these findings has not yet been fully appreciated, but they have been partially acknowledged in the one important recent addition to the demographically driven story line: the recognition that there were economic booms and rising living standards in preindustrial settings outside Europe. However, these are always treated as temporary flowerings that either proved vulnerable to political shifts or played themselves out as productivity-enhancing innovations proved unable to stay ahead of the population increases that prosperity encouraged.[17]

Such stories are an important advance over much earlier literature, which argued either implicitly or explicitly that the whole world was poor and accumulation minimal until the early modern European breakthrough; among other things, it has forced scholars to look at "the fall of Asia"[18] as well as the "rise of Europe." However, these versions of the story are often anachronistic in at least two crucial ways.

First, they tend to read too much of the nineteenth- and twentieth-century ecological disasters that have afflicted much of Asia (and the underlying problem of dense population) back into earlier periods and present eighteenth-century Asian societies as having exhausted all the possibilities available to them. Some versions attribute this condition to all of an artificial unit called "Asia" circa 1800; but, as we shall see, India, Southeast Asia, and even parts of China still had a good deal of room to accommodate more people without either a major technological breakthrough or a decline in the standard of living. Probably only a few parts of China and Japan faced such a situation.

Second, such stories often "internalize" the extraordinary ecological bounty that Europeans gained from the New World. Some do so by assimilating overseas expansion to the pattern of "normal" frontier expansion within Europe (e.g., the clearing and settlement of the Hungarian plain or the Ukraine, or of German forests). This ignores the exceptional scale of the New World windfall, the exceptionally coercive aspects of colonization and the organization of production there, and the role of global dynamics in ensuring the success of European expansion in the Americas.[19] The clearing of new agricultural lands in Hungary and the Ukraine had parallels in Sichuan, Bengal, and many other Old World locales; what happened in the New World was very different from anything in either Europe or Asia. Moreover, because nineteenth-century

---

[16] Hajnal 1965, 1982.
[18] Abu-Lughod 1989; Frank 1998.

[17] Jones 1988; Elvin 1973; Powelson 1994.
[19] See, e.g., Jones 1981: 70–74.

Europe found enormous ecological relief beyond its borders—both acquiring resources and exporting settlers[20]—such accounts rarely consider whether some densely populated core regions in sixteenth- through eighteenth-century Europe faced ecological pressures and options not radically different from those of core regions in Asia.

Thus, the literature that incorporates the "fall of Asia" tends to do so with the aid of an oversimplified contrast between an ecologically played-out China, Japan, and/or India, and a Europe with plenty of room left to grow—a Europe that, in one formulation, had the "advantages of backwardness"[21] because it had not yet developed enough to make full use of its internal resources.

In an attempt to move beyond such impressionistic claims, chapter 5 offers a systematic comparison of ecological constraints in selected key areas of China and Europe. This inquiry shows that although some parts of eighteenth-century Europe had some ecological advantages over their east Asian counterparts, the overall pattern is quite mixed. Indeed, key Chinese regions seem to have been better-off than their European counterparts in some surprising ways, such as available fuel supply per capita. Moreover, Britain, where industrialization in fact began, had few of the underutilized resources that remained in various other parts of Europe. Indeed, it seems to have been no better-off than its rough counterpart in China—the Lower Yangzi Delta—in timber supply, soil depletion, and other crucial ecological measures. Thus, if we accept the idea that population growth and its ecological effects made China "fall," then we would have to say that Europe's internal processes had brought it very close to the same precipice—rather than to the verge of "take-off"—when it was rescued by a combination of overseas resources and England's breakthrough (partly conditioned by geographic good luck) in the use of subterranean stores of energy. If, on the other hand, Europe was not yet in crisis, then in all likelihood China was not either.

In making this argument this book parallels some of the arguments in work on global development by Sugihara Kaoru—work I discovered too late in my writing to deal with in great detail.[22] Sugihara emphasizes, as I do, that the high population growth in east Asia between 1500 and 1800 should not be seen as a pathology that blocked "development." On the contrary, he argues, this was an "East Asian miracle" of supporting people, creating skills, and so on, which is fully comparable as an economic achievement to the "European miracle" of industrialization. Sugihara also emphasizes, as I do, the high standard of living in eighteenth-century Japan and (to a lesser extent in his view) China, as well as the sophistication of institutions that produced many of the beneficial effects of markets without the same state guarantees for property and contract

---

[20] Crosby 1986: 2–5, 294–308.
[21] Frank 1998: 283, playing on Gerschenkron.
[22] Sugihara 1996.

that many Westerners believe is the precondition of markets.[23] He also argues—a point consistent with my argument though beyond the scope of this book—that in the long run it has been a combination of western European and east Asian types of growth, allowing Western technology to be used in societies with vastly more people, which has made the largest contribution to world GDP, not a simple diffusion of Western achievements.

Sugihara does, however, suggest that a basic difference between these two "miracles" is that as far back as 1500, western Europe was on a capital-intensive path and east Asia on a labor-intensive path. By contrast, I argue—in keeping with the finding of surprising similarities as late as 1750 and with my determination to take the question "Why wasn't England the Yangzi Delta?" as seriously as "Why wasn't the Yangzi Delta England?"—that Europe, too, could have wound up on an "east Asian," labor-intensive path. That it did not was the result of important and sharp discontinuities, based on both fossil fuels and access to New World resources, which, taken together, obviated the need to manage land intensively. Indeed, there are many signs that substantial regions in Europe were headed down a more labor-intensive path until dramatic late eighteenth- and nineteenth-century developments reversed that path. We will find such evidence in aspects of agriculture and proto-industry throughout Europe (including England) and in almost everything about Denmark.[24] The East-West difference that developed around labor-intensity was not essential but highly contingent; the distribution of population growth (as opposed to its aggregate size) turns out to be one crucial variable, which in turn has much to do with market *distortions* in sixteenth- through eighteenth-century Europe and with migration to the New World in the nineteenth century.

In both China and Japan population growth after 1750 was heavily concentrated in less-developed regions, which then had smaller surpluses of grain, timber, raw cotton, and other land-intensive products to "vent" through trade with resource-hungry cores; and since part of the increased population of these peripheral areas went into proto-industry, they also had less need to trade with core regions. In Europe, on the other hand, it was largely areas that were already relatively advanced and densely populated that had large population increases between 1750 and 1850. Most of eastern Europe, for instance, only began to experience rapid population growth after 1800, and southern Europe (especially southeastern Europe) began to catch up even later. Chapters 5 and 6 will have much more to say about the political-economic and ecological bases of these differences and their significance for industrialization. Meanwhile, it is worth emphasizing that they are not differences that reflect a greater

---

[23] It is worth noting, however, that in recent years many Western economic historians have also become interested in describing institutional arrangements that made contracts easily enforceable, and thus permitted efficient markets, even in the absence of much state involvement in guaranteeing property rights. For a helpful summary, see Greif 1998: 597–633.

[24] See for instance Ambrosoli 1997; Levine 1977; Kjaergaard 1994.

overall strain on resources in east (much less south) Asia as compared to Europe. Let us move, then, from arguments about quantities of resources available—either those already accumulated or those left untapped—to arguments claiming that European institutions *allocated* resources in ways more conducive to long-term self-sustaining growth.

Other Europe-Centered Stories: Markets, Firms, and Institutions

A second group of arguments—evident in somewhat different ways in the work of Fernand Braudel, Immanuel Wallerstein, and K. N. Chaudhuri, and in a very different way in that of Douglass North—pays less attention to *levels* of wealth. Instead, these arguments emphasize the emergence of institutions in early modern Europe (or some part of it) said to be more conducive to economic development than those existing elsewhere. The focus of these arguments is generally on the emergence of efficient markets and property-rights regimes that rewarded those who found more productive ways to employ land, labor, and capital. A common, though not universal, companion to these arguments is the claim that economic development was stifled elsewhere (especially in China and India) by a state that was either too strong and hostile to private property or too weak to protect rationalizing entrepreneurs when the latter clashed with local customs, clergy, or strongmen.[25]

Potentially consistent with these arguments—though quite distinct from them—is the work of Robert Brenner, who explains divergent development paths within Europe as the result of class struggles that altered property-rights regimes. In Brenner's interpretation, western European peasants won the first round of a struggle with their lords in the century or so after the Plague, establishing their freedom from forced labor; eastern European peasants lost, and the ruling class lived for centuries thereafter by squeezing peasants harder, without ever modernizing agriculture or introducing labor-saving innovations. Within western Europe, Brenner continues, a second round of struggle ensued, with lords who now owned only the land seeking the freedom to manage it so as to maximize profits, often by removing unproductive or "excess" tenants. French elites lost this battle, according to Brenner, and France was stuck thereafter with an agricultural system based on millions of smallholders neither able nor very interested in innovations that would make some of them unnecessary. But in England the lords won, invested in innovations that made it possible to cut labor costs, and expelled huge numbers of unneeded workers from the land. At least some of these dispossessed farmers eventually became En-

[25] Wittfogel 1957; Jones 1981: 66–67, 118, 125; Jones 1988: 130–46; Mokyr 1990: 233–34, 256–60; Powelson 1994.

gland's industrial workforce, buying food from the agrarian surplus created by their expulsion and marketed by their former lords.

In Brenner's argument, class struggle, rather than either Malthusian pressures or the "natural" emergence of more perfect markets, supplies the motor of the story; the destination, however, is similar. How much a society winds up resembling neoclassical models determines how productive it will be thereafter; in particular, England, the country where land and labor wound up most sharply separated (and most completely commodified) is presumed to have *therefore* developed the most dynamic economy. In this, Brenner winds up rather oddly aligned with Douglass North, who—while rejecting class struggle as the explanation of property-rights regimes—also argues that economies became increasingly capable of development as they evolved increasingly competitive markets for commodified land, labor, capital, and intellectual property.

Both North's and Brenner's arguments focus on the institutional settings in which the great majority of people operated: markets for day labor, tenancy contracts, and for products that ordinary people both produced and consumed. In this they resemble the arguments discussed above, which argue that preindustrial Europeans were already uniquely prosperous and productive, and tend to merge with those arguments.

However, the other major set of institutionalist arguments—those of Braudel and his school—focuses more on the profits accumulated by a few very wealthy people; the institutions that facilitated this kind of accumulation often involved special privileges that interfered with neoclassical markets. Consequently, these scholars have paid more attention to profits based on the use of coercion and collusion. And because many of the great merchants they focus on were involved in long-distance trade, these scholars have paid more attention to international politics and Europe's relations with other areas. Wallerstein, in particular, treats the growth of trade between "feudal" eastern Europe and "capitalist" western Europe as the real beginning of a world economy, and he emphasizes that continued accumulation of profits in the free-labor "core" of that economy has required the continued existence of poor, generally unfree "peripheries."

But nonetheless, the motor of Wallerstein's story is western Europe's unique combination of relatively free labor, large and productive urban populations, and merchants and governments that facilitated long-distance trade and the reinvestment of profits. The international division of labor that emerged from this trade increased the difference in wealth between western Europe and everyone else, since peripheries increasingly specialized in those goods for which cheap, often coerced, labor was more important than the tools and institutions needed for high productivity—but it was based on preexisting socioeconomic differences that enabled western Europe to impose on others in the first place.

Problems with the Europe-Centered Stories

This work borrows from these arguments—mostly those of the various "institutionalists"—but ultimately argues for different propositions. First, no matter how far back we may push for the origins of capitalism, *industrial* capitalism, in which the large-scale use of inanimate energy sources allowed an escape from the common constraints of the preindustrial world, emerges only in the 1800s. There is little to suggest that western Europe's economy had decisive advantages before then, either in its capital stock or economic institutions, that made industrialization highly probable there and unlikely elsewhere. The market-driven growth of core areas in western Europe during the preceding centuries was real enough and was undoubtedly one crucial precursor of industrialization—but it was probably no *more* conducive to industrial transformation than the very similar processes of commercialization and "proto-industrial" growth occurring in various core areas in Asia.[26] The patterns of scientific and technical development that were taking shape in early modern Europe were more unusual, but we shall see that they still did not, by themselves, guarantee that western Europe would wind up on a fundamentally different economic path from, for instance, east Asia.

Second, European industrialization was still quite limited outside of Britain until at least 1860. Thus, positing a *"European* miracle" based on features common to western Europe is risky, all the more so since much of what was widely shared across western Europe was at least equally present elsewhere in Eurasia.

Part 1 of this book calls into doubt various contentions that Europe had an internally generated economic edge before 1800. It substitutes a picture of broad similarities among the most densely populated and commercialized parts of the Old World. Chapter 1 draws on evidence from numerous places to show that Europe had not accumulated a crucial advantage in physical capital prior to 1800 and was not freer of Malthusian pressures (and thus more able to invest) than many other large economies. People in various other areas seem to have lived as long and as well as Europeans and to have been at least equally willing and able to limit fertility in the interest of household-level accumulation. The second half of the chapter then examines the possibility that Europe had a crucial technological edge even before the Industrial Revolution. Here we do find some differences that mattered—but which would have had smaller, later, and probably qualitatively different effects without both the fortunate geographic accidents essential to the energy revolution and Europe's

---

[26] Sugihara and Hayami (1989) see the "industrial" and "industrious" revolutions diverging already in the seventeenth century, Arrighi in the eighteenth century. Although there are indeed signs of such a divergence that far back, I will argue that it was not sealed until the turn of the nineteenth century, when the New World plus coal made it clear that such a land-using, resource-intensive path would remain sustainable for a prolonged period.

privileged access to overseas resources. Technological inventiveness was necessary for the Industrial Revolution, but it was not sufficient, or uniquely European. It is unclear whether whatever differences existed in the *degree* of technological inventiveness were crucial to exiting a Malthusian world (technological breakthroughs could have been spread over a slightly longer period), but it is clear that the differences in global context that helped ease European resource constraints—and so made innovation along particular (land-using, energy-using, and labor-saving) paths a fruitful, even self-reinforcing, process—were significant.

Chapter 2 turns to markets and related institutions. It focuses primarily on a comparison between western Europe and China. It shows that western European land, labor, and product markets, even as late as 1789, were on the whole probably *further* from perfect competition—that is, less likely to be composed of multiple buyers and sellers with opportunities to choose freely among many trading partners—than those in most of China and thus less suited to the growth process envisioned by Adam Smith. I begin by comparing laws and customs governing the ownership and use of land and the extent to which agricultural producers could choose to whom to sell their output. The next section concerns labor: the extent of compulsory labor, restrictions on (or encouragement of) migration, restrictions on changing occupations, and so on.

The last and most complex section of chapter 2 treats the relationships between households as units of consumption and as institutions that allocated labor—particularly that of women and children. Some scholars have argued that Chinese families were more prone than western European ones to keep women and children working beyond the point at which their marginal output sank below the value of a subsistence wage, thus producing an "involuted economy"; I will show that there is little reason to believe this.[27] Rather, labor deployment in Chinese families seems to closely resemble the reorientation of labor, leisure, and consumption toward the market that Jan DeVries has called Europe's "industrious revolution."[28] In sum, core regions in China and Japan circa 1750 seem to resemble the most advanced parts of western Europe, combining sophisticated agriculture, commerce, and nonmechanized industry in similar, arguably even more fully realized, ways. Thus we must look outside these cores to explain their subsequent divergence.

Building a More Inclusive Story

Part 2 (chapters 3 and 4) begins by moving away from survival-oriented activities to examine new kinds of consumer demand, the cultural and institutional changes that accompanied them, and the possibility that differences in demand

---

[27] P. Huang 1990: 11–17; for a related argument see also Goldstone 1996.
[28] DeVries 1994b.

had important effects on production (chapter 3). Here we find differences that
may well have differentiated China, Japan, and western Europe from other
places, but not very much from each other. The differences in both quantities
of goods available and "consumerist" attitudes among these societies seem
small and of uncertain direction. (For instance, mid-eighteenth-century Chinese almost certainly consumed more sugar than Europeans, and people in the
Lower Yangzi core may have produced as much cloth per capita in 1750 as
Britons did in 1800.) And institutions in all these societies (though not necessarily elsewhere) seem to have been such that increased production routinely
created demand, while it is much less clear that increased demand could create
supply. Finally, those differences in consumer behavior that did favor Europe
seem to have been heavily influenced by extra-European elements—for example, the extraction of New World silver and the demand for it in Asia, which
sucked other "exotic" goods into Europe, and the system of production shaped
by New World plantations and slavery.

Chapter 4 then follows the merchants and manufacturers who brought the
new "luxuries" of chapter 3—whether imported, imitated (e.g., Wedgewood
"china"), or purely homegrown—to market. In doing so, it moves away from
the "typical" household and the sorts of markets for land, labor, and consumer
goods in which they participated. Instead it looks at actors who operated on a
larger scale, examining markets in the last factor of production—capital—and
arguments about a distinctive European capitalism. It thus moves away from
institutional arguments focused entirely on the growth of allegedly more perfect markets within western Europe to those that pay more attention to external
connections, find advantages for certain crucial actors in imperfect competition, and so also pay more heed to extraeconomic coercion.

Chapter 4 begins by rejecting various arguments that either the general
structure of society or the specific rules surrounding commercial property gave
European merchants a crucial advantage in amassing capital, preserving it
from the state, or deploying it rationally. Although some financial assets may
have been better defined and more secure in Europe (or at least in England,
Holland, and the Italian city-states), such differences are too small to bear the
explanatory weight assigned to them by scholars as diverse as Fernand
Braudel, K. N. Chaudhuri, and Douglass North—and even harder to link to the
early Industrial Revolution, which was not very capital intensive. Certainly
some of the larger Chinese firms, for instance, regularly assembled sums of
capital adequate to implementing the major technical innovations of the pre-
railroad era.

Western European interest rates were probably lower than Indian, Japanese,
or Chinese ones; but it turns out to be very hard to show that this made an
important difference to relative rates of agricultural, commercial, or proto-
industrial expansion, and even harder to show much impact on the early rise
of mechanized industry. And it is significant that where eighteenth-century

Europeans' supposedly superior commercial organizations had to compete with merchants from other Old World regions without using force, their record was mediocre. Only in overseas colonization and *armed* trading did Europe's financial institutions—nurtured by a system of competing, debt-financed states—give it a crucial edge.

Even more important, as Braudel himself emphasizes, is the point that capital was not a particularly scarce factor of production in the eighteenth century.[29] Constraints connected to energy, and ultimately to quantities of land (particularly the shrinking forests of core areas throughout Eurasia), were a far more important looming impediment to further growth. The essence of development was that both labor and capital became more plentiful relative to land, but producing any of Malthus's four necessities of life—food, fiber (clothing), fuel, and building materials—still required land.

To some extent, capital and labor could create more land (reclamation) or make land yield more food and fiber through irrigation, fertilization, or extra-careful weeding, but this was quite limited compared to what late nineteenth-century chemical industries would make possible. And when it came to producing fuel and building materials before the massive use of fossil fuels, the ability of labor and capital to substitute for land was very limited indeed. Thus, even if Europe had an edge in assembling investment capital, this would not by itself have solved the ecological bottlenecks faced by all the most "developed" proto-industrial regions. Certainly there are enough examples of capital-rich but late industrializing areas even within Europe to make any link between greater capital accumulation and a transition to industrialism dubious. Northern Italy and Holland are obvious examples, despite their highly sophisticated commercial economies, and so, in a different way, is Spain, where a huge flood of silver into a less-developed economy may well have retarded growth.[30]

Braudel did not systematically explore how his own insight about the relative abundance of capital before 1800 might affect explanations of European distinctiveness; instead he turned back to unverified claims that European fortunes were more secure.[31] However, the Braudelian family of arguments does direct our attention toward long-distance trade and toward phenomena—the state, colonial ventures, and nonmarket extraction—which I think played a greater role in the European breakthrough than is visible in most recent studies. In particular, I will argue that while neither the new forms of property created in early modern Europe (e.g., corporations and various securitized claims on future income streams) nor the domestic policies of Europe's competing and revenue-hungry states made pre-1800 Europe itself a significantly better environment for productive activity, the projection of interstate rivalries overseas

[29] Braudel 1977: 60; DeVries 1976: 210–14.   [30] Flynn 1984; Hamilton 1934.
[31] Braudel 1977: 60–75.

did matter. Similarly, joint-stock companies and licensed monopolies turned out to have unique advantages for the pursuit of armed long-distance trade and the creation of export-oriented colonies—activities that required what were for the time exceptional amounts of capital willing to wait a relatively long time for returns. When we combine this notion of European capitalism, in which links to the state and the right to use force and preempt certain markets loom large, with the idea that advanced market economies everywhere faced growing ecological problems, a new picture emerges of what Europe's most significant differences were.

Part 3 (chapters 5 and 6) then sketches a new framework for thinking about the relationships between internal and external factors in Europe's development path. Chapter 5 begins by arguing for serious ecological obstacles to *further* growth in all of the most densely populated, market-driven, and commercially sophisticated areas of Eurasia. These were not so acute as to cause major food crises, but they made themselves felt in shortages of fuel and building materials, to some extent in shortages of fiber, and in threats to the continued fertility of some areas' soils. After examining these constraints, the last part of chapter 5 examines the attempts made by all these core areas to address these shortages through long-distance trade with less densely populated Old World areas; it argues that such trade could not provide a fully adequate solution. The high cost of transport before the age of steam was one reason, but others are rooted in the political economies of many of the "peripheral" regions, the relatively low levels of demand there, and the resulting difficulties of sustaining an exchange of core manufactured goods for raw materials without either a colonial system to enforce it or the much larger interregional differences in manufacturing productivity (often based on relatively immobile factors such as capital equipment embodying new technology) that emerged from the late nineteenth century onward.

Chapter 6 then considers the dramatic easing of Europe's land constraint during industrialization. It looks briefly at the shift from wood to coal—an important story, but one well covered elsewhere—and then turns to the ecological relief provided by Europe's relations with the New World. This relief was predicated not merely on the natural bounty of the New World, but also on ways in which the slave trade and other features of European colonial systems created a new *kind* of periphery, which enabled Europe to exchange an ever-growing volume of manufactured exports for an ever-growing volume of land-intensive products.

A crucial part of this complementarity, up through the early industrial era, was the result of slavery. Slaves were purchased from abroad by New World plantations, and their subsistence production was often limited. Thus, slave regions imported much more than, say, eastern Europe and southeast Asia, where the producers of export crops were born locally, met most of their own basic needs, and had little cash with which to buy anything else.

The plantation zone also differed in critical ways from free labor peripheries such as the Chinese interior. Exporters of rice, timber, and raw cotton in east Asia had more purchasing power than did peasants in regions of coerced cash-cropping and had greater flexibility and incentives to respond to external demand. But the same system of more or less free labor that produced these dynamic peripheries also allowed people to shift away from activities with diminishing returns. With time, these areas tended to undergo significant population growth (partly due to rising incomes) and proto-industrialization of their own; this decreased both their need to import manufactures and the surplus of primary products that they could export.

By contrast, the circum-Caribbean plantation zone showed much less tendency to diversify its production or to cease needing imported slaves and provisions. And since Europe acquired most of the slaves it shipped to the New World in return for manufactures (especially cloth), while much of the grain and timber sent to the Caribbean came from British North America, enabling those colonies to buy European manufactures, all of the New World's import needs—even those for grain and humans—helped Europe use labor and capital to solve its land shortage. Finally, we will also see in chapter 6 that dynamics set in motion during the colonial period created the framework for a flow of resources to Europe from both slave and free areas that accelerated throughout the nineteenth century, despite independence and emancipation.

In the process, chapter 6 also shows how differing long-term core-periphery relations could shift the significance of a feature common to various core regions in Eurasia. That feature is "proto-industrialization": the massive expansion of nonmechanized industries, mostly composed of rural laborers producing for (often distant) markets through the mediation of merchants. Historians of Europe, who created the concept, have been divided about the relationship between proto-industrialization and industrialization proper. Some have argued that proto-industrialization contributed to the accumulation of profits and/or the development of market-oriented activity, specialization, and tastes for products hard to make at home. And Joel Mokyr has shown—in an argument I would claim is as applicable to parts of Asia circa 1750 as for his own European cases—that the development of a large pool of "pseudo-surplus labor" in proto-industrial occupations could make a crucial contribution to industrialization, without many of the complications that arise if we look for industrial workers to emerge from "surplus labor" in agriculture.[32]

But Mokyr's model of proto-industrialization assumes that proto-industrial areas will be able to keep expanding their handicraft exports and agricultural imports without affecting relative prices in whatever "world" they are a part of. Considering the limits of this assumption brings into focus another side of proto-industrialization.

[32] Mokyr 1976: 132–64; compare Lewis 1954: 139–91.

Proto-industrial growth has generally been associated with significant population increases (though the exact nature of the connection is hotly disputed); and in many cases, rapid population growth in proto-industrial areas has been associated with a vicious cycle of very low piece rates, increasing output from workers struggling to buy enough food and often without much access to land, and still lower piece rates. Any shift in relative prices—whether created by an increased proto-industrial population glutting the export market while needing to import more food, or by diminishing external supplies and markets—will intensify this pattern of immiseration. And more generally speaking, population growth—whatever its relationship to proto-industrialization—could place serious pressure on the land needed for raising fuel, fiber, and other necessities of industrial development. Unless these goods can be acquired by trade, the only way to keep increasing output is by working the land more intensely, which with the technologies then available meant higher farm-product prices, lower per capita productivity, and a drag on industrial growth.

Signs of both serious ecological bottlenecks and spiraling poverty among too-numerous proto-industrial workers and underemployed farm laborers are as evident in many regions of mid-eighteenth-century Europe as in comparable parts of China or Japan—indeed, perhaps more so. But then, I will argue, Europe and east Asia changed places.

China's Lower Yangzi, for instance, had increasing trouble selling enough cloth and importing enough food and timber to sustain either proto-industrial growth or the relatively high living standard of its workers. This was not because of any internal "flaw" in the region but because the areas it had traded with were undergoing their own population and proto-industrial booms and so were becoming less complementary to it. To some extent, the Yangzi Delta compensated as a leading area should—moving up the value-added ladder by specializing in higher-quality cloth—but this was not enough. In short, markets worked well within China's eight or nine macro-regions (each larger than most European states), encouraging people in much of the interior to devote more time to making cloth and the like as they filled up the land, felled the trees nearest the rivers, and so on. But these smoothly functioning regional markets and interdependencies conflicted with the growth of empire-wide markets, especially after about 1780; this made it harder for one or two leading regions to keep growing and to avoid having to adopt even more labor-intensive strategies for conserving land and land-intensive products. Thus, freedom and growth in the peripheries without dramatic technological change led the country as a whole toward an economic cul de sac.

By contrast, northwestern Europe became able, in the century after 1750, to specialize in manufactures (both proto-industrial and industrial) to an unprecedented degree and to make its spectacular population growth during this period an asset. A big part of this transformation was, of course, a series of impressive technological advances in manufacturing (which made huge amounts of relatively cheap goods available to exchange for land-intensive products) and in transportation, which greatly facilitated specialization. But these relatively well-known developments are not the whole story. Western Europe could also increase its population, specialization in manufacturing, and per capita consumption levels—when even eighteenth-century levels had seemed to many people near the limits of ecological possibility—because the limits imposed by its finite supply of land suddenly became both more flexible and less important. This was partly because its own institutional blockages had left significant unexploited agricultural resources that could be tapped after the French Revolution and post-Napoleonic reforms in Germany; partly because far more extreme institutional blockages (above all serfdom) in eastern Europe (the counterpart to, say, China's Upper Yangzi or southwest) had left lots of slack there; and partly because new land management techniques were brought home from the empire in the early nineteenth century. In all these ways, one might argue, Europe was catching up with China and Japan in both best and average practices in agro-forestry, rather than blazing new trails. Even so, Europe's transformation also required the peculiar paths by which depopulation, the slave trade, Asian demand for silver, and colonial legislation and mercantilist capitalism shaped the New World into an almost inexhaustible source of land-intensive products and outlet for western Europe's relatively abundant capital and labor. Thus, a combination of inventiveness, markets, coercion, and fortunate global conjunctures produced a breakthrough in the Atlantic world, while the much earlier spread of what were quite likely better-functioning markets in east Asia had instead led to an ecological impasse.

Thus, chapter 6 locates the significance of the Atlantic trade not in terms of financial profits and capital accumulation, nor in terms of demand for manufactures—which Europe could have probably generated enough of at home[33]—but in terms of how much they relieved the strain on Europe's supply of what was truly scarce: land and energy. And because it helped ease these fundamental, physical constraints, Europe's overseas extraction deserves to be compared with England's turn to coal as crucial factors leading *out* of a world of Malthusian constraints, rather than with developments in textiles, brewing, or other industries, which, whatever their contributions to the accumulation of *financial* capital or development of wage labor, tended to intensify, rather than ease, land and energy squeezes in the core areas of western Europe. And, indeed, a preliminary attempt to measure the importance of this ecological windfall suggests that until well into the nineteenth century, the fruits of overseas exploitation were probably roughly as important to at least Britain's economic transformation as its epochal turn to fossil fuels.

---

[33] On capital accumulation within Europe versus "exotic sources" see DeVries 1976: 139–46, 213–14. On demand, see ibid., 176–92; Mokyr 1985b: 21–23; and Mokyr 1985a, which questions the significance of demand factors in the Industrial Revolution more generally.

Comparisons, Connections, and the Structure
of the Argument

Thus part 1, which is essentially comparative, argues that although a combination of relatively high levels of accumulation, demographic patterns, and the existence of certain kinds of markets may separate out a few places—western Europe, China, Japan, and perhaps others—as the most likely settings for a dramatic shift in economic possibilities, they cannot explain why that shift in fact occurred first in western Europe, or why it happened anywhere. Nor can technological differences explain very much before the nineteenth century (when Europe closed the gap in land management and took a wide lead in many other areas)—and even then, only when Europe's complex and often violent relations with other parts of the globe are added to the story.

In part 2, intercontinental comparisons continue, but in a context in which intercontinental connections also begin to be important. It argues that as we move toward kinds of economic activity less directly tied to physical necessity—and involving a smaller share of the population—some possibly important western European differences in culture and institutions do appear, even vis à vis other "core" regions. However, these differences are ones of degree rather than of kind, quite limited in strength and scope. They certainly do not justify any claim that western Europe, and western Europe alone, had either a "capitalist mode of production" or a "consumer society," and they cannot themselves explain the dramatic divergences that *would* emerge in the nineteenth century. Moreover, it is striking that where significant differences are discernible, they are consistently related to *deviations* from simple Smithian market dynamics—especially to state-licensed monopolies and privileges, and to the fruits of armed trade and colonization.

Part 3 begins with comparison again, showing that whatever advantages Europe had—whether from a more developed "capitalism" and "consumerism," the slack left by institutional barriers to more intensive land use, or even technological innovations—were nowhere near to pointing a way out of a fundamental set of ecological constraints shared by various "core" areas of the Old World. Moreover, purely consensual trade with less densely populated parts of the Old World—a strategy being pursued by all the core areas of Eurasia, often on a far larger scale than pre-1800 western Europe could manage—had limited potential for relieving these resource bottlenecks. But the New World had greater possibilities, in large part due to the effects of global cojunctures. First, epidemics seriously weakened resistance to European appropriation of these lands. Second, the transatlantic relations that followed conquest and depopulation—mercantilism and especially the African slave trade—made the flow of needed resources to Europe self-catalyzing in ways that consensual trade between Old World regions was not: it anticipated, even before industrialization, the self-perpetuating division of labor between primary products exporters and manufacturing regions in the modern world. Thus the world's first "modern" core and its first "modern" periphery were created in tandem—and this global conjuncture was important in allowing western Europe to build something that was truly unique upon the base of an advanced market economy whose main features were not unique. We end, then, with connections and interactions explaining what comparison alone cannot.

A Note on Geographic Coverage

Having sketched the book's main ideas, a brief warning is in order about its geographic coverage. While joining the burgeoning field of "world history," this book treats the world's regions very unevenly. China (principally east and southeast China) and western Europe are treated at some length; Japan, south Asia, and the Chinese interior much less so; eastern Europe, southeast Asia, and the Americas still less; Africa even less, except through the slave trade; and the Middle East, central Asia, and Oceania are barely mentioned. Moreover, China, Japan, south Asia, and western Europe are treated in terms of both comparisons and connections. In other words, they are treated both as places that were plausible enough sites for fundamental economic transformations that their experiences illuminate the places where such a transformation did occur, and in terms of the reciprocal influences between themselves and other regions.

Eastern Europe, southeast Asia, the Americas, and Africa, on the other hand, are treated largely through their interactions with other regions. This does not imply that they were only acted *upon*—on the contrary, the argument sketched insists that what was possible in the areas we think of as "cores" was conditioned by the development paths and internal dynamics of "their" peripheries. Nor should it imply that the regions I treat comparatively were the only ones where important changes could happen. Industrial growth is just one part, albeit a vital one, of what we call "modernity": others may have other geographic origins. Nor, for that matter, can we afford to understand only those areas that were the seedbeds of what we now take to be the dominant characteristics of our age; to do so would greatly increase the risk of taking those features to be inevitable. In short, adding a few Chinese and Japanese foils to a European story does not make it "world history."

But there are reasons besides my finite energies for focusing as I do here. Some have to do with the stories I want to question and some with the story I want to tell.

First of all, it is China, more than any other place, that has served as the "other" for the modern West's stories about itself, from Smith and Malthus to Marx and Weber. Thus, two crucial aims of this book are to see how different

Chinese development looks once we free it from its role as the presumed opposite of Europe and to see how different European history looks once we see the *similarities* between its economy and one with which it has most often been contrasted.

Second, the processes emphasized in my own argument direct us to densely populated parts of the world and their trading partners. On the one hand, ongoing specialization is fueled by high population density; one cannot generally support oneself doing certain tasks that each person needs done only occasionally unless there are many people within one's market area.[34] Population density is not the sole determinant of Smith's "extent of the market," nor is it impossible for even sparsely populated areas to have elaborate arrays of specialists who subdivide certain tasks that the culture deems important. But for elaborate specialization to be developed in many areas of economic activity—food production, clothing production, building, transport, and exchange itself—there is ultimately no substitute for having many people within an affordable physical and cultural distance. (This is also true for specializing in the investigation of the natural world and the quest for new ways to manipulate it—the Smithian component of the much less predictable, but obviously crucial, process of generating technological change.)

Meanwhile, the ecological pressures that are also central to my argument are even more closely linked to demography.[35] Of course, areas that are sparsely populated in an absolute sense may also come under heavy ecological pressure if they are simply not capable of supporting very many people, or if people use their environment in certain ways. Thus in part 3 I make a distinction between densely populated areas and what I call "fully populated" ones—areas that have little room left for extensive growth without significant land-saving technological change, institutional improvements, or increased access to land-intensive commodities through external trade, even though they may have fewer people per acre than some other area. (Thus eighteenth-century Britain, for instance, could be more "fully populated" than Bengal, even at a lower population density, given its far lower per-acre yields and higher standard of living.) But this criterion, too, leads to a focus on western Europe, China,

---

[34] It should be noted in this connection that "specialization" is not the same as "division of labor," much less "complexity." One could imagine, for instance, a society with extremely complex rules of exchange determining who baked the bread each week, but in which no one person was a full-time baker. Such a society could certainly be as complex as any, and its people each master of a very complicated set of skills, but precisely for that reason, it would not have the same economic dynamics as one in which people are continually driven to focus on just a few tasks for which they in particular can find a market.

[35] I call these dynamics quasi-Malthusian because I do not argue that population densities were necessarily about to lead to a decline in the standard of living in any of the core areas I discuss, but only that worsening land/labor ratios were a serious obstacle to large amounts of further growth given the technologies of the preindustrial revolution, and that while early industrial technologies alleviated this constraint, they were not by themselves sufficient.

Japan, and, to a lesser extent, India. Further arguments might be made about dense populations, the pooling of information, and the likelihood of certain kinds of technological and institutional changes, though these are less straightforward.

A final, though less intellectually defensible, point is that my own training has equipped me better to write about China, Europe, and Japan than about other places and to access the relatively large piles of existing research on them. What James Blaut refers to as "uniformitarianism"—the idea that at a certain point (in his analysis, 1492), many interconnected parts of Afro-Eurasia had roughly similar potential for "dynamism" in general, and thus for "modernity"[36]—is a useful point of departure, but has limits we must discover empirically. It would be a remarkable coincidence if it turned out to be applicable everywhere, and there is much evidence that it is not. My own guess, as made above, is that population density will turn out to be extremely important, and thus that it is more likely that, say, north India will turn out to belong with China, Japan, and western Europe than, say, central Asia or even the Ottoman Empire.[37] (It is worth remembering in this connection that anyone attempting to write a book like this ten years ago would have had a much harder time finding literature to support the case I make for China than I have; twenty-five years ago it would have been hard even for Japan.) But with the literature available now—both based on my own limits and the limits of our knowledge—the geographic emphases in this book seem adequate to at least put new questions on our agendas. The places I look at relatively closely are not the world, nor does the rest of the world only matter as it interacts with them, or when it serves as a negative example, illuminating, for instance, how eastern Europe shows what China and western Europe share by being much more different from both China and western Europe than China and western Europe are from each other. But this is, I think, a reasonable distribution for rethinking where our current industrialized era came from.

[36] Blaut 1993: 42, 124, 152.

[37] On Ottoman population, which seems to have been both relatively sparse in most of the empire and declining for most of the eighteenth century, see McGowan 1994: 646–57.

PART ONE

A WORLD OF SURPRISING RESEMBLANCES

ONE

EUROPE BEFORE ASIA?

POPULATION, CAPITAL ACCUMULATION,

AND TECHNOLOGY IN EXPLANATIONS OF

EUROPEAN DEVELOPMENT

THERE IS no consensus on how Europe became uniquely wealthy by the mid-nineteenth century. However, Eric Jones's *European Miracle* probably comes closest to enunciating the current "mainstream" position. Jones's argument is eclectic, and many Europeanists would reject or question many of his claims; but several of his general propositions nonetheless command wide assent. For our purposes, the most important of these general statements—one also found in any number of other works—is that industrialization was not the point at which European economic history departed from other Old World trajectories; instead, it represents the full flowering of differences that had been more subtly building for centuries. In fact, many scholars simply take this for granted; since Jones explicitly argues for the proposition, his work serves as a useful point of departure.

According to Jones, "Europeans"[1] were already uniquely wealthy before industrialization. In particular, they had vastly more capital at their disposal, especially livestock,[2] which they accumulated by "holding back population growth a little below its maximum." This in turn allowed Europeans to "hold their consumption levels a little above those of Asia."[3] Moreover, their capital stock was less liable to destruction, because Europe suffered fewer natural disasters and began sooner than other places to build with fire-resistant brick and stone.[4] Thus, less of Europe's annual surplus above subsistence was needed to offset depreciation, and its advantage in capital stock grew steadily with time, even before the Industrial Revolution.

But in fact there is little evidence to suggest a quantitative advantage in western Europe's capital stock before 1800 or a set of durable circumstances—demographic or otherwise—that gave Europe a significant edge in capital accumulation. Nor is it likely that Europeans were significantly healthier (i.e.,

---

[1] It is not always clear whom Jones includes in this term; in some cases it embraces the whole continent, in others just western or even northwest Europe.

[2] Jones 1981: 4–5.   [3] Ibid., 14   [4] Ibid., 22–35, 40–41.

advantaged in human capital), more productive, or otherwise heirs of many years of slowly accruing advantages over the more developed parts of Asia.

When we turn to comparisons of the technology embodied in the capital stock, we do find some important European advantages emerging during the two or three centuries before the Industrial Revolution; but we also still find areas of European backwardness. Europe's disadvantages were concentrated in areas of agriculture, land management, and the inefficient use of certain land-intensive products (especially fuel wood). As it worked out, some of the areas in which Europe had an edge turned out to be important for truly revolutionary developments, while the particular areas in which other societies had better techniques did not. But even Europe's technological leadership in various sectors would not have allowed a breakthrough to self-sustaining growth without other changes that made it much freer than other societies of its land base. This was partially a result of catching up in some of the land-saving technologies in which it lagged, a process that was greatly facilitated by knowledge gained through overseas empire, and partly a matter of serendipity, which located crucial resources (especially forest-saving coal) in particularly fortunate places. It was also partly due to *global* conjunctures. Those global conjunctures, in turn, were shaped by a combination of European efforts (many of them violent), epidemiological luck, and some essentially independent developments. (One example of the latter is China's switch to a silver-based economy, which helped keep New World mines profitable and sustain Europe's colonial presence during the long period before other products were developed.)

These global conjunctures allowed western Europeans access to vast amounts of additional land-intensive resources. Moreover, they could obtain these resources without needing to further strain a European ecology that was already hard-pressed *before* the great nineteenth-century boom in population and per capita resource use, and without having to reallocate vast amounts of their own labor to the various labor-intensive activities that would have been necessary to manage their own land for higher yield and greater ecological sustainability. Without these "external" factors, Europe's inventions alone might have been not much more revolutionary in their impact on economy and society than the marginal technological improvements that continued to occur in eighteenth-century China, India, and elsewhere.

Agriculture, Transport, and Livestock Capital

Europe did indeed have more livestock per person than most other settled societies, and *within a European system of farming* that livestock constituted such valuable capital equipment that more farm animals usually meant more prosperity. And in a few places in Asia a shortage of livestock did interfere with cultivating more land. In parts of eighteenth-century Bengal, for instance, landless laborers were unable to take advantage of empty, fertile land because they lacked access to plow animals; but this was less because of an absolute shortage of livestock than because landlords, fearing the loss of their labor force, took care to monopolize the necessary animals.[5] The very fact that unused land was still plentiful makes it unlikely that Malthusian pressures were to blame for people not having livestock.

In some other Asian societies, human populations had reached densities at which they restricted the availability of livestock; but nothing in those cases indicates that a shortage of farm animals inhibited agricultural production. Indeed, had a shortage of animals been a crucial problem, it is hard to see why at least larger, wealthier farmers would not have raised and used more of them; yet for the period in which we have reasonable data, there is no observable difference between large and small North China farms in animal power used per acre.[6] Moreover, what by European standards was a tiny number of animals sufficed to do all the work needed to keep virtually all usable land under cultivation. Moreover, in this region—with a crop mix and ecology more like Europe's than that of the rice-growing south—my best estimate is that even with relatively few draft animals, late eighteenth-century Chinese placed considerably more—and higher-quality—manure on the soil than did their European contemporaries.[7] The resulting yields supported an exceptionally dense population for a dry-farming region,[8] at living standards that, as we shall soon see, were probably comparable to that of western Europe. Meanwhile, in the rice regions of Asia, even smaller numbers of draft animals coincided with the highest agricultural yields in the world; rice farming simply does not require as much animal power, and post-harvest operations also require much less power than does making wheat flour.[9] Subtropical and tropical regions elsewhere, such as Meso-America, also supported dense populations with few or even no plow animals. If even with more animals European farming was not exceptionally productive, it is hard to see this as a crucial advantage.

Of course, plow animals can also pull other loads. The huge preponderance of land transport in preindustrial Europe probably results in part from the availability of so many farm animals, who had to be fed everyday but were only needed part-time for farming. Did Europe then have a crucial advantage in capital equipment for land transportation? Perhaps so, compared to east

---

[5] Van Schendel 1991: 42; Marshall 1987: 7, 23.

[6] Huang 1985: 145.

[7] For calculations, see appendix B.

[8] The population figures in Huang (1985: 322) for Shandong, for instance, give us 400 people per square mile circa 1750—supported without net food imports—versus roughly 160 even for the Netherlands (based on McEvedy and Jones 1978: 62–63), with the help of substantial food imports.

[9] Bray 1984: 48, 198–200 (comparison with Europe); Palat 1995: 60 (on milling).

Asia, where pasture land was so scarce, but the remarkable development of water transport in China and Japan surely offset this and represented an at least equally valuable form of capital in transport; east Asia's overall advantage in transport was noted at the time by Adam Smith.[10] And in parts of Asia where, as in Europe, there was lots of meadow and grassland, rural transport was probably just as highly developed. The enormous bullock trains of north India, sometimes including 10,000 beasts,[11] are a powerful, if anecdotal, example. Quantitative estimates are fraught with many uncertainties, but what we can piece together suggests that the animal-borne freight-hauling capacity of eighteenth-century north India was not wildly different, on a per-person basis, from Werner Sombart's estimate for Germany in 1800.[12] And both China and India had long purchased warhorses and some other livestock from central Asia, which had enormous amounts of pasture. After 1700, the Qing dynasty controlled much of this territory and bred its own warhorses. Had the Chinese needed to import other animals, this would have been ecologically feasible, too.[13]

Nor do we see other signs of a shortage of transport capital in Asia. Such a shortage would presumably inhibit marketing, particularly of bulky goods such as grain. Yet in one of the most crowded societies of all—China—the share of the harvest that was marketed over long distances seems to have been considerably higher than that in Europe. Wu Chengming has conservatively estimated that 30,000,000 *shi* of grain entered long-distance trade in the eighteenth century,[14] or enough to feed about 14,000,000 people.[15] This would be more than five times a generous estimate of Europe's long-distance grain trade at its pre-1800 peak[16] and over twenty times the size of the Baltic grain trade in a normal year during its heyday.[17]

Furthermore, Wu's figure includes only the largest of many grain-trading routes in China and uses cautious estimates even for those. He omits, for instance, Shandong province, which had a population of about 23,000,000 in 1800[18]—slightly larger than that of France—and was neither particularly commercialized nor particularly backward. It imported enough grain in an average eighteenth-century year to feed 700,000–1,000,000 people—more than the Baltic trade fed—and exported roughly the same amount.[19] Thus, if we treat the grain entering and exiting this nation-sized piece of China as the equivalent of "international trade" in Europe, we find that this one province engaged in a

[10] Smith 1937: 637–38.   [11] Habib 1990: 376–77.   [12] See appendix A.
[13] See, for instance, Gardella 1992b: 101–2.
[14] Wu 1983: 277. Ond *shi* was approximately 103 liters; a *shi* of rice weighed about 160 pounds.
[15] Perkins 1969: 297–307; Marks 1991: 77–78.
[16] Braudel 1981: 127.
[17] Jones 1981: 81; DeVries 1974: 170.
[18] Huang 1985: 322.
[19] Xu Tan 1995: 86.

grain trade comparable to all of Europe's long-distance grain trading; and there must have been quite a bit of grain trading within the province as well, since even this volume of imports could not have met the demand from its urban areas (not to mention its cotton and tobacco growers).

Nor was China unique. Many cities in various parts of Asia (and probably one or two in precolonial America) were larger than any European city before eighteenth-century London, and several were larger than London as well. It has been estimated that 22 percent of Japan's eighteenth-century population lived in cities, versus 10–15 percent for western Europe;[20] and the Malay archipelago, though sparsely populated overall, may have been 15 percent urban.[21] Many of these cities—as well as some in south Asia and the Middle East—were heavily dependent on long-distance shipments of bulky foods.

Overall, then, it seems very hard to find evidence of a European advantage in transportation. A last possibility would be that European animals provided a crucial difference by providing power for industrial activities, such as turning millstones. But the rice-eating parts of Asia needed less milling to begin with, since rice (unlike wheat) was often eaten without being turned into flour. When rice was to be pounded into flour, this was generally done in very small quantities at a time, but not for lack of animal power; rather, it was the nature of rice itself, which spoils very rapidly once unhusked, which called for handprocessing small daily amounts.[22] Moreover, most mills and other industrial facilities, whether in Europe or Asia, were small; they also took many days off due to limited demand, customary restraints such as holidays, and other shortages (e.g., of fuel for forges). Thus, large numbers of animals were not generally needed, and there is nothing to suggest that a shortage of animal power was a significant brake on industrial development anywhere.

So if Europe's animals made a difference, it would not have been as a "capital good," but only as an item of consumption: i.e., as a source of protein for which other areas had no adequate substitute. Europeans certainly ate more meat and far more dairy products than most peoples in Asia. But this advantage was declining, not growing, in the early modern period, and doing so rapidly: meat consumption in Germany, for instance, fell by about 80 percent between the late Middle Ages and 1800.[23] Furthermore, meat was not an irreplaceable source of protein: many Meso-Americans and North Americans seem to have gotten the most important amino acids in meat from corn, beans, and squash, and east Asians from bean curd.

More generally, any argument based on one aspect of diet—or one other feature, such as having more brick and stone buildings—is shaky. How are we to decide which differences constitute being "ahead in standard of living"?[24]

[20] Smith 1958: 68.
[21] Reid 1989: 57.
[22] Bray 1984: 53; Palat 1995: 60.
[23] Braudel 1981: 196.
[24] Jones 1981: 7.

Why emphasize Europe's probable edge in housing, rather than, say, the remarkable supply of safe drinking water in much of Japan, China, and southeast Asia?[25] Or the greater comfort and durability of cotton, which was available to even the poor through most of Asia and preferred by even the rich in Europe once it became available? The only definitive answer would be that Europeans' particular mix of material goods made them healthier, longer-lived, or more energetic—and our admittedly limited evidence indicates no such thing. Paul Bairoch, projecting backward from twentieth-century data, has generated estimates of per capita income for most of the world circa 1800. In his figures "Asia" as a whole is very slightly behind western Europe but ahead of Europe as a whole, and China remains ahead of even western Europe.[26] But Bairoch's exercise is also fraught with many difficulties. Rather than rely on the single number he generates for each economy, I will build my own case for the economic "ordinariness" of eighteenth-century Europe, proceeding topic by topic.

Living Longer? Living Better?

Life expectancy at birth in England (perhaps the most prosperous part of Europe) was about thirty-two in 1650 even for the children of peers; it passed forty only after 1750.[27] John Knodel finds life expectancy for the people of fourteen west German villages to have fluctuated between thirty-five and forty throughout the eighteenth and nineteenth centuries, a figure which, as we shall see, is higher nineteenth-century aggregates for larger German populations.[28] The massive study by Wrigley and Schofield of English villages gives life expectancies in the mid- to high thirties throughout the eighteenth century, climbing to forty in the nineteenth century and not going much above that level until after 1871.[29]

Although these figures suggest that England as a whole had, rather surprisingly, a life expectancy only slightly worse than that cited by Stone for the sons of peers, we should not leap to that conclusion. Other scholars suggest that Wrigley and Schofield have not fully corrected for the underreporting of births and deaths among the common folk before 1780; this would increase the distance between commoners and the better-documented peers by decreasing the calculated life expectancies of ordinary folk. Peter Razzell estimates that true English infant mortality between 1600 and 1749 may well have been anywhere from 60 percent to 100 percent higher than Wrigley and Schofield's numbers indicate.[30] This alone would depress a life expectancy at birth of 37

---

[25] Hanley 1997: 104, 110–11, 117, 119–20; Reid 1988a: 36–38, 41.
[26] Bairoch 1975: 7, 13, 14.   [27] Stone 1979: 58.
[28] Knodel 1988: 68–69.   [29] Wrigley and Schofield 1981: 230, 708–13.
[30] Razzell 1993: 757–58.

to somewhere between 31.6 and 34.0, and Razzell suggests that other age-specific mortalities should also be adjusted upward, especially for the earlier part of this period.[31] Life expectancy for France's much larger population was significantly lower: between 27.5 and 30 at birth for both sexes between 1770 and 1790.[32] Figures for slightly later (1816–60) in various parts of Germany are roughly comparable to those for France: 24.7 in east and west Prussia, 29.8 in the Rhine province, and 31.3 in Westphalia.[33]

Various groups of Asians seem to have lived at least as long as these western Europeans. Hanley and Yamamura estimate mean life expectancies at birth in two Japanese villages of 34.9 and 41.1 for males and 44.9 and 55.0 for females in the late eighteenth and early nineteenth centuries.[34] Smith, Eng, and Lundy calculate the total life expectancies of those who made it to age one in a well-documented eighteenth-century village as 47.1 for males and 51.8 for females.[35] Thus it appears that rural Japanese—a group that does not include aristocrats, who were legally required to live in castle towns—lived at least as long as Europeans, and probably longer.

Chinese longevity is less impressive but still quite comparable to European longevity. The case can be made for other Asian populations as well. Telford's study of genealogies from a relatively prosperous area suggests a mid-eighteenth-century life expectancy of 39.6 at birth, though with a decline to 34.9 (still comparable to estimates for England) by the early nineteenth century.[36] Lee and Campbell, working with unusually good data for a village in rural Manchuria in the years 1792–1867, arrive at an expectancy of 35.7 for one-year-old males and 29 for one-year-old females.[37] These figures are a bit lower than Telford's numbers for the mid-eighteenth century, though for females they may be depressed by what seems to have been an unusually strong preference for sons in this population. At any rate, they are still comparable to those for prosperous parts of rural Europe. Lavely and Wong find many reasons to doubt any late eighteenth-century decline in life expectancy; they also assemble measures of Chinese life expectancy from various studies and find

[31] Ibid., 759–63; calculations of adjusted life expectancies are my own.

[32] Blayo 1975: 138–39.

[33] Nipperdey 1996: 89.

[34] Hanley and Yamamura 1977: 221–22.

[35] Smith, Eng, and Lundy 1977: 51 give figures of 46.1 and 50.8 in the table, which is of *future* life expectancy. It should also be noted that here, as in recent Chinese studies, the finding of high rates of infanticide (often *not* due to terrible scarcity) produces an unusually large gap between life expectancy at birth and at age one, and makes the latter a better guide to overall conditions. Anyone unable to believe that infanticide could be anything but a desperate measure should not only consider its prevalence among well-to-do Chinese and Japanese, but the persistence among well-off urban Europeans of sending their infants to rural wet-nurses long after it was clear that this greatly increased infant mortality.

[36] Telford 1990: 133.

[37] Lee and Campbell 1997: 60, 76–81.

them to be generally greater than those for comparable groups of northwest Europeans until the nineteenth century.[38]

Recent studies of the Qing imperial lineage—perhaps the best-documented large premodern population anywhere, and not a universally well-to-do one—present a mixed picture, but one that generally supports the idea that "Chinese"[39] lived as long as western Europeans. Life expectancies at birth seem low, in part because of very high rates of infanticide—perhaps as many as 25 percent of female newborns were killed, with the rate peaking in the eighteenth century.[40] (Infanticide was widely used as a family planning device, and the unusually good records for this population make it possible to see just how widespread it was.) However, life expectancies for those who made it to age one were at or slightly above forty by the late eighteenth century,[41] which makes them quite comparable with the best-off among the western European populations discussed above. That Chinese life expectancies were comparable to European ones can also be inferred from other demographic data. As we shall soon see, China's birthrates appear to have been lower than European ones, while its population growth rate was first higher (1550–1750) and then comparable (both China and Europe roughly doubled 1750–1850): this is only possible if Chinese death rates were also lower than European ones. (Europe had more emigration, but not enough to make an important difference until the end of this period.) Granted, further research may suggest higher birth- and death rates for China than those found so far (especially if we find good data for poorer parts of the country), but our European data are also drawn disproportionately from relatively prosperous areas.

The rough comparability of life expectancies in better-off parts of eighteenth-century China and Europe (with perhaps a slight advantage for China) are also mirrored by our scattered data on nutrition. We should not assume too close a correspondence between mortality rates and nutrition, a practice that assumes preindustrial populations had few ways of consciously influencing death rates, leaving fluctuations in available resources (and exogenous crises such as plague or war) as the main influence. Lee and Wang, for instance, have made a good case that new public health measures (e.g., the spread of smallpox invariolation), long-standing patterns of personal sanitation (using soap, boiling water), and changes in popular attitudes (about everything from seeking medical care to killing or neglecting certain infants) may have had more impact on eighteenth-century Chinese life expectancies than we would expect from research on premodern European populations. But even so, the basic Malthusian insight that per capita food supplies affect death rates cannot be

[38] Lavely and Wong 1998, especially pp. 721–24.

[39] The members of the imperial lineage were Manchus, but were living in China and were in many ways quite assimilated.

[40] Li Zhongqing 1994: 7.   [41] Ibid., 9.

ignored; it is thus reassuring to find that Chinese, who lived relatively long lives, seem to have had relatively abundant food.

Braudel finds a huge variety in European reports of calorie intake before 1800 and notes that most come from sources on the lives of the privileged; he suggests 3,500 calories per day for people doing hard physical labor (e.g., crews in the Spanish fleet) and around 2,000 calories per head for the "great urban masses."[42] Nineteenth-century English data assembled by Clark, Huberman, and Lindert run 2,000–2,500 calories *per adult male equivalent* for various groups of non-farm laborers' households, and almost 3,300 for rural farm laborers in the 1860s.[43] Ming-te Pan, working backward from the rations reported for farm laborers in a seventeenth-century agricultural manual from the Yangzi Delta, notes that these rations would have worked out to 4,600 calories from grain alone.[44] Estimates of grain consumption for the entire Chinese population in the eighteenth-century vary, but they average about 2.2 *shi* of rice equivalent per day,[45] yielding roughly 1,837 calories per person per day. If the age structure of the population was the same in the eighteenth century as it was in John Buck's samples from the 1920s and 1930s,[46] this would convert to 2,386 calories per adult equivalent, plus whatever nongrain consumption they had. Conversion to adult *male* equivalents, though desirable for comparability with England, is complicated by the fact that the differences between adult male and female consumption in both seventeenth- and twentieth-century rural Chinese data are considerably larger than in English samples; but if we use the late nineteenth-century English ratio, then our Chinese figure becomes 2,651 calories per adult male. This compares well with all but one of the various British samples, including those from the much more prosperous late nineteenth-century, and quite far above Braudel's estimate for the "great urban masses" of Europe as a whole.[47]

Data for southeast Asia are extremely spotty, but a parish register from early nineteenth-century Luzon suggests a life expectancy at birth of forty-two.[48] Other scattered evidence suggests that between 1500 and 1800, elite southeast Asians may have lived a bit longer than their European peers, and European

[42] Braudel 1981: 129–30.
[43] Clark, Huberman, and Lindert 1995: 223–26.   [44] Pan, unpublished: 10.
[45] Marks 1991: 77–78.   [46] Cited in Perkins 1969: 300.
[47] For England, see Clark, Huberman, and Lindert 1995: 226n. 25. Pan 1994: 327 and accompanying notes makes a reasonable case for estimating adult male consumption as *double* that for adult females. If this were true, Chinese consumption per adult male equivalent would be an even more impressive 3,181 calories from grain alone, but such a lopsided distribution of calories between men and women would make "adult male equivalents" a somewhat deceptive standard of comparison. Data for 1930s Shanghai, however, suggest that the grain consumption of adult females was 77 percent of average adult male consumption (Shanghai shehuiju 1989: 183); this is quite close to the .733 conversion ratio used by Clark, Huberman, and Lindert with their English data.
[48] Ng 1979: 56, cited in Reid 1988a: 48–49.

visitors in this period often remarked on how healthy the indigenous population was.[49] For many other areas, we simply lack data.

Only in India are the calculated life expectancies that we have markedly
inferior to most of those for northwest Europe: probably somewhere between
twenty and twenty-five at birth circa 1800, based on shaky data from one
area.[50] As we shall see repeatedly, a combination of enormous variety and
weak data make it particularly hard to generalize about south Asia, or even to
make the sorts of statements about subregions that are possible for China,
Japan, and Europe. In this case, it is particularly noteworthy that India had a
much greater variety of labor regimes than the even larger (but politically more
unified) Chinese empire; the range of variation seems at least as broad as it was
across Europe and thus much greater than it was in western Europe alone. It
would not be surprising if this led to equally large differences in income distribution and living conditions, even among areas with similar natural endowments. (This was, of course, the case in Europe, too, while in China the relationship between regional ecologies and standards of living seems to have
been more direct.) Meanwhile, even a life expectancy of twenty-five is only
slightly below Blayo's figure for France; moreover, a recent study suggests
that the food-purchasing power of at least south Indian laborers (both agricultural and artisanal) in the mid-eighteenth century generally exceeeded that of
the English working class.[51]

Birthrates

If European death rates were not exceptionally low, neither were their birthrates; and thus European families had no special advantage in preserving their
patrimonies. When John Hajnal first outlined the ways in which the European fertility regime, with its high rates of celibacy, of adolescents and
young adults spending years away from home as servants before they could
marry, and relatively late marriages, would produce birthrates lower than those
in a "preindustrial demographic regime" (in which nothing was done within
marriage to prevent procreation), it was widely assumed that most, if not all,
of the rest of the world was characterized by such a "premodern" system.[52]
There were, indeed, few large societies outside Europe that had comparable institutions to delay marriages or depress the rate of people ever married, and comparativists looking outward from Europe were simply not pre-
pared to find effective fertility control *within* marriage before the time it began
to appear in Europe (roughly, the end of the eighteenth century). But it is

[49] Reid 1988a: 45–50.
[50] Visaria and Visaria 1983: 472–73.
[51] Parthasarathi 1998: 79–109.
[52] Hajnal 1965, 1982; see especially 1982: 476–81.

now clear that Asians (or at least east Asians) did have some control over marital fertility.

Data from Japan were the first to show surprisingly low birthrates. Much of this seems to have been an indirect—and perhaps inadvertent—result of customary arrangements in which young women were employed away from their home villages, often for years at a time, thus producing effects on fertility similar (though more pronounced) to those observed by Hajnal for Europe.[53] Moreover, we also have unmistakable evidence of more direct human efforts to control the number and sex of children a family had, including abortion and infanticide, and perhaps contraception and abstinence as well. Still more revealing, it has become increasingly clear that these direct methods—including infanticide—were not only used as survival strategies in times of economic hardship, but as part of accumulation and mobility strategies in good times as well.[54] Indeed, there is evidence that Japanese infanticide was actually more common among the well-to-do than among the poor.[55]

Evidence from southeast Asia is sparser and less compelling, but also strongly suggests that couples made various sorts of efforts to control fertility—particularly the many families in which women engaged in migratory trade.[56] Most recently, it has become clear that Chinese families of various classes, and in both good and bad times, employed a variety of strategies to limit their family size, space their children, and select their genders.[57] The most widely used strategies appear to have been delaying pregancy in marriage and then preventing pregnancy after establishing a family; recent research suggests that this made the reproductive careers of Chinese women significantly shorter, on average, than their European peers, despite virtually universal early marriage.[58] The result was birthrates per marriage and per woman that were well below those of western Europe throughout the 1550–1850 period.[59]

In sum, it appears that various groups of Asians were at least as able and determined as any Europeans to keep birthrates down for the sake of maintaining or improving their standards of living.[60] Moreover, the evidence of Chinese and Japanese birthrates lower than European ones supports the evidence for lower death rates (and thus a fairly high standard of living), and vice versa. And if east Asians were as well- or better-off than Europeans, there is no prima facie reason to think they engaged in less household-level accumulation of capital; the next section considers arguments that various macro-level factors made Europeans' efforts more effective, nonetheless.

---

[53] Cornell 1996: 43–44; Hayami, cited in Goldstone 1991: 405.
[54] Smith, Eng, and Lundy 1977: 107–32.
[55] Skinner, cited in Goldstone 1991: 407.
[56] Reid 1988a: 16, 160–62.
[57] Li and Guo 1994: 1–38; Li Bozhong 1994a: 41–42, 46–52.
[58] Lee and Wang forthcoming: 20–21; Lee and Campbell 1997: 90–95.
[59] Li Zhongqing 1994: 3.   [60] Li Bozhong 1994a: 57–58.

Accumulation?

There seems, then, little reason to think that most Europeans—even northwest Europeans—were uniquely well-off, even as late as 1750. It thus seems unlikely that their capital stock was more valuable, since it does not seem to have enabled them to produce a better standard of living for themselves. Yet another possibility suggested by Jones—that Europe's capital stock suffered less depreciation—deserves separate attention. There are possible scenarios in which a more durable capital stock was for a long time offset by other differences (e.g., a lower rate of gross investment or lack of skilled labor) but gradually made itself felt later when those other differences became less important. At present, though, there seems little reason to place much weight on any such scenario.

Europe's buildings may well have weathered disasters better than those in China and Japan, both of whom used less brick and stone. However, we lack adequate data to say that Europe led all other societies in this respect, or that no other compensating differences in the vulnerability of capital stock existed.

Jones also argues that Europe's most common disasters—principally epidemics, wars, and harvest failures—mostly destroyed labor, rather than capital, while earthquakes and floods, which were more common in many parts of Asia than they were in Europe, were more likely to destroy capital. But again, there are reasons to doubt that this gave Europe any significant advantage.

True, populations usually recovered from all but the worst disasters within a generation or two, while some destruction of capital stock had longer-lasting effects: the centuries-long decline of parts of Iran and Iraq after thirteenth-century warfare destroyed the irrigation system may be the most famous example.[61] But if the basic fabric of a society was not destroyed, even elaborate kinds of infrastructure could often be rebuilt in little more time than it took for populations to recover from epidemics. For instance, the water-control systems throughout China's Yangzi Valley were rebuilt fairly quickly once stability returned after years of warfare, plague, depression, and depopulation in the seventeenth century[62] and within just a few years after comparable absolute (though not proportional) levels of destruction in the mid-nineteenth century.[63] And floods and earthquakes are presumably no more likely to destroy a society's basic fabric than is plague or drought. Thus, unless basic social order suffered more from warfare in Asia than it did in Europe—a hard case to make given the frequency of war in early modern Europe, its much lower incidence in at least China and Japan, and the limited extent of physical destruction in most southeast Asian wars[64]—the argument that Europe benefited from lesser depreciation of its capital becomes very shaky. (In a later work, Jones shifts his

[61] Abu-Lughod 1989: 193–97.   [62] Will 1980; Perdue 1987: 211–19.
[63] Bernhardt 1992: 129–34.   [64] Reid 1988a: 121–28.

emphasis from differences in actual physical destruction to a claim that the legacy of the Mongol era saddled Asia with particularly conservative regimes, a claim we will deal with later.[65]) And finally, Jones gives us no reason to think that it was necessarily more burdensome to replace ruined physical capital than to replace the human capital that Europe seems to have lost at least as rapidly as China, Japan, and perhaps Southeast Asia.

Nor is there any sign that Europe's weavers, farmers, or other workers were significantly more productive than their peers in various parts of Eurasia—as they should have been if they had either more or better capital. We have already seen that they do not appear to have lived longer or better—a point not only significant in itself, but because it suggests that in competition between European and Asian goods, European manufacturers were not disadvantaged by paying higher *real* wages. So had their workers been more productive, they should have been able to sell their products in Asian markets. But as all accounts agree, European merchants had far more difficulty selling their goods in Asia than in finding markets at home for Asian goods, both for elite and mass consumption. (It is possible that despite eating just as well, Asians had less of other goods than did Europeans, but we shall see in chapter 3 that the Chinese and Japanese probably did as well.) True, the largest single source of Asian manufactured exports to Europe—the Indian subcontinent—was also one large Asian region for which many scholars believe that workers' living standards were unusually low (as much because of very unequal income distribution as because of actual levels of per capita production, as we shall see in chapter 3). But Chinese textiles and other goods also found a significant Euro-American market (and not only among the rich) throughout the eighteenth and much of the nineteenth centuries.[66]

What about Technology?

By 1850, at least northwest Europe already had a marked technological advantage over the rest of the Old World, and this cannot be entirely a nineteenth-century creation. But as the previous sections make clear, it seems unlikely that eighteenth-century Europeans were, on the whole, more productive than, say, Chinese or Japanese; and that means we need to carefully circumscribe claims of overall European "technological superiority" circa 1750 and target our explanations accordingly. The results admit the importance of cultural and institutional factors that helped spread a "scientific culture" but leave open, pending further research, how unique this culture was. They also tend to minimize the role of more specifically politico-economic factors (from patent law

[65] Jones 1988: 130–46, especially 145–46.

[66] Hao 1986: 28; Morse 1966: II: 61, 180, 256, 266, 322, on the size of the American market in particular, and on the relatively modest price of the cloth.

to near-constant war-making to the high cost of British labor) highlighted by many other scholars. Meanwhile, such results increase the prominence of knowledge gained overseas for certain crucial technologies and of a set of "permissive factors" related to geography and resource availability.

If Europeans were, as I have argued, not ahead in overall productivity in 1750, then it is unlikely that the average level of technology they deployed was superior; but it is more plausible that the best available technologies deployed anywhere in Europe (mostly in Britain, the United Provinces, and parts of France) for various important sectors were already the world's best. The spread of those technologies over the next century would have then narrowed the gap between Europe's best and average technologies and created much of the productivity advantage we see by 1850. (Clearly, for instance, Newtonian mechanics allowed Europeans in 1750 to devise some pumps and canal locks better than any in existence elsewhere, but the ubiquity of, say, Chinese canals probably gave them a continued edge in the average degree to which they had exploited the possibilities of inland waterways until somewhat later.) And even if one insists on the alternate position—that all of Europe's advantage in 1850 sprang from post-1750 inventions—one would want to ask what basis existed for this sudden burst of inventiveness.

Much of the credit for both the accelerated diffusion of best practices after 1750 and the burst of new innovations must go to elements of the "scientific culture" that Margaret Jacob and others have seen emerging, especially in England, in the 150 years before 1750: increased literacy and printing, the spread of scientific societies, relatively accessible public lectures, and so on. Behind these phenomena stood a strong sense that the investigation of a mechanical nature was to be encouraged, because it offered both material benefits to the individual and a socially stabilizing alternative to two other epistemologies with political implications: dogmatic "priestcraft" and/or popular assertiveness based on intuitive, revealed, or magical knowledge of a living nature, God, and social order.[67] Some parts of this configuration were indeed unique to northwest Europe, but not all of them were. It is worth noting, for instance, that Chinese interest in the physical sciences and mathematics increased markedly in the seventeenth century, especially afer the Manchu conquest in 1644[68] and that publishers found that medical books were a particularly good way to sell lots of books, fulfill a commitment to improve the world through their work, and steer clear of the post-conquest minefields of political controversy.[69] More generally, the European configuration, however fruitful it proved, did not represent the only path to technological progress. Other areas still led or

---

[67] See especially Jacob 1988: 27–30, 58–59, 64, 77, 81–82, 89, 110, 123, 150–51, 158, 209, 223.

[68] See, for instance, Henderson 1984; Kawata 1979.

[69] Widmer 1996: 95–99, 103–4, 107–8, 113–15.

stayed even in various technologies and continued their own patterns of both invention and diffusion.

In many areas, various non-European societies remained ahead. Irrigation, which we have already mentioned, was perhaps the most obvious; and in many other agricultural technologies, too, Europe lagged behind China, India, Japan, and parts of Southeast Asia. A Welsh agricultural improvement society founded in 1753 took this as a truism, dedicating itself to bringing closer the day in which Wales might be "as flourishing as China."[70] Indeed, once we have seen that life expectancies were similar—making it unlikely that Europeans were vastly better nourished—the huge differences in population densities between Europe and east Asia stand as impressive testimony to the size of that difference.[71] To this we might add the ability of Chinese and Japanese agriculture to also keep up (as European agriculture stopped doing after 1800) with soaring demand for textile fibers and evidence (to be discussed in chapter 5) that even relatively backward North China was doing better at conserving the fertility of its soil better than, say, England or France. As we shall see later, Europeans groping for ways to combat deforestation and soil degradation in their tropical colonies near the end of the eighteenth century found much to learn in both India and China, but they did not apply the lessons at home in any systematic way until well into the nineteenth century. Take away the enormous amounts of extra land that Europe gained across the Atlantic (through luck, smallpox, and violence, as well as navigational and commercial skills) and it is easy to imagine Europe's marked technological backwardness in the largest sector of eighteenth-century economies having a significance as great as whatever advantages it had in other sectors.

There were also other sectors in which late eighteenth-century Europeans still had catching up to do. In many areas of textile weaving and dyeing, western Europeans were still working on imitating Indian and Chinese processes; the same was true of manufacturing porcelain. As late as 1827 and 1842, two separate British observers claimed that Indian bar iron was as good or better than English iron, and the price quoted for 1829 was less than half that of English iron in England.[72] Various parts of Africa also produced large amounts

[70] Bayly 1989: 80–81.

[71] The difference between the population densities supported by Shandong and the Netherlands, discussed in note 7 above, is a particularly interesting example, since irrigation was not a significant factor in Shandong agriculture. On Chinese agricultural technology generally, see Bray 1984. For a non-Chinese example (which does involve irrigation) consider the fact that in the Kaveri delta in South India, cultivators gave up about 94 percent of their output, but survived (Van Schendel 1991: 44). This suggests that one farmer could feed sixteen people (though probably not very well)—suggesting that productivity per worker, not just per acre, could be dramatically higher in parts of Asia than anything found in Europe.

[72] On iron, see Dharampal 1971: 243–44, 246–47, 260; for English iron prices (and conversion from pig iron to bar iron), see Deane and Cole 1962: 222n. 5, 223 n. 1. On weaving and dyeing, see Mitra 1978: 13.

of iron and steel that were of a quality at least as good as anything available in early modern Europe, though shortages of wood (for fuel) limited production to certain areas and could make iron quite expensive in areas distant from the forests.[73] Medicine was probably not terribly effective anywhere in the world, but east (and probably southeast) Asian cities were far ahead in crucial matters of public health, such as sanitation and the provision of clean water.[74] One of the few important medical advances of the seventeenth and eighteenth centuries—smallpox prevention—seems to have been developed independently in Europe, China, and India.[75] Recent studies have suggested that at least in the area of maternal and infant health, Qing medicine—popular knowledge of which seems to have been spreading rapidly—remained superior to its European counterpart, despite making (as far as we know) no basic conceptual breakthroughs comparable to Harvey's work on circulation.[76] The list could go on much further.

Overall, then, arguments that Europe in 1750 already enjoyed a unique level of technological sophistication need significant qualification. Even in the generation and use of energy—probably Europe's most important advantage in the nineteenth century (as I will argue later)—the situation was much less clear a hundred years earlier. Smil estimates that energy use per capita was probably comparable in China and *western* Europe circa 1700.[77] And though the efficiency of individual power-generating machines (from waterwheels to—soon—steam engines) was probably one of Europe's greatest areas of advantage, China had an equally marked advantage in the efficiency of its stoves, both for cooking and heating.[78]

In retrospect, it is clear that given Europe's nineteenth-century switch to available and abundant fossil fuels, European advances in finding ways to use heat had a greater revolutionary potential than China's edge in capturing heat efficiently—but only in retrospect, and only with the advantage of favorably located coal. Had fuel shortages slowed Europe's industrial growth and a breakthrough occurred elsewhere first, the wastefulness of European hearths might not appear as a minor "exception" to a story of growing technical superiority but as a prime example of technological weakness that had held this area back. Or had the New World not provided enormous amounts of textile fibers, European precocity in mechanizing spinning and weaving might seem more like interesting curiosities than the centerpiece of a great transformation, and we might be invoking the low level of per-acre agricultural yields in Europe as a sign of serious technological weaknesses that necessitated keeping

---

[73] Thornton 1992: 45–48.

[74] See Hanley 1997: 104–5, 110–11, 119–20; Reid 1988a: 38.

[75] Dharampal 1971: 141–64 on India; Du Jiaji 1994: 154–69 on China.

[76] Xiong 1995 on infant and maternal care; Unschuld 1986: 183–97; Widmer 1996: 95–115, and Bray 1997: 311 on the popularization of printed medical works.

[77] Smil 1994: 234.   [78] See, e.g., Anderson 1988: 154.

most land in food crops, and thus had caused these clever but nonetheless insufficient inventions to languish until they were imitated elsewhere.

We will return to the crucial examples of steam and spinning—and their relationship to resource windfalls—near the end of this chapter. The point to emphasize for now is that non-European societies retained significant techno- logical advantages in many areas even in the late eighteenth century, and it was not inevitable that they would turn out to seem relatively unimportant in the long run. Nor, even once European technology began to advance faster and on a broader front, was it inevitable that this would overcome remaining weak- nesses in land management, conservation, and market extension, or do so soon enough so that development would not be directed, with lasting effects, along paths requiring precisely the sorts of labor-intensive solutions found in east Asia and a few atypical parts of western Europe (such as Denmark).

Nor should we assume that these areas of non-European advantage were merely the lingering effects of once great, but now stagnant, traditions. While eighteenth-century Asia produced none of what Joel Mokyr calls "macro- inventions"—radical new ideas that suddenly alter production possibilities all by themselves—Europe produced few of these during the period from 1500 to 1750, and even during the years usually defined as the Industrial Revolution (1750–1830).[79] Meanwhile, smaller technical improvements of various sorts continued to be made in many different geographic and technological areas. European dyes that briefly enjoyed a strong vogue in China were then imitated by native innovators,[80] just as happened with many Asian products in Europe. In the seventeenth century, somebody discovered that a certain kind of cellar would trap enough humidity to allow cotton-spinning during the many dry months in cotton-growing North China; this innovation spread like wildfire over the next hundred-plus years, allowing a region with a population far ex- ceeding that of any European country to produce its own textiles and greatly reduce seasonal unemployment. Just as it is only the rise of fossil fuels (which made getting the most out of every ounce of combustible material much less important than before) that made the efficiency of Chinese stoves a footnote rather than a crucial fact, it is only because we know that within another cen- tury home-based textile production of any sort would come to seem "back- ward" that these cellars do not appear as a simple but vital technical break- through, disseminated at an impressive rate.[81]

The example of spinning cellars is also revealing because though we know extremely little about how this innovation was disseminated, we know it was. Though the design was simple, the people who needed to learn about it were among the poorest, most dispersed, and least literate members of society. That this sort of diffusion could occur fairly rapidly over a large area with the mech- anism being invisible to us should make us cautious about asserting that in the

[79] Mokyr 1990: 13, 57, 83.   [80] Greenberg 1951: 87.   [81] Bray 1997: 217–20.

absence of scientific societies and Newtonian clergymen, China (and other societies) lacked adequate means for spreading new and useful knowledge. At this point, we know relatively little even about scientific discussions among the elite, and, as Benjamin Elman and others have shown, these discussions were far livelier in the eighteenth century than we have generally supposed.[82] Granted, the discussion proceeded mostly in classical Chinese and largely by the exchange of letters rather than in more institutionalized settings, but these letters were not really private documents and the discussions in them were wide-ranging, sophisticated, and often quite practical. Without organized scientific societies, the popularization of complex findings was likely to be slower than it was in England or Holland and might well have made cross-pollination between elite science and artisanal knowledge more difficult. But much remains to be learned about the possible contribution of vernacular publications in science and technology, especially now that we have become aware of a lively trade in vernacular medical texts (admittedly a more prestigious subject than other kinds of science or technology). Moreover, unlike in Europe, where these formal scientific societies were often essential to protecting science from a hostile established church, in China there was no such powerful and hostile body, and it is not clear why the particular kinds of institutions that developed in Europe should have been the sine qua non of scientific or technological progress everywhere. So rather than search for reasons why Chinese science and technology "stagnated" in general—which they did not do—we need to look at why the paths on which they continued to progress did not revolutionize the Chinese economy. By the same token, while giving full credit to the institutions that helped European science and technology advance unusually rapidly and on a broad front, we also need to think about which particular paths of development proved economically critical and look for factors that allowed them to be so. To borrow Joel Mokyr's metaphor (though with a different aim) we must compare not only the motors of technological change, but also the steering wheels—and the terrains over which different societies steered.

Not only did western Europe not lead in all areas of technology, but of the areas in which they did lead, only some had long-term importance. For instance, western Europeans had the world's most efficient waterwheels by this time,[83] but this alone did not give the European industries that used water power a competitive edge capable of overcoming high transport costs (or high costs in other aspects of production) and conquering markets elsewhere. And at any rate, this was an advantage that could be deployed at only a limited number of sites and could not be expanded indefinitely even at those sites. The same was true of many, many other technologies, whether created in Europe or elsewhere.

[82] Elman 1990: 79–85.   [83] Smil 1994: 107.

Later in this chapter, I will argue that the most important innovations for creating sustained growth were land-saving ones in one way or another, particularly those associated with fossil fuels, which reduced reliance on forests for energy. But it has been far more common to argue that the crucial phenomenon was the rise of a *labor*-saving emphasis in European technological innovation. The common argument is that economic differences (principally the fact that western European laborers were free and allegedly received relatively high wages) caused Europeans (or in some versions of the argument, Britons) to focus their attention on labor-saving innovations, while other societies saw little or no need to economize on labor. (The reliance of this argument on Hajnal's demographic argument and/or Brenner's institutional one, both discussed above, should be fairly clear.) The unique western European need to cut down on the use of expensive labor, so the story goes, ultimately led to machinery, modern industry, and vastly improved per capita productivity and living standards, while other societies were more interested in looking for innovations that economized on land, capital, or some specific scarce material. Thus, Europeans were not necessarily more creative, but high wage costs steered their efforts in the one direction that led to a real transformation. Versions of this argument have been put forward by scholars as diverse as J. B. Habbakuk (Britain versus continental Europe), Mark Elvin (China versus Europe), David Washbrook (India versus Europe), and Andre Gunder Frank (Asia generally versus Europe);[84] and it dovetails with the common claim that Europe was already richer than the rest of the world before industrialization. But the argument does not work, except perhaps in one or two specific industries.

First there are empirical problems. As we have seen in the first half of this chapter, it seems likely that average incomes in Japan, China, and parts of southeast Asia were comparable to (or higher than) those in western Europe even in the late eighteenth century. If this is true, then the case that European manufacturers faced higher wage costs would have to rest on one of two possibilities. It is conceivable that the distribution of income could have been more equal in western Europe (or at least Britain, if one accepts that the Industrial Revolution began there), so that workers were receiving a larger share of a comparable average per capita income than workers elsewhere. Alternatively, a society could have had a system of unfree labor such that even though workers received fairly high aggregate payment for working, they received no incremental payment for working harder and could not seek other work if their patrons have no productive work for them to do. In such a scenario, despite what appear to be high wages, it would make more sense for elites to try to squeeze more hours of labor out of their subordinates than to invest in labor-saving technology.

[84] Elvin 1973; Frank 1998; Habbakuk 1962; Washbrook 1988.

This latter scenario may well describe the situation in certain parts of southeast Asia, where highly skilled artisans, though scarce enough that they were often well rewarded for their work, were bound to aristocratic patrons who "protected" them and monopolized their output.[85] It may apply to some parts of India as well; but formally free or semi-free (if often poorly paid) artisans seem to have been more common there, at least until British rulers legislated against various techniques weavers had used to maintain autonomy vis à vis those who advanced them their working capital.[86] And such a model has little relevance for most Chinese artisans even in the 1400s, and virtually none once the system of government-designated hereditary artisans collapsed in the 1500s. As we shall see in the next chapter, Chinese labor may well have been "freer" than early modern European labor; it was certainly not much less so. The bound-labor scenario might at first seem more relevant to Tokugawa Japan, in which various occupational statuses, restrictions on mobility, and hereditary patron-client relationships were supposedly fixed by edict; but as we shall see in the next chapter, the reality was very different from the statute books.

The argument about very cheap wage labor is knottier. In chapter 3 we shall see some evidence that the distribution of income in Qing China and Tokugawa Japan was actually more equal than that in western Europe in general and late eighteenth-century Britain in particular. (For India, on the other hand, the bulk of the anecdotal evidence presented in chapter 3 suggests that income distribution *was* more unequal than it was in Europe; quantitative evidence is scarce, with some pointing in each direction.) However, even the east Asian evidence is far from conclusive and mostly suggests that the very top of society claimed no more of national income in China and Japan than Europe's elite did; China and Japan could nonetheless have had a larger layer of desperately poor people than western Europe did, who pushed unskilled wages down to a level significantly below those in Europe. Although I see no particular reason to think that this was the case—and the anecdotal testimony of most Europeans visiting east Asia before 1840 suggests the opposite[87]—the possibility cannot be dismissed.

Moreover, there is a distinct but related—and more likely—scenario that would reconcile high living standards in Chinese and Japanese cores with wage bills lower than those confronting at least Dutch and English employers. Despite the rural location of much Dutch and English industry in the mid-seventeenth and eighteenth centuries, there is strong evidence that by this time relatively few workers in those countries moved seasonally between farm and

---

[85] Reid 1989: 61, 69–71; Reid 1988a: 135.

[86] Mitra 1978: 37–41; Hossain 1979: 324–38; Arasaratnam 1980: 259–60, 263, 265, 268, 272, 278.

[87] See, for instance, Staunton 1799: II: 138.

non-farm labor.[88] Before this period, many industrial laborers had worked in agriculture at peak season, at least in the Netherlands, and earned relatively high wages for doing so. As the agricultural and industrial labor markets became more separated, day wages had to rise to enable what were now less fully employed workers to survive; such a wage increase indeed occurred, but at the price of increased unemployment.[89] By contrast, many Chinese and Japanese handicraft workers were almost certainly less fully detached from agriculture; thus at least in theory, they could earn less for their weaving, spinning, or tile-making and still enjoy a standard of living as high or higher than their Dutch and English counterparts. Such a scenario is plausible, though far from established, and if correct, it would reconcile our other findings with a particularly strong incentive for at least some European employers to find ways to use less labor. (It would also mean that English employers would have had less trouble keeping their factories going all year-round than employers whose workers also farmed. Thus they would have more incentive to invest in centralized plant and equipment.) European employers also faced the problem of relatively high food prices, which meant that even if they did not have to pay higher real wages, they did pay higher cash wages than many, if not all, of their Asian competitors.[90]

But even if we grant provisionally the argument that western European wages were higher than any Asian ones, there are problems with inferring that this stimulated the technological changes of the Industrial Revolution. Indeed, under early modern conditions, high wages could as easily discourage technological innovation in general as it could encourage labor-saving inventions. Joel Mokyr suggests this seemingly paradoxical conclusion based on a model that seems fairly close to eighteenth-century realities.[91] Assume, he says, that new technology must be embodied in new capital equipment, which must be paid for. Assume further that wages make up the bulk of most manufacturers' costs and that there are few *ex ante* differences in technology large enough to give a firm or country with a higher wage bill lower total production costs for a particular product. Thus, those with higher wage bills will generally have lower profits than their competition. If—as was also generally true until well into the nineteenth century—bank financing for the purchase of new capital equipment is either nonexistent or, to the slight extent that it exists, dependent on a firm's earnings, then any equipment embodying new technology will

---

[88] "Relatively few" is, of course, a relative term. While DeVries and Allen, comparing the Netherlands and England to other parts of western Europe and to earlier periods, are struck by how little workers moved between proto-industry and agriculture according to the season, Sokoloff and Dollar 1997, comparing England to the United States, are struck by how *many* English people worked part-time in both agriculture and industry, even in the late nineteenth century. We will return to the U.S. example and its implications in chapter 6.

[89] DeVries 1994a: 57–62, Allen, cited in Postel-Vinay 1994: 72.

[90] Parthasarathi 1998: 101–2.   [91] Mokyr 1991: 177–81.

have to be financed out of retained earnings—and those with higher wages will be less able to do that. Thus, rather than stimulating labor-saving technical innovations, a high wage bill may just as plausibly discourage any sort of new technology. And though this model may seem counterintuitive today, it appears to work for earlier eras: it has been used, for instance, to help explain why the very sophisticated and very high-wage Dutch economy was remarkably late to adopt mechanized industry.

Furthermore, though the industrialization of the last two-hundred years has generally been labor saving and capital demanding, it is anachronistic to assume that this was always the reason for the major innovations. The application of coal and steam power to all sorts of processes eventually led to enormous labor savings, but the eighteenth-century innovations that made coal usable in making iron, glass, beer, and so on were aimed at saving money on fuel (coal was cheaper than wood), not at saving labor; and the steam engines that pumped water out of coal mines did not substitute for men doing the same work so much as they simply made it possible to exploit certain mines that no number of men could otherwise have used. Other developments in glass-blowing, iron-making, and so on were not particularly concerned with saving on any factor of production—they were concerned with making a higher-quality product. If the makers of the Industrial Revolution were primarily economizing on expensive labor, they were unaware of it. In a study of eighteenth-century English patentees, Christine MacLeod finds that most declared the goals of their innovation to be either improving the quality of the product or saving on *capital* (a goal that makes more sense when we remember that unlike post-1870 technological change, the first one hundred years of the Industrial Revolution mostly came embodied in relatively cheap capital goods); only 3.7 percent cited saving on labor as a goal.[92] And if inventors were not particularly intent on saving labor, those who judged their inventions were even less so; as late as the 1720s, it apparently counted against a patent applicant if he said that his machine saved labor.[93] The long-run results of change were no doubt labor saving; but for an argument that high wages focused efforts in a particular direction, conscious motivations would seem to be the heart of the matter.

And finally, since most of the capital goods involved were relatively low-cost ones themselves, even a producer who enjoyed a fairly low wage scale would have had an incentive to try them; indeed, it has been hard to show that low wage costs inhibit the adoption of labor-saving technology, even in our own age of much more expensive capital goods.[94] (Such arguments sometimes have sometimes held up where the differences in labor costs are vast—e.g., contemporary Pakistan and Germany—but not where the wage differentials were real but not huge—e.g., Victorian Britain versus the United States. And

---

[92] MacLeod 1988: 158–81.   [93] Jacob 1988: 92–93.   [94] Mokyr 1990: 166.

immense wage differentials are hard to find before the mid-nineteenth century, since differences in national wealth were not nearly what they are today.[95]) If pre-nineteenth-century entrepreneurs were profit maximizing then the only innovations they should have passed up because of cheap labor were ones that provided only marginal labor savings anyway; to pass up something like cotton-spinning on these grounds alone, a manufacturer would have had to enjoy virtually costless labor. In chapter 2 we will see various examples of Chinese farmers spending money in order to save themselves labor, even though Mark Elvin and other proponents of the wage incentive argument would claim that Chinese manufacturers ignored labor-saving devices because Chinese labor (unlike European labor) was so cheap.

But the high wages hypothesis might still be relevant for one crucial sector: cotton textiles, for which both Braudel and Frank assert its importance.[96] Here there was very little ambiguity about what innovations in spinning did: they cut, perhaps by over 90 percent, the amount of labor needed to spin a given amount of yarn.[97] And while such enormous savings should have been attractive to employers paying virtually any wage rates, they may well have been particularly attractive to English makers of cotton textiles, who faced much higher nominal wage bills than the Indian producers with whom they competed for various price-sensitive markets (in west Africa, the Middle East, and especially the New World, where slaves wore the cheapest cottons). The textiles that China exported in this period (and increasingly, even the ones that Jiangnan, China's leading textile region, sold in other parts of China) were fairly high quality and did not compete primarily on price;[98] but British cotton manufacturers could not possibly compete against Indian cottons in the Middle East, Africa, and the New World, unless they cut their wage bills.

Of course, British textile producers could easily have failed do so and lost this battle with Indian producers; necessity does not always yield invention. And for Britain *as a whole* the issue of whether its textiles makers would conquer these markets need not have seemed crucial *ex ante*, since the East India Company marketed their rivals' goods: even though these textile markets were quite strategic, any "necessity" operating here was a necessity for the textile producers themselves, not for "England." (The most strategic of these markets was west Africa, since a ready supply of desired textiles was essential for buying slaves there. But at least some of the cloth needed there was expensive, high-quality material, and British slave traders were less concerned with the price of this cloth than with getting enough of it—first from India and only later from the mother country.[99])

---

[95] Lazonick 1981: 491–516; Bairoch 1975: 3–17 on the scale of differences in national income circa 1800 and the much larger gaps that exist today.

[96] Braudel 1982: 522, 575; Frank 1998: 289–91.

[97] Chapman, cited in Mokyr 1990: 98–99.

[98] Li Bozhong 1998: 108.   [99] H. Klein 1990: 291–93.

So even here, the "high wage/necessity" argument faces problems. Nonetheless, in this restricted but important case, it may well have some merit; it at least suggests how the patterns of *world* textile trade and the ways in which English manufacturers competed against Bengal in particular—which was both a low-wage economy (or at least a low cash-wage economy) to start with and one in which the East India Company used increasing amounts of violence to enforce below-market prices for textiles after 1757[100]—may have intensified the search for mechanized spinning and weaving. Furthermore, it does illustrate, among other things, how important it is to look for explanations of particular innovations, rather than of "industrialization" in general, to root those explanations in the specifics of the relevant industries and in what people at the time thought certain innovations could accomplish—while also trying to choose examples that were critical to the broader phenomenon of emerging European supremacy.

Armed with knowledge of how the Industrial Revolution did happen, one is tempted to look for European advantages connected to its two most important and dynamic sectors: textiles and the coal/steam/iron complex, especially the latter. And one does find some relevant European advantages, but often in surprising places.

In textiles, the Chinese had long had machines that differed in just one crucial detail from both Hargreaves's spinning jenny and Kay's flying shuttle.[101] Thus, one could hardly say that western Europe had any significant lead in technology for this sector until those inventions were actually made. Nor can one conclude that just because the last piece needed in both cases seems simple in retrospect, its absence shows that technological innovation in China stopped altogether. Much of eighteenth-century European technology was almost developed 150 years earlier, but the intervening wait does not indicate technological "stagnation";[102] we must remember that what now seems obvious was often anything but obvious beforehand.

Moreover, English textile innovations could easily also have become footnotes to history rather than major milestones. At the time that the British pioneered major improvements in cotton-spinning, cotton was a minor fabric in Europe; the mechanization of flax-spinning and wool-spinning took significantly longer. And, as we shall see in chapter 5, there were serious ecological and social obstacles to the further expansion of either wool or flax production in Europe. Cotton came from abroad and was available only in fairly limited quantities throughout most of the eighteenth century; indeed, the increased demand for raw cotton that the new spinning technology created

---

[100] See Mitra 1978: 46–47, 51, 63–66, 75–92, 113–15, 126–27, 14–15; for wage comparisons, see Chaudhuri 1978: 157, 273.

[101] See, e.g., Mokyr, 1990: 221.

[102] E.g., Hobsbawm 1975: 38.

produced very sharp price rises, which would have greatly limited the usefulness of this technology without the rise of cotton-growing in the American
South.[103]

This problem can be phrased in a more general way. Histories of technology
often imagine one breakthrough creating a "bottleneck" that concentrates efforts on a specific problem and so leads to another breakthrough, as when
advances in weaving created incentives to speed up spinning. But such bottlenecks are just as often addressed by allocating more resources, without any
change in techniques, and the longer that process of reallocation of resources
continues, the less incentive remains to find a technological solution. (A good
example is the massive increase in the number of coal miners in the late nineteenth century, as the uses of fossil fuels for all sorts of processes soared without much change in the productivity of mining itself.)[104] In the case of mechanized textile production, a bottleneck was created in the growing of cotton (and
other fibers), which required the application of more land and more labor.

As we shall see in chapters 5 and 6, it is unlikely that the necessary land
to relieve this bottleneck could have been found in Europe. (Though sheep-
raising did expand in Poland and Russia,[105] it was nowhere near enough, and
cotton production remained minimal.) Meanwhile, the labor that was applied
to this bottleneck was largely that of African slaves: to the extent that European labor was applied to this bottleneck, it was labor used in sailing, trading,
coercing, and manufacturing (of goods swapped for slaves in Africa and for
the cotton itself). As chapter 6 will show, that particular way of reallocating
labor to solve this bottleneck was far more advantageous to Europe in the long
run than it would have been to increase the agricultural labor force in order to
grow more fiber at home, even if the land to do that had been available. (China
and Japan both went this route, squeezing more food and fuel out of some land
in labor-intensive ways while converting some lands from both forest and food
crops to fiber-growing, but they did so at considerable long-run cost.) And
while the case of cotton is unusually clear-cut, various other growing industries, and the rising population's demand for food, also created bottlenecks that
were ultimately solved without using more European land or putting more
labor onto that land. While Parthasarathi sees industrialization as in part Britain's way of escaping a vicious cycle of low per-acre yields⇒ costly food⇒
high cash wages⇒ competitive difficulties,[106] it is well to remember that industrialization alone could not solve the problem that allegedly induced the
technological gains in industry unless it could also meet the agricultural needs
of industries and workers. And since, as we will see, British yields per acre did

---

[103] See, for instance, Bruchey 1967: table 2-A (unpaginated).
[104] W. Parker 1984: 38; Mokyr 1985a: 107–8.
[105] Gunst 1989: 73–74.
[106] Parthasarathi 1998: 107.

not rise much between 1750 and 1850, that solution had to involve trading partners who could bring large amounts of additional land into play.

But still more basically, it is quite possible to imagine a huge productivity increase in cotton-spinning and weaving that did not lead to a fundamental break with the ecological constraints of the eighteenth century. The fiber needed for textiles still needed land, and competition for land among Malthus's four necessities—food, fuel, fiber, and building materials—was growing ever more intense in much of eighteenth-century Europe. As long as food and fuel prices rose faster than wages,[107] as they did in most of eighteenth-century Europe, it is hard to see how demand for textiles could grow indefinitely—even with weaving and spinning costs falling—and the new textile technology had no clear application to other sectors. These developments in cotton textile production could easily have led to just an intensification of processes (to be discussed further in chapter 2) that the long-standing growth of rural "handicraft industries" already represented—processes that included accelerating population growth, increased pressure on the land, greater labor intensity, stagnant real wages, and probably an eventual ecological dead end rather than a breakthrough.

Eighteenth-century western Europe faced serious ecological pressures (which will be discussed much more thoroughly in chapter 5). Briefly, the demographic and economic expansions of the "long sixteenth" and eighteenth centuries (especially the second half of the latter) led to massive deforestation in western Europe, with levels of forest cover and per capita wood supplies falling below even those in densely populated China, not to mention India. And deforestation brought other problems in its wake. Archaeological evidence from France and Germany suggests that the eighteenth century was one of the two worst in history for soil erosion; documentary evidence confirms this and adds several other deforested areas, which experienced massive dust storms, declining yields, and other signs of serious ecological stress.[108] Studies of erosion in modern times suggest that it tends to be the most visible sign of a much broader set of soil problems.[109] The late eighteenth century also witnessed an unusual weather pattern known as the "European monsoon"—a pattern in which unusually long droughts alternated with brief, unusually violent rains. When such rainfall came it was both unusually erosive and of little use to crops, especially since Europeans (unlike, say, Indians) did not have massive irrigation systems to store and channel it. It is not clear what caused this climatic episode, but it appears more often in badly deforested areas,[110] since trees moderate the seasonality of local rainfall patterns. One of the few temperate zone areas that has such a "monsoon" climate today is badly deforested

---

[107] Goldstone 1991: 186; Labrousse (1984): 343, 346–47.

[108] Blaikie and Brookfield 1987: 129–40, especially 138; Kjaergaard 1994: 18–22. For more details, see chapter 5.

[109] Blaikie and Brookfield 1987: 139.   [110] Ibid., 133.

North China.[111] (North China is also much further south, and thus closer to tropical pressure systems, than is northern Europe.)

These ecological pressures did not add up to a Malthusian *crisis*, in which European living standards were about to collapse. On the contrary, they were brought about in some areas by rising levels of per capita consumption as well as population growth. But they did, as we shall see, pose substantial impediments to further growth. Yet in the nineteenth century, while European population and per capita consumption accelerated, ecological variables stabilized. Western Europe's forest cover stabilized some time between 1800 and 1850, after four hundred years of decline, and even increased throughout the nineteenth century in Britain, France, Germany, and Belgium;[112] erosion decreased and soil fertility stabilized or even improved; and the European "monsoon" disappeared and a more typical rainfall pattern returned.[113]

Clearly, then, a big part of the European achievement in the Industrial Revolution was to escape a long-standing pattern in which all growth placed significant incremental demands on the land. And with a few exceptions (such as Denmark), this achievement did not rely on using large amounts of additional labor to make an acre yield more while protecting its fertility (in the manner famously described by Esther Boserup); in the late nineteenth century, labor inputs per acre even fell substantially. Yet the breakthroughs in chemistry that today allow capital to substitute for land (and labor) to an astonishing degree (above all through using synthetic fertilizer and through making synthetic materials that are not grown at all) belong to the very late nineteenth and twentieth centuries. How, then, did sustained European growth become ecologically sustainable?

To understand how self-sustaining growth became possible, one must look, as E. A. Wrigley has argued, for developments that eased the pressures on the land. Wrigley emphasizes increased use of coal, which yielded far more power per unit of surface than wood ever could.[114] To this I would add the adoption of New World food crops, particularly the potato, which yielded what for Europe were unprecedented amounts of calories per acre; improvements in ecological understanding and land (especially forest) management which, as Richard Grove has shown, owed much to colonial experiences; and the enormous resources gained by applying existing techniques to vast new territories overseas.

The last of these developments was not principally technological and will be the focus of chapter 6; for now suffice it to say that the New World yielded both land-intensive products (cotton, sugar, and later grain, timber, meat, and wool) and land-restoring products such as guano. The potato, ecological

[111] Chao 1973: 22–25, 30–31.

[112] M. Williams 1990: 181. For some specific countries, see Darby 1956: 203–4 and compare with Cooper 1985: 139n. 2 (France) and M. Williams 1990: 181 (Germany).

[113] Blaikie and Brookfield 1987: 132–33.   [114] Wrigley 1988: 80–81.

learning, and coal are part of this chapter's technology story, as is the general setting that made them so important.

The potato produced far more calories per acre than existing European crops. The potato was also adopted in eighteenth-century China and Japan, but almost exclusively as a crop for the highlands, since rice already produced enormous amounts of food per lowland acre. In Europe, where grain yields were much lower (both per acre and relative to seed), the potato also conquered the lowlands in such densely populated areas as Ireland and Belgium (replacing 40 percent of cereal calories in Flanders by 1791)[115] and, somewhat later, in much of central and eastern Europe.

A less widely known factor was, like the potato, a technological advance: in the nineteenth century, Europeans began to apply principles of scientific conservation to their forests and to understand the importance for the ecosystem as a whole of protecting trees. The path to this particular breakthrough has been carefully traced by Richard Grove. Interestingly, although this advance owed much to the application of European science—Newtonian mechanics played an important role in understanding how trees recycled water and affected local climates—some ideas popular in Europe were hindrances: even in the early nineteenth century, many European doctors and botanists blamed forests for disease-bearing "miasmas" and recommended clear-cutting woods as a public health measure.[116]

The solidification of European ecological understanding—just in time, it would appear, to help stabilize northwestern Europe[117] before it suffered the fate of parts of the Mediterranean, or even northern China—was related to empire in two crucial ways. First of all, it was on tropical islands that Europeans were able to observe the relationships among changing land use, climate (especially desiccation), and changes in soil quality unfolding at a speed that resolved debates that they could not resolve theoretically; and it was in newly colonized parts of India (where European demand and changes in property rights produced rapid shifts in land use) that they began to see that the same dynamics could affect a continental land mass, too. Moreover, the colonial botanists, surgeons, and officials (often the same people) who worked out these relationships learned an enormous amount about how to manage ecosystems from south Chinese and especially south Indian practices, which were in many ways more advanced than their own. (Japanese practices may have been still better, but they were much less accessible to curious foreigners.)[118] Fi-

---

[115] Braudel 1981: 170.   [116] Grove 1995: 408.

[117] As we shall see in chapter 5, continental western Europe was for the most part still better forested than Britain but suffered from more serious fuel shortages and more rapidly rising wood prices in the eighteenth century because most areas lacked any equivalent to Britain's growing use of coal.

[118] On European borrowing from Indian ideas and practices (which Grove argues were "more important . . . than any set of ideas imported from outside India" (382), at least before 1857, see

nally, the much weaker property rights in the colonies and the relative independence of colonial regimes from local property owners allowed British, French, and Dutch colonial officials to actually experiment with environmental regulation schemes, some of them quite radical, in a way they could not have done back home. This knowledge from overseas, once brought to Europe (and the United States) in the nineteenth century, became the basis for forestry services, for how-to books on using trees to help maintain or improve arable land, and so on.[119] Thus, empire helped Europe erase its technological disadvantage in agro-forestry (through the potato, through ecology, and through numerous important influences on botany[120]), providing crucial imports of knowledge along with the imports of resources that we will discuss later.

There was, however, no extra-European dimension in the last of our great land-saving technological shifts: the increasing use of coal (especially in Britain) both to replace fuel wood and as the basis for whole new processes.

Coal was central to earlier views of the Industrial Revolution. Only cotton, iron, steel, and railways got comparable attention, and except for cotton, these other main sectors depended on coal. But more recently, coal has often been deemphasized. People have noted, for instance, that more early factories were powered by water than by coal and that most of England's coal was used for the unglamourous and not particularly innovative tasks of home heating and cooking. E. A. Wrigley has reasserted the centrality of coal by calculating that it would have taken 15,000,000 acres of woodland (21,000,000 had he used a less conservative conversion) to match England's annual energy yield from coal by 1815,[121] but it is not obvious what this figure tells us. In the absence of the coal boom, England would not have consumed that much additional wood (nor does Wrigley say it would have) since it did not have it; nor can we say for sure that some specific number of forges would have closed, glass gone unmade, or homes unheated. The adjustments would have involved some complex combination of people being colder, buying more clothes, producing less iron, and so on, and we cannot be sure that particular industrial advances— much less industrialization more generally—would have ground to a halt without coal.

Nonetheless, at least a partial return to the earlier emphasis on coal seems warranted, both for Wrigley's reasons and for others. Water may for a time have powered more mills than coal, but it was geographically restricted, nonportable, and often seasonally unreliable. Moreover, it was no substitute for

---

Grove 1995: 387–88, 406, 440, 471–72; on Chinese influence, see 187; on earlier periods, see 77–80. For some of the insights and limits of official understanding of ecology in China, see Dunstan 1997. On Japanese silviculture, see Totman 1989.

[119] Grove 1995: 435, 463–64, 471–72, 480.

[120] Morton 1981: 118–21.

[121] Wrigley 1988: 54–55; for more on the conversion issue, see chapter 6, p. 276, n. 50.

combustion in all sorts of chemical and physical processes (from brewing to metallurgy to dye-making), nor in the transport revolution that gave such a boost to the division of labor. In the critical iron sector (and thus also steel, railways, and so on) it is hard to see what alternative to fossil fuels could have been found. True, Hammersley has shown that—contrary to some earlier claims—England's iron industry in the 1660–1760 period did not contract, and probably was not critically short of affordable fuel: he estimates that forest covering 2 percent of the land of England and Wales would have sufficed to supply England's iron industry in this period.[122] But by the end of the eighteenth century, only 5–10 percent of Britain was forest.[123] Thus even under ideal conditions, the maximum possible output of charcoal pig iron in Britain would have been roughly 87,500–175,000 tons; but by 1820, actual British iron output reached 400,000 tons.[124] And aside from needing some wood for other purposes, it was not feasible to mobilize all wood for charcoal iron-making. Forges also needed to be close to both iron and water power (to drive the bellows), and charcoal for iron production could not be transported more than ten to twelve miles (preferably under five): the furnaces needed large chunks of charcoal, but it tended to break into small bits (or even dust) when moved very far.[125] So while Hammersley does show that iron production at 1760 levels did not face an "energy crisis"—and a fortiori that deforestation did not *cause* the breakthrough to coal-based iron—the same figures show that the iron industry's further growth did require coal.

In most other British industries, development of coal-based processes came earlier than it did in iron-making[126] and thus substantially predates the enormous steam-engine-powered expansion of coal output. Thus the coal/steam engine boom could not have caused those innovations, but that does not make it irrelevant to the growth of those industries. Even if coal was mostly used for home heating, fuel for industry would have been far more expensive had less coal been available. Granted, real English charcoal prices seem to have stabilized in the 1700–1750 period after rising sharply for 1550–1700 (though all wood and charcoal prices must be treated with considerable caution).[127] And even before steam engines allowed deeper mining, cheap coal was gradually

[122] Hammersley 1973: 602–7; see also Flinn 1978: 139–64.

[123] M. Williams 1990: 181.

[124] Harris 1988: 25, 56. Flinn (1978: 145) also points out that without coal, charcoal shortages could have hobbled the growth of English iron production *after* 1750; his emphasis is on showing that the earlier rate of output was sustainable and that there was no worsening charcoal crisis that *caused* the development of coal-based iron-making.

[125] Harris 1988: 26; Flinn 1958: 150.

[126] Harris 1988: 26.

[127] Hammersley 1973: 608–10 points out that high transport costs made wood prices vary enormously by locality, and often one seller or buyer dominated a particular market, making prices a poor guide to scarcity. Moreover, charcoal prices included a significant labor cost, and so were only loosely related to wood prices.

becoming more widely available thanks to road- and canal-building; but as we shall see shortly, those gradual improvements were quite small compared to those made possible by steam (especially after 1750) and would soon have reached their limits. Moreover, real charcoal prices rose again after 1750, probably due to increased iron output, even with more coal coming on line.[128] Vastly more expensive fuel would certainly have put a crimp in the quantitative expansion of many industries, and it is not hard to see it limiting innovation as well. As we shall see, even the steam engine itself was at first sufficiently bulky, fuel-hungry, and dangerous that experimenting with it might not have seemed worth it if its fuel had cost much more and if the coal mines themselves had not been an ideal place to use it. We will have more to say about deforestation (and continental Europe) in chapter 5; for now it suffices to see how essential coal was to Britain's breakthroughs, especially in iron, steel, steam, power, and transport.

Moreover, though it would be too teleological to see in the early nineteenth-century coal boom all the ways in which cheap fossil fuels have *eventually* relaxed pressures from a finite land supply (even in farming itself, thanks to energy-intensive fertilizers), it was clearly a crucial step; water power, no matter how much the wheels were improved, simply did not have the same potential to provide energy inputs that would significantly outpace a rapidly growing population for decades to come or to permit chemistry to substitute for land. Thus it seems sensible, after all, to look at the mining and uses of coal as the most likely European technological advantage that was purely home-grown, crucial to its nineteenth-century breakthrough, and (unlike textiles) not dependent for its full flowering on European access to overseas resources.

Steam engines were crucial here, both as machines that used coal to power other processes and as the power source for more effective water pumps which permitted a huge expansion of coal-mining itself. M. W. Flinn has noted that despite the many ways in which wind, water, gravity, and horses were used to drain mines, none of these would have been much use at the depths where most of the country's reserves were. Thus, without steam, "mining in Britain could scarcely have expanded [beyond 1700 levels of annual output] and must probably have begun to show diminishing returns."[129] Instead, output grew by roughly 70 percent over the next 50 years and by almost 500 percent more between 1750 and 1830 (making the total increase roughly 900 percent), as steam engines for mining became both more numerous and more effective.[130]

Steam engines of a sort had been developed in various societies before the eighteenth century, though without ever becoming much more than a curiosity.[131] The Chinese had long understood the basic scientific principle

[128] Flinn 1978: 143–45, 147–48; Hammersley 1973: 608–10.
[129] Flinn 1984: 114.
[130] Flinn 1984: 26, 121–28.
[131] For China see, e.g., Needham 1965: 255.

involved—the existence of atmospheric pressure—and had long since mastered (as part of their "box bellows") a double-acting piston/cylinder system much like Watt's, as well as a system for transforming rotary motion to linear motion that was as good as any known anywhere before the twentieth century. All that remained was to use the piston to turn the wheel rather than vice versa. (In a bellows, the jet of hot air moved by the piston was the goal, not a step toward powering the wheel.) A Jesuit missionary who showed off working miniature models of both a steam turbine-driven carriage and a steamboat at court in 1671 appears to have been working as much from Chinese as from Western models.[132] In a strictly technological sense, then, this central technology of the Industrial Revolution *could* have been developed outside of Europe, too; thus we can never say definitively why it was in fact developed first in Europe. We can, however, identify some reasons why Europe—more specifically Britain—was a particularly likely site for the series of linked developments in coal and steam central to the Industrial Revolution. And when we compare England to the Yangzi Delta—where similar incentives existed to relieve pressure on the local wood supply, and where advanced technology and a highly commercialized economy were also present—Europe's advantage rested as much on geographic accident as on overall levels of technical skill and much more than on any (probably nonexistent) advantage in the market efficiency of the economy as a whole.

The relevant skills in which western Europe led the eighteenth-century world were ones in which Britain led. One of these was mining itself, but the others are not ones whose relevance is immediately obvious: clock-making, gunmaking, and navigational instruments.

The story of Chinese mining in general, and coal-mining in particular, is somewhat puzzling. North and northwest China have huge coal deposits, and in the long era when the north included China's political, economic, and demographic center of gravity, China developed a huge coal and iron complex. Indeed, Hartwell estimates that Chinese iron production around the year 1080 probably exceeded that of non-Russian Europe in 1700. Moreover, this iron and coal complex was not merely large but sophisticated: Chinese ironmakers, for instance, seem to have known things about the creation and use of coke (purified coal) that would not be discovered elsewhere for centuries.[133] But in the years from 1100 to 1400, North and Northwest China were hit by a staggering series of catastrophes: invasions and occupation (by the Mongols and others), civil wars, enormous floods (including a major shift in the Yellow River), and plague. The Jurchen invaders of the twelveth century often demanded that some of the most skilled artisans in the capital region be turned over to them as a price for (temporarily) halting their siege; it is unclear

---

[132] Needham 1965: 135–36, 225–26, 369–70, 387.
[133] Hartwell 1967: 102–59.

how many ever returned.[134] By the time the area began to enjoy some stability again after 1420, China's demographic and economic center had shifted irrevocably to the ecologically more hospitable south; much of North China needed to be repopulated by government-led transfers of people during the fifteenth century.[135]

We now know that, contrary to what was once thought, iron-mining and iron-working did recover from the Mongol invasion. New centers of production arose in Guangdong, Fujian, Yunnan, and Hunan, and there was some recovery of production in the northwest as well. Total output reached a new high of at least 45,000 tons by 1600, and there were some new developments in production techniques.[136] Huang Qichen's study, which has shown us this post-Mongol revival of iron production, says very little about fuel, but it is striking that all the new centers of production—which he estimates had over 70 percent of iron production—were far from coal sources, leading one to suspect that this iron was largely made with wood and charcoal fuel.[137] We still know very little about what happened to iron production in the seventeenth and eighteenth centuries, though this same study suggests (based on very slight evidence) that it declined.[138] If it did—or even if it just failed to keep growing—a shift *away* from reliance on fossil fuel as a result of the post-Mongol relocation might well have been quite fateful.

As for coal production and use more generally, there is still much we do not know. Hartwell's claim that the industry never recovered from the Mongol invasions and related catastrophes may some day be seriously challenged, as his parallel claim about iron has been. But as yet this has not happened; and even if it turns out that coal did not decline as dramatically as he thinks, it certainly was never again a cutting-edge sector of the Chinese economy.

It is unclear how much knowledge about the extraction and use of coal was wiped out amid the catastrophes of the twelfth through fourteenth centuries—a distinct possibility, since (both in China and Europe as late as the nineteenth century) it was often passed orally from master to apprentice rather than written down—and how much ceased to be used or developed further as the area housing most of China's coal became a backwater, far from major markets and far from invigorating interaction with other sorts of craftsmen. Although coal-mining remained significant in China, it was never again a cutting-edge sector: instead, various fuel-saving innovations (including stir-frying in a wok instead of boiling food in heavier vessels) became increasingly important.

The eighteenth-century Lower Yangzi region—China's richest region, and one of its most deforested—stretched its supplies by trading along riverine and coastal routes for wood and beancake fertilizer. (The fertilizer allowed people

[134] Needham 1965: 497.
[135] Huang 1985: 114–15; Ho 1959: 136–37.
[136] Huang Qichen 1989: 1–2, 46, 84.
[137] Ibid., 2, 70–72.
[138] Ibid., 2.

to burn grasses and crop residues for fuel that would otherwise have had to be returned to the soil.) Though such trade-based palliatives did not rule out simultaneous experimentation with fossil fuels—the two coexisted elsewhere and could easily have done so in the Lower Yangzi without leaving many traces in the documents—it was hardly likely that coal in particular would have attracted much attention from the Lower Yangzi's artisans and entrepreneurs: there was little coal either in the region itself or in places easily accessible to its traders. China's nine southern provinces have just 1.8 percent of contemporary China's coal reserves, and its eleven eastern provinces 8 percent; by contrast, the northwestern province of Shanxi plus Inner Mongolia have 61.4 percent.[139] Some coal mines did operate in various parts of south China and within marketing range of Beijing in the north[140]—they were mostly small and poorly positioned to take advantage of China's richest and most fuel-hungry market. They were also hampered, at least intermittently, by inconsistent government policies.[141] By far the largest deposits, which theoretically might have justified major investments in production and transportation improvements, were those in the northwest.

Although the returns to linking those northwestern coal deposits with the Yangzi Delta seem so huge in retrospect that it is tempting to imagine some people making an enormous effort to do so, it is not clear what that could have been; and most of the returns to such a project that we can now imagine, given what we know about the uses of coal, were invisible *ex ante*.

Meanwhile, northwestern coal miners, operating in a generally backward region, were not particularly likely to learn of technical developments elsewhere that they might have been able to apply to their problems and had little chance of encountering artisans who had learned precise workmanship in specialized luxury crafts such as clock-making. Such artisans did exist, and their skills, if not their numbers, seem to have been not far behind their Western counterparts—but they were almost all in the Yangzi Delta or along the southeast coast, where there was a veritable craze for clocks and mechanical toys with elaborate jack-work.[142] And even if mine operators had seen how to improve their mining techniques, they had no reason to think that extracting more coal would allow them to capture a vastly expanded market: seemingly insuperable transport problems would still have separated their mines from the rich but ecologically needy fuel users of China's major cities.[143]

[139] Sun Jingzhi 1988: 93.

[140] See, for instance, Huang Qichen 1989: 70–72 for a seventeenth-century list.

[141] Huang Qichen 1989: 109–40.

[142] See Needham 1965: 513–15, 522, 525–28, 531 (mentioning seventeenth-century clocks an inch across which required very fine work, clock-makers who could copy the finest of Western imports); see also pp. 285 and 296 on odometers with differential gears as early as the eleventh century.

[143] Skinner 1977a: 217 on transport costs; also T. Wright 1984: 9, citing a quintupling of the price of coal in Northwest China between the mine and the riverbank fifty kilometers away. Cf.

The mines in Xuzhou and Suxian in northern Jiangsu, not too far from the Grand Canal, might have been the best positioned among the few mines potentially within reach of the Yangzi Delta; but even in the Xuzhou mines, the cost of coal in Qing times doubled by the time it reached the county seat, which was also the canal port.[144] Like their counterparts further north, these mines had been part of a heavy industrial complex (particularly focused on iron and salt production) in Song times and seem never to have fully recovered from a series of disasters in the twelfth through fourteenth centuries. In the eighteenth century, when the government decided to encourage coal in this area with the explicit goal of alleviating the Yangzi Delta's fuel shortage, it also chose to give the mining licenses to poor and unemployed people, who mostly dug small, shallow mines.[145] Although it seems unlikely that even better capitalized mines would have achieved the major breakthroughs needed to transform China's energy, transport, and metals sectors, having such small operators in charge at one of the few sites in China where coal was within relatively easy reach of both large markets and concentrations of skilled artisans could hardly have improved the odds.

Finally, the biggest technical problem faced by Chinese coal miners, especially in the northwest, was fundamentally different from that faced by their counterparts in England. English mines tended to fill with water, so a strong pump was needed to remove that water. Chinese coal mines had much less of a water problem; instead they were so arid that spontaneous combustion was a constant threat. It was this problem—one that required ventilation rather than powerful pumps—that preoccupied the compiler of the most important Chinese technical manual of the period; and although the problem was never fully solved, at least one contemporary historian of mining has pronounced the approaches described in that manual quite sophisticated for their time.[146] Even if still better ventilation had ameliorated this problem—or if people wanted coal badly enough to pay for this high level of danger—ventilation techniques would not have also helped solve the problem of transporting coal (and things in general) as the steam engines that pumped out Britain's mines did. Thus, while overall skill, resource, and economic conditions in "China," taken as an abstract whole, may not have been much less conducive to a coal/steam revolution than those in "Europe" as a whole, the distribution of those endowments made the chances of such a revolution much dimmer.

---

also DeVries and Van der Woude (1997: 37) on Europe: "Historically, the exploitation of energy deposits has depended more on the costs of transportation than on the costs of gathering the resource itself."

[144] Yu Mingxia 1991: 27.

[145] Ibid., 19, 21.

[146] Sun Yingxing 1637: *juan* 11, cited in Yu Mingxia 1991: 23. Water appears to have been a lesser problem, even at the Xuzhou mines, which were in a much wetter area than the Northwest. See ibid., 27.

In contrast, some of Europe's largest coal deposits were located in a much more promising area: in Britain. This placed them near excellent water transport, Europe's most commercially dynamic economy, lots of skilled craftspeople in other areas, and—to give the problems of getting and using coal some additional urgency—a society that had faced a major shortage of firewood by 1600 if not before.[147] And although timber and timber-based products were imported by sea, this was far more expensive than receiving logs floated down a river, as the Yangzi Delta did; the incentives to use (and learn more about) comparatively accessible coal were correspondingly greater. Indeed, from 1500 on most demand for coal in England was for home heating; people used it because it was cheap, though its smoke and fumes were serious drawbacks.[148] Industries, from brewing to glass-making to iron-making, could not tolerate the impurities this smoke introduced until a series of eighteenth-century innovations solved the problem.[149]

Much of the knowledge about how to extract and use coal had been accumulated by craftsmen and was not written down even in the nineteenth century. Indeed, John Harris has pointed out that there was far less written about how to mine and use coal for industry in English than in French during the eighteenth century, precisely because the people in England who needed to know the fine points—artisans—passed this knowledge along orally. Harris shows that French attempts to copy various coal-using processes foundered, even when they reproduced the equipment, because the production of, say, a heat-resistant crucible required very detailed knowledge and split-second timing acquired through experience—and the financial losses from making a mistake could be very large. The crucial details of how long to hold things in the fire, at what angle, and how it should look at various points were so ingrained in men used to working with coal furnaces, but so completely different from what people used to wood furnaces experienced, that an artisan from one tradition would not even know what needed explaining to one from the other.[150] Only when whole teams of English workers were brought over (mostly after 1830) was the necessary knowledge effectively transferred.

Thus we see that technological expertise was essential to Europe's coal breakthrough, but the development of that expertise depended on long experience (and many failures along the way) with abundant, cheap supplies. This experience was possible because artisan skill, consumer demand, and coal itself were all concentrated near each other. Without such geographic good luck, one could easily develop lots of expertise in an area with a limited future (e.g., in using and improving wood furnaces) and not proceed along the track that eventually led to tapping vast new supplies of energy. And the Chinese situation—in which coal deposits were far further removed from the Yangzi Delta

---

[147] For details, see chapter 5 and Nef 1964: 174, 263–64.
[148] Nef 1932: 156–58; Wrigley 1988: 77–78.
[149] Nef 1964: 158, 183, 203; Nef 1932: 215–24.
[150] Harris 1992: 18–33, especially 21–23, 27, 30–31.

than they were from, say, the Paris basin—throws England's good fortune into still sharper relief.

The steam engine represented an even more important breakthrough than the slow and steady progress in tunneling for coal or learning how to keep its smoke from spoiling beer, glass, and iron. We have already seen that in this sense, Britain was fortunate to have the mining problem it did—a need to pump out water, rather than prevent explosions—since it led to engines with many other crucial applications. But the steam engine did not invent itself, and here, too, location mattered to technological progress.

What made the steam engine effective were, again, incremental improvements from numerous craftsmen—including some in rather unexpected lines of work. As Mokyr puts it, Europe's real technological edge in the eighteenth century—and Britain's within Europe—was not in tools or machines, but in *instruments*—clocks, watches, telescopes, eyeglasses, etc. Though these gadgets had some application as producer goods—principally in ocean-going navigation[151]—their principal uses were as amenities for the well-to-do, especially the urban well-to-do.[152] Yet it was the transfer of precision boring and calibrating skills from instrument-making (and to some extent from gunmaking) that made Newcomen's original steam engine work reasonably well and then allowed for Watt's improvements, which quadrupled the engine's efficiency.[153] Living after two-hundred-plus years of gradual improvements that have made engines much safer, much more fuel efficient,[154] and much less bulky than either of these prototypes, we tend to assume that the potential of even the crudest steam engine would be so obvious that people would adopt it rapidly; but this is true only in retrospect. Even with the advantages conferred by spillovers from precision tool-making for weapons and instruments, the cost, bulk, and other problems of these machines meant that there were only 2,500 built during the eighty-eight years (1712–1800) following Newcomen's first installation;[155] other industries and inventors mostly placed their bets on improved waterwheels. Indeed, Von Tunzelmann suggests that the costs of energy per unit of power for steam-run textile machinery did not decline precipitously until after 1830, so that, water (where available) remained competitive until then.[156]

---

[151] Again, a British specialty within Europe and a European one in the world. Though maritime transport was very well developed in Asia—and in some ways even in advance of that in Europe—it involved far more sailing relatively close to the shore and far less time spent in the open ocean, where relatively small initial navigation errors could prove disastrous. Here the technological needs of shippers crossing the Atlantic—a kind of voyage with no parallel among Asia's long-distance mariners—were no doubt significant, as were the demands of armies and navies for instruments that would help in the aiming of cannon.

[152] E. Thompson 1967: 66–70.

[153] Mokyr 1990: 85, 103–4.

[154] Efficiency quadrupled again between Watt's model and those available by the 1870s—see Mokyr 1990: 90.

[155] Ibid., 88.   [156] Von Tunzelmann 1978: 224, 289.

Only in the coal fields (where there were 1,000 in use in 1800) were steam engines' advantages so obvious that they spread rapidly and transformed an entire industry within a few decades.[157] At a mine, the bulk of the steam engine did not matter, and the cost of its prodigious fuel intake, which rose rapidly with distance from the mine, was no problem either. In fact pit-head steam engines often used inferior "small coals" so cheap that it probably would not have paid to ship them to users elsewhere, making their fuel essentially free.[158] Take away some of the incremental advantage conferred by skill transfers from nearby artisans in other fields, the learning by doing made possible by the application to nearby coal fields, and the low cost of coal itself, and—as incredible as it seems to us today—the steam engine could have seemed not worth promoting.

The bridging of the social distance between artisans, entrepreneurs, and the sources of scientific knowledge was a triumph of Jacob's "scientific culture"— in which Europe may have had a significant edge (though we need more research to be sure). But, even so, if it had been Europe that faced a huge geographic distance between its coal and its concentrations of mechanically skilled people, and China that had had only a small distance to bridge, it is possible that the results in either place might have been vastly different; certainly the history of China's earlier coal/iron complex suggests as much.

A surge in European technological inventiveness was certainly (in fact, tautologically) a necessary condition of the Industrial Revolution, but before we elevate that creativity to a place far above that of other eighteenth-century societies, and reify it as *the* cause of Europe's subsequent primacy, we should bear in mind how crucial accidents of geography and juxtaposition were in making British coal and steam engines the cutting edge of industrialization. If, in retrospect, Europe backed the right horse, the factors that led to that particular winning bet seem critically connected to fortuitous, and specifically English, conditions (mostly geographic ones). European science, technology, and philosophical inclinations alone do not seem an adequate explanation, and alleged differences in economic institutions and factor prices seem largely irrelevant. Finally, as we shall see in later chapters, even this energy breakthrough could have been swallowed up by Europe's population boom in the late eighteenth and nineteenth centuries if certain other resource problems had not also been solved, in large part thanks to Europe's conquests in the rest of the world. Without both coal and colonies, neither one would have been nearly as significant; and without the relaxation of resource constraints they allowed, other European innovations alone would not have created a new world where having finite land did not prevent indefinitely sustained per capita growth.

[157] Mokyr 1990: 88, 90.   [158] Von Tunzelmann 1978: 62–63.

TWO

MARKET ECONOMIES IN EUROPE AND ASIA

IF WESTERN EUROPE was not uniquely prosperous in 1750, could its institutions have been better suited to rapid development beginning around that date? If we define "institutions" broadly enough, this argument *must* be true at least for northwestern Europe. Yet the most common version of this argument—that western Europe grew fastest because it had the most efficient markets for goods and for factors of production—is quite unconvincing.[1] There are, of course, scholars who argue for very different institutional advantages, including directly contrary ones: i.e., that it was precisely the ways in which Europe deviated from free markets that allowed the accumulation and concentration of capital, protected ecologically vital "slack" resources, and so on. We will deal with these arguments in later chapters. For now, let us focus on more orthodox arguments in which markets are assumed to have been conducive to growth, and Europe is said to have had the most perfect markets.

To be sure, even these market-oriented stories are actually more nuanced. Few economic historians would argue that western European realities closely resembled the abstractions of introductory economics textbooks, and many would agree that in some specific cases, deliberate (though usually temporary) deviations from perfect competition—e.g., protection in the nineteenth-century United States and Germany—can be quite helpful to the growth of particular economies.[2] But such imperfections cause losses elsewhere—e.g., in a Britain that would otherwise have sold more to the United States, or to unsubsidized industries whose potential consumers were taxed to subsidize some particular industry—so that it is hard to argue on neoclassical grounds that deviations from perfect markets were a net long-run benefit to an economic system that includes all actual and potential trading partners. Thus, to the extent that scholars treat Europe as a whole (especially if they also minimize its links with other continents), it is hard for them to see much advantage to mercantilism and other interferences with markets.

By the same token, recent explanations of European dynamism that emphasize small-scale productivity improvements and capital accumulation by millions of ordinary people are much more likely to emphasize *relatively* perfect markets, which made all these producers compete, rather than any systematic distortions, which could only have benefited some producers at the expense of others. Consequently, many stories about European development stress the

---

[1] See e.g., North and Thomas 1973, especially pp. 157–58; North 1991: 35.

[2] See, e.g., Senghaas 1985: 28–30, 65.

decline of state intervention and arbitrary taxation, lordly and ecclesiastical monopolies, bound labor and customary restrictions on land use, occupational mobility, and so on; and they assume that these trends went further at an earlier date in Europe than elsewhere. This chapter, however, argues for a very different claim: that eighteenth-century China (and perhaps Japan as well) actually came closer to resembling the neoclassical ideal of a market economy than did western Europe.

By far the largest sector of both economies was agriculture. Thus, we begin with markets for land and for agricultural products. These will be followed by comparing restrictions on the use of one's labor (in the form of compulsory occupations and services, barriers to migration, and debarment from certain activities), then by a discussion of the freedom to engage in industry and/or commerce, and finally to a comparison of households as institutions that powerfully affected the functioning of labor markets. Markets for capital will be discussed in chapter 4.

Land Markets and Restrictions on Land Use in China and Western Europe

Naturally, both China and western Europe had enormous variations across space and time, but more and more parts of both places moved during the sixteenth to eighteenth centuries toward what Marc Bloch called "agrarian individualism." Overall, China was closer to market-driven agriculture than was most of Europe, including most of *western* Europe.

It is important here to think about how to compare different deviations from an imaginary economic ideal. Philip Huang, for instance, has made much of customary restrictions on the land, labor, and product markets of the Yangzi Delta: those trying to sell, pawn, or rent out their land often had to offer it first to kinfolk and/or fellow villagers. Thus these markets were far from perfectly competitive;[3] Huang then reminds us that the mere existence of active markets need not usher in "transformative growth."[4] But since perfect markets have not been the historic precondition for transformative growth anywhere, this does not by itself explain the failure of that economy to grow as fast as that of western Europe; to do so would require both evidence and criteria no one has provided.

Restrictions on whom one could sell or rent to may have often cost landowners money and could prevent land from going to the most efficient user; the greater the restrictions, the greater the loss of efficiency. We can never know the size of such losses, but we can place them within a certain range. It is unlikely, for instance, that the difference between what even the most tal-

---

[3] P. Huang 1990: 108.   [4] Ibid., 114.

ented farmer would have achieved on a given plot and what a less-skilled farmer favored by custom could produce would be very large, given a generally shared knowledge of basic techniques and the overwhelming use of rental arrangements (either sharecropping or fixed rent) that gave tenants incentives to maximize output. And not every transaction restricted by custom directed land toward a less-skilled farmer.

Ideally, one would want sources that not only described imperfect markets, but recounted truly peculiar outcomes, such as large price differences between specific plots that did not reflect differences in the land's productive capacity but did correspond to social relations between buyer and seller. Although we do have such examples for even fairly advanced parts of Europe, such as late seventeenth-century northern Italy[5] we as yet have none for China; and it is unlikely that enough documents will ever appear for either China or western Europe to allow a systematic comparison of how much customary rules caused land markets to deviate from neoclassical expectations.

Alternatively, we could look for evidence that market imperfections produced some large negative effect in one place that had no parallel elsewhere. The most likely such case would be the ways in which restrictions on land use in much of Europe interfered with the adoption of known technological innovations—innovations capable of making a much larger difference in productivity than any plausible difference caused by occasionally diverting a parcel from the highest potential bidder to a lower-bidding relative.

The overwhelming majority of land in all parts of China was more or less freely alienable. The early Ming (1368–c. 1430) had confiscated a good deal of land in the Yangzi Valley, but these lands always drifted back toward private status; in the mid-1500s, the government gave up and recognized all taxpaying land as otherwise unencumbered.[6] Some land, mostly in the north, still theoretically belonged to the state and was leased to hereditary groups of soldiers or Grand Canal boatmen; the crown itself had an estate of about 700,000 acres in Qing times. But even on paper, all such land never amounted to more than 3,500,000 acres, or perhaps 3 percent of total arable.[7] Moreover, much of this land came to be treated as private property anyway, with its supposedly hereditary tenants selling or mortgaging it and protesting indignantly (and successfully) when the government later tried to make them pay to formally remove it from state ownership.[8]

Somewhat more land was rendered inalienable by being placed in private "charitable estates," which were meant to provide for the widows, orphans, and ceremonial expenses of corporate lineages, or for the upkeep of temples and schools. These estates were important in a few areas—they may have held as much as 35 percent of the arable in Guangdong province—but they were

---

[5] See the discussion of the land market in a Piedmontese village in Levi 1988: 79–99.

[6] R. Huang 1974: 99.   [7] P. Huang 1985: 87.   [8] Pomeranz 1993: 240.

trivial in most of the country.[9] A twentieth-century survey estimated that 93 percent of all Chinese farmlands were held in fee simple.[10] Moreover, even where inalienable estates were common, it is not clear that they were *used* any differently from other lands.

Regardless of its owners, much land was farmed by tenants or even sub-tenants, and here further restrictions could come into play. Exactly how much land overall was rented is difficult to say, even for the better-documented twentieth century. In North China, rented land probably did not exceed 15–20 percent of the total;[11] in the highly commercialized and relatively wealthy Yangzi Valley, probably close to half of land was rented.[12] In a few places in southeast China, most of the land was rented.[13]

Customary law often specified that tenancies first be offered to kinsmen, or to people within the village. In the southeast, where lineages were particularly strong, kinship probably did often limit the possible buyers and renters for land—though since many kinship groups there were quite large, even "kin first" rules allowed many people to compete for any given plot.[14] Furthermore, some twentieth-century informants reported that kin and non-kin could rent lineage land on the same terms.[15] In other parts of the country, we know about customary restrictions favoring kin partly from documents indicating that such offers had been but the land had ultimately been sold to an outsider;[16] the quantity of land in many Chinese villages that somehow passed to outsiders indicates that these customs were rarely an insuperable barrier. Finally, at least from the eighteenth century on, we find numerous cases in which junior kinsmen leased clan land to outsiders for new and irreversible kinds of development, as if it were unencumbered; this was illegal but often seems to have been recognized once it became a fait accompli.[17]

A much more complex set of problems concerns the extent of tenants' rights and their relationship to investment in the land. Where owners did not farm themselves, tenancies, with the tenants usually making the crucial decisions about cultivation, were far more common than "managerial farms" in which the owner (or his agent) made decisions and used hired labor.[18] Thus, much debate has centered on whether tenants enjoyed enough security to encourage them to improve the land and so be as productive as managerial farmers could have been.

---

[9] Chen 1936: 34–35.

[10] Buck 1937: 192.

[11] Jing and Luo 1986: 34–35; P. Huang 1985 :103.

[12] P. Huang 1990: 103—45 percent.

[13] Marks (1984: 44) shows that most land was freehold, though a few areas had concentrations of tenants; Chen (1936: 19) indicates 68 percent of land was tenanted in a few very exceptional villages.

[14] Naquin and Rawski 1987: 100–101.   [15] Watson 1990: 247.

[16] E.g., P. Huang 1990: 107.   [17] Osborne 1994: 11–13, 15, 19.

[18] P. Huang 1985: 79–81; P. Huang 1990: 58–75.

The evidence on how secure tenants were is mixed. Most extant tenancy contracts suggest that tenants were fairly secure in their cultivation rights,[19] but archival material from landlord-tenant disputes suggests that these provisions may have been hard to enforce.[20] The rapid commercialization of the eighteenth century accelerated the shift toward purely contractual landlord-tenant relations, though not without significant resistance from those who continued to see land as an inviolable patrimony rather than a mere commodity.[21]

But even if we take the dimmest possible view of these relationships— namely that tenant insecurity and high rents left them in a poor position to make productivity-enhancing investments—we need to bear in mind two crucial points. First, in such a scenario, the failure to adopt improvements would be the consequence of increasingly strong markets, not of "tradition." Second, we are at most dealing with additional risks faced by cultivators who invested in land improvement—and many apparently chose to proceed anyway. (After all, long tenures were very common, even if not guaranteed.) Nowhere do we see customary rights making it impossible for otherwise willing farmers to make improvements—a situation which, as we shall soon see, was more common in western Europe. Even in relatively poor North China, where managerial farms were more common than elsewhere and tenancies less so—perhaps indicating that tenants there were less able to maximize productivity than elsewhere—managerial farms do not seem to have been significantly more productive than those of either tenants or smallholders.[22]

Much of western Europe's farmland was far harder to buy or sell than that of China. Even in the nineteenth century, about 50 percent of all land in England was covered by family settlements, which made it all but impossible to sell.[23] In eighteenth-century Spain "entail allowed so little land into the market that its purchase price was too high to encourage investment. . . . Improving capitalists and peasant proprietors were alike starved of land."[24] Fewer French estates were entailed, but the practice was not absent.[25] While some parts of western Europe did have virtually free land markets in the seventeenth and eighteenth centuries—Holland, Lombardy, and Sweden[26]—the entailed estates of England and Spain alone would make up a far larger proportion of western European land than was held off the market in China.

A lively rental market could do much to compensate for limits on the sale of land, allowing even an inept landowner to have his patrimony managed by the person who could use it best (and thus offer the highest rent while still

---

[19] Myers 1982: 290–91; Rawski 1985: 6, with a useful literature summary in the note; Bernhardt 1992: 24–26.

[20] Zelin 1986: 510–514.   [21] Buoye 1993: 54–57.

[22] P. Huang 1985: 139–45.   [23] F. Thompson 1963: 68.

[24] Carr 1967: 51.   [25] Forster 1960: 120, 162–63.

[26] On Holland, see DeVries 1974: 33, 38, 44–78, 54; on Lombardy, J. M. Roberts 1967: 68–69; on Sweden, M. Roberts 1967: 142, 146.

making a profit for himself). But in some parts of Europe, landowners were still responsible for making capital improvements, in which case even a strong rental market might not fully compensate for restrictions on transfers of ownership. There were also western European locales where land use was as restricted as land transfer—and sometimes even more so.

In England, landlords managed to end most hereditary guaranteed tenancies in the course of the fourteenth and fifteenth centuries.[27] In the northern Netherlands, such rights had never been well established, and much of the land farmed in the sixteenth century and thereafter was newly reclaimed anyway.[28] By the mid-1600s, those two areas had Europe's most productive agriculture and highest per capita incomes,[29] and they bulk large in accounts of the European breakthrough. But between them, Holland and England had less than half the population of France, even in 1750, and there, hereditary tenures were dominant and gaining *more* legal protection throughout the sixteenth, seventeenth, and eighteenth centuries.[30] And since the most important new investments available to European agriculture during these centuries required the cooperation of an entire community and/or a scale of investment that only a landlord (or his agent) could make, secure tenants were (unlike in China) more likely a barrier than a boon to improvements.

Hereditary tenures made it very difficult to consolidate plots, and without consolidation, enclosure was both far too expensive and of too little use. And enclosure was necessary for the single most important technical change available to European farmers before the late nineteenth century: planting fodder crops on the one-third to one-half of land kept fallow (both to preserve its fertility and to provide pasture for livestock) in any given year. By the sixteenth century, many northern Italian, Dutch, and British farmers had found that if land could be enclosed to keep the village herds off of it, sowing it with certain fodder crops would protect its fertility as well as fallowing did and make it possible to feed more livestock. The dung from that enlarged herd, in turn, made possible much higher yields on one's entire farm.[31] A recent study has argued that at least in England the extra manure from enlarged herds was not added to crop lands, so that per-acre yields on the best arable land were not increased any further. But since the increased productivity of pasture lands (including some that had previously been quite marginal) allowed more of the best land to be reserved for grain, the process nonetheless raised total farm output.[32]

But the "new husbandry" generally required one of two types of "enclosures," both of which often ran contrary to custom. One was dividing into private plots the common fields the village had used as a collective source of fuel and fodder. The other was the consolidation and fencing of land that was

[27] Bloch 1966: 127–28; Brenner 1985a: 47–48.   [28] DeVries 1974: 27–28, 31–32.
[29] DeVries 1974: 152, 243; DeVries 1976: 36.   [30] Bloch 1966: 128–92.
[31] See ratios in DeVries, 1976: 39–40.   [32] Ambrosoli 1997: 393–94.

already privately owned but had previously been subject (as virtually all land was) to the obligation that it be kept fallow one of every two or three years so that the village herds could graze it. This second kind of enclosure is less-often discussed, but it involved far more land and so is more important to our story. The plots to be enclosed were not necessarily large,[33] but enclosing very small plots was not worthwhile, and squarish plots were more profitable than the long, thin strips that were common in much of France.

Both kinds of enclosure progressed quite slowly in eighteenth-century France. The boom in legislation authorizing the partitioning of common fields came after 1750, and particularly after 1769; the biggest years for legislation allowing landowners to enclose land they already owned were 1767–1777.[34] And even once this right was granted in theory, entrenched hereditary tenures often made it useless in practice. In England, virtually every act of enclosure involved a compulsory redistribution of scattered tenancies to create plots worth enclosing; in France, this kind of coercion was "out of the question."[35] Even where local courts allowed the ouster or transfer of a particular tenant, French communities continued well into the nineteenth century to apply "severe sanctions" against both landlords who ousted such tenants and any new tenant trying to farm the plot.[36] Thus, restrictions on land use in western Europe's largest country were sufficiently strong to greatly slow the spread of the new husbandry: i.e., of techniques known to allow per-acre yields roughly 60 percent higher than those commonly achieved by the techniques used in most of France, northern Germany, and Italy circa 1800.[37] In Spain, crown edicts were even more successful in halting enclosures; attempts to fix rents and wheat prices further interfered with any movement to invest in a more productive agriculture.[38] In most of Germany, the three-field system still prevailed until at least the Napoleonic era, in large part because commonage and various traditional and protection rights remained intact; of 18,000,000 hectares of farmland, about 4,000,000 were fallow in any given year. We get a sense of how much these institutions mattered when we see what happened after their demise. By 1850, fallow had virtually disappeared, large amounts of common and previously untillable land had become arable, 25,000,000 hectares were in annual use, and output per hectare was up, too. (In parts of the southwest, however, where commonage lasted longer, the rise in productivity was likewise postponed.)[39]

Overall, according to a standard account, the areas of western Europe that practiced the new husbandry in 1800 were not much more numerous than they

[33] Parker and Croot 1985: 80–81.
[34] Bloch 1966: 221–22.
[35] Ibid., 233.
[36] Ibid., 179–80.
[37] DeVries 1974: 152; DeVries 1976: 64–67. On the widespread suppression of fallowing in northern Italy, see Zangheri 1969: 33–37.
[38] J. Elliott 1961: 62–64; see also J. Klein 1920.
[39] Nipperdey 1996: 123, 131, 134.

were in 1600—the technological "agricultural revolution" was largely a nine-teenth-century phenomenon.[40] There is no remotely comparable example in China of custom or law delaying the spread of the best known agricultural practices on such a massive scale.[41]

Some recent work has questioned whether enclosures actually led to major increases in productivity.[42] Gregory Clark, for instance, suggests that the increase in rents due to enclosures was under 40 percent in England (and probably France as well), rather than the 100 percent claimed in many sources.[43] The much larger gains in output often cited are attributable to the increased labor and capital often applied to fields after they were enclosed, not to the enclosure itself and to the fact that labor and capital were diverted from other productive uses. Thus, these scholars argue, the gains in total factor produc-tivity—the ratio of output to the value of all the land, labor, and capital em-ployed to produce the output, and thus a measure of overall efficiency—are not that impressive. And once the capital cost of enclosing is subtracted from the 40 percent rent increase, the gain in total factor productivity becomes smaller still.[44]

Such arguments suggest that even the most widely cited case of medieval and early modern European "market failure"[45] did not really matter much. Yet for our purposes, the problem remains. Using total factor productivity as a

[40] Slicher Van Bath 1977: 71; F. Thompson 1968: 63–73.

[41] The heated controversies over *why* "agrarian individualism" triumphed much later in France than in England, and of the relationship of various patterns of agricultural change to a "capitalist" class structure, regime, and mentality, need not detain us here; the point is the time lag itself and the essential connection between the relative slowness of this transition and the relatively slow introduction of new techniques (Bloch 1966: 197–98). A more serious problem would emerge if one could raise doubts about the superiority of British over French agriculture in the eighteenth century: i.e., about how much difference the freedom to employ the new techniques made. Some doubts of this sort have been raised, principally by Patrick O'Brien (1977: 174) and F. M. L. Thompson (1968: 71). However, their argument rests on suggesting that even Britain did not adopt the new techniques quite as fast as we once thought, not on denying their superiority; and revised research on the size of Britain's population has tended to push our estimates of British agricultural growth back up again (cited in Cooper 1985: 141–42). While O'Brien is right to caution us against seeing agricultural differences large enough to explain Britain's earlier *industrial* breakthrough, this does not vitiate the point that France remained "stuck" for over two centuries at an apparent population ceiling, suffering recurrent subsistence crises (Ladurie 1974, 1976) at a population den-sity lower than that of England, the Low Countries, western Germany, or northern Italy (Cooper 1985: 138–39), while custom blocked the transition to a more productive agricultural regime.

[42] Allen 1982; McCloskey 1975a, 1975b, 1989; Clark 1998.

[43] Clark 1998: 77, 87–94.

[44] Ibid., 94–97; see also McCloskey 1989: 159.

[45] For McCloskey et al., however, the market did not fail at all: open fields were rational as a way of reducing risk (by holding a "portfolio" of several small plots) when interest rates were too high to allow most people to insure against famine by keeping back the surplus grain they would otherwise sell and stockpiling it; once this condition changed, the inefficiencies of open fields were no longer offset by this insurance function and people moved to eliminate them.

measure of the gains from enclosure assumes a world in which the labor and capital that were applied to enclosed farms in increased amounts would otherwise have found employment at roughly the same prices elsewhere had these enclosed fields not existed.[46] This seems questionable for the extra capital employed in fence-building and post-enclosure improvements, and even more so for labor. Put another way, using total factor productivity as our measure assumes that land—the factor whose output was increased by enclosures—was not significantly more scarce than labor and capital, the two factors that were spent when enclosures and the new husbandry were used to raise the land's yield. But as we shall see below—and in much greater detail in chapter 5—it is more likely that land scarcity was becoming serious in various parts of Europe so that measures that increased per-acre yields were output enhancing, even if they used rather large amounts of labor and capital. Without such measures land scarcity would likely have caused more people (and perhaps money as well) to be unemployed or destructively employed, rather than used on other productive tasks.

Much early modern European wealth went to such unproductive uses as the purchase of new titles (and so, indirectly, war, the main activity of most governments) rather than into expanding production. Indeed, it has often been argued that a shift toward deploying a larger portion of available wealth in increasing production and trade, rather than the pursuit of various religious, artistic, or other signs of status, gradually made certain European economies "capitalistic," while others remained "pre-capitalist."[47] Some of this shift may indeed have reflected an emerging "spirit of capitalism." However, another part was the emergence of new outlets for productive investment, including outlets that required little direct managerial involvement by the investor (who often remained more interested in other kinds of status-seeking activities).[48] Enclosures were just one of these slowly emerging outlets for investing capital; in the interim, large sums continued to be invested in other, economically less productive ways. There is no reason to think had enclosure remained legally difficult the capital used to enclose and improve land would necessarily have been invested productively. Thus a measurement that assumes it would have understates the contribution of enclosures to total output: and so, total factor productivity *understates* the costs of institutions that stood in the way of enclosures.

[46] McCloskey (1975b: 155–56) mentions this as a possible problem, but asserts that the payment to other factors of production did equal their true opportunity costs.

[47] The locus classicus for this view is Max Weber, *The Protestant Ethic and the Spirit of Capitalism*. Numerous other explanations, some more focused on changing ideas and others on material forces, have followed, but there is wide agreement on the importance of the phenomenon. Two of the most important treatments with the latter emphasis are those of Fernand Braudel and Jan DeVries, discussed below.

[48] See, e.g., DeVries 1976: 219–26, 232–35.

The same argument applies even more strongly to demand for labor. The changes that followed enclosure—turning pasture into crop land, draining marshes, and reducing fallow—all absorbed labor: but does the market wage accurately reflect the opportunity cost of that labor? The market wage is unlikely to sink below subsistence, since there is little reason to work if it will not enable you to live, but there will not always be work for everyone at that wage. Much of early modern Europe—including England and Ireland, where population growth was especially rapid[49]—suffered unprecedented levels of rural underemployment and unemployment.[50] And, as Arthur Lewis argued in his classic work on "surplus labor" economies,[51] wages of those who are employed in such economies are unlikely to fall all the way to the (very low) level of the workers' opportunity costs—i.e., the economic value of what they would probably be doing if their current job did not exist. Therefore, wages paid to the additional labor employed on enclosed farms also overstate what must be deducted from their output when measuring the net gains from enclosures; and total factor productivity thereby understates the costs to many western European economies of barriers to enclosure.

It is unclear where early modern Europe stood on a continuum between Lewis's pure "surplus labor" scenario and one in which labor was fully employed and earned its marginal product. Certainly unemployment and underemployment were chronic problems in much of the sixteenth through the eighteenth centuries in Europe. And a detailed study of the labor market in the Netherlands strongly suggests that despite substantial unemployment in the seventeenth century and falling international wage levels, both urban and rural wages rarely declined.[52] On the other hand, Joel Mokyr has argued that at least some of this unemployed labor may be explained by factors other than an actual excess of willing workers over worthwhile tasks: e.g., a stronger preference for leisure than in the modern world and seasonality of work coupled with high transportation and information costs.[53] And efforts to find pure surplus labor—people who could be removed with no loss to total product—have been unsuccessful, even in very poor and crowded twentieth-century locales.[54] It seems likely in early modern Europe that the opportunity cost of the extra labor absorbed by enclosures was above zero, but well below the observed market wage. And if leisure was indeed more highly valued than it is today this, too, would suggest that a use of labor that was only marginally profitable

[49] See Wrigley 1990: 107–11.
[50] See, e.g., Phelps Brown and Hopkins (1956: 306 and 1957: 289–99, especially p. 296), noting the inability of agriculture to absorb the full increase in the labor force and the resulting flood of people into part-time and ill-paid by-employments. Note also that close to 5 percent of European males 15–40 were under arms during much of the eighteenth century (DeVries 1976: 204) without creating noticeable labor shortages.
[51] Lewis 1954: 139–91.
[52] DeVries 1994a: 61.
[53] Mokyr 1985a: 107–8.
[54] Schultz 1964: 61–70.

(because it cost a lot to lure laborers who valued leisure highly) may nonetheless have added significantly to output. Thus, the true measure of gains from enclosures probably lies somewhere in between what is suggested by total factor productivity calculation and those suggested by ignoring the costs of inputs other than land; this would still suggest a market failure due to unclear property rights in land far exceeding anything one can find in China.

Other improvements were also foregone because of European land laws. Both the draining of marshes and the irrigation of existing farm land in eighteenth-century France were greatly retarded by customary rules and legal procedures that made it almost impossible to buy off those threatened by such improvements—even where it would have been very profitable to do so. It took the Revolution to abolish the privileges and simplify the procedures involved.[55] By contrast, the customary arrangements for compensating those who provided irrigation and adjudicating water-rights disputes in eighteenth-century China, Japan, and perhaps in the sixteenth through the eighteenth centuries in India—where reclamation and irrigation grew apace—seem more efficient.[56]

To be sure, French farmers found other ways to raise output. At least in northern France, many late eighteenth-century farmers (and some earlier ones) who had the opportunity to buy and sell in urban markets responded by gradually implementing changes in crop mix and technique that raised total output significantly. Moreover, the potential gains from further specialization without technological change were by no means exhausted on the eve of the Industrial Revolution.[57] But by the same token, these gains were not yet exhausted because so many possibilities for Smithian growth remained unexploited. And if France's food supply picture was not quite as bleak as some *Annales* historians have suggested, it was still certainly bleak enough—and enough of a cause of concern to powerful merchants, politicians, and other urbanites[58]—that substantial rewards awaited even remote farmers who could increase their output. Yet progress remained slow, and the rest of the ancien régime continued to be marked by urban food shortages in which merchants and officials were willing to go far afield in search of grain.[59] As James Goldsmith—a strong critic of notions of an immobile countryside—puts it: "There can be little doubt that the fragmentation of the land and the antique provisions of seigneurial law slowed down the reorganization of the countryside, but they were not insurmountable

[55] Rosenthal 1992: xii, 43, 48–50, 60, 70, 93, 120, 165.

[56] Chen and Myers 1976; Marks 1997: 105–10, Perdue 1987: 165–74, 181–96 (noting that the problem became the *over*-building of irrigation works, not underbuilding like that noted by Rosenthal for France); Kelly 1982: 89–103, 118–95 (esp. 192–95), 204–19; Ludden 1985: 87–89; Stein 1982a: 109–16; Fukuzawa 1982a: 200.

[57] See, e.g., Grantham 1989c: 43–72.

[58] Tilly 1975: 392–93, 397–400, 409–14.

[59] Kaplan 1976: 252–99; Tilly 1975: 424–28; Meuvret 1977: vols. 4–6 passim.

obstacles. ... The evidence suggests an underutilization of resources, not a Malthusian impasse."[60] In sum, the relatively slow spread of various productivity-enhancing innovations—enclosures, swamp drainage, and so on—still appears as a "market failure" requiring institutional explanations (such as Rosenthal's). For eighteenth-century China, we have much less need to invoke such arguments.

Labor Systems

If western Europe's property rights in land were not unusually efficient, what about its labor markets? Let us first review how the issue of "free labor" is related to those of economic efficiency and development. From the perspective of the economic system—as opposed to that of the unfree person—the issue is whether those who control the unfree laborers employ them in activities less productive than the ones they would engage in if free. They are particularly likely to force such people to persist in relatively unproductive tasks, which seem worth doing only to an overlord for whom an extra hour of a bound laborer's time has no marginal cost in cash and quite likely an artificially depressed opportunity cost as well.[61] If the bound laborers, once released, would actually shift to some more productive work, then the system of compulsory labor actually depresses total production: this is the scenario in which, for instance, formerly bound tenants expelled from the holdings of "improving" landlords become the workforce for new industries. (The "improving" landlord may actually *produce* less, but *nets* more because he no longer supports such a large group of bound laborers restricted to relatively unproductive tasks; and the economy as a whole benefits as these workers are hired for some other job, where they produce more than their subsistence costs.)

But such a scenario is generally a long-run one, since new industries rarely develop overnight. In the meantime, many such laborers are likely to be underemployed, and total output may well decline as old tasks that had made *some* contribution to output go undone, even if the contribution were not enough to justify paying a living wage (e.g., doing further weeding on a plot with few weeds left). Thus, in the short to medium term, unfree labor can either raise or lower total production.

These issues arise in the context of various kinds of bound labor: slavery,

---

[60] Goldsmith 1984: 186, 187.

[61] An extra hour of such a laborer's time spent on anything in particular still has an opportunity cost for the lord—the value of some other task that the laborer could have been compelled to do in that time. But where there are few alternative tasks—e.g., on an agricultural estate where due to lack of capital, owner's predilections, or other reasons, there is no industrial production or all the labor needed for it is already assigned—this cost, too, might be very low. And at any rate, the cost to the overlord of having the laborer do something if the alternative is letting them have leisure is effectively zero, which is not the case for an employer who must lure free labor out of that leisure. We will discuss this in more detail in chapter 5, particularly in the context of eastern Europe.

serfdom, and so on. Some scholars have analyzed the labor of peasant women and children in the same way. They argue that where culture and/or institutions kept such people from working away from home, but they did produce salable commodities within the home (in addition to re-producing the labor force through cooking, child care, etc.), the peasant family functioned like a very small estate with a handful of bound laborers. Since family members had to be fed anyway, any amount they earned was a net gain to the household, even if the implicit hourly "wage" earned by such labor was below subsistence. An "involuted" society in which such labor is widespread may well display many of the same economic (if not social or emotional) characteristics as one featuring slavery or serfdom: use of extremely labor-intensive techniques, a very small market for purchased consumer goods, and very little interest in labor-saving technical innovations.[62] We will return to family labor after first considering institutions in which people were bound to non-kin.

Scholars disagree as to when servile labor became economically trivial in China. The state had long sought freeholding subjects whom it could tax and draft directly rather than having to work through powerful local magnates—but the state did not always get its way. Japanese scholars have done the most to document the persistence of hereditary servile farm labor, especially on estates in the Yangzi Valley.

However, such estates were losing ground by the late fifteenth century—if not earlier—to estates that hired wage labor. And by the early 1600s, "managerial" farms with either wage or servile labor in the Yangzi Valley were giving way to small plots farmed by either peasant freeholders or contractual commoner tenants. Most laborers who were still bound when the Ming-Qing transition commenced (c. 1620) were freed during the wars, chaos, and subsequent labor shortages of the next fifty years. Even those who most strongly emphasize bound labor in the Yangzi Valley generally agree that it was unimportant by the eighteenth century.[63] (Most of the non-farming "mean" people who remained—musicians, actors, and some government clerks—became regular commoners by the 1730s.)

Elsewhere, bound labor generally became trivial earlier. In North China, for instance, many agricultural workers were legally below the status of other commoners during the Ming (1368–1644), but they were not bound to the land. By the late eighteenth century, such laborers were rare, even on the very small minority of acreage (less than 10 percent) that was farmed with non-owner, non-tenant labor.[64] The last legal handicaps facing North China tenants

---

[62] Lewis 1954; Chayanov 1966: 53–117; P. Huang 1990; Geertz 1963.

[63] Elvin 1973: 235–67.

[64] In Jing Su and Luo Lun's sample of 331 "managerial landlords," only 20 percent of their holdings were farmed with non-tenant labor (1986: appendixes 1 and 2), and it is unlikely that such landlords held more than 20 percent of total land farmed (see, e.g., P. Huang 1985: 104), which would suggest that perhaps 4 percent of all land was farmed with predominantly non-owner, non-tenant labor.

and agricultural workers disappeared in the 1780s—roughly the same time as in western Europe—but for a long time before that they had applied to only a very small number of people.[65] While a few exceptions—notably the Huizhou area in Anhui—still featured estates with bound labor into the nineteenth and even twentieth centuries, these oddities affected perhaps a few thousand families amid a Chinese population of perhaps 300,000,000 in 1780.[66] Manchu bannermen were entitled to keep slaves, but by the eighteenth century, probably most of even this small population group could not afford to do so. Moreover, even in the seventeenth-century heyday of the Manchus, their slaves were usually personal servants (often treated as quasi-kin), not farmers or artisans.[67]

This timetable is not radically different from what we see in western Europe. Full-blown serfdom was very rare west of the Elbe by 1500, so that most peasants could legally marry, migrate, and own land.[68] Yet a few serfs remained, even in eighteenth-century France;[69] and forced labor and villeinage remained quite significant in the Danish states.[70] Moreover, in both France and western Germany, a wide variety of seigneurial dues and restrictions remained, often including lordly monopolies on the milling of grain, peasant service obligations, and lordly control of local justice: these powers must have made many peasants hesitate to assert any of their rights.[71] Even in early nineteenth-century England, where villeinage had been gone for centuries, the Poor Laws made people eligible for relief only if they stayed in their original parishes; this made even short migrations too risky for many people, making them a captive labor pool for a few—or even one—nearby large estates.[72] And long-distance migration within Europe was greatly discouraged by a variety of legal barriers, language differences, and other obstacles—much more so than in China, as we shall now see.

Migration, Markets, and Institutions

One would expect poor laborers to migrate (if they can move at all) in one of two directions: toward places where the land-to-labor ratio is higher (typically frontiers) or toward places (often, but not always, cities) where the capital-to-labor ratio is higher and there are jobs in construction, services, or manufactur-

---

[65] P. Huang 1985: 85–105. [66] Ye 1983: 232–33, 239–40, 291.
[67] M. Elliott 1993: 346, 383 (most slaves of Manchus were household servants); more generally Wei, Wu, and Lu 1982: 77–91.
[68] Slicher Van Bath 1977: 113–14.
[69] Soboul 1966: 159–61.
[70] DeVries 1976: 58–59; Kjaergaard 1994: 148–49, 154–55; 167, 221–23.
[71] Soboul 1966: 168–79; Behrens 1977: 606–7; Mooser 1984: 99–103.
[72] Brundage 1973: 2–5.

ing. In the sixteenth through the eighteenth centuries, the former pattern could still absorb far more people than the latter; and it was far better developed in China than in Europe.

Europeans seeking more plentiful land might theoretically have looked either toward east-central and eastern Europe or across the Atlantic. However, a variety of institutional arrangements (often lumped together under "manorialism," "feudalism," or "the second serfdom") meant that very few people from crowded parts of western Europe could improve their conditions by moving east; instead they would have had to accept a less free legal status and uncertain title to any land they staked out (not to mention such common frontier problems as limited capital and market access). Although some free Germans did move to Russia and Prussia, Dutch to Lithuania, and so on under specific deals that granted them secure legal status, these were the exceptions. Overall, migration to the relatively empty and potentially fertile areas to the east was very small compared to either what we would expect in an imaginary unified Europe or what occurred across similarly large distances in China. (We will have more to say about this in chapter 5.) Generally, the filling up of those places would have to await both big legal changes and eastern Europe's own population boom in the nineteenth century.

Even the pre-1800 movement of Europeans to the land-rich New World pales in comparison to Chinese migration. Total European migration to the Americas before 1800 was probably under 1.5 million.[73] Moreover, close to two-thirds of those from England came as indentured servants[74] while policies in various colonies made it artificially difficult for poor people to remain free while taking advantage of New World opportunities.[75] The flow of free European migrants was a trickle compared to the surplus of laborers in Britain alone and came nowhere near equalizing the life chances of free whites on both sides of the Atlantic, as a labor market that was clearing would have done. Going to New England, for instance, increased a young Englishman's life expectancy by roughly a decade circa 1700,[76] but no great flood of migrants came until after 1800.

In the case of the New World (unlike eastern Europe), the high cost of migration relative to poor people's earnings and savings was presumably a bigger barrier than any legal problems. Still, it is worth noting that most people could only meet these costs of migration by accepting indentured servitude

---

[73] Kulikoff 1992: 185–86.   [74] Ibid., 191.

[75] E.g., Morgan 1975: 215–34.

[76] Greven (1970: 26–27, 109, 193) gives a further life expectancy at 20 of 44.2 for males and 41.6 for females in the late seventeenth century (dipping slightly under 40 in later cohorts), plus an unusually low death rate for those under 20. Razzell (1993: 765) gives figures for various (mostly elite) English populations, which suggest that those who reached 25 could expect to live 25–31 years more in the seventeenth century, though this number moved closer to 35 (and thus near-parity with Massachusetts) in the middle and late eighteenth century.

and the terms on which even that bargain was offered were crucially shaped by both the limits of big export-oriented planters' demands for labor and the alternative they had of employing slaves if indentured servants became too expensive.[77] Certainly there was no real European counterpart to the Chinese state's repeated efforts to *facilitate* mass migration to areas where labor was scarce and to do so on terms that allowed cultivators to remain independent.

These Chinese efforts often included providing travel costs, start-up loans, seeds, help in obtaining plow animals, basic information, and grants of land.[78] Long-distance migrations to underdeveloped parts of China (and those depopulated by seventeenth-century wars) during the late seventeenth and eighteenth centuries alone easily surpassed 10,000,000, with most of the colonists establishing freehold farms;[79] those who became tenants were almost always free tenants.[80] And although we lack sufficient data to show how close these migrations came to equalizing earnings across regions, the anecdotal evidence suggests that Chinese lands of opportunity quickly filled up to the point at which migration to the frontier was no longer an obvious avenue for advance. Thus it seems likely that Chinese migrations, for whatever reason, did much more to clear regional gluts of labor than did European ones.

On the other hand, migration toward plentiful capital may have been easier in Europe. People in the most capital-scarce parts of Europe (e.g. Russia) were, to be sure, quite immobile; and as we saw, institutions like the English Poor Laws might artificially inhibit even a migration from a poor English parish to London (or later Manchester). But many seventeenth- and eighteenth-century Europeans did move short to medium distances toward core areas (e.g. Germans and Scandinavians toward the Netherlands, Irish toward England).

The Chinese state, always suspicious of "vagrants" and much more enamored of farmers than proletarians, took no steps to move poor people toward jobs in the cores the way it helped them seek farms in the peripheries; in fact, some of its policies discouraged such movements. Organizing famine relief so that people received their rations close to home was one such example; attempting to make neighbors responsible for each other's behavior through the *baojia* system was a much more ambitious project with a similar aim, but probably had little real impact on migration. Custom and the social structure of Chinese industry probably mattered more.

The biggest industrial sector in both eighteenth-century China and Europe was textiles, and in both places, most production was rural. In China, the bulk of the producers were female—in part because spinning and weaving were considered to be the epitome of "womanly work." But few single women

---

[77] See Galenson 1989: 52–96; Morgan 1975: 295–315; we will have more to say about this in chapters 4 and 6.

[78] J. Lee 1982: 284, 293; Sun Xiaofen (1997: 30–34) on Sichuan; Marks (1997: 291) on Guangdong to southwest.

[79] Lee and Wong 1991: 52–55.   [80] Zelin 1986: 518.

would undertake migration alone in China, where even women on brief religious pilgrimages risked their reputations if not escorted by kinfolk; in fact, there remains significant opposition to women migrating for work in parts of rural China even today.[81] For a woman to migrate with her husband, they needed housing, and he, ideally, needed access to a piece of land: there were various jobs for male wage workers, but the notion that a male household head should have his own (owned or rented) farm was strong enough to discourage most potential migrants. The Lower Yangzi and some other regions were full of rural weavers and spinners but not of couples composed of two textile workers, as one so often found in western Europe, and not of great landlords interested in settling such people on their land as cottagers in order to gain access to their labor. In short, what we might call the "proletarian migration option" was difficult in China because the normative spinner or weaver was not a proletarian—she was part of a household that had, if not its own land, at least the money for a tenant's rent deposit.

Here, then, is one place where European institutions may have been more conducive to migration that would (theoretically) create equilibria by moving people from labor-glutted areas to capital-rich ones. And in the nineteenth century, when the population of China's peripheries soared, while that of its most prosperous areas grew very little, this particular difference may have been significant; we will return to it in chapter 5. But in the mid-eighteenth century it is hard to imagine that even the great prosperity of the Yangzi Delta would have drawn many immigrants looking for wage work, regardless of their gender norms and other cultural values. The delta already had over 1,000 people per square mile,[82] while the mostly fertile and well-watered Middle Yangzi province of Hunan had about 175;[83] and, of course, far more people (especially men) knew how to farm than knew anything else. Under the circumstances, it is hard to imagine massive migration toward capital in China even if it had not been discouraged by custom and the state had not encouraged migration toward land. In Europe, after all, institutions interfered quite a bit with land-seeking and much less with seeking employment by plentiful capital, but the flows of people toward eighteenth-century jobs were still fairly modest. Certainly, we would have no grounds for arguing that the customary barriers toward going to capital-rich regions were as severe an "imperfection" in the eighteenth-century Chinese labor market as the barriers we have described for land-seekers in Europe. Of course, neither China nor western Europe was a smoothly functioning neoclassical labor market; it is enough for our purposes that China was probably somewhat *closer* to this model, and certainly not much further.

[81] See, e.g., Judd 1994.
[82] Y.C. Wang 1989: 427.
[83] Calculated from Perdue 1987: 25, 40.

Markets for Farm Products

Moreover, those farmers who sold much of their output on the market were less likely than at least their counterparts around London and Paris to confront a monopsonistic buyer. Both the English and French monarchies, eager to provision their capitals at almost any cost, allowed the growth of a "private market," in which established regulations against "forestalling"—buying up grain before it reached the marketplace—were ignored. Increasingly, merchants purchased grain directly from peasants, in one-on-one transactions that prevented the grain from ever entering a physical marketplace where the seller could consider offers from several contending buyers.[84] As Braudel emphasizes, such transactions, in which the merchant brought superior knowledge of distant markets and ready cash, were "inherently unequal"[85] and often led to a self-perpetuating cycle of peasant indebtedness and a lack of choice about when and to whom one sold one's crop.

By contrast, the Qing state was very concerned to make sure that local marketplaces had *multiple, competing* buyers and sellers for basic items—until the 1850s, this was in fact the main goal of their system of licensing merchants and brokers.[86] There is much evidence to suggest that this system generally (though not always) worked for grain and for cotton, which made up the bulk of farm goods sold. True, merchants often did use credit to secure the peasant products they sought, but it appears that—again, at least prior to 1850—peasants rarely lost their ability to choose to whom they sold.[87]

Rural Industry and Sideline Activities

Moreover, Chinese peasants were considerably freer than many of their European counterparts to engage in commercial handicraft production and to sell these manufactures to competing buyers. For simplicity, let us focus on textiles.

Early Ming China still had hereditary artisan families, including about 3 percent of the population in 1393,[88] but that system fell apart over the next two hundred years: the wages for these bound workers were so low that many

---

[84] Everitt (1967: especially 543–63, 568–73) on England; on France, see Kaplan (1976: 69–70) on attempts to force grain to be traded only at markets with multiple buyers present, on the abolition of those rules 90–91 and on how normal "forestalling" became 289–90. See also Usher 1913: 306.

[85] Braudel 1977: 53.

[86] Mann 1987: 42, 45.

[87] Pan 1994: 130–201, especially 173–87; see also Lu 1992: 488–90.

[88] Wu and Xu 1985: 112–15.

fled their duties, while peasant families increasingly sold cloth and other hand-icrafts.[89] By the end of the Ming, the system was dead, and the new Qing dynasty officially abolished it in 1645. Though guilds were common, those in textiles were of no importance, and there was no urban monopoly on legal textile production. On the contrary, the Qing strongly encouraged rural women to spin and weave, both to bolster the economic stability of tax-paying peasant households and because the example of a mother at her loom was considered good for the moral education of her children. Officials distributed cotton seeds, printed instructional pamphlets, encouraged the teaching of relevant skills, and promoted the "man plows, woman weaves" division of labor as the basis of strong families.[90]

Generally speaking, these policies worked. Almost every rural household in the Lower Yangzi did some textile work for the market by the early 1600s. Much of North China followed suit in the seventeenth and eighteenth centu-ries, along with Lingnan, and important pockets of production also developed in the Middle Yangzi and elsewhere.[91] Where local production did not de-velop, it was a lack of appropriate local resources—and handicraft imports from more developed areas—that stopped it.

Western Europe's urban guilds also lost control of textile production—but much more slowly. Though the cost advantages of using rural labor were obvi-ous, urban artisans were widely agreed to have legitimate rights to their privi-leges—rights that could be regulated, but not lightly abolished.[92] Enlighten-ment thinkers began to question the legitimacy of this sort of property, but not until after 1789 did legal codes reflect their views. European governments—which were most concerned with keeping order in *cities*[93]—knew that any rapid dissolution of urban monopolies would lead to massive unrest, and they frequently enforced bans on rural production. In much of Germany, seven-teenth- and eighteenth-century states sought to *strengthen* urban monopolies.[94] Many German guilds actually became more powerful (de facto or de jure) during the eighteenth century and continued to hunt "ground rabbits"—rural interlopers in their trades—well into the nineteenth century.[95] In spite of such efforts, rural industry continued to spread, and some masters turned from try-ing to exclude rural laborers to employing them. Nonetheless, millions of other country dwellers were still legally blocked from industrial activities by urban privileges.

---

[89] Ibid., 116–18.

[90] An especially clear discussion of these issues can be found in Mann 1992.

[91] Li Bozhong 1998: 107–8; Lu 1992: 480–81; P. Huang 1985: 118–20; Marks 1997: 171–73.

[92] Sewell (1980: 117–21) on France; Walker (1971) on Germany.

[93] Wong (1997) makes this point very forcefully and explores its implications for how the kinds of economic dislocations European states would and would not respond to differed from those in China.

[94] Kellenblenz 1974: 59.   [95] Walker 1971: 88–107.

Other barriers existed within the countryside itself. The dukes of Rutland (in England, the heartland of both liberalism and European textiles) apparently concluded (with some justice) that the spread of rural knitting led to competition for agricultural workers, higher birthrates, and ultimately higher assessments to support the poor: and as owners of three fourths of the village of Bottesford and buyers of most of its marketed output, they were able to prevent the development of such evils. As late as 1809, Pitt described their policy thusly: "A numerous and able-bodied peasantry is here supported, no stockingers, and care taken there shall be none." It is not surprising that while textile development boomed in much of Leicestershire, it was often absent in villages that were dominated by a single noble family and weak in areas of concentrated landownership.[96] In some parts of Germany (especially outside Prussia) guilds effectively barred many workers (especially women) from cloth production well into the nineteenth century;[97] meanwhile, assorted servile obligations caused problems for weavers, and for innovators, as late as 1848.[98]

In still other cases, rural industry did grow significantly, but only at the cost of imposing a restrictive guild system on the countryside, too. In these cases, rural and urban guilds often acted together (with state support) to successfully resist technological change; surveying the German record, Sheilagh Ogilvie concludes that the institutional legacy of proto-industrial development and corporate privilege still "constituted a direct and enduring obstacle to economic and social change" in the nineteenth century.[99]

We should not, however, simply list deviations from an idealized open and integrated labor market: those can be found anywhere and do not mean that there was no meaningful labor market. For some European cases, however, we also have some outcome measures—which show that labor-market integration was quite limited and intermittent.

The famous wage series produced by Phelps Brown and Hopkins for England clearly points to durable rigidities. Nominal wages for various non-farm work remained unchanged for decades, even centuries, despite frequent changes in both supply and demand; and differences between the wages of skilled and unskilled workers also remained quite steady over extremely long periods.[100] We now have similar findings for parts of France and Germany.[101] Meanwhile, unemployment—a likely result when wages do not adjust to fluctuations in demand—was quite serious in England in the sixteenth through the eighteenth centuries. It also appears that despite serious *seasonal* unemployment, few farm laborers did off-season industrial work in eighteenth-century

---

[96] Levine 1977: 19–20.   [97] Ogilvie 1996: 128–29.
[98] Kriedte, Medick, and Schlumbohm 1981: 143, 182, 197–98.
[99] Ogilvie 1996: 136.
[100] Phelps Brown and Hopkins 1981: 3.
[101] Cited in DeVries 1994a: 40–42.

England; and despite relatively high harvesttime day wages, there was also very little seasonal movement into agriculture.[102] This strong separation between agricultural and industrial labor markets helped sustain a hefty difference between urban and rural wages: urban wages were 154 percent of rural ones at the end of the eighteenth century.[103]

Dutch labor markets may have been much more flexible, at least during the Golden Age of the late sixteenth and early seventeenth centuries. Nominal wages and skill differentials changed far more often, and casual laborers clearly moved back and forth between agricultural and non-agricultural tasks, helping to integrate those labor markets.[104] But after about 1650, changes in wages and skill differentials became less frequent; various organized urban trades were able to keep wages high (and even increase them in real terms as world prices fell after 1670), despite falling profits and increasing unemployment;[105] various seasonal kinds of non-farm labor were increasingly supplied by temporary migrants from German and Scandinavian farms. Meanwhile, many poorer and less secure Dutch workers were no longer able to patch together enough days of casual labor, both because public projects (e.g., canal-digging) contracted and because farms increasingly hired year-round servants. Large numbers emigrated, going abroad as sailors or soldiers for the Dutch East India Company—an employer of last resort, but one that was growing in the eighteenth century. In effect, then, the Netherlands came to have three rather sharply separated wage labor markets, with entry to the most desirable one carefully limited, while people in the other two markets could not live in the country continuously.[106]

Nor were labor markets necessarily becoming more integrated in the late eighteenth century, or even through most of the nineteenth century. England's urban-rural wage gap (54 percent in 1797) rose dramatically during the 1820s–1850s (as is common during early industrialization), peaking at 81 percent in 1851 and only gradually diminishing (with periodic reversals) over the next several decades.[107]

France's labor market seems at first to have been more integrated, but this turns out to have been temporary. It had long been common for French rural industries to close in the summer because they could not compete with peak-season agricultural wages, and many industrial workers moved increasingly into full-time farming once they passed thirty-five or so and the wages they

[102] Allen, cited in Postel-Vinay 1994: 72.

[103] Williamson 1990: 183.

[104] DeVries 1994a: 45, 53, 56.

[105] Ibid., 61–62.

[106] Ibid., 57–60, 62.

[107] Williamson 1994: 162, 166; Williamson 1990: 182–83. The English figure is a weighted average of a much larger southern gap and a much smaller northern one; conversion from index numbers on p. 182 for 1797 and 1851 to percentages is my own.

could earn in industry began falling. This large overlap between farm and non-farm workers (25–40 percent of the French farm labor force also worked in manufacturing circa 1800) produced a more integrated labor market than that of Britain, at least outside the cities. Moreover, the increasing commercialization of French farming between 1750 and 1870 meant that this integration increased, at least in many areas.[108] However, this integration depended on much of French industry's being exceptionally non-capital intensive (which made summer shutdowns financially tolerable) and low wage (making shutdowns necessary when agricultural wages rose each summer). Such industries became increasingly uncompetitive as steam-powered factories advanced in the last third of the nineteenth century; and as harvesttime wages collapsed in the agricultural depression of the 1870s, seasonal flows of labor from industry to agriculture ceased. The result was a sharp increase in both urban-rural and regional wage differentials in late nineteenth-century France.[109] By the twentieth century, France's labor market was characterized by new patterns of segmentation, rather than a secular trend toward integration.

There is no scholarly consensus on why large and growing wage differentials between sectors and regions persisted so long into Europe's industrial era. The explanations no doubt vary and include many factors that cannot be considered "defects" in labor markets.[110] Nonetheless, there is widespread agreement that such defects played some role in perpetuating the gap. And however one weights the different components of an explanation, it is striking that here we are again faced with the need to explain a major European deviation from Smithian efficiency—both in the early modern period and in the industrial era itself—which has no close parallel that we are aware of in east Asia.

Unfortunately, we have no reliable wage series from China with which to compare these results, but we will see later in this chapter that, at least in the eighteenth century, earnings of agricultural laborers and rural textile workers were probably fairly close. And we know there were no restrictions on moving between these sectors comparable to those in much of Europe. Individual Chinese landlords almost never possessed the power of the duke of Rutland; they were, at any rate, more likely to prefer that their tenants have extra income to help them pay rents that were increasingly due in cash. And urban craft guilds, as we have seen, had no real power to exclude rural competitors. More informal arrangements, such as routing both seasonal and permanent hiring of migrants through native-place organizations, meant that the labor market was certainly segmented in many ways, but without the additional effects of legal restrictions, it seems unlikely that this produced labor markets less integrated than those of early modern Europe.

[108] Postel-Vinay 1994: 65–66, 72–74.   [109] Ibid., 78–79.

[110] Williamson (1990: 193) estimates that various differences in living costs, disamenities of city life, and the greater availability of poor relief in the countryside explain away more than half of the wage gap, but he concludes that they still leave a substantial labor-market failure to explain.

In Japan, where a multitude of legal restrictions on both migration and side-line activities persisted until the 1860s, one might expect a pattern of labor-market segmentation more like those observed in Europe. However, informal arrangements often seem to have circumvented these restrictions quite effectively, at least in commercialized regions. Saito Osamu has shown that from the 1750s on, day laborers in the towns of the Kinai region earned about the same as rural day laborers, suggesting a well-integrated labor market;[111] Nishikawa Shunsaku has similarly shown that the marginal productivity of labor in nineteenth-century Choshu, which should roughly equal the farm la-borer's wage, closely matched the wages of workers in nearby salt manufacturing firms.[112] So while much work remains to be done, the evidence we have so far does not suggest that European labor markets conformed more closely to neoclassical norms than did those of Japan or China.

Family Labor in China and Europe: "Involution" and the "Industrious Revolution"

Consumption and Output

However, Philip Huang has argued that Qing China's economy was nonetheless "involuted" in a way that that of western Europe was not. The expansion of production and exchange rested, Huang argues, on the ever-greater application of unpaid family labor, which earned small (and shrinking) amounts per unit of labor. Such earnings helped the household meet its more or less fixed consumption needs, but at considerable cost: the combination of low profits and a near-zero implicit wage made it pointless to invest in labor-saving machinery, kept people locked in low-productivity tasks, and left only a small market for "other than subsistence products." Under such circumstances, rural industry could grow, but labor productivity could not. Thus "this was the commercialization of small-peasant production and subsistence, not of incipient capitalist enterprise." Underlying this dynamic was the near exclusion, due to "cultural constraints," of women from labor outside the home;[113] these constraints encouraged families to treat women's labor as costless, much like that of slaves or serfs that an estate had to feed no matter how much or how little they worked.

Assuming for the moment that Huang's picture of China is correct, how much would it differ from western Europe before the late eighteenth century? In Europe, too, there is abundant evidence that the expansion of output that occurred between 1500 and 1800 resulted largely from the application of much larger amounts of labor, rather than any breakthrough in productivity; the trend was so general, basic, and long-lived that Jan DeVries has proposed that we

---

[111] Saito 1978: 92.   [112] Nishikawa 1978: 81–82.   [113] Huang 1990: 91, 110.

reconceptualize the period as one of "industrious revolution."[114] And, as suggested in chapter 1, it is unclear whether all that extra labor was improving the living standards of ordinary western Europeans very much. As we shall see in chapter 3, there is abundant evidence that non-elite Europeans had more possessions in 1800 than in 1500, but they did not eat any better—in fact, they may have eaten less well.

We have already seen that per capita European meat consumption declined between the late Middle Ages and 1800. Meanwhile, per capita bread consumption in Paris showed no long-term trend between 1637 and 1854;[115] evidence for other cities is similar. And as time went on, the amount of work required to earn that bread *increased*. In Strasbourg between 1400 and 1500 the amount of manual work needed to purchase a month's worth of wheat for a family of four fluctuated between 40 and 100 hours; it was usually in the 60–80 hour range. By 1540, it was well above the 100-hour line and was not to dip below that level again for three centuries; data for France in general show that it was not until the 1880s that a month's grain could again be bought with 100 hours' work.[116] Trends for German workers were roughly similar: the buying power of workers' wages measured in grain fell roughly 50 percent between 1500 and 1650.[117] In England, buying power began falling a bit later, and there was one peak (around 1740) at which builders' wages again bought as much bread as in the sixteenth century; but otherwise they, too, only recovered their sixteenth-century grain-buying power well into the nineteenth century.[118] Given how central grain was to people's diets—over half the calories even for upper-class urbanites and perhaps 80 percent of the calories for the poor[119]—it is likely that real *per hour* returns to people's labor were falling during this period. (Some people kept up the calorie-buying power of their wages by switching from bread to potatoes, but this was widely considered to be a step down in quality of diet.)

Small farmers—whether freeholders or tenants—fared only slightly better. Though they experienced cyclical gains when grain prices rose and tended to gradually accumulate more cookware, furniture, etc., their diets did not improve. Essentially, the large increase in peasants' numbers consumed much of the increase in their output, and the gradual disappearance of empty spaces in which discontented peasants might resettle helped elites and the state appropriate more of whatever surplus there was. To be sure, some new items entered people's market baskets, but given what was lost, it is not obvious that the new market basket was much superior to the old one—and people worked many more hours than their forebears had to obtain this market basket. Had agricul-

---

[114] DeVries 1994b: 249–70.   [115] Braudel 1981: 132.   [116] Ibid., 134–35.
[117] Calculated based on Abel 1980: 136, 161, 191.
[118] Clark 1991: 446.
[119] Braudel 1981: 131–33.

tural real wages been rising or even stable, there would not have been the glut of rural laborers that helped push down the better-documented real wages.[120]

Research on "proto-industrialization"—the enormous growth in rural handicrafts in early modern Europe—leads to a similar conclusion. David Levine's work on rural textiles in England makes clear that the earnings of a single rural textile worker could not support a family; even the earnings of two such people were often inadequate without some farm income and/or contributions from child labor. Nonetheless, the possibility of a couple's surviving on textile work—plus, perhaps, a very small piece of land—allowed more couples to marry without waiting to inherit a patrimony. The result was earlier marriages, higher birthrates, overpopulation in textile districts, and further downward pressure on wages. Falling wages forced many people to work more hours, accelerating the spiral.[121] Proto-industrialization, Levine suggests, was thus no harbinger of the industrial future but a dead end from which England (though not all of its textile workers) was rescued by an exogenous technological breakthrough.

The relationship between proto-industrialization and more rapid population growth no longer seems as clear as it did to the model's earliest proponents. Increased availability of agricultural wage labor, which also made it possible to earn a living and marry without inheriting land rights, could have the same effects on population as those attributed to proto-industrialization;[122] and it, too, led to a proliferation of families that needed at least two money earners to survive. Nonetheless, Levine's basic point—that proto-industrialization could as easily have led to a dead end as to a major breakthrough—still seems quite sound. It also reminds us that proletarians—who theoretically confronted the market as individuals, rather than as part of a family which was both a unit of production and consumption and might still own some land—could nonetheless deviate from neoclassical expectations in an equally "involutionary" way.

Peter Kriedte, Hans Medick, and Jürgen Schlumbohm, in a study of proto-industrialization in portions of present-day Germany, France, England, and Belgium, suggest that through the profits and organizational techniques accumulated by *merchants*, proto-industrialization may indeed have contributed to the subsequent rise of factories.[123] Nonetheless, the picture they paint of the economic and demographic consequences for workers closely resembles Levine's argument: a pattern of involution, stagnant living standards, and *increasing* overall pressure on available resources.[124] Proto-industrialization also

---

[120] Kriedte, Medick, and Schlumbohm 1981: 28–29.
[121] Levine 1977: 58–87. See also Kriedte, Medick, and Schlumbohm 1981: 57, 77–86.
[122] See the summary of the literature in Ogilvie and Cerman 1996: 1–11.
[123] Kriedte, Medick, and Schlumbohm 1981: 100–101.
[124] Ibid., 77–88, 139.

seems to have been accompanied by large population increases in the relevant parts of eighteenth- and early nineteenth-century Germany, despite local attempts to legislate marriage restrictions; massive underemployment and wage cuts to below-subsistence levels were widespread, especially in the 1840s.[125] Overall, living standards in Germany showed no signs of improvement before 1850 at the earliest. Between one-quarter and one-half of German artisans are said to have lived below the "poverty line"; the percentage of males in Frankfurt with enough property to be citizens fell from 75 percent in 1723 to about 33 percent in 1811.[126]

Thus, an increase in labor with relatively small gains in standard of living was probably at least as characteristic of western Europe as of China in the sixteenth through the eighteenth centuries. However, another part of DeVries's characterization of European changes does differ sharply from Huang's picture of China: "The industrious revolution was a process of household-based resource *allocation* that increased both the supply of marketed commodities *and* labor and the *demand for market-supplied goods*."[127] In other words, as Europeans worked more hours producing for the market, they used some of the cash they earned to buy finished or semi-finished household goods that they formerly made themselves: bread, candles, and so on.[128] Though total hours of labor still rose,[129] spending money to decrease housekeeping labor indicates that women's time was not assumed to have a zero opportunity cost.

By contrast, Huang suggests—though he does not say so explicitly—that Chinese peasants did not significantly reduce the amount of their domestic labors. Thus, no rural market for industrial goods developed because family (especially female) labor was simply increased, rather than increased and reallocated, as DeVries describes for Europe. If true, this would be a crucial contrast, but it lacks empirical support. Instead, it appears that DeVries's picture of western Europe describes advanced areas of China as well.

Some increase and some reallocation of labor occurred in both settings. Many of the new items rural Europeans started buying—coffee, tobacco, sugar (on which rural *artisans* spent more, proportionate to their income, than any other group of Europeans,[130] though most peasants probably bought very little)—were not simply purchased versions of things once made laboriously at home; indeed, most were not even heavily consumed at home until the nineteenth century.[131] Thus, it seems unlikely that they saved much home-labor time, unless we see them as a compensation for the decline in much-coveted (and labor-intensive) cooked meat. Other goods that became more common in peasant households—furniture, plates, wall decorations, and so

[125] Nipperdey 1996: 91–93.
[126] Ibid., 121, 144, 150, 183, 192, 197.
[127] DeVries 1994b: 249 (emphasis added).
[128] DeVries 1993: 107–21.
[129] DeVries 1994b: 257.
[130] Kriedte, Medick, and Schlumbohm 1981: 64–65, 68–69; Medick 1982: 90–92.
[131] On sugar, see Mintz 1985: 132.

on—also seem unrelated to saving labor. Instead, they may mark a reevaluation of minimum levels of subsistence and perhaps of the utility of owning certain goods relative to leisure.[132] It is also possible that accepted standards of subsistence were not rising but changing: i.e., that owning a chest of drawers came to seem more important to holding one's head up and eating meat frequently less so. But other increasingly common goods—bakery bread, brewery beer, and tailor-made clothes—clearly did save household labor time. (In fact, if we think of all production for home use as pure "labor," some of it quite unremunerative, the increased specialization involved in the industrious revolution might even have led to an increase in average returns to all labor hours, despite falling per-hour wages. On the other hand, the issue is complicated considerably in that some kinds of household labor [cooking, child care, and so on] may be experienced as at least partially "leisure.")

Chinese, like Europeans, also bought increasing amounts of sugar and tobacco—in fact, we shall see later that they probably ate more sugar before 1830. Laboring to finance these purchases clearly marked an increase in, rather than a reallocation of, labor. And since both grain and meat consumption seem to have held steady[133] with very little change in preparation styles, it seems unlikely that much household labor was saved there (though research on Chinese food-processing industries might require a reevaluation of this picture). Perhaps most important, what little data we have suggest that the amount of labor needed to buy a given quantity of rice increased steadily between about 1100 (when cultivated-land-to-population ratios were at their most favorable) and at least 1800,[134] a pattern much like that of post-plague Europe. (In eighteenth-century China, as in Europe, some people switched to less-preferred foods, especially New World food crops;[135] but, again, this does not change the general pattern of rising food costs.)

China also resembled Europe insofar as people began to purchase more non-food items, even as the cost of getting enough calories rose. There is some evidence for increased ownership of furniture, jewelry, and other items among the general population. Since we lack anything comparable to the inventories taken of Europeans' possessions at death, it is extremely difficult to compare the upward creep in the perceived value of various goods (and thus of money) relative to leisure in China with that in Europe, but the direction of change seems similar. We shall examine what evidence there is in chapter 3 and see that the resemblance to Europe is a fairly close one. For the purposes of our current question—whether the increased labor of Chinese was clearly more involutionary than in Europe—it is enough to say that there was *some* increase

---

[132] DeVries 1976: 179–80; DeVries 1993: passim and 107–14.

[133] Perkins 1969: 71.

[134] Zhao 1983: 55–57.

[135] See Ho (1955) on the spread of New World food crops generally, noting that they were most important in marginal areas.

in non-food purchases and no known loss of preferred foods comparable to the decline in European meat eating.

Chinese also seem to have sharply increased their purchases of services, perhaps more so than Europeans, who seem to have favored the sorts of durable goods that show up in death inventories. There is, for instance, abundant evidence of a large increase in the hiring of ritual specialists and professional entertainers in the sixteenth through eighteenth centuries, even by very humble people: indeed, a fee-for-service ritual and entertainment sector had been growing since at least the eighth century. By contrast, established churches and unpaid community groups continued to handle most life-cycle rituals in much of Europe without fee-for-service arrangements. The commercialization of leisure was a fairly new phenomenon, even for the middle classes in relatively prosperous, urban and "bourgeois" England, until the late seventeenth and eighteenth centuries.[136] Given numerous cultural differences, it would not be very surprising if Chinese consumers allocated their growing purchasing power differently from northwest Europeans. Such a difference between Chinese and European consumer preferences, if it existed, might have had long-term significance, but it would hardly be evidence of "involution."[137] But by the same token, with no drop in meat consumption comparable to that in Europe, it seems more unambiguous that the increase in other forms of consumption in China represented a net gain in the standard of living achieved by this increase in work.

Thus, neither living standards nor labor inputs in general (so far as we can tell) justify opposing an "involutionary" China to an "industrious" Europe, nor does what we know about household dynamics and labor more specifically.

If rural China was truly an involuted economy—one in which the opportunity costs for at least women's and children's labor were so low that they would almost never forgo a chance to work more and earn even a pittance more—one would also expect that their households would almost never spend any money in order to reduce women's work—but they did. For instance, cotton clothing almost completely replaced hemp clothing between 1350 and 1850, and Huang himself notes that hemp, with its short fibers, requires "a rather elaborate process" to create thread suitable for making clothes; cotton

---

[136] On China, see Teiser (1993) and the essays in Johnson, Nathan, and Rawski 1985; on England, see Plumb 1972.

[137] Nor, I hasten to point out, would such a difference necessarily mean that Chinese (or other non-Europeans) were necessarily more "other-worldly" or more inclined to "waste" resources on "unproductive" rituals. A local performance or funeral procession uses the same resources—people's time, food, the material in costumes, etc.—regardless of whether professionals or amateurs do it. Nor are "ritual" expenditures *necessarily* less economically productive than others. Carving memorial tablets creates economic demand just as smoking tobacco does, and neither does much physically that makes the purchaser a better producer: within a given context, either might be psychologically important to maintaining somebody as an effective producer and member of the community.

was much easier to work with.[138] The purchasing of candles increased throughout China, as it did throughout Europe, evidence of a willingness to use money to reduce the labor needed to run the household. As we shall see shortly, Chinese families spent more money to save time in their production of goods for sale, too.

Some special goods were still produced for home use in defiance of market-based notions of efficiency. For instance, since embroidery skills became an increasingly critical sign of womanliness in late imperial China, strong pressures remained for young women (at least those of some status) to include in their dowry chest some items they had embroidered themselves—even though that skill took quite a bit of time to learn and many young women no doubt could have done better financially by working full-time at weaving or silk-reeling for the market and buying embroidered goods. (Some did so, in spite of these values.)[139] But some such resistance to a completely market-driven life (or, to put it differently, the culturally expressive use of some production processes) exists in all societies. The homogeneous category of "home-produced goods and services" is in fact composed of many specific goods, and people in any given culture feel more strongly about continuing to produce some of them for themselves and their families than others. The same is even more true of another abstract homogeneous category that is traded off against the family members' work for the market: "leisure." This term includes all sorts of activities (doing crossword puzzles, listening to or making music, having sex, attending another family member's birthday party, and so on); in any culture, some can be more acceptably sacrificed to produce more income (and thus opportunities for purchased gratification) than others.

Thus, the presence of some household activities that were not transformed in the "industrious revolution"—however significant they may be for understanding Chinese culture—do not show that this process was weaker in China than in Europe, unless there were far more of them or they concerned far more basic items. (A society, for instance, in which feeding somebody was considered too intimate to be done for strangers for mere cash would have a far more powerful barrier to the "industrious revolution" than in either China or Europe.) Instead, the differences between China and Europe in these matters seem to run in both directions, with no clear net "advantage." For instance, Chinese peasant women, being more likely than Europeans to live in extended families, probably had easier access to free child care from people too old to work in the fields or at a loom. European peasant women would have had fewer such opportunities and a far less powerful claim than Chinese women had that their mothers-in-law should help with this as a matter of course.

[138] P. Huang 1990: 44; see also Warden (1967) for a description of problems making yarn from flax (638–39) and hemp (48–49).

[139] Bray 1997: 256, 260, 263, 265.

And turning child care over to non-kin was both costly and (in some periods) stigmatized.

At this point, then, we cannot say from output or consumption patterns whether China or western Europe saw more of an "industrious revolution"— including reallocation as well as extension of family labor and an increase in time-saving consumption—or which place saw something closer to pure "involution." It seems safest to place both in the same category and to acknowledge the growing relevance of labor markets, markets for both time-saving and other goods, and demographic pressure at both ends of Eurasia. To clinch the case for comparability, let us look as directly as we can at the valuations of people's labor time implicit in various production arrangements. We will first look at male labor, and then at women, who, having fewer employment options, are the most likely to have been trapped in an involutionary economy.

Production Decisions and Labor Allocation

We lack adequate data on small-farm production decisions. But male agricultural wages never fell below the cost of feeding the worker, and those who had access to land they could farm themselves are unlikely to have faced worse than rural proletarians. Moreover, the sharp increase in purchases of soybean cake fertilizer—which cost much more than manure (especially, of course, self-supplied manure) but could be applied with much less labor—is quite suggestive. One could, in fact, infer from wage and price data that households that bought beancake were implicitly valuing male labor at a rate that was roughly in line with the market wage.[140] Finally, since estimates of the number of labor days used to cultivate one *mu* (or one-sixth of an acre) of rice in the Yangzi Delta are virtually identical for the 1600s, the 1800s, and the 1930s,[141] while output per *mu* rose[142] and rents as a percentage of output probably fell,[143]

---

[140] According to Pan (1994: 36–38, 110–13; see also Adachi, 1978) a given weight of beancake substituted for anywhere from thirty to fifty times as much properly diluted manure and so could be applied with less labor; it also saved a large amount of labor that would otherwise be needed to gather fertilizer. A family that spent three *taels* to purchase enough beancake to provide the supplementary fertilizer on five *mu* of paddy was spending three-fifths of the annual cash wage of a long-term hired hand, but closer to one-fourth of his total cash and in-kind wage. The difference between the cost of beancake and purchased manure was probably about one month's total wage for a laborer (erring on the side of high wages) and reduced the amount needed to be hauled out to the fields by about 4,800–6,200 pounds. Depending on how scattered one's plots were, this might have saved a substantial portion of a month's labor. Adachi focuses on soybean cake purchases by wealthy farmers but specifically says that they made these purchases in large part to save on wages; it appears that a similar logic applied to smaller farms, too. (A five *mu* plot was probably toward the small end of the "average" range for the lower Yangzi Valley in the eighteenth century: see Pan [1994: 521–24], for a good discussion of plausible "average" plot sizes.) Comparisons to the average wage of day laborers are less favorable, but day laborers' wages had to be well above subsistence, since there were many days on which such people could not find work.

[141] Pan 1994: 41–43.   [142] Perkins 1969: 21.   [143] Bernhardt 1992: 228.

we actually have less indication of *agricultural* involution for at least this part of China than for early modern Europe, with its increasing working hours and arguably falling real returns for unskilled labor.

Nor do comparisons involving female labor clearly mark Europe as more "revolutionary" and China as more "involutionary." Cultural objections to women's working outside the home were stronger in China than in Europe, but that does not necessarily mean that female Europeans sold their labor in a freer market than that in which Chinese women sold their homemade products. As we have already seen, guild rules often kept European women out of product markets. Those rules were part of more general cultural norms that encouraged men to have their wives concentrate as much as possible on production for the home (however unrealistic this was for most of the population), and thus they could be at least as hostile to female enterprise as Chinese preferences, which held that women should preferably stay within the family compound but saw nothing wrong with them engaging in market-oriented production there. It is probably no accident that European Enlightenment monarchs imitated the Chinese ritual of having the emperor plow the year's first furrow, but not the practice of having empresses publicly gather mulberry leaves and patronize the silkworm goddess.[144] Certainly the idea of celebrating female production for the market as well as for home use and considering these tasks an *aid* to women's task of raising moral children[145] would have seemed quite foreign to a great many Europeans.

Of course, Chinese women rarely marketed or directed their production by themselves. They were generally supervised by husbands or mothers-in-law, who quite plausibly undervalued their leisure time and kept them at work even after the returns to further labor had sunk well below the market wage. However, the mere fact that more European women sold their labor directly to non-kin does not mean that they were not pushed by similar forces within their households to sell more of this labor than they would have wished—and without relief from low-return housework.

Moreover, when Chinese families sold the textiles their women made, they did so in a world of multiple, competitive buyers: though accounts of the relationship between peasant households and merchants vary, all agree that peasants themselves continued to enter the market with their goods.[146] By contrast, the European putting-out system—in which merchants provided the raw

[144] For French and Austrian monarchs imitating Chinese imperial farming rituals, see Ledderose 1991: 245–46. On the Qing Empresses' involvement in the silkworm goddess cult—"the only public function at which women presided as imperial officials"—see Mann 1992: 79–81.

[145] Chinese thinkers often argued that by observing their mothers at these tasks, children learned diligence, frugality, and discipline. Thus even women who could afford to not produce any cash income were often encouraged to do so, while European women were often urged to avoid working for pay if they could afford to. See Mann 1992: 86–89.

[146] Tanaka 1984: 90–92; Nishijima 1984: 61–62; Lu 1992: 490.

materials and often the equipment and an advance on wages, so that the worker had no product to sell—meant that these employers were often able to bypass a competitive labor market in much the same way that the emerging "private trade" in grain did. Merchants often divided territories so as not to compete with each other; this allowed them to bind workers to a single employer in a system that was quite close to debt peonage, or at least to continue adding workers without driving wages up.[147]

Finally, our admittedly sparse wage data suggest that China may well have been less "involuted" than western Europe. Huang relies heavily on one survey of eighteenth-century Henan wage contracts in which it appears that husband-wife teams were paid less cash (above and beyond their board) than a husband who hired out alone. Accepting such a deal would indicate that these families considered it a good idea for women to continue working even for sub-subsistence wages, and that the other things women could do (such as cotton-spinning and weaving) paid as badly or worse. But a few contracts from a poor province with limited commercial textile production are not much on which to hang an argument about rich, textile-producing areas; moreover, the contracts themselves are somewhat ambiguous.[148] Finally, Huang's estimates of the earnings of female spinners and weavers are based on late seventeenth-century prices, which, as we shall see shortly, do not represent average conditions.

By contrast, Pan Ming-te has constructed a series of hypothetical but plausible peasant-family budgets for the mid-eighteenth century. They suggest that an adult woman and her nine-year-old daughter could add 11.73 *taels* (Chinese ounces of silver) per year to the income of a fairly poor peasant family in Jiangnan by raising silkworms and weaving the thread they produced and still get the housework done; if the family could finance this production without borrowing, they could earn 13.73 *taels*.[149] A male farm laborer in this area would earn at most 5 *taels* per year, plus some meals for himself,[150] even if he managed to get twelve months of work (not a very likely scenario); if he was a year-round laborer rather than being hired by the day or month, he might have had all his meals taken care of but would have earned only 2–4 *taels* of silver.

Thus, these estimates of the earning potential of women's "extra" labor appear to be at or above the market wage for unskilled male labor. Even the 11.73 *taels* would represent about 85 percent of a male laborer's wage circa

[147] Kriedte, Medick, and Schlumbohm 1981: 50–51, 102–4.

[148] P. Huang 1990: 65, citing Li Wenzhi et al. 1983: 407, 413–17. The contracts for husband and wife laborers may often have included board for children as well as the parents; or the contracts for the husband alone may have involved fewer meals (on the assumption that his wife would prepare some for him). Either of these possibilities would invalidate Huang's inference.

[149] Data from Pan 1994: 97–101. I have added additional calculations.

[150] Zhao 1983: 55–56.

1750 if the male worked all twelve months at monthly rates *and* received all of his food in addition to the cash wages. And since, on average, our hypothetical silk-raising mother-daughter team would have eaten about 90 percent of an adult male's rice consumption,[151] they earned a surplus above their own subsistence essentially equal to his. Granted, this surplus reflects the work of two people, but one, a nine-year-old, could hardly be expected to earn as much as an adult. Each would have been devoting far less of her time to this work than our hypothetical twelve-month male farm worker; and we have made generous assumptions about the male's earning power while assuming the women had to borrow at the highest rates recorded (10 percent per *month*) to finance their efforts.

Women's earnings in the much larger cotton sector were also well above an "involutionary" level. Lu Hanchao's study of the Lower Yangzi suggests that a woman weaver in the late seventeenth century could earn enough to feed three or four people if her husband supplied the raw cotton.[152] But, like those of Huang, Lu's estimates are based on the 1690s. China was just emerging from a brutal depression, and the relative prices of different commodities seem to have been quite unusual. Our main price source for 1696, for instance, reports that cotton cloth prices were low that year, while the price of raw cotton was at its highest level in eight years, a situation that would make the earnings of weavers and spinners unusually low. And for somebody to say that cotton cloth prices were unusually low during the 1690s is quite striking in light of what would have been in their recent memory: prices in the 1680s had reached a fifty-year low and were far below those that had prevailed during most of the Ming dynasty.[153] By the mid-Qing, on the other hand, prices for medium-grade cloth were close to double those of the seventeenth century; prices for high-grade cloth were also up, though not quite as much. (We lack adequate data for the lowest grades of cloth, but the Lower Yangzi produced less and less of this anyway.)[154] And it is this period, taking in most of the eighteenth and early nineteenth centuries, which is most important to us.

But one might suspect that the demographic boom of the eighteenth century would raise grain prices faster than those for handicrafts. It was therefore necessary to estimate the real earning power of spinners and weavers at a later date. I have done so for the 1750s in appendix E, using two different sets of data for raw cotton and cloth prices. I have then relied in the text on the lower set, which seemed more reliable, and which yielded significantly lower real earnings.

I have also—among other things—continued to assume that the male farm workers found a full twelve months of work, while calculating women's earnings based on a work year of 200–210 days. In reality, it would probably make

---

[151] Pan 1994: 348.
[152] Lu 1992: 482–83.
[153] Zhang Zhongmin 1988: 207.
[154] Ibid., 207–8.

more sense to assume that it was the women weavers and spinners who could work year-round; a twentieth-century survey in the heart of the Lower Yangzi cotton country estimated 305 days of work per year.[155]

Women who only spun cotton did indeed earn very little, at least using our low-price scenario, enough to buy about 1.3 *shi* of grain, or barely half the needs of an adult female. But as Huang himself points out, very few women who only spun were adults; and even 1.3 *shi* would exceed the food intake of a preteen girl (who did much of the spinning) for the days that she actually spun. Moreover, this is the one case in which using the lower set of price data may build in a serious pessimist bias. And the high-price scenario still shows such women making well above subsistence rates.[156]

For women who wove as well as spun cotton, earnings were much better, and our case therefore becomes clearer. Such a woman could earn about 12 *taels* in a 210-day mid-century year, or about 7.2 *shi* of rice. This is slightly above the midpoint of a range for the earnings of male agricultural workers under our best-case scenario and enough to feed an adult female and as many as five small children; or, more realistically, an adult female, an elderly parent-in-law (who perhaps could handle some of the housework), and two or three children. Indeed the combination of this woman's lower food needs and higher earnings meant that her surplus above her own subsistence was 1.6 to 3 times that of a male agricultural laborer.

Finally, a rare woman who could purchase yarn and focus completely on weaving could theoretically earn 24 *taels* even in our low-price scenario: roughly double the earnings of either the weaver/spinner or a male agricultural laborer, and probably close to the earnings of the (mostly male) urban weavers who made very high quality fabrics.[157] Li Bozhong has also argued that a woman able to concentrate on weaving could earn more than a male laborer, and far more than the cost of subsistence, though his methods, dates, and estimates are different from those here.[158] In sum, forcing Chinese women to do their work for the market from within the home may have been more socially and culturally confining than the world of female work in Europe, but it does not seem to have artificially depressed productivity much.

That Chinese women at home apparently earned not much less than male proletarians (and perhaps more) becomes important when we consider a provocative new version of the "involution" hypothesis, offered by Jack Gold-

---

[155] Xu Xinwu 1992: 469.

[156] See appendix E. On the reasons why the low-price scenario may be too pessimistic here, see pages 321–22 in particular.

[157] For some wage figures for these weavers in the 1730s and 1740s, see Zhao 1983: 57. These wages actually appear to be lower than 16 *taels* for three of the four cases he cites, but the figures once again seem to include only cash earnings, while the workers almost certainly also received meals, perhaps lodging, and some other benefits.

[158] Li Bozhong 1998: 150–51.

stone.[159] Goldstone, unlike Huang, does not claim that China was more over-populated or had less-developed labor markets (at least for males) when compared to Europe. Indeed, much as I have done here, he uses the work of Levine and others to paint a picture of a Europe with a labor surplus (in a loose sense), mostly in proto-industry, comparable to that of China; he then continues to treat the two areas as similar, arguing (without ever using the word "involution") that in *both* places one found a large number of people, mostly women, whose opportunity costs (and thus the wages one needed to pay them) were well below those of unskilled men.

Goldstone then argues that this very cheap female labor cut into the potential profit of any employer who would have to compete with it using male labor—even if that employer could use machines to make his workers far more productive. Thus, Goldstone claims (here resembling Huang) that self-exploiting women in Chinese peasant homes made building factories less attractive than it would have been without their competition. (Note that for Goldstone what matters is the male-female wage gap. Thus, even if women, who ate less than men, earned their subsistence—eliminating "involution" in Huang's sense—Goldstone's argument could still hold.) The difference in Europe, he argues, is that women could leave the home to work. Thus the nascent mills could hire the same very cheap labor they were competing with and realize the profit-making potential of their new machinery. Therefore, keeping Chinese women at home—even though they produced for the market there—mattered greatly. It kept China almost factory-less even though every other factor—available capital, technological inventiveness, and so on—made it as good a candidate for industrialization as Europe.

Some of the issues Goldstone raises are dealt with elsewhere in this book. For instance, we have already seen in chapter 1 some problems with looking for blockages to explain the failure of a technological breakthrough to occur, as if it could be logically expected once a society has most of the necessary elements. And we have already seen some reasons to doubt that mechanizing textiles alone could have launched any society into self-sustaining growth; we will have much more to say about this in chapters 5 and 6. But Goldstone's major question remains: were gender norms a major impediment to textile industrialization in China, but not in Europe or Japan?

Certainly the Chinese preference for keeping women within the family compound was a strong one—strong enough to make even many poor families hesitate to send their daughters into factories. But it seems likely that there would still have been enough women (or decision makers in their families) willing to violate this taboo in return for a modest increase in their earnings, had the factories existed. Li Bozhong has shown that however strong and ancient the *ideal* of men plowing and women weaving may have been, it was not

[159] Goldstone 1996: 1–21.

nearly so well established in practice. Numerous texts from the Lower Yangzi region refer to men helping with textiles and women working in the fields in the late Ming (seventeenth century); such references are still fairly plentiful in the mid-Qing and disappear completely only after the Taiping Rebellion (1850–1864).[160] Moreover, the slowly growing implementation of this ideal seems to have been closely intertwined with practicalities, rather than running roughshod over them. Thus, men stopped helping with textile work in part because their skill levels were too low[161]—and their inadequacy presumably got worse as multi-cropping gave them less time to practice anything besides farming—while at the same time, Jiangnan's cloth production became more focused on higher-quality fabrics. Moreover, women disappeared from the fields in areas that combined rice with silk production sooner and more completely than in areas that combined rice with cotton; the reason for this appears to have been that much silk production shifted from home-based to town-based sheds, making it harder for women to make brief trips back to the fields (and making the sheds more like many early factories).[162] And in the tea country of Anhui and the sugar regions of Guangdong and Fujian, women continued to work side by side with men throughout the nineteenth century.[163]

If women could work at all these sites, why not in factories? As Goldstone himself notes, twentieth-century factories did find enough women, though sometimes only with difficulty. One study of contemporary south China argues that this prejudice worked in favor of factory employment for women, since men felt that "their" women were less "exposed" in such jobs than in many others and that the discipline of the factory was more consistent with maintaining "femininity" than were the looser routines of many other jobs.[164] In other words, people have found ways to see cultural norms and factory work as perfectly compatible, rather than clinging to a rigid definition of female modesty. Goldstone assumes that popular attitudes would have posed a much greater barrier in earlier years, arguing that late nineteenth-century foreign influences had probably softened this taboo a good deal. Given how little we know about gender roles and cultural change among non-elite families in late

[160] Li Bozhong 1996: 102–6.

[161] Ibid., 105. Bray (1997: 206–72) argues that men actually took a much greater role in textile production in the late empire—a point that would in many ways further strengthen my claims about the division of labor not being overly constrained by ancient norms. However, her argument is in large part restricted to *representations* of exemplary skills at textile work and to weavers at the very high end of the market (see, e.g., 239–41, 257), a situation perhaps a bit like that of elite male chefs in the West, whose existence did not by itself do much to change the fact that most cooking was done by women.

[162] Li Bozhong 1996: 105. This difference may also help explain the final disappearance of references to farming women in Jiangnan after the Taiping, since it was also at this time that Jiangnan made a very large-scale switch away from cotton and into sericulture (P. Huang 1990: 120–22).

[163] Gardella 1994: 172; Bray 1997: 221–22.   [164] C. K. Lee 1995: 385.

imperial China, this argument cannot be completely dismissed, but Li's evidence of a *less*-pronounced gender division of labor in the Ming and early Qing makes it seem unlikely.

Another question about how powerful this supposedly rigid taboo was comes from Goldstone's own account of the silk industry. Steam-powered filatures—which, like mechanized spindles and looms, required a workforce larger than an individual household could muster—caught on more quickly than cotton technology did. Goldstone notes that this happened first in southeast China, where lineages and *extended* families were unusually strong. He then argues that these extended families could put together a large enough workforce to operate the new machines without having to expose their wives and daughters to non-kin. Thus, he argues, the relatively rapid adaptation of machines too large for a nuclear family in this area just goes to show that it was concern to keep women *within* the family that inhibited the otherwise likely creation/adoption of other new technology. Yet Guangdong produced lots of cotton yarn and cloth as well as silk; in fact, from the sixteenth century on it was probably second only to the Lower Yangzi in both kinds of textiles. Why then did the opportunity for larger female work units presented by the area's kinship structures not manifest itself in cotton production, too?[165] (We do in fact have one report of a number of large urban workshops making cotton cloth in Foshan, Guangdong, in 1833, though at least one historian thinks the source must be incorrect.[166])

The most telling evidence against Goldstone's hypothesis, however—at least for the period before 1800—are the earnings comparisons developed above, which suggest that hypothetical factories would not have suffered from being forced to employ men. Moreover, as Huang points out, most of the females who did cotton-spinning full time in the Lower Yangzi were children—and preteens of both sexes were commonly seen in public.[167] Thus, Goldstone's link between female seclusion and the lack of factories in China seems weak, at least for the eighteenth century. The problem Goldstone describes would indeed have existed had Englishwomen been forced to stay home, since differences in male and female earning power appear to have been far larger there than in the Lower Yangzi.[168] But our evidence suggests that despite a desire to keep them secluded, Chinese women trailed their men in earnings far less than Englishwomen did. And in China, there would also have

---

[165] Goldstone might argue that the kinship structure was flexible enough to allow for adoption of a technology that had already proved its worth, but not enough to encourage somebody to imagine and introduce a new machine that required stretching the limits of existing gender norms. This is not impossible, but it involves us in attributing a very precise degree of effect to a factor that is inherently unquantifiable—and thus makes the argument unfalsifiable.

[166] Chao (1977: 30–31) dismisses this document. Robert Marks, who has done more recent work on Guangdong textiles, is not so sure.

[167] P. Huang 1990: 95.   [168] Horrell and Humphries 1995: 102–3.

been cheap male labor available for industry during non-peak agricultural times; a phenomenon which, as we have seen, powered much of early French industry (though it was apparently rare in northern England, the birthplace of factory industrialization). Finally, we should remember that once people grasped the productivity differences made possible by mechanization, it is almost impossible to imagine a wage differential that, by itself, could make mechanization unprofitable. After all, English yarn conquered the Indian market in the nineteenth century, despite a wage difference larger than any we are likely to see within any single society, plus fairly high transport costs.

But even with all this, it is worth noting that Goldstone's hypothesis might be significant for some parts of the long period between the Chinese switch to cotton cloth (in the 1300s, at which time they already had spinning equipment for ramie very close to the machines that revolutionized English cotton spinning four hundred-plus years later) and the twentieth century, when Chinese spinning was finally mechanized. Indeed, we shall see in chapter 6 that the real earning power of Chinese weavers relative to farm workers fell sharply in periods of especially serious population pressure, such as the early nineteenth and early twentieth centuries; under these circumstances it will be worth returning to some of Goldstone's questions. But it seems unlikely that Goldstone's hypothesis explains much about why industrialization began when and where it did.

Overall, then, it seems that the use of labor in China, like that of land, conformed to the principles of "market economy" at least as well as it did in Europe and likely somewhat better: the "industrious revolution" seems to have been common to at least the two ends of Eurasia. It is possible, of course, that European institutions that developed over the course of the early modern period allowed the returns to certain narrow but significant classes of activity to match more closely the contributions of those activities to the economy than was the case in China. It has been plausibly argued, for instance, that the development of patent law in eighteenth-century England allowed inventors to capture something closer to the full value of their work and thus may have influenced the technological breakthroughs of the Industrial Revolution.[169] But even if true, these arguments would become important only toward the end of our period. And even then, we need to remember how little of western Europe's economy (both in terms of geography and of economic sectors) was transformed by new technology before the mid-nineteenth century and how dependent (as we saw in chapter 1) even the most important inventions were on accident and conjunctures outside Europe for their revolutionary impact. Thus, a difference in the institutions governing the market in inventions would be far too narrow to explain Europe's eventual economic lead at any point before 1830—at the earliest.

[169] E.g., North 1981: 164–66.

Conclusion to Part 1:
Multiple Cores and Shared Constraints in
the Early Modern World Economy

To this point, then, we have examined a variety of arguments that emphasize internally generated European advantages in productivity before the mid-nineteenth century and found them all dubious. Western Europe's demographic-marital system, though unique, did not produce superior fertility control, nor did western Europeans live longer than people in various other areas. There is little to suggest that western Europe's capital stock was significantly larger or embodied decisively superior technology across the board. Its factor markets for land and labor seem no closer to Smithian ideas of freedom and efficiency than do those of China, and perhaps a good deal less so. Moreover, China's much-maligned patterns of family labor use seem, upon closer examination, to have been as responsive to shifting opportunities and price signals as those of northwestern Europe. Far from being unique, then, the most developed parts of western Europe seem to have shared crucial economic features—commercialization, commodification of goods, land, and labor, market-driven growth, and adjustment by households of both fertility and labor allocation to economic trends—with other densely populated core areas in Eurasia.

Furthermore, there is no reason to think that these patterns of development were leading "naturally" to an industrial breakthrough anywhere. Instead, all these core areas were experiencing modest per capita growth, mostly through increased division of labor, within a context of basic technological and ecological constraints that markets alone could not solve. In part 2, which explores activities further removed from physical survival and reproduction, we will look more closely at patterns of "unnecessary" consumption, and we will compare one last set of institutions that shaped a factor market—the legal and social regimes governing large accumulations of commercial and financial capital. Here, too, we will find some differences, but not enough to explain the unique rise of Europe. That, in turn, will lead us, in part 3, to a more detailed look at the shared ecological constraints alluded to in the first two chapters, to relationships between being able to continue the sorts of growth discussed here and embarking on a new, much more dramatic kind—and the role in this transition of conjunctural factors, including those that gave European cores an unprecedented ecological windfall in the New World at the very time that east Asian cores were finding their peripheries increasingly unable to play their accustomed roles in market-driven growth.

PART TWO

FROM NEW ETHOS TO NEW ECONOMY?

CONSUMPTION, INVESTMENT, AND CAPITALISM

INTRODUCTION

IN CHAPTERS 1 and 2 we considered a series of widely accepted arguments that use the institutions of pre-1800 western Europe to explain that region's early entry into industrial growth and found that none of them was convincing in light of recent literature on other areas. There turned out to be little reason to think that western Europeans were more productive than their contemporaries in various other densely populated regions of the Old World prior to 1750 or even 1800. And when we turned to factor markets for land and labor we found, surprisingly enough, that China seemed to conform to neoclassical ideas of efficient economic institutions at least as well as pre-1800 western Europe.

We were left then, with a variety of early modern core regions with roughly comparable levels and trends of development in their everyday economies—the resources, skills, institutions, and activities through which the vast majority produced, bought, and sold the necessities of life. There was no western European advantage sufficient to explain either nineteenth-century industrialization or European imperial success. It seems more likely that no area was "naturally" headed for the drastic discontinuity of industrialization, escape from shared resource constraints, and a role as "workshop of the world."

It is time, then, to move up the social and economic hierarchy. The arguments considered so far refer either to capital accumulation, resource allocation, and market demand in the economy as a whole, or to the institutions that shaped the decisions of the vast majority of households. Despite an apparent lack of important differences in these areas, there could be differences affecting the ability and inclination of a crucial minority of well-to-do households to accumulate capital or to stimulate economic change through changes in what they wished to buy. Many scholars claim that such differences did indeed exist, springing from culturally specific changes in European ideas about the self, the cosmos, and other subjects exogenous to the economy. The most famous cultural explanation for a unique European development path is Max Weber's discussion of the "Protestant ethic" and "ascetic" capitalism, but many more recent scholars focus instead on the stimulatory effects of certain European attitudes toward consumption (especially luxury consumption); and some arguments attempt to combine these seemingly contradictory positions by arguing for a uniquely European "materialism."[1] Still other arguments, based less on culture, claim that the European political economy was uniquely hospitable to commercial capital and allowed financial resources to be more easily gathered, better preserved, and more productively employed than elsewhere.

[1] E.g., Mukerji, 1983.

Despite their diversity, these arguments have much in common. All of them focus on the "commanding heights" of the economy, rather than on the activities of the vast majority of producers (though some also emphasize the eventual spread of upper-class ideas or practices to a larger portion of society). All of them focus on the production, consumption, and distribution of goods whose perceived value had relatively little to do with their contribution to satisfying basic, biological, subsistence needs, except as refracted through *social* expectations (e.g., access to certain luxuries as a precondition for marriage and legitimate procreation within certain circles). Moroever, the value of such goods was often based on being "exotic." Thus long-distance trade, which has been marginal to our discussions so far, plays a more prominent role in this section.

Long-distance trade before steamships raises other issues. The extremely long lag between the start of such ventures and the final sale of the goods obtained means that financial mediation becomes a crucial part of the story. Therefore, issues relating to the status of abstract wealth (i.e., wealth held in the form of paper money, precious metals, or IOUs, rather than in land, stored grain, or other immediately usable items) become crucial, too, as do variations in people's propensity to store that sort of wealth (rather than immediately convert it), in the extent to which it was convertible into other kinds of resources and protected by law or custom (which could, of course, be very different from the degree of protection accorded other assets). Along with abstract wealth we must consider various sorts of rights often connected with long-distance trade, such as legal grants of monopoly and other special privileges.

Because long-distance trade involved producers and consumers who would never meet, this commerce also allowed the relative few who occupied strategic positions the possibility of profit rates much higher than were possible in more local, multi-sided, and face-to-face markets. Thus, as Fernand Braudel emphasizes, the "capitalism" of the greatest merchants in the fifteenth through the eighteenth centuries flourished where conditions *least* resembled those of perfect markets. He nonetheless calls systems in which this sort of exchange was particularly well developed "capitalist," since in such societies credit and financial instruments play a large role, capital is generally deployed in order to accumulate more of it, and because such societies are likely to be gradually reshaped in ways that facilitate such accumulation. Thus both the culture and the political economy of "capitalism" must be treated separately from the worlds of daily life and market economy that we have discussed so far. What unifies the "cultural" and "institutional" arguments about capitalism—aside from the fact that culture and institutions are never really separate from each other—are the ways their concerns differ from those in the arguments about markets, subsistence, and ordinary people we discussed in part 1.

But we will see that most of these arguments also fail to decisively differentiate western Europe's prospects from those of China and Japan, though they may well separate these three from the rest of the world. (India is a complex intermediate case.) Some differences do appear but they seem too small to explain much, except in one way. Both luxury demand and the political economy of capitalism (in a broad sense that I will explain in chapter 4) had much to do with allowing Europe to gain control over the New World (though other, conjunctural factors were also critical). And the New World turned out to be vital—not so much for capital accumulation (as some scholars have argued), but because its resources helped Europe move off a path of ecologically constrained, primarily labor-intensive development (which it shared with China and Japan) onto a far more transformative path that used prodigious amounts of both energy and land.

In part 3 we will begin with those ecological constraints (and thus return to the world of ordinary people) in chapter 5. Chapter 6 will then examine institutional, ecological, and conjunctural reasons why it was Europe that was able to ease those constraints, examine their significance for the Industrial Revolution, and look briefly ahead at the "East-West" divergence that followed, examining both western Europe's fate and the fate of those areas that continued down the labor-intensive, resource-saving path on which western Europe had recently been just another traveler.

THREE

LUXURY CONSUMPTION AND
THE RISE OF CAPITALISM

More and Less Ordinary Luxuries

ARGUMENTS ABOUT the rise of "luxury" or "consumer society" after about 1400 fall into two rough groups. The first emphasizes the growth of luxury consumption among the very wealthy, usually arguing that a new emphasis on the deployment of expensive, often durable manufactured objects—silks, mirrors, elegant furniture, etc.—replaced earlier ways of expressing status, such as maintaining large retinues, which did less to stimulate production; Werner Sombart called this the "objectification" of luxury.[1] As part of this shift, luxuries became increasingly available to anyone who had enough money to buy them, rather than being restricted to those who also met certain social criteria for owning prestigious goods.

But this new luxury only translated into status if these objects were deployed according to canons of taste, which began to change more rapidly than they did in the past: these canons were partly a defense by old elites against too simple a translation of new wealth into status through consumption. This rise of "fashion" dictated that even those who owned large amounts of such durable goods as furniture or crystal would feel increasingly pressured to buy new goods, so that demand for these goods, while still experienced as *socially* necessary, became even more unmoored from any sort of physical necessity.

And finally, these arguments continue, these high-status consumption patterns were imitated by "lesser" folk. This imitation was facilitated by urbanization, which also created concentrated markets. It was further encouraged by new conceptions of the self and increased fluidity in social structure, which allowed not only the nouveaux riches but the "middling sort" and even some of the poor to use their money to claim social niches through proper kinds of consumption.

A second family of arguments—which includes Sidney Mintz's famous discussion of the growth of sugar consumption in the early modern and modern West—also *begins* at the top of society but emphasizes the transformation of what had once been luxuries into everyday goods for the middle class and eventually even the poor. It is not surprising that here, the focus is much less on substantial, durable luxury items and more on goods available in small

---

[1] Sombart 1967: 95.

units and often consumed quickly. These might include a silver hairpin or a framed picture, but they mostly consisted of what Mintz calls "the drug foods": sugar, cocoa, tobacco, coffee, and tea, all of them exotic luxuries in any part of sixteenth-century Europe but commonplace in much of western Europe by the late nineteenth century.[2]

Though these two phenomena overlap, those who focus on upper-class luxury emphasize different links to industrialization than those who focus on humbler folk and the "drug foods." Arguments about popular consumption usually claim that the demand for these sorts of goods, unobtainable except through the market, made ordinary people more hungry for cash: they thus encouraged people to work more, more intensely, and more for the market, rather than preferring to stop working for money once they had enough to meet their basic subsistence needs. Or, to put the matter differently, they redefined "subsistence" so that it included more purchased goods—some of which could not possibly be produced at home—thus contributing to the "industrious revolution" we discussed in the previous chapter. (If a customary requirement that one bring to one's marriage a quilt one had made oneself slowed a household's full acceptance of the market as arbiter of how to use their daughter's time, so a requirement that one have tea or cigarettes to offer visitors pushed one toward fuller adherence to comparative advantage; but neither one of these was clearly more a matter of "social constraint" as opposed to "individual choice" than the other.) And quite apart from changing social expectations, several of the new foods were mildly (or not so mildly) addictive and well-suited to the routines of increasingly disciplined work, which was increasingly likely to be done away from the worker's home. All of them were stimulants, easily packaged, and thus available with minimal on-site preparation to provide a break and "pick-me-up" at intervals during the workday.

Thus, these arguments focus on how the consumption of these commodities expanded aggregate demand and how that demand changed the way that ordinary people behaved as *producers*. Moreover, the Europeans affected were influenced in their capacities as producers of all sorts of *other* items—from grain to wagons to clothing—but they did not produce the drug foods themselves. Sugar, tobacco, etc., were grown outside Europe, often by slaves or other sorts of unfree laborers: such workers were not being offered an increased variety of consumer goods in hopes of making them more productive. These extra-European labor systems mattered to the European story because they increased the availability and lowered the price of the drug foods, not because they exemplified the new motivations that would fuel expanded production in Europe.[3]

---

[2] Mintz 1985: 108.

[3] Mintz (1985: 57–60) does suggest that New World plantations may have prefigured European factories in their scale of operation, intensity of work, and need for close supervision and coordination, but he is quite clear about distinguishing the direct coercion used to intensify work in the New

The arguments that focus on more durable and expensive luxuries are quite different. One could argue that the need for cash to buy these luxuries drove members of the elite to deploy whatever productive assets they owned more rationally and thus to bring more grain or other humdrum goods to market—but such arguments are hard to prove and must be balanced against cases in which purchasing baubles interfered with funding, say, the draining of a swamp. And older forms of elite behavior, including the support of retainers, also created demand.

On the other hand, many of these durable luxuries were produced largely in Europe, and the emergence of urban centers where such demand was concentrated did create important incentives for producers to expand production, realize economies of scale, and introduce new techniques. There were great opportunities, but only for those with enough working capital to buy expensive raw materials, pay skilled workers, and wait until their often powerful but cash-short customers finally paid their bills; thus a certain subset of luxury producers became successful capitalists, while others gradually became wage workers. Consequently, while discussions of elite, durable luxury consumption may mention aggregate demand for the whole economy, their focus is elsewhere—on how growing luxury markets changed the ways goods were produced, fostering new institutions and differentiating among the producers.

Thus, for our purposes, the arguments about drug foods and popular luxuries look backward toward issues raised in the last chapter: popular participation in markets, labor allocation, and popular standards of living. The arguments about durable but more exclusive luxuries, on the other hand, point toward issues that belong with the discussion of capitalism in chapter 4: changes in the structures of firms; increased control of production by those able to provide credit; and accumulation of profits by a relatively small number of people with strong incentives to reinvest. Thus, although elite consumerism came first chronologically, it makes more analytical sense to begin with everyday luxuries.

Everyday Luxuries and Popular Consumption in
Early Modern Europe and Asia

Ideally, we would not compare consumption of individual goods but of entire market baskets; and ideally, we would know that preferences were similar enough across cultures that differences in consumption were a matter of pur-

---

World from the consumerist motivation that constitutes the really revolutionary aspect of these new luxuries for European production. Moreover, though he does show certain ways in which plantations resembled factories, he does not show that any direct "learning" occurred, and there are many other institutions from which the relevant features could have been adapted.

chasing power. The realities of eighteenth-century data mean that we have no such assurances and so must be careful about the meaning of the following comparisons. Still our estimates (in chapter 1) of similar life expectancies and (later in this chapter) of the similar portion of household budgets taken up by basic calories suggest that comparisons of other kinds of consumption have some significance for our larger project.

It is important to remember the limits of the boom in "everyday luxuries," at least before the mid-nineteenth century. The list of new foods, fabrics, beverages, and the like after 1400 is dazzling, and many could be addictive. But they all spread rather slowly until at least the late eighteenth century and generally until well into the nineteenth century: huge percentage increases generally reflect tiny initial bases, even in the wealthiest parts of Europe. Even England consumed only about one pound of tea per person per year circa 1800, and 1.4 pounds in 1840; it was *after* this that prices fell dramatically and ordinary people became everyday consumers. (Consumption reached about 5 pounds per person per year by 1880.)[4] And for the rest of Europe, figures were far lower. Non-Russian Europe reported about 22,000,000 pounds of tea per year in the 1780s;[5] this would suggest that the whole continent consumed perhaps 2 ounces per person and non-English Europe considerably less. Even in 1840, the 80,000,000–90,000,000 pounds of tea exported to Europe would have provided barely 4 ounces per inhabitant per year.[6]

Chinese consumption was significantly higher. Wu Chengming has estimated the domestic tea trade at about 260,000,000 pounds in 1840, and his other estimates of Chinese internal commerce have generally been on the low side.[7] If there were 380,000,000 Chinese at this date,[8] this would be just under 11 ounces per capita—even in the unlikely case that Wu's estimates did not miss any significant local or regional circuits of tea trading.

Of course, tea consumption is an unfair comparison. High shipping costs, tariffs, and monopolies made tea far more expensive in Europe than in China, and Europeans consumed various beverages (coffee, cocoa, wine from grapes) that China lacked. Still, it is striking how long we must wait before European consumption of this "everyday luxury" outstrips that of China. We have no figures for tobacco, but both Staunton and MacCartney, British envoys to China in 1793, were struck by how much the Chinese smoked; their assertions are corroborated by a Chinese letter claiming that in Zhejiang (a generally

---

[4] Braudel 1982: 252, citing Staunton; Gardella 1994: 38.

[5] Braudel 1982: 251.

[6] Based on export figures in Gardella (1994: 6) and population figures in McEvedy and Jones (1978: 28).

[7] Wu 1983: 99.

[8] Estimates of Chinese population on the eve of the mid-nineteenth-century catastrophes have generally been in the area of 425–450 million, but more recent work by G. W. Skinner suggests that a figure of around 380 million may be more accurate (1987: 72–76).

TABLE 3.1
Sugar Consumption per Capita (in pounds)

	Europe	Europe ex-Britain	Britain
1680	1.0	.85	4
1750	2.2	1.90	10
1800	2.6	1.98	18

prosperous province, but not one where tobacco was a major crop) "even children two feet high" smoked.[9]

Even in the case of sugar, a European advantage emerges much later than one might expect. Though English consumption was already about 4 pounds per person by 1700 and had reached 18 pounds by 1800,[10] the rest of Europe was far behind. A good estimate for continental Europe in 1800 is a bit under 2 pounds per capita; this would roughly match Braudel's estimate of one kilo per person for France in 1788.[11] Moreover, outside of Britain, the upward trend in consumption is not all that marked, as table 3.1 suggests.[12]

This does not mean that the growth in sugar consumption was entirely a British story. "Europe ex-Britain" is too crude a category; at least the Netherlands and the areas around Paris, Bordeaux, and Hamburg would show much sharper growth than the rest of the continent, if not nearly as much as Britain. (As late as 1846, Parisian consumption was a bit under 8 pounds per capita.[13]) Moreover, an 1800 date—in the midst of the Napoleonic Wars—depresses consumption figures. (Indeed, sugar shortages in Paris had led to popular agitation in an earlier stage of the French Revolution.[14]) Nonetheless, these figures are worth pondering.

First of all, despite using slave labor to grow cheaper sugar, consumption was *not* on a steady upward trend throughout Europe. Today, when Europe's per capita consumption dwarfs that of England in 1800, sugar's "conquest of the world"[15] appear inexorable once specialized, cost-conscious plantations were growing it for an emerging "consumer society." And sugar, as Mintz makes clear, was not just any commodity. It had been sought by Europeans for centuries, exchanged by kings and popes, and had behind it a lore and mys-

[9] Staunton 1799: II: 48; Cranmer-Byng (Macartney) 1962: 225; letter cited in Dermigny 1964: III: 1253.

[10] Mintz 1985: 67.

[11] Using Mintz (1985: 73) for Europe as a whole and subtracting out for Britain (Mintz 1985: 67). For the French estimate, see Braudel 1982: 226.

[12] Production figures from Phillipps (1990: 58–61) for Portuguese and Spanish colonies and Steensgaard (1990a: 140) for French, Dutch, and English colonies. European population figures from McEvedy and Jones 1978: 26–29. British consumption figures from Mintz (1985: 67, 73) using 1700 figure for 1680.

[13] Braudel 1982: 226.   [14] Ibid., 227.   [15] Ibid., 224.

tique that more newly discovered tobacco or cocoa could not match; it was eagerly promoted by powerful investors and mercantilist governments who stood to gain from increased consumption; and it can be physically addictive.[16] Given all this, a fifty-year pause in the growth of European consumption—during a general economic upturn—suggests that imagining an irreversible "birth of a consumer society"[17] before 1850 may be seriously misleading. By the same token, arguments that make too much of pauses in the growth of "luxury" consumption elsewhere may be taking something quite normal and treating it as an anomaly that points to interference with a process that would otherwise "naturally" continue.

Second, the table reminds us that before 1850 we mostly have an English revolution, not a European one. Both in absolute and relative terms, the gap between Britain and most of Europe was growing, not shrinking. Sidney Pollard's point about *production*—that several noncontiguous regions in Europe, not Europe as a whole, had a ninteenth-century revolution—seems to hold for consumption, too.[18] Both this geographic unevenness and the halting pattern of consumption growth need to be kept in mind when we compare other areas to an idealized "European" story.

Sugar had important ritual uses among the upper class in China (principally in Buddhist ritual) as far back as the Tang dynasty, and it was also used medicinally.[19] By the succeeding Song dynasty (960–1279), sugar use among the rich had spread beyond special occasions: "Sugarcane products had become fully integrated into the lifestyle and food habits of the wealthy."[20] In the sixteenth and seventeenth centuries, a number of European visitors remarked on how much *more* extensive sugar use was among the well-to-do of China than among their European counterparts.[21] Meanwhile, sugar use on special occasions seems to have reached the general population: an account from Guangdong province circa 1680 tells us that sugar was molded into the shapes of people, animals, and buildings, and sugared plums were a crucial part of marriages, "whether the girl was rich or poor." The wealthy would prepare feasts at which "several thousand jars" of these were served. The amount of sweetness dispensed was said to influence the experience the new wife would have when she gave birth, and "if there are any who fail to invite people [to a sugar plum feast], everyone calls them 'sugar plum beggars.'"[22] Another source from roughly the same time notes that even the very poor ate sugar biscuits at New Year's and that large amounts of candied fruits were such an essential part of weddings that some families went broke meeting this need.[23] These uses for sugar, a combination of medicinal and ceremonial usage and of

[16] Mintz 1985: 16–18, 138–39, 164.
[17] McKendrick, Brewer, and Plumb 1982: 1–6, esp. 4–5.
[18] Pollard 1981: 84–106, 111–23.   [19] Daniels 1996: 55, 59, 62–63, 70–71.
[20] Mazumdar 1984: 62.   [21] Ibid., 64.
[22] Chu 1968: 14:20b–22a.   [23] Daniels 1996: 73, 75, 80–81.

imitative consumption—with the rich using sugar frequently and the poor doing so on special occasions—seem much like those that Mintz has pointed to in early modern Europe, which paved the way for sugar's nineteenth-century emergence as a major source of calories for ordinary people. This further transformation never occurred in China—but that cannot be explained by anything about eighteenth-century patterns of consumption.

We have no totals for Chinese sugar consumption in the mid-eighteenth century, but even the fragmentary data we have yield remarkably high estimates. The vast majority of Chinese sugar output was in Guangdong, Fujian (including Taiwan), and Sichuan. Fortunately we do have reasonably good figures for Taiwanese sugar shipments to the mainland circa 1720: about 104,000,000 pounds. Though there was no dramatic further growth in Taiwanese sugar output until after the Opium War, a slow, steady increase seems to have continued. Thus it seems safe to use the 1720 figure as a conservative estimate for 1750.

We have no overall output estimates for Guangdong. We have what seems to be a fairly conservative estimate of output per acre on Guangdong cane "plantations"—2,400 pounds[24]—but no direct figures for the extent of land under sugar. But Mazumdar records at least 15 counties in the province (out of 92) that were eighteenth-century centers of cane production;[25] in 3 of them 40 percent of land was reportedly under sugar, and in another 60 percent.[26]

Recent work by Robert Marks suggests an alternative approach. He estimates that at least 24,000,000 *mu* (4,000,000 acres) of Guangdong and Guangxi farmland had to be devoted to cash crops circa 1753; the figure may have been as high as 41,500,000 *mu*. Guangdong had over 70 percent of the total cultivated acreage in the two provinces at this time and an even larger share of non-grain crops. (Guangxi's major cash crop was rice, which was sold in Guangdong.) Thus an estimate that Guangdong had 70 percent of the area's non-grain farmland would be conservative: at least 16,800,000 *mu* (2,800,000 acres) and perhaps as many as 29,050,000 *mu* (4,841,666 acres). Marks has

---

[24] Mazumdar 1984: 297. Mazumdar makes a good case that Chinese sugar yields were unlikely to be much lower than in other parts of Asia. Henry Botham, a late eighteenth-century planter with experience in both the East and West Indies, would have concurred: he testified that Chinese free labor raised sugar more efficiently than bound laborers in Europe's Asian and American colonies (quoted in Daniels 1996: 93); other Westerners argued as late as the 1840s for the superiority of the sugar-growing methods that Chinese brought with them. Shepherd (1993: 159) has a significantly lower estimate of output per-acre for Taiwan, but there was much less pressure to maximize per-acre yields in such a sparsely populated frontier zone than there was on the mainland. Moreover, all of Taiwan's sugar land was still dry-cropped, while much of the sugar in Guangdong and Fujian was grown with irrigation, which permits much higher yields (Daniels 1996: 105, 236). Eugene Anderson (1988: 80–81) gives a range for late imperial sugar yields of anywhere from 1,600 to 3,200 pounds per acre; Mazumdar's figure of 2,400 would be exactly in the middle of that range.

[25] Mazumdar 1984: 280–81.   [26] Cited in ibid., 272.

suggested that a good guess would be that half of Guangdong's cultivated land—21,500,000 *mu*—was in non-grain crops,[27] so using 16,800,000 *mu* seems cautious.

Sugarcane probably occupied more land than any other non-grain;[28] if it was not first, it was second (behind mulberries) or at least third. (Guangdong imported most of its cotton and grew very little tobacco; tea and fruit are the only other plausible contenders for second place on this list.[29]) But even one-tenth of our minimum figure for Guangdong non-grain crops circa 1753 is 280,000 acres; that would place 3.9 percent of the province's total cultivated area in sugar. Multiplying by Mazumdar's estimate of yield per acre, we would get 672,000,000 pounds of sugar per year for Guangdong. Adding Taiwan makes the total 776,000,000 pounds in 1750, without considering Sichuan, the mainland part of Fujian, or the many places where smaller amounts of cane were planted.[30]

A seventeenth-century source estimated that Fujian (including Taiwan) and Guangdong accounted for 90 percent of China's cane crop. This would suggest that we raise our total by at least a further 86,000,000 pounds (one-ninth of Fujian and Guangdong production). In fact, we should probably raise this figure by a larger factor to reflect cane's dispersion by 1750: cane generally spread where Fujianese migrated (both in other parts of China and in Southeast Asia), and these migrations were much greater in the 1700s than they were in the 1600s.[31] Nonetheless, I will omit all production outside Guangdong and Taiwan. Finally, except when the Dutch controlled Taiwan, Chinese sugar exports were quite small before the 1840s;[32] on the other hand, China imported about 80,000,000 pounds of sugar per year from Vietnam in 1730s.[33] (I omit the much smaller amount from Thailand.[34]) Adding these imports gives us Chinese consumption of about 856,000,000 pounds per year at mid-century.

With China's population in 1750 probably 170,000,000–225,000,000,[35] this would suggest a per capita sugar consumption of 3.8–5.0 pounds per year. Adding in other Chinese production would add at least another .4–.5 pounds per year; using the absolute bottom of Anderson's broad range of late imperial

[27] Marks, personal communication, August 1996.

[28] Ibid.

[29] Mazumdar 1984: 271, 372.

[30] See map on p. 90 of Daniels 1996, which includes prefectures in six other provinces that produced some cane.

[31] Daniels 1996: 97, 105.

[32] Mazumdar (1984: 357, 374, 376), gives a 1792 figure of 65,000 piculs, or roughly 8.6 million pounds from Canton, plus another 2.6 million or so pounds to Japan. Even in 1833, exports from Canton had risen only to 34 million pounds.

[33] Nguyen, cited in Reid 1988a: 31.

[34] Cushman 1975: 105.

[35] The official total for 1741 was 141,000,000, but Ho (1959: 36–46) argues that this must be at least a 20 percent underestimate. Others have suggested even higher figures.

yield estimates would subtract 1.1 to 1.4 pounds. Raising the percentage of Guangdong land under sugar even slightly would make the estimates soar.

These estimates far exceed European averages for 1750 and even 1800. Chinese sugar was lower in sucrose content than what Europeans ate, which by today's standards would make it an inferior good. But until the nineteenth century, many people preferred their sugar with *more* impurities, and thus more flavor.[36]

At the late eighteenth-century Beijing price—presumably a relatively high price even for this highest grade, since all sugar came from the far south—a soldier would have needed between 3 and 4.5 days' wages to buy this much white sugar.[37] This does not seem implausible. An agricultural laborer would have needed almost a month's worth of his *cash* wages, which does sound like too much for this one item. But cash was only one part of the income of agricultural laborers; if we were to use the estimates of total cash and in-kind earnings a male farm laborer from chapter 2 (which are admittedly somewhat generous), then even he earned the equivalent of 10,800 copper cash per year at mid-century. Five pounds of top-grade sugar would then represent only about 4 percent of his annual earnings, a high figure, but not completely im-plausible given Fang Xing's estimate that about one-quarter of the income of the rural poor went to non-grain foods.[38] And since landless laborers were among the poorest Chinese, we would expect their sugar consumption to be lower than average.

Chinese aggregates, like European ones, also conceal enormous regional differences. Shepherd puts consumption at roughly ten pounds per person per year on Taiwan, where the sugar must have been at its cheapest.[39] Both the routes taken by sugar boats and the taste of regional dishes (especially candied fruits and various sweet sauces in the south and southeast) suggest far, far more consumption in south and east China than in the north.[40]

It thus seems quite likely that Chinese sugar consumption in 1750 was higher than that in continental Europe, even in 1800. Even if our Chinese estimates for 1750 were *double* the real figures, China would still be much closer to most of Europe than most of Europe was to Britain.

But at some point China's per capita consumption of sugar declined, while Europe's grew explosively after 1840. John L. Buck's survey in the 1930s found Chinese sugar consumption to be about 2.2 pounds per person: 60 per-cent of our lowest estimate for 1750.[41] And since Chinese sugar production

[36] Daniels 1996: 276.

[37] These figures are calculated based on prices cited in Mazumdar 1984: 64. Additional impreci-sion results from uncertainty over whether the *jin* measurement cited in this source is the "customs catty," equal to about 1.1 pounds, or the "market catty," equal to about 1.3 pounds. For our purposes this is not a large enough range to make much difference.

[38] Daniels 1996: 93, 97.   [39] Shepherd 1993: 482n. 78.

[40] Ng 1983: 134–35; Ng 1990: 306.   [41] Cited in Daniels 1996: 85

probably grew once the calamitous 1850s and 1860s were over (though much of the new production was exported), it seems most likely that this drop in sugar consumption occurred between 1750 and 1870.

Tea consumption did not plummet, but it may have stagnated. One 1912 estimate came in at 2.6 pounds per capita, which would represent impressive growth; but this seems too high, since a heavily urban sample taken in the same decade came up with just over 2 pounds per person. Chang Chung-li cites a 1930s national estimate of 1.1–1.3 pounds (18–21 ounces) as more likely.[42] That would still far exceed 1840's 11 ounces, but the earlier figure, as we said, is probably an underestimate. Per capita tea consumption in the much more prosperous China of 1987 is slightly *below* the 1840 figure;[43] though since tea now competes with beer, soft drinks, and other beverages this is an unfair comparison. Overall per capita consumption of the "drug foods" certainly grew more slowly in the nineteenth and early twentieth centuries, if it did not in fact shrink. There was nothing necessarily self-sustaining about eighteenth-century China's growing appetite for everyday luxuries—and by the same token, what was about to happen to European consumption was not inevitable either. But it is not enough to note that Europe could conceivably have followed China's path, as the continent may in fact have been doing between 1750 and 1800; we need to explain the divergence that did eventually occur.

This divergence was greatly exaggerated by demographic trends. As we shall see in more detail later, China's post-1750 population growth was heavily concentrated in relatively poor areas. Thus, even if consumption in each region remained at 1750 levels, national averages would have declined. This is especially true of sugar, since eighteenth-century consumption was especially heavily concentrated in three prosperous macro-regions connected to the sugar fields by water transport: Lingnan, the Southeast Coast, and the Lower Yangzi. These three regions may have accounted for almost all of China's sugar consumption in 1750 (except for one other small concentration near the capital), when they had about 40 percent of the population.[44] In 1843 (and 1953), these same three macro-regions were probably only 25 percent of China's population.[45] This alone would cause the national average for sugar consumption to fall 37.5 percent, accounting for most of the difference

[42] Chang 1955: 303.

[43] This figure is derived by subtracting exports from total production in the table in Gardella (1994: 8) and dividing by a population of 1.2 billion.

[44] This heavy concentration is suggested by the character of the regional cuisines, by what we know of shipping routes for sugar, and by anecdotes remarking on the heavy use of sugar here and its relative absence elsewhere. Had these regions literally consumed *all* of China's sugar in the mid-eighteenth century and had the national consumption been at the low end of the range I have estimated above, people in these areas would have had to use 10.7 pounds of sugar per person per year—a rather high figure, but not a completely implausible one, in view of estimates that people in the Taiwan sugar country itself ingested ten pounds per year (Shepherd 1993: 482n. 78).

[45] Based on Skinner 1977a: 213, adjusting for the findings in Skinner 1987.

between our low-end estimate for 1750 and Buck's early twentieth-century findings (2.2 pounds of centrifugal sugar, plus some processed in other ways, and some eaten raw in the sugar-producing regions). This demographic factor also helps explain how such a fall in consumption could occur without occasioning much comment about a decline in living standard: if consumption was not falling much in any particular place, there would be little reason for anyone to notice a decline. And this distribution of population growth stands in sharp contrast to the European situation, where, at least between 1750 and 1850, population generally grew fastest in relatively prosperous parts of the continent (plus Ireland).

But population trends explain only part of the divergence in consumption. Consumption of cotton cloth, for instance, could not have been nearly as geographically concentrated as that of sugar; and there is evidence of an absolute decline in cotton output for North China. (Even, here, though, there may have been little or no fall in local consumption, but just a decline in the cotton North China had previously exported to the Lower Yangzi. The data and their limits are discussed further in appendix F.) And, of course, European consumption did not just avoid falling between 1750 and 1900—it grew more rapidly than ever, though mostly after about 1840.

As we shall see in chapter 4, the structure of trade in these new "everyday luxuries" differed in possibly significant ways. In China, sugar, tobacco, and tea were overwhelmingly domestic products; the trade in them was a highly competitive one that involved many fairly small merchants and had relatively low profit margins.[46] Moreover, this trade did not produce significant revenues for the state. Consequently there were no particularly powerful interests promoting increased consumption of these goods, while there were officials within the government who actively discouraged them.[47] In Europe, too, we find some officials and moralists who attempted to discourage these new tastes (and for that matter in Japan, the Ottoman Empire, and India as well). But here there were also very powerful interests who wished to encourage increased consumption: revenue-hungry officials, plus merchants and colonial planters who had made large investments in productive capacity and monopoly privileges. And even so, consumption rose slowly in most of continental Europe and among the poorer Britons until the great price decline of the middle nineteenth century.

It has been suggested that the English sweet tooth could be partially a result of what was otherwise a rather simple cuisine and that, conversely, the much lower consumption of sugar in China, for instance, can be partially explained by China's complex cuisine, with its multitude of other sweeteners and spices.[48] But in view of our high figures for eighteenth-century Chinese sugar

---

[46] Ng 1983: 99, 157; Ng 1990: 305–6.
[47] Ng 1983: 184–86, 190.   [48] Daniels 1996: 87; Mintz 1985: 190.

consumption, this cannot bear too much explanatory weight. Sugar made the transition from medicine to heavily used "spice" quite successfully in China, paralleling the period in which Mintz sees Europeans of all classes learning to love sugar; what never happened was the transition from heavily used and highly desired "spice" to staple carbohydrate. And for that transition, the most important differences probably had to do less with tastes or distribution than with production, prices, and colonies.[49]

Attitudes alone could not sustain growing consumption of "popular luxuries" indefinitely, in part because these crops inevitably competed with other uses for land. It is noteworthy that much of the growth in Chinese sugar production occurred where sugar did not compete with other foodstuffs. On Taiwan, still a sparsely settled frontier well into the nineteenth century, sugar and rice cultivation advanced hand in hand—the mainland did not have to export grain in order to get its sugar. In Guangdong, many of the same peasants who grew increasing amounts of sugar in the seventeenth and eighteenth centuries also pioneered sweet potato and peanut production (often clearing hills previously thought unsuitable for farming); thus they also generated their own food supply. In still other cases, sugar production took over land once used for cotton, a switch that made sense in terms of relative prices and the growth of trade with Bengal and the Yangzi Delta.[50] But China increasingly ran short of places in which sugar (or tea, or tobacco) production could keep expanding without reducing grain output. And as we shall see later, cotton (and perhaps tobacco) production in one key region—north China—probably fell significantly between 1750 and 1900, as a burgeoning population needed more land for food.

At the very least, the need for food land prevented cash-crop output from continuing indefinitely its rapid growth of the sixteenth through the eighteenth centuries. And unless production kept growing, per capita consumption would fall, since China's population roughly doubled between 1750 and 1850. By contrast, Chinese grain production apparently *did* keep pace with population growth, even before modern agricultural inputs became available.[51] It thus seems likely that food production squeezed out at least some production of other crops, especially in North China where population growth was especially rapid and per-acre yields were relatively hard to raise.

Europe, however, grew almost all of its sugar, tobacco, and coffee in its colonies and purchased its tea with silver from the Americas; in a sense then,

---

[49] Of course, this need not have been true everywhere—one can readily imagine, for instance, that the very different way in which the exchange of food was socially coded in certain parts of India could have been quite important in shaping the use (or lack of use) of sugar among large parts of the population. But in the cases of China and Europe no such obvious candidate for a cultural factor likely to profoundly shape the reception of sugar presents itself.

[50] Mazumdar 1984: 80, 284–85, 287, 372.

[51] The classic statement of this thesis is Perkins 1969.

growing drug food consumption did not press against Europe's grain supply nearly as much as it did in China. Most of its cotton also came from either colonies or ex-colonies.

Moreover, the growth of sugar consumption came at an opportune time, particularly for Britain. As we shall see in chapter 5, English agriculture had reached a point by the late eighteenth century at which further increases in output were almost impossible without a major technological breakthrough, which would not even begin until the mid-nineteenth century: the use of large amounts of chemical fertilizer (first, mined phosphates and imported guano, and then, in the twentieth century, synthetic fertilizers). Meanwhile, England's population soared, making domestic grain supplies inadequate for the first time; and the long-term solution to this shortage—huge amounts of North American grain—was also still decades away. In the intervening half century, which is more or less that of the Industrial Revolution, England imported more grain from the rest of the United Kingdom, but this was not a complete solution either.[52] An environment in which calories were unusually scarce and many of the poor were also struggling to adapt to new rhythms of work (including having their midday meals at their job) was a perfect one for the penetration of sugar into the core of the English diet. In east Asia, sugar may have done comparably well at establishing itself as an important condiment, but since the production of grains *did* keep up with population, there was no particular reason for sugar to become part of what Mintz calls the "carbohydrate core."

The structure of colonial production also placed great pressure on planters to increase production of sugar and tobacco even when farmgate prices were falling—something that was much less true of Chinese sugar-growers, who also grew subsistence crops. Colonial plantations were often very heavily specialized in their particular cash crop; this meant that they imported everything else—from food to manufactured goods to their slave laborers themselves—and so had fairly high cash outlays to meet, even in years of low prices for their output. (We shall have much more to say about this in chapter 6.)

The very specialized nature of colonial plantations may seem to undermine the immediately preceding claim that drug foods produced overseas did not compete for scarce European farmland the way that further Chinese sugar and tobacco production would have. Swapping manufactured goods (which used more of Europe's relatively abundant labor and capital than of its relatively scarce land) for sugar did not conflict with domestic food needs; the same was true when manufactured goods (or goods acquired in Asia) were traded for the African slaves who grew New World produce; and the same was true when New World silver purchased Chinese tea. But when New World plantations

[52] Thomas 1985a: 142–47.

had to be fed from Europe, that was a different story. As Abbé Raynal put it, "To feed a colony in America it is necessary to cultivate a province in Europe."[53] Or at least this was true for the French Caribbean.

But Britain had *other* New World colonies—in North America—which produced surpluses of grain, meat, timber, and cod that could be sold to the sugar colonies. The North American colonies in turn bought manufactures from Britain, so that Britain effectively turned abundant labor and capital—not scarce land—into sugar through this route, just as it did through the African slave trade and through its direct sales of manufactures to the Caribbean. (Brazilian sugar plantations mostly consumed food produced within Brazil. Thus, like Britain, Portugal did not need to send much food from Europe; but it did not monopolize its colony's trade the way Britain did either.) We shall have much more to say about land shortages and ecological pressures in chapters 5 and 6. For now, it is worth noting that the late eighteenth-century stagnation of per capita sugar consumption in non-British Europe, which makes much of the continent look more like China than like Britain, may in part reflect similar constraints; and that part of the explanation for Britain's spectacular growth in sugar consumption may lie in *North* America.

Consumer Durables and the "Objectification" of Luxury

An internally generated European advantage seems more plausible for more durable goods: furniture, silverware, linens, and so on. But here, too, there are reasons for caution, particularly vis à vis China and Japan.

These comparisons are made particularly difficult by differences in the sources available: there are no Asian counterparts to European probate inventories, for instance. Nonetheless, changes in elite consumption seem roughly comparable across a number of societies between, say, 1400 and 1800. In Europe, China, Japan, and India, one finds a striking increase in the quantity and variety of home furnishings, elaborate clothes, eating utensils, and what would today be called "collectibles" among the wealthiest people. The display of material possessions became a more important determinant of status, while repeated attempts to make consumption conform to ranks not defined by wealth achieved only limited success. Meanwhile, the importance of personal retinues as a sign of status declined, and many old elite families found that they could not afford to continue status competition through consumption. But we need to look beyond such very general similarities.

The development of luxury consumption was not exactly alike in any two societies. Nor can this book investigate all the ways in which the *meanings* of

---

[53] Quoted in Braudel 1982: 226.

consumption varied among societies. What matters for us is that the qualitative shift in *how* goods were deployed for status competition in various societies was similar enough to propel a shared increase in the quantities employed.

The possession and exchange of objects has been an important marker of status in any number of societies. This has made it all too easy to assume that growing numbers of people with numerous possessions simply reflect a universal impulse to accumulate things, which had previously been frustrated by overweening elites or feeble productivity. In such formulations desire for more luxuries is timeless and needs no explanation; only production and income distribution change.

Alternatively, one can dismiss the possession of luxury goods by a handful of people in earlier societies as too rare to matter much and argue that the upsurge in nonessential consumption in the early modern period marks a radically new "materialist" way of life. This latter approach is very important for the way in which it treats the modern phenomenon of infinite demand as created, not natural; but it, too, has problems. Most serious for our purposes, it can too easily slide into creating a dichotomy between societies in which "commodities" and "markets" determine social relations, and exchange is conceived as the individualistic pursuit of gain, on the one hand, and those in which social relations regulate the economy, status governs consumption, and people are concerned with reciprocity, on the other.[54] When these dichotomies are applied to history, the result tends to be a division between a Europe that became "materialist" first and the rest of the planet, which because it had not yet crossed this divide, had to have "commodities," "materialism," and "economic man" introduced from outside.

But more recent literature has framed these issues with more subtlety. In one useful formulation, Arjun Appadurai creates a continuum that runs from "fashion systems" on the one hand to "coupon" or "license" systems on the other. In fashion systems, an enormous number of status-conferring goods may be purchased by anyone with enough money; the complete and immediate transmutability of money into status is mostly limited by the ever-shifting social rules that make some consumer behaviors "vulgar" and others "refined." In coupon systems certain crucial, often sacred, items can only be legitimately possessed and exchanged by those who are socially "licensed" to hold them. In both cases, social status and the exchange and possession of goods are mutually constituting, but through opposite methods:

> Where in the one case status systems are protected and reproduced by restricting equivalences and exchange in a *stable* universe of commodities, in a fashion system what is restricted and controlled is *taste* in an *ever-changing* universe of commodities, with the illusion of complete interchangeability and unrestricted

[54] E.g., Polanyi 1957.

access. Sumptuary laws constitute a intermediate consumption-regulating device, suited to societies devoted to stable status displays in exploding commodity contexts, such as India, China, and Europe in the premodern period.[55]

This formulation avoids placing societies completely in one camp or another—in fact, Appadurai finds some "coupon" goods even in the contemporary West—and so makes it clear that we have both "economy" and "culture" in all societies.[56] It also prevents consumption from being subsumed, as it sometimes has been, under a supposedly unique Western "individualism," and thus from treating strong communities as necessarily opposed to increased consumer demand.

Although it erases overly simple dichotomies, Appadurai's sketch still highlights differences between fashion and coupons as distinct modes of interplay between status and consumption. Moreover, the differences between them are clearly enough defined that we can see how a shift in one direction or another would have enormous consequences for economic development, and we can look for explanations of such shifts.

A weakening of "coupon" systems, by allowing more people to purchase a highly charged good, will mean increased recourse to the market; so will the entry (probably from an "exotic" source) of a new status-conferring good. And the closer a system is to being a fashion system, the faster people will turn over their personal stock of goods, thus increasing demand. Moreover, a coupon system, by definition, discourages the imitation of a higher status group's consumption by groups below them; in something closer to a fashion system the elite responds not primarily by forbidding such imitation, but by shifting to new goods (or ways of displaying them) and labeling the old ones as "vulgar." Thus, this sort of system leads to the continuing pursuit of goods by those at every level seeking to maintain social distinctions and those seeking to bridge (or leap over) them. It is also likely to lead to the production of explicit canons of taste, and to their commodification in turn, as printed works and hired tutors help people pursue this competition.

Even this brief sketch gives us some concrete things to look for: an increase in the variety of goods charged with social significance and the velocity with which they changed; an increase in how many people were allowed to possess them, and in the extent to which they could be acquired from strangers; a sharp increase in imitative consumption, and proliferation of different kinds of status goods for different levels of people; and a proliferation of discussion about the "proper," "tasteful" way to use various commodities.

All these phenomena are *best* documented for various urbanized regions of western Europe: Renaissance (northern) Italy; Golden Age Spain; Holland; some parts of France; and England. Each case included a transformation of

---

[55] Appadurai 1986: 25 (emphases in original).   [56] See also Sahlins 1976.

upper-class homes and their purposes. In the countryside, castles that were more suitable for military defense and for the entertainment of large groups of retainers (having, for instance, one dominant, central banquet hall with a few very long benches) gave way to estates with more rooms (and hallways) allowing privacy, more design features oriented toward personal comfort, and vastly more decoration.[57] More families acquired multiple residences. Sometimes this was because centralizing states required at least part-year attendance at court, sometimes because more rural notables had enough business in cities to require a second residence there, and sometimes, perhaps, because of a changing sense of self. There seems to have been more willingness to build a home (generally not one's first home) for one's own use and enjoyment, rather than to serve as the enduring base for the dynasty one belonged to, and to locate and style it accordingly.[58] Urban houses were likely to be much less spectacular than rural ones, but these, too, were built in increasing numbers, with increasing solidity, and were increasingly designed to meet new "needs" for comfort, privacy, and a place to display the possessions that indicated one's wealth and one's taste.[59] Royal palace-building may have led this trend, but it quickly spread to wealthy nobles, merchants, and others.

As important as the houses themselves—perhaps more so, especially in urban areas—was a proliferation of objects within them. Mirrors, clocks, furniture, framed pictures, china, silverware, linen, books, jewelry, and silk clothing, to name just a few items, all became increasingly "necessary" signs of status for well-off western Europeans. Moreover, it became increasingly important that these goods be "fashionable" as well as numerous and well-made;[60] thus stocks of luxury goods were depreciated culturally much faster than they decayed physically, and further luxury consumption was increasingly unimpeded by existing inventories. Large numbers of writers complained that these trends drained the wealth of society, bankrupted noble families, and undermined more important measures of status and human worth. Throughout Europe, governments and religious institutions tried, at least intermittently, to arrest these tendencies—but with little success. Increasingly, people defined themselves through the tireless accumulation of possessions.

But this rise of "consumer society" was not unique. Craig Clunas has shown that upper-class homes in Ming dynasty (1368–1644) China also became increasingly crammed with paintings, sculptures, fine furniture, and so on. Moreover, he finds that—just like in Europe—it became increasingly important to have the right sort of luxury good for a particular setting, person, or purpose. Thus, for instance, elegantly carved beds began to be marked as appropriate for either men or women in China before the same specialization

[57] Hoskins 1953: 44–59; Stone 1979: 169–70, 245–46.

[58] Sombart 1967: 97, 100–105.

[59] Schama 1988: 311.   [60] Braudel 1982: 311–33.

existed in Europe;[61] the very rich might also have different beds and chairs for different seasons of the year.[62] Meanwhile, the most prestigious luxury goods—pieces known to have been produced by great artists—were increasingly commodified: i.e., they were available to anyone with enough money, rather than circulating only among intimates.

And as wealth could increasingly be converted to status *through consumption* (rather than through buying office, or land, or education for one's children), published guidebooks began to offer advice on how to evaluate and display such objects properly. Some books showed older elites how to reassert their status through taste, even if the "vulgar" might have more money for luxuries; some other manuals targeted the nouveaux riches, advising them on the proper way to acquire and display these objects.

These discourses—one of them self-consciously titled "A Treatise on Superfluous Things"—began to appear slightly earlier than their European counterparts; new ones continued to be written and older ones reprinted throughout the Ming period.[63] And while the early Ming state promulgated various sumptuary laws, attempting to regulate in great detail the dress, tableware, and so on of various social groups, these laws seem to have had little effect and soon became hopelessly outdated and irrelevant; only one new item was added after 1500, even though new luxuries and styles proliferated.[64] Meanwhile, sumptuary laws continued to be promulgated in seventeenth-century Italy and Spain, and attempts to reinvigorate such laws were made even in such "bourgeois" places as Holland and England.[65]

Similar evidence could be adduced for Muromachi and Tokugawa Japan, where both complaints from moralists and a series of ineffective sumptuary laws list all kinds of goods being "improperly" used by people of the "wrong" rank. By the eighteenth century these included strictures against "gold, silver, and ivory" decorations in the homes of *peasants*[66] and complaints about how samurai and even daimyo had been ruined attempting to keep up with the consumption habits of wealthy commoners.[67] At least one scholar of European consumerism has concluded from this that Chinese and Japanese developments seem strikingly like contemporaneous ones in western Europe.[68]

The Indian evidence is more ambiguous. To be sure, there was a significant increase in luxury consumption in Mughal India. Numerous Europeans—many fresh from London, Paris, or Amsterdam—noted a dazzling array of luxury goods for sale in Indian cities.[69] And as the eighteenth-century break-up of the Mughal empire made various *regional* courts more important, these

[61] Clunas 1991: 54–55.
[62] *Jin Ping Mei*, 692.
[63] Clunas 1991: 8–39.
[64] Ibid., 151.
[65] Ibid.
[66] Hanley and Yamamura 1977: 89.
[67] Yamamura 1974: 41–47.
[68] P. Burke 1993: 148–61, especially 158.
[69] E.g., Tavernier 1925: I:52; Raychaudhuri 1982a: 180–81; Raychaudhuri 1982b: 266–67; Bayly 1983: 206, 266.

capitals often became regional centers of imitative elite consumption, much like the multiple courts of Europe.[70] Indeed, growing luxury consumption, partly fueled by the increased commercialization of the perquisites of government office (see chapter 4), appears to have been one of the principal motors of the Indian economy in this period.[71]

However, we do not have, at least so far, the same kind of evidence that we have for China, Japan, and Europe of an emerging "fashion system" with broad participation from many classes: e.g., guides to the proper and tasteful deployment of commodities. Though merchants and "service gentry" grew more important in seventeenth- and eighteenth-century India,[72] luxury demand seems to have been very heavily concentrated among aristocrats.[73] Conversely, we have more evidence for India than for western Europe or east Asia that older "coupon" systems, in which status has a relatively stable role in rationing access to a relatively stable set of special commodities, retained much of their force.[74] It thus seems likely that "consumerism," though certainly present, made less headway in India than in either east Asia or western Europe.

This seems logical if we think of the "objectification of luxury" as an alternative to the marking of status through the size of one's personal retinue. In both China and western Europe, a sharp decline in the number of bound servants and tenants from at least the sixteenth century, plus the growing urbanization of the elite, was making it harder to maintain large retinues; and though Japan did not experience comparable *legal* changes, social and economic forces there pushed in the same direction. The decline in the centrality of personal retinues, it should be noted, also made elites more likely to complain about popular consumption. When servants of various sorts were fully incorporated in the households of their masters, putting at least the more visible ones in finery was part of the elite family's own demonstration of wealth; but once servants were inferior but independent, any display they made was likely to be condemned as improper and even dangerous self-assertion.[75] Thus the plethora of documents condemning popular consumption in China, Japan, and Europe represent both economic changes and the extent to which elites in these places had stopped claiming to directly encompass those below them—and thus how much more they themselves had come to mark status relations among humans in terms of goods.

In India, by contrast, bound labor clearly remained quite important, even if there is disagreement over just how important,[76] and both office-holding no-

---

[70] Bayly 1983: 201–4; Bayly 1989: 51.

[71] Bayly 1983: 201–2, 204–6, 266.

[72] Ibid., 466–67.

[73] Ibid., 206, 268.

[74] E.g., Dumont 1970.

[75] See, for instance, Stansell 1986: 164–65. See also Adshead (1997: 25–26) for a slightly different interpretation, but with similar practical implications.

[76] Perlin 1979, 1985; Washbrook 1988.

bles and rural zamindars were legally obliged to have many retainers.[77] Indeed, much "aristocratic" luxury demand probably reflected the need to give gifts to favored retainers. Using expensive gifts with established symbolic meanings to maintain such relations seems to have remained central to Indian social and political competition,[78] but this probably did less to promote "fashion" than did purchases for more strictly personal use.

The Indian elite was relatively urban, probably more so than in China, though perhaps less so than in western Europe and certainly less so than in Japan. However, foreign observers were struck by how often even large Indian cities resembled immense camps, with people grouped around the people they served.[79] If this sort of personal service and dependency was stronger, both as fact and as norm, than in either western Europe or China, we would expect less of a shift toward social competition through "fashion." Nor were urban luxury markets growing as steadily in India as they were in China, Japan, and western Europe. As Bayly puts it, Benares and Lucknow in 1780 represented huge concentrations of luxury demand, but they were not very different in this respect from Delhi and Agra in 1680, when Mughal power and aristocratic residence had been more concentrated.[80]

The same arguments apply still more strongly in southeast Asia. Here, too, we find intriguing signs of an "objectification of luxury" between about 1450 and 1650, especially in the cities; and certain luxury goods were as lavish in their use of expensive materials as those from anywhere. Nonetheless, there was not a sustained shift toward "objectification of luxury" and "fashion" on a European or east Asian scale. Personal dependency remained the central organizing principle of society,[81] and even most large cities were agglomerations of encampments, with people grouped around their patron to make up a more or less separate village within the city. And (unlike in India) almost all nonreligious buildings were fairly simple. Everything about such arrangements emphasized the prestige of having adherents over that of having possessions.[82]

It seems, then, that China, Japan, and western Europe were more like each other than any of them was like India or southeast Asia; the same would probably be true if we compared them to eastern European, Middle Eastern, or African societies. Or, to make a more modest claim, at least the Chinese and Japanese cases show that the new elite consumerism in Europe was not unique in kind. But we must also consider whether there were significant differences in degree.

[77] Moosvi 1987: 175–76; Bayly 1983: 199, 266; Raychaudhuri (1982b: 181) on the vast size of retinues.

[78] Bayly 1983: 266.

[79] Tavernier 1925: I:105; Hambly 1982: 438–42.

[80] Bayly 1983: 199.

[81] Reid 1989: 60, 64, 69, 71.

[82] Reid 1993: 87.

Developments in housing *were* quite different. In much of Europe, the boom in the construction of palaces, chateaux, townhouses, and other residences for the rich seems to have continued (though with cyclical ups and downs) right through the end of the eighteenth century. In both China and Japan, however, the great boom in palace-building accompanied seventeenth-century political transitions (the rise of the Qing and Tokugawa respectively), rather than emerging earlier.[83] At least in Japan, the widespread building of really durable homes appears to have been a sixteenth- and seventeenth-century development.[84] And while the quality of homes definitely improved during the sixteenth through eighteenth centuries, the differences seem less marked than in Europe and do not suggest a basic shift in the idea of what a home was for.[85] In China, too, the purpose of homes changed relatively little in the late empire. The home remained, for instance, an important location for work and religious activity as well as for eating, sleeping, and cooking. It continued to be thought of (at least among elites) as belonging to multiple generations (including the ancestors whose altar and tablets it housed) more than as expressing the achievements and tastes of its current inhabitants. With the idea of the home not changing much, building styles also changed much less than they did in Europe.[86]

Moreover, the preferred building material in both China and Japan remained wood, and both building booms tapered off when stands of the most desirable woods began to give out in the eighteenth century.[87] (There are some indications of increased use of stone for houses,[88] but this remained unusual.) In Japan's prosperous Kinai region, for instance, the wages of both urban and rural building workers fell relative to those of most other kinds of workers (including farm laborers) from at least the mid-eighteenth century on, strongly suggesting that demand for *new* housing was not particularly robust.[89] This slackening of the building boom did not indicate a general economic slowdown, nor an inability to use stone. In Japan, at least, the preference for wood had much more to do with suitability for the climate and the threat of earthquakes; indeed, the ease with which Japanese homes could be "aired out" seems to have reduced respiratory illnesses in a humid climate and likely contributed to the relatively high life expectancy of urban Japanese relative to Europeans.[90] And as Francesca Bray points out, Chinese had many cosmological and ritual reasons for preferring wood to stone in home-building, even though they knew how to use stone and even though wood became increasingly expensive in Ming and Qing times;[91] some of the beliefs behind these

[83] Menzies 1992a: 64; Osako 1983; Totman 1992: 22.
[84] Hanley 1997: 25–35.
[85] Ibid., 36.
[86] Bray 1997: 59–172, esp. p. 71.
[87] Totman 1992: 23; Totman 1995: 84; Osako 1983: 132–35; Menzies 1992a: 64, 69.
[88] See, for instance, Perdue 1987: 109–10.   [89] Saito 1978: 98.
[90] Hanley 1983: 188–89.   [91] Bray 1997: 77.

preferences had wide currency in Japan, too. Whatever the reasons for these preferences, they meant that "keeping up with the Joneses" in east Asia required far less investment of capital in one's home; the same was even more true in southeast Asia.[92] Massive investment in home construction (and the use of stone) was probably more common for elites in India, but I know of no way to measure its extent.

But differences in other kinds of spending are harder to pinpoint, in part because there was so much diversity within these huge units: differences, at the very least, among classes and regions. Though we cannot analyze either thoroughly, some beginnings are possible.

At least in some parts of Europe, even rather humble people bought "luxuries." Not only wealthy merchants and well-established master artisans, but even very vulnerable journeymen bought some "luxuries": belts, shoes, and waistcoats with silver and gold buttons, brewed and distilled beverages, coffee, tea, sugar, and so on. In fact, the sharing and/or display of such goods became a crucial part of an urban "plebian culture."[93] Hans Medick argues that artisans spent more of their total budgets on such "minor luxuries" than did any other social group.[94] He has also assembled evidence of similar behavior among Europe's *rural* artisans, and not only in England and Holland: he cites such examples as ribbon-makers in rural Saxony who aped urban fashion to distinguish themselves from peasants, and Wurttemburg artisans who, in the words of a contemporary, could afford little besides potatoes "but would consider themselves less than human if they were compelled to give up their morning coffee."[95] Merely establishing that such consumption existed is significant, and some of it (such as coffee and tea) must have been new in the sixteenth through the eighteenth centuries. But it remains unclear how much "luxury" consumption there was among plebians, or how new it was; non-elite consumption of "luxuries" probably drew disproportionate comment from their "betters," even when the total amount, as we have seen with tea and sugar, remained quite small. And not all new consumption habits marked *lasting* additions to aggregate demand: the spectacular rise of gin consumption in early eighteenth-century England, for instance, was followed by an almost equally dramatic decline in the second half of the century.[96]

Peasant demand is still harder to pinpoint and likely quite different from habits among rural artisans.[97] However, Jan DeVries's work on Friesland between 1550 and 1750 establishes that, at least in this unusually prosperous

[92] Reid 1988a: 62–73.   [93] Medick 1982: 86, 90–95.

[94] Kriedte, Medick, and Schlumbohm, 1981: 64–65, 69; Medick 1982: 90.

[95] Medick 1982: 94–95.

[96] See, e.g., Medick 1982: 103–4.

[97] Note that Medick's Saxon ribbon-makers wished to look *different* from peasants, not to look like better-off peasants; and note, too, that Medick's argument that rural artisans adopted various sorts of new consumption as ways to mark status in the absence of the land ownership so crucial for the rest of rural society would have less relevance for peasants.

region, rural smallholders and even tenants purchased a wide variety of non-essential goods. He also shows that inventories of high-quality furniture and other wooden goods, tableware, home decorations, and some other goods increased substantially (though unevenly) over time.[98] (One would, of course, expect some increase in the stock of very durable items even if the rate of further purchases was slow.) Yet it is also significant that certain types of stocks do *not* seem to have increased much—most notably those of textiles, the largest "industrial" sector of this era and the leader in the eventual Industrial Revolution. That people did not own more textiles is particularly striking since most cloth prices declined relative to those for other goods between 1550 and 1750.[99] Moreover, the inventories of consumer goods grew more slowly than those of capital goods.[100] Overall, then, as DeVries himself notes, neither the scale of increased peasant demand in this prosperous area nor its exact components seem quite right for explaining the Industrial Revolution[101]—and much of the demand for *cotton* textiles in particular would come from outside Europe.[102]

Even so, the mass consumer demand in Europe could have been enough greater than the demand elsewhere to merit some role in explaining Europe's eventual divergence from other "advanced" economies. Unfortunately, we lack truly comparable records of possession in other societies. We can, however, guess whether large differences were likely, in part by seeing whether non-elites elsewhere were less *able* to buy nonessentials.

The evidence we can use to compare income distribution across societies is also distressingly spotty. What we do have, however, runs contrary to Jones's contention that income—and thus effective demand for "everyday" luxuries—was far more evenly distributed in Europe than in the major economies of Asia.[103] A real gap may have existed between India on the one hand and China, Japan, and western Europe on the other, but what little evidence we have suggests no great differences among these three areas.

For China, virtually the only quantitative estimate of income distribution before the twentieth century is that of Chang Chung-li. Chang's nineteenth-century Chinese "gentry"—broadly defined to include most wealthy merchant families as well—was about 2 percent of the Chinese population and received about 24 percent of the national income.[104]

No comparable figure that I am aware of exists for Europe as a whole, but we do have contemporary estimates of income distribution for England and

---

[98] DeVries 1975: 220–24.　　　　　　　　　　[99] Ibid., 218–20.
[100] Ibid., 234–35.　　　　　　　　　　　　　　[101] Ibid., 236.
[102] Braudel 1984: 575.

[103] Jones 1981: 110. Jones's evidence for this point actually comes from India, for which, as we suggested earlier, he is quite likely right; but his sweeping claim about "Asia" and "Europe" is much weaker.

[104] Chang 1962: 326; more generally, see pp. 296–331.

Wales in 1688, 1759, and 1801–3. As revised by Peter Lindert and Jeffrey Williamson, these estimates suggest that the top 2 percent of the population in 1688 (excluding the royal family) received 19 percent of the national income; in 1759, 22 percent; and in 1801–3, 23 percent.[105] And the unit of "England and Wales," of course, takes in only a small and relatively prosperous part of Europe, while the Chinese figure above takes in a range from China's London to China's Bulgaria. Certainly the vastly more equal distribution of land in China—still the most important productive asset at either end of Eurasia—suggests that a more properly matched comparison might well show greater income equality in China. Returns to the ownership of land must have been far more equally distributed across China's population than they were in Europe, even if European rental markets reduced the disparity in access to land so that opportunities to work were as widely and evenly distributed as they were in China. The share of income held by the lower 98 percent of the population is of course only a very partial picture of overall income distribution and an even less adequate guide to the distribution of purchasing power,[106] but as the only quantitative indicator available to us, it is well worth considering. Also striking is George Staunton's comment (unlike those of Smith and Malthus), based on his travels over a long trip from Peking to Canton in the 1790s, that he had seen little serious poverty.[107] A recent reconstruction of peasant budgets in the Lower Yangzi suggests (based on fragmentary evidence) that a "typical" farm family would spend 55 percent of its total income (in cash and kind) on grain in the seventeenth century, 54 percent two hundred years later.[108] Basic calories often consumed about the same share of peasants' and artisans' earnings in late eighteenth-century England.[109] The Chinese study almost certainly undercounts non-grain consumption, thus biasing this comparison against China.[110]

[105] Calculated from data in Lindert and Williamson 1982: 393, 396–97, 400–401.

[106] The amount of income available to purchase non-necessities is inevitably much less evenly distributed than total income. Moreover, inequalities in *wealth* further cloud the picture, as any debt-burdened peasant whose income each year went partly to offset his negative net wealth could tell us; and we know next to nothing about how distributions of wealth would compare between China and Europe.

[107] Staunton 1799: II: 134, 141.

[108] Fang 1996: 93, 97.

[109] Phelps Brown and Hopkins 1981: 14: 53 percent of outlays on grains for poor families in England in the 1790s.

[110] Fang 1996. Lacking any independent estimate of rural laborers' incomes, Fang works from what agricultural manuals say about what such workers needed to be given and calculates the values of five basic categories of consumer goods—grain, other foods, fuel, housing, and clothing—and the families' production expenses. His sources leave out infrequent but very large expenses such as life-cycle rituals, jewelry (though it appears that even poor women often had a little), entertainment and incidental food (i.e., snacks bought on trips to the market), and any items that, purchased with money earned by, say, a textile-weaving wife, escaped detection by people concerned with the hiring, supervision, and pay of the farm workers themselves.

The largest non-agricultural sector of the economies of both Europe and east Asia was textiles; and textile consumption has regularly been one of the first kinds of consumption to increase during industrialization. Though our data are spotty, they suggest comparable levels of textile production and consumption at the two ends of Eurasia.

For China's premier cloth-producing region—the Lower Yangzi—we can generate estimates of raw cotton and silk output in much the same way that we estimated sugar output in Guangdong. Indeed, the exercise is more accurate in this case, since our land-use data are much better than what we had for Guangdong. This exercise suggests that just the eleven extremely commercialized prefectures on the south side of the Yangzi Delta produced almost 16 pounds of ginned cotton per capita, and about 2.0 pounds of high-quality raw silk.[111] Some cotton was exported to Lingnan before spinning, but raw cotton was also imported from North China. By 1850 Jiangnan was a net exporter of raw cotton, since Lingnan's demand kept rising while imports from North China fell off, but it is hard to know by how much; and in 1750 any net exports would have been much smaller.[112] Thus, I have assumed that Jiangnan spun and wove all its raw cotton, except what was used for padding: 1.3 pounds per person in the twentieth century[113] and probably about the same in the eighteenth century. So 14.5 pounds of cotton and 2.0 pounds of silk cloth per capita seem plausible (though perhaps somewhat high) estimates for Yangzi Delta textile production.

By comparison, the United Kingdom's production of cotton, wool, and linen together comes to 12.9 pounds per person in 1800,[114] when the transformation of textile technology was well underway. (Since both linen and wool cloth are generally lighter per square foot than cotton, amalgamating these different kinds of textiles biases the comparison against China.) Unfortunately, we do not know how much cloth the Yangzi Delta exported—the share may well have been even higher than the United Kingdom's proportion (about one-third of output),[115] thus reducing the area's cloth *consumption* below U.K. levels. But even roughly comparable per capita cloth consumption in the most productive regions of China and Europe is quite suggestive, especially when we remember that these Yangzi Delta prefectures had almost twice the population of the United Kingdom. Moreover, Chinese cotton cloth outfits seem to have been considerably more durable than their British-made counterparts, at least in the nineteenth and early twentieth centuries.[116] Unfortunately, the data for both China and Europe are very spotty, and production was much too geographically dispersed to allow us to concentrate on a few key areas. One

---

[111] For details of method and calculation, see appendix F.
[112] The reasons for these suppositions are explained further in appendix F.
[113] Chao 1977: 233.
[114] Deane and Cole 1962: 51, 185, 196, 202. Population estimates from Mitchell 1988: 8–10.
[115] Deane and Cole 1962: 196, 202.   [116] Huang 1990: 137.

exception to this is silk, where the Lower Yangzi likely had the majority of China's output, perhaps more than three-fourths.[117] Thus total production was likely under one pound per person—not nearly as significant as cotton but not trivial for a luxury fabric and still far higher than the figures for Europe.

Unfortunately, the methods used to generate our cotton, sugar, silk, and Yangzi Delta cotton estimates, which work well for relatively contained but highly commercialized areas, break down in vast but less commercialized areas. In such cases small changes in assumptions can easily double or triple our estimates of the amount of land available for cotton (from, let us say, 3 percent to 9 percent of a very large total acreage). The best alternative is probably working backward from later figures.

In 1870, shortly after the Nian and Taiping rebellions were suppressed, China grew roughly 1,850,000,000 pounds of cotton:[118] probably a bit over five pounds per person, though population estimates in the aftermath of the mid-century wars are quite shaky. This figure then fell to about 1,500,000,000 pounds by 1900, but then it began a new and so far continuous rise. Examining China's major cotton areas one by one suggests what may at first seem surprising: that China's 1750 output was not much lower than it was in 1900, and was thus much higher per capita.

First of all, it is important to note that there were not many large new cotton regions that emerged after 1750.[119] Though the Middle Yangzi provinces did increase their cotton cultivation after 1750, they never became very large producers. Meanwhile, some important producing areas in Sichuan and Shaanxi switched to a different cash crop in the nineteenth century—opium poppies—largely at the expense of cotton;[120] some of this occurred before 1870 and some after. While many other pockets of cotton cultivation were scattered all over China, the most important areas both in 1750 and 1870–1900 were the Lower Yangzi and North China.

There is little reason to believe that Lower Yangzi cotton output expanded much in the nineteenth century. Population grew little and cultivated acreage not at all between 1750 and 1850 in the most commercialized parts of the region and not much in the rest of it. The mid-nineteenth-century catastrophes reduced population and acreage considerably; they may have recovered by 1900, but they did not grow much further until after 1949.[121] Meanwhile, the portion of land devoted to cash crops in this area in 1750 was probably already

[117] So (1986: 81n. 2) cites Guangdong as contributing one-fourth of China's silk *exports* before 1840. Exports are a far-from-ideal proxy for total output, but since Guangdong included the country's only port open to foreign trade and was hundreds of miles further from China's principal domestic luxury markets than the Lower Yangzi (which was itself the largest such market), it seems unlikely that it was less export oriented than Jiangnan; and if that is true its share of exports should serve as a rough ceiling on its share of total output.

[118] Kraus 1968: 158–59, 162–64, 167.   [119] Chao 1977: 23.
[120] Ibid.   [121] Skinner 1977a: 213; Ho 1959: 244–47.

as high as it would get over the next two centuries—indeed, rice imports to the area were probably lower in the 1930s than in the 1750s,[122] suggesting that some land may have even turned back to food production. If anything, *cotton* acreage may have declined by 1900, as more land shifted into mulberries after 1870. Although our yield figures are very spotty, they do not suggest any marked increase for Yangzi Valley cotton between 1750 and 1900; nor would one expect one, since there was no major change in techniques and (with no increase in population) probably not much change in labor inputs.

This brings us to North China, where data are particularly scarce and cropping patterns may well have fluctuated more than they did elsewhere. On the one hand, Richard Kraus suggests that Shandong and Hebei together had only 3,000,000 *mu* under cotton in 1900, rising to 5,000,000–6,000,000 *mu* by the 1920s (despite significant damage done by warlords in this area) and still higher in the 1930s.[123] (Shandong and Hebei are two of North China's three major cotton-growing provinces; I have found no useful data on the third province, Henan.) This rise was likely a recovery to earlier levels: we have already seen that national cotton output fell between 1870 and 1900, and in North China, which endured horrendous late nineteenth-century droughts, it would have been very logical for people to reduce acreage of this very thirsty crop. And even Kraus's 1920s figure amounts to barely 3 percent of cultivated acreage in the two provinces.

On the other hand, Zhao Gang quotes a mid-eighteenth-century source which claims that 20–30 percent of the cultivated land in Hebei (then known as Zhili) was under cotton: this would be 14,000,000–21,000,000 *mu* in that province alone.[124] Though this seems implausible, another source's claim that 20–30 percent of the province's acreage south of Baoding was in cotton is more likely.[125] That would have equalled 7,000,000–15,000,000 acres in Zhili, depending on precisely what area the source meant to include.[126] If even 10 percent of Shandong and Zhili farmland grew cotton, that would be 17,000,000–24,000,000 *mu*, or six to eight times the 1900 figure.[127] This is also the approximate acreage available for non-food crops in the two provinces if we use the estimating methods used above for other regions, accept the unrealistically low official estimates of cultivated acreage, and assume per capita food consumption of 2.2 *shi* per year.[128] If we instead accept Huang's claim that cultivated acreage in the 1750s was already close to 1930's levels, the acreage available for non-food crops balloons to 70,000,000–90,000,000

---

[122] Skinner 1977a: 234–35, 713nn. 30–32.   [123] Kraus, cited in P. Huang 1985: 128.

[124] Chao 1977: 23.

[125] Fang Guancheng quoted in Zhang Gang 1985: 99.

[126] See appendix F for details.

[127] For official figures on cultivated acreage, which are far too low, and a plausible correction to them, see P. Huang 1985: 325.

[128] Marks (1991: 77), noting estimates that range from 1.74 to 2.62 *shi* per person, uses 2.17 for Lingnan, which was more prosperous than north China.

mu, depending on whether we assume food consumption of 2.2 or 2.5 *shi* per person; and cotton was North China's largest non-food crop.[129] Thus, there are various reasons to believe that North China grew considerably *more* cotton in 1750 than in 1870 or 1900.

Other data also suggest such a scenario. The population of Shandong and Zhili/Hebei increased over 40 percent between 1750 and 1870, and by about 80 percent by 1913, while cultivated acreage increased far less. Dwight Perkins has suggested, in fact, that this acreage did not increase at all.[130] This strikes me as too extreme—for instance, these provinces probably had significantly more forest even in 1800 than was left by the 1930s (see chapter 5). But even the discredited official figures for the 1750s are only 4 percent lower than for 1873 and 45 percent below the 1930s; and these "increases" include long-cultivated land added to the tax rolls.[131] Elsewhere in China, the worsening person/land ratios were offset by large gains in per-acre yields, created by greater use of fertilizer (both manure and beancake), more multi-cropping, and additional labor per *mu* (e.g., extremely careful weeding). But North China did not grow anything that would respond to additional labor as impressively as rice does; additional inputs of fertilizer were largely limited to manure, since the more effective beancake was also more expensive; and the relatively short growing season placed limits on multi-cropping. Moreover, worsening problems of waterlogging and soil salinity after the Yellow River shift in 1853 quite likely caused yields to fall on millions of acres in Shandong and eastern Henan.[132] Consequently, the amount of food North China needed probably grew *much* more than its cultivated area did between 1750 and 1870, 1900, or even 1930.

Thus, it seems likely that North China cotton output fell significantly, as Sichuan and Shaanxi output did, while Lower Yangzi output stayed about the same; only the Middle Yangzi and (conceivably) Henan—two much less-important cotton areas—increased their output. It would then follow that total Chinese cotton output circa 1750 was at least as high as it was in 1870, or certainly 1900.

If we take the lowest of the figures (1900), subtract cotton used for wadding, and then divide by the much smaller population (170,0000,000–225,000,000) of 1750, we get an average consumption per capita of about 6.2 pounds; using the 1870 figure gives us almost 8.0 pounds per person. How does this compare with European figures? U.K. consumption (including Ireland) in 1800 appears to have been about 8.7 pounds per capita of cotton, wool, and linen combined.[133] French linen production in the 1780s appears to have been about 6.9 pounds per capita, and cotton a trivial .3 pounds.[134] Data for wool exist

---

[129] For more details, see appendix F.   [130] Perkins 1969: 233–34.

[131] P. Huang 1985: 326–27.

[132] Huang (1985: 53–69) surveys many of the problems with the soil.

[133] Calculated based on Deane and Cole 1962: 51, 185, 196, 202.

[134] Mitchell 1980: 30, 449, 478.

only in square yards rather than pounds, and an exact conversion naturally depends on the type of cloth made; but 1.2 pounds per person for the end of the eighteenth century seems reasonable.[135] It thus seems likely that French textile output per capita on the eve of the Revolution was a bit above the high end of our conservative estimate for China, and one-third above the low end. German output figures are significantly lower: wool output in 1816 was a mere 1.1 pound per person, cotton output in 1838 still only .6 pounds per person, and linen output in 1850 about 3.3 pounds per person, making a total of 5 pounds of textiles per person.[136] Imports from England raised German consumption above its production, but it still seems likely that early nineteenth-century Germans—hardly the poorest Europeans—used less cloth each year than Chinese (averaging in the entire empire) had seventy-five years earlier.

Thus, Chinese textile consumption stacked up quite well against that of Europe in the mid- to late eighteenth century. Moreover, anecdotal evidence suggests that even the peasantry made many other non-food purchases, with both the variety and the quantities involved increasing in at least the sixteenth and eighteenth centuries. For instance, several texts from the Lower Yangzi refer to peasant smallholders and tenants pawning the gold and silver hairpins of their womenfolk to finance sericulture.[137] Disapproving accounts of popular religious cults, including some from very poor rural areas, refer to the excessively gaudy clothes, make-up, and jewels worn by even peasant women at some of these celebrations.[138] Pilgrimages themselves were a booming business. By the early 1600s, Mt. Tai alone probably drew close to a million visitors a years—with no major city nearby. Package tours that handled all expenses en route for a flat fee seem to have been marketed even in rather "backward" rural districts—much to the disgust of elite moralists.[139] Meanwhile, the very gentry who claimed to scorn religious pilgrimage were increasingly traveling themselves, not only for business but for education and enjoyment. As Timothy Brook puts it, "Travel had been absorbed into the gentry project of cultural refinement."[140]

A parallel boom in commercialized eating places extended even to rural market towns, at least in the Yangzi Delta. An early nineteenth-century source cites one town of "a few thousand households" with 45 wine shops and over 90 teahouses, plus three others nearby with 40, 65, and 80 teahouses respectively. The patrons, who included both town residents and people from

---

[135] Data from Markovitch 1976: 459; information on measures on 497. To convert to pounds, I used Chao's (1977: 234) estimate of the weight of coarse cotton cloth and Jenkins and Ponting's observation (1977: 11–12) that wool yarn weighed 1.5 times as much as cotton yarn of the same length and fineness.

[136] Mitchell 1980: 30, 449, 478.

[137] Cited in Pan 1994: 85.

[138] Chen Hongmou 1962: 68:5a–6a.

[139] Dudbridge 1991: 226–52; Pomeranz 1997a: 188–91; Wu Peiyi 1992: 39–64.

[140] Brook 1998: 181.

the surrounding villages, came to get price information, see performers, and gamble: i.e, for commercialized entertainment, commercialized eating, and commerce tout court.[141]

There was also a huge boom in the sixteenth through the eighteenth centuries in the printing of religious texts, medical manuals, and almanacs using simplified language and aimed at a popular audience. In about 1600, the missionary Matteo Ricci believed that books were cheaper and more widely available in China than in Europe.[142] While Chinese book owners were probably less common than Bible owners in the more prosperous parts of seventeenth- and eighteenth-century Protestant Europe (which enjoyed the cost advantages of movable type in alphabetic languages), their numbers still testify to a large and growing popular demand.

Housing is one of the areas in which China and Japan both probably had their greatest disadvantage vis à vis Europe. Eric Jones, as we saw earlier, takes housing as a crucial sign of greater European prosperity. But even in housing and home furnishings, China did not necessarily lag far behind Europe before 1800. European visitors to urban China in the sixteenth through the eighteenth centuries were still greatly impressed, as their forebears had been, at the massive public buildings and monuments, especially in Beijing and in the great cities of the Lower Yangzi Valley. The relatively small number who went to more out-of-the-way places were also struck by the homes of the very rich there: Galeota Pereira and Gaspar Da Cruz, who were exiled to remote Yunnan after incidents near Canton in the 1560s, were particularly struck by the lavish homes of imperial princes in Guilin.[143] But lavish homes existed in India, the Near East, and eastern Europe as well. Consequently, Da Cruz's observations on the homes of Chinese outside the tiny nobility and the scholar/ gentry are of greater interest, all the more so since Da Cruz never visited either the Yangzi Valley or the capital region.

Da Cruz first observes that Canton (Guangzhou) is "far inferior in buildings" to other Chinese cities, including several smaller ones,[144] but then goes on to describe the houses of magistrates there as "very sumptuous."[145] He continues, "The houses of the [urban] common people in the outward show, are not ordinarily very fair, but within are much to be admired"; he praised the mason work, the fine timbers and dyes used, and especially the "great cupboards finely wrought, which take up the curtain-wall of the house."[146] Even more interesting is his description of the homes of "rich husbandmen"—apparently neither gentry nor merchants—in rural south and southwest China:

In the unwalled villages, there are some houses of rich husbandmen, the which when a man sees them from afar (for they are among fresh tree groves, so you

[141] Fan 1990: 279–81.
[142] Cited in Rawski 1985: 17.
[143] Galeote Pereira 1953: 40; Da Cruz 1953: 109.
[144] Da Cruz 1953: 92.   [145] Ibid., 96–97.   [146] Ibid., 99.

cannot see any other houses but these) on account of the groves of trees a man might think he is looking at country manors in Portugal, noble and high. . . . These houses are very high, with three or four stories. The tiled roofs cannot be seen, because the walls run up above them, very well finished, and water is thrown outside by projecting gutter-pipes. These are strong holds and have great and noble portals of stonework. . . . Entering in the first of these houses (which is large) it has therein some huge cupboards very well wrought and carved, but the work is more for strength and durability than for show. They have likewise chairs with shoulder-backs, all made of a very strong wood and very well made, in such wise that their furniture is durable and of great repute and credit, which endures for their sons and grandsons.[147]

To be sure, such households sound much less lavish and fashion-conscious than those of the merchant princes of Yangzhou, Surat, Osaka, or Amsterdam, or the nobles of Beijing, Delhi, Edo, and Paris; quite likely they also lagged behind the social-climbing Lower Yangzi landlords who read *Advice to the Householder* and other guides to connoisseurship. But as members of what we might call a rural "upper-middle" class, rather than a true upper class, they point to a substantial market for high-quality purchased goods even in villages that were off the beaten track[148] and part of China's most backward macro-regions; from what little we can tell, they seem more like than unlike the better-off among DeVries's Friesland farmers.

Unfortunately, the earliest actual survey of what Chinese peasants of all economic levels and regions owned is that of John L. Buck and his associates in the 1920s. Moreover, the survey has some significant flaws. Among other things it overrepresents larger farms,[149] and it tells us virtually nothing about the *quality*, as opposed to quantity, of the items in question. Still, it has some interest.

The sample included over 30,000 farm families from all over China. Moreover, the late date may not be as big a problem as it initially appears to be. Chinese rural living standards probably did not improve much (if at all) between 1800 and 1850. The next twenty-five years were catastrophic, featuring no less than four major civil wars, massive floods, droughts, and other calamities: the death toll of these events was likely upward of fifty million. The last quarter of the nineteenth century and beginning of the twentieth century probably saw recovery to 1850 levels and the beginnings of some growth beyond mere recovery, but not much more. Indeed, some reconstructed "typical"

[147] Ibid., 106.

[148] Note that these houses were in villages, not the market towns or walled county seats to which landlords in the most commercialized parts of the country were moving by the sixteenth century. Moreover Da Cruz particularly associates these houses with areas that had significant banditry problems—generally the less economically advanced parts of the countryside.

[149] Esherick (1981) and Stross (1985) provide two useful, though divergent, views of the limitations of the Buck data.

TABLE 3.2

Average Number of Goods per Rural Household

	China Wheat	China Rice	Friesland Inland	Friesland Coastal
Tables	4.1	4.6	1.3	2.6
Benches	4.0	12.0	2.5	4.3
Chairs	2.1	4.0	6.7	13.5
Mirrors	.4	.3	1.0	1.2
Beds	3.4	4.1	3.3	5.2
Chests	2.2	2.7	1.0	1.2

budgets suggest that peasants of the 1920s and 1930s in both North China and the Lower Yangzi Valley were worse-off than their forebears of the 1750s;[150] our reconstructions of cloth, tea, and sugar consumption per capita also suggest a decline in the living standards of at least some large population groups. Another study suggests that Lower Yangzi landlords were receiving far less income from their holdings in 1937 than they did in 1840,[151] and less in 1840 than in the late 1700s. So it is therefore not completely outlandish to suggest that eighteenth-century village dwellers had most of what those in the 1920s had.

Most of Buck's data concern furniture. Furniture almost certainly became more expensive relative to other goods between the eighteenth and twentieth centuries, because wood became so much more scarce. A rough guess would be that wooded acreage per capita in 1937 was between 6 percent and 8 percent of what it had been in 1700.[152] Thus, it seems unlikely that the amount of furniture Chinese were purchasing each year would have increased over this period—or even the shorter period since 1800—even if there was a slight improvement in overall standard of living. Meanwhile, the immense destruction of the mid-nineteenth century would have wiped out much of the stock accumulated in earlier decades.

Buck's figures are presented as a set of averages for eight climatic regions and then aggregated into two huge "wheat" and "rice" regions, which correspond roughly to China north and south of the Huai River. Table 3.2 juxtaposes the figures for these two huge regions with DeVries's seventeenth-century figures for one inland Friesland village and two coastal ones: all the categories for which both Buck and DeVries give data are included.[153]

[150] See, e.g., Pan 1994: 325–26, 382–83, 394–97.

[151] Bernhardt 1992: 50–52, 135–36, 219–23.

[152] Based on figures for forested area from Ling (1983: 34–35) and a population of 100–120 million in 1700 and 450–500 million in 1937. Deforestation and trends in harvestable wood supply per capita per year are discussed in much greater detail in chapter 5.

[153] DeVries 1975: table 6–16; Buck 1937: 456.

We should not make too much of these numbers. Many of the Dutch furnishings listed above were quite elaborate,[154] while much of the Chinese furniture was probably fairly crude: only 36 percent of it was painted.[155] It has not been possible to control for household size and complexity, though it seems unlikely that they bias the comparison much.[156] And, of course, these data cover only one part of rural families' household goods. Nonetheless, they should undermine stereotypes of a Spartan rural China versus European homes stuffed with new goods.

In Japan, the socioeconomic changes of the early Meiji were so far-reaching that working backward from late nineteenth-century figures is useless. However, we do have a study of twenty-nine late Tokugawa villages which suggests that at least 20 percent of *peasant* income in the area studied was available for savings or truly discretionary nonsubsistence spending; some other work suggests even higher figures.[157] And by the late eighteenth century one finds people in farm villages buying furniture, medicines, and other specialized luxury goods from far away, while village stores stocked a variety of ready-made perfumes, hair oils, incense, and paper.[158] Eighteenth-century sumptuary edicts complained of peasants eating too well, using expensive specialty woods, and having overly decorative clothing, umbrellas, and gold, ivory, and silver ornaments.[159] One particular village store in the early nineteenth century stocked a variety of writing implements, serving dishes and cookware, tobacco products, and "other daily necessities."[160]

There are signs that Indian income distribution was significantly more unequal (and so popular consumption more limited) than it was in China, Japan, or western Europe. A study of Mogul land taxes for 1647 finds that 445 families received 61.5 percent of all revenues, which were about 50 percent of gross agricultural output, and that roughly one-quarter of the revenue flow to those families represented actual personal income. (The rest was consumed in various expenses of office.)[161] If this is accurate, these 445 families—

---

[154] DeVries 1975: 220–24; Schama 1988: 311, 316–20.

[155] Buck 1937: 457.

[156] The average household sizes were 5.5 people for the China Wheat sample and 5.2 for the China Rice sample (Buck 1937: 370). DeVries does not have household size figures for his data, but it seems likely that they were on average as large or larger, given our general demographic data. On the other hand, north European households tended to be less complex than Chinese ones—i.e., to contain fewer people other than a single married couple and their children. Since co-residents not part of the main conjugal family might be more inclined to need their own bed, and perhaps some other things of their own, this would tend to offset the effects of having more people in the household in the first place.

[157] See summary in Hanley and Yamamura 1977: 357–58. See Nishikawa (1978: 76–79) and Saito (1978: 85, 93, 99) on a general increase in real wages and narrowing of both regional and skill differentials.

[158] Hanley 1983: 190.

[159] All quoted in Hanley and Yamamura 1977: 88–89.

[160] Crawcour 1965: 41.   [161] Raychaudhuri 1982c: 266.

presumably less than .002 percent of the population—would have received an income from their offices alone equal to 7.5 percent of total agricultural output, or perhaps 6 percent of the society's total income![162] An estimate based on Shireen Moosvi's reconstructions for 1595[163] is similar: it suggests that 1,671 Mughal nobles would have had a net personal income from their claims on government revenue alone equal to about 7 percent of total empire-wide output. Although the records Moosvi worked from have been questioned, her calculations could be off by quite a bit and still confirm our general picture. And while at least some European visitors to China commented on a lack of severe poverty there, Europeans in India seem to have been struck by its extremes of wealth and poverty.[164] It is thus no surprise that Bayly's discussion of Indian luxury demand refers almost exclusively to *aristocratic* demand.[165] Habib's estimate of 3,000,000–4,000,000 pounds of silk produced in the mid-seventeenth-century Mughal empire[166]—less than one-fifteenth of our estimate for mid-eighteenth-century China—also suggests a rather narrow market for such a vast empire (though China's own production in 1650 would have been much lower than it was in 1750, too).

It is risky to stake too much on the comparison of any one good or on the amount of income going to a small elite. Moreover, Prasannan Parthasarathi's recent work makes a provocative case that Indian laborers were far from impoverished and may have faced fewer obstacles to effective bargaining than their British counterparts did.[167] Perhaps, then, it will turn out that Indian income distribution has both a heavy concentration at the very top and relative adequacy at the bottom, with the middle strata being the groups whose share of income and consumption lagged behind their Chinese, Japanese, and western European peers. But despite the new evidence it still seems too early to speak of rising popular consumption in India as comparable to that in those other places.

Growing numbers of rural Indians were producing cash crops or crafts, but these were often extracted from them directly. Thus an increase in the production of commodities need not entail an increase in peasants' participation in the market; indeed, the brisk market in rights to extract various peasant dues and goods coercively ultimately depended on those rights—which preempted the peasants' own participation in the market—remaining enforceable.[168]

[162] Moosvi (1987: 303–4) argues that urban areas accounted for perhaps 17 percent of total value added in the Mughal empire c. 1595: the method used is very rough, but seems serviceable for these purposes.

[163] Moosvi 1987: 108, 129, 131, 221, 278.

[164] Hambly 1982: 440.

[165] Bayly 1983: 201–6.

[166] Habib 1982b: 224.

[167] Parthasarathi 1998: 82–101.

[168] Perlin 1978: 183–84, 188; Perlin 1985: 440–43, 448n.83, 452; Bayly 1983: 195.

Some subordinate groups in India were able to flee or modify their obligations by taking advantage of demand for their skills; in fact, labor demand in
general was strong for much of the eighteenth century, and the *state* did not
intervene to prevent mobility or otherwise deny Indian workers the benefit of
that situation (as it did in many other places, some in Europe).[169] In particular,
castes that farmed dry land or worked in occupations suited to the dry zones
(such as well-digging) had considerably more mobility, since such land was
far more plentiful and harder to monopolize than was land with complex irrigation systems. Moreover, since members of the castes associated with dry-
land cultivation often undertook their migration in groups, they often formed
more or less autonomous single-caste communities in which switching occupations became easier. But in other cases (especially in wet zones), restrictions
on both geographic and occupational mobility did hold, and the imbalance of
economic power between landowners and tenants was extreme.[170] If this division between wet- and dry-zone patterns, which Ludden derives from one
south Indian region, was true more generally, then the parts of India yielding
the largest surpluses may have also had the most unequal distribution of income and thus relatively narrow participation in markets for non-necessities.
Even subordinate groups who improved their position through migration
might have been less prone to accumulating goods than similar groups elsewhere who could more easily bargain while staying put.

To be sure, recent research shows that in addition to aristocrats, Indian
towns and cities from the fifteenth through the eighteenth centuries featured
growing numbers of clerks, small to medium-sized merchants, and others who
often purchased non-necessities.[171] And at least by the 1820s, silver jewelry
and savings seem to have been common even among peasants.[172] But it still
seems likely that far fewer people were regular participants in these markets
than they were in Japan, China, or western Europe. Bayly suggests that circa
1850 direct peasant purchases from town markets were still largely restricted
to salt and iron goods.[173] Thus, even if Indian "luxury" and "fashion" resembled Japanese, western European, and Chinese developments more closely
than I have argued here, its social relations and labor systems probably ensured
that such impulses affected a much smaller proportion of the population. The
same argument applies at least as strongly to southeast Asia in this period.
There was probably less poverty there than in India, but bound labor remained
a central institution.[174]

But in China, Japan, and western Europe, consumer demand reached
broadly across classes. Its diffusion across space is a very complex problem;

[169] Parthasarathi 1998: 92–96, 99–101.   [170] Ludden 1985: 46–52, 59–67, 81–96.
[171] Bayly 1983: 194, 370–71, 466–67; Perlin 1978: 191.
[172] Bayly 1983: 242.
[173] Ibid., 347; but for a contrary view see Perlin 1985: 468–70.
[174] Reid 1988a: 129–36; Reid 1989: 64–71.

we have already seen, for instance, how enormously the use of sugar varied across both China and Europe. People in less-commercialized regions not only consumed less but produced more of what they did consume themselves. Thus, regional differences in market demand were even larger than those in standard of living. DeVries, for instance, found a fourfold difference in the value of household goods between the more prosperous parts of Friesland and the inland parts of the province, as well as a huge difference in the number of specialized craftsmen; even these inland areas were far from poor in the broader European scheme of things.[175] "Backwardness" affected even the demand of the local rich, since a tiny market meant high prices and limited selection for specialized goods. The fall-off in demand beyond the very richest areas seems to have been quite sharp. In Pont St.-Pierre, even substantial farmers did not begin to acquire clocks until after 1750—sixty years after many peasants in Friesland began to do so—yet Pont St.-Pierre was in Normandy, one of France's more prosperous rural areas, and was linked by river to both Paris and the coast.[176] Given such variation even within the more prosperous parts of northwestern Europe, there is little chance of systematically comparing levels of demand across the far more internally heterogeneous units "China," "Japan," and "Europe."

Consequently, the following paragraphs have a more modest aim: to suggest that we have little reason to think that the gaps between richer and poorer regions were larger in China and Japan than they were in Europe.

In Japan, demand was probably less geographically uneven than it was in Europe. Japan is, of course, smaller than China or Europe, and much of it has access to coastal shipping. Since from the mid-seventeenth century on every daimyo in the country was forced to spend roughly half his time at the shogun's court in Edo, accompanied by numerous family members and retainers, the spread of new tastes was encouraged at least among the elite. And since each daimyo also held court at his own "castle town"—unlike, say, some French nobles who were rarely at their ostensible home—there would have been ample opportunities for local notables to see and imitate the habits brought back from Edo. Moreover, the transportation network built to move elite families to and from Edo served other travelers, too, creating at least rudimentary national markets and well-developed regional (as opposed to purely local) markets for a wide variety of goods. Wage differentials between more and less "advanced" parts of Japan seem to have been narrowing from at least the mid-eighteenth century on.[177]

The Chinese case is considerably more complex. Here, too (as we shall see in chapter 6), income differentials between the most advanced regions and a

[175] DeVries 1975: 231 and table 6–16.
[176] Dewald 1987: 72; DeVries 1975: tables 6–8 to 6–10.
[177] Saito 1978: 99.

middle group of developing areas probably narrowed somewhat between 1750 and 1850, but it seems likely that the poorest regions fell further behind. Still, it seems unlikely that the gap between regions was growing as fast as it was between the northwestern core and the rest of Europe.

Nonetheless, the distribution of "luxury" demand might have been much more skewed than income distribution. Craig Clunas, for one, has suggested that the new interest in "superfluous things" may have been largely an affair of the Lower Yangzi Valley, where the guides to elite consumerism he has analyzed were written.[178] And China lacked the numerous royal courts that served as outposts of the fashionable world even in relatively poor parts of Europe—though in the Ming, it did have several princely courts.

On the other hand, the fact that these guides to luxury consumption were all written in the Lower Yangzi tells us much less than a similar concentration would in Europe: since China shared one written language, these books, like others published in Jiangnan, probably circulated more widely. Indeed, since both merchants and officials in China traveled extensively—indeed it was a commonplace that any ambitious person had to leave his native place[179]—new elite tastes were likely to spread quickly and widely. Timothy Brook argues that although in the 1560s it was still possible to imagine gentry who were out of the Jiangnan-dominated "fashion circuit," this was virtually impossible a century later.[180]

Tastes certainly spread quickly from Jiangnan to Beijing and vice versa. An eighteenth-century official in Fuzhou, on the southeast coast, thought that the lifestyle of elites in that city was as lavish as in the richest cities of the Yangzi Valley.[181] Canton, the principal city of the Lingnan macro-region was, among other things, widely considered to be the producer of some of the country's finest furniture, which had a following among members of the elite hundreds of miles away.[182] The seventeenth-century novel *Golden Lotus*, which provides some of the most detailed accounts of fabulously varied and expensive food, furniture, clothing, decorations, and even sexual gadgetry, is set in Linqing, a medium-sized city in North China. (In 1843 it was the tenth largest city in that relatively rural macro-region,[183] though it probably had a higher ranking in the seventeenth century.) This novel also provides some of the clearest examples of the rule of "taste," by which older elites defended themselves in a new world of consumerism: its merchant protagonist continually undercuts himself by consuming in exactly the ways that Clunas's guidebooks marked as vulgar.

A less well-known seventeenth-century novel, *A Marriage to Awaken the World*, takes place in Wucheng, an utterly insignificant North China county

---

[178] Clunas 1991: 173.
[179] See Skinner (1971, 1976) for a fuller explanation.
[180] Brook 1998: 221–22.   [181] Guo Qiyuan 1962: 36:21a.
[182] Clunas 1988: 66–68.   [183] Skinner 1977a: 238.

seat. Yet in the first four short chapters alone the protagonist (whose father has suddenly become rich) buys several gauze-curtained beds with silk coverlets, a wide assortment of embroidered silk and damask clothing, ivory chopsticks and carved lacquer cups with silver inlays, brocade shoes bound in lambskin, decorative swords and knives, elaborate drapes, quilts, and "extravagant decorations," a gold lacquer writing table, a number of books, gold fans, damask socks, and a vast array of medicines and aphrodisiacs made with rare ingredients.[184] This is a picture of excess, but of excess that is supposed to be plausibly obtainable in a fairly short time in a town of perhaps two to three thousand people: surely not even among the five hundred largest in the empire.[185] In our discussion of housing we saw some signs of what we might call "middle-class luxury" even in the southwest, one of the two poorest of China's nine macroregions; and our twentieth-century furniture survey presented averages for the entire nation.

As for Europe, we have already seen several examples of how unevenly new durable goods spread even in such relatively prosperous locales as northern France and Holland. The same was true of smaller luxuries. As we have seen, there was no sustained surge in continental per capita sugar consumption until after 1830, when prices declined sharply.[186] In many parts of rural France, coffee remained enough of a luxury to be an appropriate gift for special occasions until the twentieth century.[187] Even in England, it seems unlikely that working-class consumption of tobacco, tea, and sugar was of much significance before the 1840s; certainly overall consumption rose much faster after that date than before.[188] That the English poor purchased more alcohol, clothing, and reading material by the early nineteenth century than one or two years before is beyond doubt, and certainly they used some tobacco. But is this enough to really show that desires for new purchased goods were strong enough to change old work habits? Or does it make more sense to see this consumption as compensatory—a new way of marking social being that became more important faute de mieux as changes forced on workers by changing systems of production eroded old claims and identities and as old status goods like meat became more scarce?[189] And since the much poorer and less

---

[184] Nyren 1995: 8, 11, 17, 18, 23–24, 46–47.

[185] In 1843, China had 1,653 towns of over 2,000 (Skinner 1977a: 229) and though the population had grown a great deal by then, the *proportion* of people living in urban places had not.

[186] I have not found Europe-wide consumption data, but a large mid-century increase can be inferred from production data. Mitchell (1993: 511) shows a surge in Brazilian output, combined with the appearance of sugar beets starting in the 1850s–1870s in most of continental Europe (1993: 255–312).

[187] E. Weber 1976: 143.

[188] Mokyr 1988: 74–75, 79–90.

[189] See, for instance, the differing emphases even within the work of one of the principal students of "plebeian culture" in this period: Kriedte, Medick, and Schlumbohm 1981 versus Medick 1982.

market-involved lower classes of, say, Italy, Portugal, and Ireland—not to mention millions of eastern European serfs—were far less involved in the new consumer society, we should not make too much of the uneven spread of new goods across the even larger space of China.

Exotic Goods and the Velocity of Fashion: Global Conjuncture and the Appearance of Culturally Based Economic Difference

But even if the accumulation of actual goods by western Europeans, Chinese, and Japanese seems very similar, there are also intriguing differences. The growth and transformation of European consumption seems to have persisted through periods of rising and falling real incomes and gathered additional speed in the mid-eighteenth century. Comparable trends in China and Japan do not show the same ongoing acceleration. Clunas, for instance, notes that once China's new Qing dynasty was firmly established (by roughly 1683) and began drawing elites back into the sorts of public service roles that many had avoided in the late Ming, new publications about luxury fell off sharply. With an older way of establishing rank and identity reestablished, he suggests, "talking about things had become superfluous," and the development of a "consumer society" stopped short of attaining a "critical mass."[190]

Eighteenth-century Chinese texts are at least as full of complaints about luxury as those of the sixteenth and seventeenth centuries, while novels provide ever more extensive catalogs of baubles. One suspects that if we had inventories of possessions, they would on average be greater for the eighteenth century than for the sixteenth or seventeenth century (which, as we have seen, is not necessarily the case for Europe). However, a slowdown in new guides to taste might well indicate a slowdown in the rate at which *new* commodities and styles were becoming de rigeur for the socially ambitious. Shen Congwen's monumental history of Chinese clothing also suggests such a possibility: though many late Ming innovations in clothing and jewelry styles continued to spread downward from the top of society during the early Qing[191] and the new dynasty mandated a number of changes of style for officials, there seems to have been much less change in the clothing styles of ordinary people in the Qing than in the Ming,[192] and much less than in late eighteenth-century Europe.[193]

In Europe, on the other hand, the pace of change in fashion kept accelerating, especially for clothing. Virtually all the studies of European (and North American) probate inventories show that the share of consumer goods

---

[190] See also Brook (1993) and Peterson (1978); Clunas 1991: 169, 173.
[191] Shen 1992: 489.   [192] Ibid., 488.   [193] Staunton 1799: II: 180.

in the total value of estates *declined* over time; even the absolute value of such goods declined in many studies. To reconcile these findings with the overwhelming evidence of growing consumer demand in sixteenth- through eighteenth-century Europe, and of a greater *variety* of goods owned, it seems almost necessary to conclude that various consumer goods were being discarded faster so that more purchases over a lifetime did not always mean a greater stock of things at any one moment (such as the one captured in death inventories).

Why would the life span of goods decline? Some, like cloth, became (relatively) cheaper, making them easier to replace. In other cases the new goods may have been less durable than the old ones (drinking glasses and porcelain, for instance, presumably broke more often than pewter, tin, or wooden tableware).[194] Yet increased fashion consciousness also seems to have played a role. It was, after all, in eighteenth-century Europe that wars were interrupted to allow safe passage to the "wooden mademoiselle": a mannequin wearing the coming season's Paris fashion, which circulated from St. Petersburg to Boston.[195] This greater triumph of fashion may well have meant that annual European *demand* for luxuries grew faster than Chinese or Japanese demand, despite our provisional hypothesis that inventories of these goods (and attitudes toward them) were changing in very similar ways.

This suggests that a comparison of European and east Asian levels of spending on possessions might show a larger gap than a comparison of possessions themselves; and that, in turn, limits what we can infer from either one. For our current purpose—to explore the possibility that Europeans purchased more goods each year and so pushed the "industrious revolution" a little further than others—a comparison based on the velocity of purchase is valid; but it is much trickier to argue that such a pattern shows a "higher standard of living." It may instead show a difference in tastes or in available materials.[196] Given our

---

[194] DeVries 1993: 101–4. [195] Jones 1981: 113–14.

[196] The problem becomes apparent when we place goods on a continuum from the least physically durable (food and drink) to the potentially most durable (such as housing). Clearly the right measure of how well people eat is the annual *flow* of food that they obtain, since no food benefits you unless you "depreciate" it totally; a measurement of the stock of food on hand at any given moment is pointless. But with housing, it is the *stock* available that measures welfare (since one uses that stock every day while depreciating it only very marginally). If one were to find that, say, Japanese spent more in an average year on housing than English people, because their wood homes needed more frequent repair and replacement than stone ones, it would surely be perverse to argue that this showed that the Japanese were necessarily better housed. But what does one do with things that lie in between houses and loaves of bread in durability—from clothes to furniture—especially if their obsolescence is determined as much by fashion as by actual wear and tear? In general, we have accepted the modern notion that these goods are inherently short-lived and so have counted annual flows of production (and acquisition) of them, without bothering to subtract their "depreciation" from national income. But in many poorer economies, differences in the rate at which such goods depreciated may have had a significant impact on people's well-being, which would be inversely related to the level of their spending (and thus to their *apparent* well-being if

comparisons for sugar, tea, and cloth, we should remember that we are not even sure that Europeans did spend more on non-necessities each year. But if they did, despite being no richer than Chinese or Japanese, it is worth considering whether this socially induced "depreciation" was what kept European consumption growing unusually strongly through changes in economic cycles, relative prices, political stability, and so on.

Why would differences in the speed with which still-usable goods were discarded (or relegated to the back of closets) appear in the first place? Comparative social history provides some hints. For China, Japan, and western Europe alike, the seventeenth century was a time of enormous political and social instability, but the Qing and Tokugawa regimes that came to power in mid-seventeenth-century China and Japan probably gave those societies greater stability in the eighteenth century than most of western Europe enjoyed. Of course important parts of Europe—particularly Britain, where the new consumerism was most evident—also enjoyed relative peace (at home) in the eighteenth century, but the state did not throw itself as energetically into the preservation and/or revival of traditional roles and statuses as the Qing and Tokugawa did. This could conceivably have made it less important for people to define themselves and compete with each other through fashion; thus one would have had the sort of accumulation of goods and opulence that is associated in both China and Japan with the "prosperous age" of the eighteenth century, but with less interest in turnover of one's inventory for turnover's sake.

At least in China, it is worth thinking about the rise of fashion as part of a very long, slow, and by no means linear process in which status competition and self-identification among elites became gradually less closely tied to government service and official ranks. One important period in this trend was the late sixteenth and early seventeenth centuries, in which the growing uncertainties and frustrations of official career paths seem to have encouraged a search among elites for other life activities and (at least implicitly) for ways of ranking themselves that did not depend as directly on the state-sponsored examination system. This quest, plus growing private wealth, helped fuel not only the rise of fashion and conspicuous consumption that we have discussed, but such other activities as increased elite patronage of Buddhist monasteries and increased interest in privately organized textual scholarship.[197]

---

we ignore depreciation). After all, any expenditure you must make to just stay where you are has the same effect on you, whether it represents interest on a debt, repairs to offset physical depreciation, or a socially induced need to replace daily goods that are still physically functional. Moreover, when we subtract depreciation for classes of goods (e.g., housing) that may have been more durable in Europe while ignoring it for classes of goods that may have depreciated more rapidly there, we are making Europeans look richer, and Asians poorer, than they really were.

[197] Brook 1993; Peterson 1978.

From this perspective, the Qing success in not only reestablishing order after 1644 but in restoring some of the luster of public service (both in official positions and through philanthropy that the state encouraged but did not run) as an ideal and a status marker may well have stopped the growth of fashion, as it apparently did to monastic patronage. Any argument that the revival of the public career had broad psychological effects that slowed the growth of fashion must remain speculative, but at least one fairly direct connection can be suggested. The strict regulation of *official* dress was the one kind of sumptuary legislation that did remain effective in the Qing dynasty,[198] and awarding the right to wear various pieces of clothing otherwise restricted to officials (buttons, caps, etc.) was one visible way that the state rewarded merchants, landlords, and literati who provided meritorious assistance in public projects ranging from famine relief to road-building. Wearers of such items certainly had no interest in seeing them depreciated or made available to those who had not done comparable service. In this sense the Qing revitalization of the state, while certainly not crushing the "sprouts of capitalism" in the wider economy the way some scholars once thought, may have done enough to reinvigorate a "coupon" system to somewhat slow the growth of "fashion."

Qing order had equally important effects on elite women, despite their exclusion from government office. Exchanging poems—which had become an absolutely crucial means of both self-expression and social competition for elite women in the Ming, at least in the Lower Yangzi—became even more entrenched in China's "long eighteenth century," reflecting prosperity, an intensely competitive marriage market (in a land without hereditary aristocrats), and what may have been a greater-than-ever stress on writing as the sine qua non of civilized personhood (which accompanied the surge in textual scholarship).[199] This form of competition and self-expression required less purchasing than did European fashion. The collection of verses from women in more backward regions, including newly conquered areas, even gave these women a way to participate vicariously in Qing empire-building and a Manchu-Chinese "civilizing mission"[200]—a very different way of mastering the frontier than by consuming its exotic products. At the same time, the moralism of high Qing culture encouraged these women to limit their physical comings and goings much more than in the Ming and to draw a sharper line between themselves and the women of the urban pleasure quarters. Social occasions and exchanges of writing between elite married women and courtesans, quite common in the late Ming Lower Yangzi, became much less so in the Qing,[201] and as these two ceased to mix, the commercialized and fashion-conscious entertainment quarters presumably had much less influence on the larger, wealthier, and more important group of elite married women.

---

[198] Shen 1992: 516.
[200] Ibid., 212–16, 219.

[199] Mann 1997: 16–18, 76–120.
[201] Ko 1994: 266–78; Mann 1997: 121–28.

Here, too, then, a return of political and social "order" may have made people less interested in defining themselves through the ever-more rapid purchase and discard of consumer goods. But any such arguments must be re-
garded as extremely speculative—we know far too little about elite dress for
different sorts of occasions (not to mention household budgets) to go much
further at this point. For further clues, we need to problematize the extraordinary acceleration of European fashion, which needs at least as much explanation as any "failure" of Chinese and Japanese tastes to change quite so
dizzyingly.

Part of any explanation must surely lie in very general changes of attitudes,
as many authors have suggested. The increased prominence in eighteenth-
century western Europe of a person's perceived range of choice—in everything from marriage partners to careers to religious worship—as a defining
mark of status and personal dignity[202] seems likely to have also raised the
importance of consumer choices as a form of self-representation and thus
given an additional fillip to the growing European "fashion system." While
some scholars have seen a roughly contemporaneous increase in the weight
accorded to personal choice among Chinese elites (in marriage decisions, for
instance), they have wisely also stopped short of pronouncing these trends to
be equally pronounced and have noted that they do not represent the same sort
of ideological primacy for the "individual" as a choosing being.[203]

To look at the matter somewhat differently, sixteenth- through eighteenth-
century European states grew partly by clipping the wings of great extended
families (by, for instance, outlawing feuds and extending standardized law).[204]
In the process, they almost certainly diminished the centrality of extended kin
networks in defining people's identities, and so arguably also increased the
tendency to mark who one was through new relationships with purchased
commodities (as opposed to both kin and inalienable patrimonies). By contrast, both the Tokugawa and the Qing restored order through a partnership
with local institutions in whose hands they left much of daily administration;
extended kin groups occupied a prominent place among these institutions, particularly in China, and the state promoted both their power and ideological
centrality far more often than it sought to curb them. Perhaps where such
institutions and identities remained more prominent, people had less incentive
to be constantly defining themselves through making and displaying choices
about commodities[205] and thus less need to replace items that were physically
still serviceable.

---

[202] For a sensitive treatment of both the degree to which choice was real and the degree to which
it became the defining mark of status in at least part of English society, see Handler and Segal
1990: especially pp. 43–63.

[203] E.g., Rowe 1992: 2–3, 5–6, 32–34.

[204] See, for instance, Stone 1979: 93–107, especially 99–100.

[205] Cf. Sahlins (1976: 216): "Money is to the West what kinship is to the rest."

But because the perceived value of personal choice and of group member-
ship could be inflected in so many different ways in different societies and
encouraged in some spheres while inhibited in others, it behooves those of us
looking for explanations of a more specific phenomenon to do most of our
hunting at a more specific level. In this case, that involves looking more
closely at just what *kinds* of objects were involved in the accelerated growth of
Europe's "fashion system" and at factors affecting their production and distribution around the globe.

If indeed European tastes changed faster than those in China and Japan, part
of this difference seems attributable to a difference in the degree to which
exotic goods, especially exotic *manufactured* goods, became prestigious. After
all, Indian and Chinese textiles, Chinese porcelain, and so on all became very
important to European fashion, even down to a fairly humble level, while no
Western good became equally important in east Asia. True, seventeenth-
century Chinese guides to connoisseurship listed various foreign-made goods
as prestigious collectibles,[206] and various other Chinese and Japanese writings
of the period indicate an interest in Western products. Western eyeglasses and
other accoutrements provoked interest in the late Ming and early Qing, and
"Western ocean jackets"—with very expensive cloth that imitated the patterns
on a tower for a Ming imperial retreat by an Italian visitor—achieved a lasting
vogue, being adopted by Chinese palace women in the seventeenth century
and by fashionable women in the Lower Yangzi in the eighteenth century.[207]
Also in the eighteenth century, exotic furs—first Russian, then American—
became very popular. But nothing from abroad ever had the impact on Chinese
and Japanese style and consumption patterns that Asian textiles, for instance,
had on Europe. Why?

It has been a commonplace of Western scholarship on east Asia (especially
China) that the people of these countries were uninterested in foreign goods
because they were so convinced of the superiority of their civilization; and
some documents do support such a claim. Probably the most famous statement
reflecting this attitude came from Chinese Emperor Qianlong, who told English emissaries in 1793 that China produced all that it needed and had no
interest in the clever toys that the West had to offer; consequently, he saw no
reason for broader trade relations.[208] For many historians, this statement has
epitomized a long-standing "Chinese" attitude that was held to be the opposite
of the curious, acquisitive, dynamic "Western attitude." Even more subtle
scholarship, which has noted how imperial attitudes fluctuated between em-
bracing exotica (as part of the throne's pretensions to *universal* sovereignty) in
some periods and excluding them (as part of an assertion of Chinese cultural
superiority) in other, has tended to treat these imperial postures as synecdoches

---

[206] Clunas 1991: 58–60, 110, 137.   [207] Shen 1992: 491.
[208] Teng and Fairbank 1954: 19–21.

for "Chinese" attitudes toward foreign goods more generally.[209] Thus from such a perspective, Europe's greater interest in foreign fashions would be no coincidence. It would indicate that European divergence was, after all, rooted in a basic attitudinal difference, one perhaps linked to a greater willingness to take risks and innovate in general.

Yet once we stop taking Manchu emperors to represent China, much simpler explanations of the country's lesser tendency to import mountains of exotic goods come to mind. After all, China imported just as much as it exported (by definition, given the foreign trade institutions of this period), and its commerce with Southeast Asia in particular was full of exotic primary products: sharks' fins and birds' nests for gourmet eating (as well as enormous amounts of less exotic black pepper), pearls for jewelry, incense transshipped from the Middle East and various Pacific islands, and rare woods.[210] Demand for all these imports rose sharply in the eighteenth and even early nineteenth centuries: certainly British merchants, who carried many of these products from the Malay archipelago to Canton, found that their problem was securing enough supply, not glutting the market.[211]

None of these exotic imports experienced booms comparable to those in English tobacco, tea, and sugar imports, but it is hard to see how they could have. Even as it was, the search for sandalwood and other exotic imports prized in China did massive ecological damage to a number of Pacific islands, from which they were only rescued, ironically enough, when China-bound ships began to be filled with opium.[212] Moreover, except for pepper, virtually all these exotica were items that were *gathered* rather than planted: and that simple fact ruled out an intensification of production (and decline in unit price) comparable to what was accomplished on New World plantations, with huge numbers of slaves working very intensely under close and brutal supervision. One could not plant more sharks or create more jungle habitat for the birds who made the desired nests the way one could clear more land for sugar. Attempts *were* made to increase the number of gatherers by raiding for slaves—especially in the Sulu kingdom, in what is today the southern Philippines[213]—but the dispersed nature of this work meant that even slaves retained significant bargaining power; nothing like a Caribbean plantation was possible.

Sugar and tobacco consumption did soar, but (as we have already seen) they were largely produced within China by free peasants: this meant that they competed not only with other uses for land but other possible uses of the

---

[209] E.g., Sahlins 1994 (1989).

[210] For a list of the wide variety of luxury items imported from Thailand alone, see Cushman 1975: 105–6, 200–204; on imports from the tropical jungles of maritime Southeast Asia, see Warren 1982: 419–20.

[211] Warren 1982; McNeill 1994: 319–25.

[212] McNeill 1994: 325–36.   [213] Warren 1982: 419–34.

producers' time (including leisure). It is hard to see in these patterns any evidence that the Chinese were not interested in exotic luxuries: it seems more likely that most of the exotica they bought were not easily converted into cheap "everyday" luxuries. (The same was true, of course, of the cloves and fine spices that Europeans sought in southeast Asia; sugar and tobacco were exceptional among Europe's exotic imports, too.)

Any case for a relative Chinese indifference to exotic goods would have to point to paucity of *manufactured* imports. Even here, as Clunas points out, Chinese connoisseurs did include various foreign products among their prized possessions.[214] While Qianlong may have had little interest in European manufactures, the same was not true of elites in coastal Guangdong and Fujian, some of whom did accumulate clocks and other Western curiosities.[215] Still, there can be no question that China's per capita imports of manufactured goods were very small and had little impact on notions of appropriate dress and home decoration. Moreover, since Europe had little besides manufactured goods to offer, China's imports from the West, unlike its imports from Southeast Asia, did have a startling monotony. Roughly 90 percent of its imports from Europe and European colonies before the opium boom consisted of silver, and it is from this that historians have taken the impression that China as a whole (not just the court) lacked an interest in things foreign. But there is a much better explanation of why silver so dominated Western cargos to China, one evident in recent works by Richard Von Glahn, Dennis Flynn and Arturo Giraldez, and Andre Gunder Frank.

From roughly 1400 on, China was essentially remonetizing its economy after a series of failed experiments with paper and a grossly mismanaged copper coinage under the Yuan dynasty (1279–1368) had left the country without any widely accepted monetary medium. In this process, silver was becoming the store of value, the money of account (and often the actual medium) for large transactions, and the medium of state payments for this huge and highly commercialized economy. The enormous demand for silver this created made it far more valuable in China (relative to gold and to most other goods) than anywhere else in the world: and China itself had few silver mines. Consequently, China was already importing huge amounts of silver (mostly from Japan, and to some extent from India and Southeast Asia) in the century *before* Western ships reached Asia.

When Westerners did arrive, carrying silver from the richest mines ever discovered (Latin America produced roughly 85 percent of the world's silver between 1500 and 1800[216]), they found that sending this silver to China (whether directly or through intermediaries) yielded large and very reliable

---

[214] Clunas 1991: 58–60.

[215] Idema 1990: 467–69 (examples from literature); Waley-Cohen 1999.

[216] Barrett 1990: 224.

arbitrage profits—profits so large that there was no good reason for profit-maximizing merchants to send much of anything else. (The tribute missions to Beijing, which Marshall Sahlins has analyzed to understand "Chinese" attitudes, were unaffected by this, since they were essentially symbolic exchanges between sovereigns at administered prices. Profit-seeking often played a decidedly secondary role in these exchanges, though the missions were generally accompanied by profit-seeking "private" trade.[217])

Various Western intellectuals and politicians, who would have rather kept this silver at home (as a stockpile to pay for wars, for instance), were constantly arguing that other goods should be sent to Asia instead. The prominence of their protests in the written record has often made it appear that "the West" was desperately trying to get "Asians" to buy other foreign goods, while the Chinese were simply too ethnocentric (or Westerns artisans too unskillful) for this to work. But to focus on these polemics is to mistake the opinions of a few political leaders for the preferences of a whole society, just as focusing on the pronouncements of Chinese emperors about the proper forms and limits of tribute trade does. And in both cases, the actual decisions about what to trade were made by merchants embedded in markets.

The tendency to see China's import preferences as a sign of cultural conservatism has been further reinforced by treating silver as modern "money"—in other words, a residual store of abstract value transferred to make up Europe's "trade deficit." Instead, we need to see silver itself as a good: a refined product with a mineral base, which was well suited to an important function and which the West could produce far more cheaply than any place in Asia (excepting, in certain periods, Japan); the accidents of geology were such that China could barely produce it at all. It was, moreover, one of the few manufactured goods in which the West had an advantage not only in its supply of raw materials but in the technology of further production: European minting produced better and harder-to-copy coins than anything available in Asia.[218] Since the Chinese used silver in bar form, this advantage in minting mattered little to them, but it mattered a great deal to south Asian and other users who were often the initial purchasers of European silver, subsequently sending much of it to China through their own trade networks.[219]

The arbitrariness of treating silver as "money" in the modern sense, which was sent to east Asia *in lieu of goods*, rather than as a good the Chinese used as a monetary medium, becomes obvious once the issue is raised. After all,

---

[217] Wills 1995 (unpublished; cited with permission); Hamashita 1988: 16–18; Sahlins 1994 (1989).

[218] Perlin (1991) does not speak of an absolute advantage (this seems assumed, given European advantages in printing and metal stamping), but does emphasize that market forces were sufficient to cause production of many coins in Europe specifically for eventual use as domestic currency in Asia.

[219] Flynn 1995: 429–48.

many prestige goods—silk, pepper, opium, cocoa beans—have also performed monetary functions in one place or another but are nonetheless treated as goods. Moreover, much silver went back and forth between being used as money and as decoration (when jewelry was pawned or melted down, for instance). Treating silver as one more specific good, rather than as the equivalent of modern dollar bills, helps us make sense of the fact that significant amounts of gold flowed from China to both Europe and India during the same period that silver was flowing in.[220] Finally, the tendency to see silver as a residual store of value sent to China to pay for consumer goods has been reinforced by a long-standing tendency among Western scholars to see the West as the active (and desiring) agent in the knitting together of the world. But once we think about the dynamic created by changing the monetary base of perhaps as much as 40 percent of the world's economy in this period (once we add in China's tributary states, which were also "silver-izing"), it becomes hard not to see China's silver demand as every bit as much an "active" force in creating a global economy as was the West's demand for porcelain, tea, and so on.

We will treat New World silver more broadly in chapter 6. What is important here is a more specific point: that the West's huge comparative advantage in the export of silver sucked in trendsetting prestige goods from Asia. This helps explain why so many other exotic goods flooded into Europe—they paid for silver and made the wheel of fashion spin faster here than elsewhere. (We will discuss some other reasons for the influx in chapter 4.) It roots this unique influx in an economic conjuncture spanning Europe, Asia, and America, rather than in any uniquely European "materialism"[221] or "curiosity." And, given the way Europe acquired and ran the American silver mines, it reminds us of the tremendous significance of coercion in generating Europe's economic edge. (Advances in technology also mattered, but they would not have without the seizure of the mines and the imposition of labor obligations on the population.) In this particular case, the fruits of external coercion may have been significant for the way in which they accelerated changes in fashion and thus a consensual market-based trade within Europe; but it is crucial that the direction of explanation runs from coercion abroad to an extra boost to Smithian dynamics (and later to import-substituting industrialization) at home, *not* from more efficient marketing and industrial production at home to the power to coerce people abroad.

Finally, we must remember that even with whatever extra boost to the fashion mechanism silver-induced luxury imports provided, it is only a hypothesis that European demand for "non-necessities" was sufficiently more vigorous than Chinese or Japanese demand to make a real economic difference—not the

---

[220] For a far more detailed explanation of this, see Flynn and Giraldez 1996; Von Glahn 1996: 83–142, 224–37; Perlin 1991: 315–48.

[221] Mukerji 1983.

certainty that Sombart, Braudel, and others have taken it to be. As we saw earlier, there is no compelling reason to think that Europe's "industrious revolution" and popular participation in Smithian dynamics were much more pronounced than that of China (or probably Japan), regardless of what was happening to luxury demand at the top of society. It remains to consider the second significance sometimes accorded to the new luxury demand—that it led to new accumulations of capital among successful merchants and artisans, new advantages for bigger operators, and thus the emergence of capitalist firms employing proletarianized workers. Our final section turns to these arguments, and the next chapter looks at financial institutions and "capitalism" more generally.

Luxury Demand, Social Systems, and Capitalist Firms

Werner Sombart's classic work on luxury and the origins of European capitalism argues that the growing demand for luxuries produced new sorts of artisans and merchants. Given the expense of the materials, the time needed for fine craftsmanship, and the problem of collecting from customers who were often powerful but short of cash, most artisans could not produce these goods independently.

This in itself was nothing new. Much luxury production had always involved working capital beyond what an artisan could summon, and this problem had been solved by having the eventual owner commission and finance the work; often the artisan did his work at the estate of the patron, which prevented absconding with advances and allowed the patron to intervene in design choices along the way. Now, however, the growing volume of demand for these goods and the concentration of demand in cities meant that a producer (or dealer) who could finance production himself could take advantage of economies of scale and thus produce goods more cheaply than artisans working under the old system.

Thus, Sombart argues, a few independent shops emerged, which would first produce and then sell articles to anyone with enough money. These few very successful artisan-merchants then began to produce on a larger scale and employ the far more numerous artisans, who, lacking adequate capital, could never become independent producers; instead, they gradually became proletarians.[222]

Such cases did occur, but we should not overestimate their numbers. One did not have to go very far outside major urban centers to find the older style of commissioned work predominating, even in the late eighteenth century.[223] By the same token, one finds the same phenomena described by Sombart for

---

[222] Sombart 1967: 134–35.   [223] E.g., Dewald 1987: 195.

Europe—such as ready-made luxury goods—in the major cities of China and Japan as well, side by side with commissioned work.[224]

Elsewhere, meanwhile, artisanal, bespoke production was perfectly able to meet a huge surge in luxury demand. The same Europeans who noted that virtually everything one could imagine was available in major Indian cities noted that these goods were often obtained by coercing artisans to undertake specific commissions, rather than by purchasing them from independent shops.[225] Again, the pattern is not consistent across the subcontinent: many rural Indian weavers had considerable independence from any one buyer/ patron. S. Arasaratnam's study of eighteenth-century southeastern India makes clear that even weavers who had received cash advances for their work (as most did) retained considerable control over the disposition of their product, unlike Europeans who received raw materials through the putting-out system; and in weaving villages that were close to ports or other areas with many potential buyers, this translated into considerable autonomy.[226]

This, then, was a long way from artisans serving and being directly dominated by a few immensely wealthy patrons. But in most cases these weavers dealt with merchants through quasi-hereditary head weavers (and sometimes other layers of mediation as well) rather than directly. These head weavers, who "exercised a paternal control over a group of weavers but had no economic control over the fruits of their labor,"[227] seem to have arranged for vastly expanded production, often of very high quality, without becoming capitalists with direct control of production or creating proletarians directly supervised by those who financed and marketed their goods.

In Southeast Asian cities, too, aristocratic consumers still called the tune. Skilled artisans were in perpetual danger of being brought to court against their will and often found working under the aegis of a particular noble or rich merchant to be their best protection.[228] Even seventeenth-century Melaka—at 200,000 people bigger than all but a handful of European cities—was apparently well provided with all sorts of luxuries without the growth of "capitalist" artisan-merchants. Although the scarcity of southeast Asian artisans often allowed them to negotiate rather good terms for themselves, they did not move away from a patronage system and bespoke production (even in capital-intensive goldsmithing) until near the end of the nineteenth century, well after European colonial regimes had put an end to legal personal servitude (but not to the cultural importance of patron-client ties).[229]

Moreover, the logic of production of various non-luxury goods could present different and equally compelling reasons to shift toward a capitalist

---

[224] Clunas 1988: 65–72; Clunas 1991: 155–56; for Japan, see the variety of ready-made goods sold in shops even in Niigata, a middle-sized port in the seventeenth and eighteenth centuries: Takekoshi 1967: 3:11.

[225] Raychaudhuri 1982b: 266.   [226] Arasaratnam 1980: 259–60.   [227] Ibid., 265.

[228] Reid 1988a: 135–36.   [229] Reid 1989: 64–71.

organization. Chinese lumbering, for instance, moved in this direction due to the long waiting time beyond venturing into the forests and finally being paid for logs, plus the need for fairly large teams of lumberers. By the nineteenth century, lumbering firms employed thousands of wage workers, rather than purchasing timber from smaller independent operators.[230] An even clearer case arose in late Tokugawa fisheries.

Hokkaido fishing had long been a commercial operation; most of the catch became fishcake fertilizer sold to richer but ecologically harder-pressed areas. Demand boomed in the late Tokugawa along with the continuing commercialization of agriculture in many parts of Honshu. At the same time, a major famine at the northeastern tip of Honshu greatly increased the availability of wage laborers in sparsely populated Hokkaido, allowing large contract fisheries to make widespread use of a new and efficient, but expensive, net that required fifteen to twenty laborers to manipulate it. With this, the contract fisheries gained a competitive advantage over the region's numerous independent fishing households and changed their relations with them. Big fish merchants had long lent money to the smaller operatives and then purchased their catch, but in a world of scarce labor and rising demand they had had neither the incentive nor the power to proletarianize these suppliers; even fishers in default on last year's loans typically received new credit to carry on as independent operators. But this changed once more workers and the new nets were available: it now made sense to foreclose, buy more nets, and turn the defaulting fishermen into wage laborers. In short, capital moved from trade into production itself, wage labor increased, and centrally coordinated production with more fixed capital became the norm, all in an industry with one of the humblest product lines imaginable.[231] And it is worth remembering, once again, that the one area in which European luxury consumption does clearly stand out as opposed to China, Japan, and southeast Asia (though perhaps not India)—housing—was one of those in which the artisanal structure of production was particularly slow to break down and in which the production of many identical units with resulting economies of scale did not occur until the twentieth century.

The conclusion, then, seems inescapable: there was nothing about the scale or nature of luxury demand per se that created shopkeepers with pre-produced baubles and numerous employees rather than other systems of production. It was, rather, a matter of growing demand (and occasionally economies of scale) within societies where product and factor markets were becoming more important in general. Without that context, the growing demand from the noble customers of Parisian artisans (whose desire to use their power to escape their bills Sombart cites as a reason why only the best-capitalized artisans could survive) could as easily have reinvigorated older relations of production as transformed

---

[230] Wu and Xu 1985: 437–39.   [231] See Howell 1992: 271–78.

them. The demand from merchants, "rich husbandmen," and others with less political power than nobles may have been more significant in stimulating a new kind of workshop for ready-made goods, but as we have seen, there is good reason to think that "luxury" demand was at least as dispersed among various classes of Chinese and Japanese as it was among Europeans. And as we have already seen at some length, when it came to matters of "free labor" and markets in the overall economy, Europe did not stand out from China and Japan; indeed, it may have lagged behind at least China. At the very least, all three of these societies resembled each other in these matters far more than any of them resembled India, the Ottoman Empire, or southeast Asia.

Thus, at least so far, we would seem to have similar conditions in these three societies for the emergence of the new kinds of firms that we generally think of as "capitalist." It is time, then, to consider why we so often hear that such firms—and "capitalism" more generally—emerged only in Europe.

FOUR

VISIBLE HANDS:

FIRM STRUCTURE, SOCIOPOLITICAL

STRUCTURE, AND "CAPITALISM"

IN EUROPE AND ASIA

A NUMBER OF historians, most of them influenced by Fernand Braudel, look to the big firms at the apex of the economy for explanations of European uniqueness. These varied arguments (like those about consumption) are sometimes less precise than the arguments discussed in part 1, which referred to an explicit and fairly simple model of "perfect" markets and/or to quantifiable measures of wealth. They argue instead that the ideal conditions *for concentrated* capital accumulation—a.k.a. "capitalism"— included the widespread development of property rights (including secure rights in financial assets) and competitive markets, but also arrangements that allowed some people to profit by circumventing competitive exchanges, limiting their liability, and securing rights in such nonmarket or anti-market privileges as monopolies and tax farms.

Because these arguments invoke a complex mixture of contradictory tendencies as "just right" for capital accumulation, they are difficult to operationalize and discuss comparatively. While the arguments about markets in chapter 2 could be refuted by reference to a single Asian society, arguments about an exclusively European "capitalism" require comparisons to a wider range of cases. Moreover, we do find some genuine European organizational advantages here—but they seem applicable to very few endeavors in the pre-1800 world besides war, armed long-distance trade and colonization. Thus a discussion of these issues will eventually direct our attention toward the political economy of extra-European trade and colonization. As I will argue in part 3, extra-European activities *were* crucial—not so much because they led to *financial* accumulation, but because they vastly increased supplies of *physical* resources.

Braudel himself has documented at length how many features were shared by big merchants throughout the preindustrial Old World. These include virtually all the practices that he labels "capitalist": operating outside "transparent" competitive markets, focusing on transactions in which producer and consumer knew little about each other, using credit to prevent cash-hungry parties (from hungry artisans to overextended princes) from dealing with possible competitors, and moving repeatedly among high-return activities, so that the capitalist specialized in the "insertion of capital into the ceaseless process of production [or perhaps distribution?]," rather than in any particular line of goods.[1]

One reason for this restlessness is that in the preindustrial world, no single sector had enough economic possibilities for the most successful merchants: "The merchant did not specialize because no one branch of the commerce available to him was sufficiently developed to absorb all his energy. It has too often been accepted that the capitalism of the past was small because it lacked capital. . . . In fact, the correspondence of merchants and the memoranda of chambers of commerce reveal capital sums looking vainly to be invested."[2] This glut of capital only changed with the rapid technological change of the nineteenth century, which made it profitable to invest large sums in buying equipment that transformed actual production processes. Until then, the most successful capitalists faced a constant problem of where to reinvest their profits—a problem exacerbated by the tendency of imitators to introduce competition to once-safe preserves, reducing their originally high returns. (This also made various status-enhancing but unproductive ways to use one's profits all the more attractive—a point others emphasize more than Braudel.)

Thus, Braudel argues, capitalism developed slowly and could only become truly powerful where a very stable social order in which ownership was considered sacrosanct allowed capitalist families to build their holding over many generations—conditions Braudel claims were met only in Europe and Japan.[3] In both China and the Islamic world, he argues, the state was simply too powerful for rich nonrulers to enjoy any real security; in India, caste restrictions on occupation gave the great merchants some security, but not enough, while simultaneously limiting their access to new activities.[4]

K. N. Chaudhuri makes similar, if somewhat narrower, claims about differences between European and Asian treatments of property. In his early work, Chaudhuri highlighted certain post-1500 European business forms—the deposit-accepting public bank and the joint-stock company—that facilitated investment.[5] In making these arguments, Chaudhuri built on Weber, who argued that only western Europe developed the ideas and accounting systems that kept the resources of firms, principals, and agents reliably separate, made it possible to compute true profitability, and thus maximize capital accumulation.

But recent research has undermined these claims. Chinese accounting, for instance, was far more sophisticated than Weber supposed; it also turns out that remarkably few Western firms adopted the most "rational" of Western

---

[1] Braudel 1977: 47.
[2] Ibid., 60.
[3] Ibid., 69–71.
[4] Ibid., 72–74.
[5] Chaudhuri 1981: 40, 45; Chaudhuri 1985: 212.

accounting systems until large "managerial" firms came to the fore in the *late* nineteenth century.[6] And many Chinese firms survived for centuries, despite the ups and downs of the lineages from which they were indeed imperfectly separated. Records of commercial dynasties are particularly scant, as this kind of success was rarely flaunted,[7] but some examples have survived nonetheless. The Ruifuxiang Company, which operated a number of piece-goods stores, lasted over three hundred years, while the Yutang Company, a food-processing concern, survived from 1776 until after 1949.[8] Tianjin had several merchant dynasties that thrived from the eighteenth century (or even the late seventeenth) into the twentieth century.[9] And if one looks at family dynasties more generally one finds several that survived a thousand years or more even though China had few hereditary offices and (as we have seen) little inalienable land.[10]

Moreover, even those firms that were predominantly associated with one lineage often attracted some capital from others and hired professional managers.[11] Many raised enough capital to operate across large geographic areas, enter multiple lines of business, and even achieve a substantial degree of vertical integration.[12] Each of the great lumbering companies in early nineteenth-century Shaanxi reportedly employed from 3 to 5 thousand workers.[13] This made them some of the largest firms in the preindustrial world and certainly suggests that they could raise enough money to manage any preindustrial or early industrial process. By the nineteenth century numerous firms in the major entrepot of Hankou were organized on joint-stock principles, with investors from diverse parts of the country; the same was true for firms that made and sold salt from the giant salt yards in Furong, Sichuan.[14] Complex commercial partnerships involving many non-kin investors were also common among the *banjara* and *banya* merchant groups in north India[15] and elsewhere. No doubt these firms still fell short of Weber's ideal type, but it is not clear that most actual Western firms came much closer.

In some of his subsequent work, Chaudhuri has focused less on his earlier

[6] Chandler 1977; Gardella 1992a: 317, 331 and especially 321.

[7] Mann (1987: 91–93) provides an excellent example of the way in which traditional Chinese sources understate the importance of commerce to prestigious lineages and of some of the code words used to present commercial success as an achievement of a different, more prestigious kind. See also Pomeranz 1997b: 19.

[8] On Ruifuxiang, see Chan 1982: 218–35; on Yutang, see Hai 1983: 48–78, 90–106 and Pomeranz 1997b.

[9] Kwan 1990: 260–72, 290–94; Zhang Xiaobo 1995: 67–72.

[10] Beattie 1979: 1–23, 127–32; Dennerline 1986: 173–79, 194–207; Rowe 1990: 51–59, 63–65; Watson 1990: 247.

[11] Chan 1982: 219–22.

[12] See, e.g., Pomeranz 1997b (on Yutang).

[13] Wu and Xu 1985: 439.

[14] Rowe 1984: 72–73; Zelin 1988: 79–80, 86–90, 96–101; Zelin 1990: 87–88, 91–95, 106.

[15] Habib 1990: 389.

arguments about rational business organization[16] and more on an alleged lack of security for commercial capital in Asia.[17] Unlike Braudel, who at times suggests that this reflects a generally more arbitrary system of rule in Asia, Chaudhuri suggests that *persons* and *landed wealth* were not necessarily more insecure in Asia than in Europe. But the capital of merchant firms was not treated separately from people in Asia, as it came to be in Europe, and so remained insecure:

> The merchants and bankers in these trading nations of Asia could not turn their investments into spheres of public interest protected by law and encouraged by the state. Members of the public who invested their money in the bonds of the republics of Venice or Genoa or the Bank of Amsterdam were not free from financial risks. But the bonds had the qualities of legal recognition and of mortgage value. The Indian and Chinese merchants lending money to the ruling elites or helping with the realization of taxes were unable to institutionalize their public credits into marketable assets.
>
> The concept of private property in land was not limited in Asia either by size or by the type of owner. . . . This was never the case with trading capital. The merchant and his working stock remained indivisible. Capitalism as a commercial activity was universal in the Indian Ocean. There was little social or legal admission of capital's productive role as distinct from its owners.[18]

This lack of separation between capital and capitalists, Chaudhuri argues, derived from the fact that the ruling elites of Asia's great empires, unlike those of European city-states, did not engage in commerce either for the government's account or their own:

> Other factors of production, land and labour, were considered socially divisible; anyone who possessed sufficient purchasing power could buy land and employ labor. But capital utilized in trade and industry remained firmly in the hands of mercantile groups. *The notion that the possession of title to commercial investments yielding permanent income might be better than the direct taxation of merchants does not seem to have suggested itself to Asian rulers.* Had it done so, the other necessary condition would have followed: the need to define such titles and rights under the law. Because it remained legally undefined and socially misunderstood (being associated with usury, engrossing and monopolies) the area of the social ownership of capital, and of its specific utilization, management, and accumulation, also remained confined. (emphasis added)[19]

Consequently, "the specter of arbitrary expropriation was never far off."[20]

However, it is unclear whether big Asian merchants actually suffered more expropriations than their European counterparts did. Such a claim seems

---

[16] See Chaudhuri (1978, 1981) for the earlier view.
[17] Chaudhuri 1985: 210–15, 226–28; Chaudhuri 1990: 386.
[18] Chaudhuri 1985: 210, 214. [19] Ibid., 228. [20] Ibid., 213.

particularly dubious once we add in the de facto expropriation that occurred when European monarchs defaulted on their loans: as we shall see, at least some south Asian merchants had significant protection against this, and Chinese merchants were largely spared this problem because the state borrowed very little. Merchants in Tokugawa Japan, whom Braudel suggests enjoyed the same *advantages* as their European counterparts, probably suffered more de facto expropriations (through aristocratic and domainal defaults and debt cancellations legislated by the shoguns) than did merchants in China or India, though they became less frequent later in the period.[21]

Moreover, although some level of security for property is clearly necessary for functioning markets, it is not certain that every additional increment of security automatically lowers risk premiums, cheapens capital, and increases economic growth. Gregory Clark finds that although interest rates on public debt did respond to political crisis and stability over the long haul between 1540 and 1837, the rates of return demanded in private transactions generally did not. Moreover, major changes in the political regime that enhanced the security of property against both confiscation and taxation (e.g., the cementing of parliamentary control over the government budget) had no discernible effect on the price of capital in private transactions. Thus, he doubts that a gradual "perfecting" of the institutional environment was an important prelude to the Industrial Revolution; at least in this respect, English institutions were stable enough at least as early as 1540, with the subsequent development of a less arbitrary and corrupt political system of little importance to the capital market.[22] If the differences between the security of property in England circa 1540–1660 and 1690–1760 did not make much difference in the cost of capital, it becomes still less clear why the differences between eighteenth-century Europe and east Asia (and perhaps south Asia as well) should have made a crucial difference.

But even if the state did not threaten Chinese or Indian merchants much more than their European counterparts did, a less-complete separation between commercial capital and its owners might still matter. Some have argued that in China the claims of extended kin groups on any member who became rich inhibited long-term capital accumulation, draining off profits to landed "charitable trusts" that supported widows, education, and office-seeking. However, recent work shows that successful Tianjin merchants had little trouble separating their assets from those of their brothers' families, and even less so over time.[23] Alternatively, the "charitable trust" could itself be a vehicle for long-term accumulation of mercantile capital. We are uncovering more and more cases in which these theoretically inalienable trusts were lent to entrepreneurs or owned some commercial or industrial enterprise, rather than

---

[21] Totman 1993: 333 (forced loans), and 519 (some defaults continuing as late as 1831).
[22] Clark 1996: 587–88.
[23] Kwan 1990; Zhang Xiaobo 1995.

land.[24] Here the ties of kinship and communal property worked for long-term capital accumulation, allowing each branch of the family to receive a stream of income from the business while making it very difficult for any branch to take out its principal; the managers (who were sometimes hired from outside the lineage) seem to have had broad powers to set the payout rate of the firm, retaining earnings as needed, much like modern corporate managers.[25] And, unlike the great Yangzhou merchants studied forty-five years ago by Ho Ping-ti[26]—whose high living and eagerness to join the literati have long shaped our picture of late imperial China's merchant elite—neither the Tianjin nor the Furong merchant dynasties made much effort to send their sons into official-dom until the increased politicization of the twentieth century made this neces-sary.[27] Finally, we should remember that the family firm also dominated all but a few sectors of European economies until the late nineteenth century—well into the factory era.

Western European and east Asian business organization may have been most different in the one sector that Europeans saw the most of—overseas commerce. It was largely for purposes of long-distance trade and colonization that Europeans created new forms of partnerships and, ultimately, joint-stock companies. These forms did institutionalize a new degree of separation be-tween capital and its owners and in doing so facilitated unified management of trading voyages and cargos too big for a single investor.

By contrast, a Chinese junk trading in southeast Asian waters typically car-ried the stock of many different merchants, and those merchants or their agents were onboard serving as crewmembers and receiving cargo space in lieu of wages. One scholar has described these ships, with their holds subdivided into many compartments, as "resembling a Canton suburban market set afloat," while others have concluded that such trade could only be part of a "back-ward," "peddling," "petty" capitalism.[28] But, as we shall see below, merchants who worked this way competed successfully with Europeans on most routes, as long as the Europeans did not use force. (They could, of course, have gained markets by accepting lower profits, but we have no evidence of that, and the higher cost of capital in China makes it unlikely.)

Indeed, such a system made perfect sense in light of the monsoon winds on these routes. Since one could not return home until the winds reversed them-selves, one could not drastically reduce the amount of time spent in port(s). A group of land-based entrepreneurs who used all the cargo space themselves or

[24] Zelin 1988: 87–95, 97–109; Zelin 1990: 86–88, 92, 95, 98; Kwan 1990: 271–72, 290–300; Pomeranz 1997b.

[25] The exception to this resemblance, as Kwan notes (1990: 272 n.2), was the absence of an equity market reconciling liquidity for particular investors with the firm's need for paid-up capi-tal—but the Yutang Co. seems to have found a way to finesse that, too (Pomeranz 1997b).

[26] Ho 1954.

[27] Zelin 1990: 99–100, 105; Zhang Xiaobo 1995: 88–91; Kwan 1990: 175–87, 262–76.

[28] Ng 1990: 315; for the classic description, see Van Leur 1955.

rented it for cash would have found themselves paying enormous wage bills to support professional sailors during long stays on shore. It made more sense to make many shorter stops and have crewmembers who could and did occupy themselves in buying and selling cargo at each port.

By contrast, shipping costs fell dramatically in the Atlantic during the eighteenth-century because various groups of European shippers, who *did* pay wages to their crews, found ways to cut port time—e.g., from over one hundred days gathering cargo in the Chesapeake before returning circa 1700 to under fifty days circa 1770[29]—and so could make two round trips a year rather than one. But the wind patterns in south, southeast and east Asia ruled out any such breakthrough there, at least as long as ships relied on sails. Thus, the lesser physical separation between the merchant and his capital that we see in this case was in no way irrational; it was adaptive for a world whose winds were different from those of the Atlantic.

The overland tea trade between south China and Russia—which involved a relatively uniform commodity (which, like Chesapeake tobacco, could be readily collected at a central place before the ship or caravan arrived) and in which winds were no constraint—was organized on much more "European" principles. Gardella describes a tea trade with some large firms (though more small ones), complex partnerships, advance financing, a market for shipping space (allowing investors to be physically separate from their cargos), spot and forward wholesale markets, and so on; the partnerships seem to have roughly resembled early modern European companies for long-distance trade (e.g., the English Muscovy Company) in many ways.[30] They did lack some further refinements of seventeenth-century corporations—particularly unlimited life—but there was no particular need for them to have this feature. Like the earlier trading companies in Europe, they embodied the degree of impersonality needed for the business they did—and as we shall see later, it was only in very special contexts that a further separation of managers and owners had real advantages.

The argument that European capitalists had more investment options seems more promising, but only as long as the field of comparison is restricted to China and southeast Asia. Unlike dry goods, soy sauce, or lumbering, heavy involvement in overseas trade might bring a Chinese firm unwanted state attention, particularly if the principal stayed overseas for more than a single trading season at a time. Thus within this limited but important sphere, Chaudhuri's previously cited strictures about the insecurity of Asian mercantile fortunes might apply.[31] Chinese remained heavily involved in overseas trade, despite one interlude (during the political instability of the seventeenth

---

[29] Shepherd and Walton 1972: 87.
[30] Gardella 1994: 34–35; Gardella 1992b: 101–7.
[31] Wills 1995; Godley 1981: 60–61.

century) when the government made serious efforts to stop this trade; even this interruption does not seem to have had much long-term effect on the growth of China-based trading networks. However, the Chinese state did not use force to promote Chinese commerce overseas, where rates of profit may have been unusually high. The Qing did, as we shall see, show some concern for Chinese "guest merchants" who visited southeast Asia annually, but they were indifferent or hostile to Chinese who *settled* overseas; this latter group would have been crucial to a trading post or colonial empire. Nor would any Chinese regime license the development of private armed trading from a Chinese base. The Qing roughly doubled China's size between 1680 and 1760, but their focus was on central Asia, which was of little interest to coastal merchants. Chinese political economy was, then, less favorable to the growth of one particular capitalist endeavor than were the competing states of early modern Europe.

Moreover, the Chinese state borrowed very little, did not involve merchants very much in revenue-forwarding, and sold relatively few offices (though many exam degrees) before the mid-nineteenth century.[32] And while it did create one domestic monopoly—salt—from which a few licensees became extraordinarily rich, and some smaller monopolies, too, it did much less of this than European states did. There were no Chinese monopolies on sugar, tobacco, alcohol, or the other increasingly popular "little luxuries" that made so much money for both European rulers and the merchants they favored. Thus, public finance—which not only yielded large profits to many of Europe's richest capitalists but also served as a laboratory for new financial institutions[33]—offered far fewer opportunities for great Chinese merchants.

Thus, at least for China, one could argue that a state that was usually able to live off current land-based revenues *interfered* less with its merchants than its European counterparts, but also *created* fewer opportunities and privileged niches for them; we shall return to this possibility later. Perhaps the concessions that Europe's biggest firms got from involvement with the state were well worth the interference they suffered, and so Europe's political economy was more conducive to capitalist accumulation than China's was. But such a claim remains to be proven.

Another possibility is that the institutional innovations created in response to state financial needs in Europe led to the development of more efficient capital markets in general. This seems plausible, but we need to be very careful in specifying for which activities more sophisticated capital markets mattered. Before turning to that task, we need to deal a bit more with some very broad-

[32] On Ming public finance, see R. Huang 1974: 5, 24, 49–50, 80, 104, 112, 114, 119, 148, 150, 203; on merchant involvement in revenue forwarding, see Zhang Xiaobo 1995: 94–98; on the sale of offices, see Ho 1962: 33, 47–50; and on the relatively small involvement of merchants in government finance generally, and a comparison with early modern Europe, see Wong 1997.

[33] Van der Wee 1977: 345, 352, 368, 373.

gauged claims that credit-hungry European states offered unique security to financial assets. Examining some Asian cases beyond China with very varied relationships between public finance and private markets will raise questions about any simple link from the state's need for credit to security for capital to cheap and abundant credit more generally.

In Southeast Asia, most precolonial states were fairly weak by either European or Chinese standards; though some mainland states were growing stronger,[34] this was less true in the more commercialized island world. Many southeast Asian states were eager sponsors of cross-border trade and actively recruited merchants to anticipate, collect, and manage government revenue.[35] Nonetheless, the shares of these states in their societies' surpluses were relatively small,[36] so that the opportunities they provided for making large profits through buying financial or commercial privileges were smaller than those in early modern Europe.

But that public borrowing developed much more slowly in China and southeast Asia than in western Europe does not mean that private debt and financial assets in general were less secure than elsewhere. Meanwhile in much of south Asia and the Middle East, intense military competition among near equals was more common and created fiscal needs analogous to those of early modern European states;[37] and in some of those areas one finds financial institutions developing that seem as sophisticated as those of Europe.

Much recent scholarship has described a south Asian capitalism that burst precisely those limitations that Chaudhuri emphasizes. Frank Perlin, for instance, has shown that beginning in the fourteenth century, great families in various parts of India accumulated village headships, taxing rights, and other shares in the produce of the land. These rights were often acquired through lending to the state, to other important families, and, increasingly, to peasants themselves.[38] In the process, these separable shares in peasant output became institutionally defined and the extent of their protection agreed upon: even the king could not revoke them,[39] and an owner could sell or borrow against them. In other words, they were as much "securities" as the European bonds or liens on future revenues that Braudel and Chaudhuri refer to.[40] Indeed, in India, public financial management seems to have evolved from private innovations, not the other way around.[41]

[34] Lieberman 1990: 79–80.
[35] Subrahmanyam 1993: 18–25; Reid 1993: 116, 120.
[36] Reid 1988a: 120–21, 126–29, 145.
[37] See Bayly (1989: 52–55), for a general account of "military fiscalism" in the Mughal, Safavid, and Ottoman empires.
[38] Perlin 1985: esp. 422, 431–32, 442–46; Perlin 1979: 179, 187–92.
[39] Perlin 1985: 448n. 83, 452.
[40] Ibid., 442–48, 452; see also Wink 1983: 606–8.
[41] Perlin 1985: 431–32.

While Perlin and Andre Wink concentrated on north and central India, Sanjay Subrahmanyam found even stronger evidence of the interpenetration of capital-accumulating families and commercialized public finance in south India. Subrahmanyam traces the careers of what he calls "portfolio capitalists": men who combined an ever-shifting mix of interests in long-distance trade (mostly high-profit luxury goods); loans, bill-forwarding, and other financial activities; the purchase or leasing of tax rights and government monopolies (e.g., diamond mines); capital-intensive land reclamation (often purchasing the tax rights to frontier areas, financing settlement and irrigation, and then using the leverage provided by credit and taxing rights to become the sole purchaser of locally produced export goods); service as local purchasing agents to the British and Dutch; and service as a courtier or general, and military supply officer.[42] And here, too, rights to future income streams won strong customary and sometimes formal protection; eventually they became tradable, heritable, and mortgageable, much like the equivalent interests in most of Europe.

More recently, Subrahmanyam has generalized from south India to much of what he calls "early modern Asia,"[43] arguing that two particularly large and important groups of "portfolio capitalists" fanned out across the enormous littoral of the Indian Ocean and its adjacent seas. Iranians inserted themselves into trade, revenue-collection and forwarding, finance, and high-profit kinds of production (e.g., government mines) from coastal east Africa to the Middle East, south Asia, and (later) parts of southeast Asia. Meanwhile, Chinese from coastal Guangdong and Fujian fanned out across southeast Asia. Both groups brought methods first developed in private business and finance to the project of state revenue collection, while using state connections to gain lucrative concessions, acquire privileged information, and otherwise further their mercantile interests, much the way Perlin describes.[44]

The activities of "portfolio capitalists" and the generally mercantilist attitude of the states they penetrated are best documented for a series of city-states that lived off their positions as commercial entrepots (Melaka, Hormuz, etc.) and needed to offer a favorable climate for mobile merchants.[45] These states alone would constitute a zone of activity and security comparable to those enjoyed by early modern European capitalists—note that Chaudhuri refers to the clear legal status that creditors of Venice, Genoa, or Amsterdam enjoyed, not the more uncertain position of those who had lent to the kings of France, Spain, or other large European states. (Even in England, the most pro-mercantile of Europe's national states, the government defaulted on substantial debts

---

[42] Subrahmanyam 1990: 298–342.
[43] Subrahmanyam 1993: chap. 1.
[44] Ibid., 20–26; Subrahmanyam 1990: 298–342; Perlin 1979: 172–237.
[45] Subrahmanyam 1993: 16.

during the Civil War period, and uncertainty about whether some other royal debts would ever be repaid lingered for decades.[46])

Subrahmanyam then argues that the great landed empires of south and Southeast Asia were increasingly following the lead of these city-states, while some of the city-states were gaining control of substantial hinterlands. Thus there was a convergence of the previously separate patterns of state finance in the great agrarian states and the merchant-dominated city-states of the Indian Ocean, and a vast expansion of the territories in which "portfolio capitalists" could operate securely and profitably.[47]

The eighteenth-century merchants who served as intermediaries for state revenues in some of these landed empires may have attained legal protections for their interests even greater than those enjoyed by most of their European peers. Take, for instance, Bengal—which, with close to 20,000,000 people before the horrendous 1770 famine,[48] was more populous than any European state besides Russia or France. The Jagat Seths, bankers to the regime, customarily advanced revenues to the *nawab* (ruler) in return for a right (which they in turn contracted out) to collect the taxes they had anticipated. If the ruler was toppled by internal or external enemies, their claims apparently remained intact—an important factor in their willingness to conspire against a *nawab* trying to revoke various privileges his predecessors had sold.[49] Their contemporaries who loaned to European monarchs often lacked this option, much as they might have wanted it.

It is striking that we find these portfolio capitalists flourishing in India, where the general population was probably less involved in the market than it was in China, Japan, or western Europe: their presence sets in especially sharp relief the need to distinguish between conditions for the growth of a capitalist class and conditions under which society as a whole is transformed. In a work that predates Subrahmanyam's, C. A. Bayly suggests at least two factors that limited the transformative potential of early modern Indian capitalism.[50]

Bayly emphasizes that the traffic in various revenue-collection rights, monopolies, and other privileges—what he calls "the commercialization of kingly power"—was premised on excluding much of the population from the market. Such rights would not have had a secure enough existence to be widely traded had purchasers not been confident that they could continue preempting the growth of more competitive markets for various goods and services. In that sense, a certain kind of capitalism, far from going hand in hand with the growth of market economy, could be quite inimical to it, and thus to a more general economic transformation.

But Bayly also makes an argument about what we might call the spirit of

[46] C. Hill 1980: 188–89.
[47] Subrahmanyam 1993: 18–27; Subrahmanyam 1986: 357–77.
[48] Van Schendel 1991: 38.
[49] Marshall 1987: 40, 51, 59, 71, 75–79.   [50] Bayly 1983.

Indian capitalism—an attempt to pursue Weber's notions of a link between religious belief and economic activity, but based on far better evidence than Weber had for any non-European case. Though we cannot do full justice to that argument here, it is worth briefly sketching it and considering how economically important these differences are likely to have been.

Bayly argues that the majority of north Indian merchants were disinclined to imitate the great portfolio capitalists—either in becoming deeply involved in ventures (mostly state-connected) that involved high profits, high risks, and the rapid turnover of capital, or in getting closely involved in the management of land—because aspects of these activities clashed with ordinary bazaar merchants' ideas of what they should be. In particular, Bayly argues, ordinary Indian merchants were concerned to protect the family's "credit"—financial, social, and spiritual. That credit could be endangered by risky ventures, by high living, or by merely *having* the kind of wealth that would be likely to lead one (or one's children) into high living. Thus ordinary merchants built their status through cautious business practices, a relatively slow turnover of capital, and a relatively ascetic lifestyle—all inconsistent with life as a high-flying courtier-merchant. Moreover, a number of cautionary tales that circulated among merchants suggested that directly managing land or land revenue was especially dangerous, since it enmeshed one in complex patronage obligations and risky gambles on the harvest. In an economy where popular purchasing power was limited, it was always tempting to become involved in managing state revenues, long-distance trade, and other areas of potentially high profit, but the ethos of most Indian merchants pointed away from such activities. The portfolio capitalists themselves were sometimes admired and envied, but they were also often taken as negative models by their more conservative fellow merchants.[51]

It is hard to question this description of merchant culture, but also hard to know how much it explains. After all, the cautious merchant who frowns on his higher-flying colleagues is not only an Indian figure. He is to be found even in a hotbed of early capitalist gambling like Amsterdam. There, as Simon Schama has suggested, the stock exchange was for many burghers a symbol of wholly inappropriate speculation, while the extremely cautious municipal bank symbolized worthy commercial activity.[52] Moreover, Bayly himself cites the fascinating example of pious north Indian merchants who lived in humble, unadorned houses near the bazaar but also maintained palatial Persian-style residences on the outskirts of town, from which they presumably conducted a more high-flying kind of business.[53] Often, then, piety may have dictated what one boasted of more than what one actually did; this was also the case with scholar-gentry families in China who quietly maintained substantial commercial investments.

[51] Ibid., 383–87.   [52] Schama 1988: 347.   [53] Bayly 1983: 387–88.

Even if many merchants were truly kept out of high-risk, high-return ventures by their sense of themselves, it is not clear how much difference this made to the economy as a whole. There was room for a limited number of participants in those sectors anyway, and the lure of high profits seems to have moved enough people that such activities were not starved for capital. The contrast with more obvious economic implications would appear to be a structural one—that in at least some European states, lending to the government *eventually* came to be the epitome of cautious investment, while involvement with the state remained a gambler's activity amid the turmoil of eighteenth-century India. (A similar change in the *relative* valuation of the risk in public and private lending is suggested by the English interest-rate movements cited by Clark and discussed above.) Indeed, as we shall see shortly, investment in certain quasi-state activities—including war-waging—through competing East and West India Companies actually gave birth to new forms for amassing *patient* capital in Europe, while elsewhere investment in violence remained a more short-term and speculative activity. But the reasons for this contrast were not primarily cultural, and the applicability of these new financial instruments to activities other than colonial settlement and armed trading seem to have been limited.

There is some evidence that western European capital markets were the most efficient in the eighteenth-century world, though there are also reasons for caution. Dutch interest rates, at 3 percent for the best borrowers, were probably the lowest in the seventeenth- and eighteenth-century world, with British rates falling to 4–5 percent during the eighteenth century.[54] Interest rates were about 7 percent for the best borrowers in late seventeenth-century Surat and seem to have been falling all over seventeenth-century India.[55] Japanese interest rates fell, too, but from a higher initial level. Interest on loans to daimyo—who defaulted enough that they were hardly ideal borrowers—fell from an average of 12.45 percent in 1707–1740 to 8.68 percent in the 1860s (despite enormous political turmoil in the latter decade).[56] In China, our fragmentary evidence suggests that nominal interest rates were about the same as Japan's in the eighteenth century, and higher in the nineteenth century. Tianjin "banks" seem to have charged 10 percent per year to both the government and a few very solid merchants in the late eighteenth century,[57] while pawnshops considered state loans at 12 percent attractive enough that they would in turn obey various state regulations.[58] This would seem to suggest that places where "military fiscalism" was more pronounced and public credit more developed (south Asia and above all Europe) did develop better methods for delivering

[54] DeVries 1976: 211; Clark 1996: 567.
[55] Habib 1982d: 376–77; Chaudhuri 1981: 45; Perlin 1990: 269.
[56] Hanley and Yamamura 1977: 345.
[57] Zhang Xiaobo 1995: 97.
[58] Pan 1985: 40–55; Pan 1994: 103–30.

capital to the economy more generally. But we should not quickly conclude that even China suffered from expensive credit.

First, since we do not know the inflation rate in eighteenth-century China we do not know its real interest rates. Second, interest rates vary with the borrower, and differences between societies in the rates charged on riskier loans might not always be the same as those on loans for the best borrowers. Moreover, if borrowers were sometimes judged on criteria other than credit-worthiness, low interest rates may not always reflect a market price for credit. English court records, for instance, show that seventeenth-century lenders faced considerable pressure to lend to (and not foreclose on) their social superiors, even when they were known to be insolvent.[59]

More important, the interest rate was not the only nor even necessarily the most important influence on people's willingness to borrow for investment. For instance, it was extremely hard in China to seize land used as collateral; if the owner defaulted one could make him a rent-paying tenant, but it was very hard to evict him or to terminate his option to someday repay the debt and reclaim the land. Viewed from one perspective such (customary) rules represent a serious imperfection in property rights, which undoubtedly raised the interest rate that lenders demanded. But the borrowers' perspective was likely different. The millions of peasant households deciding whether to borrow to buy a loom, procure mulberry leaves to feed an extra rack of silkworms, or even finance a wedding (and thus the acquisition of another laborer) may have been *more* willing to take the plunge at high rates with almost no chance of losing all access to their land than they would have been with lower rates but more severe penalties for default. This seems especially likely for those in sericulture, where the borrowing period was generally short, and both the return on a good crop and the risk of failure quite high.

In Europe, on the other hand, the working and fixed capital for rural industry generally came from putting-out merchants, rather than the workers; and these generally more solvent investors were probably less risk averse, preferring lower rates with harsher consequences in the relatively unlikely event that they defaulted. But unless we find evidence that Chinese interest rates reflected an absolute shortage of capital, or that these rates made certain crucial activities not worth doing, we cannot assume that they impeded either further proto-industrial and agricultural growth or mechanization. And as we shall see shortly, neither of these scenarios is likely.

None of our core areas suffered from an absolute insufficiency of capital for industrialization. As Braudel points out, in the quotation cited on p. 167, the limitations on earlier "capitalisms" did not result from too little capital.[60] They resulted from a lack of adequate outlets for capital in an era before the technologies were available for transforming production processes by investing large

---

[59] L. Hill unpublished.   [60] Braudel 1977: 60.

sums in fixed plant and equipment. Or to be more precise, the problem was a lack of enough outlets that were more attractive to rich people than investing in titles and other assets that were economically unproductive (though some were personally profitable nonetheless).[61] Since even China—which had the highest interest rates of the regions discussed here—nonetheless had productivity and standards of living comparable to those in Europe, it seems unlikely that it had a serious shortage of capital stock or lacked adequate institutions for mobilizing capital. Most early industrial projects in Britain were financed by the entrepreneurs or their kin, without recourse to financial institutions; since it appears that the top 2 percent of the Chinese population received about the same share of total income as the elite did in England and Wales,[62] it is hard to see why the same could not have occurred in China. Research on later, better-documented periods also shows a substantial surplus potentially available for investment.[63] In Japan, where interest rates were only slightly lower than in China and higher than in either Indian ports or western European cities, a study of two towns and twenty-nine villages in the 1840s suggests a savings rate among *peasants* of roughly 20 percent.[64]

Still, differences in interest rates should have had some effects. As it turns out, the most likely scenario is that northwest Europe's cheaper capital and more sophisticated capital markets made it easier for this particular core region to gain steadily increasing supplies of needed primary products from remote places, while higher rates *may* (though this is quite speculative) have impeded this in China. But before looking at this hypothesis, let us consider the possibility that differences in capital costs directly affected the productive capacity of the cores themselves.

It is unlikely that these differences made a crucial difference for agricultural or proto-industrial developments in the cores. Ming-te Pan's work has shown how peasants in the seventeenth- and eighteenth-century Lower Yangzi (and in North China as well) increased their incomes substantially by borrowing to go into sericulture, cotton-growing, home-based textile production, and the like, even at prevailing high interest rates—in fact, often even at the highest rates quoted for essentially unsecured credit. He makes clear that what mattered was access to some source of credit that did not trap the peasant into dependence on a single patron (either a landlord-creditor or a monopsonistic putting-out merchant) and thus prevent the would-be producer from buying and selling in competitive markets; most peasants apparently could avoid such dependence.[65] As I suggested before, peasants may even have been actually *more* willing to undertake these activities than they would have been had interest rates been lower but the penalties for default more dire.

[61] DeVries 1976: 213–31.
[62] See discussion in chapter 3 above.
[63] Riskin 1975: 65–80, especially 75.
[64] Cited in Hanley and Yamamura 1977: 357.
[65] Pan 1994: chap. 3.

One might nonetheless expect that more looms, spindles, and so on would be purchased in Europe, where merchants could acquire them with much cheaper credit than was used for this purpose by Chinese peasants. But this would only make it worthwhile for more people to spin or weave if the merchants passed on their gains from cheap credit to the producers, rather than keeping those gains as profit or using them to cut prices. Given the very competitive markets for textiles in early modern Europe and the much less perfect nature of markets for rural proto-industrial labor, with many laborers facing monopsonistic or oligopsonistic purchasers of labor in their district,[66] this seems rather unlikely.

It is even harder to see why Sino-European differences in capital costs or business forms should have been decisive for early mechanized industry. Most technologies of the early Industrial Revolution were cheap. Early textile mills did not require much fixed capital and were easily financed by family firms. The British coal industry, which made possible the most important break with preindustrial constraints, raised its capital almost entirely from families and local contacts until the mid- to late nineteenth century.[67] The corporate form was almost never used in these sectors of the early industrial economy.

Moreover, the returns on investment for the early industrial innovators were high enough that interest rates higher than those in Britain should not have been a deterrent. Conversely, seventeenth- and eighteenth-century Holland[68]—with what was probably the world's cheapest credit—did not produce an energy breakthrough: peat, the most promising local source of subsurface energy, simply turned out to be inadequate in both quantity and quality, despite much investment in experiments and in infrastructure to ship it cheaply.[69] Thus, it seems unlikely that differences in capital markets were terribly significant for *production* before the *Second* Industrial Revolution, in the late nineteenth century.

In local and regional commerce, it is likely that Europe's cheaper credit made some difference, but it is hard to tell how much; given the extensive marketization of all the societies discussed here, it is hard to see how a small disadvantage in trade caused by higher interest rates would have been the decisive "blockage" in China, Japan, or even India. And with the important exception of armed, intercontinental trading and settlement, the business forms used in commerce were not much different among the various Eurasian cores;[70] certainly the corporate form was barely used by merchants before the mid-nineteenth century.

[66] See chap. 2, pp. 87–89.
[67] Griffin 1977: 43–59; Morris and Williams 1958: 137–49.
[68] DeVries 1976: 211.
[69] Ibid., 165–67, 252; de Zeeuw 1978.
[70] See Braudel (1982: 585), though he claims these activities were less common in Asia than Europe; Gardella 1992a: 319–21; Perlin 1990: 258–301.

If emerging capitalist firms in western Europe had unique advantages, one would expect these advantages to show up where European firms competed with Asian merchants. But a European edge appears primarily where geography and local politics favored using force to create monopolies or near-monopolies (mostly on spices). In those instances, Europeans did oust their Asian competitors and reap large profits: the Moluccas ("Spice Islands"), Sri Lanka, and (intermittently) the Straits of Melaka, Hormuz, and the Red Sea are prime examples.[71] In the coffee trade, on the other hand, Europeans failed to dominate a competitive trade based in the Middle East. When they eventually succeeded in the 1700s, it was by creating new production centers in their own colonies: Java, St. Domingue, Reunion.[72] Political and military power, rather than superior commercial organization, also seem to have been crucial to the way in which European merchants wrested control of some (though still by no means all) trades from indigenous merchants in India and from Chinese merchants in the Philippines.[73] Europeans did gain control of the important textile trade along parts of the Coromandel (eastern India) coast in the mid-seventeenth century without using much force, but this was because *local* wars had exhausted the resources of indigenous merchants and the losers allied with the foreigners in a desperate attempt to recoup their positions.[74] Generally, where weapons could not provide a trump card, Europeans found themselves losing out to Chinese, Gujarati, and other Asian merchants—or joining up with them—at least as often as they defeated them.[75] Moreover, the Dutch and English East India Companies, supposedly the most advanced capitalist firms in Europe,[76] often could not pay their dividends and needed periodic rescues from bankruptcy, even with the aid of various privileges.[77]

Railway-building, with its much higher capital requirements and longer wait before profits began, was a different story, for which the corporate business form and access to cheap capital did matter. But railroads were only built once the Industrial Revolution was well underway. The crucial breakthrough in land transport was technological, not financial; the mid-century railway boom was hardly the result of entrepreneurs' finally figuring out how to finance lines that had long been understood to be both possible and profitable. Undoubtedly, railway construction proceeded much faster *once it began* be-

[71] Subrahmanyam 1993: 62–74, 136; see also Bayly 1989: 67–74.

[72] Ukers 1935: 1–5; Chaudhuri 1985: 92, 198–99.

[73] Habib 1990: 398; Wang Gungwu 1990: 421.

[74] Brennig 1977: 326–38, 331–32.

[75] Subrahmanyam 1993: 186; Subrahmanyam 1990: 193–218; Blussé 1986: 97–99, 116, 120, 123–29, 154, 165; Ng 1990: 311–12; Bayly 1989: 69; Lombard 1981: 179–80; Pearson 1991: 108.

[76] Chaudhuri 1978, 1981; Steensgaard 1982.

[77] Chaudhuri (1978: 444–52) on the East India Company in the years before 1760; Bayly (1989: 98, 120) on after 1760; Glamann (1981: 249–50, 264–65) and Gaastra (1981: 69) on the VOC. More generally, see Lombard 1981: 179.

cause a large pool of investors (many of them made rich by cotton mills, coal mines, and other early industrial enterprises) were seeking safe ways to reinvest large profits and would accept relatively modest returns (especially after being burned on loans in newly independent Latin America).[78] With lots of money seeking secure outlets and many branches of industry still not using much fixed capital, Braudel's era of plentiful capital seeking adequate outlets was not quite over, though it was about to be as new technologies created profitable ways to place huge sums for long periods.[79] Thus, the Western corporate form and Western financial institutions more generally may not have been absolutely necessary even for the railroads,[80] though they probably helped. What *was* unquestionably necessary was Britain's unique success with coal, partly conditioned by geography.

Transport more broadly may have been one area in which cheap capital and sophisticated financial institutions were important, at least in England. Numerous turnpikes and canals were built with private money in England, linking producers, inputs (including coal and grain), and markets. And though none of these efforts required capital on the scale that railroads would, they did share with railroads a relatively long time lag between initial investment and the realization of revenues—a much longer turnover time than for the capital in virtually any kind of production before 1850 or any trade within a single continent. Consequently, these infrastructural improvements were sensitive to the efficiency of instruments for assembling capital, including those that allowed some investors to liquidate their shares before the enterprise had borne fruit. When Britain began to rely heavily on primary products from the Americas in the nineteenth century, transport infrastructure became even more important, opening up the interior of these continents; and those projects, whether publicly or privately financed, did require organized capital markets that pooled investments from large numbers of strangers.[81]

[78] Hobsbawm 1975: 109–15.

[79] Braudel 1977: 60. The situation may be thought of as analogous to that which Schultz postulated for many "underdeveloped" areas as late as the 1960s: the limit on investment in new agricultural techniques, he argued, was not set by an inadequate supply of savings, as some had suggested, but by an inadequate supply of new technologies and other investment opportunities that had proved their worth in the particular setting in which landlords and other wealth-holders were considering their options. See Schultz 1964: 83–90, 96–101.

[80] Roy (1997: 78–114) makes a provocative argument that the corporate form was not functionally necessary even to the growth of the much larger American rail network—however, once used to maximize the gains of financiers from railroads, it became an institutional norm to which other firms were expected to conform and often did so even though the form was not intrinsically any more efficient a way to organize the kind of work they did.

[81] For North American examples, see Majewski (1994: 47–105, esp. 50–51, 93–94, 109ff.) on the importance of private finance and the corporate form (even for projects that never paid dividends). On the increased importance of banks once railroads came along, see also D. Klein and Majewski 1991: 12–18. On the crucial role of government subsidies (and thus markets for public debt) even before the railway era, see Goodrich 1960: 51–65.

But to show that organized and efficient capital markets (on both sides of the Atlantic) helped create the transport infrastructure Britain needed is not the same as showing that China's less-developed capital markets left Jiangnan and Lingnan lacking the transport capacity needed for either further proto-industrial growth or mechanized industrialization. In both the Yangzi and the Pearl River Deltas, a remarkable network of rivers and canals gave almost everybody access to cheap water-borne intra-regional transport. And the navigability of most of China's major rivers (most of the Yellow River being the big exception), plus the fourteen-hundred-mile government-built Grand Canal, gave China as a whole a considerable advantage over Europe in water transport, as Adam Smith noted.[82] Certainly Jiangnan, at the head of a river system that still drains the homes of over one-third of China's population (and also sits at the end of the Grand Canal and along the Pacific Coast), was extremely well served. Most of the one crucial item that Jiangnan could not get in large quantities by water—coal—was, as we have seen, so many landlocked and mountainous miles away that without modern construction equipment and motor vehicles, no financing mechanism could have solved the transport problem.

But one plausible possibility remains. As we will see in the next chapter, nineteenth-century Jiangnan no longer got as much cheap rice, timber, and other primary products from the Middle and Upper Yangzi as it had in the mid-eighteenth century, a development that placed important limits on its further growth and its specialization in manufacturing. For the most part, as we shall see, this change was a product of population growth and proto-industrial development in these hinterland regions themselves. Population growth presumably would have occurred in any case, but it is not immediately clear why, for instance, the Middle Yangzi began to develop its own handicrafts, rather than exporting that much more rice and importing that much more cloth. Many factors were involved, transport costs perhaps among them.

Most of the later-settled areas were ones further from the Yangzi itself, so that high transport costs between these new communities and the riverbank would have encouraged more self-sufficiency and less trade: and these costs might have been reduced had either the local government or private parties had easy access to cheap credit. Many Chinese roads do seem to have been quite poor, despite adequate road-building knowledge[83] and were designed more for personal travel (and postal couriers) than for the transport of bulky goods. Even some roads connecting fairly important towns were not much wider or better than purely local roads.[84] In some areas, roads simply could not compete

---

[82] Smith 1937: 637–38.

[83] As late as the early nineteenth century, MacAdam could still make a large contribution to European road-building techniques by bringing back from China the process that today bears his name: see Heske 1938: 24.

[84] Schran 1978: 30–31.

with the superb system of waterways, but where that was not a factor, we might want to assign some role to the financial system. In the logging of the Northwest, Upper Yangzi, and Southwest, it is also possible that easier credit might have helped keep exports growing a little longer before they leveled off: logging does, after all, involve unusually large sums of working capital for a preindustrial activity.

But most likely this was a fairly small factor in both the rice and the timber cases. Timber was hauled long distances to the riverbank in any case (further than timber was ever hauled overland in Europe), yet the very limited evidence I have found suggests that the final price of trees in Jiangnan was a smaller multiple of their price on the stump than was the case for Baltic timber making its way to England.[85] The ultimate constraint on the timber trade was most likely either the size of the forests themselves or the kinds of transport problems (e.g., very steep mountainsides) that no premodern technology could have conquered, however generously financed. And though transport problems may have had something to do with the stagnation of the rice trade, we will see in chapter 5 that other factors were probably much more important.

It seems unlikely, then, that we can pinpoint any way in which Chinese capital markets were the crucial problem in maintaining Jiangnan's relations with its peripheries. But this exploration of how Chinese credit institutions might have done more to help sustain needed flows of primary products from afar does help focus our attention on where Europe's financial institutions—in fact the political economy of capitalism (in Braudel's sense) and military fiscalism in general—were probably most important: namely in organizing western Europe's trade with remote peripheries.

The rest of this chapter will focus on these relationships. I look first at arguments that the New World, the slave trade, and overseas coercion generally were crucial to European capital accumulation: these arguments cannot be dismissed, but neither are they compelling. We then proceed to what seems to be a stronger link among capitalism, overseas coercion, and industrialization: namely that the political-economic institutions of European capitalism and violent interstate competition, combined with some very lucky (for Europe) global conjunctures, made European (especially British) relations with the rest of the Atlantic world unique among core-periphery relationships. These relationships, in turn, gave Britain a unique advantage in access to some of the land-intensive products that all the major Eurasian cores were, by the late

[85] Albion 1965: 103 (citing a final price of twenty times stump price) vs. Li Bozhong 1994b: 93. The sources Li cites here are rather vague and impressionistic, but they seem to suggest that something closer to ten times the stump price was typical. Of course, these multiples might have been different for other source areas or for different kinds of timber; but at the very least, this evidence would seem to place the burden of proof on those who would argue that lack of transport infrastructure was a particular problem for Chinese lumbering.

eighteenth century, finding it difficult to secure enough of. This argument will then take us into part 3 of this book, where we look in more detail at common ecological problems and Europe's escape from them.

Overseas Extraction and Capital Accumulation: The Williams Thesis Revisited

Various scholars primarily concerned with non-European locales have argued that the financial assets accumulated through slave-trading, piracy, and similar activities were crucial to the funding of the Industrial Revolution; Eric Williams's version of this argument is the most famous one. A few Europeanists, most notably Fernand Braudel, have agreed that New World mines, plantations, and slave-trading gave Europe an important ability to live better and invest more than its own productivity would have allowed.[86] But most have maintained that these profits were unimportant for at least one of three reasons. Some deny that coercion allowed above-average profits in the first place. Others concede at least the possibility of above-normal profits but argue that the accumulation of these profits was trivial compared to the accumulation of profits from economic activity within Europe itself. And others point, as I have above, to the relatively small capital requirements of the early Industrial Revolution and argue that this makes whatever above-normal profits there might have been largely irrelevant to industrialization.

The validity of the last argument—that the stock of capital available for fixed investment was not decisive in creating an industrial revolution—depends on exactly what argument is being refuted. Take away the profits of the slave trade and New World mines, and some people in Britain still could have built cotton mills and breweries; even the much larger capital requirements of railroads could have been met once the profits of the cotton revolution rolled in. But a more general argument might still be tenable. In view of the considerable difficulties that parts of Europe were having in providing for their growing eighteenth-century populations—and the difference to Europe's long-run path it might have made had the necessary output been generated by further increasing labor intensity rather than capital intensity (a subject we will consider at length in chapters 5 and 6)—a reduction in available financial resources could have had profound implications.

It seems unlikely that there were no excess profits from coercion overseas. Clearly, slave-trading, New World mining, piracy, and so on could be spectacularly profitable; and though various failed attempts brought down the average returns significantly, some great accumulations of wealth were built on the continued pursuit of these activities. True, some humdrum activities within

---

[86] Braudel 1982: 196–205.

Europe were equally profitable, but it is by no means clear that in the absence of coercion-intensive opportunities overseas, European wealth-holders would have consistently drained more swamps rather than buying more titles, tulips, or Titians. Indeed, even in relatively "bourgeois" England it was much easier to attract upper-class investment to trading ventures that mentioned piracy in their prospectuses than to those that did not.[87] It is undoubtedly true that "the key to understanding the growing power of capital in the European economy is not to be found by searching for esoteric sources of capital; rather it rests with the solution to the problem of preserving and keeping productive the capital stock already in existence."[88] But we cannot overlook the fact that some of the "productive" uses existed and made money largely because of extra-European coercion. Though a whole complex of cultural and institutional changes contributed to gradually increasing the propensity of Europeans to invest their wealth in economically productive enterprises, we should not completely ignore the lures of patriotism, exoticism, and vicarious conquest in inducing at least some people to take advantage of the new opportunities for passive investment created by joint-stock companies and other new institutions. In short, overseas coercion must have made some contribution to western European capital accumulation—but was it large enough to matter?

By any measure, extra-European profits were dwarfed by those earned in less-spectacular activities within Europe; but that need not settle the issue. Patrick O'Brien has calculated in an often-cited article that the fruits of overseas coercion could not have been responsible for over 7 percent of gross investment by late eighteenth-century Britons (though a later article leaves open the possibility of a higher figure); and for Europe as a whole the figure would have been far less.[89]

But in a preindustrial world, this could have been quite significant. Typical rates of growth in output were much slower than in most industrial economies today, and it has been suggested (though not proved) that preindustrial capital goods were on average far less physically durable than they are now (being made of different materials and more often exposed to the elements). This would suggest that a much smaller proportion of the year's production that was not consumed became *net* capital accumulation than is the case today: most went to offset the high rate of depreciation in the capital stock. Simon Kuznets once estimated that by using a lower annual growth rate for the economy as a whole (.4 percent vs. the 2.5 percent he took to be normal for industrial

---

[87] Rabb 1967: 35–48; Andrews 1984: 18–19.

[88] DeVries 1976: 213.

[89] O'Brien 1982: 17. In a later essay (O'Brien 1990: 171, 176–177), he allows that profits from extracontinental trade could have funded one-fifth to one-sixth of gross capital formation, but he declines to estimate what percentage of that might be due to coercion of various sorts. Thus it seems more prudent to stick with his original figure.

economies), shortening the average life span of the capital stock from forty to thirty years, and raising current maintenance needs (from 1 percent to 2 percent of output) to account for these differences, one arrived at a model "preindustrial" economy in which only 6 percent of gross savings became net capital accumulation, as compared to 76 percent in his model modern economy. Making further adjustments, he arrived at a hypothetical premodern economy which, even if it saved more in gross terms (26 percent) than his modern one (24.9 percent), achieved a net increment to its capital stock equal to only 1.32 percent of its annual output (versus 19 percent).[90]

In such a context, even a relatively small "free lunch"—an increment to gross savings that was not purchased at the expense of consumption—could lead to a very significant increase in net capital accumulation. For instance, if we imagine an economy that conformed exactly to Kuznets's second model of a preindustrial economy (gross investment of 26 percent of production, net of 1.32 percent), raising gross investment by the 7 percent O'Brien concedes was possibly due to "super-profits" would more than *double* the year's net increase to the capital stock. Conversely, one would not have to lower the amount of gross capital formation by very much to wipe out most or even all net capital accumulation; either way this hypothetical 7 percent addition could have been very important.

Granted, one must say "could have been," not "was." For the purposes of this argument, O'Brien has stipulated that commerce with the periphery was twice as profitable as "normal" commerce, while he rightly points out that nobody has yet shown any such thing.[91] And while much of the cost of coercion was paid by the chartered companies—and thus is already accounted for in O'Brien's exercise—some further costs were not and would need to be deducted in any thorough version of this thought experiment. (Such an exercise would also face once again the question of how to assess the opportunity costs of labor in early modern Europe—would, say, the Scandinavian migrants and Dutch rural unemployed who signed up with the Dutch East India Company otherwise have found something productive to do at home?[92] Many might not have.) But if coercion yielded *some* additional profits for Europeans, as seems likely, and small increases in gross investment may have meant large changes in net investment, it seems premature to dismiss the contribution of extra-European coercion to Europe's ability to finance growth. Nonetheless, it would be at least equally risky to assume that these extra profits were crucial. A better point, it seems, is that with or without a contribution from overseas coercion, late eighteenth-century Europe still did not have an edge in the way it amassed, protected, or deployed commercial capital (from whatever source) that can explain very much about its long-term path.

[90] Kuznets 1968: 47–50.
[91] O'Brien 1982: 17.   [92] DeVries 1994a: 58–60.

The Importance of the Obvious: Luxury Demand,
Capitalism, and New World Colonization

Where European luxury demand, consumerism, and a capitalist political economy obviously did matter is in stimulating the growth of New World economies and the African slave trade. But even here it was a combination of European political economy and demand from both Europe and Asia—especially
China—that drove New World settlement.

Despite some religiously and politically motivated colonists, it is hard to
believe that Europe's New World colonies would have grown much had the
colonists not found goods that they could sell in either Europe or Asia. Most
colonization was privately financed by people seeking profits. Many *settlers*
may have sought a piece of land on which they could live relatively self-
sufficiently, rather than a place from which they could participate in a fluctuating export economy;[93] but less than a third even of white settlers before 1800
financed their own passage, and those who did pay for migration were interested in using the immigrants' labor to create exports, not in helping them
realize dreams of self-sufficient security.[94]

Furthermore, the cost of emigration, already high relative to the savings of
the poor, would have been far higher had the Americas not exported so much
tobacco, sugar, etc.: shippers of these products, faced with near-empty ships on
their return voyage, competed aggressively to carry emigrants.[95] Indeed, exports were so important that some economic histories of colonial North America make falling ocean shipping costs—which allowed settlers to move further
inland and still sell to the European market—the principal motor of the growth
in the white population and the territory it controlled.[96] And above all, the flow
of Africans to the circum-Caribbean region (including southern North America and Brazil)—which until 1800 was a much larger flow than that of
whites—was clearly driven by the expansion of European luxury demand.

The mechanism was a bit more complicated for the Spanish empire. There,
by far the most important export was silver—and the most important demand

---

[93] On the wild ups and downs of tobacco, see Morgan 1975: 185–86, 197; on desires for security and limited participation in the market, see Kulikoff 1992: 17–18, 27–28, 35, 39.

[94] Galenson (1989: 56–64) has estimates for the number of people who arrived as indentured
servants and shows that the cost of the voyage was well beyond the means of most unskilled
laborers—especially young ones; presumably this would have held all the more forcefully for
emigrants from Germany or other parts of Europe, where wages were generally lower than in
England.

[95] Galenson 1989: 57.

[96] For a general treatment of the importance of European demand in driving the economic
development even of colonial North America—the least export-dominated part of the New
World—see McCusker and Menard 1985, especially the general statement of issues on pp. 17–34;
also Shepherd and Walton 1972.

came not from Europe, but China, where the world's largest economy was converting to a primarily silver-based system after a series of ultimately unsuccessful experiments with paper money and very debased copper coins. (Indian demand for monetary silver was also growing, though not as much. It had a smaller population, was less thoroughly monetized, and used an even wider variety of monetary media—including gold—than did China.) In the late 1300s, when China began drawing in huge amounts of Japanese silver, its gold-to-silver ratio was between 1:4 and 1:5. When New World silver began to arrive, China's ratio was still only 1:6, versus 1:11 or 1:12 in Europe, 1:10 in Persia, and 1:8 in India.[97] With arbitrage so lucrative, somewhere between one-third and one-half of all New World silver wound up in China. Dennis Flynn and Arturo Giraldez have shown it was this enormous Chinese demand that allowed Spanish kings to levy heavy mining royalties without pricing most of the New World's silver production out of the market. Indeed the huge European inflation of the sixteenth and early seventeenth centuries suggests that even with China (and, to a lesser extent, India and the Near East) drawing off so much of the Atlantic world's silver (and supplying in return goods for the silver that remained in Europe to chase) the value of that silver was falling rapidly. Without Asian demand, the mines of the New World would probably have ceased within a few decades to be able to keep earning a profit while paying the rents that kept the Spanish empire functioning.[98]

This was not primarily a luxury demand. Since silver became the Chinese economy's principal store of value, its principal means of paying taxes, and an important (though far from exclusive) medium of circulation, it was frequently used by all but the very poorest people. (The copper coinage was restabilized in the 1700s, creating a bi-metallic system that lasted into the twentieth century.) In fact, the silver that stayed in Europe—where people increasingly turned to copper coins for daily use in the seventeenth century[99]—had more of the character of a premodern luxury trade, albeit on an unprecedented scale. The silver trade represented something new—a truly global, large-scale trade in an item used regularly by ordinary people—and Chinese demand, nurtured by various unusual circumstances, represented both the quantitative and qualitative cutting edge.[100]

---

[97] Von Glahn 1996: 214.   [98] Flynn and Giraldez 1996: 321–29.

[99] See the citations for numerous European countries in Flynn 1984: 47.

[100] By designating this the "cutting edge" of global trade, I do not mean to imply that other exchanges on a similar scale were likely to follow close behind. It could be argued that given the distribution of mining, printing, and other relevant technologies at the time, and the distribution of ore deposits, monetary silver was, for China, a good with virtually no close substitutes: a highly unusual situtation that would have made silver virtually unique among goods for a mass market in its capacity to bear high markups and intercontinental transport costs. (In a recent conversation, my colleague R. Bin Wong suggested that perhaps the only other potential European export before 1850 that would have had both comparably few close substitutes and the potential for very large sales in China would have been advanced armaments.) If this line of speculation is accepted, it would make the role of contingency and conjuncture in the rise of Europe greater still.

But the growth of luxury consumption and "consumerism" in Europe still plays an important role in the silver story. For Asian demand for silver to be effective demand, other goods had to flow from Asia to the Atlantic world: Chinese silks, porcelain, and other goods, and Indian and Southeast Asian cottons and spices. Indeed, Andre Gunder Frank has argued that New World silver, by allowing Europe to become a market for Asian products (otherwise Europe would have had little to exchange), explains much of the growth of Asian "proto-industry" between 1500 and 1800, and thus also much of its population growth.[101] At least for China, I am inclined to doubt that European luxury demand was a crucial stimulus to increased production; even with silk, domestic demand dwarfed exports and so presumably called forth most of China's increased output and demand for labor. But certainly the influx of silver, by oiling the wheels of the Chinese economy, had some stimulatory effect. And, as we saw in chapter 3, it is less likely that India or especially Southeast Asia would have experienced comparable growth without external demand.

Because Frank is particularly concerned to discredit theories that place all agency in Europe, he tends to treat European desire for Asian goods as a given. He emphasizes two things: how New World silver allowed Europeans to convert far more of those desires into effective demand than they otherwise could have; and how the dynamism of Asian economies allowed them to meet this demand and to absorb unprecedented net imports of monetary media. As a corrective to Eurocentric views, these emphases are helpful. Still, one cannot explain growing European demand for Asian goods simply as a matter of greater ability to pay and timeless or unexplained desires.

If one imagines, for instance, a world in which Europeans had reached Mexico and Peru, but in which all of Europe had had social structures like Romania or even Prussia, it seems unlikely that as much silver would have been shipped to China. Or to take a less-extreme counterfactual, simply imagine that Europe's leading states had enforced sumptuary laws more effectively than they in fact did. In either case, Asian demand for silver would have been harder to hitch to New World supply; and without that, as Flynn and Giraldez show, Spain would have had great difficulty in sustaining its New World presence.

My point here is not to assign a unique motivating force to European fashion and luxury demand, which, though *perhaps* quantitatively greater per capita than in China or Japan, was not unique in kind. Rather, I would emphasize that this demand mattered only in conjunction with the New World silver itself, the productive capacity of Asian proto-industries, and the unprecedented demand in those economies for huge imports of an item of daily use (silver). But surely the growth of European demand—both in its familiar and unusual features—needs to be *part* of the story, even for silver-dependent, and thus China-dependent, New Spain.

[101] Frank 1998: 158–64.

For the circum-Caribbean region and North America, of course, the argument that *European* luxury demand drove the expansion of settlement is much more straightforward. After all, Asia grew its own sugar, tea (which largely preempted any market for coffee or chocolate), and before long its own tobacco as well. Thus the feedback mechanism driving Caribbean and North American growth was an Atlantic circuit, even if that circuit rested within a larger global economy. European demand made it profitable to expand New World production; growing production and shipping volumes helped push down per-unit transaction costs and thus made it worthwhile for private parties to finance settlement further from the original ports and to import more people (slave, indentured, or free), expand port facilities, and so on.

Meanwhile, the duties on these exports financed the government needed for growing settlements; this created the preconditions for the much more rapid expansion of both settlement and exports that would begin later. In that later more rapid phase of growth, the principal exports would be staples—cotton, increasingly cheap sugar, and (after mid-century) wheat. But for the first two-hundred-plus years, most of the non-silver exports of the New World were luxuries: Brazilian gold, North American furs, and tobacco and sugar. In short, European luxury demand was crucial to priming the pump that would eventually supply the far larger flows of resources that were indispensable for Europe's nineteenth-century industrial and population booms.

Overseas exploration, settlement, and trade—not proto-industrialization or early factories—were the most capital-hungry activities of the period. And Europe's new financial institutions and the broader patterns of military fiscalism were well suited to organizing armed settlement and trade overseas. Indeed these activities, rather than production or trade within the core itself, were where these institutions mattered most.

It is tempting to draw a direct line between early colonial corporations and modern multinationals, but their differences are equally striking. Perhaps most important, these were firms that specialized territorially and aimed (much like a state) to exclude everyone else from their geographic niche, rather than specializing in a particular range of products or services across many places. In short, they were as much quasi-governments as proto-multinationals, and they were often chartered as much for military/political ends as for economic ones.[102] Indeed, Niels Steensgaard has argued that it was precisely the unique challenges of carrying out long-distance armed trading to Asia—challenges roughly similar to those involved in conquering, settling, and carrying out armed trade with New World colonies—that caused the Dutch East India Company (Vereenigde Ostindische Compagnie, or VOC) to become a more "modern" kind of enterprise than anything that had previously existed.

Briefly, Steensgaard argues that the huge fixed costs of the VOC's military/commercial empire in Asia—costs it bore internally, rather than relying on a

[102] See, for instance, Arrighi 1994: 73.

separate, nonprofit government—made it impossible to follow earlier practices in which trading partnerships were completely liquidated after a preset period of time, with all assets distributed back to the partners. Instead it became necessary to treat much of the company's capital stock as permanent and to retain as much of the profit as possible for circulating capital; this alone made it possible to spread large fixed costs over a sufficiently large volume of trade and adequately compensate investors whose original capital could never be liquidated for return to them. And finally, because not all investors were willing to be patient enough for this sort of enterprise, ownership and control of the firm had to be firmly separated, with a market in shares that allowed dissatisfied owners to exit a permanent arrangement in which they were increasingly denied a voice on policy.[103]

We have seen reasons to doubt Steensgaard's further claim that this new sort of firm was more efficient *as a purely economic enterprise* than the various Asian firms it competed with. But this form of organization was tailor-made for creating commercial empires in both the East and West Indies. Indeed, what is most interesting about Steensgaard's argument for our purposes is that it shows the Western corporate form evolving from the needs of coercion-intensive *colonial* trade; only much later (with railroads) was it needed for a project at home.

In the meantime, the need of these companies to increase the volume of "exotic" imports back to Europe may well have had various significant effects. For one thing, it meant that some very powerful mercantile and political actors had a large stake in promoting tastes for tobacco, sugar, and the like; just how much of an interest will be discussed below. And while desires to promote new tastes were often counterbalanced (among politicians if not merchants) with concern about luxury imports draining the national wealth and character, no such worries interfered with the acquisition of goods for reexport to the rest of Europe. With several companies (and governments) attempting to do this and with borders impossible to seal, the new luxuries received a powerful boost.

With some goods, the new companies had at least one further effect that they surely did not intend. By aggressively promoting fashions for new products that remained expensive (in part due to high tariffs, in part due to monopoly or oligopoly pricing power), the Indies companies encouraged the development of new import-substituting industries, from Delft, Wedgewood, and Meissen "china" to late eighteenth-century imitations of Indian textiles. As I will argue in chapter 5, such industries alone could not have fueled a self-perpetuating process, given constraints on supplies of various land-intensive commodities: that breakthrough required that western Europe also receive ecological relief through coal and colonies. But they certainly did give an added

---

[103] Steensgaard 1982: 235–58; see also Gaastra (1981: 57) on the state helping VOC directors fend off shareholders who wanted a rapid wind-up of the company. The "exit" and "voice" terminology is from Hirschmann 1970.

boost to the processes of increased consumption, specialization, and "industrious revolution" in Europe; in that sense, the colonial trading companies may have contributed to European growth by being both well organized for armed trading and *non*-competitive with domestic imitators of their wares, against whom they could not use force.

Interstate Competition, Violence, and State Systems: How They Didn't Matter and How They Did

This further suggests that the *political* economy of early modern Europe—in particular the constant expensive military competition—may well have mattered more than either entrepreneurial talents or curiosity about exotic goods per se in making Europe's overseas commercial expansion distinctive. Moreover, it suggests that Europe's military competition probably made its greatest *positive* contribution to European economic growth not through the way that war-making, bureaucratization, and so on affected the economic environment within Europe (e.g., by promoting technological change or the granting of new property rights by rulers hard-pressed for cash), but through the extension of this competition beyond Europe. And the payoffs were largest where coercion mattered most: in the burgeoning Atlantic economy.

But before we turn to the significance of extending European state-making and war-making overseas, it is worth considering arguments about the effects of these activities within Europe. Such arguments have proposed three possible benefits of war-making for European development: technological spillovers, stimulus from increased demand, and incentives for governments to change their institutions in ways that fostered increased output (and thus state revenue).

Since the reasons for technological change are not well understood, we cannot completely dismiss arguments that warfare promoted technical innovations. But prior to the nineteenth century, the number of military-sponsored innovations that had civilian applications is surprisingly small. Advances in food preservation made in the nineteenth-century Royal Navy were an early example of what has since become an expected pattern of such spillovers, but before the advent of industrialized warfare, such events were relatively rare.[104] Nor is there much reason to think that preindustrial warfare increased the total effort that went into seeking new ways to manipulate nature; earmarked research and development budgets did not exist, and though occasional prizes were offered for solving particular problems it seems more likely that they diverted inventors from one task to another than that they drew additional people into technological experimentation. There were some learning-by-

---

[104] Mokyr 1990: 140, 184–86.

doing effects, in which, for instance, learning to do precision boring for gun-making proved useful for doing the precision boring required to improve steam engines; but other kinds of artisanship (e.g., watch-making) also taught those skills, and there is nothing to suggest that war-related tasks provided especially good training. If anything, the net effect of warfare on technological innovation is likely to have been negative, drawing skilled people away from projects with greater civilian applications, while disrupting the flow of information, killing potential inventors, and so on.[105]

Similar arguments can be applied, with greater certainty, against the claim that warfare provided a crucial stimulus by increasing demand. Contracts for munitions, uniforms, and the like did stimulate particular industries at particular times, but all such demand was ultimately financed through taxation, thereby reducing private demand. As we have already seen, western Europe (like east Asia) seems to have developed an institutional and cultural framework in which consumer demand kept expanding over the long term (despite cyclical ups and downs) and in which the payments made for middle- and upper-class consumer goods themselves generated demand from the producers. In short, there is nothing to suggest that inadequate aggregate demand was a problem at either end of Eurasia, except during periods of natural disaster (when food soaked up most of people's buying power). Without a problem, military demand can hardly have been the solution.

Arguments that interstate competition led to institutional arrangements uniquely favorable to economic development are more complex. Most such arguments note that monarchs often granted greater security of property—the sine qua non of a market-based economy—in return for short-term revenue, which they needed to meet military emergencies; thus, they conclude, increasing security of property was a by-product of ceaseless military competition.[106] But if this was indeed how property rights became more secure in Europe, it was not the only possible route to that result. Those who assume it was, though, argue that where states did not face as much pressure to constantly increase their military spending, they had less need to negotiate with their wealth-holders and so had no reason to grant them rights. The Chinese empire, which faced no neighbors of comparable size and wealth, is sometimes said to be the classic example.[107] Chaudhuri's claim—seconded by M. N. Pearson—that because the major Asian empires did not rely on commercial revenues (which they would have needed to tap had military competition been more intense) they never needed to grant security to commercial property is a narrower but similar formulation.[108]

[105] Ibid., 183–86.   [106] North 1994: 263.

[107] For an influential example, see Braudel 1977: 68.

[108] Chaudhuri 1985: 210–14; 1990: 384–86. Pearson (1991: 97–103) makes a similar argument, but with the key variable determining fiscal stress being the size of the peasantry that the empire could tax, rather than the scale of military pressures it faced.

After our lengthy discussions above about how markets functioned in China—often hewing closer to neoclassical principles than did eighteenth-century European markets—such a claim can hardly stand up if it refers to the kind of "property" described there: the largely uncontested right to sell and use productive assets. However important interstate competition may have been to moving Europe in that direction, other societies reached a comparable position in other ways.

What ongoing warfare did help to secure was something quite different: property in privileges, ranging from tax farms and venal office to state-granted monopolies and confirmations of guild privilege. We have already seen that such privileges were a common feature in militarily contested Europe and south Asia and were generally quite secure and readily transferrable in the eighteenth century.[109] By contrast, China, facing much less consistent and intense military challenges, had in Qing times only two significant nationally licensed monopolies or oligopolies (salt and the Canton trade), sold rather few offices (though many honorary titles) before the nineteenth century, had no public debt, collected taxes directly rather than contracting them out, and either opposed or stood aside from attempts by urban guilds to exclude rural competitors.[110]

The question, then, becomes, what contribution did the spread and confirmation of these particular kinds of property have on economic development. In terms of aggregate production, it is hard to see how it could have been positive. Tax farmers and purchasers of offices surely added little to output, while guilds interfered as best they could with the mobilization of underemployed rural labor. Monopolists kept the price of all sorts of goods—from sugar to tobacco to necessities such as salt—sufficiently high that they reached only a fraction of the market they would reach in the nineteenth century.[111] (By contrast, China's one major monopoly was on salt, which could be made in many domestic locations, and illicit production and smuggling made the system so leaky that it may not have depressed demand much.) The point that Perlin makes so forcefully for India—that privileges were valuable precisely insofar as they guaranteed the power to keep various other people from participating in markets on equal terms—is only slightly less apposite for Europe (where at least the rights sold less often involved access to bound labor).

More generally, this suggests the need to separate out a number of changes within certain European societies—firmer property rights, the development of

[109] For the Indian evidence, see Perlin 1979 passim; Bayly 1983: 217.

[110] Kwan 1990: 146–47; Mann 1987: 42 (the purpose of merchant licensing was to regulate markets, not to raise revenue); Mann 1992: 76–79; Zhang Xiaobo 1995: 94–98.

[111] For evidence that the increase in tea and sugar consumption in the first half of the nineteenth century was mostly an effect of falling prices rather than rising incomes, see Clark, Huberman, and Lindert 1995: 233–35; also Mokyr 1988: 74–75, 79–86.

representative government (at least for the propertied), and the spread of certain civil liberties—that have too often been lumped together under such headings as "modernization," "liberalization," and "rationalization." Since many of these concessions were granted by states seeking money for war, and all appear somehow related to licensing internal competition (for political power, in the marketplace, or in the "marketplace of ideas"), it has been too easy to assume that intense interstate competition selected for the societies that were most characterized by internal competitiveness—a logic that seems verified by the (temporary) triumph of Britain, where liberal institutions went the furthest.[112] But a closer look suggests otherwise.

First of all, as Charles Tilly reminds us, any such arguments have applicability only to those states that followed what he calls the "capital-intensive" or "coercion- and capital-intensive" paths to state-building (as opposed to what he calls the "coercion-intensive" path).[113] These states were not the only winners in early modern struggles (Russia being the obvious counterexample). Meanwhile, some states in the "coercion- and capital-intensive" category, such as Denmark, nonetheless fared poorly in the competition for political power, and the purely capital-intensive group (such as the Dutch Republic) did not fare very well at all.[114]

Second, not all of these changes had the same relationship to either warfare or internal competition. Representative government and various property rights were often granted or confirmed in return for revenue needed for war; freedom of speech, however, was usually won through paths that had little to do with military mobilizations. And it is worth remembering that even in Britain—often taken as the perfect example of how liberalization paid off in interstate competition—chronology casts doubt on any simple relationship. Britain was arguably in one of its most authoritarian periods between 1790 and 1830—and seemed until the end of 1832 to be getting more so—when it recovered from the loss of its American colonies, became the undisputed

---

[112] North (1994: 262–63), recognizes that the need for revenue produced experiments that reduced the security of property (e.g., in Spain and Portugal) as well as those that helped it, but nonetheless emphasizes that the latter approaches eventually triumphed and were necessitated by the state's revenue needs.

[113] Note that Tilly is referring to the choice between capital- and coercion-intensive strategies for raising state resources from the home population (e.g., choices between corvée and purchasing services, or between hiring mercenaries and conscription); he is not denying that everyone used coercive approaches to dealing with other states and with extra-European subjects.

[114] Tilly 1990: 134–37, 150–51. Denmark would presumably qualify for the "coercion- and capital-intensive" group, since it had one of the highest tax levels in eighteenth-century Europe—most of which went for the largest army and fleet per capita in Europe—at the same time that it also had a great deal of commerce and a full complement of chartered companies trading outside Europe. Yet in spite of these strenuous efforts, it lost what is today southern Sweden in 1658, Norway in 1814, and Schleswig-Holstein and Iceland later in the century, leaving a state with a fraction of its former territory and influence. See Kjaergaard 1994: 4–5, 14–15.

leading power in the world, and diverged (for a time) from the rest of Europe economically.[115]

Moreover, not all the property rights involved led toward economic liberalism. Many confirmed the sorts of anti-competitive privileges discussed above; and even those that were less peculiar by today's standards often interfered with overall efficiency. In France, for instance (one of the major winners in interstate competition), a perpetually cash-hungry state confirmed local "property" rights (and rights of adjudication by local courts) that included minority vetoes on the consolidation and enclosure of plots and the conversion or parceling out of commons. As we saw in chapter 2, this made numerous improvement schemes all but legally impossible until after the Revolution.[116] (Several small west German states followed similar policies without saving their sovereignty, further weakening any necessary relationship between internal liberalization and success in interstate competition.)

Even if privileges likely depressed output in the short to medium term, one could imagine that they encouraged capital accumulation and thus longer-term growth. A rather restricted form of this argument would be that the guarantee and sale of all sorts of future income streams (from tax farms and so forth) helped develop the instruments that allowed other sorts of future income streams to be securitized: thus tax farms and public debt paved the way for private bonds, the corporation, and so on.

One source of the corporation—complex partnerships—could be found all over the world. But a business combining eternal life, a separate legal personality, and structures that particularly favor the accumulation of capital within the firm does seem distinctively Western. We have seen, however, that it was not until the railway era that a technology emerged that called for quantities of patient capital too large to be assembled through the traditional (usually kin-based) networks that financed most other endeavors (including the coal and cotton sectors so central to early industrialization). Until then, as we have already seen, corporations were mostly important in overseas colonization and armed trade—which were the activities that (thanks largely to the expenses of acting as a quasi-government, including making war and building infrastructure) required the largest amounts of patient capital. In Britain in particular, family firms dominated most economic activities throughout the nineteenth

---

[115] Bayly 1989: 8, 116, 161, 195–213, 235–36; E. Thompson 1966.

[116] See Brenner (1985a, b) on the connections between French state-building and obstacles to enclosure, consolidation, etc.; and Rosenthal (1992) on local adjudication and the barriers they posed to improvement. It is worth noting here that Brenner's insistence that this policy amounted to a policy of protecting *peasants* in order to secure the regime's tax and conscription base has been challenged (cf. Cooper, Rosenthal, etc.) by people who point out that it was in fact often the well-to-do and privileged who were the holdouts against schemes to, for instance, divide the commons. To the extent that this was true it only strengthens the point being made here about how loosely one must speak to see the competitive interstate system somehow selecting for more "competitive" economic institutions within societies.

century, including the trade of a world-girdling empire. (One exception, interestingly, was trade and colonization in Africa, where substantial amounts of quasi-government activity was again contemplated and for which joint-stock companies were again chartered.[117] We shall return to colonial corporations shortly.) One must, then, take a *very* long view to find an important benefit of these new financing mechanisms per se to economic activity within Europe.

A more powerful argument, were it true, would be that the war-driven creation of privileges favored accumulation because it put wealth in the hands of people particularly likely to reinvest for maximum gain. In some places in his work, Braudel suggests as much, emphasizing (as we have seen) the importance of great family dynasties moving among a wide variety of investment vehicles. But even if such dynasties were important, it hardly follows that *all* the vehicles they found were essential; and at least some of these state-linked vehicles probably diverted capital from more productive activities. As Jan DeVries has argued, much of the capital for early modern European growth was "found" by diverting money away from various prestigious but economically unproductive outlets for wealth. The military competition that led almost every state in Europe to put more offices, tax farms, and titles on the market was an impediment to this transformation, not an aid. Geoffrey Parker has noted that even in Holland, perhaps the most bourgeois part of seventeenth- and eighteenth-century Europe, a great many bondholders were upset to see wars end, since this deprived them of a safe, lucrative, prestigious (and intellectually undemanding) place to put their money: what we would call productive investment was something that at least some people turned to faute de mieux.[118] Under the circumstances, it is hard to see how military fiscalism can be said to have contributed much to economic development within Europe itself, and the wars themselves, of course, increased the rate at which assets depreciated, skills were lost, and the costs of doing business rose.

When projected outside Europe, however, military competition did pay dividends. The framework of interstate competition drove much of the thrust overseas in the first place. Furthermore, it both accelerated and shaped New World development in ways that did much more to resolve Europe's resource bottlenecks than merely opening these depopulated areas to free emigration and trade would have done.

To some extent, of course, the overseas conquests themselves were the result of intense military competition within Europe. That competition led to significant advances in military technology and tactics, which enabled the Europeans to compensate for their very long supply lines and the limited size of their overseas forces. But we should be wary of attributing too much of Europe's overseas success to the "military revolution." Many of the Europeans' gains in Asia were as attributable to encountering foes who, not used to

---

[117] Arrighi 1994: 282–84.   [118] G. Parker 1988: 63–64.

fighting over land (as opposed to captives), abandoned territory to them (as in parts of southeast Asia),[119] or whose internal conflicts created situations in which small numbers of well-armed troops could make a big difference (as in Bengal).[120] And even so, European gains in the Old World were limited (and often subject to reversal)[121] until the end of the eighteenth century. It was above all in the New World that European adventurism paid off, and there diseases were at least as important as military technology or organization.[122]

What may have been more important are the ways in which the licensed monopolies, tax farming, and other features of a Braudelian "capitalism" linked to revenue-hungry, privilege-granting competitive states were essential to the unique economic effects of Europe's New World intrusion. We can see some of this by comparing the effects of Europe's New World empires to those of Chinese merchants who established themselves in southeast Asia without state backing. Most of southeast Asia, like the post-contact New World, was sparsely populated and capable of supplying vast quantities of land-intensive resources that were in demand "back home." Chinese went there in significant numbers, but southeast Asia never became for coastal China what the New World was for western Europe.

European colonization in the New World involved considerable costs for military protection (from Amerindians, from other Europeans, and from African slaves, who outnumbered whites in many areas) and political organization. Such costs were most easily borne by a single party (whether state or licensed monopolist) that could take a cut on all exports and avoid "free rider" problems. (A man working in Virginia's tobacco fields in the 1670s earned more for the crown than he did for either himself or his master.[123]) Thus, monopoly arrangements made it more worthwhile for people in Europe to finance further settlement by others than it would have been had New World producers been part of a more open market.

The colonial companies, which had put up the start-up costs for the colonies, did what they could to promote tastes for their products back home.[124] So, at least in some cases, did officials. Though we read more about European mercantilists who disliked any imports of "luxuries," we should remember that England, Holland, and France strongly supported their companies' acquiring such goods for reexport to the rest of Europe. And if people were going to consume exotic goods anyway, even the most mercantilist official could easily be convinced that it was best that they do so through their own national com-

[119] See Reid 1988a: 122–23.
[120] Bayly 1989: 52–53, 67–70; Marshall 1987: 70–82.
[121] See, e.g., Marshall 1980: 15–17, 21–23, 27; Bayly 1989: 98.
[122] Crosby 1986: 71–103, 196–216.
[123] Morgan 1975: 198.
[124] See, e.g., Mintz 1985: 163–64, 170.

pany, with the government getting its own piece of the action through import duties and wartime loans from chartered companies.[125]

One could theorize that without monopolies, the market in Europe would have grown still faster, as it did after nineteenth-century liberalization reduced prices. But it is not at all clear how settlement and development would have been financed had free trade prevailed from the beginning. Sugar plantation owners might well have imported still more slaves had they had a still larger market to supply, but it was European merchants, not New World planters, who provided most of the working capital necessary for getting slaves to the New World. Even for those luxury exports where non-wealthy newcomers had a chance to get involved—tobacco, furs, and arguably even gold and silver (by the late seventeenth century there were many small private mines in operation)—most of the gains from a more open trading system would probably have accrued to European consumers, not New World producers, and it is difficult to see how the dispersed gains of those millions of consumers would have funded either expanded migration or the overhead costs of New World development.

Eventually, of course, millions of ordinary people did fund their own transatlantic migration or that of their relatives. But that story belongs to a nineteenth-century world of vastly lower information, transaction, and transportation costs,[126] plus New World governments capable of taxing their own populations to provide the military force, political order, and basic infrastructure necessary for private economic activity to flourish.

It would be foolish to argue that Europe's growing "luxury" consumption (resembling that of east Asia) and its competing states that granted monopolies to develop new territories (a pattern more like that of south and southeast Asia) "explain" why Europe alone wound up with important overseas possessions. Accidents of geography and epidemiology, navigational advances, and many other factors make this a classic case of "over-determination." Still, it is worth considering what different contexts for expansion were provided by European and Chinese political economy.

Overseas Chinese merchants came from Fujian and Guangdong primarily; those provinces also contained huge numbers of land-hungry people, many of whom did migrate to Taiwan and various inland Chinese frontiers. Laborers (mostly miners, but also some farmers) also went in fairly large numbers to various sparsely populated parts of southeast Asia before 1800—sometimes brought in by local potentates to clear land for cash-crop cultivation.[127] The places they settled in included both future sites for sugar, tea, and tobacco

---

[125] For figures on the fiscal significance of New World imports, see O'Brien (1988: 11, 15), and chapter 6 below.

[126] Galenson 1989: 67–68.

[127] See, for instance, the examples cited in Heidhues 1996: 164–82.

plantations (a Southeast Asian "Caribbean") and the Irrawaddy, Mekong, and Chaophraya Deltas (plus Luzon), which would become southeast Asian "North Americas" after 1850: i.e., enormous sources of grain farmed by overseas migrants. Wages in much of labor-scarce southeast Asia were high enough that they might have lured people even if they could not immediately get any of the region's plentiful land for themselves.[128] Turning the great mainland southeast Asian river deltas into paddy fields would have required enormous amounts of labor—mostly to level the fields—but there was no technological reason why this had to await French and British colonial regimes.

But a mass migration of farmers was never a serious possibility in the eighteenth century. The Chinese state had no interest in directly providing military and political backing for its subjects' overseas forays (as Wang Gungwu and others have pointed out[129]). This allowed Dutch and Spanish colonial authorities to prevent the large Chinese merchant communities of Manila and Batavia from buying land, to periodically encourage angry "natives" to vent their discontent in massacres of the Chinese, or to perpetrate such massacres themselves. (Batavia in 1740 and Manila in 1603 and 1764 are especially notable examples.) Under the circumstances, Chinese merchants had good reason to keep their assets liquid—so they could easily flee and/or pay bribes, rather than tie up their wealth by acquiring or improving land (which they were, at any rate, not supposed to own). For those who particularly wanted land, some could be purchased back home where property rights were more secure and kin would provide fairly reliable caretakers.

Moreover, even when Chinese merchants and Chinese farmers were both present in pre-1850 Southeast Asia, the links between them were weak. Events in Batavia make this clear.

Chinese entrepreneurs dominated the development of sugar production outside Batavia's city walls after 1690: 79 out of 84 mill owners in 1710 were Chinese, and a large percentage of the laborers were, too. However, the mill owners did not include the wealthy Chinese merchants within the city walls (who had shown their ability to cripple the city if they were mistreated). Meanwhile the rural sugar-producing Chinese communities were under a Dutch sheriff who seems to have been extremely corrupt, not under the Chinese "captain" who was responsible for the urban Chinese.[130] The VOC bought the sugar at controlled prices and sold it in Persia, India, and Europe.[131]

When these markets slumped, rural discontent followed, and the Dutch tried to deport the agriculturalists to Ceylon, where more laborers were needed. The urban Chinese only became involved in these problems when the Dutch and Javanese blamed them for a rebellion among the rural deportees-to-be and then

---

[128] See Blussé (1986: 26–27) for a good example in the area near Batavia; see Reid (1988a: 129–31) on high wages for laborers in general.

[129] Wang Gungwu 1990: 400–421.

[130] Blussé 1981: 174.   [131] Ibid., 175.

massacred them: in reality, there seem to have been very few links between urban and rural Chinese.[132]

Without a stable—much less privileged—relationship to their home market, or at least the security for Chinese life and wealth that later regimes in southeast Asia provided, there was no reason for the successful Chinese merchants within Batavia to bring large numbers of their countrymen to farm or to make the investments rural settlements would need. Thus, without home-government support, Chinese *rural* settlements abroad continued to resemble temporary camps created to exploit short-term booms, rather than becoming (as New World plantations did) the nuclei for growing communities with land-intensive exports that could repay those back home who financed further settlement.

The Qing did give serious thought to taking punitive measures in 1740. This should caution us against too sweeping a claim that China was a "world empire" that could see nothing to be gained from involvements with economies beyond its own borders.[133] Indeed, one of the major arguments in favor of a trade embargo to punish the Dutch for the massacre was that if not properly chastened, the Dutch might mistreat the next group of Chinese who came to trade, just as they had mistreated their long-term Chinese residents. The major argument against a ban was the deleterious effect it would have on the lives of hundreds of thousands of people on the south China coast. The crucial distinction was that those who remained based in China were entitled to imperial protection when they traded with and traveled to southeast Asia; but those who *settled* elsewhere were not. The Qing certainly engaged in territorial expansion, too—but in central Asia, which could not help Jiangnan and Lingnan obtain primary products the way a merchant-financed settler empire in southeast Asia could have.

Nor, given Qing notions of security,[134] their desire to keep taxes low, and (until the end of the eighteenth century) their recurring budget surpluses, were they even interested in passively licensing armed maritime trade by Chinese (by, say, granting import monopolies). Consequently, no private parties (with one short-lived exception) were ever able to be the exclusive link between the huge Chinese market and overseas luxury goods.

[132] Blussé 1986: 94–97; for the Qing understanding of what happened in this case, see Fu 1966: 173–74.

[133] For the view that "an empire pretends to be the whole. It cannot enrich its economy by draining other economies, since it is the only economy. (This was surely the Chinese ideology, and was probably their belief)," see Wallerstein 1974: 45. On the Qing discussions of retaliation, see Cushman 1978 and Fu 1966: 173–74.

[134] On the particular worries about Chinese with too many overseas ties (as opposed to the foreigners themselves) and Qing suspicion of any combination of mercantile and naval power in the same set of hands, see Wills (1979, 1995). And on the notion that the main security concern of the Qing was internal rebellion—a threat that would only have been increased by licensing violence among people who would eventually return home—see Wong 1997: 83–89.

That one exception, the Zheng family's maritime empire, became remark-ably wealthy and powerful in its seventeenth-century heyday. Its success in both commercial and naval battles with the Dutch (whom it drove off of Tai-wan and displaced from various lucrative Southeast Asian markets) casts seri-ous doubt on any claim that "the Chinese" were intrinsically uninterested in, unsuited to, or technologically ill-equipped for a European-style combination of armed trade and colonial/maritime expansion.[135] The Zheng also undertook colonization: they not only seized and expanded settlement on Taiwan, but threatened Luzon.[136]

But the Zheng empire flourished only during a Chinese dynastic crisis; far from having secure and privileged access to the markets of the mother country, it could only trade to a shifting set of constantly besieged mainland ports. Moreover, the Zheng leaders always saw overseas activities primarily as a source of funds for military operations in China (aimed at the hopeless task of restoring the Ming dynasty), rather than as a long-term project in itself. Their empire thus stands as an illuminating example of a kind of activity that suc-cessfully paralleled European armed trading and colonization but was not a normal part of the Chinese state system.

And even had Chinese overseas traders and settlers armed themselves and somehow secured trade monopolies, they would have faced other limitations. A monopoly on, say, sugar imports would have done a merchant little good, given China's huge domestic production of that same commodity. By contrast, European merchants could tack high enough margins onto sugar, coffee, tea, and silk imports (and for quite a while, tobacco, too) to recover their overseas protection costs, since there was no domestic production of these commodi-ties. (On the other hand, they could not have gotten away with heavy mark-ups on, say, wheat from North America. Thus, though Pennsylvania grain was sold in parts of Europe,[137] and people knew there was plenty more land like that a little further inland, vast new areas were not opened in order to export wheat during the colonial period. Rapid expansion of the wheat frontier had to await a much greater fall in shipping costs, the growth of large urban markets in North America itself, and the emergence of an independent government with its own reasons to pay for conquering, ruling, and integrating that frontier even without expecting much immediate revenue from it.)

Thus, Chinese overseas trade developed very differently from the state-linked capitalism of the European companies. Competitive trade with rela-tively low margins made 1730s Taiwan alone a sugar exporter equal to about one-third of the entire New World in the 1750s and earned adequate returns for a large number of small investors and shipowners.[138] It did not, however, gen-

---

[135] For a more detailed account, see Wills 1994: 223–28.
[136] Santamaria 1966: 78–79.
[137] McCusker and Menard 1985: 199.
[138] See Ng (1983: 157) on shipping costs; for volumes of sugar, see ibid. (163) and Shepherd

erate concentrations of profit that would have made, say, seizing northern Luzon worthwhile—even though, given Spain's weak eighteenth-century grip on this area,[139] its proximity to Taiwan, and the presence of an important Chinese merchant community in Manila (already larger in 1603 than New York or Philadelphia in 1770, and more than double the size of Boston in 1770),[140] it might have been perfectly logical for hypothetical Fujianese merchants armed with a license to use force and privileges in their home market (allowing them to recoup the costs of force) like those that their European counterparts had. By the end of the 1700s, Batavia and its environs could conceivably have had 100,000 Chinese: more people than New York, Boston, and Philadelphia in 1770 put together.[141] But colonization was out if there was no way to make consumers of exports pay for it. In that sense, both Southeast Asian sugar and Southeast Asian rice were more like New World wheat than they were like tobacco or sugar—and so the great future rice bowls on the Southeast Asian mainland, like the great breadbaskets of the Americas, had to wait longer before the capital and labor needed to develop them could be imported.

Moreover, the state had no revenue interest in "everyday luxuries." With 90 percent of China's sugar and all of its silk and tobacco crossing no borders and generating no duties (until the creation of the *lijin* (transit) tax on internal trade in the 1850s), Qing officials had nothing to gain from promoting these trades. Officials concerned that sugar shipments from Taiwan were too large were not necessarily any more "anti-market" than were European mercantilists who opposed exporting silver to buy silk; after all, they wanted Taiwan to keep selling rice to the commercial, handicraft, and tea-growing parts of Fujian, not to make either place autarkic.[142] Qing officials knew that large numbers of people on the south China coast relied on overseas trade, and they wished that trade to continue, except when it exacerbated security concerns. But when some officials did see security concerns and wished to curtail "luxury" imports, they were not, like European silver hawks, confronted by treasury, military, and colonial officials with powerful contrary interests.

It was not only the relationship among extracontinental trade, colonial expansion, and military fiscalism that made European colonialism unique. Even

1993: 156–66 vs. Deerr 1949: 193–203, 235–42, Phillips 1990: 59, 61, and Steensgaard 1990a: 140.

[139] See, for instance, deJesus (1982: 21–37) for a case study of how weak Spanish control in this area was. And though Spanish control was stronger near Manila, there the Chinese population outnumbered Spaniards by a wide margin.

[140] There were perhaps as many as 30,000 Chinese in the Manila *parian* on the eve of the 1603 massacre (Bernal 1966: 51) while Philadelphia in 1770 had 30,000 people, New York 25,000, and Boston 16,000 (McCusker and Menard 1985: 131).

[141] Blussé (1986: 97) claims that there were 100,000 Chinese in Batavia and its immediate hinterland by 1800.

[142] For these concerns, see Shepherd 1993: 162–68.

had China had more "European/Indian" style mercantilism, or India more "European/Chinese" style mass demand for exotic imports, they still would probably not have made of southeast Asia what Europeans (and African slaves) made of the New World. For one thing, they had no biological advantage comparable to the Old World/New World disease gradient. But had Europe not benefited from a remarkable confluence of factors—epidemiology, European warfare, military fiscalism and luxury demand, Chinese silver demand, and so on—it could not have used the New World as it did, either. Alfred Crosby rightly argues that any Old World people arriving in the Americas with their crowd diseases would have depopulated large areas, but pathogens alone would not have replaced the societies thus destroyed with export-oriented economies and large-scale migration financed in anticipation of those exports. And, as we shall soon see, New World exports were a crucial, though not sufficient, condition for continued and accelerated growth—especially in Britain. Here, then, we have a context and mechanism through which European capitalism and consumerism might have mattered far more than they could have without two new continents in which to operate.

Conclusion to Part 2:
The Significance of Similarities—and of Differences

It would appear, then, that as late as the mid-eighteenth century, Western Europe was not uniquely productive or economically efficient. But we cannot jump from the finding that many other parts of the Old World were just as prosperous and "proto-industrial" or "proto-capitalist" as western Europe to the huge counterfactual assertion made by some scholars—that certain Asian societies were headed toward an industrial breakthrough until Manchu or British invaders crushed the "sprouts of capitalism." What seems more likely is that no part of the world was necessarily headed for such a breakthrough: indeed, even in Europe, the major economic thinkers of the late eighteenth century saw nothing of the kind coming.[143]

Rather, the most "fully populated" (i.e., densely populated relative to the carrying capacity of the land using available technologies)[144] and economi-

---

[143] This point is made by Wrigley (1988) and elaborated on in Wong (1997).

[144] Note that as used here, a "fully" populated area is not synonymous with a densely populated one: north India, for instance, had more people per square mile than western Europe, but its ecology also allowed it to support considerably more people. A relatively "fully" populated area is one supporting about as many people as it probably could have without a major breakthrough in technology. Such areas are likely to face looming ecological crises and be places in which elites who control a relatively scarce factor of production (land or perhaps capital as well) may be less likely to insist on binding (abundant) labor to themselves; they are thus areas with relatively good conditions for the emergence of labor markets, and thus factor markets in general. These conditions would seem to characterize China, Japan, and western Europe in the late eighteenth century:

cally developed parts of the Old World all seem to have been headed for a common "proto-industrial" cul de sac, in which even with steadily increasing labor inputs, the spread of the best known production practices, and a growing commercialization making possible an ever-more efficient division of labor, production was just barely staying ahead of population growth.[145] Whether it would have continued to stay ahead indefinitely—producing a European duplicate of what Sugihara calls the "East Asian miracle" of sustained growth based on labor intensity—or whether it would have fallen behind, creating a truly Malthusian impasse, is unknowable. But neither of those results bears much resemblance to the capital-intensive, energy-intensive, land-gobbling "European miracle" that in fact occurred. The growing production and consumption of textiles, though often cited as the onset of "industrialization," could not by itself have changed that path, since it offered no solution to a basic quandary: that the production of food, fiber, fuel, and building supplies all competed for increasingly scarce land. Indeed, to the extent that forests disappeared in favor of fiber crops (or worse yet, sheep, who needed far more land per pound of yarn), the energy needed for more basic breakthroughs in transportation or heavy industry was becoming more and more inaccessible.

Thus, rather than looking at other advanced economies in the sixteenth through eighteenth centuries as cases of "Europe *manqué*," it probably makes more sense to look at western Europe in this period as a none-too-unusual economy; it became a fortunate freak only when unexpected and significant discontinuities in the late eighteenth and especially nineteenth centuries enabled it to break through the fundamental constraints of energy use and resource availability that had previously limited *everyone's* horizons. And while the new energy itself came largely from a surge in the extraction and use of English coal, we shall see in the next two chapters that Europe's ability to take advantage of a new world of mineral-derived energy also required flows of various New World resources. It was through creating the preconditions for those flows that European capitalism and military fiscalism—as part of a large global conjuncture—really mattered.

---

all three had reached unprecedented population levels by this time, which they would not greatly surpass until the onset of industrialization (imminent for western Europe; two more generations for Japan; over a century later for China), and greatly increased rates of population growth. By contrast, some places that are now almost synonyms for population pressure, such as India, Java, and Vietnam, appear to have had much slower population growth to this point and to have seen the onset of very rapid growth in the early or middle nineteenth century; for eastern Europe, rapid population growth began even later.

[145] Compare Levine (1977) and Kriedte, Medick, and Schlumbohm (1981) with Elvin (1973) or P. Huang (1990); this similarity is also pointed to in Wong 1997.

PART THREE

BEYOND SMITH AND MALTHUS:

FROM ECOLOGICAL CONSTRAINTS TO SUSTAINED

INDUSTRIAL GROWTH

FIVE

SHARED CONSTRAINTS:

ECOLOGICAL STRAIN IN WESTERN EUROPE

AND EAST ASIA

HAVING SEVERED industrialization from any "natural" working out of early modern economic processes in *any* area, we can now suggest ways in which a developing pattern of relations between certain areas gave western Europe important advantages on the eve of industrialization. These were not advantages that *had* to lead to an industrial breakthrough, but advantages that greatly increased that possibility and made such a break-through much easier to sustain. These advantages helped address a major problem shared by Old World cores: that before synthetic fertilizer, synthetic fibers, and the cheap mineral energy that makes synthetics economical, there were limits on the ability of labor and capital to substitute for land. These limits made it difficult to continue to expand populations, raise per capita consumption, and increase an area's degree of specialization in industry simultaneously, much less to do so at the accelerating rates of the nineteenth century. Trade helped, as we will see, but it could not solve these problems. Labor-intensive land management could support more people and perhaps sustain modest improvements in living standards, but probably no more than that; and it would tend to lower, not raise, the percentage of the population able to work outside agriculture.

Europe's advantages in escaping these constraints were largely ecological. Some stemmed from slack resources in Europe itself—and were ironic benefits of barriers to the earlier development of these resources—but these were largely offset by east Asian advantages in the efficient use of land and fuel. Others, already discussed in chapter 1, were related to the fortunate location of coal deposits and skill at exploiting them. Others were based on the bounty of the New World and the particular conjunctures that shaped its relationship to Europe: this part of the story will be the focus of chapter 6. These favorable resource shocks, in turn, bought time for the emergence of other innovations; together they transformed Europe's world of economic possibilities. That does not, of course, mean that having this extra breathing room explains technological creativity—but the two factors worked hand in hand, each increasing the rewards of the other.

Thus, in this chapter, I first recap briefly how western Europe's prospects compared to those of other regions, emphasizing what it shared with other densely populated areas. Then I sketch a set of common eighteenth-century ecological challenges and find that, despite being less densely populated in absolute terms than either China or Japan, western Europe faced comparably serious ecological problems. Both in western Europe and east Asia, there was relatively little room left by the late eighteenth century for further extensive growth to occur without significant institutional change, new land-saving technologies, and/or vastly expanded imports of land-intensive commodities. While Japan still had some peripheral domains in which, if institutional changes could be made, growth could be realized by applying existing best practices to land that was not yet used intensively, and Europe much larger areas (especially in eastern Europe) of this kind, China had relatively few. All three areas also had cores (the Yangzi Delta and Pearl River Delta, Britain and the Netherlands, the Kinai and Kantō) where only major technological change, vastly increased trade with peripheries, or both could sustain further growth in population and consumption.

Theoretically, Europe had more room left than did east Asia to sustain further population growth by increasing the labor intensity of its land use; but the nature of European farming made it unlikely that it would ever fully exploit these possibilities. Moreover, such a path was unlikely to lead to large further increases in per capita consumption, much less industrialization. When we look at one European country that did more or less develop in this direction—Denmark—we will see that increased labor intensity allowed it to stabilize its fragile ecology and *maintain* its standard of living: but population and per capita consumption stagnated, and no foundation for a major breakthrough was laid.

Finally, I examine the extent to which all these core regions attempted to alleviate their problems through trade with various less fully populated Old World areas. In each case, such trade was only a partial solution, not only because of technical limits (e.g., high transport costs) that might have been surmounted eventually, but because of social and economic limitations that were inherent in the nature of consensual trade between more and less "advanced" parts of the Old World.

It seems reasonable to assume that only those areas that combined relatively dense populations, productive agriculture, extensive and sophisticated commerce, and extensive handicraft industries were even possible sites for an industrial transformation. But these criteria would still leave China, Japan, and perhaps India—especially north India—in the same category as western Europe.

Upon further consideration, India comes to seem a less likely site than the other regions. Though it had a large, dense population in absolute terms, it was still far from its peak preindustrial carrying capacity. Population growth appears to have been much slower in Mughal India than in China, Japan, or western Europe over the same period; estimates for 1600 to 1800 vary from .1 percent to at most .3 percent per year, with more rapid growth beginning only after 1830.[1] Moreover, the caste system, where operative, gave fairly tightly knit groups of specialists exclusive control of certain resources and (at least theoretically) made those people and their descendants dependent on those resources in perpetuity; this may have worked against the rapid depletion of resources more common in China, Japan, and Europe, where restraints on overuse were harder to enforce and people could more easily escape reliance on a depleted resource through occupational or geographic mobility.[2] While caste seems to have often been honored in the breach even where Europeans claimed it was important, it may well have acted as some sort of a brake on economic growth, on population growth (which is more likely where wage labor and occupational mobility allow people to marry without inheriting an existing economic niche), and on resource exhaustion.

For whatever reason, India's political economy and ecology look different from those areas that were already very near their preindustrial population peaks and well above any previous cyclical peaks. Certainly, late eighteenth-century India still had very large amounts of forest: even densely populated Bengal was still about one-third uncultivated woods and swamps in the mid-1700s.[3] The most common mode of peasant self-defense—individual and collective flight—was one that had long since become impractical in most of China, Japan, and western Europe. Granted, recent research has undermined the idea that precolonial Indian rulers carefully maintained an ecological equilibrium before British timber and cash-crop demand, fee simple property rights, and nineteenth-century population growth upset the balance. But the same evidence that has undermined the romantic image of the precolonial ecological regime—including accounts of the authorities burning forests in order to deny sanctuary to tax evaders, rebels, and robbers[4]—reminds us that India still had a degree of ecological slack and a style of peasant resistance that had become much rarer at the ends of Eurasia.

With empty land still relatively plentiful, Indian elites often relied on bound labor, though there was also a large "free" rural proletariat that worked for others because they could not acquire land.[5] Thus, as we have seen, even though vast amounts of both Indian farm and artisanal goods entered the market, the producers often did not—and that meant they also bought fewer

---

[1] Moosvi 1987: 402, 405; Subrahmanyam 1990: 358–60; Habib 1982a: 166–67; Visaria and Visaria 1983: 463–65.

[2] Gadgil and Guha 1993: 91–110.

[3] Van Schendel 1991: 38.

[4] See, e.g., Rangarajan 1994: 149–52.

[5] Raychaudhuri 1982a: 180–81; Habib 1982a: 168; Habib 1982c: 249; Fukuzawa 1982b: 251–52; Raychaudhuri 1982b: 284, 304; Raychaudhuri 1982c: 335; Arasaratnam 1980: 259–60.

goods and faced fewer of the time-allocation issues central to the "industrious revolution."

One consequence of these patterns of land use and class relations was a surprisingly limited internal market for the everyday goods used by commoners. Indeed, for as far back as we can trace, India appears to have exported far more goods than it imported (exclusive of precious metals).[6] Changes in external and elite demand loom far larger in explanations of its economic fluctuations than they do for China, Japan, or western Europe, where it is generally assumed (at least after 1500 or so, or after 1000 in China) that any increase in production would create its own demand through payments to the producers.[7] Where production and elite incomes can be increased by driving bound laborers harder and/or bringing unused land under the plow, elites are not very likely to invest in attempts to develop new production processes.[8] There was also no assured market for innovations that could expand the production of ordinary goods, despite the vast population and relatively good transportation; too many people had very limited money. Moreover, a clever Indian artisan had little assurance he personally would benefit from an innovation. Finally, given the valorization of hierarchical reciprocity embedded in many patron-client relationships, the quest for financial profit itself, though certainly present, may have been less powerful than it was in China, Japan, or western Europe.

Thus, India was not a very likely site for an industrial breakthrough, despite its sophisticated commerce and technologies. It is worth recalling again how varied the Indian scene was, especially in the politically fluid eighteenth century. Social arrangements in some areas seem to have been moving in the same directions as in the "fully populated areas." Tokugawa Japan, in which what were on paper very elaborate and restrictive legally binding roles were increasingly circumvented, seems a plausible analogy for these areas. We should probably not think of India as a place on a completely different economic track from China, Japan, or western Europe, but as one in which the tendencies I have described for those areas were quantitatively weaker and the forces push-

[6] Chaudhuri 1978: 155–56; Latham 1978a: 50.

[7] Compare, for instance, Raychaudhuri (1982b: 306), Bayly (1983: 204–6, 251, 266, 272, 290), and Prakash (1981: 196–97) with standard accounts for China, Japan, and western Europe.

[8] David Washbrook (1988) has made roughly this point in trying to argue that eighteenth-century India was "capitalist," but in a way that would not lead to industrialization: he focuses on the cheapness of labor rather than the fact that it was so often *bound*, which I consider at least equally important, and does not discuss the issue of cheap idle productive capacity. This other part of the scenario has been developed as the "vent for surplus" model of foreign trade, largely for application to countries that still had lots of open land in the late nineteenth and twentieth centuries. (See Myint 1958; Lewis 1954.) Among the points these economists make is that under such circumstances, growth requires very little capital, at least for a while; for our purposes, we might reformulate this insight by saying that in such settings, elite profits can grow through exports with relatively little investment and certainly without much investment in transformative technology.

ing in other directions a good deal stronger. Which tendencies would have prevailed in the absence of colonialism must remain conjectural—and growing long-distance trade could potentially have contributed to either direction.[9]

Elsewhere in the Old World, population was much further still from its eventual preindustrial maximum than it was in India, and the case for a path of development fundamentally different from that of western Europe and east Asia correspondingly stronger. From southeast Asia to eastern Europe, sparse populations meant that elites could not easily give up bound labor, and they often tightened it in response to new markets for their products.

This leaves us with China, Japan, and western Europe. Not coincidentally, these were the areas that "shattered the biological Old Regime"[10] and reached new levels of population density prior to 1800.[11] At least in their core areas, dense populations and substantial accumulations of capital allowed elites— who were relatively free to deploy productive assets as they wished—to do without bound labor and still get workers at rates that left room for profit. And by the same token, these were the areas that had the least empty land, misallocated labor, and other forms of "idle capacity."

Thus, these three regions had the greatest *need* for an industrial breakthrough and the institutions that maximized incentives to transform production processes—but need alone could not create results. Thus, these "fully populated" areas all faced a common potential cul de sac.

None of these areas faced an immediate shortfall in food production, but other kinds of biological stress were evident. In China and Japan, output of both food and fiber crops kept up with population growth, but at the cost (at least by the nineteenth century) of serious deforestation, hillside erosion, and a concomitant increase in flood dangers; and without important new farming tools (such as lots of mined or manufactured fertilizer), even this sort of ecologically costly labor-intensive expansion might have been nearing its limits. The same was generally true in western Europe, but with two important differences.

On the one hand, as we have seen, various ways of intensifying western European agriculture remained underutilized, even in 1800. Consequently, there were somewhat more "slack" resources than there were in East Asia that could be tapped if institutional and price changes made it profitable, and this was slowly happening. George Grantham's work on France, for instance, shows that gradual improvements in market access induced peasants to change their crop mixes, use previously underutilized household labor, and shift their own consumption patterns in ways that allowed them to sell far more grain by 1850 than in 1750, even without much technical change. Similar patterns are

---

[9] This point is made especially forcefully by Perlin 1994: 83–85; Perlin 1985: 468–73.

[10] The phrase is Fernand Braudel's (1981: 70).

[11] On China, see Ho (1959); on Japan, Saito (1985: 185–88); on Europe, McEvedy and Jones (1978: 26–30).

found in Germany, beginning a bit later: after 1800, when the end of Old
Regime restrictions on land use led to an enormous reduction in fallowing,
there was a marked switch to new crops and much more market-oriented agriculture.[12] To the extent that it left such improvements to be realized in the
future, eighteenth-century European farming left more room to continue
growth before encountering Malthusian constraints than was present in east
Asia.

But on the other hand, this "slack" could not be quickly and easily mobi-
lized to meet the new population and other pressures of the nineteenth century.
Grantham's data shows that the turn to more productive farming occurred very
unevenly, even across relatively advanced northern France. French farming, as
he argues elsewhere, remained undercapitalized even in the 1860s, though
there was no shortage of capital in the economy as a whole; the problem was
very slowly changing institutional arrangements, which influenced the choice
of techniques in farming.[13] France continued to feed itself, but its population—
especially its urban population—grew much more slowly than that of England,
Germany, and nineteenth-century Europe as a whole.

Meanwhile England, where both industrialization and population growth
were most rapid, probably had very little of this slack left to exploit even in
1750, since the stimulus of marketing opportunities and favorable institutional
arrangements had become widespread far earlier than in France. Consequently,
English agricultural productivity seems not to have changed much between
1750 and 1850.[14] Improvements in fodder crops allowed more middling-
quality land to be used for pasture and meadows so that top-quality land could
be devoted more exclusively to cereals, but the result was a stricter division
than before between land for grain and land for animals, with the extra manure
generated by better-fed livestock kept entirely in the improved pastures. Grain
land was no better nourished than before. Thus, per-acre and total yields from
arable land remained flat and the threat of decline constant,[15] until Britain
began mining, importing, and later synthesizing fertilizer, mostly after 1850.
Mauro Ambrosoli's work indicates that though the English studied continental
practices, classical agricultural manuals, and their own experiments very in-
tently, much of what they learned about how best to maintain soil fertility
while increasing yields was not actually applied in England, because it involved highly labor-intensive methods and English capitalist farmers (unlike
continental peasants, Ambrosoli suggests) were intent on labor-cost minimiza-
tion and profit maximization. The methods they adopted instead, which raised
labor productivity, represented a fundamental break with much of the literature
on best farming practices and actually interfered with preserving soil fertility
in many cases; it was in part because of these strategies that increasing

---

[12] Nipperdey 1996: 126–27, 130–31.   [13] Grantham 1989b: 147, 151.
[14] E.g., Clark 1991: 454–55.   [15] Ambrosoli 1997: 367, 374, 392–95, 412.

amounts of off-farm phosphates and nitrates were needed in the nineteenth century just to keep yields from declining.[16] In other words, without the new industrial inputs that came to its rescue, England might have had a hard time even maintaining its yields without putting far more labor into the soil. As we shall see, many other places took the labor-intensive path, but it did not lead to industrialization.

Even when these new inputs became available, it was difficult to do much more than maintain output for several decades, while consumption soared. F. M. L. Thompson estimates that English farm output grew perhaps 50 percent per laborer between 1840 and 1914, but since the number of laborers fell, this represented an increase in total output of perhaps 12 percent in seventy-five years; grain production actually fell between 1866 and 1914. And since the contribution to output of machinery plus feed and fertilizer from off the farm—still quite small in 1840—had reached 45 percent by 1938–39, it is clear that most of these productivity gains involved technologies that were simply not available circa 1800. What was available at that point within England itself were very limited gains from further market-induced rationalization in what was already a very market-oriented agriculture,[17] some of which actually decreased total agricultural output (though it released labor for other work) and did nothing to shore up soil fertility.

Moreover, since overall European population roughly doubled between 1750 and 1850,[18] whatever slack capacity was being brought into play on the continent was meeting local needs. Northwest Europe as a whole was deficient in bread grains by 1836[19]—a point at which continental industrialization had barely begun. In Germany, despite a gain of close to 80 percent in cultivated acreage in the fifty years after Napoleon began tearing down the old regime, output just barely kept pace with soaring population (also produced in part by the end of the Old Regime, which had restricted both marriage and the movement of people into the proto-industrial and other wage-labor jobs that often made marriage possible). Indeed, growing rates of emigration during "the hungry 40's" and thereafter indicate that food supply growth here may have lagged a bit behind population.[20] The European mainland did not have growing surpluses to sell to Britain.

Britain's own grain and meat output were becoming inadequate, as indicated first by a sharp rise in the price of wheat relative to other products (40 percent between 1760 and 1790)[21] and then by intense problems during the Napoleonic Wars. For relief, it turned first to imports from Ireland, subsidized at about 10 percent of value by the Irish Parliament from 1784 on.[22] These

[16] Ibid., 412.
[17] F. Thompson 1989: 189, 193; Ambrosoli 1997: 395, 412.
[18] McEvedy and Jones 1978: 28–29; Grantham 1989a: 43.
[19] Thomas 1985a: 149.   [20] Nipperdey 1996: 92–93, 97.
[21] Thomas 1985a: 141.   [22] Ibid.

imports were equal to about 10 percent of Britain's own output from agriculture, forestry, and fishing combined by 1824–26 (surpassing combined imports from Germany and Poland), and still more in the 1830s (when statistics become unavailable),[23] but they could not grow much further; soon, Ireland would fail dramatically to feed itself, and its farm exports would fall sharply (without stopping altogether). As Britain's food deficit kept growing, it came to depend heavily on the New World and to a lesser extent on Russia and Oceania.

Meanwhile, Britain's nineteenth-century food consumption did not grow as fast as its increases in both population and per capita income would predict. As Clark, Huberman, and Lindert note, all available estimates show that British foodstuff supplies per capita stagnated or declined in the nineteenth century, even with the imports we have already discussed and the huge surge in sugar imports that we will discuss in chapter 6.[24]

The reasons a more prosperous population did not consume more calories per head had to do, in various ways, with industrialization itself. Fewer people worked outdoors, which lessens food requirements. Agricultural workers' families in 1863 consumed almost 50 percent more calories per adult male equivalent than families of urban workers and spent more on food than urban workers with the same incomes.[25] Fewer people did heavy, nonmechanized labor—a shift that can reduce caloric needs by one-third to one-half per hour.[26] The vast decline in the cost of cotton cloth—85 percent between 1750 and 1850[27]—and in the cost of home heating[28] also greatly reduced caloric needs.[29] Tea and sugar, which became vastly cheaper and more common in the nineteenth century relative to other foodstuffs,[30] tend to act as appetite suppressants;[31] thus their contribution to reducing British needs for cereals is even larger than is captured by the substantial share of British calories that sugar provided. (We will discuss this further in chapter 6.) It is important to note that all these changes were linked to either the coal breakthrough or to the surge in cheap imported raw materials (cotton, sugar, and tea) from extra-European sources. They thus accentuate the point that Britain did not meet its growing food needs in the way that Grantham suggests for continental Europe; and thus it strengthens our sense that without the dual boons of coal and colonies, Britain would have faced an ecological impasse with no apparent internal solution.

Moreover, Grantham's argument that the growth of urban demand increased supply by stimulating a switch to more productive crop mixes probably applies mostly to food crops. Fiber crops posed more serious problems, in large part because they demand so much from the soil, and so much labor. In most of

---

[23] Ibid., 145–46. For comparison with continental imports, see p. 141.
[24] Clark, Huberman, and Lindert 1995: 215.   [25] Ibid., 226–28.
[26] Ibid., 225.   [27] Mokyr 1990: 111.
[28] Clark, Huberman, and Lindert 1995: 233.   [29] Ibid., 235.
[30] Ibid., 233.   [31] Ibid., 234.

England, flax and hemp were essentially garden crops, grown on a very limited scale. Even numerous government subsidies failed to induce the increases in output that would have been necessary to make Britain self-sufficient in these crops. And self-sufficiency in these crops would still have been a far cry from self-sufficiency in fibers, since in the late eighteenth century Britain began to import ever-growing quantities of cotton.[32] In France, fiber crops were rarely grown in regular crop rotations because they took so much out of the soil. Hemp cultivation did expand a bit between 1750 and 1850, but only near cities, where plentiful supplies of human and animal manure were available. The extent of land close to cities was of course limited; and since peri-urban areas offered many employment opportunities, these farms rarely had the plentiful underutilized labor that would have been needed for a large expansion of labor-intensive fiber crops.[33] (At the other extreme, flax-growing did expand in Russia, where it was easy to rest the soil between crops—but neither the labor problem nor transport problems were so easily solved.) Thus, although European agriculture may have been able to meet increased demand for food without further deforestation, soil depletion, or technological breakthrough, it had far less flexibility with regard to fiber. When cloth production skyrocketed in nineteenth-century Europe, that continent found itself importing vastly more of its fiber than either China or Japan had to, or probably could have.

And if fiber supply was less price elastic than food supply, supplies of building materials and fuel—the last two of Malthus's four necessities—were considerably less so than either. Silviculture can raise wood yields per acre above those of natural stands. However, such efforts were still fairly rudimentary everywhere, with Japan probably a bit more advanced than either China or Europe as of 1800.[34] Though the European experience in the tropics and the East India Company's takeover of Indian forest reserves were yielding valuable knowledge about both the importance and the methods of afforestation techniques, this knowledge was not applied in Europe until after the 1840s.[35] Certainly nothing in the late eighteenth or early nineteenth century suggested that any of the core regions of the Old World could increase production of wood very much: instead all of them faced rising demand for wood, shrinking local acreage on which to grow it, and little change in yields per acre. Here, then, was a severe ecological threat to accelerating growth for both western Europe and east Asia. It is worth examining further.

---

[32] On imports, see Bruchey 1967: table 2-A; on subsidies for flax and their limited effects, see Warden 1967: 362–64.

[33] Grantham 1989a: 49–71; on limited prospects for increasing continental flax output, see Warden 1967: 724.

[34] Totman 1995: 104; Totman 1989: 116–70; Li Bozhong 1994b: 88; Osako 1983: 132, 135, 142; Menzies 1996: 651–54.

[35] Grove 1995: 187, 199, 261, 264–66, 299–300, 332–36, 365, 382, 387–406, 409, 427, 435, 440, 463–64, 471–72.

Fuel shortages were a major problem in the most developed parts of Europe, China, and Japan as forest land gave way to arable. Timber shortages in Europe were, unsurprisingly, the worst in areas of intensive cultivation—from Sicily to Denmark—but they were reported almost everywhere on the continent; by the Napoleonic era, the timber shortage was perceived as an acute Europe-wide crisis.[36] This perception was surely inaccurate for, say, Scandinavia and Russia, but its existence demonstrates how habitual it had become to worry about timber supplies.

If we accept Braudel's estimates, overall European fuel supplies were still sufficient to supply roughly .5 tons of coal equivalent (tce) per person per year.[37] This would have left Europe on average comfortably above contemporary estimates of the minimum (.33 tce per capita) amounts required by farm families in Asia.[38] But given northern European winters, Europe's more energy-intensive methods of cooking, and its inefficient hearths, Braudel's figure may not represent greater comfort than the contemporary "minimum" for rural Asia. Kjaergaard's figure for total fuel use in late eighteenth-century Denmark[39]—which converts to .55 tce per person per year—roughly matches Braudel's guesses for France and for Europe as a whole. That level of fuel consumption made the years 1740–1840 the worst in Danish history for indoor temperatures—and for tuberculosis.[40]

Averages understate the problems, since timber could not be moved long distances over land and local fuel shortages were common. Even in relatively well-forested France, there were areas where "timber [could] no longer be found" and "the poor [did] without fires" in the eighteenth century. And the situation was getting worse with population growth.

The rise in fuel prices in eighteenth-century Europe generally seems to have greatly outpaced other price increases.[41] In France, Labrousse estimates that the price of fuel wood rose 91 percent between 1726 to 1741 and 1785 to 1789—the largest increase for any commodity in his huge study. This rise was particularly rapid after 1768 and continued into the early nineteenth century, when it attained a "remarkable force."[42] In Britain, firewood prices had already risen 700 percent between 1500 and 1630 and three times as fast as the general price level between 1540 and 1630;[43] for much of the country the seventeenth century was a period of energy crisis.[44] After 1750, the country was perpetually short of wood, charcoal, naval stores, and bar iron (made with charcoal). The price of bar iron doubled between 1763 and 1795 and imports from Swe-

---

[36] Kjaergaard 1994: 18–19, 89–91.   [37] Braudel 1981: 367.

[38] For such an estimate, see, e.g., Asian Development Bank 1982: 114, 360. These minima would probably be somewhat higher in Europe, given the cooking methods used there, and would of course be higher still in the colder parts of northern Europe. (By contrast, most of contemporary Asia's poor, except in North China, live in relatively warm climates.)

[39] Kjaergaard 1994: 123.   [40] Ibid., 97.

[41] Goldstone 1991: 186.   [42] Labrousse (1984): 343, 346–47.

[43] Nef 1932: I: 174, 263.   [44] Nef 1964: 262–64.

den and Russia soared despite tariff protection and the beginnings of substantial growth in coal-based production.[45] Over half the total shipping tonnage entering British ports in the 1750s was timber; and fir imports grew a further 700 percent from 1752 to 1792.[46]

Even where adequate fuel for cooking could be scrounged up, it was not necessarily adequate for industrial uses; iron forges in various parts of eighteenth-century Europe regularly operated for just a few weeks a year due to fuel shortages.[47] Indeed, crude estimating techniques suggest that by 1789, just maintaining the fuel consumption figure estimated by Braudel would have required over 90 percent of the sustainable yield of France's woodlands.[48] Thus even if no wood were wasted and all of it could be easily transported to where it was needed, there could have been precious little wood available for an expansion of kilns, breweries, or forges, or to make more paper, boats, or houses. Increasing use of coal—to which we will return later—provided significant relief in much of Britain, in Belgium, around Lyon, and (through imports) in Denmark,[49] but not before 1850 in the rest of western Europe.[50]

The Netherlands is an interesting intermediate case, having run for quite a while on what we might call a semi-fossil fuel: peat. Heavy investments in digging peat and in canals to transport it provided the Netherlands in the sixteenth through the eighteenth centuries with unusually plentiful and cheap energy supplies. In the long run, however, peat would not be adequate for truly sustained and large-scale industrial growth.[51]

This is not to say that the troubles of Dutch industry were caused by fuel-supply problems. DeVries and Van der Woude show that energy supply cannot be seen as the limiting factor in the Dutch economy, since much peat still remained unexploited while industries declined (nineteenth-century peat output rose considerably). Moreover, imported coal could reach Holland at a price not that far above its cost in London. Lack of fossil fuels was not the limiting factor in Dutch growth. Instead, they argue, peat production stagnated because demand did; Dutch industry slumped for various reasons, but not because it lacked fuel.[52]

These arguments are quite logical. And peat is, of course, mined rather than grown annually. But the stagnation of Dutch population, industrial production, and per capita energy use for one hundred fifty years makes the Netherlands a special case. So does its unusual niche as an exporter of commercial, financial, and insurance services to much of western Europe, and the fact that it had long relied on imports of both grain and timber while it met its own needs for fiber

---

[45] But note that Sweden and Russia's competitive advantage in iron involved low labor costs and high-quality ore, not just plentiful fuel (Flinn 1958: 151).
[46] Thomas 1985a: 140; Thomas 1985b: 729.   [47] Braudel 1981: 367.
[48] See appendix D.   [49] Kjaergaard 1994: 120.
[50] Nef 1932: I: 169.   [51] De Zeeuw 1978: 23–25.
[52] DeVries and Van der Woude 1997: 709–10, 719–20.

and fuel. We do not need to show that a shortage of some sort of raw material was pressing hard on every advanced economy regardless of other circumstances; and certainly other, institutional causes of stagnation might intervene before fuel became a constraint, as was apparently the case in the Netherlands. But if any large economy was to sustain both further growth in population and in output per capita, it would need fossil fuels and/or some other dramatic easing of the land constraint. By the 1780s, even the Netherlands, with its stagnant population and plentiful peat, was importing coal equal to about one-third of its peat production.[53] Had the Dutch population doubled between the early eighteenth and early nineteenth centuries, as Britain's did, then even the rapid growth in peat production that occurred in the nineteenth century would only have sustained a per capita energy supply of 2,000,000 kcal per year; the British economy was already using over 8,000,000 kcal of coal-based energy per person in 1815, *before* most of the boom in steam engines.[54] And if even large supplies of peat were inadequate to fuel the new economy, the annual growth of trees was much less so.

Meanwhile, better quality timber for things like ship's masts was in even shorter supply. Such shortages led Britain to try to reserve for the navy all suitable trees in its New England colonies and to shift much construction of merchant ships to its heavily forested colonies from Quebec to Madras. On the eve of the American Revolution, one-third of Britain's merchant fleet had been built in the American colonies alone.[55]

Nor were British—much less French—timber shortages unusually severe for Europe. Perhaps 16 percent of France was still forested in 1789, versus over 33 percent in the mid-sixteenth century.[56] Michael Williams has estimated that most of the rest of "insular and peninsular Europe"—Italy, Spain, the Low Countries and Britain—was down to 5–10 percent forested by 1850.[57] Denmark's forests—20–25 percent of its land area in 1500—were only 4 percent of its land area by 1800,[58] despite massive fuel conservation measures. This, as we shall see, is about the same percentage of forest land to which China's Lingnan macro-region, an area second only to the Lower Yangzi in commercial development and population density, would gradually decline by the *1930s*.[59] Much of Scandinavia, some parts of eastern Europe, and huge

[53] Ibid., 709n. 18.

[54] Dutch figures based on ibid. (subtracting the contribution of imported coal) and observation on p. 719 that nineteenth-century peat production equaled that of the seventeenth and eighteenth centuries combined. British coal production figures from Mitchell (1988: 247); energy content for coal based on Smil (1985: 36), and assuming a 50–50 mix of soft and hard coal.

[55] Lower (1973: 36) on Quebec; Cronon (1983: 109–10) on New England; Gadgil and Guha 1993: 119; Albion 1965: 161; Thomas 1985a: 140.

[56] See Cooper 1985: 139n. 2.

[57] M. Williams 1990: 181.

[58] Kjaergaard 1994: 15.

[59] See Ling (1983: 35), for estimates of forested area.

parts of Russia were still heavily forested, but as we shall see, their capacity to relieve shortages in more "advanced" parts of Europe was limited. The area that became Germany and Austria still had more forest than France, perhaps as much as 25 percent overall.[60] Regional shortages were nonetheless severe in parts of Germany, even before the great nineteenth-century surge in population and cultivated land; and annual consumption appears to have exceeded forest growth for Germany as a whole even in the late eighteenth century, resulting in *both* timber imports and unsustainable amounts of tree-felling within Germany.[61]

Meanwhile, growing food demand also threatened another kind of European energy supply: the fertility of the soil. Sheep and cattle herds appear to have been diminishing (as suggested by the long-run decline in meat consumption discussed earlier) as former pasture land was turned into arable.[62] Dwindling forests also made it more expensive to keep pigs, and these herds seem to have declined as well.[63] In Denmark, where forests were becoming especially scarce, cattle were banned from the forests in the eighteenth century;[64] this allowed more tree seedlings to survive but greatly increased the cost of keeping cattle and so decreased the supply of manure.

Consequently, the amount and quality of manure applied per acre of farm seems to have fallen in much of Europe during the late seventeenth and eighteenth centuries, even in some areas where cropping was becoming more intensive;[65] at least in France, the pace of decay seems to have accelerated after 1750.[66] In Denmark, the price of manure rose by 500 percent between 1700 and 1759, while crop prices rose very little. And while clover at first seemed such a panacea that it was planted on 40–70 percent of the land in some late eighteenth-century Danish rotations, this produced its own problems: "clover fatigue" in the soil, rapidly spreading clover disease in the plants themselves, and declining yields that necessitated further changes.[67]

In England, where a very market-oriented agriculture and a high rate of literacy produced an enormous literature on agricultural improvement, animal herds were, on the contrary, probably increasing; but the outlook for soil fertility was still far less rosy than is suggested by some accounts of the "Agricultural Revolution." A 1787 report from Norfolk made it clear that the famous "Norfolk rotation" had not solved problems of soil degradation, at least on light soils; the clover came in patchy and the land showed signs of fatigue.[68] Imported clover varieties and other fodder crops had their greatest effect in making it possible for some second-rate land to be turned into good pasture, allowing the best soils to be reserved for cereals. But the manure generated on

[60] M. Williams 1990: 181.
[61] Ibid.: Heske 1938: 5, 25–26.
[62] Slicher Van Bath 1977: 90.
[63] Ibid., 89.
[64] Kjaergaard 1994: 107.
[65] Slicher Van Bath 1977: 95.
[66] Blaikie and Brookfield 1987: 131–32.
[67] Kjaergaard 1994: 60, 85–86.
[68] Ambrosoli 1997: 374.

these new pastures had to be kept there if they were to be sustainable, so the system brought no relief to either grain land or the grain supply; it increased total farm output (grain plus animal products) but not crop output.[69]

Overall, then, despite gradually improving land management knowledge, some of the most intensely farmed soils of Europe (including in England) faced serious depletion by the early nineteenth century. (However, England does not seem to have faced the serious erosion problems which, as we shall see shortly, plagued parts of the continent, perhaps due to convertible husbandry and the early exit from agriculture of many producers without adequate resources for reinvestment.[70]) Without the boom in nineteenth-century fertilizer imports (especially guano), mined phosphates, and, later, synthetic fertilizers, the situation could have been disastrous.[71]

Finally, where deforestation was followed by overgrazing, the soil itself could disappear: sand drifts and huge dust storms (sometimes carrying soil over thirty miles) were common in suddenly treeless parts of eighteenth-century Hungary, Prussia, Sweden, Denmark, England, Holland, and coastal France.[72] Other former forests became waterlogged (since other vegetation neither absorbs water as well as trees nor provides as good a surface for re-evaporation) and highly acidic; enormous amounts of labor-intensive marling and ditch-digging were needed to offset this.[73] Archaeological studies of parts of France and Germany suggest that the eighteenth century was one of the two worst in European history for soil erosion and that the problem reached its worst level ever in this period.[74] Moreover, serious erosion usually indicates the presence of further soil problems,[75] which are confirmed by reports of stagnant or declining yields in many parts of continental western Europe after 1750.

Much of the lowland erosion in Europe was reversed in the nineteenth century. (Many upland areas, however, never recovered.[76]) This took a combination of better plowing and manuring techniques (with improved plows much like those long common in China), reforestation efforts (aided by new ecological knowledge, increased availability of non-wood fuels, and later in the century, North American timber), and the abolition of the remaining common fields (which became badly overused as they shrank and population grew). Migration to the cities (and to the Americas) by marginal farmers in the nineteenth century probably also helped. And the increased availability of farm products from overseas and off-farm fertilizer (first mined, then synthesized) was also essential to allowing more Europeans to eat better in the 1800s, while

[69] Ibid., 392–94.

[70] Blaikie and Brookfield 1987: 140.

[71] Hobsbawm 1975: 106; F. Thompson 1968: 62–77.

[72] Kjaergaard 1994: 20–21.

[73] Ibid., 21, 40–41, 50–56.

[74] Blaikie and Brookfield 1987: 129–31, 138, 140.

[75] Ibid., 137.   [76] Ibid., 136.

checking the decline of soil quality. Without these multiple sources of relief, in which the New World bulked large, the nineteenth century could have seen a downward ecological spiral—as seems to have occurred in some parts of China—or avoided that fate only at the cost of much slower growth in population, lower living standards, and a need to keep a far larger share of the population on the land, engaging in very labor-intensive land-saving techniques rather than providing cheap labor for industry.

There is even some reason to speculate—though we can do no more—that western European deforestation had begun to have deleterious effects on climate. The normal European pattern is for precipitation to be spread relatively evenly throughout the year, but the late eighteenth century witnessed "the European monsoon," in which brief periods of violent, concentrated (and often highly erosive) precipitation alternated with relatively long seasons of drought.[77] While we do not know why this occurred, deforested areas are much more prone to such weather patterns. Indeed, as we have seen, Europeans were just beginning to learn this from the changing weather in several colonial possessions where forests had been overcut to create plantations and/or provide naval timber.[78] One of the few temperate zone regions with such a climate today is severely deforested North China, to which we shall turn shortly. Moreover, even where deforestation may not go so far as to affect the climate, it can have the same effects on the soil that would occur if the climate did become more extreme. Peak temperatures at surface level can rise significantly when land goes from forest to cultivated field (by 10–11 degrees in some experiments in New England), while minimum temperatures become lower. Moreover, because land with fewer trees does not hold snow as well, it loses a protective blanket and tends to freeze to a greater depth than before. Average wind speeds increase, with potentially serious consequences for erosion, and runoff becomes more rapid, accentuating both floods and droughts and lowering the water table, even without any change in the atmospheric weather.[79] To the extent that parts of Europe that already had little agricultural output to spare stood on the brink of such changes—or of needing to devote far more labor to avoiding them—they faced an ecological crisis with the potential to seriously retard industrialization.

Deforestation and Soil Depletion in China: Some Comparisons with Europe

Quantitative data on rural China is scarce, but we do know that regional resource depletion was often serious. In the Yangzi Delta, timber shortages caused the price of large buildings and ships to soar. The cost of wood for a

[77] Ibid., 133; see also Lamb 1982: 235–36. [78] Grove 1995.
[79] For a useful summary of these relationships, see Cronon 1983: 122–23.

seagoing ship may have risen 700 percent between 1550 and 1820 (while rice rose perhaps 100 percent); much of the building of junks for overseas trade relocated from the Yangzi Delta, Fujian, and Guangdong to Southeast Asia.[80] As much as possible, people in various parts of China avoided burning precious timber for fuel, turning to crop residues, grasses, and dung.[81] By about 1750, at least three macro-regions—Lingnan, the Southeast Coast, and above all the Lower Yangzi—depended on outside supplies of various ecologically sensitive goods. All three of these regions imported significant amounts of food (13–18 percent of total supply for the Lower Yangzi); all three imported timber; and at least the Lower Yangzi, a major producer of soil-depleting cotton, also imported large amounts of beancake fertilizer from Manchuria.[82] (Lingnan imported most of its cotton and also began to import much more beancake in the nineteenth century, when its population, unlike that of the Yangzi Delta, continued to grow.)

Indeed, given China's high population densities, it is tempting to assume that Chinese ecological problems were considerably worse than those in Europe; but that is not actually clear. Though China may have had less chance than Europe to expand construction and fuel-intensive industries, it probably did not face a much greater threat to its ability to reproduce its existing standard of living than a hypothetical Europe without the Americas would have faced; indeed, it may have been slightly better-off.

Wet-rice farming—in which water, rather than the soil, carries most of the nutrients, and one year's algae can replace the nitrogen depletion caused by twenty-four successive paddy crops[83]—made intensive cropping in south China quite sustainable; and the number of pigs (a major fertilizer source) seems to have kept increasing.[84] Per-acre food yields in Lingnan's irrigated rice farming kept growing with the help of ever-more beancake fertilizer and may have doubled between 1750 and 1900. In the Lower Yangzi, where beancake was already heavily used in the eighteenth century, yield increases slowed after 1800, but some apparently continued even into the 1930s, without much use of new technologies. (Synthetic fertilizers and pesticides only began appearing after 1900 and were not widely available until the late 1960s.)[85]

Dry-farming areas were more fragile ecologically, but still compared surprisingly well to those in western Europe. The crude estimate I have generated

---

[80] Li Bozhong 1994b: 86–89, 94; Viraphol 1977: 180.

[81] Marks 1997: 320. Li Bozhong (1998: 48, 200n. 23) notes a shortage of manure in Jiangnan and a switch to off-farm sources of fertilizer. He emphasizes, however, the advantages of the new fertilizers rather than the use of dung for other purposes.

[82] Y. C. Wang 1986: 90–95; Y. C. Wang 1989: 427; Adachi 1978; Marks 1991: 76–79.

[83] For a classic description of the ecology of paddy rice, see Geertz 1963: 29–37. For the capacity of dried algae placed on the field to restore nitrogen losses, see Smil 1985: 140.

[84] Perkins 1969: 71–72.

[85] Marks, personal communication, on Lingnan; Perkins (1969: 21) on Lower Yangzi.

for a predominantly wheat and sorghum-growing dry-farming area in North China circa 1800 suggests that perhaps 40–60 percent more manure was applied per cropped acre than in western Europe. We know little about the quality of this manure, but there are reasons to think it was better than that in use in western Europe and was applied in ways that preserved its nutrients better.[86] More important, a typical North China farm would receive three crops of nitrogen-fixing soybeans over an average six-year rotation as opposed to two nitrogen-fixing clover crops every six years in a hypothetically average mixed husbandry rotation. (Actual rotations were very varied, in China and in Europe.) Appendix B estimates nitrogen depletion rates on a sample North China wheat farm and an English wheat farm. Though this exercise is far from exact, it suggests that soil nutrients were being better preserved in North China— except perhaps on its cotton lands—than in the heartland of "advanced" European farming.[87] Moreover, the loess soil that covers much of North China has an important advantage. Because such soil has remarkably good capillary action, it draws up water and minerals from unusually far below the surface; this makes it, in the words of one geographer, effectively "self-fertilizing" as long as it remains moist.[88] Since what evidence we have strongly suggests that crop yields per acre continued to rise in much of nineteenth-century China, even without imported or artificial fertilizers, there is little reason to think that soil problems were critical outside a few particular areas. By contrast, many English and other farmers would have been unable to sustain their circa 1800 yields much longer without imports of guano and other mined fertilizers.[89]

Fiber shortages were potentially more serious at both ends of Eurasia. In China, as we have seen, per capita cotton production may have fallen significantly between the mid-eighteenth and late nineteenth centuries, but not total production. The costs to the soil of even that achievement may have been serious, however, at least in areas that did not get large inputs of soybean cake fertilizer from Manchuria. The big difference for Europe, of course, was that beginning in the late eighteenth century it would massively increase its imports of fiber—above all American cotton, but also Indian and Egyptian cotton, and later wool from Australia and New Zealand.

China's problems with forest cover and fuel supply were more serious, but probably not as bad as we often think, and—surprisingly—not clearly worse than those of western Europe. Ling Daxie has estimated the overall share of forested land circa 1700 at 26 percent of the empire.[90] If we subtract four remote and sparsely populated areas that had little to do with the rest of the

[86] See explanation of calculation in appendix B.

[87] See appendix B.

[88] Chi 1963: 14–15.

[89] Rossiter 1975: 149–53, 172; Ambrosoli 1997: 395; Hobsbawm 1975: 106; F. Thompson 1968: 65–70. See also appendix B.

[90] Ling 1983: 34.

empire—Tibet, Xinjiang, Qinghai, and Outer Mongolia—the figure for the rest
of China would be 37.2 percent. Moreover, Ling's estimates for much of the
North China plain are likely too low.[91]

However, Ling's figures are for 1700, when the great Qing population boom
was just beginning; how much worse was the situation in 1800? Certainly, a
vast amount of what had been forest became farms in the eighteenth century,
particularly once the dissemination of maize, sweet potatoes, and other imported crops allowed people to farm previously uncultivable lands; and in the
long run, the clearing of hillsides was ecologically disastrous. Meanwhile, the
ever-increasing reclamation of land from lake and riverbeds led to slower-
moving rivers, rising siltation rates in riverbeds, and growing flood problems.
Yet these problems took many years to become critical; in 1800 they were
quite likely no worse than in other densely populated regions. The pattern by
which highland settlement led to erosion and increased flooding, for instance,
was also quite evident in Japan's highly developed Kinai and Kantō regions
and seems to have reached a stage of near-permanent flood danger at least fifty
years before the Yangzi Valley did.[92]

Let us begin in the Lower Yangzi, the macro-region most comparable to rich
but ecologically strained areas such as England and the Netherlands in Europe,
or to the Kantō and Kinai regions of Japan. Complaints about excessive lowland reclamation were common by the mid-eighteenth century in both the
Lower and Middle Yangzi, but this was generally at the expense of water, not
forests, and its effects (mostly on drainage) were not yet critical.[93] There are
few complaints about ecological problems caused by highland clearance before the 1780s.[94] (Complaints about social problems were another matter—
many of those who cleared highlands were migrants from other regions, and
clashes between "native" and "immigrants" were frequent.) Much of the
Yangzi Delta, having been reclaimed from sea and swamp rather than by clearing forest, had always had fewer trees than most of south China; Jiangsu province, including much of the Delta, is the only southern province that was apparently less than 50 percent forested (46 percent) even in 2700 BCE.[95] Ling
Daxie estimates that by 1700, Jiangsu—which consisted largely of part of the
Yangzi Delta plus a southern extension of the north China plain—was roughly
5 percent forest: this made it comparable to the worst parts of North China and
to eighteenth-century England.[96]

But forests were not far away. Large areas of the Zhejiang hills, which lay
just beyond the southern half of the Yangzi Delta, were still forested as late as

[91] See below, pp. 234–35, and appendix C.
[92] Compare Totman 1992: 22, with Schoppa 1989: 147–67; Perdue 1987: 227, 230; Will 1980;
Osborne 1994: 30–31.
[93] Compare Schoppa 1989: 120–39 with 147–63; see also Perdue 1987: 196, 202, 219–33.
[94] Osborne 1994: 30.   [95] Ling 1983: 33.   [96] Ibid., 34.

1802, and new clearing continued to occur through the 1840s; in fact, the rate of clearance accelerated after 1820.[97] And the very first case of flooding attributed to hill clearance does not appear in the records until 1788.[98] Parts of Fujian on the southeast coast—like Jiangnan a very crowded area, and also a major center for boat-building—appear to have had serious problems of hillside deforestation, increased erosion, and flooding as early as the sixteenth century, but the situation seems to have stabilized later, rather than getting steadily worse.[99]

Serious problems were building in the ecology of the Lower Yangzi, but it was probably not until well into the nineteenth century that they became more severe than problems in core regions in Europe and Japan. And by that time, as we shall see, the most developed parts of Europe had obtained significant ecological relief from underground *and* overseas; to a lesser extent, so had Japan, which increasingly relied on food and fertilizer from far-flung fishing expeditions.[100] And even with this relief, Japan's population stagnated from roughly 1720 to 1860. Some scholars also argue that Japan's per capita income stagnated beginning in the mid-eighteenth century, albeit at an exceptionally high level.[101]

A more quantitative measurement of deforestation and fuel-supply pressures is possible for Lingnan, probably China's second most commercialized and densely populated macro-region. And though this area was certainly ecologically troubled by the late eighteenth century, it had larger remaining wood supplies than much of "insular and peninsular Europe" did. Quite likely, it was even in better shape than France, which is often singled out within Europe as a contrast to developed but deforested Britain.[102] (Lingnan had 17,500,000 people circa 1753 and reached 30,500,000 by 1853;[103] France had 26,000,000 people in 1789 and a land area about 40 percent greater than that of Lingnan.)

Ling Daxie gives a circa 1700 figure of 54.5 percent forest cover for the coastal province of Guangdong and 39 percent for Guangxi, the adjacent province that was becoming Guangdong's rice bowl.[104] As elsewhere in China, the population boom that was just beginning in 1700 took a great toll on the forests; and unlike in the Lower Yangzi, Lingnan's population growth continued unabated right through the nineteenth and twentieth centuries. By 1937, Guangdong's forest area can be reliably placed at about 10 percent and

[97] Osborne 1994: 36.
[98] Ibid., 30–31.
[99] Vermeer 1990: 141–47, 156, 161.
[100] Totman 1992: 23.
[101] Hanley and Yamamura (1977: 16–28) survey this view and criticize it; L. Roberts (1991: 88–95) suggests the need for a more complex breakdown and argues that the old view may indeed apply to some periods and regions.
[102] See, e.g., M. Williams 1990: 181–82.
[103] Marks 1997: 280.
[104] Ling 1983: 34. Robert Marks, author of the first comprehensive survey of the ecological history of Lingnan, finds these figures generally plausible.

TABLE 5.1
Forest Area in Lingnan, 1753–1853

	Forested area (hectares)			Percent forested		
	Guangdong	Guangxi	Lingnan	Guangdong	Guangxi	Lingnan
1753	9,000,000	6,500,000	15,500,000	45	35	40
1773	8,200,000	6,020,000	14,220,000	41	32	37
1793	7,440,000	5,660,000	13,100,000	37	30	34
1813	6,560,000	5,240,000	11,800,000	33	28	30
1833	5,760,000	4,940,000	10,700,000	29	26	28
1853	4,880,000	4,700,000	9,580,000	24	25	24

Guangxi's at a mere 5 percent.[105] But we lack figures for the dates in between, and we need to make some estimates.

One simple way is to make use of trends in population. Using figures compiled by Robert Marks, we can compute an average relationship between population growth and the disappearance of forest: each additional person in Guangdong meant a reduction of roughly .4 hectares of forest, and each new person in Guangxi a reduction of .6 acres.[106] (This difference makes sense since Guangdong reclaimed coast as well as clearing forests, had lots of very intensively farmed paddy, and, unlike Guangxi, also imported rice.) We can then use those averages to compute how much forest would have been lost by certain dates, given Marks's population estimates at twenty-year intervals. While the method is crude, it probably biases our results in the direction of making the situation look very bad at an *earlier* date than was really the case.[107] The results are given in table 5.1.

The steady downward trend is obvious, yet Lingnan still had almost 25 percent forest cover in 1853, when it had roughly 77 people per square kilometer; by comparison, France had already declined to 16 percent forest cover in 1789, when its population density was still under 50 per square kilometer.[108]

Precisely because Lingnan was much more densely populated than France, its higher percentage of forest land might still mask a greater scarcity of wood. To investigate this, I have created two simple though artificial measures. One,

---

[105] Ling 1983: 35.   [106] Based on Marks 1997: 280.

[107] In fact, we would expect each additional person to cause a smaller reduction in the forest in the earlier part of our period and a larger one later. Better land is likely to be settled first, so earlier additions to the population probably required fewer acres than did later ones (though rising land productivity could offset this). Further, in earlier years the additional fuel needs of new population could be met without exceeding the year's annual wood growth; but as population became very dense, cutting for fuel could exceed sustainable yields, setting off a downward spiral in at least some areas.

[108] French population statistics from McEvedy and Jones 1978: 59.

sustainable fuel supply per capita, is an estimate of how much heat (in tce) could be harvested each year without cutting more than the normal growth of woodlands. The second, industrial wood supply per capita, is an estimate of how much wood would be available for other uses (from paper-making to construction to firing forges) assuming that basic home fuel supply needs were met but not exceeded and that no wood was wasted.

It might seem obvious that France would come out better than Lingnan on these measures, with so many fewer people relying on each hectare of forest. But at least four factors suggest otherwise.

First, fuel needs per capita in south China were probably significantly lower than those in France: less heating was needed in a warmer climate; Chinese cooking methods were much faster and more fuel efficient than European ones; and Chinese stove design was much more efficient, both for cooking and home heating, than the stoves and (especially) open hearths common in Europe. I have made some adjustments for these differences in my calculations for Guangdong (see appendix C) but in a way that almost certainly underestimates their impact.[109]

Second, the general pattern of tree cultivation and fuel-wood gathering in China—characterized by small clumps of trees in or near each family's courtyard and more linked reliance on harvesting consolidated blocks of forest—meant that transport costs were minimal. Thus, it was worthwhile to gather twigs and other small bits of combustible material that would be left on the forest floor and wasted in Europe. I have no way of knowing the size of this difference and will omit it from the calculations, but it fits a general pattern in which Chinese farm families used a little extra labor (often that of women and children) to make the most of resources and offset the ecological costs of a denser population.[110] (The relative lack of large blocks of forest also fits another pattern in which Chinese elites—far less taken with hunting and riding than most Eurasian ruling classes—did less to reserve large blocks of land for low-intensity uses than did the dominant groups of most other settled societies.[111] The result was greater efficiency, but fewer of the slack resources that would later become "advantages of backwardness" for Europe.)

Third, the annual growth of each tree was almost certainly greater in subtropical Lingnan than in France. This difference could be estimated and added

[109] On stove design, stir-frying, and other matters affecting the fuel efficiency of cooking, see Anderson 1988: 149–51, 154. See also appendix C, pp. 308–9.

[110] On this pattern of tree cultivation and its difference from that in Europe, see Menzies 1996: 663, 667.

[111] Such a generalization refers much more to the ethnic Chinese gentry, merchants, and landlords than to the Manchu conquerors who set up the Qing dynasty; but the latter were never numerous, except in Beijing and Manchuria. Moreover, while many Manchus became less "martial" in their cultural interests and abandoned hunting and riding, very few Han Chinese adopted either hunting or horseback riding.

to the calculations, but I have not done so; this is one more way of making sure that these comparisons are, if anything, biased against China rather than Europe.

Fourth, and perhaps most important, Chinese farm families got much of their fuel supply not from wood, but by burning crop residues. Thus, while each hectare of forest turned to farmland in France was a total loss to the fuel supply, in China, land put under the plow still produced fuel, too. Burning crop residues was not environmentally costless, but it was not necessarily a big problem, either. It entailed a loss of organic matter that would otherwise be returned to the soil (as worms, bacteria, and fungi broke up the plant matter into nutrients accessible to plants), though our estimates of nitrogen fluxes suggest that this would not have been a crucial problem. Another incalculable but perhaps more serious problem is that the removal of crop residues tends to increase the loss of soil to wind erosion. This would more likely have been a serious problem in North China, which we will consider later, than in Lingnan, since the North had generally lighter soils and a much longer interval between harvest and the next appearance of plants with roots stong enough to help hold the soil. For current purposes, I will ignore these costs, at least in Lingnan, and proceed to estimate the value of this practice in meeting the area's fuel needs.

Less than half the weight of pre–Green Revolution rice plants (and other small grain plants) was edible; we will certainly not be overestimating the amount of crop residue if we assume it was equal to the output of edible rice, which is reasonably well known. Some of these residues, however, were also used to feed farm animals, especially pigs. Although we have no census of farm animals for any part of China before the 1920s, there are reasons to think that the ratio of pigs (the primary source of meat) to people did not change much; this enables us to project backward from twentieth-century to eighteenth-century figures. I have assumed that other farm animals, who would have been used primarily for work, were roughly as numerous per human as they were in twentieth-century north China; this is almost certainly an overestimate, since Lingnan peasants farmed much smaller plots than northerners. (For more details on sources, assumptions, and calculations, see appendix B.)

Applying this method to Lingnan's food output in 1753 (as reconstructed by Robert Marks) leads to the conclusion that crop residues available for burning would have generated at least .08 tce per capita, or roughly one quarter of the Asian Development Bank's estimate of minimum needs today; a much more likely figure is .16 tce per person. (It is unlikely that eighteenth-century peasants used much more fuel than is considered necessary today, and it would be paradoxical to assume that they did and therefore faced a terrible fuel crisis.) And just in case this estimate still contains some upward bias, I have completely ignored any crop residues from land planted with crops other than grains, sweet potatoes, and beans—and other crops were very widespread.

TABLE 5.2
Total "Fuel" Supply per Capita
If Wood Had No Other Uses (in tce)

1753	1.75	1813	.99
1773	1.45	1833	.83
1793	1.19	1853	.70

TABLE 5.3
Supply of Wood Above and Beyond Domestic Fuel Needs

	Forest Land (hectares)	Forest Needed for Fuel	Remaining Forest	"Non-fuel" Wood per Capita (tons)
1753	15,500,000	1,650,000	13,850,000	2.85
1773	14,220,000	1,675,000	12,545,000	2.25
1793	13,100,000	2,260,000	10,840,000	1.73
1813	11,800,000	2,469,000	9,331,000	1.32
1833	10,700,000	2,956,000	7,744,000	1.00
1853	9,580,000	3,339,000	6,241,000	.74

Marks has estimated that all the food consumed by the population of Lingnan in 1753 could conceivably have been grown on as little as 30 percent of its cultivated acreage. Thus, even in the unlikely case that Marks's yield estimates need to be halved, the amount of land devoted to other crops throughout Lingnan must have been over 40 percent of total acreage; ignoring residues from those lands almost certainly overcorrects for any optimism in the estimate of heat obtained from residues.

We can now move on to the fuel supply in 1753 and thereafter. Adding the population gained in Lingnan at twenty-year intervals, plus an appropriate number of animals, assuming (falsely) that the additional land brought under cultivation did no more than meet the food needs of that population and using the figures calculated above for the disappearance of forests, generates tables 5.2 and 5.3. Table 5.2 shows how Lingnan's potential fuel supply per capita changed. Table 5.3 shows how much wood was available for other uses if only the sustainable yield of the woodlands was taken each year and if the amount needed to meet the gap between available residues and minimum home heating and cooking was subtracted in advance of other uses.

Imprecise though they are, these figures illustrate two very important points. On the one hand, we see how quickly population growth could eat away at wood supplies even in an economy that used resources efficiently. When we remember that the "non-fuel" wood in Table 5-3 was used for many buildings, carts, boats, and other essentials, it is clear that the energy supplies needed for growth in any industry (even textiles, which use fuel for bleach and dye production) were dwindling fast. Thus, it would appear that insofar as the growth of market handicrafts helped power population growth, those same forces could eventually close the ecological window within which the "industrious revolution" could lead to an industrial revolution: unless, that is, there was a massive turn to fossil fuels and/or imported primary products. An ecological bottleneck was at hand, which in retrospect (though only in retrospect) appears as a severe constraint on further population growth, per capita income growth, or movement out of agriculture.

On the other hand, these figures do not suggest an imminent Malthusian crisis, even as late as 1853. Lingnan's situation seems more benign than that faced much earlier by France (again, hardly the most deforested part of western Europe). Around 1550 France probably had a total potential fuel supply per inhabitant of 2.3 tce per inhabitant or 3.6 tons of harvestable wood per capita above basic fuel needs; by 1789, almost all of this surplus had disappeared. Fuel supply would be about .64 tce per capita if all harvestable wood were burned, leaving about .29 tons of wood per person for other uses if fuel consumption were kept at Braudel's estimate of .5 tce per person. Far from having uniquely severe ecological problems, even some of China's more densely populated parts seem better-off than economically comparable parts of Europe.

Finally, though, we need to consider North China. This dry-farming region lacked the advantages of paddy rice, and the burden of supporting China's capital (always one of the world's largest cities) has been considerable. By 1900, much of North China *was* an ecological disaster area, and there has been a widespread tendency to assume that this had been true for a long time. Ling Daxie's figures for 1700 suggest that two north China provinces—Shandong and Henan—were already very severely deforested (1.3 and 6.3 percent forest, respectively). The third province entirely in the North China macro-region, Zhili, was in much better shape (22.7 percent), as was Shanxi, which is partly in North China (18.8 percent). Nonetheless, this would still be a very worrisome situation.

Overall, the North and Northwest China macro-regions probably had China's most serious ecological problems. Since Northwest China was sparsely populated, we will ignore its worsening problems here—important as they were locally—and focus on its much more populous neighbor. Indeed, North China, as we saw in chapter 3, is the one Chinese macro-region in which the production of non-food crops probably fell in absolute as well as per capita terms between 1750 and 1900, as more and more of its land was needed for food. But even in North China, the overall picture circa 1800 was not uniformly grim: prospects for raising living standards were limited, but stable living standards and some continued population growth were still ecologically plausible.

Traveling along the Grand Canal in 1696, the French missionary Du Halde mentioned vast forests in southern Shandong, one of the most densely populated parts of North China's most deforested province.[112] And throughout the eighteenth century, the area near Yanzhou—near the forests Du Halde saw—continued to send firewood up the canal to the imperial brickworks at Linqing. Though the amounts involved were small, this also tends to suggest that Shandong was not as devoid of woodlands as Ling's figures suggest.[113] Even as late as 1793, George Staunton, a member of a British mission to Beijing, presents a mixed picture. While noting that trees were "scattered thinly" on most of the North China plain,[114] he also noted large groves in some places, usually near cemeteries.[115] In general, he believed that the rural North Chinese he saw, though often poor, did not lack basic necessities. He also noted that the roots of North Chinese sorghum, usually burned to use the ash for fertilizer, were burned at home "*when* fuel is scarce."[116] Finally, he notes that the Grand Canal itself in North China was lined for miles and miles by willows and other trees planted to strengthen its banks.[117] Though not numerically significant in themselves, these trees suggest that the fuel shortage was not yet critical: in the twentieth century, when people had become truly desperate, it proved impossible to defend such trees from illicit cutting.[118]

Any quantitative estimates must be very rough, but some reasonable guesses are possible by working backward from twentieth century data. As a sample area, I chose twenty-seven counties in southwestern Shandong, with a probable 1800 population of about 5,000,000. This particular portion of North China had one of China's most desperate fuel shortages by the 1930s—with a fuel supply of perhaps .09 tce per person per year, worse than the worst parts of contemporary Bangladesh or the Sahel.[119] So it is striking that even this area seems to have been fairly livable circa 1800—much as Staunton's testimony suggests.

Crude but very conservative estimating techniques give this region a fuel supply at that date of .62 tce per year: about 20 percent above Braudel's estimates for French energy use at the same time, and almost double contemporary estimates of a minimum viable supply. Probably over 40 percent of that fuel supply would have come from crop residues, but it seems likely that the area was still at least 13 percent woodland in 1800.[120] This would not have left

---

[112] Pomeranz 1993: 134. [113] Xu Tan 1986: 138.

[114] Staunton 1799: I: 279, II: 46. [115] Ibid., I: 266; also II: 46, 169.

[116] Ibid., II: 138, 141. [117] Ibid., II: 142.

[118] On twentieth-century fuel shortage and illicit tree cutting, see Pomeranz 1993: 124–25, 143–45.

[119] See Pomeranz 1993: 125; Pomeranz 1988: appendix F.

[120] See appendix C. The woodland figure is significantly higher than Ling's figure for the province as a whole (1983), but I can see only two ways that it could be too high. One would be if I have seriously overestimated crop yields per acre, but that would require the unlikely conclusion that growth in yields during the ecologically calamitous and technologically unimpressive nineteenth century grew much faster than even the rapidly growing population. The other would be if I have significantly underestimated the amount of land under non-food crops in this area, which seems to have been (as it would be in the twentieth century) heavily concentrated in wheat

much wood for other uses—rural housing, for instance, made heavy use of sundried brick—much less for industrial growth; and the burning of crop residues might have taken a long-term toll in increased erosion and loss of soil nutrients (particularly in combination with further deforestation in later decades, and a falling water table, which we will discuss later). As of 1800, however, the overall situation seems no worse than in large parts of western Europe.

So despite its dense population, Chinese pressure on the land was probably not much worse than that in Europe (or Japan) in 1800. And at least with respect to trees and soil, the rate of decay in China was probably slower than that seen in eighteenth-century western Europe.

In other areas Europe may have had a greater ecological cushion. For instance, the greater use of multi-cropping in east Asia made that area more vulnerable when the Northern Hemisphere experienced cooler temperatures (i.e., an unexpected shortfall of solar energy) in the first half of the nineteenth century.[121] Less speculatively, Europe still had large amounts of grasslands and pasture that were sufficiently well watered to be converted to arable. Almost two-thirds of the farmland added in non-Russian Europe between 1700 and 1850 came from these pasture lands, and both demographic and institutional histories suggest that most of that conversion came after 1800. But in China (or, more accurately, Chinese central Asia), most remaining grasslands were semi-arid, and almost all additional farmland had to come from clearing forests or reclaiming land under water.[122] Thus, a relative abundance of water (as a matter of original endowments) may have given Europe extra room for dealing with the pressure on its land.

Land and water problems were related in other ways, too. Although the careful gathering of twigs, crop residues, etc., in China solved fuel shortages just as well as clearing less land and leaving more trees, it was not as good in other ways. Deforestation eventually led to soil erosion and flood dangers; the former, as already noted, may have been no worse in eighteenth-century China than it was Europe, but the latter probably were. Deforestation also leads to desiccation (since deforested areas get less rainfall and have higher rates of evaporation from ground and low plants exposed to the sun). North China in particular has a pattern of highly seasonal rainfall and aridity more like some Mediterranean and tropical locations than like northern Europe,[123] a pattern

---

and sorghum, with relatively small amounts of tobacco and cotton. This is more possible—I have argued in chapter 3 that North China as a whole probably grew more cotton in the late eighteenth century than one hundred years later—but if my woodland figures are wrong for this reason it would mean that there were even more crop residues available for fuel than we thought and that China circa 1800 was even more prosperous than I have suggested.

[121] Marks 1997: 224.

[122] For European figures, see Richards 1990: 164.

[123] See, for instance, maps I-17 and I-23 in Hsieh (1973), showing average annual precipitation of roughly 500 millimeters for most of North China, with 250 mm. of that coming in July and

that was probably exacerbated as its forests disappeared. Moreover, as loess soil becomes increasingly dry it can no longer provide plants with extra nutrients from below through its unusually strong capillary action. Most important of all, because loess soil is very light, it is particularly vulnerable to erosion as deforestation removes badly needed windbreaks. (Much of the soil lost in the American Great Plains during the 1930s dust bowl was also loess.)

Thus, Europe's way of coping with its fuel shortages (even before the coal boom) may have been better for other kinds of conservation than China's method. It should be emphasized that this was not because Europeans were consciously trying to prevent desiccation by maintaining tree cover. Though such efforts were beginning in a few of Europe's tropical possessions (where the effects of deforestation on climate were much more obvious), these ideas (in part learned from Chinese and Indian sources) had no impact in Europe itself until later: tree conservation, to the limited extent it was practiced in eighteenth-century Europe, was aimed solely at securing adequate timber for construction (especially of ships) and fuel.[124]

Lack of water may have been developing into a serious problem by 1800 in parts of late eighteenth-century North China, though our current knowledge does not allow a definitive conclusion. The last two centuries have seen a large, dangerous decline in the water table; indeed, today many North Chinese cities face both water shortages and serious subsidence problems.[125] But in the late eighteenth century, these problems were probably not yet critical. True, North China peasants were finding it necessary to drill deeper and more expensive irrigation wells, especially if they wanted to plant cotton. (In the long run, of course, this made matters worse.)[126] However, a survey of the area immediately south of Beijing in 1771 still showed 117 springs and 5 large lakes, almost unchanged from what had been found in 1420.[127] The disappearance of surface water near Jinan (Shandong's capital) and in southwest Shandong also seems to have been primarily a late nineteenth- and (especially) twentieth-century phenomenon. An 1839 prefectural gazetteer listed 7 lakes, 150 springs, 11 wells, 14 ponds, and 18 bays in Licheng county; it specifically mentioned that 2 of the 72 springs for which the county had been famous were gone, and listed 7 other springs and 2 lakes that had been recorded in the past (sometimes the distant past) but had since disappeared. (The previous gazetteer for the area was done in 1785.)[128] This suggests some decline in the water

---

August alone, and 150 at most in October through April. For a northern European comparison, see Wallen 1970: 63, 114, 162–92, 227–39.

[124] Grove 1995: 56–59, 155, 199, and passim.

[125] Smil 1994: 38–49; *China News Digest*, May 21, 1998.

[126] Pan 1994: 57–59.

[127] Zuo and Zhang 1990: 476. This area was, however, unusual since much of it had been kept as an imperial preserve.

[128] *Jinan fuzhi* 1839: *juan* 6. The specific references to water that has disappeared are on 6:24a–b, 6:32a, 6:33b, 6:35a, 6:36a–b, 6:40b, and 6:42b.

table, but not a sharp one. By the 1920s, however, a county gazetteer for Licheng, which is far more detailed in almost every way, mentioned only 5 lakes,
40 springs, 5 ponds, and 4 creeks; it specifically said that fewer than half of the
72 famous springs (70 still active in 1839) still existed and listed numerous
other bodies of water that had disappeared or shrunk considerably.[129] It thus
seems likely that any eighteenth-century problems with wells and a declining
water table were an early and relatively mild sign of a problem that would
accelerate greatly sometime after 1850.

Nonetheless, with the advantage of hindsight, we can see some important
differences in the nexus between ecological and economic problems in China
and Europe. Europe had little chance of expanding its supplies of clothing fiber
and wood from within its own borders, given its relatively non-intensive agriculture and (compared to east Asia) limited labor supply (which would have
interfered with increasing flax production, more careful fuel gathering, and use
of crop residues), and perhaps not even of expanding its food supply at a rate
that could match nineteenth-century population growth. However, it turned out
to be possible to address these shortages through long-distance trade (first
cotton, guano, sugar, wooden ships, and naval stores and later grain, meat, and
logs). China and Japan met more of these needs domestically through labor-
intensive methods and (as we shall see later) internal trade; and they did so
without placing themselves in an immediate ecological bind. But in the long
run, at least China did so at the price of reducing its margin of safety in water
supply and (perhaps) vulnerability to cold weather, problems that could not be
solved by either trade or any technology readily available even today.

The relatively thin margin of ecological safety in China's peripheries also
made them vulnerable to any decline in the efficiency or commitment of the
state, which helped manage these problems—and a sharp decline occurred in
the mid-nineteenth century. The rich Yangzi Delta, which had long been expected to manage most of its own water control and other ecological tasks, was
much less affected by this decline, though it was greatly affected by the nineteenth-century civil wars and soaring opium imports that also accompanied the
state's new problems and new orientation.[130]

Finally, once the people who were involved in and supported by this more
intensive agriculture and fuel-gathering were there, there was no easy way to
backtrack and exchange the problems that this route created for those of Europe's path, which proved to be solvable through colonies, technology, and
chemistry.[131] Even under contemporary conditions, moving China's popula-

---

[129] *Xuxiu Licheng xianzhi*: *juan* 10–12; the reference to the 72 springs is on 10:44a.

[130] See Pomeranz 1993: chaps. 3–5.

[131] Sugihara (1997) reads this same phenomenon more optimistically, arguing that while the
adoption and adaptation of Western technologies to the large population bases left by the later east
Asian "miracle" has thus far produced only one country (Japan) whose standard of living rivals the
richest Western nations, it has brought benefits to millions not paralleled in the rest of the non-

tion into export-oriented industry and importing more primary products (as Europe did) has proved very difficult to do on a sufficient scale. This is true not only because the numbers of people involved are so large, but because many of these "surplus" workers, unlike "surplus" workers in proto-industry, *cannot* in fact be moved to factories without worsening the shortfall of agricultural output.

In short, none of the changes that combined to arrest western Europe's ecological decline during the nineteenth century was operative in China. There was no slack from highly inefficient land-use patterns such as commonage, three-field systems, or pastures reserved for horse-loving nobles. There were no gains from the spread of heavier iron plows (deep plowing retards erosion), which had been common for centuries, nor from the importation and further development of ideas and techniques for afforestation. Marginal farmers had neither industrial cities nor the Americas as an alternative, and, as we saw in chapter 2, customs reduced even the much more limited relief that peripheries might have realized from migrants seeking higher earnings in the proto-industrial Yangzi Delta. There was neither a coal boom to substitute for firewood nor vast quantities of land-intensive goods from the New World. And though Chinese population growth was probably slower than that in Europe between 1800 and 1850 (and about the same from 1750 to 1850), it was concentrated in regions such as north China and the Middle and Upper Yangzi, which had been important exporters of primary products to the Yangzi Delta. So if one adds together the ways in which China circa 1800 may have already become more ecologically vulnerable than Europe (partly by remaining self-sufficient in fibers), as well as the absence of institutional slack, of relatively easy-to-realize improvements in land management, and of any equivalent to the Americas as both population outlet and source of primary products, a sudden divergence becomes much less surprising. We can see how an ecological situation that was not much worse than that in Europe circa 1800, especially in core regions, and even seemed to be worsening more slowly, could rapidly become much worse in some Chinese regions, all at the same time that Europe's situation was stabilizing. And so, conversely, it seems possible to imagine that without all (or at least most) of its multiple sources of relief—some generated by new technology, some through catching up, and some through the New World windfall—Europe, too, could have wound up with much less economic transformation and much more environmental travail.

In this context, it is revealing to look again at Denmark, a western European case that looks in some ways more like parts of China and Japan than like England. Despite a vigorous expansion of both its navy and its merchant marine in the sixteenth through the eighteenth centuries (at considerable cost

---

European world and has been responsible for more total growth in twentieth-century world GDP than the West's own growth.

to its forests) and the chartering of companies for overseas trading and colonization on the Anglo-Dutch model, Denmark did not ultimately gain much
from overseas expansion, and its land, fuel, and soil fertility problems became
acute in the eighteenth century. However, it did far better than most of Europe
at stabilizing its ecology through domestic measures: massive campaigns of
marling, reclamation of sand dunes, ditch-digging, systematic forest management, convertible husbandry with the planting of huge amounts of clover, and
so on. These were very labor-intensive measures—Kjaergaard *very* conservatively estimates a 50 percent rise in per capita working hours for rural laborers[132]—and in many cases required massive mobilizations of forced villein
labor (which was still common in eighteenth-century Denmark).[133]

Though these efforts placed agricultural prosperity on a new and ecologically sounder footing, Denmark saw no increase in the share of its population
living in cities between 1500 and 1800 and witnessed only limited growth of
proto-industry;[134] certain fuel-intensive products, including glass, were virtually all imported, despite the transport problems involved.[135] These patterns
persisted well into the nineteenth century, even though Denmark had reasonable amounts of capital, good transport, participated in European science, and
had plenty of nearby and culturally similar models for industrialization. Moreover, labor remained overwhelmingly concentrated in agriculture even though
these very labor-intensive approaches to farming, fuel conservation, and land
management produced a substantial long-term decline in the physical productivity of labor: Kjaergaard estimates an increase in agricultural output of at
most 100 percent between 1500 and 1800 (a rising share of which had to be
sold to pay for imports like fuel), while labor inputs increased over 200 percent.[136] (When returns to labor in Denmark did begin to rise, in the late nineteenth century, this was at first less because physical productivity improved
than because its neighbors became increasingly industrial, raising the prices
Danes could get for their farm goods.)

Thus, the path of ecological near self-sufficiency through rural labor intensification, once adopted, was not easily abandoned, at least until twentieth-
century chemistry and machinery made possible a far more radical transformation of farming. In that sense, Denmark's path resembled that taken by various
parts of eighteenth- and early nineteenth-century east Asia more than that of
England or even Flanders. (It is, as well, the "peasant" path that Ambrosoli
sees England diverging from, in a gamble that could have been ecologically
catastrophic had guano and other off-farm fertilizers not become available.)

---

[132] Kjaergaard 1994: 151. In fact, since he finds a probable increase of 50 percent in the length
of the work week and more weeks of work per year, the likely increase is larger than 50 percent.
See also the discussion of marling on pp. 55–56, where he calculates that 110 labor days per *tonde*
(.55 hectare) was likely, but then does further calculations based on 50 days per *tonde*.

[133] Kjaergaard 1994: 37–38.   [134] Ibid., 151–54.
[135] Ibid., 123.   [136] Ibid., 158.

And even with this huge application of labor to land management, the result was only *near* ecological balance: coal imports rose steadily after 1740, and especially after 1820.[137]

But it is only in hindsight that Europe's problems appear more solvable than those of China, and solvable only with a combination of technological change, institutional catching-up, and New World resources. In the late eighteenth century, east Asia could not be judged "overpopulated" compared to Europe, since its larger number of people were living just as well and in some ways straining their ecology less than Europeans were.

Even the further growth of Chinese population—by at least 150,000,000 and perhaps even 225,000,000—between 1800 and the 1930s was accomplished without any clear decline in nutritional levels. Even in the early twentieth century itself, when social misery was particularly acute and Malthusian ideas seemed particularly appropriate, there may have been a small upward creep in the average height of young adults, an often-used (though controversial) proxy for general nutrition.[138] Average consumption of nonessentials probably did decline, but much of this was, as we saw in chapter 3, an effect of population growth being concentrated in less-developed regions, so that the relatively high-living people of Jiangnan and a few other places came to have less weight in national averages for consumption. With the possible exceptions of North and Northwest China, there is little to suggest a decline in the living standards of any particular place, except during the mid-nineteenth-century disasters. Thus, there is little to suggest either "overpopulation" or imminent "ecological crisis" in 1800 (much less 1750), if by this we mean a threat to existing expectations. At most we could argue that there was an ecological "bottleneck" constraining any sharp further improvement in living standards, as well as some hints of more serious problems in the future for North and Northwest China.

Overall, then, both ends of Eurasia were in serious trouble. Any difference in the degree to which they were in trouble (based on domestic resources alone) would probably turn out to be fairly small. And most of Europe's advantages consisted of slack left by institutional barriers to intensive land use, not the gradual accumulation made possible by superior economic arrangements. What seems more significant than any differences, as long as we restrict ourselves to these areas' internal resources, is how quickly population growth and proto-industrialization seemed to be closing the ecological window in which a much more radical change in economic life and per capita resource use would be possible anywhere. Massive windfalls of fuel, fiber, and perhaps even food would have to be found somewhere for an industrial revolution to occur and be sustained, or even for proto-industrial growth to continue much longer.

---

[137] Ibid., 127–28.   [138] Lee and Wang forthcoming: 6, 10.

But to understand the full significance of these rather sudden windfalls, we must first look at one last area of general similarity. I have argued above that thanks to extremely efficient (and often labor-intensive) ways of using resources, Chinese and Japanese cores did better at finding *local* palliatives for shortages of land-intensive resources; but these solutions were far from complete (especially for timber) and they depended on importing other non-local resources (e.g., Manchurian beancake to relieve cotton-growing soil). In short, both European and Asian core areas needed to obtain land-intensive resources through long-distance trade with less densely populated areas. To the extent that this long-distance trade was consensual trade with other parts of the Old World, cores at both ends of Eurasia faced comparable opportunities and limits; but, a good case can be made that Chinese cores used this kind of trade more successfully than their western European counterparts did.

Trading for Resources with Old World Peripheries: Common Patterns and Limits of Smithian Solutions to Quasi-Malthusian Problems

Import Substitution in Free Labor Peripheries

Core areas in China, Japan, and Europe all imported land-intensive commodities (especially forms of energy) from more sparsely populated zones. For western Europe, this meant first the Baltic and eastern European grain, timber, and cattle trades, and later a plethora of New World products. For Lingnan, there were some imports from Southeast Asia and even India, but Jiangnan relied primarily on rice and timber from upstream on the Yangzi and its tributaries, and, beginning around 1680, on timber and soybeans from Manchuria. In Japan, a large sixteenth- and early seventeenth-century foreign trade was seriously restricted by the state after 1640, leaving little except some traffic in silver and silk by 1700.[139] However, a pattern of internal exchange developed between core regions (what Susan Hanley and Kozo Yamamura call "Region I") and the rest of the country (Hanley and Yamamura's "Region II"). Region I, which appears to have reached the maximum population it could support by 1720, exported nails, tiles, tools, leather shoes, and above all textiles. Region II imported manufactured goods and exported rice, timber, horses, and other land-intensive products. The outer areas, especially in the far north, were also major sources of fish, which became increasingly important both as food and as fertilizer in core regions from the mid-eighteenth century onward, and which was sought further and further afield.[140]

---

[139] Sugihara 1996: 38.
[140] Hanley and Yamamura 1977: 19–28, 132–36, 163–71; Howell 1992: 271–75.

Land-intensive imports had to be paid for, and all our core regions sought to do this by selling manufactures, particularly textiles. But that pattern of exchange faced at least two possible limitations.

One was that raw materials exporters often began a process of import substitution, in which they themselves began to make the manufactured goods they had previously imported. And as diminishing returns set in in the production of the area's main exports—as, for instance, exporting more lumber began to involve hauling logs further and further to the riverbank—people turned to other work. In the twentieth century, many Third World governments have adopted import substitution as a conscious strategy for industrialization, often with rather poor long-term results.[141] Consequently, economists tend to view import substitution as an effort to push against the "natural" tendencies of the market, using tariffs, subsidies, and the like to artificially improve the competitive position of nascent industries. But two-hundred plus years ago, the technological gaps between cores and peripheries were often fairly small, and whatever gaps there were were not guarded by internationally recognized patents; very few production processes required large initial investments of fixed capital; and relatively high transport costs (especially for high bulk-to-value items of daily use) provided a certain amount of "natural" protection. A few kinds of production (e.g., silk-rearing and weaving) were so complex that it was very hard to compete with established producers,[142] but many others were simple. Thus, import substitution was not a "forced" process in the pre-1800 world: it seems to have occurred fairly naturally in those peripheries where people were free to switch into new kinds of production and to decide which goods to produce for themselves and which to purchase with the cash earned from their other labors (i.e., to participate in DeVries's "industrious revolution"). The process was blocked only when some special raw material was missing, where particularly complex skills were involved, or where government or lordly monopolies interfered.

Indeed, import substitution eventually spread through most of that part of China with which the Lower Yangzi and Lingnan traded. The development of proto-industry cut into the Middle Yangzi's rice surplus (both because population grew and because some land switched into cotton to supply local spinners and weavers), which had previously gone to the Lower Yangzi, and it also made that area less dependent on cloth from Jiangnan.[143] North China had begun to make more of its own cotton textiles in the seventeenth century and, as this process continued in the eighteenth century, it exported less raw cotton to Jiangnan.[144]

North China's decline as a raw cotton exporter was probably more severe than that of the Middle and Upper Yangzi as rice and timber sources, because

[141] Of course, many more open economies have also fared poorly.

[142] Borah 1943: 85–101; Schurz 1939: 44–45, 364–66.

[143] Li Bozhong 1998: 108.   [144] Lu 1992: 482–83.

it appears to have had fewer built-in brakes on its population growth and ultimately far more severe ecological problems. Like the Middle and Upper Yangzi, North China's population growth exceeded the empire's average between 1750 and 1850. But in the Middle Yangzi, population growth seems to have been self-regulating, much as it was in the Lower Yangzi. It slowed considerably in the last few decades before the mid-nineteenth-century civil wars, as land and water shortages mounted; it then probably took fifty years to recover from those wars.[145] And although pressure on the region's land and water was serious, the slowdown in population growth seems to have come soon enough to avert major ecological or economic crises. The surface area of Dongting Lake—the second largest in China—is one useful proxy for population-driven ecological stress in the Middle Yangzi, since much land was reclaimed from the lake, greatly increasing flood dangers. This area seems to have declined by almost 800 square miles (13 percent of the lake's previous size) between 1825 and 1850, but then held roughly steady for the rest of the century.[146]

In North China, on the other hand, population growth continued with barely a pause, right through to the still faster population growth that began in the 1950s: and it did so in spite of a series of genuine ecological catastrophes with lasting effects. And both before and after 1850, the most rapid population growth within North China appears to have been in Henan, generally the poorest province in the macro-region.[147] It is not clear why this should have happened. But recent studies of fertility control elsewhere in China may provide some clues.

James Lee and Wang Feng's pathbreaking new work on the Chinese demographic system emphasizes the role of extended kin groups, acting through lineage organizations or through the household heads of joint co-resident families. Such groups were essential for enforcing restraints on procreation within marriage, arranging the adoptions that compensated for such restraint, and providing reasonable guarantees of old-age security and ritual continuity in cases where a given conjugal unit failed to produce a male biological heir.[148] More generally, it has been argued that social arrangements in which bonds between married brothers remain strong provide a form of insurance that reduces the need to hedge risk by having more children to call upon.[149] Lineage

---

[145] Perdue 1987: 219–33; Skinner 1987: 67–77.

[146] Perdue 1987: 204.

[147] Liang 1981: 396–97, 400–404 (pre-1850); Lin and Chen (1981: 39) for 1774 and for later dates, disregarding 1842 figures, which are suspiciously high for all the provinces they list, and the 1711 Henan figure, which is impossibly low (but would make that province's subsequent growth rate still more impressive).

[148] See Lee and Wang forthcoming, especially chaps. 7 and 8; on adoption in particular, see also Waltner (1990) and Dennerline (1986).

[149] Cain 1982: 173.

organizations were especially strong in south China (though the households that composed them were no more complex on average than in the north[150]); joint households were particularly common in Liaoning, the other major source of Lee and Wang's rural data.

But lineages were generally weak in North and Northwest China, joint households seem (based on admittedly spotty data) to have been much less common than in Liaoning, and essentially independent nuclear families were much more common. When brothers divided the family property in the north (whether a parent was still alive or not) they were far less likely to leave or create any property that belonged to a supra-family unit than was the case in the south.[151] Even the room that had housed the family's ancestral tablets and altar was likely to be turned into housing and/or divided; each brother maintained his own separate altar thereafter, even if the brothers' homes still fronted on a common courtyard.[152] Under such circumstances, it is hard to imagine that the extended family, either as material force or as ideal, could shape fertility decisions made within the nuclear family as strongly as it apparently did in Jiangnan and in Liaoning. It may be, then, that a different kinship system made the household-level mechanisms that were central to demographic restraint in some other parts of China relatively weak in the North and Northwest, leaving them closer to the population dynamics that Malthus, Hajnal, and others have mistakenly attributed to all of China.

Whatever the causes of North China's population boom, its population density probably exceeded that of the Middle Yangzi by 50 percent in the 1840s—despite having less water, a shorter growing season, and other disadvantages.[153] By 1953, North China's population density exceeded that of the Middle Yangzi by 70 percent. Under the circumstances, North China—unlike the Middle and Upper Yangzi—almost certainly decreased its per capita production of non-food crops somewhere between 1750 and 1900; it may even have suffered a fall in absolute production levels. And if raw cotton output fell while more of it was spun locally, the fall in exports to Jiangnan would have been very large. (For more on these scenarios, see appendix F.)

Whether these processes of development in the peripheries reached a relatively benign equilibrium, as they seem to have done in the Middle and Upper Yangzi, or failed to do so, as in North and Northwest China, they limited the ability of more advanced regions to keep growing and to specialize further in manufacturing. Before we return to those consequences, however, it is worth looking further at causes of the process.

Thus far, I have described this as a "natural" process, to be expected if peripheries had more or less free labor and no special restrictions (e.g.,

---

[150] See, for instance, Buck 1964: 367.
[151] Wakefield 1992: 224–29, 254.
[152] Wakefield 1994: 201, 227–28.
[153] Skinner 1977a: 213, 226, adjusting for Skinner 1987.

colonial monopoly systems). But the reality is more complex. We are still far from understanding what caused population growth in any of these peripheries, though external demand for their products and increasing opportunities to earn a living surely played some role.

Nor is the link between rising population and falling raw materials exports a simple one. In dry-farming North China, where increased labor inputs alone could not raise yields dramatically, population growth and environmental strain are probably a pretty good explanation for why so much of the area's additional labor power went into handicrafts and raw cotton exports fell.[154] Population growth alone would also explain much of the decline in exports from timber-producing regions; food and forest compete for land, and knowledge of how to raise per-acre wood yields was still rudimentary.[155]

But in the Middle Yangzi, where additional labor could easily raise rice yields, it is not as certain why, as the labor force grew, the extra workers did not concentrate on growing even more rice than they did and trading for cloth, rather than producing cloth themselves. Indeed, Perkins's scattered data suggest that per acre rice yields in some of the most export-oriented counties in the Middle Yangzi province of Hunan did rise sharply as the province filled up: they were about 60 percent of Lower Yangzi levels in the eighteenth century and caught up during the nineteenth century.[156] Cultivated acreage also rose significantly—presumably mostly in less-advanced areas.[157] Since Hunan's population grew about 40 percent between 1775 and 1850 (it probably grew faster on a per annum basis between 1750 and 1775, but the data are very poor)[158] the province probably could have maintained its per capita food output and so increased the absolute size of its exportable surplus. Since those exports fell instead, we must conclude that the yield increases of the leading export counties were not matched in many other places where they could have been, at least in part because people chose to use their labor differently. Many Qing officials believed as much; several blamed failures in their campaigns to encourage double-cropping on the unwillingness of peasants to put in the necessary labor, even where the local environment was suitable.[159] And the people who put more of their labor into non-grain production—whether they were lowland women weaving cloth or highland men and women growing tea—still consumed rice, decreasing the exportable surplus. These reallocations of labor were not inevitable.

Despite diminishing physical returns to the labor engaged in producing any particular export, primary-product prices could certainly rise enough to make continued specialization more rewarding than diversification. While premodern transport costs could encourage regional self-sufficiency, riverine and

---

[154] For a further discussion, see appendix F.
[156] Perkins 1969: 21, 315, 318–19, 321.
[158] Perdue 1987: 56–57.
[155] Menzies 1996: 619–22, 644–65, 659–63.
[157] Ibid., 234.
[159] Ibid., 129, 132.

coastal shipping rates were often modest. Since China's peripheries did continue to ship large (though declining) amounts of high bulk-to-value goods to Jiangnan and Lingnan, one would think that shippers, needing return cargoes, would have offered attractive shipping rates for Jiangnan's exports (though adding weight was a greater problem when going back upstream than it was going down to Jiangnan). So we need further explanations of Middle Yangzi proto-industrialization, either through forces that *discouraged* further export growth or forces that *encouraged* intraregional diversification.

One logical possibility—though one for which we have little data—would involve local transport costs. Within a macro-region, people first filled up the most fertile and accessible regions, closest to the rivers that served as major transportation arteries; later growth would be disproportionately located away from these arteries, from which shipping bulky goods was expensive. And since China had fewer large domesticated animals per person than Europe or India did, it is possible that—although (as argued in chapter 1) it was at no disadvantage in *overall* transport capacity—transport costs may have risen unusually steeply as one moved away from riverbanks. But at most this would help explain why exports did not keep rising in step with population, cultivated area, and total output in the peripheries. It does not explain why the people already settled near good transport would have exported less in the nineteenth century, unless we can show that they began trading their primary products for goods produced in later-growing areas.

This would have made sense for some groups among those who settled outside the main river valleys—the rapidly growing number of people who cleared and cultivated hillsides in late eighteenth- and early nineteenth-century China. This hillside settlement has long been linked to the Chinese adoption of foreign food crops (potatoes, sweet potatoes, etc.) that would grow on highland and inferior soils.[160] This places hillside clearance in a Malthusian context, with population growth forcing people onto inferior land and the new crops providentially allowing them to survive there, or with new food lands allowing population to grow further. Such poor highlanders scratching out a living with inferior foods would be irrelevant to the export surpluses of the more fortunate farmers in the valleys.

But highland farming had another face, which is relevant to our story. Much of what was grown on hillsides and former wasteland—tea, peanuts, and various oilseed crops—were in greater demand because of increased prosperity, not just rising population. In fact, in a recent article Fang Xing rests his case for an improved standard of living in the Lower Yangzi between the seventeenth and nineteenth centuries precisely on evidence that more non-grain foods were consumed.[161] Although we do not yet have comparable studies of

---

[160] For the classic statement, see Ho 1955: 192, 196–97.
[161] Fang 1996: 97.

diets in the rest of China, it seems likely that the lowland rice growers of the Middle and Upper Yangzi, whose terms of trade and land productivity were both improving,[162] would have spent some of their increased incomes on condiments of various sorts. If they did, they would have become customers of their upland neighbors and probably sent them at least some rice in return. The literature has reasonably emphasized how Chinese producers of non-grain cash crops often grew food, too—so that, say, tea and sweet potatoes might advance in tandem—which made them less dependent on purchased food than the very specialized producers of "drug foods" in the Caribbean.[163] The spread of secondary grains in the late eighteenth and nineteenth centuries even turned a few former food-deficit counties in Hunan into net exporters.[164] But it still seems likely that some of the rice that used to go downriver now instead went up into the hills.

So far, I have restricted this discussion to economic factors, adding details specific to the way that market forces played themselves out in China, rather than invoking any other causal forces. Still more economic factors could be added to explain still more of Jiangnan's increasing shortage of crucial imports. Water transport between North China and the Yangzi Valley deteriorated after 1800, further inhibiting raw cotton shipments; the rise of opium as a cash-cropping alternative to cotton in the Upper Yangzi, Northwest, and Southwest could not have helped either, though this came after 1850.[165] But other influences, related to culture and to state policy, need to be considered as well.

One such possible factor is the system of state and charity granaries, which, at least in the eighteenth century, were fairly effective at dampening both seasonal price fluctuations and price increases in bad harvest years. As Pierre-Etienne Will and R. Bin Wong point out, this lessened the risk of going into non-grain production and buying food from the market.[166] The granary system was at its height in the eighteenth century; it fell on hard times thereafter. But many local granaries continued to work well even later, while the government could no longer make large interregional grain transfers to meet episodic crises. Thus, the nineteenth-century granary system may have continued to buffer the risks for some peasants in grain surplus areas who chose to diversify, while no longer doing as much to buffer the risks of interregional specialization.

A more deep-seated factor may have been Chinese gender norms. It was much more "proper" for women to work indoors (above all, spinning and

---

[162] Perdue 1987: 113–35; Perkins 1969: 21.

[163] Mazumdar 1984: 269–70; Gardella 1994: 32.

[164] Perdue 1987: 134.

[165] On the decline of the north-south Grand Canal, see Hoshi 1971: 223–27; Pomeranz 1993: 154–64. On opium replacing cotton in some regions, see Chao 1977: 23.

[166] Will and Wong 1991: 496–97.

weaving) than in the fields. Had this preference (and one for wives with bound feet) not existed, hinterland families might have sought larger plots or farmed even more intensively—thus having a larger surplus to sell—and made less cloth.

We have already discussed (in chapter 2) some of the problems in assessing how much these norms constrained economic choices, and we have seen that even in Jiangnan, women did not completely leave the fields until after 1850. We also saw that, at least at mid-eighteenth-century prices, one need not invoke cultural preferences to explain that rural women in this period did weaving rather than farming. (Relative prices presumably favored weaving even more in the Middle Yangzi, where rice was cheaper.) But the most parsimonious explanation does not always give the best account of actual motives, and the idealized "man plows, woman weaves" division of family labor—one that became more common during the Ming and especially Qing, with state encouragement—probably did encourage import substitution in the interior.[167]

Since the "man plows, woman weaves" division of labor was an ideal that was sometimes overridden by practicality, one might even see it as a coveted lifestyle (much like restricting women to homemaking in some Western countries during certain periods when men earned enough to allow this) that more Middle Yangzi families would have adopted as the area became more prosperous in the later eighteenth century. And since cultural preferences do not automatically enact themselves—Hunanese men had to learn how to grow cotton and Hunanese women how to spin and weave it—Qing efforts to encourage the farmer/weaver household by disseminating knowledge presumably made some difference.

Furthermore, these gender norms probably also mattered in the mid-nineteenth century—once internal frontiers had largely filled up (except in Manchuria)—in discouraging people from migrating back toward Jiangnan. As long as land was still available in the interior and most people's skills (and self-images) were tied to farming, there probably would not have been much migration toward the coast anyway. But despite its nineteenth-century troubles, Jiangnan still had the highest per capita income in China, and as land became scarce elsewhere, one could imagine people without enough land migrating toward the handicraft and service jobs of the Yangzi Delta—and thus restarting its population growth, lowering its wages, making its cloth exports cheaper, and so on. That is, one could imagine such migrations if women had been able to migrate alone (toward textile-making jobs) without stigma, and had weaving not been seen as ideally done by women who were part of a household in which the husband had secure access (through ownership or long-term rental) to farmland. But since these preferences did exist—even tenancies in Jiangnan usually required a significant deposit—no migration of poor

[167] Mann 1992: 75–96; Li Bozhong 1996: 99–107.

rural households to the core was likely. It took the rise of urban factory-based industry (some of which included dormitories for single women workers) and a proletariat in the European sense after 1900 to create such a movement; and then it was halted again when the People's Republic banned migration to the cities after the mid-1950s.

The Qing favored population growth and handicraft development in less-developed regions not only as parts of a cultural ideal but also as a way of maximizing the number of ordinary households prosperous enough to pay their taxes reliably. And the Qing did not simply trust market dynamics to create these developments. We have already seen how the state encouraged migration to less-populated areas, providing information, infrastructural investment, and sometimes loans. And land-tax policies—both the de jure assessment of heavy tribute quotas on Jiangnan and a few other rich areas that were not levied elsewhere and the de facto policy of allowing much newly settled or resettled areas to stay off the tax rolls—certainly favored "peripheral" development, while probably restraining that of the empire's foremost core.

The state also made considerable if sporadic efforts to promote the spread of best practices in both agriculture and handicrafts: introducing new crop varieties and hiring Jiangnan weavers to come teach people in other areas, for instance.[168] (Having officials who never served in their home territory and rotated frequently facilitated these efforts.) And in both North and Northwest China, the Qing made major efforts to make subsistence secure in ecologically marginal areas. The biggest such project, the Yellow River conservancy (which served other purposes as well), probably consumed over 10 percent of total government spending in the early nineteenth century: more than some governments spent on all expenditures beyond war, debt repayment, and official salaries.[169]

We cannot measure precisely the impact of Qing policies; and they probably did not fundamentally alter the dynamics of development. But surely they had some effect: one that worked with markets to spread an agricultural, handicraft, and commercial economy across the empire. That effect, however, was probably not constant over time, and it would be well worth examining when and why it changed.

As R. Bin Wong has pointed out, late Ming and Qing officials had before them two models of economic expansion across the empire. One stressed interregional trade and specialization; the other, the multiplication of largely independent, self-sufficient cells. Both kinds of expansion usually involved some

---

[168] Mann 1992: 86; Wong 1997.

[169] For a lengthy account of this system as a subsidy to ecologically fragile North China—which, however, emphasizes that the subsidy was withdrawn near the end of the nineteenth century (so that it cannot account for continued rapid population growth in the twentieth century), see Pomeranz 1993.

state effort in their early stages, but the latter required considerably less on-going attention from higher levels of the state.[170] (Or at least it was thought to: if one considers the long-run ecological effects of regional or local autarchy, this may not remain true. The picture is also complicated by the many different levels at which we can talk about degrees of interdependence or self-sufficiency, from the empire through Skinnerian macro-regions and down to local marketing communities.) The post-1750 period in which, I have argued, the reality on the ground shifted strongly in the direction of "separate cells" was also one in which (especially after 1800) the state seems to have been more reluctant to handle large projects and was less effective when it did so. To what extent the prevalence of different ideas changed to reflect a changing sense of what was possible, or vice versa, and exactly how shifting official visions, specific policies, and broad trends in the economy were related all remain to be fleshed out by further research.

Japan, meanwhile, shows somewhat similar patterns of development with very dissimilar central government commitments. Growth in Japan's major cores was very limited after about 1720—in fact, population in both the Kantō and the Kinai *fell* in the late eighteenth and early nineteenth centuries—while population and handicrafts took off in various peripheral areas after about 1780.[171] The Tokugawa did not encourage the peripheries at the expense of the cores. But after about 1760 they at least gave the leaders of some peripheral domains tacit permission to undertake new measures that enabled these domains to diversify their economies and support growing populations less precariously than in the past.

For instance Tosa, a relatively poor lumber-exporting domain, was badly deforested during the seventeenth-century construction boom, stripping entire mountains to provide lumber for Osaka (and to pay for the very high expenses that the lords of Tosa incurred for service to the shogunate and attendance in Edo). Subsequent attempts to farm the cleared land failed to keep up with population growth and were dogged by massive floods descending from bare hillsides. The eighteenth century was harder than the seventeenth century in Tosa; the popular diet appears to have gotten sparser and the 1750s were years of famine.[172]

But population growth resumed and hardship eased a bit in Tosa late in the century; this was largely due to the abolition of domainal monopolies, which led to an enormous boom in small-scale production of exports such as high-quality paper. This relaxation of monopolies, in turn, was possible because the lords of Tosa greatly reduced their expensive establishment at Edo and their

[170] Wong 1997: 139; see also 224–29.

[171] On the stagnation of core area populations, see Saito (1985: 211) compared to Iwahashi (1981: 440). On the continued growth of population in peripheries—despite serious famine in the mid-eighteenth century—see L. Roberts 1991: 87–91.

[172] L. Roberts 1991: 88–100, 115–21.

service to the shogunate—changes that the central government had to agree to before the burdens of this particular periphery could be lightened and its economy freed from harmful fiscal pressures.[173]

As it became fiscally possible to abolish harmful monopolies and labor obligations and thus support a larger population in the peripheries, that population growth itself also worked to reinforce tendencies toward liberalization. Population growth in outer domains was accompanied by greater double-cropping of paddy rice, and the increased use of that very labor-intensive and hard-to-supervise cropping system seems to have encouraged a trend toward smaller farms and greater tenant autonomy. The same changes in the land system had appeared two centuries earlier in the Kinai region, when it was experiencing both population growth and increased planting of double-cropped paddy rice.[174]

So although the Tokugawa did not, like the Qing, promote a more even spread of population and proto-industry across the landscape, they did eventually eliminate policies that had encouraged the concentration of people and handicrafts in cores. Meanwhile, at least some European states were doing the opposite, fighting (not always successfully) against markets to maintain the privileged position of specialized core regions. For whatever reasons, proto-industry in Japan, as in China, came to show a much less marked regional division of labor than proto-industrial England, and a more marked familial division of labor.[175]

Development in Old World hinterlands did not cause immediate shortages in the more advanced regions that bought primary products from them. Even the densely populated Lower Yangzi continued to find markets where it could exchange its industrial exports for raw materials—partly by going further afield and partly by specializing in certain niches, such as higher-quality fabrics, in which other regions could not yet compete. But these processes had limits.

By 1800, China's timber merchants had penetrated every corner of the empire, and some lumber floated over one thousand miles to its final destination. In low-wage Shaanxi, some trees were hauled sixty-five miles just to get to the river—further than Europeans hauled logs overland except in the very peculiar case of supplying Madrid.[176] But the quantities of free labor required for such tasks ultimately made such timber too expensive even for Jiangnan. As an eighteenth-century source put it, "Whether a tree is worth 100 *taels* or 1,000

[173] Ibid., 271–99.   [174] Smith (1959) quoted in Palat 1995: 62.
[175] Saito 1983: 40–43.

[176] Wu and Xu 1985 435–46; Li Bozhong 1994b: 93; Braudel 1981: 365–67. On Madrid, see Ringrose 1970: 27. Madrid could afford unusually expensive resources (and thus grow to a size that its immediate hinterland could not supply) because of its position as tax collector and way-station for New World silver, not from any goods it produced to exchange for primary products or even any rents and taxes owed it from its immediate surroundings.

taels, it will still cost 1,000 *taels* to harvest."[177] Moreover, high transport costs could have the paradoxical effect of increasing the depletion of forests without benefiting importing regions: a pattern exactly opposite to the efficiencies achieved when fuel was gathered from trees near the family courtyard. In the 1920s, for instance, high transport costs from the forests of northwest China meant that only the most valuable parts of the tree were worth shipping: the effect was not to slow logging, but to increase the size of stumps and quantity of "waste wood" that loggers left on the ground, slowing the forest's regeneration.[178] Late eighteenth-century lumbering probably became similarly wasteful as it moved into more remote areas. Thus, despite the remarkable efficiency of China's long-distance product markets, they could not provide raw materials for growing coastal regions indefinitely.

The trade between Japan's Region I and Region II was running into similar problems in the eighteenth century, though perhaps not as rapidly. Import substitution in Region II was gathering steam, and peasants in these domains were becoming more involved in the cash economy, though both processes were still slowed down somewhat by daimyo monopolies.[179] Thus, by the nineteenth century, many of Region I's still unchallenged export niches were in the sale of luxury goods for Region II's rather small elite. Meanwhile, population growth in the hinterland (which continued long after it had stopped in Region I) was reducing its surpluses of land-intensive products. Lumber output, for instance, stagnated in the eighteenth century.[180] Overall, as Conrad Totman puts it, "Tokugawa society encountered unprecedented difficulty in expanding its ecological base."[181] And this occurred despite zero population growth in core regions, liberalization of the timber and rice trades,[182] and a geography that gave most of the country some access to water transport.

Less Free and Flexible Peripheries

Western Europeans trading with eastern Europe faced a different set of constraints. Unlike the Chinese interior, eastern Europe was full of estates managed with varying degrees of forced labor. While peasants in Prussia could sometimes sue in defense of their rights, the Junkers controlled the courts, and success would not come easily;[183] peasants in Mecklenburg, Poland, and Russia had even less recourse to justice. And while this still left the possibility of

---

[177] Quoted in Li Bozhong 1994b: 93.   [178] Menzies 1996: 634.

[179] Hanley and Yamamura 1977: 19–23, 131–46. The greater effectiveness of daimyo control in Region II seems to have been partly a matter of different administrators—Region I was largely ruled by the Tokugawa themselves, who tended to handle their domains more loosely than did many of the "outside" daimyo—and partly due to the lesser development of towns, trade, and opportunities for off-farm employment in Region II.

[180] Totman 1995: 104.   [181] Ibid., 102.

[182] Ibid., 105–7.   [183] Hagen 1985: 114; Hagen 1986a: 71–72.

running away, those who did so risked losing whatever few rights they did have,[184] as well as serious reprisals. Russian serfs who fled were often returned. Though estate owners could not stop flight, they seem to have coordinated their responses far more than the "owners" of labor obligations in India and Southeast Asia, with considerable deterrent effect. Polish peasants fled fairly successfully for a time, but this became increasingly difficult in the eighteenth century.[185] Though recent scholarship has made it clear that even eastern European lordship was "negotiated" rather than simply imposed, it nonetheless created very different dynamics than those in freer areas. These differences meant that population growth and import substitution were slower than in the Chinese interior. But as we shall soon see, they limited exports in other ways.

Landlords who relied heavily on compulsory labor were much slower to experience diminishing returns to export production than were owner-cultivators or employers of wage labor. At least in theory, an extra hour of a serf's time cost his lord nothing, so that even hard-to-reach timber need not have sold at sky-high prices. And cultivation with bound labor could expand under circumstances that would be perverse in a world of free labor (even low-wage free labor): output, for instance, sometimes expanded in response to falling prices in order to maintain the lord's income.[186]

In fact, labor was not simply extracted from a passive peasantry. As William Hagen has shown, at least in Prussia, the huge additions in compulsory labor extracted during the sixteenth-century grain boom were partially offset by decreases in the in-kind and cash payments required of peasants; thus this labor did have a significant cost to the estate holder. Moreover, peasants accepted these increases (grudgingly) in part because they stayed within bounds that still allowed the peasant enough time (and use of his horses) to cultivate his own plot; this suggests that earlier images of a peasantry crushed by these increased labor impositions may well be exaggerated. Indeed, peasants seem to have increased the cultivation of relatively labor-intensive garden crops on their own land. This was in part, no doubt, a necessary measure brought on by the shrinkage of those plots as population grew and lords used various advantages to gobble up additional farmland for themselves, but it also probably reflected the decrease of in-kind (grain) and cash payments, which meant that the peasant could get by with a smaller grain harvest.[187] If people worked more hours growing export crops for their lords and took a more labor-intensive approach to their own shrinking plots, it seems likely that total labor input was being increased—probably more than it would have had export demand

---

[184] Hagen 1985: 114; Hagen 1996: 308; Hagen forthcoming: 38–39.

[185] Blum 1961: 309–10, 552–54; Hagen 1996: 307; compare Reid 1988a: 129–30; Fukuzawa 1982b: 251; Habib 1982c: 248; Ludden 1985: 42–50, 80–84.

[186] Kochanowicz 1989: 100–102.

[187] Hagen 1985: 104, 107, 111; Hagen 1986b: 154; Hagen forthcoming: 38–39, 43.

pushed up peasant earnings per hour and allowed them to choose more leisure and/or more consumption. In this area, then, "negotiated lordship" may well have had an impact not too different from what we would expect from older models of a unilaterally imposed "serfdom." And in Mecklenburg, most of Poland, Lithuania, Russia, and many other places something close to the old image of serfdom may yet apply.

Meanwhile, the rather weak development of towns and of proto-industry in eastern Europe also prolonged export orientation and decreased the potential for the sort of import substitution that we saw in east Asian peripheries. Explanations for the stagnation and destruction of towns in late medieval and early modern eastern Europe vary. Some stress competition from other commercial and industrial centers, some the impact of numerous wars, some a backward agriculture that limited town size in the first place, some the conscious efforts of nobles to break the power of the bourgeoisie at any cost (and deny to peasants the possible refuge of cities), and some the grain boom itself, bringing with it a new division of labor between eastern and western Europe.[188]

Whatever the reasons, textile production went into at least relative decline in eastern Europe as early as the fifteenth century, and it declined in absolute terms while grain exports were rising.[189] There were some exceptions, where textile production grew rapidly: eighteenth-century Silesia and parts of Bohemia and Alpine Austria. But such growth usually occurred in the interstices of lordly power—i.e., in mountain districts where good land was scarce but where there was little compulsory labor.[190] On most of the great plains of eastern Europe, estates were more powerful, and rural industry lagged far behind that of western Europe.[191] In the Hungarian parts of the Habsburg Empire—which were not Baltic and not major *grain* exporters to the West until later but did export cattle, wine, and other land-intensive goods beginning in the "long sixteenth century"—over 80 percent of the labor force was in agriculture until the 1860s or 1870s.[192]

Moreover, neither the export boom nor proto-industrial development in this region had quite the same demographic impact as did prosperity in freer areas,

[188] See the historiographic summaries in Hagen 1988 and Hagen forthcoming.

[189] Pach 1990: 183, 186–88, 190; Kisch in Kriedte, Medick, and Schlumbohm (1981): 178–99.

[190] Kriedte, Medick, and Schlumbohm 1981: 14, 19. Good (1984: 22) makes the same point for Austria-Hungary, associating proto-industry with low soil fertility and an absence of estate agriculture.

[191] Gunst 1989: 64, 69. Bohemia did have both great estates and highly developed proto-industry, but the estates were unusual in at least two ways. First, the peasantry had unusually strong rights by eastern European standards. Second, because a strong mining sector had existed *before* most of the estates were formed—and had given rise to a relatively large town population and an unusually monetized economy—most of the surplus of the estates was targeted at local markets (and was mostly in the form of rye and hops for brewing, rather than food grains, anyway) rather than export to the West.

[192] Good 1984: 23.

where, via wage labor, they often led to earlier marriages and more children. Prussian lords responding to a renewed rise in grain prices after 1763 did eventually use more wage laborers, as attempts to further increase compulsory labor ran into increasing resistance and inefficiency: in doing so, they settled additional people on their land as independent cottagers, allowing more rapid formation of new families.[193] But so far as we know this was not a common pattern elsewhere east of the Elbe—indeed, compulsory labor generally increased in the eighteenth century, sometimes to six days a week—and even in Prussia it belongs primarily to the last half-century before emancipation.[194] Furthermore, even in this case, the preemancipation turn to wage labor was not a steady trend. On the contrary, as wage laborers grew more numerous, they also became more like the older labor force of encumbered peasants. In 1763, these day-laborers paid 9.5 *taler* (a silver coin, roughly equal to a week's cash wages for a rural day laborer) for their houses, gardens, and grazing rights; were paid in kind for threshing and in cash for various other tasks; and rendered only six days of unpaid labor per year. By 1808, their cash rent had been cut to 5 *taler*, but they each owed sixty-five days per year of unpaid labor (plus threshing, plowing, and other heavy work): about 40 percent of the obligation of a "full peasant" given a much more substantial piece of land.[195]

Proto-industrial development also was less likely to lead to easier marriage and more rapid demographic growth in eastern Europe than in western Europe. In one area studied intensively by Jürgen Schlumbohm, even the growth of a large linen industry in the eighteenth and nineteenth centuries provided relatively few opportunities to the landless. Instead, most of the labor for this industry came from "full-holding" farmers, who already had enough land to support a family, and their dependent cottagers. The large-holding patrons continued to control the right of these cottagers to form families, and they did not want too many of them. Population grew, but not at the booming pace that Schlumbohm, in his earlier writings, associated with proto-industrialization.[196] Looking at eastern Europe in general circa 1800, Werner Rosener estimates that 10–15 percent of the rural population were household servants on large estates who were generally unable to form families.[197] In Austria-Hungary it was not until 1781 that peasants could marry without lordly interference.[198]

This kind of regime also kept immigration to the east low, even when land was relatively uncrowded. There were colonization schemes—especially in Prussia, where perhaps as many as 300,000 colonists were brought in to drain and occupy wetlands, but also in parts of Galicia, Lithuania, and Russia. To secure these new tenants, rulers usually had to assure them of their personal freedom and grant them hereditary rights to their farms and various exemp-

[193] Hagen 1986a: 73–90.   [194] Rosener 1994: 113.   [195] Hagen 1986a: 88.
[196] Hagen 1997.   [197] Rosener 1994: 154.   [198] Good 1984: 34.

tions from the usual dues.[199] But these were exceptional arrangements and involved what had been waste land; the best land drew no migrants, since it was farmed under conditions few Westerners would have agreed to. Moreover, though the wave of (mostly German) emigration to eastern Europe, which dated back to the twelfth century, continued into the eighteenth century, it came to have less and less influence on local conditions. Earlier emigrants had brought both new farming techniques and ideas about the rights of cultivators, which influenced their Slavic neighbors in Prussia, Bohemia, and parts of Poland, but the eighteenth-century migrants to points further east (mostly Bukovina and Russia) had little impact: they were too few relative to the surrounding population and too isolated.[200] Thus, just when demographic trends in western Europe would lead us to expect more people (and with them ideas) to move east, the flow instead dwindled.

Thus the institutional forces slowing any trends toward population growth, proto-industrialization, and a turn away from exports were far stronger in eastern Europe than in Japan's peripheries, and far, far stronger than in the Chinese interior. The chance for western Europe to perpetually trade manufactures for primary products here was correspondingly enhanced. We get some sense of the trans-European differences in purchasing power, resources, and opportunity costs when we consider that Baltic timber reaching English dockyards cost about twenty times what it cost on the stump, without any further processing; the very limited and imprecise data I have for wood prices in Jiangnan and remote Chinese hinterlands suggests a ratio of more like ten to one.[201]

But this kind of trading partner posed different problems for western Europe. First, institutional rigidities limited eastern Europe's ability to increase output. Second, it was not much of a market for manufactures, which limited western Europe's ability to pay for its primary products. Consequently, bound labor helped stabilize a pattern of east-west exchange in Europe but also kept it on a fairly small scale, one that was increasingly inadequate to western Europe's appetite for land-intensive goods. Let us look first at the obstacles to increasing output and then at the problems resulting from eastern Europe's relatively limited demand for western European goods.

Forced labor tended to be unproductive, and neither lords nor peasants invested much in improvements. It is significant, that when the Junkers began to invest more heavily in capital for their farms, they also began to use more wage labor.[202] It is also worth remembering that the seigneurial systems of eastern Europe (like the much milder ones in much of western Europe) were not only

---

[199] Rosener 1994: 130–32.   [200] Gunst 1989: 63–64.

[201] Albion 1965: 103 versus Li Bozhong 1994b: 93. It should be emphasized, though, that some of the price reports Li quotes are vague, using terms such as "several *taels*" or "several tens of *taels*."

[202] Hagen 1986a: 86–92.

relationships between a lord and individual peasant households, but also between a lord and a village community. As such, they helped reproduce various kinds of common property—woodlands, common pasture, and open fields—on which, as we have seen, it was extremely difficult to make changes. By maintaining this "slack," eastern European institutions may have set aside an exportable grain surplus for the future; but in the shorter run these institutions made it very hard to mobilize this land for grain-growing, regardless of price incentives.[203]

In Germany, as we saw in chapter 2, the end of commonage made massive output increases possible, but only after Napoleon. In the Habsburg lands, where emancipation was slower, so was the decline of fallowing: from 33 percent of land circa 1750 it declined only as far as 25 percent by 1850.[204] The replacement of fallowing with new crop rotations was just beginning in mid-nineteenth-century Poland and Hungary. In fact, even the two-field system was not completely gone from these regions until the mid-nineteenth century, while in Russia, Romania, Bulgaria, and Serbia it persisted, well beyond the introduction of railroads linking farm areas to ports and the opening of the Bosporus to Russian ships in 1829. In parts of Russia, the two-field system lasted until after the emancipation of the serfs in the 1860s.[205] In general, the further East one got, the slower new techniques were to spread. Thus there were supply-side reasons for grain exports from preemancipation eastern Europe to stagnate at a level far below what was ecologically possible. As we shall now see, there were demand-side problems as well.

Eastern (and far northern) Europe did not buy very many western European manufactures. Most eastern European peasants bought almost no imports, being largely outside the cash economy; townspeople were few, and a relative handful of rich lords did not by themselves create a very large market. In Prussia, at least the "full-holding" peasants seem to have sold enough grain of their own to enable them to buy significant amounts of linen and other manufactured goods; but even in Prussia, such families were greatly outnumbered by poorer "half-holders," cottagers, and servants. In Poland, commoners who could buy much in the way of manufactured goods seem to have been rare indeed.[206] In most of Scandinavia, the farmers and foresters were free, but there just were not enough of them to buy very much; thus opportunities to buy from them were likewise limited.[207] While western Europeans did manage to sell both their own and extra-European luxury goods (Asian spices and silks, and later New World sugar) to the upper class, about one-third of their imports from eastern Europe had to be paid for with silver.[208] And even demand for

[203] Rosener 1994: 172–84.   [204] Good 1984: 70.
[205] Gunst 1989: 76–77.   [206] Hagen forthcoming.
[207] Blum (1961: 132–34) on limits of the money economy in Russia; Jeannin (1969: 94) on Scandinavia; Kindleberger (1990: 58–59) on Norway.
[208] Glamann 1977: 262–63.

silver could easily be glutted in an economy where monetization was limited (as in Russia), or where monetization was occurring, but in a small economy (as in Norway).

Similar demand-side problems dogged western Europe's trade with southeast Asia, though the distances involved would have limited any pre-steamship trade in bulky products anyway.[209] (And here, too, there was much land that later supplied exports going unexploited in the eighteenth century, as we saw in chapter 4.) The trade of China and Japan with southeast Asia presents a more complex picture, with various monetary media flowing in different directions (indicating that arbitrage, rather than the settlement of trade balances, was the principal motivating force)[210] and many Chinese goods being purchased for resale to points further west. Nonetheless, everyone selling to southeast Asia per se seems to have found only a fairly small market, so that a large cargo of any given commodity could easily glut the market in a particular port.[211] Meanwhile the primary products that left south and southeast Asia for China and Japan (Vietnamese and Thai sugar, Indonesian pepper, and so on) had much broader markets and faced no comparable "glut" problem. Indeed, a good deal more of some of these commodities probably could have been sold were it not for restrictions placed on the participants by authorities at both ends of these routes.[212]

Once again, India presents a complex and intermediate picture, on both the import and export sides. In its trade with China, India exported farm products primarily—cotton, indigo, and later opium—and reexported some of the silver it received from further west. From China it received gold and a variety of luxury fabrics (some but not all of which were then reexported). The gold in question certainly had monetary and quasi-monetary uses (jewelry, for instance, was often melted down when needed) but more as a store of value than as a medium of either state payments or (least of all) daily transactions; indeed, much of it probably circulated sufficiently slowly that demand for it could be seen as largely a hoarding rather than a transactions demand. In its trade with China, then, India looks almost like a larger southeast Asia or eastern Europe—which would fit with our earlier observations about how many Indians were still largely outside the cash economy and with an apparently very uneven distribution of income.

But India's eighteenth-century trade with other areas looks very different. Here the exports were much more varied, and by far the largest one—cloth—was a manufactured good. Though the British were beginning to show an interest in India's forests, this was still largely in the form of having ships built at Madras and Bombay. Timber exports still lay in the future, as did the cotton,

[209] Barrett 1990: 250–51.   [210] Von Glahn 1996: 132.

[211] Van Leur 1955: 67, 135–36, 162, 197–200.

[212] Cushman 1975: 105–6, 124, 200–211; Viraphol 1977: 107–21, 181–209.

indigo, and eventually wheat exports of the nineteenth century.[213] It is true, as Charles Kindleberger notes, that India bought few European-made goods in volume other than coins made of New World metals in the eighteenth century; but this often reflected either local competition or transport difficulties rather than an inert economy.[214] Moreover, the coins imported from Europe (and the cowries imported from Oceania) were widely used for ordinary transactions by ordinary people, not just as a store of value for the rich.[215] Various Indian states also imported large amounts of European-made arms and war horses from central Asia and Arabia;[216] these are not consumer goods, but they are further evidence that stereotypes of India as an economy of "hoarders" rather than "spenders" are seriously overdrawn. Thus, India does not seem to have posed the same "small-market problem" for its European trading partners that eastern Europe and Southeast Asia did, but the particular commodities traded did little to meet western Europe's need to trade manufactures for land-intensive products: that pattern of exchange would come later.

Finally, the parts of Africa that traded extensively with early modern Europe present a picture somewhat like that of southeast Asia, though in some ways even less promising as a source of primary products. Here, too, we find a relatively sparse population (though not in some parts of Senegambia) and a social structure in which bound labor played a major role. (Though, like southeast Asia's bound labor, bound Africans were generally freer than eastern European serfs.) Meanwhile, local industries were perfectly capable of meeting the vast majority of local needs, with imports largely confined to luxuries. John Thornton has argued persuasively that the iron that Europeans sold to Africa in the sixteenth and seventeenth centuries cannot have accounted for more than 10–15 percent of iron use, even in the importing coastal regions, while cloth imports cannot have been above 2 percent of those regions' cloth use: what imports there were were probably used mostly as exotica for elite display. Meanwhile, Africa also sold significant amounts of cloth to Europe.[217]

Moreover, since Africa (here unlike southeast Asia) also had large amounts of gold, there was relatively little besides luxury manufactures that Europeans could use to acquire goods here. And Africa's principal primary-product exports—pepper, gold, and ivory—did little to substitute for European land, anyway; it was not until much later that Europeans had the military power (and disease resistance) with which to force Africans to grow what Europe needed.[218]

---

[213] See Wadia (1955) on ships; Rangarajan (1994) on forests; McAlpin and Richards (1983) on cotton acreage and deforestation; Latham and Neal (1983: 271–73) on wheat.

[214] Kindleberger 1990: 68–69; for a list of European goods sold to India, see Chaudhuri 1978: 475–76.

[215] Perlin 1987: 248–314.   [216] Chaudhuri 1990: 278–83.

[217] Thornton 1992: 45–54.   [218] Ibid., 112–25; Crosby 1986: 136–42.

Eventually, of course, one African export did reach a huge scale: slaves. But the growth of the slave trade does not indicate that Europeans could unilaterally shape their trade with Africa, even though from a contemporary standpoint this traffic suggests a relationship of complete dominance. The external slave trade took advantage of the fact that the relevant societies not only allowed a kind of property in people, but did not have private property in land. Thus, ownership of people became a way of storing accumulated wealth,[219] and Europeans who bought slaves were allowing their owners to convert this stored wealth into inanimate (and thus more secure, if less productive) prestige goods: goods that Europe had to continually scramble to find enough of as the slave trade expanded.[220]

To summarize, then, we should avoid projecting back into earlier eras the twentieth-century pattern in which the terms of trade usually favor industrial exporters over raw materials exporters, making "agrarian" almost synonymous with "poor."[221] This pattern only became set once primary-product production itself began to require more manufactured inputs and once even poor people began to purchase many non-farm goods and/or farm goods produced with the aid of industrial inputs. Consequently, "underconsumption" emerges here as a very different phenomenon from the one often presented by scholars (mostly, though not exclusively, Marxists) working on the late nineteenth and twentieth centuries. In most such accounts, inadequate demand is seen as a problem of core areas, created when the huge leaps in productivity made possible by mechanization far exceeded the purchasing power of poorly paid workers; thus, some have argued, the need for additional markets motivated a new, peculiarly capitalist wave of *late* nineteenth-century imperialism. Here, however, underconsumption emerges as a problem created by social structure and demographic conditions in some preindustrial peripheries themselves (which is why *they* exported more than they imported) and is seen to have hampered the efforts of preindustrial cores (which were short of certain supplies, not of consumers) to obtain the land-intensive goods they needed.

For western Europe in particular, eastern Europe represented a peripheral trading partner that was *ecologically* capable of exporting vast quantities of grain, wood, and other land-intensive products. And thanks to institutional rigidities, that capacity was not being diverted to internal growth at the same

---

[219] Thornton 1992: 85–90.

[220] On the difficulties in procuring enough Indian cloth for this trade (which helped spur the English cotton boom), see Hobsbawm 1975: 57–58; Chaudhuri 1978: 273–75.

[221] One finds this assumption most fully elaborated in dependency and world systems analyses, which emphasize how infrequently countries that have become part of the world economy's periphery have been able to close the gap with the core. However, the same assumptions also underlay a variety of development projects and perspectives that emphasized the need to move resources out of agriculture and build an industrial base as quickly as possible, even when the latter theories, unlike the former, often praised in principle the effects of participation in global markets.

rate as in east Asian peripheries. But the same rigidities meant that eastern Europe's trade with western Europe peaked rather quickly and at levels that, as we have already seen, were minor compared with the long-distance flows of grain, timber, and fertilizer in China.[222] The relatively restrained cutting of abundant Baltic timber, despite strong demand, rising prices, and generally good water transport, is also striking. We lack the data to do a quantitative comparison with China's lumber trade, but Baltic lumbering seems to have been much more restrained than timber-cutting in, for instance, eighteenth-century New England and Canada, which had few other exports and imported most of their manufactures. It certainly pales next to nineteenth-century lumbering.[223]

World-systems theorists generally see these exchanges between "feudal" eastern and "capitalist" western Europe[224] as a transformative moment, from which a global division of labor unfolded. What we have seen here, however, is that those exchanges were not unusual in kind or in scale and that there were crucial built-in limits on their growth: limits that were also limits on western Europe's ability to expand its stock of food, fuel, fiber, and building supplies through these exchanges. Merely finding "less-advanced" trading partners did not solve any core's problems, at least not for long.

In the late nineteenth century, it may have become an advantage for western Europe that eastern Europe had not undergone massive population growth (either by natural increase or by immigration[225]) and import substitution at an earlier date, the way the Chinese interior and Japan's "Region II" had. This had the effect of leaving more of eastern Europe's land-intensive products available for export in an era in which the massive capitalization of production and productivity increases of the Industrial Revolution had made both the Habsburg lands and Russia places where one could sell everything from cloth to rolling stock. Thus here, too, Europe (if considered as a whole) may eventually have reaped certain "advantages of backwardness" that resulted from institu-

---

[222] See pp. 34–35, 226 above.

[223] Lower (1973: 22, 31–32) and McCusker and Menard (1985) on the late eighteenth-century Baltic, New England, and Canada; on nineteenth century, see Lower 1973: 59–134; Tucker and Richards 1983: xii–xvii.

[224] Wallerstein 1974: 71–89.

[225] In the case of immigration, we have another way in which the existence of multiple states maintaining multiple social systems mattered to Europe—but again by impeding short-term efficiency, not by pressing the race for it forward. Certain czars might occasionally lure Germans to their country by making special promises, but given the legal status of most Russian land and cultivators, even the Black Earth belt would not lure people from overcrowded Westphalia or East Anglia the way that Sichuan or the Jiangxi highlands lured Fujianese, or Manchuria the Shandongese. Instead, these people stayed where they were until the New World attracted them—at the cost of a *temporary* loss of freedom if they went in the seventeenth or eighteenth century, but for the much smaller and rapidly falling cost of a place in steerage if they went in the nineteenth or early twentieth century.

tional barriers to more intensive use of the land at an earlier date. But those advantages could not yet be reaped in the technological and institutional climate of the eighteenth or early nineteenth century. At that point, when emancipation and the parceling out of the commons were just starting to spread across central and eastern Europe, ordinary people in much of eastern Europe still bought very few manufactures, and expensive capital goods were still rare. Consequently, trade between eastern and western Europe circa 1800 remained where it had been since the mid-seventeenth century, which was far short of meeting the west's needs. Thus, in 1800, the ecological pressures described earlier in this chapter remained unresolved for western Europe, as they did for China and Japan. Those pressures could have either stopped growth altogether or forced it down a more labor-intensive, "east Asian" (or perhaps "Danish") path that involved no dramatic breakthrough. Eventually, the ecological "advantages of backwardness" discussed here made a major difference, but they took time to become available.

In the interim, the coal breakthrough provided one important form of ecological relief—but even that was not enough, given the variety of land-intensive products required. If western Europe was to undergo a large further increase in its industrial production and primary-product consumption beyond the levels of the mid-eighteenth century—even a total increase, much less a per capita one—it would need a new kind of trading partner. And that, as we shall see, was uniquely possible in the New World.

SIX

ABOLISHING THE LAND CONSTRAINT:

THE AMERICAS AS A NEW KIND

OF PERIPHERY

ONE CORE, western Europe, was able to escape the proto-industrial cul de sac and transfer handicraft workers into modern industries as the technology became available. It could do this, in large part, because the exploitation of the New World made it unnecessary to mobilize the huge numbers of additional workers who would have been needed to use Europe's own land in much more intensive and ecologically sustainable ways—if even that could have provided enough primary products to keep ahead of nineteenth-century population growth. The New World yielded both "real resources" and precious metals, which require separate treatment. Let us begin with real resources; they, in turn, begin with plantation products from the Caribbean, northeastern Brazil, and later the southern United States.

The New World's farm exports were largely slave grown. The plantations were almost all either on islands or near the coast. Consequently, exports from the circum-Caribbean plantation zone did not plateau the way that exports from the Chinese interior to Jiangnan and Lingnan did when free laborers ran into diminishing returns and switched more of their efforts to handicrafts; nor were they beset by the soaring transport costs that Old World foresters faced once they moved away from the riverbanks. And because the proprietors of New World plantations (unlike those of eastern European estates or southeast Asian pepper fields) purchased most of their labor force from abroad and often curtailed their subsistence production, western Europe's trade with this area also escaped the "small-market problem" that had dogged its trade for eastern European raw materials. Exports had to be high enough to cover the costs of buying slaves and much of the cost of feeding and clothing them.

There were many reasons why African slaves became the principal workforce in so many New World colonies. First and foremost are the astonishing death rates among New World peoples after contact, mostly from disease. Few of Europe's poor, as we have seen, could pay their own passage before 1800, and they were only worth transporting if one could force them to produce exports. With outright enslavement of Europeans unacceptable, this meant indentures that would end with freedom and a grant of land. As survival rates for Europeans (and Africans) in the New World began to improve, this became too expensive for most plantation owners; they preferred to pay more money up front and get a slave who never had to be freed.[1] The surviving New World peoples were sometimes enslaved (especially in Brazil), but Africans were preferred for several reasons. New World peoples were seen as fragile because so many died upon contact with Europeans; and at least some Europeans opposed their enslavement on humanitarian grounds (but not that of Africans).[2] Amerindians also would have found it much easier to flee and to make common cause with unconquered native peoples nearby (though Africans sometimes did this, too). And since the conquest of native peoples slowed down considerably after the first half century (once smallpox had done its worst damage and various indigenous peoples had acquired guns and horses), acquiring indigenous slaves was not always easy.[3] By contrast, the large internal slave trade in Africa made it relatively easy for Europeans to acquire slaves there, as long as they had goods that the slaveholders wanted. Meanwhile, the Spanish and the Portuguese crowns preferred the transatlantic slave trade to New World slave-raiding, because the former was much easier to monitor and tax than local slave-raiding.[4] This was yet another way in which interstate competition and military fiscalism indirectly helped accelerate the repopulation of the New World from overseas and helped place the settlers in a context in which they (unlike, say, settlers on the Chinese frontier) would find it hard to switch away from a focus on export production. The slaves had no choice at all, and even their owners may have had little choice, since they (unlike a hypothetical group raiding locally for slaves) had to pay for their purchased workforce.

Slave imports to the British West Indies equaled roughly one-fourth of sugar export revenues between 1760 and 1810; imports from Britain itself covered about one-half, and food and wood from British North America (above and beyond the amounts swapped directly for sugar) covered the remaining quarter.[5] French Caribbean sugar exports were about 15 percent below those of Britain just before the French and Haitian Revolutions, and its slave imports were almost identical to those for the British Caribbean throughout the eighteenth century: so here slave imports should have covered roughly 30 percent of sugar revenue.[6] And in Brazil, the world's largest slave importer, the prices paid for imported slaves in 1821–26 (the first set of several consecutive years for which I found figures) equaled the country's total export

---

[1] Galenson 1989: 52, 76; Morgan 1975: 215–16, 296–99.

[2] Thornton 1992: 135–36.

[3] Ibid., 138–41.

[4] Ibid., 136–37.

[5] Calculations based on slave prices from Miller 1986: 70; British import data based on Mitchell 1988: 462–64 and Deerr 1949–50: 1: See also appendix D.

[6] For export volumes, see Deerr on the British Caribbean (1949–50: I: 193–203) and the French Caribbean (I: 235–42); for slave imports, see Curtin 1969: 216.

revenues for those years.[7] Since the 1820s saw an unusually high volume of high-priced slave imports, this is no doubt atypical: the late eighteenth-century average was probably closer to one-fourth the value of all exports, much as in the British and French West Indies.[8] Thus, the slave trade helped make Euro-American trade fundamentally different and more expandable than the more direct exchanges of raw materials for manufactured goods and silver between Old World cores and peripheries.

Furthermore, though nearly all bound cash-crop producers in the Old World also grew what was needed for their subsistence, many New World slaves had little or no opportunity for subsistence farming. And since for a long time plantation owners purchased very few women slaves (and manumitted more of them than they did men), many slaves also lacked families, who helped supply the subsistence needs of compulsory cash-crop workers in many Old World settings.[9] Thus, despite their poverty, the everyday needs of slaves created a significant market for imports; in this, slaves were unlike most of the unfree populations in Old World peripheries. These goods (above all cheap cotton cloth for slaves to wear) were a large part of the manufactured imports that took up almost 50 percent of sugar export proceeds in the British Caribbean. Some of these goods were always made in Europe; others came at first from India via Europe but were later replaced by British imitations.

Grain and wood from British North America (above and beyond an unknown amount obtained in direct barter for sugar) took up the remaining one-quarter of Caribbean sugar revenue. And since this trade enabled the mainland to pay for its own imports of British manufactures,[10] it represented an indirect route through which Britain turned still more of its relatively abundant capital and labor into land-saving imports. Slave plantations in Brazil and British North America acquired more of their supplies locally than those in the Caribbean, and Brazilian plantations in particular also economized by providing exceptionally skimpy food and clothing to their slaves;[11] thus they purchased less from abroad, but these needs were still non-trivial.[12] Moreover, the Brazilian strategies that limited supply purchases—from skimpy diets to unbalanced sex ratios—increased the need to replenish the supply of slaves themselves with fresh purchases from Africa.

[7] Figures for 1821–26 from Miller (1986: 70) and Ludwig (1985: 107, 314), using a rough price of 250,000 *reis* per slave (toward the low end of Miller's range); calculation methods the same as for West Indies.

[8] For slave purchases and prices, see Miller 1986: 70; Ludwig 1985: 107, 314; Curtin 1969: 216. Brazilian export figures for 1796 and 1806 from Morineau 1985: 177–78.

[9] See, e.g., Schwartz (1985: 354–58, 385) on sex ratios and marriage rates in Brazil.

[10] See Shepherd and Walton 1972: 43–44; Richardson 1987: 765–66.

[11] See, e.g., Schwartz (1985: 136–38, 296, 436, 441–42) on Brazil.

[12] See, e.g., Subrahmanyam (1993: 182–85 on the cheapest cloth being shipped to Brazil for slave clothing.

Thus, slavery helped make Euro-American trade unlike any between Old World cores and peripheries. A free-labor periphery like southwest China would not have served Europe as well, even if it had been just as ecologically bountiful; nor would a periphery like eastern Europe (or later Java) in which participants in a still-functioning subsistence-oriented economy were forced into part-time export production. Silver exports from Potosi, which fell as the native population recovered and a more self-sufficient regional economy reemerged,[13] remind us that European demand alone did not ensure a continued flow of a commodity to Europe without either massive force or the *reproduction* of local needs for European goods. We will return to silver shortly. What needs emphasizing here is that it was not only ecology that made so much sugar, tobacco, and later cotton flow from the circum-Caribbean region: the region was also sociologically and politically set up to "need" almost everything else. Indeed, one of Britain's advantages was that unlike France, Holland, or Denmark, it did not need to ship *food* from Europe to its sugar colonies but could rely on continental North America to do so, which in turn bought English manufactures (employing labor and capital rather than land).

Thus, a combination of depopulation and repopulation with slaves made the circum-Caribbean region a perversely large market for imports and a source of land-intensive exports. In fact, it became the first periphery to assume a now familiar "Third World" profile: that of a large importer of both capital goods (in this case, walking, talking, kidnaped ones) and manufactured goods for daily use, with exports that kept falling in price as production became more efficient, capital intensive, and widespread. By contrast, the prices of most forms of energy produced in Europe, including food, rose throughout the eighteenth century, relative to both wages and other goods.[14] Thus the plantation areas of the New World were a new kind of periphery: one that would import enough to keep its trade with the core fairly balanced. Moreover, its imports and exports stimulated each other: more sugar exports consistently led to more slave imports, more food and clothing imports, and (often) more plantation debt, which led to selling more sugar next year, at whatever price.[15]

Meanwhile, concentration on one or two exports in most plantation areas greatly facilitated a crucial improvement in trade itself. Transatlantic shipping costs fell roughly 50 percent during the eighteenth century, even without substantial technological change. Part of the decline was due to political change:

[13] Lang 1975: 61, 65–66. See also Stern (1988) for a more general discussion of the reemergence of economies with a significant degree of internal coherence and autonomy in the Spanish-ruled New World.

[14] See, for instance, the chart in Goldstone 1991: 186; also Thomas 1985a: 140–41.

[15] Richardson (1987: 745–46) shows a direct relationship between the exports of sugar from the British West Indies in any given year and the area's demand for slaves in the following year, which in turn produced more sugar.

the British Navy repressed most piracy, which reduced insurance rates and allowed more freight to travel on unarmed ships with smaller crews.[16] However, the other major component (briefly discussed in chapter 4) was a sharp decline in the time spent acquiring cargo. This meant a faster turnover of working capital, more intensive use of ships, and large savings in sailors' wages (who had to be paid for every day away from home, even if they were waiting in port while a cargo was purchased). This reduction in port time was achieved by having a local agent collect the desired goods in a warehouse before the ship arrived, rather than having the ship visit many plantations and spend time haggling. Such delegation of responsibility was much easier when each area only sold one or two exports, rather than the numerous possibilities in, say, an Indian Ocean port.[17]

Thus, while seeking more primary products from many Old World peripheries meant exhausting the most accessible sources, facing higher transport costs, and working against the logic of import substitution, an opposite dynamic was at work in much of the New World. With political and sociological factors working against import substitution, export monocultures brought down transatlantic transport and transaction costs. This in turn allowed Americans to incur higher local transport costs—i.e., expand further inland—and still sell enough in Europe to pay for manufactures and repay start-up costs. This dynamic operated whether the labor in question was slave, indentured, or free but in need of start-up money, and it played a crucial role in populating North America.[18] It also helped the transatlantic exchange of manufactured goods (and kidnaped "capital goods") keep expanding, unlike the Baltic trade or the trade from the Chinese interior.

In other words, a demographic catastrophe, colonial legislation, and slavery combined to create a periphery that was an ever-expanding source of raw materials in an era before most production required expensive capital goods and when most people still had some connection to subsistence production. Indeed, this situation proved temporary even in much of the New World; as population levels recovered in Peru and Mexico, more self-sufficient economies reemerged and exports fell.[19] Without the peculiar conditions created in the circum-Caribbean region, the mere existence of trade between a rich, free labor core and a poorer, bound labor periphery would not have had such epochal effects; western Europe's trade with eastern Europe, for instance, was in no way more important or dynamic than that between the Lower Yangzi and its various free labor peripheries. The form of labor control on the periphery was indeed crucial, as world-systems theorists insist, but we oversimplify

[16] Shepherd and Walton 1972: 81–84.

[17] Ibid., 52–53, 87. On the enormous diversity of cargo carried on any given merchant ship in the Indian Ocean, see Van Leur 1955: 132, 253; Chaudhuri 1978: 204–8.

[18] Shepherd and Walton 1972; especially McCusker and Menard 1985: 18, 23, 28–30.

[19] Lang 1975: 61, 65–66.

greatly if we lump together all kinds of "coerced cash-crop producers." New World slavery and colonialism were different in very important ways.

Earlier arguments about the importance of slavery in European (especially British) industrial growth have often focused on export markets as a stimulus for burgeoning industries; they have thus been vulnerable to the "internalist" argument that domestic markets were growing, too, and off a much larger base. Such debates may be inherently inconclusive—if Caribbean demand accounted for 12 percent of the growth of British industrial output between 1748 and 1776,[20] is the proverbial glass half full or half empty? By contrast, the argument here emphasizes that some markets mattered more than others. For the New World and the slave trade offered what an expanding home market could not have: ways in which manufactured goods created without much use of British land could be turned into ever-increasing amounts of land-intensive food and fiber (and later timber) at reasonable (and even falling) prices.

Another New World, Another Windfall: Precious Metals

Meanwhile, Mexico, Peru, and later Brazil sent Europe vast amounts of precious metals. Some of this was the direct result of colonial extraction, such as the Spanish and Portuguese kings' cut of all mining in their domains. Legally, this share was at least 27.5 percent—and perhaps as much as 40 percent—of all shipments prior to 1640.[21] Since these rates quickly led to widespread smuggling, the crown's actual share of output was never that high, and the legal rates were gradually lowered to try to reduce contraband; even so, the crown probably received one-tenth to one-fifth of registered output.[22]

A substantial further portion of the flow was only slightly less directly based on coercion. Forced labor quotas lowered the costs of mining, whether indigenous people actually did the labor themselves or bought their way out of it, subsidizing the wages of others.[23] While the direct beneficiaries of these quotas were mining entrepreneurs resident in the New World, they clearly increased the output possible at any given price; and since many people—from big and medium-sized mine operators to "sharecropping" miners themselves—had gold and silver to sell,[24] they could not keep from passing along these savings to European buyers. Meanwhile, colonial legislation greatly reduced competition among those bringing European and Asian goods to exchange for precious metals—and at least attempted to restrict production of local alternatives to these imports. Thus both the scale of this trade and the prices at which it

[20] Richardson 1987: 768.
[21] Hamilton 1934; Flynn and Giraldez 1996: 321–29.
[22] Morineau 1985: 102, 121, 289.
[23] Stern 1988: 849–52; Tandeter 1993: 15–85.
[24] Stern 1988: 852–54.

occurred were distorted, making some unknown further portion of gold and silver exports a "gift" to Europe.

Some of this "gift" stayed in western Europe. Those metals probably did little for Europe's economic development, since they financed numerous wars, including Spain's nearly successful assaults on the emerging core economies of northwest Europe.[25] Nonetheless, the metals may have helped grease the wheels of European trade, and they certainly played a role in the growth of more effective militaries. Meanwhile, much New World treasure went further east, bringing other commodities to Europe. It can be roughly divided into three separate streams.

One substantial stream of New World gold and silver exports went to various ecologically rich small market zones in the Old World—from Southeast Asia to parts of the Near East to eastern Europe—making it possible for Europe to expand its imports of real resources from these peripheries. In these cases, silver or (less often) gold were used like modern currency reserves: they were a residual store of value transferred to cover an otherwise unbalanced trade with areas that had limited demand for the goods Europe sold. But one could also see these metals, which were usually coined before transshipment from Europe, as the one European manufactured good for which these zones had fairly large markets and (lacking the proper raw materials) limited local production.[26] In economies that were monetizing rapidly (e.g., much of Scandinavia), this manufactured good was at least partially an item of popular use; in the least marketized peripheries, such as eastern Europe, it was essentially a luxury good. Either way, it made it possible to obtain more primary products from these areas than would have been possible otherwise.

But, since precious metals do not wear out or get used up (unlike cloth, or grain), it was hard to create an *expanding* (or perhaps even enduring) market for them if only a tiny part of the society used them. True, wealthy people could add to their silver or jewelry hoards; but at some point they had enough for all conceivable obligations, and silver as a form of conspicuous consumption must have begun to lose value relative to silk, porcelain, paintings, and so on. Thus, New World silver helped western Europe obtain more raw materials than they could have had the fifteenth-century "bullion famine" continued,[27] but could not by itself indefinitely expand western Europe's trade with less-monetized Old World economies.

The second stream also helped Europe obtain land-intensive goods, but less directly. This flow was exchanged for various Asian (mostly Indian) manufac-

[25] Flynn 1984: 43.

[26] Perlin (1994: 113–18, 147–74) emphasizes the point that coins in this period are often more usefully thought of as a manufactured good than as "money" that stands opposed to "goods." Perlin (1991: 239–373, esp. 248–49, 268–80) examines the production of coins as goods often designed for remote target markets.

[27] Day 1978: 3–54.

tured products, which then covered much of the cost of procuring slaves for the Americas. Indian cloth alone made up roughly one-third of all the cargo by value exchanged by English traders for African slaves in the eighteenth century and may have made up over half of the goods that French traders (whose industries were slower to produce good imitations of Indian fabrics) used to acquire slaves.[28] Much Portuguese imperial trade went directly from Asia to Africa to Brazil, stopping in the mother country only to deliver New World goods.[29] In other words, this portion of the metals flow facilitated the process we have already described, in which New World slave areas became an important complement to labor and capital rich, land-poor Europe.

In India, as we have seen, there is a strong case for seeing much of the flow of gold and silver coins as meeting a broadly based transactions demand, rather than as a store of wealth that covered a "trade deficit." But despite impressive evidence of ongoing monetization in India, it does not necessarily follow that in the absence of New World metals, India would simply have imported more of other Euro-American goods. Much of the population still only entered the market to obtain a few necessities, meet occasional ceremonial expenses (e.g., for weddings), and raise cash to pay taxes and other dues; and to the extent that they did purchase other goods, it is not clear that European manufactures would have been competitive. And the greater prestige of Chinese fabrics and ceramics, Southeast Asian delicacies, and specifically Islamic goods from the Middle East meant that European luxury goods would not have found a large market either. So even if we treat precious metals flowing to India as just another product, they were probably special in another sense: they were about the only European good that one could imagine India buying on such a huge scale. (The one possible alternative that comes to mind is arms; it is unclear what effect a large further increase in this already substantial trade might have had in the period spanning Mogul decline and British ascendancy.)

Finally, the third stream of metals was for decades the largest of all; but this flow of silver probably did the least to ease pressures on Europe's land. It went to densely populated, heavily commercialized parts of Asia, where it was used as a medium for transactions involving every class in society; and in return, various consumer goods flowed to Europe and to the Americas themselves. This description, as we have seen, may fit some of the Indian trade, but it refers above all to the enormous flow of silver to China, where millions of ordinary people used silver to pay their taxes and for many ordinary purchases.

Here silver was clearly a good, not residual wealth used to settle unbalanced accounts. Indeed, while silver flowed into China between 1500 and 1640, gold and copper left China, often ending up in Europe.[30] And though silk, the most

[28] H. Klein 1990: 291.

[29] Subrahmanyam 1993: 183–85.

[30] Flynn and Giraldez 1997: xxvii; Von Glahn 1996: 129–33, 224–29.

important "real good" among China's exports, was a fabric rather than a metal, it, too, was used as money in some places. Thus, New World silver in this trade was just one of many goods being arbitraged: items that were more plentiful in China than elsewhere (gold, porcelain, silk) were exchanged for silver, which was comparatively scarce in China[31] but in very high demand as it became the monetary and fiscal base of the world's largest economy.[32] By about 1640, this trade had brought silver to gold ratios in China and Europe into rough equilibrium; thus, having lost its raison d'être, this trade went into a sharp decline, recovering only in the eighteenth century.[33] In its first incarnation, the trade did little to supply land-intensive commodities to Europe. It had, however, been enormously profitable and yielded goods that (unlike more and more silver) could be used to make exchanges elsewhere.

In China, as in India, it may be difficult to imagine another good that would have been imported on such a massive scale had silver not been available. Thus in this case, too, New World mines were important to Europe's capacity to obtain goods in the rest of the Old World. But the Chinese case differs from the Indian one, from the importer's side, in that it is far harder to see much of the silver it imported as nonessential; thus, in the absence of that flow, we must imagine either other imports of monetary media or a large reallocation of China's own productive resources, perhaps in turn expanding demand for other imports. From the European side, meanwhile, the difference between this flow of metals and that which went to India is that this one did relatively little, even indirectly, to ease pressure on the land.

These distinctions among various uses of New World treasure are post hoc and highly imperfect, and the association of different uses with different final destinations for the metals must be seen as tendencies, not absolute rules. Even in eastern Europe—perhaps the periphery in which the general population was the least involved in the cash economy—not all imported metals represent abstract "wealth" hoarded by the elite in a stagnant economy. At the other end of the scale, there was surely some hoarding of silver even in China. What we need to recognize is that some of this behavior went on everywhere; there are no grounds for the sharp distinction some scholars have seen between western "spenders" and Asian "hoarders."[34] Moreover, the line between hoarding and transactions demand was itself vague in a world in which ordinary people did not have savings accounts, and in which jewelry and other items of display were often a crucial part of securing the marriages that reproduced productive units.

[31] For data on gold/silver ratios in different places, see Von Glahn 1996: 127.

[32] Flynn and Giraldez 1997: xix.

[33] Von Glahn 1996: 128, 232.

[34] For a recent restatement of this alleged difference and its enduring importance, see Kindleberger 1990.

But despite the approximate and fluid nature of these categories, they do show us something: New World metals were not simply "money" that Europeans turned into "real" resources by distributing them around the Old World, with European needs always driving the story. The internal dynamics of other regions could create "needs" no less real than those of Europe, such as China's need for a more usable currency, or the desire of eastern European elites to turn their grain surpluses into something easily stored and shipped and thus usable for provisioning their troops on campaign.[35] It was the *intersection* of European and other regional dynamics that determined the extent and nature of these metals' flows: the world economy remained polycentric, and forces emanating from elsewhere could shape it just as much as those emanating from Europe.

Indeed, as we saw in chapter 4, had China in particular not had such a dynamic economy that changing its metallic base could absorb the staggering quantities of silver mined in the New World over three centuries, those mines might have become unprofitable within a few decades. The massive inflation of silver-denominated prices in Europe from 1500 to 1640 indicates a shrinking value for the metal there even with Asia draining off much of the supply,[36] and the less-monetized parts of the Old World would not have indefinitely kept absorbing precious metals without also devaluing them. This is one more way in which early modern silver and gold were not quite like contemporary "money": today those who have hard currency to spend will never have trouble obtaining more resources, since contemporary peripheries have staggeringly large needs for capital.

Nonetheless, the transshipment of New World metals did allow western Europe to expand its imports of real resources far beyond what it could have obtained otherwise. Some New World silver may have had to have been converted to cloth, porcelain, or spices to keep expanding the flow of resources from some of the less-monetized Old World peripheries; but thanks to Chinese demand, this option was available, too. And as we have already noted, the combination of New World metals themselves, transshipped Asian goods that had often been obtained with silver, and exotica from the New World itself (such as sugar and tobacco) paid for more of western Europe's imports from the rest of the Old World than did manufactures created wholly within Europe.

Thus the distinction that some authors make between bullion extracted through coercion and a far more important flow of real resources obtained through consensual trade seems artificial.[37] Not only were the land and labor that produced New World resource exports very much the fruits of extra-market coercion, but it took the unique arrangements of Caribbean plantations

[35] Blum 1961: 201–4.
[36] Hamilton 1934; Flynn and Giraldez 1996: 323–29.
[37] See, e.g., Jones 1981: 83–84.

and of mercantilist policies throughout the New World to escape all the forces that caused core-periphery exchange within the Old World to plateau. Without these features, and without silver that helped pay for colonial administration and provided for Asian goods to be transshipped to Africa and the Americas, it is hard to see how the "ecological windfall" could have found its way to Europe in such quantities; nor is it clear how Europe could have obtained as much ecological relief from the rest of the Old World as it did.

Some Measurements of Ecological Relief: Britain in the Age of the Industrial Revolution

The quantities involved were vast,[38] but to discuss them usefully they must be broken down a bit. For argument's sake, let us eliminate goods that could have been obtained from Old World peripheries without major institutional changes (e.g., furs, which Russia presumably could have exported in larger amounts) and gains from Old World adoptions of New World plants such as the potato (without which neither Ireland nor Prussia could have exported grain to England). The New World's huge fisheries, for which North American landfalls were convenient but not essential, are also best left out. These belong to the New World windfall in some loose sense, but if we cast our net too widely, we are simply counting traffic across the Atlantic rather than showing that these exchanges (much less any particular mechanism behind them) were essential. So for the eighteenth and early nineteenth centuries, the discussion will focus almost exclusively on sugar and cotton, with some reflections on the larger torrent of primary products that came from the Americas in the mid- and late nineteenth centuries.

Mintz estimates that sugar made up roughly 2 percent of Britain's caloric intake by 1800, and a stunning 14 percent by 1900.[39] In fact, the real figures would appear to be even higher. Using the same estimates of per capita sugar consumption as Mintz does, and the same conversion into calories, the per-person, per-day consumption of sugar for the United Kingdom (including Ireland) comes to over 90 calories in 1800. If the average Briton consumed 2,500 calories per day in 1800 (a generous estimate),[40] then 90 calories is almost 4 percent of total intake even at that early date; the average 1901 sugar intake

---

[38] For methods of calculation throughout this section, see appendix D.

[39] Mintz 1985: 133.

[40] Clark, Huberman, and Lindert (1995: 223) assemble various surveys of per capita consumption in workers' households and come up with estimates as low as 1,500 calories *per adult male equivalent* (for a sample of the rural poor in 1787–96) and as high as 2,400 (for urban workers in 1863 and 1889–90), plus one estimate of 3,200 for rural workers in the 1860s; but even the latter figure would translate into less than 2,500 calories per person.

would have yielded over 18 percent of total calories if people really averaged 2,500 calories per day, and over 22 percent if they averaged a more likely 2,000. And although today sugar is often derided as a source of "junk" calories, it can be valuable in poorer diets, preventing scarce protein from being burned for energy.[41]

The 4 percent figure for 1800 may seem modest, but it is worth recalling that an acre of tropical sugar land yields as many calories as more than 4 acres of potatoes (which most eighteenth-century Europeans scorned[42]), or 9–12 acres of wheat.[43] The calories from the sugar consumed in the United Kingdom circa 1800 (using figures from Mintz[44]) would have required at least 1,300,000 acres of average-yielding English farms and conceivably over 1,900,000; in 1831, 1,900,000 to 2,600,000 acres would have been needed. And since the land that remained uncultivated in Europe (and especially in Britain) by this time was hardly the continent's best, we could plausibly make these numbers still larger.

Dried meat, plus ships, wood-based naval stores, and small amounts of timber and grain spared some land in the late eighteenth century and a good deal in the early nineteenth century. North American timber exports to Britain, for instance, were trivial before 1800 (though exports to southern Europe were not); but by 1825, they were large enough to replace the output of over 1,000,000 acres of European forest and soared thereafter.[45] Some savings also came indirectly, as New World silver and reexports paid for much of Britain's Baltic timber imports (which replaced the output of about 650,000 acres per year in the 1780s and 1790s). Given that the total arable land of Britain was roughly 17,000,000 acres,[46] the 3,000,000–4,000,000 New World "ghost acres" found so far are a non-trivial addition to Britain's land base, even without cotton—and before the much, much larger boom in American imports in the mid-nineteenth century.

By 1815, Britain imported over 100,000,000 pounds of New World cotton; by 1830, 263,000,000 pounds.[47] If one replaced this fiber with an equivalent weight of hemp or flax, the extra acreage needed would be comparatively

[41] Daniels 1996: 277.

[42] Braudel 1981: 170; Salaman 1949: 479–84.

[43] Mintz 1985: 191.

[44] Mintz refers here to "Britain," but since his figures match those both Deerr and Mitchell provide for the U.K., he probably meant the U.K. as well; for his purposes, it would make little difference. And since, as we have seen, England from 1770 on drew heavily on food supplies from Wales, Scotland, and Ireland—supplies that would have been reduced had those places not had some other way to meet minimum caloric needs—the U.K. figures are what we need to use for estimating the Caribbean contribution to feeding industrializing England.

[45] For methods of calculation, see appendix D; export figures from Lower 1973: 259.

[46] Mitchell 1988: 186. The figure is actually for a later date (1867), but it is the earliest one available and seems to have been fairly stable at that point.

[47] Mann 1860: 112.

modest: 200,000 acres in 1815, 500,000 in 1830. But hemp and flax—especially hemp—were both considered inferior fibers for most purposes, were much more difficult to work with, and processes for spinning them mechanically emerged later than that for cotton.[48] More important, both hemp and flax were extremely labor-intensive and manure-intensive crops: so much so that most people only grew them as garden crops. Even three centuries of government schemes and subsidies had failed to promote larger-scale production in either England or North America.[49]

This leaves wool, long Europe's main clothing fiber. But raising enough sheep to replace the yarn made with Britain's New World cotton imports by would have required staggering quantities of land: almost 9,000,000 acres in 1815, using ratios from model farms, and over 23,000,000 acres in 1830. This final figure surpasses Britain's total crop and pasture land combined. It also surpasses Anthony Wrigley's estimate that matching the annual energy output of Britain's coal industry circa 1815 would have required that the country magically receive 15,000,000 additional acres of forest.[50] If we add cotton, sugar, and timber circa 1830, we have somewhere between 25,000,000 and 30,000,000 ghost acres, exceeding even the contribution of coal by a healthy margin.

Extracontinental imports also reduced per capita food needs by changing habits, as discussed in chapter 5; this might increase our land-savings calculation significantly, but it is probably uncountable. Cheaper home heating was, of course, largely attributed to the surge in coal output. But having far more people work indoors—rather than following the "Jiangnan" or even the "Danish" route to ecological survival—was crucially dependent on *both* cheap coal-based energy and overseas supplies of cotton, grain, and other land-intensive imports; and indoor laborers appear to have consumed about one-third fewer calories per capita than outdoor ones.[51] The unprecedented amounts of cheap cloth that helped preserve warmth and further reduced caloric needs was unimaginable without American cotton. And insofar as caloric needs were also reduced by the appetite-suppressing qualities of tea and sugar, this was another hidden savings achieved in part through coercion abroad. Most sugar came from New World plantations, while tea was paid for first with New World silver and then with Indian opium. These factors together would

---

[48] Mokyr 1990: 103.

[49] See Warden (1967: 32–40) on England and its colonies.

[50] Wrigley 1988: 54–55. Wrigley actually makes "the death of George III (1820)" his cut-off date, but according to the coal production statistics in Mitchell (1988: 247) it would be 1815 when production actually reached the requisite 15,000,000 tons. More important, Wrigley's estimate that an acre of woodland produced two tons of dry wood a year is, as he notes, probably generous, and biases his estimate of coal's impact downward. Were he to use the contemporary global mean as Smil does (1983: 36) and as I have elsewhere, his estimate of the impact of coal would rise to slightly over 21,000,000 "ghost acres."

[51] Clark, Huberman, and Lindert 1995: 223 vs. 226.

add significantly to the "ghost acreage" even in the early nineteenth century and enormously in the middle and later years of the century.

Of course, the southern United States is not the only place where cotton will grow; but without that area, the early growth of Manchester would have faced very serious impediments. Some sense of how much more difficult it would have been to sustain a boom in cotton textiles without this area's particular ecological and institutional heritage can be gained by looking at the so-called cotton famine that occurred later, during the American Civil War.

Though American cotton exports were cut off only between 1862 and the middle of 1865 (during 1861 the North did not yet have an effective blockade), Britain had begun by 1850 to make considerable efforts to increase cotton supply. These efforts were almost certainly far greater than Britain would have made to find cotton supplies in an imaginary world in which U.S. exports were not available in the first place. British power was far greater at this point than it had been at the beginning of the century, and the shipping and other relevant technologies available to it were far superior. Perhaps more important, the existence of numerous mills, huge numbers of workers, and existing customers expecting products created far greater incentives to avoid a diminution of cotton supply than the imagined possibility of building such an industry could ever have created for overcoming an initial lack of cotton. Yet in spite of these efforts, "the supply of raw material . . . prov[ed] obstinately inelastic."[52]

The major focus of British efforts was India. The Indian government was pursuing a "cotton-oriented policy of annexation and railway construction" during the 1850s but with little to show for it for the first decade. A big jump did occur in 1861—much of it at the expense of domestic consumption and shipments to China rather than by expanding output—but Indian shipments were still less than half of U.S. shipments to Britain in 1861. Moreover, exports rose only 8.6 percent further after this, even though this was when the Union blockade became effective and cotton prices soared.[53]

The other relative success—with far less outside effort—came in Egypt. This was possible because the Egyptian government itself had been committed to expanding cotton output since the days of Mohammed Ali: once the mills he had ordered built proved uncompetitive, the cotton crop was available for export. Exports began in 1821, passed 27,000,000 pounds in 1824, and almost 50,000,000 pounds by the 1850s;[54] but this was less than half of what U.S. exports had been as far back as 1815. At its peak, Egyptian exports approached 200,000,000 pounds (still well short of those of the United States in 1830) before falling back very sharply.[55] These short-lived achievements came after forty years of intense pressure from above—indeed until the Civil War, Egyp-

[52] Farnie 1979: 136.
[53] Ibid., 137, 142, 145–46, 151.
[54] Issawi 1966: 362, 416–17, measurement conversion from 518.
[55] Ibid., 417.

tian cotton cultivation did not spread much beyond the estates of Mohammad Ali and his relatives—engineered by a regime that had been inspired by the example of Lancashire's success. Despite this long preparatory period, they did not represent a sustainable level of production, much less one capable of further expansion. Nor did they provide the cotton at a price Lancashire could have lived with for very long.

During the U.S. Civil War, about 40 percent of the Nile Delta was growing cotton in any given season; given the rotations being used, it appears that cotton was grown in every delta field at some point between 1863 and 1865.[56] Given the limited amount of well-watered land in Egypt, this probably represented an absolute maximum of possible cultivation without the kind of irrigation made possible by twentieth-century mega-projects. Even on this land, costs of cultivation quickly rose to levels that were profitable only at the absolute peak of prices in 1864;[57] and at those prices (in fact, even at the lower ones of 1862), raw cotton was actually more expensive than coarse yarn.[58]

Britain's less-focused efforts to stimulate exports from other promising-sounding sources—Brazil, west Africa, Queensland, and Burma—produced almost nothing,[59] even though prices soared. British cotton consumption fell 55 percent between 1861 and 1862, while prices (already up in 1861 because of the war) doubled. In relative terms, cotton had cost about one-third the price of wool in 1860, but cost more by 1864.[60] Prices would no doubt have gone higher still were it not that when the Civil War began, there was both a fairly large supply of stockpiled raw cotton and a huge glut of finished cotton goods in warehouses (thus depressing demand for more spinning and weaving).[61] Employment in Lancashire mills fell by roughly half in 1862, and the remaining operatives were working two and a third days a week by November (versus six days in 1860–61);[62] large numbers of firms (especially smaller ones, who more closely resembled the early mills in terms of cash reserves, equipment, and other resources) went bankrupt.

True, even this inadequate supply of raw cotton was well above what the United States had supplied in the early nineteenth century; but, as we have seen, it also resulted from efforts that would have been inconceivable at that time. And without twentieth-century farming tools, a substitute for the later and greater bonanza of food crops from the "neo-Europes" is considerably less likely still; there simply was no place in the Old World with anything like the same combination of ecologies that were better for European food plants than Europe itself, relatively sparse population and favorable institutional structures.[63]

[56] Owen 1966: 424.
[57] Ibid.
[58] Farnie 1979: 145.
[59] Ibid., 150.
[60] Ibid., 147, 162.
[61] Ibid., 138–39, 144–45.
[62] Ibid., 145–46.
[63] See, generally, Crosby 1986.

Comparisons and Calculations: What Do
the Numbers Mean?

One might object to these calculations in ways that parallel a common response (discussed in chapter 4) to arguments about overseas extraction and
European capital accumulation: how can we call something decisive if other
factor(s)—capital accumulation within Europe, domestic supplies of food, or
whatever—were larger? The question is important, both for this particular case
and for conceptualizing historical processes more generally.

If we are largely concerned with growth accounting for a single case,
smaller factors are minor factors. But even here, problems of categorization
arise. "New World farm goods imported to Britain" as an inclusive category
may look small next to a parallel category of "domestic (British) farm production," and "imports from the rest of Europe," but if we break these categories
down further ("food imports from Germany," "timber imports from Scandinavia," etc.) we find that some New World subcategories, such as "fiber imports from the United States," would be among the largest items on this longer
list of elements. And how narrow we make our categories depends on complex
judgments (and some further counterfactuals) about the substitutability of different products, the importance of particular sectors for the larger economy,
and so on. (This is one reason why New World resources seem more crucial
than New World profits: there were clearly alternate investments that could
yield money, but it is less clear that there were alternate ways to get huge
amounts of land-intensive goods.) Thus, unless we want to make a categorical
statement that there are *always* substitutes for any particular thing, and markets
always accurately measure the relative importance of activities, goods, etc.,
such judgments cannot be avoided. (To see some limits to these assumptions,
imagine that martians suddenly deprived the earth of all its fossil fuels. We
could estimate the impact by looking at the fairly small percentage of world
GDP that currently goes to fossil-fuel producers, but the actual impact would
certainly be greater.)

More generally, there are clearly some situations where a fairly small increment in something makes all the difference. Human genes are 98.4 percent
identical to those of pygmy chimps,[64] but few of us would disqualify an explanation of why humans have spread across almost the entire planet (while chim-
panzees survive in just a few pockets) because it focused too much on the
behaviors made possible by the remaining 1.6 percent.

The basic idea that relatively small differences can create large historical
divergences is both proverbial ("For want of a nail . . . ") and modern (as in the

[64] Diamond 1992: 23.

famous "chaos theory" example of a butterfly beating its wings in Africa and changing the weather in Greenland). It cuts against equilibrium-seeking models, in which small differences should not create large *and lasting* divergences. It thus makes for an awkward marriage between history and economics—at least schools of economics that posit a single equilibrium as the destination toward which a given system tends. Accepting the importance of small factors can also lead to intellectual anarchy. Explanations can become so cluttered that we can not grasp them; or they can become a grab bag, with everybody championing as "crucial" the factor that suits their personal agenda. But for history to matter, there must sometimes be factors with lasting effects larger than their size might suggest.

Arguing for such factors based on comparisons rests in part on how clear it is that the cases being considered are otherwise similar. History is never as neat as the chimpanzee/human case, in which 98.4 percent of the genes are absolutely identical. Instead, we have statements of rough similarity, or of advantages that seem closely tied to some off-setting disadvantage, or where it is hard to think of any mechanism that would have greatly magnified the importance of a particular difference during the period in which the larger divergence emerged.

Thus, how important coal and the New World will seem depends partly on how convinced readers are of the similarities I have suggested in other areas, as well as on the arguments about those particular phenomena. As for those phenomena themselves, I would suggest four reasons to give them special weight:

1. the calculations above show they were not small relative to some reasonable standards (e.g., Britain's domestic land base)

2. they appear at the right time to explain a crucial divergence (once we have pushed the date of that divergence back to the century surrounding 1800)

3. they affected development through relieving a constraint—the finite amount of land—which was otherwise very difficult to relieve within the knowledge base and institutions of the time

4. the examples of core regions in China, Japan, and certain parts of Europe itself (such as Denmark) provide plausible examples of how societies lacking these advantages might have looked.

They do not require us to imagine that without this relief, Europe would have suffered a Malthusian catastrophe: a situation akin to the "butterfly wings yield hurricane" scenario or to imagining that with a slightly longer ecological window, India, China, or Japan would have produced an industrial revolution. A European ecological crisis *could* have happened, but our counterfactual allows us to imagine a variety of more likely outcomes, which have in common a set of labor-intensive adjustments to land pressures that actual people in somewhat similar circumstances made successfully but would not have led to anything like the British breakthrough. Indeed, as we shall see in our last section, these labor-intensive paths may have also made it harder to imitate industrialization even once the technology was there for the copying. Thus, highlighting the factors I have chosen seems to me a reasonable, rather than reckless, invocation of the principle that not so large initial difference can lead to vastly larger future ones.

Beyond and Besides the Numbers

Having introduced the idea of dynamic effects not easily captured by equilibrium models or quantitative measure more generally, let us look briefly at some of these ways of relating the New World to Europe's divergence from the rest of the Old World. We have touched only briefly (in chapter 3) on the dynamic cultural effects of New World exports such as tobacco and coffee—in particular, their influence on consumption habits and incentives to produce for the market. Though not significant in the sorts of ecological calculations we have made, these "unnecessary" goods—and others obtained in Asia with the use of New World silver—no doubt did much to speed the "industrious revolution" so crucial to Europe's economic dynamism.

For one thing tobacco, sugar, cocoa, coffee, and tea were all somewhat addictive, easy to prepare and consume quickly, and provided short bursts of energy. This made them perfect for punctuating long work days, especially away from home: these characteristics became more important as home and workplace were separated, especially in the factory age. (In Britain in particular, the New World silver that financed the partial substitution of Chinese tea for gin and beer may also have done much to create a population better suited to rapid, sometimes dangerous work.) Moreover, these new "everyday luxuries" were all (except for tobacco) commodities that did not grow in Europe and thus could never be made within the household; consequently, they could only be obtained through producing for the market. The same was true for those desiring cotton or silk fabrics, or the popular blends thereof; and the same was true for the silver belt buckles and other small adornments that became important status symbols even among poor people.

Not only did these materials have to be purchased but in many cases their cost was an incentive to specialization. A family that might have made its own clothes out of hemp or flax would be less likely to risk ruining a fancier piece of fabric; and one would have to be quite wealthy to be willing to write off all the fabric that would be wasted in the process of training a youngster to work with silk, unless this was going to be how they made their living. Consequently, the exotic commodities that became parts of many ordinary people's lives in this period may have contributed in important though unquantifiable ways to the reallocation of labor time from production for home use to production for the market, which in turn was crucial to Europe's "internally generated" gains from increased division of labor. We have also left to one side the possible significance of the plantations themselves as laboratories for factory organization, as suggested by Sidney Mintz.[65]

Moreover, we must remember that New World treasure did more than just allow Europeans to *buy* additional goods in other parts of the New World. It also helped create European military commanders and paymasters who became influential partners of local elites and often later their colonial masters.[66] Consumption taxes on plantation-grown sugar and tobacco, as well as other colonial goods, also played a significant role in building these military capabilities. Half the increase in British government revenues (in constant prices) between 1670 and 1800 (or 1810, if one prefers to take in more of the Napoleonic Wars) came from customs revenue; and at least in 1788–92, two-thirds of customs revenue came from the duties on tea, sugar, Indian cloth, raw silk, tobacco, and "foreign spirits" (mostly rum made with Caribbean sugar—this category did not include wine).[67] Together, customs on these particular commodities made up 22 percent of the yield from all major taxes in Britain during these years.[68] And, of course, the various East India Companies, which lived off these trades, carried out many of the early European conquests in Asia themselves.

It is also worth noting that while growing military power allowed late eighteenth- and early nineteenth-century Europeans to take advantage of political instabilities in various parts of Asia, Europe was having internal upheavals of its own.[69] Jack Goldstone has drawn plausible connections between European political instability in both the mid-seventeenth and late eighteenth centuries and population-induced resource shortages and price shifts.[70] In that light, the resources from abroad loom larger, having kept these problems from being still worse. The same could be said of the state revenues gained from New World commodities, since these taxes were far less unpopular than those on domestic products and assets. This looks still more significant when we remember that Britain had a relatively smooth passage through the Age of Revolution, which for much of the continent involved major economic setbacks, and that it emerged from the period with a vastly enlarged empire.

Thus, it seems likely that the exploitation of the New World, and of the Africans taken there to work, mattered in many ways above and beyond those

[65] Mintz 1985: 46–61.   [66] Bayly 1989: 74; Washbrook 1988.
[67] Calculated from data in O'Brien 1988: 15.   [68] Calculated from ibid., 11.

[69] Bayly (1989) provides an excellent account of the importance of political crises rooted in commercialization that shook Muslim empires from north Africa to Java in opening the way for a new wave of European imperialism and notes general similarities between these crises and the "general wreck of nations" that Europeans found closer to home.

[70] Goldstone 1991 passim.

reflected in our ghost acreage figures. Taking all the indices together, it seems likely that this exploitation did more to differentiate western Europe from other Old World cores than any of the supposed advantages over these other regions generated by the operation of markets, family systems, or other institutions within Europe. Only three strong candidates would seem to exist for a factor of comparable importance in differentiating western Europe from at least east Asian cores. One, paradoxically, would be Europe's ecological "advantages of backwardness," which left unexploited resources that then provided ecological breathing room in the nineteenth century. We have seen, however, that these advantages did not extend to Britain (or to the Low Countries) or to some crucial commodities (notably fiber crops and wood), and they were offset by ecological disadvantages. The second possibility would be the fortunate location of Britain's coal deposits and its relationship to the development of the whole coal/steam complex. The third would be the wave of industrial innovations themselves—something still not fully understood and, as we have seen, of vastly greater significance because it was combined with both plentiful coal and the easing of other resource constraints made possible by the New World.

In this book's last two sections, I follow up the idea of fateful divergences in two ways. First, I carry the argument about the importance of the New World for European development further into the nineteenth century, briefly sketching how these dynamics both changed and continued as industrialization spread beyond Britain. Finally, I look back at China, Japan, and India, all places which, to varying degrees, had to adopt increasingly labor-intensive approaches to ecological stresses and to varying degrees found that these adjustments made capital-intensive, energy-intensive industrialization more difficult later. Since I have argued repeatedly that without the windfalls discussed here, Europe, too, could have been forced down a much more labor-intensive development path, these last examples are meant not just to round out a global story, but to complete the argument that the early nineteenth century represents a crucial moment of divergence with lasting effects—the moment when, thanks to all the factors we have discussed, England avoided becoming the Yangzi Delta, and the two came to look so different that it became hard to see how recently they had been quite similar.

Into an Industrial World

Land-saving New World imports would only grow in significance after 1830: for decades they kept pace with the stunning progress of fossil fuels. Britain's coal output would increase fourteen times from 1815 to 1900,[71] but its sugar

[71] Mitchell 1988: 247.

imports increased roughly eleven-fold over the same period,[72] and its cotton imports increased a stunning twenty-fold.[73] Meanwhile, Britain also began to live off American grain, beef, and other primary products; lumber imports soared; and the New World, at last, also became an enormous outlet for Europe's surplus population.

In the early nineteenth century, of course, Britain ceased selling slaves to North America and the Caribbean, and it had never sold many to Argentina. But by mid-century, new technology had made possible still larger declines in transatlantic shipping costs than in the eighteenth century, and other changes (particularly the railroad) were revolutionizing inland transport. This greatly accelerated the process discussed above, in which falling transport costs allowed European emigrants to cover their costs of passage, start-up, and manufactures by sending primary products back to Europe from ever larger parts of the Americas. (The growth of an independent U.S. government, much less concerned with getting back what it spent to secure and develop the frontier than were earlier for-profit colonial companies, also accelerated the process.)

By that time there were also mechanical (as opposed to human) capital goods that New World producers wanted from Europe and at least some patent protection for the designs. Meanwhile, cheap transport, mechanized production, and tastes brought by European emigrants meant that Europe could also now sell large amounts of consumer goods in the New World. With large inflows of capital and labor in the straightforward forms of immigrants and investment, as well as in the indirect form of manufactured goods, the land-rich, market-oriented United States were a perfect complement to an increasingly densely populated and industrial Europe.

Yet even with all these changes, at least Britain was still indirectly dependent on coercion to finance a good part of its nineteenth-century surge in imported New World resources. In fact, even at the height of its reputation as "workshop of the world," Britain rarely sold enough in the Americas to balance its transatlantic imports.[74] The situation got worse as import substitution proceeded on the European continent and North America and eventually created industries that competed in export markets as well. Consequently, European colonialism and overseas coercion—now concentrated in the Old World—continued to matter for many decades, if not as much as before 1850.

Indeed, in the last four decades before World War I, Britain balanced what had become very substantial trade deficits with the Americas and continental Europe—even after figuring in such "invisibles" as shipping, insurance, and

---

[72] Calculated based on Mitchell 1988: 709–11.

[73] Compare Farnie 1979: 7; see Mitchell (1988: 709–12) on sugar consumption and (1988: 196–201) showing no significant domestic production until the 1920s; and Bruchey 1967: table 2-A.

[74] See Latham (1978b: 69) and Hobsbawm (1975): 138, 144–45) on the trade balances; see Platt (1972: 4–5) on limits of British markets in Latin America.

interest payments—largely through huge surpluses with Asia. By far the biggest surplus was in Britain's trade with India, where legislation artificially enlarged its markets for everything from cloth to locomotives; and India in turn still financed much of that deficit through exports of opium to China and of various farm goods such as tea and indigo produced under highly coercive circumstances for export to continental Europe.[75] Meanwhile, Britain's ability to sustain large deficits with its Atlantic and continental European trading partners while still exporting large amounts of capital mattered to more than just British consumers: it also aided the next wave of industrializers, particularly the United States, who could protect their own markets, sell in an unprotected market, and receive large capital inflows.

It is true, as Eric Jones has argued, that not just any group of people stumbling on the New World (and depopulating it, as any people bearing Old World diseases would have done) could have used these continents as Europe did; but the European entrepreneurship Jones points to[76] was not the *unique* part of the equation, or one in which western Europe had surpassed developments in other densely settled parts of the globe. Western Europeans' innovations in organizing for exploration and durable conquest and in creating institutions that combined entrepreneurship with intense coercion—plus favorable global conjunctures shaped by everything from Amerindians' vulnerability to smallpox to the massive supplies of New World silver and the equally massive project of Chinese remonetization—gave them much of their edge. This, in turn, gave western Europeans a privileged position from which to endure the last century of the "biological old regime," with its multiple ecological challenges, and even continue expanding industries (from textiles to brewing to iron) that made great demands on the products of the land.

Last Comparisons: Labor Intensity, Resources, and Industrial "Growing Up"

Thus when coal, steam, and mechanization opened up vast new technical possibilities, western Europeans (especially in England) were in a unique position to capitalize on them. Vast untapped New World resources (and underground resources) still lay before them, essentially abolishing the land constraint. Moreover, what they had already gained in the New World meant they entered the nineteenth century with a higher standard of living than they would otherwise have had, enlarged military capabilities (which could force open markets in some cases and impose monopolies in others), and far more extensive handicraft industries than they could otherwise have maintained. And it was from

---

[75] See Latham 1978b 69–70, 80, 89; Farnie 1979: 325; Hobsbawm 1975: 149.
[76] Jones 1981: 84.

these proto-industrial workers, not directly from the peasantry, that most early factory workers came.

The importance of a factory workforce drawn heavily from people already working in proto-industry is brought out very clearly in Joel Mokyr's "growing up" model of European industrialization. First, despite numerous attempts to find "surplus labor" in agriculture—i.e., workers who could be removed from that sector without appreciably affecting production[77]—such cases seem rare, even in today's Third World;[78] and none of our cores could afford to have their agricultural output fall very much circa 1800. Second, factories employing former proto-industrial workers have a distinct advantage. If factory workers were drawn out of agriculture, then even if demand for them did not raise wages (in other words, if there *was* surplus labor in agriculture), there would be no reason for that wage to fall; and as the diffusion of mass-production techniques caused the price of the product made by a factory to fall, the firm would encounter declining profits and might have difficulty expanding. (Mokyr assumes that the fixed capital needed is fairly cheap, as is common in early industrialization; and since the raw materials cost roughly the same regardless of the production process, the factory's wage bill is the most important variable cost.) But if the nascent industry can draw on proto-industrial workers who made the same product as the factory did, then the same technological diffusion that places downward pressure on the factory's prices also depresses workers' alternate earnings possibilities. Thus the factory can reduce wages and still attract recruits from this sector; this allows it to maintain higher profits for longer.[79]

Thus, in this scenario, industry can result from the "growing up" of proto-industry; it does not require a *simultaneous* social and technological transformation that enables agriculture to maintain or increase output from about the same amount of land while releasing a huge number of workers. Moreover, proto-industrial workers often moved to the factory with some relevant skills and/or knowledge useful for making further innovations. All this suggests that the continued growth of proto-industry in the decades preceding and overlapping the growth of mechanized industry left Europe in a far better position than if it had been compelled to keep more people in agriculture and forestry.

To put things slightly differently: Europe's expansion of both proto-industry and many early mechanized industries required more agricultural output. Quite aside from whether Britain (or even Europe more generally) could have found enough land at home to resolve these problems, putting large additional amounts of labor into supplying these farm goods directly would have created

[77] Lewis 1954: 139–91; for later literature, see Myint 1958: 317–37.
[78] Schultz 1964: 61–70.
[79] Mokyr 1976: 132–64.

further problems later on. But instead, Europe acquired many of these supplies by having others grow them, while putting its own labor into additional soldiers, sailors, traders, and producers of manufactured goods. As factories at home needed more labor, they could draw on proto-industrial workers, with the advantages discussed above.

Over time, soldiers and sailors became more effective per capita thanks to technological change (e.g., better guns and ships) and were increasingly supplemented or replaced by "natives" hired with the proceeds of colonial taxation. Thus the overseas sector went through a sort of "growing up" of its own, which meant that this way of obtaining primary products did not absorb increasing amounts of European labor. The massive expansion of agriculture at home, which would have been needed otherwise, would have been not only ecologically difficult, but hard to reconcile with the expansion of the industrial workforce. When Britain's agricultural workforce finally began to decline in absolute numbers after 1850, it was tied both to technologies that had been unavailable earlier in the century and to massive increases in agricultural imports; production held steady as labor inputs declined, but did not rise much.[80] The contrast to the atypical (for Europe) case of Denmark, discussed in chapter 5, is striking. There, a near-stabilization of the ecology through labor-intensive methods seems to have been inconsistent with industrialization for many decades, even though the marginal returns to much of this work—and the real wages of both urban and rural laborers—were low and falling further.[81]

For a long time China and Japan, like Europe as a whole, also found ways to keep expanding their proto-industrial sectors, even without a New World to supply the needed fiber and other land-intensive inputs. These processes also involved some expansion of trade (and of fishing) to relieve local pressure on the land in cores; but compared to the European solution, they involved a greater intensification and expansion of their own agricultural sectors, particularly for fiber production. And by the end of the eighteenth century, that process seems to have been proceeding at diminishing rates and at considerable ecological cost. Japan's population stopped growing by 1750, and while China's continued growing for another century, the percentage of the population in proto-industry likely stagnated or even declined. In all probability, few areas in China that had extensive proto-industry actually underwent significant deindustrialization. What happened instead was that the heavily agricultural areas of China came to make up a much larger percentage of the population by 1850 than they had in 1750.

---

[80] Thompson (1989: 189) shows that output of food per farm worker rose about 50 percent between 1840 and the early 1900s, but the number of farm workers fell by 25 percent, making a net gain in output of 12.5 percent. Moreover, even those gains required a massive increase in the use of off-farm chemicals and other products for agriculture (see 193–99).

[81] See Kjaergaard 1994: 160 on wage trends.

The most advanced prefectures of the Yangzi Delta, which had roughly 16–21 percent of China's population in 1750, were barely 9 percent of the empire by 1850, and about 6 percent by 1950. As we shall see shortly, the percentage of these prefectures' population that worked in proto-industry may have fallen slightly, but whether or not that happened, the empire's most proto-industrial region simply ceased to have the same weight in aggregate figures. In Lingnan, the second most proto-industrial macro-region, population growth between 1750 and 1850 was about 75 percent, but China as a whole grew about 100 percent; moreover, a disproportionate share of Lingnan's growth was in Guangxi, a province largely limited to agriculture and forestry.

Thus, even though some of the heavily agricultural macro-regions were becoming more proto-industrial, their very large share in post-1750 population growth meant that China as a whole was at least as agrarian in 1850 as in 1750 and not much less so in 1950. Moreover, proto-industrial workers scattered across the farmsteads of the interior and often seen as part of an ideal agrarian household were not as easily available to move into hypothetical factories as true proletarians with no ties to the land might have been. Thus, during the two centuries or so after 1750, China became less well positioned for industrializing along the relatively easy path of "growing up" and has instead had to deal with all the problems of drawing most of its factory workers directly out of agriculture.

The United States, however, is an important reminder that not all early industrializers had large proto-industrial sectors. In fact, Kenneth Sokoloff and David Dollar, comparing the United States and England in the nineteenth century, have emphasized that the much greater seasonality of agricultural work in England slowed the development of factory-based industry. With large numbers of workers available only part of the year, but at wages far lower than what they would have required to leave the land completely, handicraft industry proved a tenacious competitor for factories, and investment in centralized plants, equipment, and supervision was less advantageous than it would have been had the agricultural and industrial workforces been more completely separate. In the United States, by contrast, very favorable land-to-labor ratios meant that farmers could supplement their grain-growing with other activities—animal husbandry, wood-cutting, fruit-raising and land-clearing, for instance—which yielded less per acre but paid well per hour; thus the rural labor force was occupied full-time without much resort to handicraft industries. Thus when factories were built, they could grow still more rapidly than in England (especially grain-growing, handicraft-producing south England).[82]

This argument is persuasive for the two cases of England and the United States. But the American case was radically different from anything in our Eurasian cores. The very favorable land-to-labor ratios meant that American

[82] Sokoloff and Dollar 1997: 1–20.

farms could easily feed a separate industrial workforce as that group emerged (whether from immigration or from rapid natural increase and rural-urban migration). It also meant that these farmers were sufficiently prosperous, even without industrial by-employments, to buy factory goods, even if those goods were made with fairly expensive labor. Long distances and tariffs, meanwhile, helped ensure that European manufactures made with what was often cheaper labor did not capture all of the United States market.

Under those special circumstances, American factories that had to find their laborers among ex-farmers (whether from Massachusetts, Ireland, or Germany) might still, contrary to the "growing up" model, expand more rapidly than English factories. But very few places in the eighteenth-century Old World could have accommodated a huge increase in population that neither raised local farm output nor brought in primary products by producing industrial *exports*; and where rural populations in Old World cores were not available for proto-industry, this was more likely due to very labor-intensive year-round multi-cropping (e.g., in parts of Lingnan) or enormous amounts of work to preserve a fragile ecology (e.g., marling, ditch-digging, and so on in Denmark) than to the sorts of lucrative but land-intensive by-employments that one finds on nineteenth-century U.S. farms.

Thus, Old World cores could not create a factory labor force in the way the United States did. For them, the choice was between pulling people out of full-time proto-industry or out of at least part-time farming. Given that, being able to draw on proto-industrial workers would still seem the most advantageous way to create Old World industrial workforces. This left England far better-off than places like the Yangzi Delta, which lacked peripheral trading partners that would complement it in the way that England's did.

This argument can also be expressed in terms of another feature of Mokyr's "growing up" model of European industrialization. The model assumes that people turn to proto-industrial activities in the first place when the marginal productivity of their labor in agriculture falls below that of proto-industry. (The former starts off higher than the latter, but falls much more rapidly, largely because the supply of land is limited.) Thus, the extra labor beyond a certain point will all go into proto-industry, as long as the area in question can continue exporting proto-industrial products in exchange for food (and, we might add, fiber and timber) without affecting the relative prices of food and handicrafts in the "world" market where it makes these exchanges.

This condition, usually called the "small-country assumption," makes perfect sense for the Netherlands and Belgium, the cases for which Mokyr developed this model—and at one point it also made sense for the Lower Yangzi and Lingnan, and the Kantō and Kinai regions. Although, as we have seen, the Yangzi Delta prefectures imported huge amounts of primary products—36,000,000 people importing 15–22 percent of their food, plus timber, beancake fertilizer, and so on—the hinterlands and marketing networks they drew on were so vast that the small country assumption still makes sense as a way of looking at the region's trade in the mid-eighteenth century. But as some of these hinterlands, such as the Middle and Upper Yangzi and North China, grew more populous, experienced diminishing returns in agriculture and developed more of their own proto-industry, the terms of trade did shift, to the marked disadvantage of proto-industrial producers.

Though silver-denominated cotton cloth prices fluctuated from year to year, there seems to have been no trend in nominal cloth prices from 1750 to 1850.[83] Raw cotton prices in Canton, for which we have relatively good data, also show no clear trend, though short-term fluctuations were often violent.[84] But silver-denominated rice prices in the Lower Yangzi rose by 40 percent over that same century.[85] That increase alone would have cut the spinning and weaving income of the hypothetical women in chapter 2 by about 30 percent, from 7.2 *shi* of rice in 1750 to 5.0 *shi* in 1850.

Moreover, fragmentary data collected by Kishimoto Mio suggest that in the Lower Yangzi itself, raw cotton prices did rise substantially between 1750 and 1800. Such a finding is consistent with trendless prices near Canton, since transport costs between these two areas fell sharply in the late eighteenth and early nineteenth centuries. It would also be consistent with seventeenth-century patterns, in which the price of raw cotton in the Yangzi Delta seems to have roughly tracked that of rice.[86] If Kishimoto's data are roughly representative for Jiangnan, then the fall in spinners' and weavers' earnings would be roughly 50 percent just between 1750 and 1794 (when her data stop), though they would be falling from a higher starting point. And if we guess that the trend in raw cotton prices followed that of rice over the long haul, the rice-buying power of our hypothetical weaver/spinner would fall 25 percent between 1750 and 1800, and 37 percent by 1840.[87] Measured in salt or probably firewood, they fell further still.

Even these depreciated earnings could still meet the subsistence needs of the woman herself and would be close enough to male agricultural wages (which were also falling in real terms) that China's "gender gap" remained less severe than that in Europe. But they do show a substantial decline in earnings from home-based textile production, even before any competition from machine-made cloth. A woman weaving very high-grade cotton cloth would have escaped these pressures, since its prices nearly doubled over this same century,[88] but these were atypical women who had unusual skills and probably produced fewer pieces each year.

---

[83] Zhang Zhongmin 1988: 208.

[84] See Dermigny 1964: IV: table 19.

[85] Y. C. Wang 1992: 42, 45.

[86] Kishimoto 1997: 139, 141; Greenberg 1951: 92; Dermigny 1964: IV: table 19. For more details, see appendix E.

[87] See appendix E for more details.   [88] Zhang Zhongmin 1988: 194.

In Mokyr's model, such a fall in returns to proto-industrial labor in the Lower Yangzi should have led to at least some labor shifting back into agriculture at what would previously have been unacceptably low returns, and thus to a combination of further agricultural intensification and some measure of de-industrialization.[89] Though any such shift would have been modest, we have one possible indication of it. Raw cotton from the Lower Yangzi seems to to have become cheaper and more plentiful in Guangzhou (Canton) in the early nineteenth century, much to the dismay of foreign merchants bringing Indian cotton to sell. Though the fall in price may have been largely a matter of improved transportation,[90] the growth in quantity suggests that perhaps less Yangzi Delta cotton was being spun and woven locally; it seems unlikely that Lower Yangzi raw cotton output rose much in this period, and imports from North China were almost certainly falling.

And yet, most Yangzi Delta women continued to spin and weave, even at lower returns; in fact, as we saw earlier, it is precisely in the nineteenth century that references to women of that region working with men in the fields finally disappear completely.[91] If some families were unwilling to move their wives and daughters back into the fields where they would be more visible—and perhaps even tried to increase cloth output to maintain income—the situation might have come to resemble the quasi-involutionary situation described by Goldstone, in which women "stuck" in very low-wage home-based spinning and weaving made it much less profitable to contemplate factory-based textile production. Any such pattern emerging in this period would be the result of a

[89] When graphed, the relationship looks roughly like this:

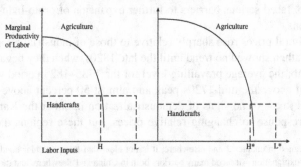

Time T = 1
Before rise in relative price
of primary products

Time T = 2
After rise in relative price
of primary products

H, H* = points at which labor switches into handicrafts
L, L* = total labor input
L – H, L* – H* = labor devoted to handicrafts

[90] Greenberg 1951: 91–92.
[91] See Li Bozhong 1996, and above pp. 103–4.

temporary conjuncture, rather than a fundamental feature of long-term Chinese development based on timeless norms (as Huang suggests) and it would be too late appearing to be the basic explanation of the nondevelopment of factories, as Goldstone proposes.[92] Nonetheless it might have helped slow the replacement of domestic textile production by factory production, even once the technology became available, as Goldstone suggests later in his essay. Either way, these women remained part of households in which the men (and to some extent children) were driven to increasingly labor-intensive strategies of farming, fuel-gathering, and land-management—not a promising precursor to industrialization.

Japan's response to similar pressures remained within the same basic framework as China's, but with some differences that may have had long-term implications. First of all, Japan's population broke through its historic ceiling, never to return, earlier than that in either China or Europe. Population reached new heights in the late seventeenth century, when both Europe and China experienced downturns, and by about 1720 it had reached a plateau that would last until about 1860.[93] This long period of zero population growth may represent a more rapid and thorough demographic adjustment to ecological constraints than the slowing, but still positive population growth of early nineteenth century China, but it could also be argued that the adjustment was sharper because the situation was even worse: after all, overall population density in Japan even circa 1860 was still much higher than it was in China.[94] And while the enormous increase in Japanese ocean fishing offered a kind of relief much less used in China (it provided both food and fertilizer), and the early development of systematic silviculture was also an important adjustment,[95] Japan, too, faced serious barriers to further expansion of proto-industry in its core regions.

Agricultural prices rose sharply relative to those of industrial goods during the 1730s, then showed no trend until the late 1820s, when they began another steep climb; the average prevailing level for the 1735–1825 period was about 20 percent above the mid-1720s peak and almost 50 percent above the 1730 trough.[96] I know of no signs of deindustrialization in either the Kantō or the Kinai in response to changing relative prices, but these regions did decline

[92] As I argued in chapter 2 and elsewhere, it is not clear that this particular nondevelopment needs much explanation—it faced many barriers both in China and elsewhere, and the more "natural" path appears to have been an exhaustion of the possibilities of proto-industrialization. What needs explaining is why parts of Europe did not follow this path, too—so that Europe can be seen as China manque (or England as Flanders manque) rather than the whole world being England manque.

[93] Saito 1985: 185.

[94] McEvedy and Jones 1978: 166–71, 179–81; note especially the low percentage of Japanese land that is arable.

[95] Totman 1989: 81–170; Howell 1992: 271–75.

[96] Saito and Shinbo 1989: 91.

in population: 16 percent for the Kantō between 1751 and 1821 and perhaps 5 percent for the Kinai, while the prefectures with impressive population growth were mostly in areas that were still relatively sparsely populated in 1870 and also still well below the national average on Saito's index of rural industrialization. (By contrast, the Kinai region had both a population density and a rural industrialization index that doubled the national averages.)[97] We have already seen that the major growth of both industry and population was in poor domains such as Tosa, where old monopolies were being relaxed; but many such monopolies persisted, as did barriers to migration. These barriers to growth in the peripheries may have spread pressure for family limitation into more peripheries than in China (though any comparison is speculative with current data), ultimately preserving some of the same sort of slack capacity that much of continental Europe had but China lacked. To put it another way, the share of Japan's most advanced regions in national aggregates declined, as it did in China, but much more gently, since peripheral growth was more modest. Labor intensity increased, but this was due almost entirely to increased hours per worker, not to population growth. And though cities and towns lost ground relative to the countryside,[98] the country's still relatively high urbanization rate also suggests that more of what Mokyr calls "pseudo-surplus" labor was stored in handicrafts (as opposed to agriculture) than was the case in China.

As we would expect, the Indian story is different again, but it still fits within the same general framework. Moreover, India's differences from China point in the opposite direction from Japan's differences and suggest more serious long-term obstacles to industrialization. India, as we have seen, began its population boom later than China or western Europe did, and much later than Japan: probably after 1830, and almost certainly after 1800.[99] The nineteenth century saw an enormous increase in cultivated land in India and few signs of serious overall shortages of food, fuel, fiber, or building materials. (Distribution was, of course, quite another matter: India exported large amounts of grain in the late nineteenth century, for instance, while it had serious hunger at home.) But despite a continuation of late precolonial commercialization, the share of India's population in non-farming occupations probably fell during early British rule. The subcontinent underwent what Bayly calls "peasantization," as both formerly migratory peoples and former handicraft workers were increasingly drawn—and pushed—into sedentary farming. The process appears to have begun before colonialism, in part because the competing successor states to the Mughal empire hoped that settling migratory peoples on the land would increase state control, public security, and state revenues; it

[97] See Saito (1985: 211) and compare with Iwahashi (1981: 440).
[98] Sugihara 1997: 153.
[99] Moosvi 1987: 402, 405; Subrahmanyam 1990: 358–60; Habib 1982a: 166–67; Visaria and Visaria 1983: 463–65.

accelerated under the British and touched increasing numbers of former urbanites as well.[100]

An intense debate has been waged about whether India deindustrialized in the nineteenth century; with inadequate data, it is unlikely to be settled.[101] However, it does seem fairly well established that the number of full-time weavers and spinners (especially those based in towns) decreased significantly beginning in the late eighteenth century. This seems to have been due at first to measures taken (especially in Bengal) by the East India Company and some other merchants who increasingly bound weavers to a single potential buyer; as this depressed earnings, many artisans fled their occupation.[102] Later, earnings came under intense further pressure from competition with Lancashire.[103] And the percentage of the Indian population living in cities declined significantly over the long term—from 13–15 percent in the late seventeenth century to 9.3 percent in 1881—though it is currently impossible to date the decline much more precisely.[104] Deindustrialization is also suggested by Habib's finding that the value of sugar, cotton, and indigo grown in India quite likely fell in absolute terms (not to mention per capita terms) between 1595 and the 1870s.[105]

While total yarn and cloth output in India may have held their own, thanks to an increase in part-time rural spinning and weaving, this would not have had the same significance for future industrialization as would the growth of a full-time proto-industrial workforce. These were not people who could later be moved into factories with no cost to agricultural output;[106] nor were they workers whose cost to a potential factory owner would fall together with the unit price of his product, since much of their income came from farming.

Thus, it could be argued, though India began the nineteenth century with a less-monetized economy than that found in China, Japan, or western Europe, it was moving in similar directions and had more ecological room for increasing population and per capita consumption than they did. But by the early twentieth century it had lost that advantage and had both the disadvantages of a densely populated zone and those of a zone with limited proto-industrial development and a limited internal market. This combination of problems had occurred not so much through the sort of (largely) market-driven regional development that seems to have led to China's cul de sac, but through the preferences of colonial (and, to some extent, indigenous) authorities for settled

[100] Bayly 1983: 219–26, 290–92; Bayly 1989: 188–89.

[101] See, e.g., Bagchi 1976; Vicziany 1979: 105–43; Bagchi 1979: 147–61; Perlin 1983: 89–95; Harnetty 1991: 455–510.

[102] Hossain 1979: 326–35; Mitra 1978: 23, 25, 29, 32, 37–38, 48–49, 56, 79–80, 84, 87–92, 132, 144, 164, 172–73.

[103] Harnetty 1991: 463–66, 505–7; Mitra 1978: 188, 194–95.

[104] Habib 1982a: 168–69.

[105] Ibid.

[106] On the absence of true "surplus labor" in Indian agriculture, even in the twentieth century, see Schultz 1964: 61–70.

populations, "customary" law, agricultural and forest exports, and a captive market for the mother country's industrial goods. The result was an *increasing* emphasis on primary-product exports even amid great population growth—primary products often produced with labor that was no less coerced (and maybe more so) than in the least free areas of eighteenth-century India.[107]

Thus, despite considerable growth in agriculture and commerce, India may have become less well positioned for industrial-led transformative growth. Compared to what at least might have happened had eighteenth-century social trends continued a bit longer while population grew and competition from mechanized goods stayed away a little bit longer, colonial India's form of "peasantization" might reasonably be labeled a "development of underdevelopment." The British probably did not frustrate an industrial breakthrough that was otherwise highly likely, as some nationalist scholars claim, but nineteenth-century changes may have made such a breakthrough even more difficult than it would have been otherwise and more difficult than the transition faced by either western European economies or east Asian ones. To put it another way, Japanese and especially Chinese cores may have faced bottlenecks due to the convergence of their peripheries toward "core" profiles, but Indian cores suffered the worse fate of converging toward a more peripheral profile.

The wonder then is that at roughly the same time that the "small-country assumption" became less applicable to east Asian cores—largely because the growth of population and proto-industry in their peripheries was making the quantity of primary products available on their "world" markets smaller relative to their needs—that same assumption remained applicable to Britain even though its population soared and its per capita demand grew (first slowly, then very rapidly after about 1840). Moreover, it remained applicable over the next century, not only to Britain, but to an ever-larger "industrial Europe." Without that wonder the combination of a much larger population, higher per capita consumption, and far *less* labor-intensive land management—all central to the "European miracle"—was not possible. Without that wonder, the achievements of Europe's preindustrial market economy—impressive though they were—could have led in the same direction as the also impressive market economies of other regions. Even that other wonder—the string of technological innovations that makes up the original history of the "Industrial Revolution"—might well have slowed to a crawl without this one.

The wonder can be partly explained by western Europe's own "advantages of backwardness," as discussed in chapter 5: domestic resources left unexploited because of institutional blockages that were only relieved in the nineteenth century and that, at that point, kept the import needs of some industrializing areas from being even larger. But as we have seen, this argument has little applicability to Britain, and little to fiber and wood. Technological

---

[107] See, for instance, Bayly (1989) on tea plantations.

catching up—e.g., in per-acre yields—also helped, but that alone can hardly explain Europe's surge ahead of the rest of the globe. Europe's wood problem was of course substantially eased by coal, but for quite a while this applied only in Britain and a few other places. Furthermore, overall timber demand kept rising even where coal was used heavily, since wood had many other uses: timber imports continued to rise throughout the late eighteenth century and at an unprecedented rate in the nineteenth century. (Though coal, as we saw, also had other dimensions, through its links to steam power, railroads, and so on.)

Thus, for a more complete explanation of what occurred in Europe's core, we must also look at its peripheries and understand why they became growing rather than shrinking suppliers of primary products to the "world" market. Part of the answer lies in institutional arrangements in eastern Europe and Russia that long inhibited population growth and proto-industrialization of the sort that occurred relatively rapidly in the Chinese interior and Japan's Region II—more "advantages of backwardness," but ones that could not be reaped on a large scale until after 1860. Much of the rest of the answer—and the bridge that got Europe through the first century of the proto-industrial to industrial transition—lay, as this chapter has argued, in the New World: not just in its natural bounty, but in the unique institutions and conjunctures that brought far more of its bounty to Europe far earlier than purely Smithian trade could have.

The institutional factors include some—like the slave trade and the mine labor systems—whose departure from market principles are obvious and which we often consign too quickly to a "premodern" world, forgetting their role in making our world possible. Others, like the corporation, are familiar, "modern," and clearly European in origin. Consequently, we tend to forget that they were created by and for extracontinental encounters and that for a long time they may have been most significant as a method of underwriting the huge fixed costs of violence: a method that then forced these enterprises to increase *volumes* of "exotic" imports (rather than focusing exclusively on profit margins, as the Venetians and Portuguese had tended to do) and thus to expand the European presence abroad. Still others, like the specialized slave plantation, are well known, but their role in creating a new kind of periphery for Europe is here placed in a new light. And beyond these institutions lie various global conjunctures that favored the expansion of the European presence in the New World: from wind patterns and disease gradients to European state competition and Chinese silver demand.

Together, these largely extra-European and nonmarket factors were essential in making transatlantic trade a uniquely self-expanding route by which Europe (especially Britain) could use its labor and capital to relieve its hard-pressed land and thus turn even a demographic and proto-industrial expansion that (unlike in east Asia) far outpaced advances in agriculture into an asset for further development. Without those factors, this demographic and proto-industrial expansion could have been the basis for a later catastrophe; or it could have been stopped by rising primary-product prices in the nineteenth century; or it could have been severely constrained by a need for much more labor-intensive approaches to exploiting and conserving a limited land base.

Thus, forces outside the market and conjunctures beyond Europe deserve a central place in explaining why western Europe's otherwise largely unexceptional core achieved unique breakthroughs and wound up as the privileged center of the nineteenth century's new world economy, able to provide a soaring population with an unprecedented standard of living. Our long journey through interregional comparisons has brought us to at least some resolution of the methodological question with which we began: it has shown that rather than pretend we are seeking the differences among truly independent entities on the eve of industrialization, we must acknowledge the importance of preexisting connections in creating those differences.

APPENDIXES

APPENDIXES

A

COMPARATIVE ESTIMATES OF LAND TRANSPORT
CAPACITY PER PERSON:
GERMANY AND NORTH INDIA CIRCA 1800

DESPITE THE considerable cost advantages of water transport, most goods in many premodern economies traveled by land: water routes were often simply unavailable or required considerable land travel to get to and from the waterside. Yet few estimates of either the actual or potential volumes of goods transported by land exist for any preindustrial economy.

A rare exception is Werner Sombart's calculation for Germany circa 1800 in *Der Moderne Kapitalismus* (volume 2, part 1, pp. 339–41). He relies on an 1846 census of horses used for transport and travel in the German customs union, which he assumes was slightly lower than the number of horses in use in 1800 (since the beginning of railroad-building had presumably begun to decrease the desirability of owning horses). He then multiplies by a plausible load and daily travel distance that each horse could handle and assumes 250 work days per year. (This last assumption is not stated, much less explained, but it is necessary to reconcile his figures.) The result is 500,000,000 ton kilometers per year or 325,000,000 ton miles per year.

In a recent article, Irfan Habib estimates the transport capacity of north India's *banjaras* (migratory ox-herding castes who carried freight for others and sometimes became traders themselves) at 821,000,000 metric ton miles per year.[1] While Habib's figure for one crucial variable—the size of the *banjaras*' herds—is based on rough inferences from unofficial observers, rather than a census, it seems as likely to be conservative as excessive.

Moreover, Habib's estimate is based on roughly 115 work days per year—less than half of Sombart's figure. *Banjaras* had no permanent homes, and the herds needed to keep moving to find food anyway—it was because they grazed along the way and rarely ate purchased feed that they were a very cheap means of transport, and for the same reason that Habib assumes they could cover only six or seven miles per day. Thus, Habib's figure for work days—chosen in order to be as conservative as possible—seems far too low for our comparison. To estimate transport *capacity*, we could simply stop estimating number of days worked and compare capacity available per day. I have chosen an alternative, which biases the results slightly (though only slightly) in favor of

[1] Habib 1990.

Germany: assuming Sombart's estimate of days worked is reasonable while doubling Habib's estimate so that it reflects roughly 230 work days per year (vs. 250 in Germany). Habib's figure then becomes 1,642,000,000 metric ton miles per year, or slightly over five times Sombart's figure. A final uncertainty in comparing capacities is that Sombart does not specify English or metric tons—if he meant the former, then the north India figure would need to be adjusted by a further 10 percent, making it 5.5 times the German one.

Finally, we need to divide by population; here, too, figures are sketchy, but we can specify plausible ranges. McEvedy and Jones give an 1800 figure for what later became the German empire (and thus was roughly the same as the area covered by the *Zollverein* horse census Sombart relies on) of 24,000,000;[2] Nipperdey gives 30,000,000 for the same time and area.[3] Estimates for India vary widely: the *Cambridge Economic History of India* lists a range of estimates for the whole subcontinent of 139,000,000–214,000,000 circa 1800. Most of the figures, however, are in the 170,000,000–190,000,000 range.[4] If we eliminate the roughly 20,000,000 in south India, which was outside *banjara* territory,[5] we have 150,000,000–170,000,000: anywhere from five to seven times Germany's population, served by 5 or 5.5 times as much land transport capacity.

This would suggest that German land transport capacity per capita may have exceeded that of north India, but not by much. Moreover, our data are probably biased against India. The *banjara* specialized in long-distance transport, which means that we are leaving out animal transport that carried goods to local markets and on other short trips; such trips were probably the great majority of land transport in a preindustrial economy. By contrast, Sombart counted all transport horses, explicitly including those used primarily for carrying people rather than goods. Given the shakiness of the data, no final comparisons are possible, but it seems likely that capacities were roughly comparable—and that there was a good deal of unused capacity available in both locations.

[2] McEvedy and Jones 1978: 71.   [3] Nipperdey 1996: 85.
[4] Visaria and Visaria 1983: 466.   [5] Subrahmanyam 1990: 360.

B

ESTIMATES OF MANURE APPLIED TO NORTH CHINA AND EUROPEAN FARMS IN THE LATE EIGHTEENTH CENTURY, AND A COMPARISON OF RESULTING NITROGEN FLUXES

TWENTIETH CENTURY data from Mantetsu surveys (which seem to be accurate in other respects) give a range of 1,800–2,000 *jin* of manure per cropped *mu* in poorer north China villages; I have treated this as an estimate of 1,900 *jin*. For a more developed North China village, they give a figure of 3,000 *jin* per cropped *mu*.[1] Converting to kilograms per acre gives us 6,600–10,600 kg/cropped acre.

To project these figures backward into the late eighteenth century, I assumed that in an economy with very few plow animals,[2] pigs and humans were the most important sources of fertilizer; I further relied on Perkins's estimate that the number of hogs roughly tracked the trends in China's human population.[3] Using figures compiled by Philip Huang for Hebei and Shandong population in 1790 and 1933,[4] late eighteenth-century manure supplies should have been about 60 percent of 1930's levels.

But these smaller eighteenth-century manure supplies were applied to less cropped land than in the twentieth century. Taking a figure halfway between Huang's figures for 1753 and 1812 (which are at any rate very close together) and comparing them with his 1933 figure gives us a multiplier of 1.4.[5]

The result of the arithmetic is a range of 5,600–8,900 kg/cropped acre, well above Slicher Van Bath's figures of 4,000–5,600 for late eighteenth-century Europe;[6] and the "European" data in question come quite disproportionately from the Netherlands, Rhineland, England, and France. And it seems likely—though unprovable—that the quality of manure in North China was equal to or better than that in Europe.

Going from crop output and manuring levels to trends in soil nutrients themselves is an extremely imprecise exercise. How much of a given nutrient is added to the soil by a given amount of manure—or, even more important, by

---

[1] All figures quoted in P. Huang 1985: 147–48.
[2] See ibid., 138–54.
[3] Perkins 1969: 71.
[4] P. Huang 1985: 322.
[5] Ibid., 327.
[6] Slicher Van Bath 1977: 94.

nitrogen-fixing crops such as legumes—depends on many factors, including some we cannot know. So many local conditions affect these things that the best estimates even for today are wide ranges rather than numbers: to take an extreme case, a crop of soybeans is said to fix 15–331 kilograms of nitrogen (kgN) per hectare.[7] Nonetheless, there is some utility comparing agriculturally induced nitrogen fluxes in western Europe and China, using the reported average results for such crucial parameters as the amount of nitrogen added by a ton of a particular crop. Nitrogen is a logical element to focus on because it is one of the three crucial plant "macro-nutrients." Levels of one of the other two, phosphorus, tend to be closely correlated with those for nitrogen. The third, potassium, presents even greater analytical difficulties: large quantities of this nutrient can be present in a soil yet unavailable to plants, and we as yet know very little about why this is so.[8] Moreover, because nitrogen cannot be stored in the soil for long periods in forms usable by most plants—except through the planting of nitrogen-fixing crops—nitrogen fluxes were, quite often, the limiting factor in premodern soil productivity.[9]

With these caveats, I compared a "typical" reconstructed North China farm with a model English farm, using Peter Bowden's estimates of various parameters.[10] In most ways, England is more comparable to the Lower Yangzi or Lingnan, China's most economically advanced regions, but the ecological differences between wheat and paddy rice are an insuperable problem. At least by using North China we are comparing similar crops, so that choosing a particular estimate of, say, the nitrogen depletion caused by growing a ton of wheat will not distort the comparison between cases. I assumed the North China farm to be on a three-crops-in-two-years rotation, with two wheat crops and one soybean crop, a typical arrangement; for the English farm I assumed one crop per year, with two years of wheat followed by a year of nitrogen-fixing clover.

It appears that a wheat crop takes roughly .0234kg of nitrogen from the soil to grow each kilogram of wheat and the straw that grows with it.[11] If the straw is plowed back into the soil, but—as typically happens—at least half the nitrogen in the straw is lost in the process,[12] then European-style farming would involve an N uptake for each kg of wheat of .0214kg. For North China, I assumed that *all* residues were lost to the soil, though that is an exaggeration, so that the nitrogen loss for each kg of wheat produced would be the full .0234 kg.

British wheat yields in the 1770s averaged about 23 bushels per acre.[13] At 8 bushels to the quarter[14] and 5 quarters to the ton,[15] this converts to

[7] Smil 1985: 140.   [8] Smil 1990: 429.
[9] Kjaergaard 1994: 22, 58, 87.   [10] Bowden 1990.
[11] Based on the per hectare figure in Smil (1985: 174); projections based on the somewhat different information in Smil (1983: 203) yield the roughly similar figure of .0209 kg N/kg wheat.
[12] Smil 1985: 218.   [13] Bowden 1990: 197.
[14] Ibid., 373, table 48, note a.   [15] Ibid., 32.

523 kg/acre. Direct figures for North China in the late eighteenth century are very hard to come by. However, a good estimate for the 1930s would be about 100 *jin* per *mu*;[16] when combined with figures for the quantity of residues per *mu* on North China wheat land in that period (140 *jin* according to *Santō no Chikuguyu*[17]), this also gives us very realistic wheat-to-chaff-ratios. If we then project backward to 1800 by using Perkins's argument that per capita food output did not change, and we adjust output per *mu* to make that true given (approximately) known trends in land farmed and in population, we get an 1800 figure of about 306 kg/acre.[18] So over the course of six years, the English farm in our model would have produced four wheat crops totaling 2,092 kg/ acre, and the North Chinese farm six wheat crops totaling 1,816 kg/acre. (It is worth noting that once one adds three soybean harvests for the North Chinese field, it becomes a much better total food producer than the English farm, though North China was a relatively poor food producer in the Chinese scale of things.)

The English wheat crops should have taken 44.77 kg of nitrogen from each acre over six years; the Chinese wheat crops 42.49 kg/acre. We can now turn to replenishment efforts, starting with manure.

Contemporary figures suggest that the nitrogen input to the soil from live-stock manure is about .9 percent of fresh weight, of which half or more is lost after application to the soil through volatilization.[19] If we applied these figures to the late eighteenth century, it would appear that both English and North Chinese farms were easily replenishing their nitrogen losses even without ni-trogen-fixing crops, but this seems unlikely; farmers in both places (and indeed almost everywhere) found that crop rotation was absolutely necessary to sus-tain high yields. And there are at least two reasons why these late twentieth-century figures are much too high for the late eighteenth century. First, they come from animals fed on commercial feeds much more nutritious than what earlier animals would have eaten. Second, the figures above are for fresh ma-nure. Manure loses its value rapidly if it is not applied quickly,[20] but labor-saving considerations meant that in both China and Europe manure was accu-mulated for quite a while before application. On some English farms, in fact, the practice was to apply a massive dressing of fertilizer less than once a year.[21]

Consequently, the gains from fertilization must have been much lower than twentieth-century calculations would suggest, but we do not know how much less. But whatever the absolute levels were, the North Chinese farms were probably *relatively* superior in this area. Not only did they apply roughly

---

[16] See, e.g., Perkins 1969: 267, 270.

[17] Minami Manshū Tetsūdo Kabushiki Kaisha 1936: 33.

[18] See appendix C and Pomeranz (1995) for more on the use of Perkins to project estimates of agricultural parameters backward from the 1930s to circa 1800.

[19] Smil 1983: 333–34, 336.

[20] Ibid., 335–36.   [21] Slicher Van Bath 1977: 94–95.

60 percent more fertilizer by weight per acre, as we have seen, but they applied it more frequently, so that nutrient loss from storage was probably smaller. Finally, most animal manure in China would have been from pigs, while most English manure came from dairy cows or beef cattle. At least today, pigs yield significantly better fertilizer: 2.0–7.5 percent nitrogen content (by fresh weight) versus .6–4.9 percent for beef cattle and 1.5–3.9 percent for dairy cows.[22] Applying more fertilizer of higher quality at shorter intervals, Chinese manuring should have benefited the soil more than British manuring.

Finally, we come to nitrogen-fixing crops. In North China, these would generally have been soybeans; in England, peas, beans, or clover. Clover is a far better nitrogen fixer than peas or beans: under contemporary conditions, the bacteria on the roots of most types of clover will fix 24–94 kgN/acre, with an average for most varieties of around 60 kgN/acre. This mean is slightly higher than that for soybeans, which is 48 kgN/acre.[23] However, since our hypothetical Chinese farm has three soybean crops over six years while the English one has two clover crops, a comparison of mean performances would again favor the Chinese farm (144 kgN/acre every six years vs. 120).

This comparison is beset by many uncertainties, but it at least shows, once again, that there is no reason to assume that China was worse-off. And, English farms that grew either peas or beans as their off-year crop rather than clover would probably have been much worse-off: for ordinary beans, the contemporary range is 4–26 kg/acre with an average of 12, and for peas 7–31 kg/acre with an average of 22 (though lentils are somewhat higher and broad beans much higher).[24] While Smil's estimates for beans correspond to a mean crop yield of about .56 tons per acre[25]—again with wide variations—Bowden's figures for bean output on actual English farms in two of the three years for which he has such figures (1737 and 1738; the third figure is from a year [1671] in which the reported yields for all crops are abnormally high) are 13.4–15 bushels per hectare;[26] this works out to roughly .144 tons per acre, or barely one-fourth of the contemporary mean. If we discount nitrogen fixation by a like factor, to 3 kg/acre, it becomes far too small to compensate for two years of wheat farming. (Incidentally, the comparison among peas, beans, and clover—the latter a crop that spread quickly on "improved" farms—suggests yet another way in which enclosures may have made a big difference, despite the recent tendency in the literature to argue otherwise.)

In sum, then, we cannot generate precise estimates of nitrogen fluxes for either England or North China. We can say, however, that all our evidence suggests that North China was no worse-off; and much of it suggests that it was better-off.

[22] Smil 1985: 153.   [23] Ibid., 142.   [24] Ibid.
[25] Ibid., 145.   [26] Bowden 1990: 374–75.

C

FOREST COVER AND FUEL-SUPPLY ESTIMATES

FOR FRANCE, LINGNAN, AND A PORTION OF

NORTH CHINA, 1700–1850

THE ESTIMATE of North China fuel supply is for southwestern Shandong, one of the most densely populated portions of the North China plain. I have previously generated a fuel-supply estimate for this area in the 1930s, based on fairly reliable data. (The basic sources and techniques used are described in Pomeranz 1988, appendix F.)

To project these estimates back into the late eighteenth century, I again used Huang's estimates of percentage changes in population and cultivated area for North China over this period, as described above; I have no detailed figures that would permit a separate estimate of changes in these counties in particular. And once again, I accepted Perkins's arguments that changes in China's pig population have roughly tracked changes in its human population, while changes in the number of plow animals roughly tracked changes in cultivated acreage.

Reducing cultivated acreage by roughly 30 percent, as indicated by province-wide figures, then requires guesses about what this land was before it was farmed. I have tried to depress my fuel supply estimates by assigning as much land as was even remotely possible to the uses in which it produced the least fuel.

For instance, my 1930s estimate placed 18.9 percent of the area's land under buildings and roads, thus producing no biomass; this was probably a high estimate to begin with. Since the amount of land under buildings and roads should roughly track population and commercialization, it would have been most plausible to assume that only 60 percent as much land was devoted to these uses circa 1800; instead I assigned 80 percent of the 1930s figure (15.1 percent) to this category.

The land that was not cropped, not under buildings or roads, and not totally useless (e.g., rocky hillsides or land so sandy that nothing would grow) needed to be assigned to one of three categories: grassland, semi-forest, or mature forest (in ascending order of their per-acre energy yield). North China has had relatively little grassland for centuries, as it has had relatively few large animals aside from those essential for plowing; and according to a 1940 survey, this area's livestock received only 7.5 percent of their food from grasslands. In order to keep my estimates conservative, I assumed that circa 1800, farm animals received fully half of their feed from grasslands: this is far higher than any of the anecdotal evidence would suggest, and required assigning 27 percent of all land in the area to this category (vs. 3.8 percent in the 1930s). I then assigned the remaining 13 percent of all land to forests, placing two-thirds of it in the lower-yielding category of semi-forest. This is roughly the proportion found in post-1949 surveys, but the share of mature forests was almost certainly higher 150 years earlier.

Finally, I adjusted the quantity of crop residues available for use downward, again guided by Perkins's assumptions. If roughly 70 percent as much land was feeding roughly 60 percent as many people and animals as in the 1930s and yielding a per capita surplus that was not much larger or smaller, then per-acre crop yields were about 85 percent of 1930s levels; I assumed that each acre similarly yielded about 85 percent as much crop residue. I further assumed that farm animals ate about as much in 1800 as they did in 1930 and that the techniques that rural families used to burn wood, stalks, etc., in 1800 were about as efficient as they were in the 1930s. The result was a fairly comfortable fuel supply, by pre–fossil fuel era standards, of .62 tce per person per year; and since the exercise is quite sensitive to land-use estimates, changing any of my very conservative assumptions about land use would quickly increase fuel-supply estimates.

The calculation for France is considerably simpler. Since crop residues and grasses were rarely used for fuel, we need not worry much about patterns of land use other than how much territory was wooded. To arrive at a rough estimate of fuel supply per capita, I simply used the approximate figures for wooded area in 1550 and 1789 cited in Cooper: roughly 18 million and 9 million hectares respectively; for the sustainable fuel yield of each hectare, I used Smil's global average figure of 3.6 tons of wood (1.8 tce) per hectare, which was also used for North China.[1] The population figures—14,000,000 in 1550 and 25,000,000 in 1789—are from McEvedy and Jones.[2]

The result is a per capita fuel supply of 2.31 tce per capita in 1550 and .64 tce per capita in 1789. Since people probably did not use more than .5 tce per person in 1550, we should think of the wood above what was needed to reach that level as available for other uses, and it was available in substantial quantities: roughly 3.6 tons of wood per person per year. But by 1789, almost all of the annual growth on wooded land would have been needed to meet Braudel's estimate of fuel consumption (.5 tce). A mere .29 tons would remain for other uses, just barely above the .24 tons of wood per capita theoretically available for non-fuel uses in North China circa 1800—one of the two most severely deforested parts of China proper. The Asian Development Bank (ADB) suggests that .33 tce per capita is the minimum sustainable fuel use per

---

[1] Cooper 1985: 139n. 2; Smil 1983: 100–101.

[2] McEvedy and Jones 1978: 59.

capita, rather than the .5 tce per capita used here for both France and North China, but most of Asia's poorest people today live in warmer climates than those found in either France or north China, and they have more heat-efficient stoves and homes than people had in the eighteenth century; many also use cooking methods that are far more fuel efficient than French, if not north Chinese, ones. If .5 tce is indeed a reasonable minimum for both France and North China, then by 1800 neither could have spared much wood for other uses without creating a serious fuel crisis for part of the population.

Lingnan, however, was in somewhat better shape than France was, despite a population density that in 1753 was already equal to that of France in 1789, and which then roughly doubled by 1853. Two factors account for most of this advantage. First, in Lingnan, as in North China, crop residues were regularly used as fuel. Second, given Lingnan's subtropical climate and use of Chinese cooking methods, it seemed reasonable to use the ADB's .33 tce per capita as the "subsistence" fuel consumption level, rather than the .5 tce used for France and North China. Smil estimates that people in the poorest tropical villages today burn only one-fifth as much fuel as poor people in temperate zones do;[3] and though Lingnan is only subtropical, I have probably understated its advantages by assuming that people there needed two-thirds as much fuel per capita as in France—particularly since they also used more economical cooking methods than Europeans did. Moreover, to avoid making too much of this climatic difference, I used the same figure for sustainable wood yield per hectare as I did for France and North China, despite the fact that trees grow much more per year in warmer climates.

The first task was to estimate wooded area at different dates. I began with the estimates of forest cover in Lingnan circa 1700 presented by Ling Daxie;[4] Robert Marks has found that these estimates generally accord with other data.[5] Ling estimates that 54.5 percent of Guangdong's 20,200,000 hectares was forest in 1700, and 39 percent of Guangxi's 18,700,000 hectares. By 1937, for which we have better data, Guangdong was down to 10 percent, Guangxi 5 percent,[6] while the two provinces had gained roughly 25,000,000 and 10,000,000 people respectively.[7] Since population growth is the primary force for deforestation, I divided the lost forest by the population increase and obtained rough averages of .4 hectares of lost forest per additional person in Guangdong and .6 hectares per person in Guangxi. (The difference makes sense, given the much greater use of high-yielding paddy agriculture in Guangdong.)

Though crude, this approach is more likely to *overstate* deforestation during the early part of this period than understate it. In the early part of the period,

[3] Smil and Knowland 1980: 119.
[4] Ling 1983: 34.
[5] Marks, personal communication, August 1996.
[6] Ling 1983: 35. [7] Marks 1997: 280.

TABLE C.1

Remaining Forested Area (hectares)

	Guangdong	Guangxi	Total
1753	9,000,000	6,500,000	15,500,000
1773	8,200,000	6,020,000	14,220,000
1793	7,440,000	5,660,000	13,100,000
1813	6,560,000	5,240,000	11,800,000
1833	5,760,000	4,940,000	10,700,000
1853	4,880,000	4,700,000	9,580,000

enough wooded area remained that there was no need to cut more than the sustainable yield for fuel or probably even construction; by the end of the period, sustaining even the most basic household needs would have made it necessary to overcut trees for wood, thus adding an additional dynamic to those undermining the remaining forests. The results appear in table C.1.

Next we need to figure out how much of the subsistence level of fuel consumption (.33 tce per capita) could be met from crop residues. To avoid overestimating the available fuel supply, I made two extremely unrealistic assumptions. First, I assumed that land that was deforested without becoming crop land yielded no fuel and very little animal feed. This ignores a huge amount of land: Marks's estimate of all land added to cultivated area in Guangdong between 1700 and 1937 equals only one-sixth of the lost forest area; for Guangxi, the figure is about one-third. Much of the rest became grassland that could not support crops (especially in hilly areas)[8] but much of that grass was collected for animal feed and other uses.

Second, I have counted only crop residues from food crops. We do not know how much of Lingnan's farmland was being used for different crops at different pre-twentieth-century dates, but we do have a fairly reliable estimate of food consumption from local sources circa 1753: 60,000,000 *shi*, or roughly 9,300,000,000 *jin*.[9] And since rice (and most other crops) produce slightly more residue by weight than edible output, we thus have a minimum figure for residues available from food crops without needing precise acreage figures. But to see how conservative an estimating technique this is, it is worth noting that Marks estimates that Lingnan's food needs could have been raised on as few as 16,800,000 *mu* in 1753,[10] while 43,000,000 were cultivated in Guangdong alone (chapter 9). Thus we are excluding much of the region's crop residues—probably a majority—from our estimates, as we previously excluded the large and growing amount of land that was neither farmed nor forested.

The last part of getting an estimate of crop residues available for fuel in 1753 was to estimate how much of the crop residues were needed for animal

[8] See ibid., 280, 319–27.   [9] Marks 1997: 251.   [10] Ibid., 250.

TABLE C.2
Wood Available for Uses Other Than Fuel in Lingnan,
1753–1853

	Lingnan Forest Area (ha)	Fuel Supply Area	Available for Other Uses
1753	15,500,000	1,650,000	13,850,000
1773	14,200,000	1,675,000	12,525,000
1793	13,100,000	2,260,000	10,840,000
1813	11,800,000	2,469,000	9,331,000
1833	10,700,000	2,956,000	7,744,000
1853	9,580,000	3,339,000	6,241,000

feed. To do this, I estimated that the numbers of livestock per person were the same in eighteenth-century Lingnan as in twentieth-century North China: roughly one cattle equivalent per six people. This may slightly underestimate the number of pigs, since Lingnan was more prosperous than North China, while Perkins estimates that the number of pigs per capita did not change much for China as a whole over this period.[11] However, it is almost certainly an overestimate of work animals, since the number of these animals needed keeps pace with cultivated acreage rather than population, and Lingnan had far less cultivated land per person than North China did. The feed consumption of livestock was assumed to be the same in the eighteenth as in the twentieth century. Finally, I assumed that roughly half of livestock food needs were met with things other than crop residues: grasses, foraging on the ground in wooded areas, human table scraps, etc. (Grass alone could have provided much more than half of these needs.) The result of all these calculations is a figure of 636 pounds (.318 tons) of residues per person available for burning in 1753, yielding .16 tce per capita, or almost half of minimum needs. The remaining fuel needs could have been met by consuming the sustainable wood yield of a mere 1,650,000 of Lingnan's 15,500,000 hectares of forest.

I then used the same conservative methods to estimate fuel supply from crop residues in future years. In other words, I took Marks's estimate of the population increment for each twenty-year period and multiplied by his estimate of food consumption per capita to get the additional residues available (ignoring, once again, that the amount of land cleared was far larger than the amount needed to grow this increment of food), added livestock food demand in proportion to human population growth, assumed constant fuel needs per capita, and then estimated how much forest it would take to sustainably meet fuel needs not met with residues. Table C.2 presents the results.

Finally, I calculated the sustainable yield of wood on the "extra" woodland, and divided by population (see table C.3). Clearly, population growth pressed

[11] Perkins 1969: 71.

TABLE C.3
"Available" Wood per Capita (in tons),
Lingnan, 1753–1853

1753	2.8	1813	1.3
1773	2.2	1833	1.0
1793	1.6	1853	.7

hard against "surplus" wood supplies, even in an ecological/economic regime
that was generally quite frugal. In a century in which population rose roughly
75 percent, forested area declined by only 40 percent, but "surplus" wood
supply fell by 55 percent, and surplus wood per capita by 75 percent. Nonetheless, both current levels and trends remained better than those in preindustrial
France. France's 1550 surplus of 3.6 tons per capita compares favorably with
Lingnan's 1753 figure but not by as much as one might expect; and because
crop land did nothing for French fuel supplies, the strain placed on the wood
"surplus" by each additional person was much greater than it was in Lingnan.
By 1789, population had increased by slightly under 80 percent since 1550—
about the same as in Lingnan from 1753 to 1853—but surplus wood per capita
had fallen by a stunning 92 percent, reaching a level just 40 percent of Lingnan's. Without a new fuel source both areas were headed for serious trouble:
but, contrary to our intuitions, it appears to have been France that faced the
tighter squeeze.

D

ESTIMATES OF "GHOST ACREAGE" PROVIDED
BY VARIOUS IMPORTS TO LATE EIGHTEENTH- AND
EARLY NINETEENTH-CENTURY BRITAIN

Sugar

SUGAR consumption in the early nineteenth-century United Kingdom was roughly 150,000 tons per year *before* the fall in duties touched off a vast increase in purchases.[1] Since 5.6 tons of sugar provides 420 calories a day for 140 people for a year,[2] 150,000 tons of sugar would provide 2,500 calories per day to 614,000 people for a year. (Figures on daily caloric intake vary quite a bit, but estimates for the common folk of Paris on the eve of the Revolution are lower than this[3]—and so are most figures for nineteenth-century English workers.[4]

How much acreage would have been needed to feed this many people otherwise? Converting 150,000 tons of sugar into total calories using Mintz's conversion yields 571,812,466,000 kilocalories. Using the same figures for English wheat yields as in appendix B, and assuming one-tenth of the crop had to be set aside for the following year's seed, a sown acre would yield 471 kilograms of wheat. With a roughly 50 percent extraction rate after milling[5] this becomes 235 kg of flour, with about 3400 kcal per kg,[6] for a total of 799,000 kcal. per sown acre. This would mean that approximately 715,000 sown acres of prime land would be needed. Moreover, according to the English farming accounts summarized by Bowden,[7] such a farm would require four oxen a year as plow animals, each of which would require the hay output of one acre of land (even assuming it got 50 percent of its intake from common grazing areas, and was stall fed only part of the year). Thus, 20 sown acres of wheat really required at least 24 acres of land; multiplying out, we find that replacing the calories in imported sugar with wheat would have required 858,000 acres. If we try to set aside enough hay to feed the plow animal all year long without the use of common grazing land, the figure rises to

---

[1] Mintz (1985: 143), erroneously using "British"; Mitchell 1988 has the actual figures.

[2] Mintz 1985: 191.

[3] Braudel 1981: 130.

[4] Clark, Huberman, and Lindert 1995: 223–26.

[5] Aykroyd and Doughty 1970: 86–88.

[6] Ibid., 89.   [7] Bowden 1990: 73, 75, 294.

1,001,000 acres; if we assume a three-field system in which 10 acres of fallow land (or, in more modern versions, of clover) had to be set aside for 20 acres that were growing wheat, with the animals grazing on those 10 acres, the figure rises to 1,072,000 acres. Finally, if we assume both 10 acres of fallow that was truly resting and 4 separate acres for hay (though this was no longer a common approach by the end of the eighteenth century in England), we get 1,215,500 acres.

An alternate approach involves recognizing that the entire United Kingdom was essentially one food market, with England drawing heavily on supplies from the "Celtic fringe" in the years between 1770 and 1860:[8] an operation that was only possible if these areas had other sources of calories. Scotland, Wales, and Ireland together had almost as many people as England in the early nineteenth century and consumed sugar at about the same rate.[9] Multiplying Deerr's average figure for U.K. consumption (roughly 18 pounds per person) by the population figures in Mitchell[10] yields the following results:

1801: 311,000,000 pounds
1811: 333,000,000 pounds
1831: 432,000,000 pounds

Using the same methods discussed before, the first figure yields 892,000–1,264,000 ghost acres. The 1811 figure becomes 950,000–1,346,000 ghost acres; the 1831 figure 1,237,000–1,752,000 acres. If we were to substitute what Braudel[11] takes to be typical continental yields (assuming England would have had to import any additional grain from elsewhere in Europe), all these numbers would almost double; if on the other hand, we assume greater use of potatoes, the numbers shrink.

Timber

Timber is the easiest case to calculate. I have used Vaclav Smil's estimate[12] of the harvestable increase in wood produced by a hectare of reasonably productive "natural" forest (i.e., not the product of silviculture), and Arthur Lower's figures[13] on the quantity of Baltic and American timber exports to Britain and the conversion of board feet to cubic feet. The result is an estimate of 646,875 acres worth of timber per year from the Baltic at the end of the eighteenth century (based on 150,000,000 board feet per year) and slightly over 1,000,000 acres worth per year from North America in the early nineteenth century (based on 250,000,000 board feet).

---

[8] See Thomas 1985a.   [9] Deerr 1950: II:532.
[10] Mitchell 1988: 9–10.   [11] Braudel 1981: 121.
[12] Smil 1983: 36.   [13] Lower 1973: 25, 39, 259.

Cotton

In 1815, Britain imported roughly 100,000,000 pounds of New World cotton; in 1830, 263,000,000 pounds.[14] Since flax yielded roughly 500 pounds per acre if well tended,[15] enough flax to replace 1815 cotton imports could have been grown on roughly 200,000 acres; enough to replace 1830 imports on roughly 500,000 acres. But flax production was subject to the difficulties described in the text and would have been very hard to expand to this level; *total* English production in the late eighteenth century may have been no more than 8,000,000 pounds on perhaps 16,000 acres.[16] And hemp, which yielded about the same amount per acre and had many of the same problems as a crop, was useless for better fabrics.[17]

Turning to wool, I have used Bowden's reconstruction of a 500-acre English sheep farm on good land in the seventeenth century.[18] He estimates that such a farm could have supported a total of 1,000 wethers (yielding 4.5 pounds of fleece per year) and 1,181 other sheep (yielding 3.5 pounds per animal): the result is a total output of 8,445 pounds of wool per year for the whole farm. At this rate of output, it would have required 11,841 such farms, or 5,920,500 acres, to replace 1815's cotton imports by weight, and 15,393,300 acres to replace 1830's. A pound of wool yielded 35,840 (64 times 560) yards of 64s fine yarn, a "key type,"[19] while a pound of cotton yielded 64 X 840, or 53,760 yards of 64s yarn: 1.5 times as much. (Most eighteenth-century cotton yarn was between 40s and 80s, though nineteenth-century machinery could spin much finer yarns.[20]) If we adjust by this factor to get enough wool to produce as much yarn as the imported cotton, we then get almost 9,000,000 acres for 1815, and over 23,000,000 for 1830.

[14] Mann 1860: 112.
[15] Warden 1967: 11.   [16] Rimmer 1960: 5.
[17] Warden 1967: 49.   [18] Bowden 1990: 86.
[19] Jenkins and Ponting 1982: 11–12.   [20] Mann 1860: 26–27.

E

ESTIMATES OF EARNING POWER OF RURAL
TEXTILE WORKERS IN THE LOWER YANGZI
REGION OF CHINA, 1750–1840

ANY ESTIMATES of how much women earned spinning and weaving cotton must be approximate, because our price information for both raw cotton and cloth is quite spotty and short-term fluctuations are often quite large. Matching peak cotton prices to trough cloth prices—or vice versa—creates very misleading results. Moreover, "cloth" was far from a uniform product, and price quotes are not always clear about what they refer to. The average quality of cloth produced in Jiangnan improved over the course of our period,[1] in part because macro-regions with lower labor costs were meeting more of their own needs for low-quality cloth.

The price data for raw cotton recorded by Kishimoto[2] and for cloth by Zhang Zhongmin[3] fit together into a picture that makes sense, and they seem to represent the most typical cases. However, Fang[4] cites much higher raw cotton prices—almost as high as the final cloth prices cited by Zhang—while the *Mumianpu*, a widely cited eighteenth-century source, cites a cloth price that makes sense in terms of those higher cotton prices but would yield fabulous earnings for textile workers if combined with Kishimoto's prices for raw cotton. (Fang's cotton prices are for North China and at remote markets, but since North China exported raw cotton to Jiangnan, the problem remains.) And the differences matter, since—given that rice prices are well known—using relatively high prices for both cotton and cloth results in higher earnings *in rice* than using low ones.

Consequently, I have done two sets of calculations: one using high prices for both cloth and cotton, and one using lower prices. The two scenarios come out fairly close in the case of a person (or household) that combined weaving and spinning, though the high-price scenario yields a higher income. For those who only spun, the low-price scenario confirms the view that such work did not pay enough to support an adult woman, though this is true only when the most pessimistic assumptions possible are made about all parameters. Otherwise, it suggests such work could support an adult female but without very much left over: not surprising, since it seems that most non-weaving spinners,

---

[1] Fang 1987: 89. [2] Kishimoto 1997.
[3] Zhang Zhongmin 1988. [4] Fang 1987.

at least in the Yangzi Delta, were young girls. The high-price scenario, on the contrary, suggests that even an adult woman spinner could have supported herself and had a bit left over: a somewhat suspicious, but not completely implausible, scenario. And for women who only wove, the low-price scenario gives us earnings that are fairly high but still plausible, while the high-price scenario yields earnings that we know exceed what most rural households had to spend.

Thus, the low price-price scenarios seem more likely, are less favorable to my hypothesis, and accord with more of the available price data. Consequently, I use only those figures in the text. In this appendix, however, I present both sets of estimates.

Mid-Eighteenth-Century Spinning and Weaving in Combination

Using High Prices

CHOICE OF DATA

For the mid-eighteenth century, the *Mumianpu* says that prices for "very good" cotton cloth (it is not clear just how unusual a quality this refers to) "did not exceed" 50 cash (a widely used copper coin, worth roughly one one-thousandth of an ounce of silver) per *chi* (a unit of surface area). Lu Hanchao[5] cites a 1677 source saying that beginning with raw cotton, a woman would need about seven days to spin and weave one 20 *chi* bolt of cloth; these estimates of physical productivity are not much different from Huang's. That bolt of cloth would be worth approximately 1,000 cash, or 1.1 *tael* at 1750 silver-copper exchange rates.

But some part of that value was the cotton in the cloth, rather than the woman's work, and cotton prices varied considerably. Kishimoto Mio's data suggest a mid-century Jiangnan price of 20–40 cash per *jin* of unginned cotton, with prices usually between 20 and 30 cash per *jin*, but exceeding even 40 cash per *jin* in drought years.[6] These are much lower than the cotton prices that Fang cites for North China, as we shall soon see. Nonetheless, when we match Kishimoto's cloth prices with her raw cotton prices, we get shares of the value of the cloth for textile labor and for the cotton itself very close to those derived from Fang.[7] This "low-price scenario" assuming both cheap raw cotton and cheap cloth, is developed on pages 319 and 321–22 below.

However, trouble ensues if we match Kishimoto's relatively low raw cotton prices with the high cloth price in the *Mumianpu*. Since one *jin* of unginned cotton yielded only .33 *jin* of ginned and cleaned cotton, Kishimoto's

[5] Lu 1992: 481.   [6] Kishimoto 1997: 139.   [7] Fang 1987: 92.

unginned cotton prices would suggest prices of 60–120 cash per *jin* of ginned cotton. At this rate, the roughly 1.33 *jin* of cotton that went into a bolt of cloth[8] would cost around 130 cash in an average year; matching this with *Mumianpu* cloth prices leaves almost 90 percent of the value of the cloth as the return to labor. This seemed implausibly high, and since I wanted to produce a conservative estimate of textile workers' earnings, I assumed that the *Mumianpu* price would only occur when raw cotton prices were also high (though it is not clear that this was so). Thus, I used instead the much higher figures of Fang Xing,[9] who gives us a late eighteenth-century North China price of 140–400 cash per ginned *jin*. Since North China still shipped some raw cotton to the Lower Yangzi in this period, I assumed that Lower Yangzi prices could not be lower than the North China price and so chose Fang's top price of 400 cash (again, in order to bias earnings estimates downward). This "high-price" scenario is developed in the following section and on pages 320–21 below.

RESULTS OF HIGH-PRICE SCENARIO

At these prices, the 1.33 *jin* of ginned cotton in a bolt of cloth would cost 533 cash, or more than half the value of the bolt. (These price fluctuations were irrelevant, though, to families who spun and wove cotton they grew themselves.) Since Fang Xing also estimated that a woman who spun cotton (a much less skilled and less remunerative operation than weaving) would usually earn 30–50 percent of the value of the cotton she started with[10]—an estimate on which Huang also relies—our estimate, which implies that a woman who both wove and spun the cotton added slightly less than 90 percent to the value of the raw material, seems quite conservative given these prices: it is far below the contemporary estimate cited by Fang that the price of cloth was generally four times that of the cotton.[11]

If a woman could thus earn 467 cash for seven days of spinning and weaving, then a 210-day work year would yield 14,010 cash per annum. (Such a work year figure is much lower than that observed for rural spinners and weavers in early twentieth-century Jiangnan, who averaged over 300 days of work a year;[12] and, as appendix F shows, it is roughly consistent with our conservative estimates of total cloth output for the region, if every woman in Jiangnan wove. Since some undoubtedly did not, it is likely that the work year for those who did was somewhat longer than 210 days and that our earnings estimates are again being biased downward.) At mid-century exchange rates, this would equal 15.5 silver *taels*. If we use Wang Yeh-chien's 31-year moving average centered on 1750 for rice prices (1.67 *taels*), it would buy 9.3 *shi*.

---

[8] P. Huang, 1990: 84.   [9] Fang 1987: 84.   [10] Ibid., 88.
[11] Ibid., 92.   [12] Xu Xinwu 1992: 469.

Spinning and Weaving Using Low Prices

The Mumianpu price cited above does not appear typical and may reflect cloth of unusual quality or an unusual year. Zhang Zhongmin[13] cites prices of .3 or .4 *taels* for cloth that was 16 *chi* long (80 percent of the length of the cloth in the *Mumianpu*), but gives no figures for weight and does not provide a date other than "mid-Qing." Fang Xing[14] tells us that cloth prices in the Qianlong period (1736–95) were on average .4 *taels* but could be as much as .7 or .8 *taels* in some years. He also gives us a weight for the cloth, saying it used 3 *jin* of raw cotton, or three-fourths of the quantity required by the standard bolt referred to in the *Mumianpu* and in Lu's and Huang's calculations. Let us use his figure of .4 *taels* and go from there.

At the mid-eighteenth-century Lower Yangzi exchange rate, .4 *taels* was roughly 360 cash. If Kishimoto's cotton price figures represent unginned cotton (otherwise, they are absurdly low and would give very high earnings estimates even with low cloth prices), the cotton content of these bolts would cost about 90 cash. These figures mesh perfectly with a source cited by Fang,[15] which says that the cost of cloth was four times that of the equivalent amount of raw cotton. The value added by labor for this piece of cloth would thus be 270 cash; if we translate this into the larger bolts that Lu, Huang, and the *Mumianpu* have in mind, the value added by labor would be 360 cash. If this was what a woman earned with seven days of spinning and weaving labor, her earnings in a 210-day work year would be 10,800 cash or 12 *taels*; about 22 percent below our estimate using high prices, but still enough to purchase 7.2 *shi* of rice at 1750 prices, and as we shall now see, fully competitive with the earnings available to male farm workers.

Comparisons to Male Earnings and to the Cost of Eating

Estimates of average rice consumption range from 1.74 to 2.62 *shi* per person per year; Marks settles on 2.17 as a good average.[16] The highest estimate I have seen is 5.5 *shi* per year for an adult male doing outdoor physical labor; Pan uses 2.5 for an adult female and considerably less for children.[17] These data help put our hypothetical woman's earnings in context.

Landless male agricultural laborers in Jiangnan in this period typically earned between 2 and 5 *taels* in cash per year;[18] the higher figure comes not from annual rates but from multiplying monthly rates by 12 and thus assumes

[13] Zhang Zhongmin 1988: 207.
[14] Fang 1987: 92.
[15] Ibid., 92.
[16] Marks 1991: 77–78.
[17] Pan 1994: 327.
[18] Zhao 1983: 57.

that such a laborer managed to find work all twelve months of the year (some-what unlikely, but not impossible). Agricultural laborers also received at least some of their meals while working. If we assume for argument's sake that they received all their nutrition free, they found work all year-round, and their diet consisted largely of 5 *shi* of rice per year (slightly below the highest available figure), then they earned in cash and rice the equivalent of 10.4–13.4 *taels* per year (or, alternatively, 6.1–7.8 *shi* of rice).

Thus, our hypothetical high-priced weaver/spinner earned 116–149 percent of the earnings of a male farm laborer, even if he worked all year-round and she "only" 210 days. If we look at the margin of income left over after feeding oneself and remember how much less women customarily ate than men (espe-cially men working in the fields), the difference grows significantly: the woman would have 6.8 *shi* of rice left over after feeding herself; the man only 1.2 to 3.0 *shi*.

The weaver/spinner in our more likely low-price scenario does not do quite as well, but still compares well to a male farmhand. Her 12.0 *taels* of earnings are just above the mid-point of the 10.4–13.4 *tael* range for male farm laborers that we calculated with very generous assumptions; and since adult women ate less than men, she, too, enjoys a significantly larger surplus above her own consumption than does a male farm laborer.

To put matters another way, the woman in the high-price scenario could feed 1.9 adult male equivalents with her work, or (if she were a widow) she could feed herself, an aging parent or parent-in-law, and three or perhaps even more young children (depending on ages and assuming, of course, that the aged grandparent handled enough child care and other housework to make the mother's textile work feasible). The woman in the low-price scenario could feed 1.4 adult male equivalents, or herself, an elderly person, and perhaps as many as two children. Though such an existence would have been difficult, it would have been no worse, and probably somewhat better, than that of a household headed by a male farmworker whose wife had died, even if he was rather lucky in other respects. Clearly, female earnings were not below subsis-tence in this period, as suggested by "involutionary" arguments.

Spinning without Weaving in the Mid-Eighteenth Century
Using High Prices

Women who only spun had bleaker prospects, though still less bleak than some scholars have suggested. An adult woman using a spinning wheel with a foot pedal could produce 8 *liang* (0.5 *jin*) of yarn a day; using a pedal-less wheel (as a young girl would have), 5 *liang* (0.31 *jin*) per day was more likely. At roughly 30–50 percent of the value of the cotton she started with (Fang

1987:88), the spinner earned the equivalent of 0.09 to 0.25 *jin* of cleaned and ginned cotton daily, depending on both her output and price fluctuations; let us use 0.16 *jin*, slightly below the midpoint of this range. If cotton prices varied from 140 to 400 cash per *jin*, and we again use a middle figure, she would earn 43 cash per day, or 8,600 cash—equaling roughly 9.5 *taels*, or 5.3 *shi* of rice—for a 200-day work year. Continuing to use mid-range figures for raw cotton prices and the spinner's earnings relative to that price, while adopting a low-end output figure, yields 6,600 cash per year, or roughly 7 *taels*: 3.9 *shi* of rice. If we maintain our generous assumptions about male farm laborers' earnings, then these women earned at most 91 percent as much (matching the highest estimate for spinners to the lowest one for farm laborers) and perhaps 52 percent (if we do the opposite). But 200 days of even these low earnings would have fed an adult woman and a child; moreover, many Jiangnan spinners who did not weave were young girls living with parents. Only if we insist on combining low-end figures for price *and* productivity does a 200-day work year yield an earnings estimate (2.0 *shi*) that was probably inadequate for feeding an adult woman, and even then she might survive on it: it would buy about 1,700 calories of rice per day.

There is another way to generate estimates of the earnings of "spinners," though it depresses those earnings excessively. Roughly speaking, producing a bolt of cloth required 7 days of work (6 in some later sources): 4 for spinning, 1 for weaving, and 2 for other tasks. Let us assign all miscellaneous tasks to the spinner, making them part of how she earned an income equal to 40 percent of the value of the 1.3 *jin* of raw cotton contained in a bolt of cloth (priced at the midpoint of Fang's range). The spinner then earned 143 cash over 6 days: 24 cash per day, or 4,800 in a 200-day work year, yielding about 3.2 *shi* of rice annually. This was still enough to feed an adult and perhaps a small child. And as we shall see, this method of calculation, which attributes the entire difference in value between yarn and cloth to one day of weaver's labor, yields ridiculously high earnings for weavers; its only usefulness is for arriving at an ultraconservative estimate of spinners' earnings. Since in reality most households combined weaving and spinning, their net results were unaffected by which family member did which subtasks.

Using Low Prices

If we continue estimating spinners' incomes at 40 percent of the value of the cotton they spun, using low-end cotton prices naturally depresses earnings. Pricing ginned cotton at about 90 cash per *jin*, a spinner processing a low-end 0.31 *jin* per day earned a dismal 11.2 cash per day, or roughly 1.5 *shi* of rice per year. If we further assume that she did all other work besides weaving, her daily earnings fall to 0.22 *jin* per day, or 1.2 *shi* of rice per year. This would be well below an adult female's subsistence, though it might still feed a pre-teen girl. It is also noteworthy that the scholar who estimated spinners' earnings as a percentage of the cotton price, Fang Xing (1987), also took our high cotton prices as typical. There is no reason to assume that this percentage was fixed regardless of cotton prices; more likely, Fang's low figure for labor's share of the value of yarn reflects the pressures that producers would have faced when raw materials prices rose while the markets in which cloth was sold remained intensely competitive, keeping prices down. It also bears repeating that households typically combined spinning and weaving; thus isolating the returns to spinning alone would mostly be relevant to a relatively few particularly unfortunate people, such as elderly widows who could no longer weave.

Weaving Only in the Mid-Eighteenth Century

At any given cloth price, the less value attributable to the spinner, the more would be attributable to the weaver. Very few rural weavers purchased all their yarn; most either spun some themselves or had a family member who spun (probably without the family ever calculating the shadow "earnings" of separate members). But for argument's sake, let us estimate the income from a 210-day year of only weaving.

It took 7 days to produce a bolt of cloth, with the spinning requiring 4 days, and the weaving 1. If we again assign all non-weaving tasks to the spinner (which is unlikely but necessary for generating the lowest of the above estimates of spinners' earnings), the entire difference between yarn and cloth prices would be attributable to one day of weaving, making that day very lucrative. Using the low price scenario above (which seems to have been the more typical one), that one day of labor would have transformed yarn worth about 168 cash (40 percent above the value of the ginned cotton) into cloth worth about 480 cash. That would mean 312 cash per day or 65,520 per year—an incredible 73 *taels*. The earnings in the high-priced scenario would be even more implausible: 640 cash each day, or a ridiculous 134,400 cash (almost 150 *taels*) per year. This reinforces the artificiality of the lowest estimates of spinners' earnings.

If we instead assign all three days of non-spinning work to the weaver, we get a high, but perhaps plausible, 24.3 *taels* per year for the weaver in a low-price scenario (roughly double the earnings of a farm laborer) and an outrageous estimate of almost 50 *taels* for the high-price scenario. But in the end, this, too, is largely a theoretical exercise: relatively little yarn was marketed, so most households combined spinning and weaving; average earnings for the whole cloth-making process are what count.

Spinning and Weaving in Later Times

Our scattered price data make it hard to be sure what happened to the earning power of spinners and weavers in the century after 1750. Because cloth prices appear to have been pretty flat, except for the fanciest cloth,[19] while rice prices (which are very well documented) rose significantly, we can be sure that the real buying power of our hypothetical spinner/weaver fell, but in order to estimate how much, we need to make some assumptions. In what follows below, I sketch four possible scenarios, which yield declines of 25–50 percent.

A

This is the simplest approach and yields the most optimistic result. It involves beginning from our high-price scenario and using trends in raw cotton prices from the Canton area; we have relatively good data for this area, thanks in large part to the presence of foreigners (many of them bringing cotton from India). Since these raw cotton prices show no secular change between 1750 and 1850[20] and the price of cloth also shows no trend, this model tells us that a textile producer's nominal earnings should also have shown no change; she would then be poorer in real terms by the increase in the price of rice, which was roughly 22 percent between 1750 and 1800 and 32 percent by 1840.[21]

B

However, it is unlikely that raw cotton prices in the Yangzi Valley were as trendless as those in the Canton area. In fact, flat prices in the Canton area themselves suggest an upward trend in the Yangzi Valley. Lingnan had long received most of its cotton from the Lower Yangzi, but in the mid-eighteenth century it also began to buy cheaper Indian cotton; when cotton from the Lower Yangzi again pushed out the Indian imports at Canton, this was widely attributed to a sharp decline in transport cost between the Lower Yangzi and Lingnan.[22] If prices at Canton were level while transport costs fell, this suggests that the acquisition cost of the cotton in Jiangnan was rising. But by how much?

[19] Zhang Zhongmin 1988: 207–8.   [21] Dermigny 1964: IV: table 19.
[20] Y. C. Wang 1992: 41–44.   [22] See, e.g., Greenberg 1951: 91–92.

Let us initially take our high-price scenario as representing 1750 conditions. If we do that, we need to use Fang's high-end price as our mid-century point of departure, but since he provides no data on trends over time, we need some proxy for how much further raw cotton prices may have risen over the next century. One very simple approach that has something to be said for it would be to assume that over the long run the price of cotton tracked the price of rice. This gains some plausibility from the fact that these two prices do seem to have moved together (though with cotton lagging by a few years) over the course of the seventeenth century.[23] It also seems reasonable in terms of either a monetary explanation for price increases, or—more central to our analysis—a hypothesis that emphasizes changing land/labor ratios and proto-industrialization in Jiangnan's trading partners, leading to more difficulty in acquiring cheap imports of either rice or raw cotton. Indeed, there are reasons to think that raw cotton would have been subject to greater inflation than grain. North China, the Lower Yangzi's main external source of cotton, had particularly high population growth during the century after 1750, and (as shown in chapter 3 and appendix F) probably reduced its cotton acreage while increasing its own spinning and weaving; thus its raw cotton exports may have fallen particularly sharply. And as the Grand Canal decayed, shipping costs between North China and the Lower Yangzi may well have risen, further interfering with Jiangnan's imports of raw cotton. Meanwhile, the fall in transport costs between the Lower Yangzi and Lingnan—a route along which Jiangnan *exported* raw cotton—probably raised the price that buyers for the Lingnan market were willing to pay. Although rice imports to the Lower Yangzi (mostly from the Middle Yangzi) fell for the same reasons as did cotton imports from North China—population growth and proto-industrialization in the relatively less-advanced area—the decline was not as sharp, and increased trade with Manchuria may have offered at least some relief through rising imports of secondary grains; the main import was soybeans that were ground up for fertilizer, but some wheat (and some soybeans that were eaten) arrived, too. Thus, though assuming that raw cotton prices rose at the same rate as rice prices after 1750 is a guess, it is probably a conservative guess.

If we use rice price trends to stand for cotton, too, then the raw cotton content of a 1,000 cash piece of cloth should have risen from 533 cash (based on Fang's work, as discussed above) to roughly 654 cash by 1800. Accordingly, the textile worker's share of the price falls from 467 cash to 346 cash, a decline of roughly 25 percent. And with rice prices rising by slightly over 20 percent over the same fifty years,[24] the decline in real earnings comes to roughly 40 percent. If we carry out the same operation for the year 1840, we find that the cost of cotton in a 1,000 cash piece of cloth has risen to 702 cash,

---

[23] Kishimoto 1997: 141.   [24] Y.C. Wang 1992: 41–44.

and the return to textile labor has accordingly fallen to 298 cash; with rice rising still further to 2.20 *taels* per *shi*, the decline in real earnings rises to roughly 52 percent over this ninety-year period.

But as we have seen, our low-price scenario is probably the more typical one, and here, too, we can generate two possibilities. The first takes Kishimoto's scattered figures for eighteenth-century cotton prices at face value; the second uses instead her finding that seventeenth-century cotton prices roughly tracked those for rice and applies it to the eighteenth and early nineteenth centuries. With the limited data available, both are only rough estimates.

C

Kishimoto has collected a number of eighteenth-century Jiangnan raw cotton prices which suggest that these prices more than doubled between 1750 and 1800 (though we again have troubles separating real trends from short-term fluctuations).[25] And, as we have seen, these prices yield reasonable earnings estimates when coupled with the mid-century cloth prices cited by Zhang Zhongmin and by Fang Xing (though very high ones when combined with those in the *Mumianpu*). If we now turn to our low-price scenario for 1750, which used Kishimoto's cotton prices and Zhang and Fang's cloth prices, and then double the price of raw cotton, the raw material share of the value of a 480 cash bolt of cloth rises from 120 cash to 240, and the spinner/weaver's share accordingly falls from 360 to 240 cash per bolt: a 33 percent decline in nominal earnings. If we then further deflate these earnings by the increase in the rice price just to 1800 (Kishimoto's cotton price data stop in 1794), the decline in real earnings is 45 percent. If we assume (in the absence of data) no further rise in cotton prices to 1840, the further increase in the price of rice nonetheless brings the decline in real earnings to almost exactly 50 percent; if cotton prices continued to rise after 1800, the fall in earning power would be even larger.

D

Finally, let us use our low-price scenario for mid-century but imagine that raw cotton prices tracked those of rice. If so, then the cost of the cotton in a 480 cash bolt rose from 120 to 158 cash between 1750 and 1840, and the spinner/weaver's share fell from 360 to 302 cash: a decrease of just under 33 percent. Wu and Xu cite a mid-nineteenth-century source which says that raw cotton sold for "3,200" (presumably copper cash) per *dan* (100 *jin*) in

[25] Kishimoto 1997: 139.

1821,[26] which would be very close to Kishimoto's prices for unginned cotton seventy years earlier; the same source, however, says that by 10–20 years later, 4,500–5,000 (cash) was a more normal price (with, as in other sources, reports of far more violent short-term fluctuations). Thus this data produce roughly the same price increase over a century as does the guess that raw cotton prices tracked those of rice, though it differs in packing all of that increase into the last twenty years of the period.

If we use the rice price index and raise the share of raw material in our cloth price from 120 to 158 cash, the spinner/weaver's share falls from 360 to 302 cash: a rather modest decline of 16 percent in nominal earnings. But coupled with the rise in rice prices, even this scenario yields a decline in real earnings of 37 percent by 1840. (The figures for 1800 would be 147 cash for the cotton and 333 for labor—the decline in earnings would thus be 7 percent in nominal terms and 25 percent in real terms.)

[26] Wu and Xu 1985: 323.

F

ESTIMATES OF COTTON AND SILK PRODUCTION, LOWER YANGZI AND CHINA AS A WHOLE, 1750 AND LATER—WITH COMPARISONS TO UNITED KINGDOM, FRANCE, AND GERMANY

Silk Production in Guangdong

I HAVE estimated silk production for the two largest producing regions only: Guangdong (mostly the Pearl River Delta) and the Yangzi Delta. For Guangdong, the method is basically the same as was used for sugar production (described in chapter 3). We begin with Robert Marks's data on cultivated land and the amount of land needed for food crops and arrive at an estimate that at least 16,800,000 *mu* of land were being used for non-grain crops in 1753. (Marks himself suggests that the number is probably about 20 percent higher than this.) We then assign one-tenth of this land—1,680,000 *mu*—to mulberries for silk-raising, just as we did with sugar. This is almost certainly an underestimate, since mulberries and sugar were by far the most common non-grain crops in the province, and since this gives us an acreage in mulberries for the entire province that is less than the amount in the three biggest silk counties in the province during the 1920s, and much lower than the figures for the delta counties as a whole. If we use Alvin So's estimate that it took 20 *mu* of mulberries to feed the silkworms who produced 1 picul (133 pounds) of high-grade silk,[1] these 1,680,000 *mu* could have generated about 11,000,000 pounds of silk per annum.

At about the same time, Guangdong produced roughly one-quarter of China's silk exports.[2] Since Guangdong had the only port in the country open to foreign trade and was hundreds of miles further from the main internal markets for high-quality silk (the Lower Yangzi and the capital region) than was the other main producing area (the Yangzi Delta itself), it seems unlikely that Guangdong's silk production was *less* export oriented than that of the Yangzi Delta. It therefore seems unlikely that Yangzi Delta silk production would have been any less than three times that of Guangdong (33,000,000 pounds) and likely that it was considerably more: a guideline worth keeping in mind as we turn to estimating that area's production.

[1] So 1986: 80. [2] Ibid., 81 n.2.

Silk Production in Jiangnan

For the Yangzi Delta, we know considerably more about cropping patterns. Wang Yeh-chien has done careful estimates of the food consumption and food imports of the fourteen delta prefectures,[3] which can be used to generate estimates of how much land must have been in food crops in order to provide the locally produced part of the food supply. I have used Perkins's figure of 1.9 *shi* per *mu* of husked rice as an average yield,[4] Wang's own population figures for each prefecture[5] (which are actually for 1778, but population was not growing much in this area after 1750), and cultivated *mu* figures from the official tax rolls (which are certainly not too high) as recorded in Perkins and Liang Fangzhong.[6] (These data come from both 1735 and 1820 and are very close together for most of the prefectures.)

I have departed from Wang in only two ways, both of which should depress my output estimates. First, I have omitted the three prefectures lying on the north side of the Yangzi River. Though these areas did produce both cotton and silk, they were also major salt producers, which complicates the task of assigning non-grain land to other crops. By omitting them completely, I naturally decrease my total output estimates. Second, I have used an estimate of 2.2 *shi* of rice or its equivalent for average per capita grain consumption, rather than Wang's 2.0: this makes my calculations consistent with those of Marks for Guangdong and means that more land had to be under grain than Wang would suggest.

This process yields the totals found in table F.1 for land under non-grain crops in the delta prefectures—figures that are generally the same or lower than the casual estimates of contemporaries cited by Wang that (for instance) half of a particular prefecture's land was in cotton.

Once we have these estimates of non-grain land, we need to allocate that land among the possible non-grain crops. In this area, such land would have been overwhelmingly devoted to cotton and mulberries, rather than to the great diversity of Guangdong cash crops; consequently we can avoid the need for such low-ball estimates such as the one-tenth of non-grain land that we allocated to sugar and silk in Guangdong. Instead, we can be guided by Wang's characterizations of these prefectures as largely cotton producing, largely silk producing, or mixed—though we will once again reduce the acreage arbitrarily (by 50 percent for some prefectures) just to be sure that our estimates are conservative.

Hangzhou, Huzhou, and Jiaxing were all primarily silk-raising prefectures

---

[3] Y.C. Wang 1989.   [4] Perkins 1969: 21.   [5] Y.C. Wang 1989: 427.
[6] Perkins 1969: 230; Liang Fangzhong 1981: 401–13.

TABLE F.1

Estimated Acreage of Non-grain Crops in Yangzi Delta Prefectures
c. 1750

Prefecture	Cultivated Acreage	Grain Acreage	Non-Grain Acreage
Suzhou	6,254,000	3,471,209	2,782,791
Songjiang	4,048,871	1,877,230	2,171,641
Taicang	3,962,671	1,263,409	2,699,262
Changzhou	5,579,264	3,222,943	2,356,321
Zhenjiang	5,200,023	1,815,028	3,384,995
Jiangning	5,233,949	1,798,866	3,435,083
Hangzhou	4,284,327	1,733,300	2,551,027
Jiaxing	4,356,442	1,538,385	2,818,057
Huzhou	6,136,678	1,406,438	4,279,640
Ningbo	4,066,059	1,290,984	2,775,075
Shaoxing[a]	3,492,271	2,955,317	536,954

[a]Shaoxing is the only case in which the 1735 and 1820 figures for total cultivated acreage are wildly disparate; the 1820 figure of 6,765,514 is almost double the one used here. Adopting it would bring the percentage of land in non-food crops for Shaoxing up to slightly less than 60 percent, a figure far more in line with the other Delta prefectures than the roughly 15 percent used here. Nonetheless, I have decided to use the lower (and almost certainly less accurate) figure in order to avoid any risk of overestimating silk and cotton output.

with very little cotton; together they had 10,098,724 *mu* of cash-crop land, capable of generating 66,651,578 pounds of high-quality silk. If, for argument's sake, we take just three-fourths of this land to be in mulberries, this would still generate approximately 50,000,000 pounds of silk. Suzhou, Ningbo, and Shaoxing were mixed cotton/silk prefectures. According to our earlier calculations they had 6,094,820 *mu* of cash crops among them. Though the figure for Suzhou seems a bit low, given the near-unanimous opinion that it was the most highly commercialized prefecture in the empire, and the figure for Shaoxing is certainly low (see note to the table above), I have further reduced this acreage by 50 percent just to be extra cautious. This gives us 3,947,410 *mu* to split evenly between cotton and mulberries; doing that would yield another 10,056,453 pounds of high-grade silk. Thus even if we make all these allowances and assume zero silk production in the rest of the delta (clearly not the case), we arrive at an estimate of roughly 60,000,000 pounds of silk per year for this region: roughly two pounds per resident. It would not be hard to justify a figure twice as high.

Generating a national figure is extremely difficult, since we have omitted so many producing areas and tried to generate low numbers even for the two we examined. Still, it is worth noting that even if the figures above represented total Chinese silk output, we would have about 71,000,000 pounds, or 5.1 to 6.5 ounces per year for each of 175,000,000–225,000,000 people—not much, but far from trivial for a luxury product.

Jiangnan Cotton

The procedures above assigned 1,523,705 *mu* to cotton in our mixed cotton/ silk prefectures, even after arbitrarily reducing their non-food acreage by 50 percent. At what appears to have been an average yield for this era of about 39 pounds of ginned cotton per *mu*, this land would give us 59,424,495 pounds of output. If we then take the acreage in the delta prefectures that were primarily cotton growing and multiply by the same output estimate, we get 547,764,778 pounds of cotton, which, added to our earlier figure, puts us slightly over 600,000,000 pounds. In the interests of again being conservative I have arbitrarily reduced this to 500,000,000 pounds. Nonetheless, this gives a total Jiangnan cotton output of slightly over 16 pounds per person.

Two further steps are needed to arrive at an estimate of how much cotton was turned into cloth in Jiangnan. First, we need to account for cotton that was used for things other than cloth (principally padding for jackets and quilts). We have no estimates for the amount of cotton so used in the eighteenth century, but in the early twentieth century, these uses amounted to about 1.3 pounds per person in China as a whole.[7] If the same was true in the eighteenth century, Jiangnan would have had about 14.7 pounds of cotton per person available for spinning and weaving; I have rounded this down to 14.5 pounds.

Second, we need to factor in the cotton that Jiangnan imported from North China, and the cotton that it exported to the Southeast Coast and Lingnan (mostly in exchange for sugar). Unfortunately, we have virtually no hard data on the size of these flows. Some anecdotal evidence suggests that Jiangnan's cotton imports were probably larger than its exports in the eighteenth century, so that we would not be inflating local cloth output estimates if we simply left these flows aside; I have adopted that as a provisional strategy and used the cloth output figures from the paragraph above. But there are some reasons to think that in spite of this anecdotal evidence, Jiangnan was a net *exporter* of raw cotton even in the 1750s; and since Lingnan demand rose and imports from North China fell over the next century, it certainly was by 1850. Unfortunately there is no direct way of measuring these flows with available data (and fortunately, they do not matter for calculating *national* output); we can only guess at how much they might affect our regional estimates.

One reason to think that Jiangnan exported raw cotton is that it would have

[7] Chao 1977: 233.

been difficult—though not impossible—for its labor force to turn as much raw cotton as it produced into cloth. If we stick by our estimates of bolt size and per woman productivity from appendix E, the 450,000,000 pounds of cotton (after subtracting what was used for padding) would have been enough to make roughly 30,000,000 bolts of cloth, which would have required the labor of roughly 10,000,000 adult female equivalents working 210 days per year. In 1750, Jiangnan had roughly 16,000,000 female residents; if the age structure of the population was roughly the same as it was in the early twentieth century, this would yield almost exactly 10,000,000 women between the ages of ten and fifty.[8] Since we know that a fair number of women worked in sericulture and others at various other tasks besides cotton-spinning and weaving, it is hard to see that there could have been enough adult females involved in cotton textiles.

Various solutions to this problem are possible. One is that there was some labor contribution (in spinning, not weaving) by nine- and perhaps eight-year-olds; this is probably true, but there cannot have been much more than 300,000 of these girls. The number of women over fifty would have been more substantial (perhaps 2,500,000) and some no doubt did spin and weave, but we do not know how many. Men did some weaving, but we have no way of knowing how much. It is possible that my rather arbitrary estimate of a 210-day work year for women in cotton-spinning and weaving is too low—it was, as we saw, over 300 in the early twentieth century—but raising it much further would yield suspiciously high female (and household) earnings. It is not impossible that these various factors could reconcile our estimates of labor productivity with the assumption that Jiangnan imported as much raw cotton as it exported, but it seems more likely that there is some residual still to be explained by exports. Some of this was probably to areas very nearby, such as the three rather prosperous prefectures directly adjacent (on the north) to Jiangnan: these prefectures, which Wang Yeh-chien includes in his definition of the "Yangzi Delta," probably had another 1,500,000 women aged 10–49.

The rest of the difference would have been exported to the Southeast Coast and Lingnan. That Jiangnan's exports were large is suggested by evidence of booming textile production in these two regions (which produced very little cotton of their own, and imported some, but not nearly enough, from India). It is also suggested by the scale of Jiangnan's sugar imports from those regions: quite likely something in the area of 300,000,000 pounds, at a price per pound (for white sugar) about the same as that for ginned cotton.[9] Contemporaries often described the Lingnan-Jiangnan trade as primarily an exchange of these two commodities, so it is tempting to simply assert that Jiangnan exported 300,000,000 pounds of ginned cotton; but we have no way of knowing that the

[8] Buck 1964: 377.
[9] See Mazumdar (1984: 64) on sugar prices; appendix E on cotton prices.

merchandise trade balanced, or about the other items involved (which included various expensive luxuries). And since the scale of imports from North China is even harder to estimate (see pages 335–37 below), it seems futile to try to estimate by how much we need to cut our Jiangnan cloth production figures; until more data surfaces, it seems best to simply say (remembering the other things I have done to try to keep this estimate down) that 14.5 pounds per capita is probably a bit high, but not wildly so.

In an important, just-published work, however, Li Bozhong has made an estimate of Jiangnan cloth output that is considerably below mine. (He does not address empire-wide output.) Interestingly, his estimates reflect estimates of output per laborer that are about the same as mine,[10] but he assumes that a far lower percentage of the Jiangnan population was engaged in spinning and weaving.

Li uses for Jiangnan an estimate of per capita cloth consumption for one of its prefectures, Songjiang, generated by Xu Xinwu; he then adds Wu and Xu's estimate of "exports" to come up with Jiangnan's total output.[11] But unless Songjiang cloth was extraordinarily heavy, Xu's estimate (in bolts) would convert to a per capita cloth consumption for Songjiang—perhaps the richest prefecture in the empire—considerably below even the cautious empire-wide average of Wu and Xu (on which, see page 337 below). Li then works backward from this output to generate an estimate of the number of women engaged in textile production.[12] He takes it as confirmation of this estimate that it is reasonably close to his estimate of how many rural households were engaged in non-agricultural activities: but that is a very risky procedure given the huge number of families that *combined* farming and textile production. In what follows, I suggest that, on the contrary, estimates based on the textile labor force are more consistent with my higher guess.

Li estimates that roughly 1.4 million households in a particular part of Jiangnan, each with a mother and daughter working in textile production, could have produced about 60 percent of what he takes to be Jiangnan's cloth output. If the rest were all produced by similar households at a similar rate, this would still give a textile labor force of about 2.3 million such mother-daughter pairs—fewer than half of all rural households—and a total of roughly 3.5 million adult equivalents producing textiles: about 19 percent of the total Jiangnan labor force. These figures seem to me far too low.

Li notes that various early and mid-Qing observers estimated the non-agricultural labor force in Jiangnan at 50–70 percent, but he believes these numbers must be too high.[13] Instead he adopts estimates in 1930s and 1940s surveys, which suggest that slightly over 10 percent of rural households did no

[10] Li Bozhong 1998: 150–51, 219n. 28.   [11] Ibid., 109.
[12] Ibid., 185n. 10.   [13] Ibid., 22–23.

farming, while suggesting that this is a conservative estimate. He further suggests that the population of Jiangnan was about 15 percent urban.[14]

Li is almost certainly right that the figure of 10 percent of rural households doing no farming is too low for the eighteenth and nineteenth centuries, probably substantially so. (He uses it anyway in order to make his estimates conservative.) For one thing, rural spinning had been devastated by urban, mechanized competition by the 1930s. For another, as discussed in chapters 5 and 6, there is substantial reason to think that the quantity of cloth production (and thus of weaving) in Jiangnan had declined by the 1930s, and some of what remained had moved into cities. Moreover, grain shipments to Jiangnan from the rest of China appear to have been lower in the 1930s than two hundred years earlier, despite the growth of substantial cities; this confirms other evidence that local grain output must have been rising, largely due to increased labor inputs. Some of that increased labor was no doubt more work from each laborer, but there are good reasons to also suspect some increase in the agricultural labor force. For all these reasons, the share of non-farming rural households in Jiangnan two hundred years earlier was almost certainly well above 10 percent. And since in some of these households both men and women would have been engaged in textile production, they would have raised the number of people producing cloth substantially. If one adds in some urban production as well as production by the women of the household in considerably more than half of all farming households (recall Li's own observation elsewhere that the Qing period finally saw the nearly complete triumph of the "man plows, woman weaves" ideal for division of labor in Jiangnan[15]), it is not hard to generate significantly higher cloth production figures for Jiangnan. The simplifying assumption made here that Jiangnan's raw cotton exports and imports balanced out may generate figures that are a bit too high, but other cautions have been built into the calculations, and I continue to think that my estimate of over 14 pounds per capita for Jiangnan cotton production in 1750 falls within a reasonable range of possibility.

Comparisons with the United Kingdom

If we accept this as a rough estimate, it is suggestive that the United Kingdom's production of cotton, wool, silk, and linen put together comes to 12.9 pounds per person in 1800,[16] well after the breakthroughs in textile technology

[14] Ibid., 20–22.   [15] Li Bozhong 1996: 99–107.
[16] Deane and Cole 1962: 51, 185, 196, 202. Population figures from Mitchell 1988: 9–10. Ideally, it would be preferable to compare the Yangzi Delta to Britain, since Ireland presumably depresses per capita figures, and the Yangzi Delta did not have a comparably large poor area within it, but I have not been able to disaggregate the U.K. numbers.

had begun to spread. (Since a pound of either linen or wool generally made fewer square feet of cloth than a pound of cotton, amalgamating these different kinds of textiles in one weight both simplifies the comparison and biases it against China.) Unfortunately, we do not know how much of its cloth the Yangzi Delta exported—the share may well have been even higher than the U.K.'s proportion (about one-third of output),[17] thus reducing the area's cloth *consumption* below U.K. levels. But the likelihood of roughly comparable production and perhaps consumption of this key commodity in the most productive regions of China and Europe is suggestive, especially when we remember that these Yangzi Delta prefectures, with 31,000,000 people in 1753, were almost twice as populous as the United Kingdom.

National Cotton Production and Comparisons with Other Parts of Europe

When we try to compare the whole of China with the whole of Europe, the data problems become much worse. Data for both China and Europe become very spotty and production much too geographically dispersed to allow us to concentrate on a few key areas. The exception to this, as we saw, is silk, where the Lower Yangzi likely had the majority of China's output, perhaps as much as three-fourths. But silk was a small portion of total textile output, and cotton production was quite dispersed.

Unfortunately, the methods used to generate our sugar, silk, and Jiangnan cotton estimates, which work well for well-defined, highly commercialized areas, break down when applied to vast but less-commercialized areas. In such cases relatively small changes in our assumptions about per capita food consumption, for instance, can easily double or triple our estimates of the amount of land available for cotton (from, let us say, 3–9 percent of a very large total acreage). Consequently, we need to try something else—working backward from later figures.

In 1870, shortly after the Nian and Taiping rebellions were suppressed, China grew roughly 1,850,000,000 pounds of cotton.[18] This figure then fell to about 1,500,000,000 pounds by 1900, but then began a new and so far continuous rise. It seems likely that 1750 output was not much lower and was thus much higher per capita. This claim may seem surprising, but it is borne out by examining China's major cotton areas one by one.

First of all, it is important to note that there were few large regions that took up cotton-growing for the first time during the Qing.[19] The Middle Yangzi

[17] Deane and Cole 1962: 185, 196, 202.

[18] Calculated based on Chao (1977: 233) and Kraus (1968: 162).

[19] Zhao 1977: 23.

provinces did increase their cotton cultivation after 1750, but they never became very large producers. Meanwhile, some important producing areas in the western provinces of Sichuan and Shaanxi switched to a different cash crop in the nineteenth century—opium poppies—often at the expense of cotton; some of this occurred before 1870 and some after.[20] While other pockets of cotton cultivation were scattered all over China, the most important areas in 1750 and 1870–1900 were the Lower Yangzi and north China. For the Lower Yangzi, there is little reason to believe that cotton output expanded much in the nineteenth century. Neither population nor cultivated acreage grew at all between 1750 and 1850 in the most commercialized parts of the region, nor much in the rest of it; after huge losses in the mid-nineteenth-century catastrophes, population and acreage may have recovered by 1900, but they did not grow much further until after 1949.[21] And since all our indications suggest that the portion of land devoted to cash crops in this area in 1750 was already as high as it would get over the next two centuries—indeed, rice imports to the area were probably lower in the 1930s than the 1750s, suggesting that some land may have even turned back to food production—one would expect that cash-crop acreage was about the same throughout. If anything, *cotton* acreage may have declined, at least by 1900, since much more land shifted into mulberries after 1870. And though our yield figures are spotty, they do not suggest any increase for Yangzi Valley cotton between 1750 and 1900; nor would one expect an increase, since there was no major change in technique and (with no increase in population) probably not much change in labor inputs.

This brings us, finally, to North China, for which data are particularly scarce and the amount of land in cotton may well have fluctuated more than elsewhere. On the one hand, Kraus's estimate suggests that Shandong and Hebei together had only 3,000,000 *mu* under cotton in 1900, rising to 5,000,000–6,000,000 *mu* by the 1920s (despite significant damage done by warlords in this area), and still higher in the 1930s.[22] (Shandong and Hebei are two of North China's three major cotton-growing provinces; I have found no useful data for the third province, Henan.) This rise was likely a recovery to earlier levels, since we have already seen that national cotton output fell between 1870 and 1900, and North China, which was hit by horrendous late nineteenth-century droughts that must have made a thirsty crop like cotton seem particularly risky, would have been a logical place for much of that decline to occur. Even Kraus's 1920s figure amounts to barely 3 percent of cultivated acreage in the two provinces.

On the other hand, Chao Kang quotes a mid-eighteenth-century source which claims that 20–30 percent of the cultivated land in Zhili (the Qing name

[20] Ibid.

[21] Li Bozhong, 1994a: 34; Skinner 1977a: 213, adjusting for Skinner 1987.

[22] Kraus (1968), cited in P. Huang 1985: 126, 128.

for Hebei) was under cotton: 14,000,000–21,000,000 *mu* in that province alone.[23] The *Mianhua tu*, also an eighteenth-century source, says that 20–30 percent of the land in Zhili south of Baoding was in cotton.[24] Depending on precisely how we interpret that statement, we get an area of 35,000,000–50,000,000 registered *mu* in 1820 (again, probably a significant underestimate of real acreage); multiplying by 20–30 percent gives us 7,000,000–15,000,000 *mu* under cotton just in this one province. If even 10 percent of land in Shandong and Hebei was under cotton, that would be 17,000,000–24,000,000 *mu*, or 6 to 8 times the 1900 figure.[25] This is also the approximate acreage available for non-food crops in the two provinces if we use the estimating methods used above for other regions, accept the unrealistically low official estimates of cultivated acreage, and assume per capita food consumption of 2.2 *shi* per year.[26] If we instead accept that cultivated acreage in the 1750s was already close to 1930s' levels, the acreage available for non-food crops balloons to a suspiciously high 70,000,000–90,000,000 *mu*, depending on whether we assume food consumption of 2.2 or 2.5 *shi* per person; in either case, cotton would have been the most common non-food crop. Thus, there are good reasons to believe that North China may have grown considerably *more* cotton in 1750 than in 1870 or 1900.

Other data indirectly suggest the same thing. The population of Shandong and Hebei increased over 40 percent between 1750 and 1870, and by about 80 percent by 1913, while cultivated acreage increased much less. Perkins has suggested, in fact, that this acreage did not increase at all.[27] This strikes me as too extreme—as noted in chapter 5, I think these provinces had significantly more forest even in 1800 than they had by the 1930s. But even the dubious official figures for the 1750s suggest an increase of barely 4 percent by 1873, and about 45 percent by the 1930s; "increases" that include significant additions to the rolls of land that had been farmed all along.[28] Elsewhere in China, the worsening person/land ratios were largely balanced by large gains in per-acre yields, created by more intensive use of fertilizer (both manure and beancake), more multi-cropping, and the application of additional labor per *mu* (e.g., through extremely careful weeding). But North China did not grow anything that would respond to additional labor as impressively as rice does; additional inputs of fertilizer were largely limited to manure, since the more effective beancake was also more expensive; and the shorter growing season ruled

---

[23] Chao 1977: 23.

[24] Quoted in Zhang Gang 1985: 99. Acreage figures for Zhengding, Xunde, Guangping, Daming, Yizhou, Chaozhou, Shenzhou, and Dingzhou, plus maybe Hejian and Baoding itself from Liang (1980: 401).

[25] For official figures on cultivated acreage, which are far too low, and a plausible correction to them, see P. Huang 1985: 325.

[26] Marks (1991: 77), noting estimates that range from 1.74 to 2.62 *shi* per person, uses 2.17 for Lingnan, which was more prosperous than North China.

[27] Perkins 1969: 219.   [28] P. Huang 1985: 322.

out a massive increase in multi-cropping. Moreover, worsening problems of waterlogging and soil salinity after the Yellow River shift in 1853 quite likely caused falling yields on tens of millions of *mu* in Shandong province. Consequently, it seems most likely that the amount of land North China needed to devote to raising its food increased considerably faster than the amount of land it cultivated between 1750 and 1870, 1900, or even 1930; this in turn suggests that this area's absolute output of cotton is likely to have shrunk significantly over this period.

Thus, it seems likely that North China cotton output fell significantly, as Sichuan and Shaanxi output may have, while Lower Yangzi output stayed about the same; only the Middle Yangzi and (conceivably) Henan—two much less important cotton areas—increased their output. Given these regional results, it seems likely that total Chinese cotton output circa 1750 was at least as high as it was in 1870, or certainly 1900.

If, for the sake of further caution, we take the 1900 figure, subtract cotton used for wadding and other non-yarn uses, and then divide by 1750's much smaller population (175,000,000–225,000,000), we get an average consumption per capita of about 6.2 pounds per person; using the 1870 figure gives us almost 8.0 pounds per person. These figures are considerably higher than Xu and Wu's estimate for 1840, which is based on reasoning backward from twentieth-century figures (a very tricky enterprise since we have no agreement on whether output and living standards rose or fell during the tumultuous century after 1840).[29] They come up with about 3.5 pounds per capita (including wadding) versus 7.5 pounds (including wadding) for even my lower estimate. But this is not actually very worrisome. If I am right that total cotton output did not change much between 1750 and 1840, while population doubled (Xu and Wu use an 1840 figure of 400,000,000), their per capita estimates for 1840 should be roughly half of mine for 1750. Thus, my range of estimates for 1750 seems reasonable, with the low end more likely than the high one.

How does this compare with European figures? U.K. consumption (including Ireland) in 1800 appears to have been about 8.7 pounds per capita of cotton, wool, silk, and linen combined.[30] French linen production in the 1780s appears to have been about 6.9 pounds per capita and cotton a trivial .3 pounds.[31] Data for wool exist only in square yards rather than pounds, and an exact conversion depends on the type of cloth made; but using what seems a fairly safe rate, circa 1800 production comes to 1.18 pounds per person per annum.[32] It thus seems likely that French textile output per capita on the eve

[29] Ibid., 322.

[30] Calculated based on Deane and Cole 1962: 51, 185, 196, 202.

[31] Data from Mitchell 1980: 30, 448, 478.

[32] Data from Markovitch 1976: 459; information on measures on p. 497. To convert to pounds, I used Chao's (1977: 234) estimate of the weight of coarse cotton cloth and Jenkins's and Ponting's observation (1982: 11–12) that wool yarn weighed 1.5 times as much as cotton yarn of the same length and fineness.

of the Revolution was similar to our higher estimate for China and one-third higher than our bottom estimate. For Germany, the earliest figures I could find suggest a significantly lower textile output than China: wool output in 1816 was a mere 1.1 pounds per person, cotton output in 1838 still only .6 pounds per person, and linen output in 1850 about 3.3 pounds per person, making a total of 5 pounds of textiles per person.[33] No doubt cloth imports from England made German consumption higher than these production figures, but it still seems likely that early nineteenth-century Germans used less cloth each year than the average Chinese had seventy-five years earlier. And Germany, of course, was still far from the poorest part of Europe—I am not aware of any useful figures for eastern or southern Europe until the late nineteenth century—while our Chinese estimates include the most remote and impoverished parts of the empire. It would appear, then, that Chinese textile consumption stacked up quite well against Europe's in the mid- to late eighteenth century.

[33] Data from Mitchell 1980: 30, 448, 464, 478.

BIBLIOGRAPHY

Abel, Wilhelm. 1980. *Agrarian Fluctuations in Europe from the 13th to the 20th Centuries*. New York: St. Martin's Press.

Abu-Lughod, Janet. 1989. *Before European Hegemony: The World System*, A.D. 1250–1350. New York: Oxford University Press.

Adachi Keiji. 1978. "Daizu kasu ryūtsū to shindai no shōgyōteki nōgyō" (The circulation of soybean cake and commercialized agriculture in the Qing). *Tōyōshi Kenkyū* 37:3. 35–63.

Adshead, S. A. M. 1997. *Material Culture in Europe and China, 1400–1800*. New York: St. Martin's Press; London: MacMillan Press.

Albion, R. G. 1965 (1926). *Forests and Sea Power: The Timber Problem of the Royal Navy*. Hamden, Conn.: Archon.

Alexander, Paul, Peter Boomgaard, and Ben White. 1991. *In the Shadow of Agriculture: Non-farm Activities in the Javanese Economy, Past and Present*. Amsterdam: Royal Tropical Institute.

Allen, Robert. 1982. "The Efficiency and Distributional Consequences of Eighteenth Century Enclosures." *Economic Journal* 92:4 937–53.

Ambrosoli, Mauro. 1997. *The Wild and the Sown*. Cambridge: Cambridge University Press.

Amin, Samir. 1974. *Accumulation on a World Scale*. New York: Monthly Review Press.

Anderson, Eugene. 1988. *The Food of China*. New Haven: Yale University Press.

———, and Marja Anderson. 1977. "Modern China: South." In K. C. Chang, ed., *Food in Chinese Culture: Anthropological and Historical Perspectives*. New Haven: Yale University Press. 317–82.

Andrews, Kenneth. 1984. *Trade, Plunder and Settlement: Maritime Enterprise and the Genesis of the British Empire, 1480–1630*. Cambridge: Cambridge University Press.

Appadurai, Arjun. 1986. "Introduction: Commodities and the Politics of Value." In Arjun Appadurai, *The Social Life of Things: Commodities in Cultural Perspective*. Cambridge: Cambridge University Press. 3–63.

Arasaratnam, S. 1980. "Weavers, Merchants and Company: The Handloom Industry in Southeastern India, 1750–1790." *Indian Economic and Social History Review* 17:3. 257–81.

Arrighi, Giovanni. 1994. *The Long Twentieth Century: Money, Power, and the Origins of Our Times*. New York: Verso.

Asian Development Bank. 1982. *Asian Energy Problems*. New York: Frederick A. Praeger.

Aykroyd, W. R., and Joyce Doughty. 1970. *Wheat in Human Nutrition*. Rome: United Nations Food and Agriculture Organization.

Bagchi, A. K. 1976. "De-industrialization in India in the Nineteenth Century: Some Theoretical Implications." *Journal of Development Studies* 12:2 (January): 135–64.

———. 1979. "A Reply [to Marika Vicziany]." *Indian Economic and Social History Review* 16:2. 147–61.

Bairoch, Paul. 1975. "The Main Trends in National Economic Disparities since the Industrial Revolution." In Paul Bairoch and Maurice Levy-Leboyer, eds., *Disparities in Economic Development since the Industrial Revolution*. New York: St. Martin's Press. 3–17.

Bakewell, Peter. 1988. *Silver and Entrepreneurship in Seventeenth Century Potosi*. Santa Fe: University of New Mexico Press.

Barrett, Ward. 1990. "World Bullion Flows, 1450–1800." In James Tracy, ed., *The Rise of Merchant Empires*. New York: Cambridge University Press. 224–54.

Bayly, C. A. 1983. *Rulers, Townsmen, and Bazaars*. Cambridge: Cambridge University Press.

———. 1989. *Imperial Meridian: The British Empire and the World, 1780–1830*. London: Longman's.

Beattie, Hilary. 1979. *Land and Lineage in China: A Study of T'ung-ch'eng County, Anhwei, in the Ming and Ch'ing Dynasties*. Cambridge: Cambridge University Press.

Behrens, Betty. 1977. "Government and Society." In E. E. Rich and C. H. Wilson, eds., *The Cambridge Economic History of Europe, Volume V*. Cambridge: Cambridge University Press. 549–620.

Bellah, Robert. 1957. *Tokugawa Religion: The Values of Pre-Industrial Japan*. Glencoe, Ill.: Free Press.

Bernal, Rafael. 1966. "The Chinese Colony in Manila, 1570–1770." In Alfonso Felix, ed., *The Chinese in the Philippines, 1570–1770*. Manila: Solidaridad Publishing. 40–66.

Bernhardt, Kathryn. 1992. *Rents, Taxes and Peasant Resistance: The Lower Yangzi Region, 1840–1950*. Stanford: Stanford University Press.

Bhargava, Meena. 1993. "Perception and Classification of the Rights of the Social Classes: Gorakhpur and the East India Company in the Late 18th and Early 19th Centuries." *Indian Economic and Social History Review* 30:2. 215–37.

Blaikie, Piers, and Harold Brookfield. 1987. *Land Degradation and Society*. London: Meteun.

Blaut, James. 1993. *The Colonizer's Model of the World: Geographical Diffusionism and Eurocentric History*. New York: Guilford.

Blayo, Yves. 1975. "La mortalité en France de 1740 à 1829" (Mortality in France, 1740 to 1829). *Population* (November–December): 138–39.

Bloch, Marc. 1966. *French Rural History*. Berkeley: University of California Press.

Blum, Jerome. 1961. *Lord and Peasant in Russia, from the Ninth to the Nineteenth Century*. Princeton: Princeton University Press.

———. 1971. "The Internal Structure and Polity of the European Village Community from the Fifteenth to the Nineteenth Century." *Journal of Modern History* 43:4 (December): 541–76.

Blussé, Leonard. 1981. "Batavia 1619–1740: The Rise and Fall of a Chinese Colonial Town." *Journal of Southeast Asian Studies* 12:1 (March): 159–78.

———. 1986. *Strange Company: Chinese Settlers, Mestizo Women and the Dutch in VOC Batavia*. Dordrecht, Holland: Foris Pubications.

Borah, Woodrow. 1943. *Silk Raising in Colonial Mexico*. Berkeley: University of California Press.

Borgstrom, George. 1972. *The Hungry Planet: The Modern World at the Edge of Famine*. New York: MacMillan.

Bowden, Peter, ed. 1990. *Economic Change: Wages, Profits, and Rents, 1500–1750.* Vol. 1 of Joan Thirsk, gen. ed., *Chapters from the Agrarian History of England and Wales.* Cambridge: Cambridge University Press.

Boxer, Charles, ed. 1953. *South China in the 16th Century.* London: Hakluyt Society.

Braudel, Fernand. 1977. *Afterthoughts on Material Civilization and Capitalism.* Baltimore: Johns Hopkins University Press.

———. 1981. *The Structures of Everyday Life: The Limits of the Possible.* Trans. Sian Reynolds. New York: Harper and Row.

———. 1982. *The Wheels of Commerce.* Trans. Sian Reynolds. New York: Harper and Row.

———. 1984. *The Perspective of the World.* Trans. Sian Reynolds. Berkeley: University of California Press.

Bray, Francesca. 1984. *Agriculture.* Part II of Vol. 6, *Biology and Biological Technology* (Vol. 41 overall). In Joseph Needham, ed., *Science and Civilization in China.* Cambridge: Cambridge University Press.

———. 1985. *The Rice Economies: Technology and Development in Asian Societies.* New York: Oxford University Press.

———. 1997. *Technology and Gender: Fabrics of Power in Late Imperial China.* Berkeley: University of California Press.

Brenner, Robert. 1985a. "Agrarian Class Structure and Economic Development." In T. H. Aston and C. H. E. Philpin, eds., *The Brenner Debate: Agrarian Class Structure and Economic Development in Pre-Industrial Europe.* Cambridge: Cambridge University Press. 10–63.

Brenner, Robert. 1985. "The Agrarian Roots of European Capitalism." In T. H. Aston and C. H. Philpin, eds., *The Brenner Debate: Agrarian Class Structure and Economic Development in Pre-Industrial Europe.* New York: Cambridge University Press. 213–327.

Brennig, Joseph. 1977. "Chief Merchants and the European Enclaves of 17th Century Coromandel." *Modern Asian Studies* 11:3. 321–40.

———. 1986. "Textile Producers and Production in Late 17th Century Coromandel." *Indian Economic and Social History Review* 23:4. 333–53.

Britnell, R. H. 1993. *The Commercialization of English Society, 1000–1500.* Cambridge: Cambridge University Press.

Brook, Timothy. 1993. *Praying for Power: Buddhism and the Formation of Gentry Society in Late-Ming China.* Cambridge, Mass.: Harvard University Press.

———. 1998. *The Confusions of Pleasure: Commerce and Culture in Ming China.* Berkeley: University of California Press.

Bruchey, Stuart. 1967. *Cotton and the Growth of the American Economy, 1790–1860.* New York: Harcourt Brace.

Brundage, Anthony. 1978. *The Making of the New Poor Law: The Politics of Inquiry, Enactment, and Implementation, 1832–1839.* New Brunswick, N.J.: Rutgers University Press.

Buck, John L. 1964 (1937). *Land Utilization in China.* New York: Paragon Book Reprint Corp.

Buoye, Thomas. 1993. "From Patrimony to Commodity: Changing Concepts of Land and Social Conflict in Guangdong Province during the Qianlong Reign (1736–1795)." *Late Imperial China* 14:2 (December): 33–59.

Burke, Peter. 1993. "*Res et Verba*: Conspicuous Comsumption in the Early Modern World." In John Brewer and Roy Porter, eds., *Consumption and the World of Goods*. New York: Routledge. 148–61.

Butel, Paul. 1990. "France, the Antilles, and Europe, 1700–1900." In James Tracy, ed., *The Rise of Merchant Empires*. Cambridge: Cambridge University Press. 153–73.

Cain, M. 1982. "Perspectives on Family and Fertility in Developing Countries." *Population Studies* 36:2 (July): 159–75.

Carr, Raymond. 1967. "Spain." In Albert Goodwin, ed., *The European Nobility in the Eighteenth Century*. New York: Harper and Row. 43–59.

Chan, Wellington. 1977. *Merchants, Mandarins and Modern Enterprise in Late Ch'ing China*. Cambridge, Mass.: Harvard University Press.

———. 1982. "The Organizational Structure of the Traditional Chinese Firm and Its Modern Reform." *Business History Review* 56:2 (Summer): 218–35.

Chandler, Alfred D. 1977. *The Visible Hand: The Managerial Revolution in American Business*. Cambridge, Mass.: Harvard University Press.

Chang Chung-li. 1955. *The Chinese Gentry: Studies on Their Role in Nineteenth Century Chinese Society*. Seattle: University of Washington Press.

———. 1962. *The Income of the Chinese Gentry*. Seattle: University of Washington Press.

Chao Kang (Zhao Gang). 1975. "The Growth of a Modern Cotton Textile Industry and the Competition with Handicrafts." In Dwight Perkins et.al., *China's Modern Economy in Historical Perspective*. Stanford: Stanford University Press. 167–201.

———. 1977. *The Development of Cotton Textile Production in China*. Cambridge, Mass.: Harvard University Press.

———. 1983. "Zhongguo lishishang gongzi shuiping de bianqian" (Changes in the historic level of wages in China). *Zhongguo wenhua fuxing yuekan* 16:9 (September): 52–57.

———. 1986. *Man and Land in Chinese History: An Economic Analysis*. Stanford: Stanford University Press.

Chaudhuri, 1978. K. N. Chaudhuri, *The Trading World of Asia and the English East India Company, 1660–1760*. Cambridge: Cambridge University Press.

Chaudhuri, K. N. 1981. "The English East India Company in the 17th and 18th Centuries: A Pre-Modern Multi-national Organization." In Leonard Blussé and Femme Gaastra, eds., *Companies and Trade*. Leiden: Leiden University Press. 29–46.

———. 1985. *Trade and Civilization in the Indian Ocean: An Economic History from the Rise of Islam to 1750*. Cambridge: Cambridge University Press.

———. 1990. *Asia before Europe: Economy and Civilization of the Indian Ocean from the Rise of Islam to 1750*. Cambridge: Cambridge University Press.

Chaussinand-Nogaret, Guy. 1985. *The French Nobility in the 18th Century*. Cambridge: Cambridge University Press.

Chayanov, A. U. 1966 (1925). *The Theory of Peasant Economy*. Homewood, Ill.: Irwin.

Chen Han-seng. 1936. *Landlord and Peasant in China*. New York: International Publishers.

Chen Hongmou. 1962 (1820). "Fengsu tiaoyue" (Agreed principles concerning customs). In He Changling and Wei Yuan, eds., *Huang chao jingshi wenbian* (A collection of essays on statecraft in our dynasty). 68:4a-6b (pp. 1752–53). Taibei: Guofeng chubanshe.

Chen Fu-mei and Ramon Myers. 1976. "Customary Law and the Economic Growth of China during the Ch'ing Period." *Ch'ing-shi wen-t'i* 3:1. 4–12.

Chi Ch'ao-ting. 1963 (1936). *Key Economic Areas in Chinese History*. New York: Paragon.

China News Digest, May 21, 1998.

Chu Dajun, ed. 1968 (1680). *Guangdong xinyu*. (A new discourse on Guangdong). Taibei: Taiwan xuesheng shuju.

Clark, Gregory. 1991. "Yields Per Acre in English Agriculture, 1250–1860: Evidence from Labour Inputs." *Economic History Review* 44:3. 445–60.

———. 1996. "The Political Foundations of Modern Economic Growth: England 1540–1800." *Journal of Interdisciplinary History* 26:4 (Spring): 563–88.

———. 1998. "Commons Sense: Common Property Rights, Efficiency, and Institutional Change." *Journal of Economic History* 58:1 (March): 73–102.

Clark, Gregory, Michael Huberman, and Peter H. Lindert. 1995. "A British Food Puzzle, 1770–1850." *Economic History Review* 48:1. 215–37.

Clunas, Craig. 1988. *Chinese Furniture*. London: Bamboo Publishers.

———. 1991. *Superfluous Things: Material Culture and Social Status in Early Modern China*. Cambridge: Polity Press.

Cooper, J. P. 1985. "In Search of Agrarian Capitalism." In T. H. Aston and C. H. Philpin, eds., *The Brenner Debate: Agrarian Class Structure and Economic Development in Pre-Industrial Europe*. New York: Cambridge University Press. 138–91.

Cornell, Laurel. 1996. "Infanticide in Early Modern Japan? Demography, Culture and Population Growth." *Journal of Asian Studies* 55:1 (February): 22–50.

Cranmer-Byng, J. L., 1962. *An Embassy to China: Being the Journal Kept by Lord Macartney during His Embassy to the Emperor Ch'ien-lung, 1793–1794*. London: Longman's.

Crawcour, E. S. 1965. "The Tokugawa Heritage." In William W. Lockwood, ed., *The State and Economic Enterprise in Japan*. Princeton: Princeton University Press. 17–44.

———. 1968. "Changes in Japanese Commerce in the Tokugawa Period." In John W. Hall, ed., *Studies in the Institutional History of Early Modern Japan*. Princeton: Princeton University Press. 189–202.

Cronon, William. 1983. *Changes in the Land: Indians, Colonists, and the Ecology of New England*. New York: Hill and Wang.

Crosby, Alfred. 1986. *Ecological Imperialism: The Biological Expansion of Europe, 900–1900*. Cambridge: Cambridge University Press.

Curtin, Philip. 1969. *The Atlantic Slave Trade: A Census*. Madison: University of Wisconsin Press.

———. 1984. *Cross-Cultural Trade in World History*. Cambridge: Cambridge University Press.

———. 1990. *The Rise and Fall of the Plantation Complex: Essays in Atlantic History*. New York: Cambridge University Press.

Cushman, Jennifer. 1975. "Fields from the Sea: Chinese Junk Trade with Siam during the Late Eighteenth and Early Nineteenth Centuries." Ph.D. diss., Cornell University.

———. 1978. "Duke Ch'ing-fu Deliberates: A Mid-Eighteenth Century Reassessment of Sino-Nanyang Commercial Relations." *Papers on Far Eastern History* 17 (March): 137–56.

Da Cruz, Gaspar. 1953 (1570). "The Treatise of Fr. Gaspar da Cruz, O.P." In Charles R. Boxer, ed. and trans., *South China in the Sixteenth Century*. London: Hakluyt Society. 45–239.

Daniels, Christian. 1996. "Agro-Industries: Sugarcane Technology." Volume 6, Part III of Joseph Needham, ed., *Science and Civilization in China*. New York: Cambridge University Press. Section 42a:5–539.

Darby, H. C. 1956. "The Clearing of the Woodland in Europe." In B. L. Thomas, ed., *Man's Role in Changing the Face of the Earth*. Chicago: University of Chicago Press. 187–216.

Day, John. 1978. "The Bullion Famine of the 15th Century." *Past and Present* 79 (May): 3–54.

Deane, Phyllis, and W. A. Cole. 1962. *British Economic Growth, 1688–1959*. New York: Cambridge University Press.

Deerr, Noel. 1949–50. *The History of Sugar*. Vols. 1 and 2. New York: Chapman and Hall.

deJesus, Eduard C. 1982. "Control and Compromise in the Cagayan Valley." In Eduard C. deJesus and Alfred W. McCoy, *Philippine Social History: Global Trade and Local Transformation*. Quezon City: Ateneo de Manila University Press. 21–38.

Dennerline, Jerry. 1986. "Marriage, Adoption and Charity in the Development of Lineages in Wu-Hsi from Sung to Ch'ing." In Patricia Ebrey and James Watson, eds., *Kinship Organization in Late Imperial China*. Berkeley: University of California Press. 170–209.

Dermigny, Louis. 1964. *La Chine et l'Occident: Le commerce à Canton au XVIIIᵉ siècle 1719–1833* (China and the West: The Canton trade in the eighteenth century, 1719–1833). 4 vols. Paris: S.E.V.P.E.N.

DeVries, Jan. 1974. *The Dutch Rural Economy in the Golden Age, 1500–1700*. New Haven: Yale University Press.

———. 1975. "Peasant Demand and Economic Development: Friesland 1550–1750." In William Parker and E. L. Jones, eds., *European Peasants and Their Markets*. Princeton: Princeton University Press. 205–65.

———. 1976. *The Economy of Europe in an Age of Crisis, 1600–1750*. New York: Cambridge University Press.

———. 1993. "Between Consumption and the World of Goods." In John Brewer and Roy Porter, eds., *Consumption and the World of Goods*. London: Routledge. 85–132.

———. 1994a. "How Did Pre-Industrial Labour Markets Function?" In George Grantham and Mary MacKinnon, eds., *Labour Market Evolution*. London: Routledge. 39–63.

———. 1994b. "The Industrious Revolution and the Industrial Revolution." *Journal of Economic History* 54:2 (June): 249–70.

———, and Ad. Van der Woude. 1997. *The First Modern Economy: Success, Failure, and Perseverance of the Dutch Economy, 1500–1815*. Cambridge: Cambridge University Press.

Dewald, Jonathan. 1987. *Pont St. Pierre, 1398–1789: Lordship, Community, and Capitalism in Early Modern France*. Berkeley: University of California Press.

de Zeeuw, J. W. 1978. "Peat and the Dutch Golden Age: The Historical Meaning of Energy Attainability." *Afdeling Agrarische Geschiedenis Bijdragen* 21. 3–31.

Dharampal, ed. 1971. *Indian Science and Technology in the Eighteenth Century: Some Contemporary European Accounts.* Dehli: Impex India.

Diamond, Jared. 1992. *The Third Chimpanzee: The Evolution and Future of the Human Animal.* New York: Harper Collins.

Du Jiaji. 1994. "Qingdai tianhuabing zhi lunchuan fangzhi ji qi dui huangzu renkou zhi yinxiang chu tan" (A preliminary discussion of the spread and prevention of smallpox in the Qing Dynasty and its influence on the population of the imperial lineage). In Li Zhongqing and Guo Songyi, eds., *Qingdai huangzu renkou xingwei de shehui huanjing* (The social environment of the demographic behavior of the Qing imperial lineage). Peking: Peking University Press. 154–69.

Dudbridge, Glen. 1991. "A Pilgrimage in Seventeenth Century Fiction: T'ai-shan and the *Hsing-shih yin-yuan chuan.*" *T'oung Pao* 77:4–5. 226–52.

Dumont, Louis. 1970. *Homo Hierarchicus: An Essay on the Caste System.* Chicago: University of Chicago Press.

Dunstan, Helen. 1977. "Official Thinking on Environmental Issues and the State's Environmental Roles in Eighteenth Century China." In Mark Elvin and Liu Ts'ui-jung, eds., *Sediments of Time.* Cambridge: Cambridge University Press. 585–614.

Earle, Peter. 1989. *The Making of the English Middle Class: Business, Society, and Family Life in London, 1660–1730.* Berkeley: University of California Press.

Elliott, J. H. 1961. "The Decline of Spain." *Past and Present* 20 (November): 52–75.

———. 1990. "The Seizure of Overseas Territories by the European Powers." In Hans Pohl, ed., *The European Discovery of the World and Its Economic Effects on Pre-Industrial Society, 1500–1800.* Stuttgart: Franz Steiner Verlag. 43–61.

Elliott, Mark. 1993. "Resident Aliens: The Manchu Experience in China, 1644–1800." Ph.D. diss., University of California, Berkeley.

Elman, Benjamin. 1990. *From Philosophy to Philology: Intellectual and Social Aspects of Change in Late Imperial China.* Cambridge, Mass.: Harvard University Press.

Elvin, Mark. 1973. *The Pattern of the Chinese Past.* Stanford: Stanford University Press.

Engerman, Stanley. 1994. "The Industrial Revolution Revisited." In Graham Snookes, ed., *Was the Industrial Revolution Necessary?* London: Routledge. 112–23.

Esherick, Joseph. 1981. "Number Games: A Note on Land Distribution in Pre-Revolutionary China." *Modern China* 7:4. 387–412.

Everitt, Alan. 1967. "The Marketing of Agricultural Produce." In Joan Thirsk, ed., *The Agrarian History of England and Wales.* Vol. 4 Cambridge: Cambridge University Press. 460–592.

Fairbank, John K. 1968. "A Preliminary Framework," and "The Early Treaty System in the Chinese World Order." In John K. Fairbank, ed., *The Chinese World Order.* Cambridge, Mass.: Harvard University Press. 1–20, 257–75.

Fan Shuzhi. 1990. *Ming Qing Jiangnan shi zhen tanwei* (An exploration of towns in Jiangnan during the Ming-Qing period). Shanghai: Fudan daxue chubanshe.

Fang Xing. 1987. "Lun Qingdai qianqi mianfangzhi de shehui fen gong" (An essay on the social division of labor in cotton textile production in the first half of the Qing Dynasty). *Zhongguo jingji shi yanjiu* 2:1. 79–94.

———. 1996. "Qingdai Jiangnan nongmin de xiaofei" (The expenditures of peasants in Qing Dynasty Jiangnan). *Zhongguo jingji shi yanjiu* 11:3. 91–98.

Farnie, D. A. 1979. *The English Cotton Industry and the World Market, 1815–1896.* New York: Oxford University Press.

Ferguson, James. 1988. "Cultural Exchange: New Developments in the Anthropology of Commodities." *Cultural Anthropology* 3:4. 488–513.

Fletcher, Joseph. 1995. *Studies in Chinese and Islamic Inner Asia.* Ed. Beatrice Forbes Manz. Brookfield, Vt.: Variorum.

Flinn, M. W. 1958. "The Growth of the English Iron Industry, 1660–1760." *Economic History Review* 2d ser. 11:2 (1958): 144–53.

————. 1978. "Technical Change as an Escape from Resource Scarcity: England in the 17th and 18th Centuries." In William Parker and Antoni Marczak, eds., *Natural Resources in European History.* Washington, D.C.: Resources for the Future. 139–59.

Flinn, Michael W. 1984. *The History of the British Coal Industry. Volume 2. 1700–1830: The Industrial Revolution.* Oxford: Clarendon Press.

Flynn, Dennis. 1984. "Early Capitalism Despite New World Bullion: An Anti-Wallerstinian Interpretation of Imperial Spain." Translation of "El desarrollo del primer capitalismo a pesar de los metales preciosos del Nuevo Mondo: Una interpretacion anti-Wallerstein de la Espana Imperial." *Revista de Historia Economica* 2:2 (Spring): 29–57.

————. 1995. "Arbitrage, China, and World Trade in the Early Modern Period." *Journal of the Economic and Social History of the Orient* 38:4. 429–48.

————, and Arturo Giraldez. 1996. "China and the Spanish Empire." *Revista de Historia Economica* 14:2 (Spring): 309–38.

————. 1997. "Introduction." In Dennis Flynn and Arturo Giraldez, eds., *Metals and Monies in an Emerging Global Economy.* Aldershot, U.K.: Variorum, xv–xl.

Forster, Robert. 1960. *The Nobility of Toulouse in the Eighteenth Century: A Social and Economic Study.* Baltimore: Johns Hopkins University Press.

Frank, Andre Gunder. 1969. *Capitalism and Underdevelopment in Latin America: Historical Studies of Chile and Brazil.* New York: Monthly Review Press.

————. 1998. *ReOrient: The Silver Age in Asia and the World Economy.* Berkeley: University of California Press.

Fu Lo-shu. 1966. *A Documentary Chronicle of Sino-Western Relations, 1644–1820.* Tuscon: University of Arizona Press and Association for Asian Studies.

Fukuzawa, H. 1982a. "The State and the Economy: Maharashtra and the Deccan." In Tapan Raychaudhuri and Irfan Habib, eds., *The Cambridge Economic History of India, Volume 1 c.1200–c.1750.* Cambridge: Cambridge University Press. 193–202.

————. 1982b. "Agrarian Relations and Land Revenue: The Medieval Deccan and Maharashtra." In Tapan Raychaudhuri and Irfan Habib, eds., *The Cambridge Economic History of India, Volume 1 c.1200–c.1750.* Cambridge: Cambridge University Press. 249–60.

————. 1982c. "Non-Agricultural Production: Maharashtra and the Deccan." In Tapan Raychaudhuri and Irfan Habib, eds., *The Cambridge Economic History of India, Volume 1 c.1200–c.1750.* Cambridge: Cambridge University Press. 308–14.

Gaastra, Femme. 1981. "The Shifting Balance of Trade of the Dutch East India Company." In Leonard Blussé and Femme Gaastra, eds., *Companies and Trade.* Leiden: Leiden University Press. 47–70.

Gadgil, Madhav, and Ramachandra Guha. 1993. *This Fissured Land: An Ecological History of India*. Berkeley: University of California Press.

Galenson, David. 1989. "Labor Markets in Colonial America." In David Galenson, ed., *Markets in History*. New York: Cambridge University Press. 52–96.

Galeote Pereira. 1953 (1555). "The Report of Galeote Pereira." In Charles Boxer, ed. and trans., *South China in the Sixteenth Century*. London: Hakluyt Society. 3–45.

Ganesh, K.N. 1991. "Ownership and Control of Land in Medieval Kerala: Janmam-Kanam Relations during the 16th–18th Centuries." *Indian Economic and Social History Review* 28:3. 300–23.

Gardella, Robert. 1990. "The Min-Pei Tea Trade during the Late Ch'ien Lung and Chia-Ch'ing Eras: Foreign Commerce and the Mid-Ch'ing Fu-chien Highlands." In Edward Vermeer, ed., *Development and Decline of Fukien Province in the Seventeenth and Eighteenth Centuries*. Leiden: E. J. Brill. 317–47.

———. 1992a. "Squaring Accounts." *Journal of Asian Studies* 51:2 (May): 317–39.

———. 1992b. "Qing Administration of the Tea Trade: Four Facets over Three Centuries." In Jane Kate Leonard and John Watt, eds., *To Achieve Security and Wealth: The Qing State and the Economy 1644–1912*. Ithaca: Cornell East Asia Series. 97–118.

———. 1994. *Harvesting Mountains: Fujian and the China Tea Trade, 1757–1937*. Berkeley: University of California Press.

Geertz, Clifford. 1963. *Agricultural Involution: The Process of Ecological Change in Indonesia*. Berkeley: University of California Press.

Glamann, Kristof. 1977. "The Changing Patterns of Trade." In E. E. Rich and C. H. Wilson, eds., *The Cambridge Economic History of Europe*. Volume V. New York: Cambridge University Press. 185–285.

———. 1981. *Dutch Asiatic Trade, 1620–1740*. 's-Gravenhage: Martinus Nijhoff.

Godley, Michael. 1981. *The Mandarin Capitalists from Nanyang: Overseas Chinese Enterprise in the Modernization of China, 1893–1911*. Cambridge: Cambridge University Press.

Goldsmith, James. 1984. "The Agrarian History of Preindustrial France: Where Do We Go from Here?" *Journal of European Economic History* 13:1 (Spring): 175–99.

Goldstone, Jack. 1991. *Revolution and Rebellion in the Early Modern World*. Berkeley: University of California Press.

———. 1996. "Gender, Work and Culture: Why the Industrial Revolution Came Early to England but Late to China." *Sociological Perspectives* 39:1. 1–21.

Good, David. 1984. *The Economic Rise of the Habsburg Empire*. Berkeley: University of California Press.

Goodrich, Carter. 1960. *Government Promotion of American Canals and Railroads*. New York: Columbia University Press.

Grantham, George. 1989a. "Agrarian Organization in the Century of Industrialization: Europe, Russia, and North America." In George Grantham and Carol Leonard, eds., *Agrarian Organization in the Century of Industrialization: Europe, Russia and North America*. Greenwich, Conn.: JAI Press. 1–24.

———. 1989b. "Capital and Agrarian Structure in Early Nineteenth Century France." In George Grantham and Carol Leonard, eds., *Agrarian Organization in the Century of Industrialization: Europe, Russia and North America*. Greenwich, Conn.: JAI Press. 137–61.

Grantham, George. 1989c. "Agricultural Supply during the Industrial Revolution: French Evidence and European Implications." *Journal of Economic History* 49:1 (March): 43–72.

Greenberg, Michael. 1951. *British Trade and the Opening of China.* New York: Oxford University Press.

Greif, Avner. 1998. "Theorie des jeux et analyse historique des institutions" (Game theory and the historical analysis of institutions). *Annales HSS* 3 (May–June): 597–633.

Greven, Philip. 1970. *Four Generations: Population, Land, and Family in Colonial Andover, Massachusetts.* Ithaca: Cornell University Press.

Griffin, Alan R. 1977. *The British Coalmining Industry: Retrospect and Prospect.* Buxton, Derbys, England: Moorland Publishing.

Grove, Richard. 1995. *Green Imperialism: Colonial Expansion, Tropical Island Edens, and the Origins of Environmentalism, 1600–1800.* Cambridge: Cambridge University Press.

Guerrero, Milagros. 1966. In Alfonso Felix, ed., *The Chinese in the Philippines, 1570–1770.* Manila: Solidaridad Publishing. 15–39.

Gunst, Peter. 1989. "Agrarian Systems of Central and Eastern Europe." In Daniel Chirot, ed., *The Origins of Backwardness in Eastern Europe.* Berkeley: University of California Press. 53–91.

Guo Qiyuan. 1962 (1820). "Lun Min sheng wuben jieyong shu" (A discourse on fundamental things and restraint in Fujian Province). In He Changling and Wei Yuan, eds., *Huang chao jingshi wenbian* (A collection of essays on statecraft in our dynasty). 36:20a–21a (pp. 929–30). Taibei: Guofeng chubanshe.

Habbakuk, John. 1962. *American and British Technology in the Nineteenth Century: The Search for Labour-Saving Inventions.* Cambridge: Cambridge University Press.

Habib, Irfan. 1982a. "Population." In Tapan Raychaudhuri and Irfan Habib, eds., *The Cambridge Economic History of India, Volume 1 c.1200–c.1750.* Cambridge: Cambridge University Press. 163–71.

———. 1982b. "Systems of Agricultural Production: North India." In Tapan Raychaudhuri and Irfan Habib, eds., *The Cambridge Economic History of India, Volume 1 c.1200–c.1750.* Cambridge: Cambridge University Press. 214–25.

———. 1982c. "Agrarian Relations and Land Revenue: North India." In Tapan Raychaudhuri and Irfan Habib, eds., *The Cambridge Economic History of India, Volume 1 c.1200–c.1750.* Cambridge: Cambridge University Press. 235–49.

———. 1982d. "Monetary System and Prices." In Tapan Raychaudhuri and Irfan Habib, eds., *The Cambridge Economic History of India, Volume 1 c.1200–c.1750.* Cambridge: Cambridge University Press. 360–81.

———. 1990. "Merchant Communities in Pre-Colonial India." In James Tracy, ed., *The Rise of Merchant Empires.* Cambridge: Cambridge University Press. 371–99.

Hagen, William. 1985. "How Mighty the Junker? Peasant Rents and Seigneurial Profits in 16th Century Brandenburg." *Past and Present* 108. 80–116.

——— 1986a. "The Junkers' Faithless Servants: Peasant Insubordination and the Breakdown of Serfdom in Brandenburg-Prussia, 1763–1811." In Richard Evans and W. R. Lee, eds., *The German Peasantry.* London: Croom Helm. 71–101.

———. 1986b. "Working for the Junker: The Standard of Living of Manorial Laborers in Brandenburg, 1584–1810." *Journal of Modern History* 58 (March) 143–58.

———. 1988. "Capitalism and the Countryside in Early Modern Europe: Interpretations, Models, Debates." *Agricultural History* 62:1. 13–47.

———. 1991. Review of Daniel Chirot, ed., *The Origins of Backwardness in Eastern Europe. Journal of Social History* 24:4 (Summer): 889–92.

———. 1996a. "Subject Farmers in Brandenburg-Prussia and Poland: Village Life and Fortunes under Manorialism in Early Modern Central Europe." In M. L. Bush, ed., *Serfdom and Slavery: Studies in Legal Bondage*. London: Longman. 296–310.

———. 1996b. Review of Jürgen Schlumbohm, *Lebenslaufe, Familien, Höfe. Die Bauern und Heuerleute des Osnabrückischen Kirchspiels Belm in proto-industrieller Zeit*. In *Central European History* 29:3. 416–19.

———. Forthcoming. "Village Life in East-Elbian Germany and Poland, 1400–1800: Subjection, Self-Defence, Survival." In Tom Scott, ed., *The Peasantries of Europe, 1400–1800*. London: Longman.

Hai Shan. 1983. "Yutang chunqiu—Jining shi Yutang jiangyuan jianshi" (Chronicles of Yutang—A short history of Jining municipality's Yutang soy sauce factory). *Jining shi shiliao* no. 1: 48–78 and no. 2: 90–106.

Hajnal, John. 1965. "European Marriage Patterns in Perspective." In D. V. Glass and D. E. C. Eversley, eds., *Population in History*. Chicago: Aldine Publishing. 101–46.

———. 1982: "Two Kinds of Preindustrial Household Formation System." *Population and Development Review* 8:3 (September): 449–94.

Hamashita Takeshi. 1988. "The Tribute Trade System and Modern Asia." *Memoirs of the Research Department of the Tōyō Bunko* 46. 7–25.

Hamashita Takeshi. 1994. "Kindai Dō Ajia kokusai taikei." (The international system of modern east Asia). In Hamashita Takeshi et al., *Chiiiki Shisutemu to kokusai kanken* (Regional systems and international relations). Vol. 4 of *Kōza Gendai Ajia* (The professorial chair for modern Asia). Tokyo: Tōdai Shuppankai. 285–325.

Hambly, Gavin R.G. 1982. "Towns and Cities: Mughal India." In Tapan Raychaudhuri and Irfan Habib, eds., *The Cambridge Economic History of India, Volume 1 c.1200–c.1750*. Cambridge: Cambridge University Press. 434–51.

Hamilton, Earl. 1934. *American Treasure and the Price Revolution in Spain*. Cambridge, Mass.: Harvard University Press.

Hammersley, G. 1973. "The Charcoal Iron Industry and Its Fuel, 1540–1750." *Economic History Review* 2d ser. 26:2. 593–613.

Handler, Richard, and Daniel Segal. 1990. *Jane Austen and the Fiction of Culture: An Essay on the Narration of Social Realities*. Tucson: University of Arizona Press.

Hanley, Susan. 1983. "A High Standard of Living in Tokugawa Japan: Fact or Fantasy." *Journal of Economic History* 43:1. 183–92.

———. 1997. *Everyday Things in Premodern Japan: The Hidden Legacy of Material Culture*. Berkeley: University of California Press.

———., and Kozo Yamamura. 1977. *Economic and Demographic Change in Pre-Industrial Japan, 1600–1868*. Princeton: Princeton University Press.

Hao, Yen-p'ing. 1986. *The Commercial Revolution in Nineteenth Century China: The Rise of Sino-Western Capitalism*. Berkeley: University of California Press.

Harnetty, Peter. 1991. "'Deindustrialization' Revisited: The Handloom Weavers of the Central Provinces of India, c. 1800–1947." *Modern Asian Studies* 25:3. 455–510.

Harris, John R. 1988. *The British Iron Industry, 1700–1850*. London and New York: Macmillan.

Harris, John R. 1992. *Essays on Industry and Technology in the 18th Century: England and France*. New York: Variorum.

Hartwell, Robert. 1962. "A Revolution in the Iron and Coal Industries during the Northern Sung." *Journal of Asian Studies* 21:2 (February): 153–62.

———. 1967. "A Cycle of Economic Change in Imperial China: Coal and Iron in Northeast China, 750–1350." *Journal of the Economic and Social History of the Orient* 10:1 (July): 102–59.

———. 1982. "Demographic, Social and Political Transformations of China, 750–1550." *Harvard Journal of Asiatic Studies* 42:2 (December): 365–442.

Hayami Akira. 1989. "Kinsei Nihon no keizai hatten to Industrious Revolution" (Modern Japanese economic development and the industrious revolution). In Hayami Akira, Saito Osamu, and Sugiyama Chuya, eds., *Tokugawa shakai kara no tenbo: hatten, kozo, kokusia kankei* (A view from Tokugawa society: Development, structure, and international relations). Tokyo: Dobunkan. 19–32.

Heidhues, Mary Somers. 1996. "Chinese Settlements in Rural Southeast Asia: Unwritten Histories." In Anthony Reid, ed., *Sojourners and Settlers: Histories of Southeast Asia and the Chinese in Honour of Jennifer Cushman*. St. Leonards, New South Wales: Association for Asian Studies of Australia with Allen and Unwin. 164–82.

Henderson, John. 1984. *The Development and Decline of Chinese Cosmology*. New York: Columbia University Press.

Heske, Franz. 1938. *German Forestry*. New Haven: Yale University Press.

Hill, Christopher. 1980. *The Century of Revolution: 1603–1714*. Walton-on-Thames: Nelson.

Hill, Lamar. unpublished "Extreame Detriment: Failed Credit and the Narration of Indebtedness in the Jacobean Court of Requests." Unpublished paper, cited with permission of the author.

Hirschman, Albert. 1970. *Exit, Voice and Loyalty: Responses to Decline in Firms, Organizations, and States*. Cambridge, Mass.: Harvard University Press.

Ho Ping-ti. 1954. "The Salt Merchants of Yang-chou." *Harvard Journal of Asiatic Studies* 17. 130–68.

———. 1955. "The Introduction of American Food Plants into China." *American Anthropologist* 57. 191–201.

———. 1959. *Studies on the Population of China, 1368–1953*. Cambridge, Mass.: Harvard University Press.

———. 1962. *The Ladder of Success in Imperial China: Aspects of Social Mobility, 1368–1911*. New York: Columbia University Press.

Hobsbawm, Eric. 1975. *Industry and Empire*. London: Penguin.

Hodgson, Marshall. 1993. *Rethinking World History: Essays on Europe, Islam, and World History*. Edited, with an introduction and conclusion by Edmund Burke III. Cambridge: Cambridge University Press.

Horrell, Sara, and Jane Humphries. 1995. "Women's Labour Force Participation and the Transition to the Male-Breadwinner Family, 1790–1865." *Economic History Review* 48:1. 89–117.

Hoshi Ayao. 1971. *Dai Unga* (The grand canal). Tokyo: Kundo shuppansha.

Hoskins, W. G. 1953. "The Rebuilding of Rural England." *Past and Present* 4. 44–59.

Hossain, Hameeda. 1979. "The Alienation of Weavers: Impact of the Conflict between

the Revenue and Commercial Interests of the East India Company, 1750–1800."
Indian Economic and Social History Review 16:3. 323–45.

Howell, David. 1992. "Proto-Industrial Origins of Japanese Capitalism." *Journal of Asian Studies* 51:2 (May): 269–80.

Hsieh, Chiao-min. 1973. *Atlas of China.* New York: McGraw-Hill.

Huang, Philip. 1985. *The Peasant Economy and Social Change in North China.* Stanford: Stanford University Press.

———. 1990. *The Peasant Family and Rural Development in the Lower Yangzi Region, 1350–1988.* Stanford: Stanford University Press.

Huang Qichen. 1989. *Zhongguo gangtie shengchan shi, shisi—shiqi shiji* (A history of Chinese iron and steel production, fourteenth to seventeenth centuries). Zhengzhou: Zhongzhouguji chubanshe.

Huang, Ray. 1974. *Taxation and Government Finance in 16th Century Ming China.* Cambridge: Cambridge University Press.

Idema, Wilt. 1990. "Cannons, Clocks and Clever Monkeys: Europeana, Europeans, and Europe in Some Early Ch'ing Novels." In Eduard Vermeer, ed., *The Development and Decline of Fukien Province in the 17th and 18th Centuries.* Leiden: E. J. Brill. 459–88.

Issawi, Charles, ed. 1966. *The Economic History of the Middle East, 1800–1914.* Chicago: University of Chicago Press.

Iwahashi Masaru. 1981. *Kinsei Nihon bukkashi no kenkyū: kinsei beika no kōzō to hendō.* (Research on prices in Japan's modern epoch: Structure and change of rice prices in the modern epoch). Tokyo: Ohara Shinseisha.

Jacob, Margaret. 1988. *The Cultural Meaning of the Scientific Revolution.* New York: Alfred A. Knopf.

Jeannin, Pierre. 1969. *L'Europe de nord-Ouest et du nord aux XVIIᵉ et XVIIIᵉ siècles* (North and northwest Europe in the seventeenth and eighteenth centuries). Paris: Presses Universitaires de France.

Jenkins, D. T., and K. G. Ponting. *The British Wool Textile Industry, 1770–1914.* London: Heinemann Educational Books.

Jin Ping Mei. 1957 (Author and date unknown seventeenth century). Shanghai: Qingyun tu gongsi. Translated by Clement Egerton as *The Golden Lotus.* London: Routledge and Kegan Paul.

Jinan fuzhi. (Provincial gazetteer of Jinan). Jinan: 1839.

Jing Su and Luo Lun. 1986 (1958). *Qing dai Shandong jingying dizhu jingji yanjiu* (Economic research on managerial landlords in Shandong during the Qing Dynasty). Rev. ed. of 1958 text. Jinan: Qilu shushe. Abridged tranlation of earlier text published as Endymion Wilkinson, ed., *Landlord and Labor in Late Imperial China.*

Johnson, David, Andrew Nathan, and Evelyn Rawski. 1985. *Popular Culture in Late Imperial China.* Berkeley: University of California Press.

Jones, Eric L. 1981. *The European Miracle: Environments, Economies, and Geopolitics in the History of Europe and Asia.* Cambridge: Cambridge University Press.

———. 1988. *Growth Recurring: Economic Change in World History.* New York: Oxford University Press.

Judd, Ellen. 1994. *Gender and Power in Rural North China.* Stanford: Stanford University Press.

Kaplan, Steven. 1976. *Bread, Politics, and Political Economy in the Reign of Louis XV*. The Hague: Martinus Nijhoff.

Kawata Tei'ichi. 1979. "Shindai gakujutsu no ichi sokumen (Sidelights on scholarship in the Qing period). *Tōhōgaku* 57. 84–105.

Kellenblenz, Herman. 1974. "Rural Industries in the West from the End of the Middle Ages to the Eighteenth Century." In Peter Earle, ed., *Essays in European Economic History, 1500–1800*. Oxford: Clarendon. 45–88.

Kelly, William. 1982. *Water Control in Tokugawa Japan: Irrigation Organization in a Japanese River Basin, 1600–1870*. Ithaca: Cornell University East Asia Papers #3.

Kindleberger, Charles. 1990. "Spenders and Hoarders." In Charles Kindleberger, ed., *Historical Economics: Art or Science*. Berkeley: University of California Press. 35–85.

Kishimoto Mio. 1987. "Shindai Bukkashi Kenkyū no Gensho" (The current state of research in Qing Dynasty price history). *Chūgoku Kindaishi Kenkyū* 5. (April): 79–104.

———. 1997. *Shindai Chūgoku no Bukka to Keizai Hendō*. (Prices and economic change in the Qing Dynasty). Tokyo: Kenbun shuppan.

Kjaergaard, Thorkild. 1994. *The Danish Revolution, 1500–1800*. Cambridge: Cambridge University Press.

Klein, Daniel, and John Majewski. 1991. "Promoters and Investors in Antebellum America: The Spread of Plank Road Fever." Irvine: University of California Irvine Institute for Transportation Studies Working Paper 91–1.

Klein, Herbert. 1990. "Economic Aspects of the 18th Century Atlantic Slave Trade." In James Tracy, ed., *The Rise of Merchant Empires*. Cambridge: Cambridge University Press. 287–310.

Klein, Julius. 1920. *The Mesta: A Study in Spanish Economic History*. Port Washington, N.Y.: Kennikat Press.

Knaap, Gerritt. 1995. "The Demography of Ambon in the 17th Century: Evidence from Proto-Censuses." *Journal of Southeast Asian Studies* 26:2 (September): 227–41.

Knodel, John. 1988. *Demographic Behavior in the Past: A Study of Fourteen German Village Populations in the Eighteenth and Nineteenth Centuries*. New York: Cambridge University Press.

Ko, Dorothy. 1994. *Teachers of the Inner Chambers: Women and Culture in Seventeenth-Century China*. Stanford: Stanford University Press.

Kochanowicz, Jacek. 1989. "The Polish Economy and the Evolution of Dependency." In Daniel Chirot, ed., *The Origins of Backwardness in Eastern Europe*. Berkeley: University of California Press. 92–130.

Kraus, Richard. 1968. "Cotton and Cotton Goods in China, 1918–1936: The Impact of Modernization on the Traditional Sector." Ph.D. diss., Harvard University.

Kriedte, Peter, Hans Medick, and Jürgen Schlumbohm. 1981. *Industrialization before Industrialization*. Cambridge: Cambridge University Press.

Kulikoff, Alan. 1992. *The Agrarian Origins of American Capitalism*. Charlottesville: University Press of Virginia.

Kuznets, Simon. 1968. "Capital Formation in Modern Economic Growth (and Some Implications for the Past)." *Third International Conference of Economic History: Munich 1965*. Paris: Mouton 1968. 1: 15–53.

Kwan Man-bun. 1990. "The Merchant World of Tianjin: Society and Economy of a Chinese City." Ph.D. diss. Stanford University.

Labrousse, Ernest. 1984 (1933). *Esquisse du mouvement des prix et des revenus en France au XVIIIe siècle* (Outline of the movements of prices and incomes in eighteenth-century France). Paris: Librairie Dalloz.

Ladurie, Emmanuel LeRoy. 1974. "A Long Agrarian Cycle: Languedoc, 1500–1700." In Peter Earle, ed., *Essays in European Economic History*. Oxford: Oxford University Press. 143–64.

———. 1976. "De la crise ultime à la vraie croissance, 1660–1789" (From the final crisis to true growth). In Georges Duby and A. Walton, *Historie de la France Rurale*. Volume 2. (Paris: Seuil). 359–575.

Lamb, H. H. 1982. *Climate, History and the Modern World*. London and New York: Methuen.

Lamoreaux, Naomi. 1994. *Insider Lending: Banks, Personal Connections and Economic Development in Industrial New England*. Cambridge: Cambridge University Press and National Bureau of Economic Research.

Landes, David. 1969. *The Unbound Prometheus: Technological Change and Industrial Development in Western Europe from 1750 to the Present*. Cambridge: Cambridge University Press.

Lang, James. 1975. *Conquest and Commerce: Spain and England in the Americas*. New York: Academic Press.

Latham, A. J. H. 1978a. "Merchandise Trade Imbalances and Uneven Development in India and China." *Journal of European Economic History* 7 (Spring): 33–60.

———. 1978b. *The International Economy and the Undeveloped World, 1865–1914*. Totowa, N.J.: Rowman and Littlefield.

———, and Larry Neal. 1983. "The International Market in Rice and Wheat, 1868–1914." *Economic History Review* 2d ser. 36. 260–80.

Lavely, William, and R. Bin Wong. 1998. "Revising the Malthusian Narrative: The Comparative Study of Population Dynamics in Late Imperial China." *Journal of Asian Studies* 57:3 (August): 714–48.

Lazonick, William. 1981. "Production Relations, Labor Productivity and Choice of Technique: British and U.S. Spinning." *Journal of Economic History* 41:3 (September): 491–516.

Ledderose, Lothar. 1991. "Chinese Influence on European Art, Sixteenth to Eighteenth Centuries." In Thomas Lee, ed., *China and Europe*. Hong Kong: Chinese University Press. 221–50.

Lee, Ching Kwan. 1995. "Engendering the Worlds of Labor: Women Workers, Labor Markets and Production Politics in the South China Economic Miracle." *American Sociological Review* 60 (June): 378–97.

Lee, James. 1982. "The Legacy of Immigration in Southwest China, 1250–1850." *Annales de Demographie Historique* 279–304.

———, and Cameron Campbell. 1997. *Fate and Fortune in Rural China: Social Organization and Population Behavior in Liaoning, 1774–1873*. Cambridge: Cambridge University Press.

———, and Wang Feng. Forthcoming. "Malthusian Mythologies and Chinese Realities." Cambridge, Mass.: Harvard University Press.

———, and R. Bin Wong. 1991. "Population Movements in Qing China and Their Linguistic Legacy." In William S-Y. Wang, ed., *Languages and Dialects of China*. Berkeley: Journal of Chinese Linguistics Monograph Series. 52–77.

Lee, Robert H. G. 1979. *The Manchurian Frontier in Ch'ing History.* Cambridge, Mass.: Harvard University Press.

Levi, Giovanni. 1988. *Inheriting Power: The Story of an Exorcist.* Chicago: University of Chicago Press.

Levine, David. 1977. *Family Formation in an Age of Nascent Capitalism.* New York: Academic Press.

Lewis, Arthur. 1954. "Economic Development with Unlimited Supplies of Labor." *Manchester School of Economics and Social Studies* 22:2 (May): 139–91.

Li Bozhong. 1994a. "Kongzhi zengchang yi bao fuyu—Qingdai qian, zhongqi Jiangnan de renkou xingwei" (Controlling increase to protect prosperity: Demographic behavior in early and mid-Qing Jiangnan). *Xin shixue* 5:3 (September): 25–71.

———. 1994b. "Ming Qing shiqi Jiangnan de mucai wenti" (Wood supply problems in Ming-Qing Jiangnan). *Zhongguo shehui jingji shi yanjiu* 1:86–96.

———. 1996. "Cong 'fufu bing zuo' dao 'nan geng nu zhi'" (From "husband and wife work together" to "man plows, woman weaves"). *Zhongguo jingji shi yanjiu* 11:3. 99–107.

———. 1998. *Agricultural Development in Jiangnan, 1620–1850.* New York: St. Martin's Press.

Li Wenzhi et al. 1983. *Ming Qing shidai de nongye zibenzhuyi mengya wenti* (The question of "sprouts of agrarian capitalism" in the Ming-Qing Period). Beijing: Zhongguo shehui kexue chubanshe.

Li Zhihuan. 1990. *Zhongguo shi tang shigao.* (A draft history of Chinese sugar). Beijing: Nongye chubanshe.

Li Zhongqing. 1994. "Zhongguo lishi renkou zhidu: Qingdai renkou xingwei ji qi yiyi" (The demographic system of historical China: Qing Dynasty demographic behavior and its meaning). In Li Zhongqing and Guo Songyi, eds., *Qingdai huangzu renkou xingwei de shehui huanjing* (The social environment of the demographic behavior of the Qing imperial lineage). Beijing; Beijing daxue chubanshe. 1–17.

———, and Guo Songyi, eds. 1994. *Qingdai huangzu renkou xingwei de shehui huanjing* (The social environment of the demographic behavior of the Qing imperial lineage). Peking: Peking University Press.

Liang Fangzhong. 1981. *Zhongguo lidai hukou, tiandi, tianfu tongji* (Historical statistics of population, land, and taxation in China). Shanghai: Shanghai renmin chubanshe.

Lieberman, Victor. 1990. "Wallerstein's System and the International Context of Early Modern Southeast Asian History." *Journal of Asian History* 24: 70–90.

———. 1993. "Abu-Lughod's Egalitarian World Order. A Review Article." *Comparative Studies in Society and History* 544–50.

Lin Man-houng. 1990. "From Sweet Potato to Silver: The New World and 18th Century China as Reflected in Wang Hui-tsu's Passage about the Grain Prices." In Hans Pohl, ed., *The European Discovery of the World and Its Economic Effects on Pre-Industrial Society, 1500–1800.* Stuttgart: Franz Steiner Verlag. 304–27.

Li Dangrui and Chen Daiguang. 1981. *Henan renkou dili zhi* (Population geography of Henan). Henan sheng kexueyuan dili yanjiusuo.

Lindert, Peter, and Jeffrey Williamson. 1982. "Revising England's Social Tables 1688–1812." *Explorations in Economic History* 19:4 (October). 385–408.

Ling Daxie. 1983. "Wo guo senlin ziyuan de bianqian" (Changes in the forest resources of our country). *zhongguo nongshi* 3:2. 26–36.

Lombard, Denys. 1981. "Questions on the Contact between European Companies and Asian Societies." In Leonard Blussé and Femme Gaastra, eds., *Companies and Trade*. The Hague: Martinus Nijhoff. 179–87.

Lombard-Salmon, Claudine. 1972. *Un example d'Acculturation Chinoise: La province du Gui Zhou au XVIIIe siècle*. Paris: École Française d'Extreme Orient.

Lower, Arthur R. M. 1973. *Great Britain's Woodyard: British America and the Timber Trade, 1763–1867*. Montreal: McGill University Press.

Lu Hanchao. 1992. "Arrested Development: Cotton and Cotton Markets in Shanghai, 1350–1843." *Modern China* 18:4 (October): 468–99.

Ludden, David. 1985. *Peasant History in South India*. Princeton: Princeton University Press.

———. 1988. "Agrarian Commercialism in Eighteenth-Century South India: Evidence from the 1823 Titunelveli Census." *Indian Economic and Social History Review* 25:4. 493–517.

Ludwig, Armin K. 1985. *Brazil: A Handbook of Historical Statistics*. Boston: G. K. Hall and Co.

MacLeod, Christine. 1988. *Inventing the Industrial Revolution: The English Patent System, 1660–1800*. New York: Cambridge University Press.

Majewski, John. 1994. "Commerce and Community: Economic Culture and Internal Improvements in Pennsylvania and Virginia, 1790–1860." Ph.D. diss. UCLA.

Mann, James A. 1860. *The Cotton Trade of Great Britain*. London: Simpkin and Marshall.

Mann, Susan. 1987. *Local Merchants and the Chinese Bureaucracy, 1750–1950*. Stanford: Stanford University Press.

———. 1992. "Household Handicrafts and State Policy in Qing Times." In Jane Kate Leonard and John Watt, eds., *To Achieve Security and Wealth: The Qing State and the Economy*. Ithaca: Cornell University Press. 75–96.

———. 1997. *Precious Records: Women in China's Long Eighteenth Century*. Stanford: Stanford University Press.

Markovitch, T. J. 1976. *Les industries lainières de Colbert à la Revolution*. (The woollen industries from Colbert to the Revolution). Geneva: Librairie Droz.

Marks, Robert. 1984. *Rural Revolution in South China: Peasants and the Making of History in Haifeng County, 1570–1930*. Madison: University of Wisconsin Press.

———. 1991. "Rice Prices, Food Supply, and Market Structure in 18th Century China." *Late Imperial China* 12:2 (December): 64–116.

———. 1997. *Tigers, Rice, Silk, and Silt: Environment and Economy in Guangdong, 1250–1850*. New York: Cambridge University Press.

Marshall, P. J. 1980. "Western Arms in Maritime Asia in the Early Phases of Expansion." *Modern Asian Studies* 14:1. 13–28.

———. 1987. *Bengal—The British Bridgehead: Eastern India, 1740–1828*. New York: Cambridge University Press.

Mazumdar, Sucheta. 1984. "A History of the Sugar Industry in China: The Political Economy of a Cash Crop in Guangdong, 1644–1834." Ph.D. diss. UCLA.

McAlpin, Michele, and John Richards. 1983. "Cotton Cultivation and Land Clearing in the Bombay Deccan and Karnatak, 1818–1920." In John Richards and Richard Tucker, eds., *Global Deforestation and the Nineteenth-Century World Economy*. Durham: Duke Press Policy Studies. 68–94.

McCloskey, Donald. 1975a. "The Persistence of English Common Fields." In E. L. Jones and William Parker, eds., *European Peasants and Their Markets: Essays in Agrarian Economic History*. Princeton: Princeton University Press. 73–119.

———. 1975b. "The Economics of Enclosure: A Market Analysis." In E. L. Jones and William Parker, eds., *European Peasants and Their Markets: Essays in Agrarian Economic History*. Princeton: Princeton University Press. 123–60.

———. 1989. "The Open Fields of England: Rent, Risk and the Rate of Interest, 1300–1815." In David Galenson, ed., *Markets in History: Economic Studies of the Past*. Cambridge: Cambridge University Press. 5–49.

———. 1991. "History, Differential Equations, and the Problem of Narration." *History and Theory* 30:1 21–36.

McCusker, John, and Russell Menard. 1985. *The Economy of British America, 1607–1789*. Chapel Hill: University of North Carolina Press.

McEvedy, Colin, and Richard Jones. 1978. *Atlas of World Population History*. New York: Penguin.

McGowan, Bruce. 1994. "The Age of the Ayans, 1699–1812." In Halil Inalcik and Donald Quatert, eds., *An Economic and Social History of the Ottoman Empire*. 2 vols. New York: Cambridge University Press. 637–758.

McKendrick, Neil, John Brewer, and J. H. Plumb. 1982. *The Birth of a Consumer Society: The Commercialization of Eighteenth-Century England*. Bloomington: Indiana University Press.

McNeill, John R. 1994. "Of Rats and Men: A Synoptic Environmental History of the Island Pacific." *Journal of World History* 5:2. 299–349.

Medick, Hans. 1982. "Plebeian Culture in the Transition to Capitalism." In Raphael Samuel and Gareth Stedman-Jones, eds., *Culture, Ideology, and Politics*. Cambridge: Cambridge University Press. 84–112.

Menzies, Nicholas. 1992a "Sources of Demand and Cycles of Logging in Pre-Modern China." In John Dargavel and Richard Tucker, eds., *Changing Pacific Forests*. Durham, N.C.: Forest History Society. 64–76.

———. 1992b. "Strategic Space: Exclusion and Inclusion in Wildland Policies in Late Imperial China." *Modern Asian Studies* 6:4 (October): 719–34.

———. 1996. "Forestry." In Joseph Needham, ed., *Science and Civilization in China*. Vol. 27. Cambridge: Cambridge University Press. 541–690.

Metzger, Thomas. 1973. *The Internal Organization of the Chinese Bureaucracy: Legal, Normative, and Communications Aspects*. Cambridge, Mass.: Harvard University Press.

———. 1977. *Escape from Predicament: Neo-Confucianism and China's Evolving Political Culture*. New York: Columbia University Press.

Meuvret, Jean. 1977–88. *Le problème des subsistances à l'époque Louis XIV* (The subsistence problem in the age of Louis the Fourteenth). 6 vols. Paris: Mouton.

Miller, Joseph. 1986. "Slave Prices in the Portuguese Southern Atlantic, 1600–1830." In Paul Lovejoy, ed., *Africans in Bondage*. Madison: University of Wisconsin Press. 43–77.

Minami Manshū Tetsūdo Kabushiki Kaisha. 1936. *Santō no Chikūguyū* (The livestock of Shandong). Tianjin: Mantetsu.

Mintz, Sidney. 1985. *Sweetness and Power: The Place of Sugar in Modern History.* New York: Penguin.

Mitchell, B. R. 1980. *European Historical Statistics, 1750–1975.* New York: Facts on File.

———. 1988. *British Historical Statistics.* New York: Cambridge University Press.

———. 1993. *Historical Statistics: The Americas.* New York: Stockton Press.

Mitra, Debendra Bijoy. 1978. *The Cotton Weavers of Bengal, 1757–1833.* Calcutta: Firma KLM Private Limited.

Mokyr, Joel. 1976. *Industrialization in the Low Countries, 1795–1850.* New Haven: Yale University Press.

———. 1985a. "Demand and Supply in the Industrial Revolution." In Joel Mokyr, ed., *The Economics of the Industrial Revolution.* Totowa, N.J.: Rowman and Allanheld. 97–118.

———. 1985b. "The Industrial Revolution and the New Economic History." In Joel Mokyr, ed., *The Economics of the Industrial Revolution.* Totowa, N.J.: Rowman and Allanheld. 1–52.

———. 1988. "Is There Life in the Pessimist Case? Consumption during the Industrial Revolution, 1790–1850." *Journal of Economic History* 48:1. 69–92.

———. 1990. *The Lever of Riches: Technological Creativity and Economic Progress.* New York: Oxford University Press.

———. 1991. "Cheap Labor, Dear Labor and the Industrial Revolution." In David Landes, Patrice Higgonet, and Henry Rosovsky, eds., *Favorites of Fortune.* Cambridge, Mass.: Harvard University Press. 177–200.

———. 1994. "Progress and Inertia in Technological Change." In Mark Thomas and John James, eds., *Capitalism in Context: Essays on Economic Development and Culture in Honor of R. M. Hartwell.* Chicago: University of Chicago Press. 230–54.

Moore, Barrington. 1966. *Social Origins of Dictatorship and Democracy.* Boston: Beacon Press.

Mooser, Josef. 1984. *Ländliche Klassengesellschaft, 1770–1848* (Rural class society, 1770–1848). Gottingen: Vandenhoeck and Ruprecht.

Moosvi, Shireen. 1987. *The Economy of the Mughal Empire c.1595: A Statistical Study.* Delhi: Oxford University Press.

Morgan, Edmund S. 1975. *American Slavery, American Freedom: The Ordeal of Colonial Virginia.* New York: W. W. Norton and Co.

Morineau, Michel. 1985. *Incroyables Gazettes et Fabuleux Metaux* (Incredible gazettes and fabulous metals). Cambridge: Cambridge University Press.

Morris, J. H., and L. J. Williams, 1958. *The South Wales Coal Industry, 1841–1875.* Cardiff: University of Wales Press.

Morse, Hosea Ballou. 1966. *A Chronicle of the East India Company Trading to China.* 4 vols. Taipei: Chengwen (reprint).

Morton, A. G. 1981. *History of Botanical Science.* New York: Academic Press.

Mote, Frederick. 1977. "Yuan and Ming." In K. C. Chang, ed., *Food in Chinese Culture.* New Haven: Yale University Press. 195–257.

Mukerji, Chandra. 1983. *From Graven Images: Patterns of Modern Materialism.* New York: Columbia University Press.

Myers, Ramon. 1982. "Customary Law, Markets, and Resource Transactions in Late Imperial China." In Roger Ransom, Richard Sutch, and Gary Walton, eds., *Explorations in the New Economic History: Essays in Honor of Douglass C. North*. New York: Academic Press 273–98.

Myint, H. 1958. "The 'Classical' Theory of International Trade and the Underdeveloped Counties." *Economic Journal* 68. 317–37.

Najita, Tetsuo. 1987. *Visions of Virtue in Tokugawa Japan*. Chicago: University of Chicago Press.

Naquin, Susan, and Evelyn Rawski, 1987. *Chinese Society in the Eighteenth Century*. New Haven: Yale University Press.

Needham, Joseph. 1965. With assistance from Wang Ling. *Physics and Physical Technology*. Vol. 4, part 2 (vol. 27 overall). In Joseph Needham, et al., *Science and Civilization in China*. Cambridge: Cambridge University Press.

Nef, John. *The Rise of the British Coal Industry*. London: Routledge.

———. 1964. *The Conquest of the Material World*. Chicago: University of Chicago Press.

Ng Chin-keong. 1983. *Trade and Society: The Amoy Network on the China Coast, 1683–1735*. Singapore: Singapore University Press.

———. 1990. "The South Fukienese Junk Trade at Amoy from the 17th to the Early 18th Centuries." In Eduard Vermeer, ed., *Development and Decline of Fukien Province in the 17th and 18th Centuries*. Leiden: E. J. Brill. 297–316.

Nipperdey, Thomas. 1996. *Germany from Napoleon to Bismarck, 1800–1866*. Princeton: Princeton University Press.

Nishijima Sadao. 1984. "The Formation of the Early Chinese Cotton Industry." In Linda Grove and Christian Daniels, eds., *State and Society in China*. Tokyo: University of Tokyo Press. 17–78.

Nishikawa, Shunsaku. 1978. "Productivity, Subsistence, and By-Employment in the Mid-Nineteenth Century Choshu." *Explorations in Economic History* 15. 69–83.

North, Douglass. 1981. *Structure and Change in Economic History*. New York: W. W. Norton.

———. 1991. "Institutions, Transaction Costs, and the Rise of Merchant Empires." In James D. Tracy, ed., *The Political Economy of Merchant Empires*. Cambridge: Cambridge University Press. 22–40.

———. 1994. "The Evolution of Efficient Markets in History." In John James and Mark Thomas, eds., *Capitalism in Context: Essays on Economic Development and Culture in Honor of R. M. Hartwell*. Chicago: University of Chicago Press. 257–64.

———, and Robert Paul Thomas. 1973. *The Rise of the Western World: A New Economic History*. Cambridge: Cambridge University Press.

———, and Barry Weingast. 1989. "Constitutions and Commitment: The Evolution of Institutions Governing Public Choice in 17th Century England." *Journal of Economic History* 49. 803–32.

Nyren, Eve. 1995. *The Bonds of Matrimony = Hsing Shih Yin Yuan Chuan*. (Translation of seventeenth-century novel, attributed by some to Pu Songling.) Lewiston, N.Y.: E. Mellen Press.

O'Brien, Patrick K. 1977. "Agriculture and the Industrial Revolution." *Economic History Review* 2d ser. 30:166–81.

————. 1982. "European Economic Development: The Contribution of the Periphery." *Economic History Review* 35:1 (February): 1–18.

————. 1988. "The Political Economy of English Taxation." *Economic History Review* 41:1 (February): 1–32.

————. 1990. "European Industrialization: From the Voyages of Discovery to the Industrial Revolution." In Hans Pohl, ed., *The European Discovery of the World and Its Economic Effects on Pre-Industrial Society, 1500–1800.* Stuttgart: Franz Steiner Verlag. 154–77.

————, and Caglar Keydar. 1978. *Economic Growth in Britain and France, 1780–1914.* London: George Allen and Unwin.

Ogilvie, Sheilagh. 1996. "Proto-Industrialization in Germany." In Sheilagh Ogilvie and Markus Cerman, eds., *European Proto-Industrialization.* Cambridge: Cambridge University Press. 118–36.

————, and Markus Cerman. 1996. "Introduction: The Theories of Proto-Industrialization." In Sheilagh Ogilvie and Markus Cerman, eds., *European Proto-Industrialization.* Cambridge: Cambridge University Press. 1–11.

Osako, Masako M. 1983. "Forest Preservation in Tokugawa Japan." In John R. Richards and Richard P. Tucker, eds., *Global Deforestation and the 19th Century World Economy.* Durham: Duke University Press Policy Series. 129–45.

Osborne, Anne. 1994. "The Local Politics of Land Reclamation in the Lower Yangzi Highlands." *Late Imperial China* 15:1 (June): 1–46.

Owen, E. R. J. 1966. "Egyptian Cotton and the American Civil War, 1860–1866." In Chalres Issawi, ed., *The Economic History of the Middle East, 1800—1914.* Chicago: University of Chicago Press. 416–29.

Pach, Z. S. P. 1990. "The East-Central European Aspect of the Overseas Discoveries and Colonization." In Hans Pohl, ed., *The European Discovery of the World and Its Economic Effects on Pre-Industrial Society, 1500–1800.* Stuttgart: Franz Steinr Verlag. 178–94.

Palat, Ravi. 1995. "Historical Transformations in Agrarian Systems Based on Wet-Rice Cultivation: Toward an Alternative Model of Social Change." In Philip McMichael, ed., *Food and Agrarian Orders in the World Economy.* Westport, Conn.: Greenwood Press. 55–76.

Pan, Ming-te. 1985. *Zhongguo jindai diandangye zhi yanjiu (1644–1937).* (Research on the modern Chinese pawnshop industry, 1644–1937). Taibei: Guoli Taiwan shifan daxue lishi yanjiu suo zhuankan #13.

————. 1994. "Rural Credit Market and the Peasant Economy (1600–1949)—The State, Elite, Peasant, and 'Usury.'" Ph.D. diss., University of California, Irvine.

————. 1998. "Who Was Worse Off?" Paper delivered at 1998 meeting of Chinese Historians in the United States, Seattle, Wash.

Parker, Geoffrey. 1988. *The Military Revolution: Military Innovation and the Rise of the West, 1500–1800.* New York: Cambridge University Press.

Parker, Willam. 1984, 1991. *America, Europe, and the Wider World.* 2 vols. Cambridge: Cambridge University Press.

Parker, David, and Patricia Croot. 1985. "Agrarian Class Structure and the Development of Capitalism: France and England Compared." In T. H. Aston and C. H. E. Philpin, eds., *The Brenner Debate: Agrarian Class Structure and Economic Development in Pre-Industrial Europe.* Cambridge: Cambridge University Press. 79–90.

Parthasarathi, Prasannan. 1998. "Rethinking Wages and Competitiveness in the Eighteenth Century: Britain and South India." *Past and Present* 158 (February): 79–109.

Pearson, M. N. 1991. "Merchants and States." In James D. Tracy, ed., *The Political Economy of Merchant Empires*. Cambridge: Cambridge University Press. 41–116.

Perdue, Peter. 1987. *Exhausting the Earth: State and Peasant in Hunan, 1500–1850*. Cambridge, Mass.: Harvard University Press.

Perkins, Dwight H. 1969. *Agricultural Development in China, 1368–1968*. Chicago: Aldine Publishing.

Perlin, Frank. 1978. "Of White Whale and Countrymen in the 18th Century Maratha Deccan: Extended Class Relations, Rights, and the Problem of Rural Autonomy under the Old Regime." *Journal of Peasant Studies* 5:2. 172–237.

———. 1983. "Proto-Industrialization and Pre-Colonial South Asia." *Past and Present* 98 (February): 30–95.

———. 1985. "State Formation Reconsidered, Part Two." *Modern Asian Studies* 19:3. 415–80.

———. 1987. "Money Use in Pre-colonial India." In John F. Richards, ed., *Imperial Monetary Systems in Early Modern India*. New York: Oxford University Press. 232–373.

———. 1988. "Disarticulation of the World: Writing India's Economic History." *Comparative Studies in Society and History* 30:2 (April): 379–87.

———. 1990. "Financial Institutions and Business Practices across the Euro-Asian Interface: Comparative and Structural Considerations, 1500–1900." In Hans Pohl, ed., *The European Discovery of the World and Its Economic Effects on Pre-Industrial Society, 1500–1800*. Stuttgart: Franz Steiner Verlag. 257–303.

———. 1991. "World Economic Integration before Industrialization and the Euro-Asian Monetary Continuum." In H. G. Van Cauwenberghe, ed., *Money, Coin, and Commerce: Essays in the Monetary History of Asia and Europe*. Leuven: Leuven University Press. 239–374.

———. 1994. *Unbroken Landscape: Commodity, Category, Sign and Identity: Their Production as Myth and Knowledge from 1500*. Aldershot, U.K.: Variorum.

Peterson, Willard. 1978. *Bitter Gourd: Fang I-chih and the Impetus for Intellectual Change in the Ming*. New Haven: Yale University Press.

Phelps Brown, E. H., and Sheila Hopkins. 1956. "Seven Centuries of the Prices of Consumables, Compared with Builders' Wage-rates." *Economica* 23:4 (November): 296–314.

———. 1957. "Wage-rates and Prices: Evidence for Population Pressure in the Sixteenth Century." *Economica* 24:4 (November): 289–99.

———. 1981. *A Perspective of Wages and Prices*. London: Methuen.

Phillips, Carla Rahn. 1990. "The Growth and Composition of Trade in the Iberian Empires, 1450–1750." In James Tracy, ed., *The Rise of Merchant Empires*. New York: Cambridge University Press. 34–101.

Platt, D. C. M. 1972. *Latin America and British Trade, 1806–1914*. London: A&C Black.

Plumb, J. H. 1972. *The Commercialization of Leisure in Eighteenth-Century England*. Reading: University of Reading Press.

Polanyi, Karl. 1957. *The Great Transformation*. Boston: Beacon Press.

Pollard, Sidney. 1981. *Peaceful Conquest: The Industrialization of Europe, 1760–1970*. New York: Oxford University Press.

Pomeranz, Kenneth. 1988. "The Making of a Hinterland: State, Society, and Economy in Inland North China 1900–1937." Ph.D. diss., Yale University.

———. 1993. *The Making of a Hinterland: State, Society, and Economy in Inland North China, 1853–1937*. Berkeley: University of California Press.

———. 1995. "How Exhausted an Earth? Some Thoughts on Qing (1644–1911) Environmental History." *Chinese Environmental History Newsletter* 2:2 (November): 7–11.

———. 1997a. "Power, Gender and Pluralism in the Cult of the Goddess of Taishan." In R. Bin Wong, Theodore Hunters, and Pauline Yu, eds., *Culture and State in Chinese History*. Stanford: Stanford University Press. 182–204.

———. 1997b. "Gentry Merchants Revisited: Family, Firm, and Financing in the Yutang Co. of Jining, 1779–1956." *Late Imperial China* 18:1 (June): 1–38.

Postel-Vinay, Giles. 1994. "The Dis-Integration of Traditional Labour Markets in France: From Agriculture *and* Industry to Agriculture *or* Industry." In George Grantham and Mary MacKinnon, eds., *Labour Market Evolution*. London: Routledge 1994. 64–83.

Powelson, John. 1994. *Centuries of Economic Endeavor: Parallel Paths in Japan and Europe and Their Contrast with the Third World*. Ann Arbor: University of Michigan Press.

Prakash, Om. 1981. "European Trade and South Asian Economies: Some Regional Contrasts, 1600–1800." In Leonard Blussé and Femme Gaastra, eds., *Companies and Trade: Essays on Overseas Trading Companies during the Ancien Régime*. Leiden: Leiden University Press. 189–205.

Rabb, Theodore K. 1967. *Enterprise and Empire: Merchant and Gentry Investment in the Expansion of England, 1575–1630*. Cambridge, Mass.: Harvard University Press.

Rangarajan, Mahesh. 1994. "Imperial Agendas and India's Forests: The Early History of Indian Forestry, 1800–1878." *Indian Economic and Social History Review* 31:2. 147–167.

Rawski, Evelyn. 1972. *Agrarian Change and the Peasant Economy of South China*. Cambridge, Mass.: Harvard University Press.

———. 1985. "Economic and Social Foundations of Late Imperial Culture." In David Johnson, Andrew Nathan, and Evelyn Rawski, eds., *Popular Culture in Late Imperial China*. Berkeley: University of California Press. 3–33.

Raychaudhuri, Tapan. 1982a. "The State and the Economy: The Mughal Empire." In Tapan Raychaudhuri and Irfan Habib, eds., *The Cambridge Economic History of India, Volume 1 c.1200–c.1750*. Cambridge: Cambridge University Press. 172–92.

———. 1982b. "Non-Agricultural Production: Mughal India." In Tapan Raychaudhuri and Irfan Habib, eds., *The Cambridge Economic History of India, Volume 1 c.1200–c.1750*. Cambridge: Cambridge University Press. 261–307.

———. 1982c. "Inland Trade." In Tapan Raychaudhuri and Irfan Habib, eds., *The Cambridge Economic History of India, Volume 1 c.1200–c.1750*. Cambridge: Cambridge University Press. 325–59.

Razzell, Peter. 1993. "The Growth of Population in Eighteenth Century England: A Critical Reappraisal." *Journal of Economic History* 53:4 (December): 743–71.

Reid, Anthony. 1988a. *Southeast Asia in the Age of Commerce: Volume I, The Lands below the Winds*. New Haven: Yale University Press.

———. 1988b. "Women's Roles in Pre-Colonial Southeast Asia." *Modern Asian Studies* 22:3 (July): 626–46.

———. 1989. "The Organization of Production in Southeast Asian Port Cities." In Frank Broeze, ed., *Brides of the Sea: Port Cities of Asia from the 16th to 20th Centuries*. Honolulu: University of Hawaii Press. 55–74.

———. 1990. "The System of Trade and Shipping in Maritime South and Southeast Asia and the Effects of the Development of the Cape Route to Europe." In Hans Pohl, ed., *The European Discovery of the World and Its Economic Effects on Pre-Industrial Society, 1500–1800*. Stuttgart: Franz Steiner Verlag. 74–96.

——— 1993. *Southeast Asia in the Age of Commerce: Volume II, Expansion and Commerce*. New Haven: Yale University Press.

Richards, John. 1990. "Land Transformation." In B. L. Turner II et al., eds., *The Earth as Transformed by Human Action*. Cambridge: Cambridge University Press. 163–78.

Richardson, David. 1987. "The Slave Trade, Sugar, and British Economic Growth, 1748–1776." *Journal of Interdisciplinary History* 17:4 (Spring): 739–69.

Rimmer, W. G. 1960. *Marshalls of Leeds, Flax Spinners, 1788–1886*. Cambridge: Cambridge University Press.

Ringrose, David. 1970. *Transportation and Economic Stagnation in Spain*. Durham: Duke University Press.

Riskin, Carl. 1975. "Surplus and Stagnation in Modern China." In Dwight Perkins, ed., *China's Modern Economy in Historical Perspective*. Stanford: Stanford University Press. 49–84.

Roberts, J. M. 1967. "Lombardy." In Albert Goodwin, ed., *The European Nobility in the Eighteenth Century*. New York: Harper and Row. 60–82.

Roberts, Luke. 1991. "The Merchant Origins of National Prosperity Thought in 18th Century Tosa." Ph.D. diss., Princeton University.

Roberts, Michael. 1967. "Sweden." In Albert Goodwin, ed., *The European Nobility in the Eighteenth Century* New York: Harper and Row. 136–53.

Rosener, Werner. 1994. *The Peasantry of Europe*. London: Basil Blackwell.

Rosenthal, Jean-Laurent. 1992. *The Fruits of Revolution: Property Rights, Litigation, and French Agriculture, 1700–1860*. Cambridge: Cambridge University Press.

Rossiter, Margaret. 1975. *The Emergence of Agricultural Science: Justus Liebig and the Americans, 1840–1880*. New Haven: Yale University Press.

Rowe, William. 1984. *Hankow: Commerce and Society in a Chinese City, 1796–1889*. Stanford: Stanford University Press.

———. 1989. *Hankow: Conflict and Community in a Chinese City, 1796–1895*. Stanford: Stanford University Press.

———. 1990. "Success Stories: Lineage and Elite Status in Hanyang County Hubei, c.1368–1949." In Joseph Esherick and Mary Rankin, *Chinese Rural Elites and Patterns of Dominance*. Berkeley: University of California Press. 51–81.

———. 1992. "Women and the Family in Mid-Qing Thought: The Case of Chen Hongmou." *Late Imperial China* 13:2 (December): 1–41.

Roy, William G. 1997. *Socializing Capital: The Rise of the Large Industrial Corporation in America*. Princeton: Princeton University Press.

Rozanov, Boris, Victor Targulian, and D. S. Orlov. 1990. "Soils." In B. L. Turner et al., *The Earth as Transformed by Human Action*. New York: Cambridge University Press. 203–14.

Sahlins, Marshall. 1976. *Culture and Practical Reason*. Chicago: University of Chicago Press.

————. 1994 (1989). "Cosmologies of Capitalism: The Trans-Pacific Sector of the World System." In Nicholas Dirks, Geoff Eley, and Sherry B. Ortner, eds., *Culture/Power/History*. Princeton: Princeton University Press. 412–55.

Saito Osamu. 1978. "The Labor Market in Tokugawa Japan: Wage Differentials and the Real Wage Level, 1727–1830." *Explorations in Economic History* 15. 84–100.

————. 1983. "Population and the Peasant Family Economy in Proto-Industrial Japan." In *Journal of Family History* 8:1 (Spring): 30–54.

————. 1985. *Puroto-Kōgyō no jidai: Seiō to Nihon no hikakushi* (The age of proto-industrialism: A comparative history of Japan and the West). Tokyo: Nihon Hyōronsha.

————. and Shinbo Hiroshi. 1989. *Kindai Seichō no Taidō* (The quickening of modern growth). Tokyo: Iwanami Shoten.

Salaman, Redcliffe N. 1949. *The History and Social Influence of the Potato*. Cambridge: Cambridge University Press.

Santamaria, Alberto. 1966. "The Chinese Parian." In Alfonso Felix, ed., *The Chinese in the Philippines, 1570–1770*. Manila: Solidaridad Publishing. 67–118.

Schama, Simon. 1988. *The Embarrassment of Riches: An Interpretation of Dutch Culture in the Golden Age*. New York: Alfred A. Knopf.

Schoppa, R. Keith. 1989. *Xiang Lake: Nine Centuries of Chinese Life*. New Haven: Yale University Press.

Schran, Peter. 1978. "A Reassessment of Inland Communications in Late Ch'ing China." *Ch'ing-shih wen-t'i* 3:10 28–48.

Schultz, Theodore. 1964. *Transforming Traditional Agriculture*. New Haven: Yale University Press.

Schurz, William. 1939. *The Manila Galleon*. New York: E. P. Dutton.

Schwartz, Stuart. 1985. *Sugar Plantations in the Formation of Brazilian Society: Bahia, 1550–1835*. New York: Cambridge University Press.

————. 1992. *Slaves, Peasants, and Rebels: Reconsidering Brazilian Slavery*. Chicago: University of Chicago Press.

Senghaas, Dieter. 1985. *The European Experience: A Historical Critique of Development Theory*. Dover: Berg Publishers.

Sewell, William. 1980. *Work and Revolution in France: The Language of Labor from the Old Regime to 1848*. New York: Cambridge University Press.

Shanghai shehuiju. 1989 (1935). *Shanghai zhi shangye* (The commerce of Shanghai). Taibei: Wenhai Chubanshe.

Shen Congwen. 1992. *Zhongguo gudai fushi yanjiu* (Research on Chinese clothing and fashion of earlier times). Hong Kong: Shangwu yinhu shuguan.

Shepherd, John Z. 1993. *Statecraft and Political Economy on the Taiwan Frontier, 1600–1800*. Stanford: Stanford University Press.

Shepherd, James F. and Gary M. Walton. 1972. *Shipping, Maritime Trade, and the Economic Development of Colonial North America*. Cambridge: Cambridge University Press.

Skinner, G. William. 1971. "Chinese Peasants and the Closed Community: An Open and Shut Case." *Comparative Studies in Society and History* 13:2. 270–81.

———. 1976. "Mobility Strategies in Late Imperial China: A Regional Systems Analysis." In Carol A. Smith, ed., *Regional Analysis*. New York: Academic Press. Vol. 1. 327–64.

———. 1977a. "Regional Urbanization in Nineteenth-Century China." In G. William Skinner, ed., *The City in Late Imperial China*. Stanford: Stanford University Press. 211–49.

———. 1977b. "Cities and the Hierarchy of Local Systems." In G. William Skinner, ed., *The City in Late Imperial China*. Stanford: Stanford University Press. 275–351.

———. 1987. "Sichuan's Population in the 19th Century: Lessons from Disaggregated Data." *Late Imperial China* 8:1 (June): 1–79.

Slicher Van Bath, B. H. 1977. "Agriculture in the Vital Revolution." In E. E. Rich and C. H. Wilson, *The Cambridge Economic History of Europe*. Vol. 5. New York: Cambridge University Press. 42–132.

Smil, Vaclav. 1983. *Biomass Energies*. New York: Plenum.

———. 1984. *The Bad Earth*. Armonk, N.Y.: M. E. Sharpe.

———. 1985. *Carbon, Nitrogen, Sulfur*. New York: Plenum.

———. 1990. "Nitrogen and Phosphorus." In B. L. Turner et. al., *The Earth as Transformed by Human Action*. New York: Cambridge University Press. 423–36.

———. 1993. *China's Environmental Crisis: An Inquiry into the Limits of National Development*. Armonk, N.Y.: M. E. Sharpe.

———. 1994. *Energy in World History*. Boulder: Westview.

———, and William Knowland. 1980. *Energy in the Developing World: The Real Energy Crisis*. Oxford: Oxford University Press.

Smith, Adam. 1937 (1776). *The Wealth of Nations*. Ed. Edwin Cannan. New York: Modern Library.

Smith, Thomas. 1958. *The Agrarian Origins of Modern Japan*. Stanford: Stanford University Press.

———, Robert Eng, and Robert Lundy. 1977. *Nakahara: Family Farming and Population in a Japanese Village*. Stanford: Stanford University Press.

Snookes, Graham. 1994a. "New Perspectives on the Industrial Revolution." In Graham Snookes, ed., *Was the Industrial Revolution Necessary?* London: Routledge. 1–26.

———. 1994b. "Great Waves of Economic Change." In Graham Snookes, ed., *Was the Industrial Revolution Necessary?* London: Routledge. 43–78.

So, Alvin. 1986. *The South China Silk District: Local Historical Transformation and World-System Theory*. Albany: SUNY Press.

Soboul, Albert. 1966. *La France à la veille de la Revolution: Economie et société* (France on the eve of the revolution: Economy and society). Paris: Société d'Edition d'Enseignement Superieur.

Sokoloff, Kenneth, and David Dollar. 1997. "Agricultural Seasonality and the Organization of Manufacturing in Early Industrial Economies: The Contrast between England and the United States." *Journal of Economic History* 57:2 (June): 1–20.

Solow, Barbara. 1992. "Why Columbus Failed: The New World without Slavery." In Wolfgang Reinhard and Peter Waldman, eds., *Nord und Süd in Amerika*. Freiburg: Rombach Verlag. 1111–23.

Sombart, Werner. 1924–27. *Der Modern Kapitalismus* (Modern capitalism). Munich: Dunckner and Humblot.

———. 1967. *Capitalism and Luxury.* Ann Arbor: University of Michigan Press.

Spence, Jonathan. 1977. "Ch'ing." In K. C. Chang, ed., *Food in Chinese Culture.* New Haven: Yale University Press. 259–94.

Stansell, Christine. 1986. *City of Women: Sex and Class in New York City, 1790–1860.* Urbana: University of Illinois Press.

Staunton, George. 1799. *An Authentic Account of an Embassy from the King of Great Britain to the Emperor of China.* 3 vols. Philadelphia: R. Campbell.

Steensgaard, Niels. 1982. "The Dutch East India Co. as an Institutional Innovation." In Maurice Aymard, ed., *Dutch Capitalism and World Capitalism.* New York: Cambridge University Press. 235–58.

———. 1990a. "Trade of England and the Dutch before 1750." In James Tracy, ed., *The Rise of Merchant Empires.* New York: Cambridge University Press. 102–52.

———. 1990b. "Commodities, Bullion and Services in International Transactions before 1750." In Hans Pohl, ed., *The European Discovery of the World and Its Economic Effects on Pre-Industrial Society, 1500–1800.* Stuttgart: Franz Steiner Verlag. 9–23.

Stein, Burton. 1982a. "Vijayanagara c.1350–1564." In Tapan Raychaudhuri and Irfan Habib, eds., *The Cambridge Economic History of India, Volume 1 c.1200–c.1750.* Cambridge: Cambridge University Press. 102–24.

———. 1982b. "State and Economy: The South." In Tapan Raychaudhuri and Irfan Habib, eds., *The Cambridge Economic History of India, Volume 1 c.1200–c.1750.* Cambridge: Cambridge University Press. 203–13.

———. 1985. "State Formation and Economy Reconsidered Part One." *Modern Asian Studies* 19:3. 387–413.

Stern, Steve J. 1988. "Feudalism, Capitalism and the World System in the Perspective of Latin America and the Caribbean." *American Historical Review* 93:4 (October): 829–72.

Stone, Lawrence. 1979. *The Family, Sex, and Marriage in England, 1500–1800.* New York: Harper and Row.

Stross, Randall. 1985. "Number Games Rejected: The Misleading Allure of Tenancy Estimates." *Republican China* 10:3 (June): 1–17.

Subrahmanyam, Sanjay. 1986. "Aspects of State Formation in South India and Southeast Asia." *Indian Economic and Social History Review* 23:4. 357–77.

———. 1990. *The Political Economy of Commerce: South India, 1500–1650.* Cambridge: Cambridge University Press.

———. 1993. *The Portuguese Empire in Asia, 1500–1700.* London: Longman's.

———. 1996. "The European Miracle and the East Asian Miracle: Towards a New Global Economic History." *Sangyō to Keizai* 11:2. 27–48.

Sugihara, Kaoru. 1997. "Agriculture and Industrialization: the Japanese Experience." In Peter Mathias and John Davis, eds., *Agriculture and Economic Growth.* Oxford: Blackwell Publishers. 148–66.

Sun Jingzhi. 1988. *Economic Geography of China.* New York: Oxford University Press.

Sun Xiaofen. 1997. *Qingdai qianqi de yimin zhen Sichuan* (Immigration to Sichuan in the early Qing Dynasty). Chengdu: Sichuan daxue chubanshe.

Takekoshi, Yosaburo. 1967 (1930). *The Economic Aspects of the History of the Civilization of Japan*. Vol. 3. New York: Macmillan.

Tanaka Masatoshi. 1984. "Min-shin Jittai no tonyasi maegashi seisan ni tsuite; iryo seisan shu to suru kenkyūshiteki oboegaki" (On credit from middlemen in Ming-Qing period manufacturing: A research note with special attention to textile manufacture). In Nishijima Sadao Hakushi kanreki kinen ronso henshu iinkai, eds., *Higashi Ajia shi ni okeru kokka to nōmin* (State and peasant in east Asia). Tokyo: Yamakawa shuppansha.

Tandeter, Enrique. 1993. *Coercion and Market: Silver Mining in Colonial Potosi, 1692–1816*. Albuquerque: University of New Mexico Press.

Tavernier, Jean-Baptiste. 1925 (1676). *Travels in India*. 2 vols. Trans. from the 1676 French edition by V. Ball. Ed. William Crooke. London: Oxford University Press.

Teiser, Stephen. 1993. "The Growth of Purgatory." In Patricia Ebrey and Peter Gregory, eds., *Religion and Society in T'ang and Sung China*. Honolulu: University of Hawaii Press. 115–46.

Telford, Ted. 1990. "Patching the Holes in Chinese Genealogies: Mortality in the Lineage Population of Tongcheng County, 1300–1800." *Late Imperial China* 11:2 (December): 116–36.

Teng Ssu-yu and John K. Fairbank, eds. 1954. *China's Response to the West*. Cambridge, Mass.: Harvard University Press.

Terada Takanobu. 1972. *Sansei shōnin no kenkyū*. (Research on Shaanxi merchants). Kyoto: Tōyōshi kenkyū kai.

Thomas, Brinley. 1985a. "Food Supply in the United Kingdom during the Industrial Revolution." In Joel Mokyr, ed., *The Economics of the Industrial Revolution*. Totowa, N.J.: Rowman and Allanheld. 137–50.

———. 1985b. "Escaping from Constraints: The Industrial Revolution in a Malthusian Context." *Journal of Interdisciplinary History* 15:4 (Spring): 729–53.

Thomaz, Luis Filipe Feirera Reis. 1993. "The Malay Sultanate of Melaka." In Anthony Reid, ed., *Southeast Asia in the Early Modern Period: Trade, Power, and Belief*. Ithaca: Cornell University Press. 70–89.

Thompson, E. P. 1966. *The Making of the English Working Class*. New York: Vintage.

———. 1967. "Work, Time and Industrial Discipline." *Past and Present* 38 (December): 56–97.

Thompson, F. M. L. 1963. *English Landed Society in the Nineteenth Century*. London: Routledge.

———. 1968. "The Second Agricultural Revolution, 1815–1880." *Economic History Review* 21:1. 62–77.

———. 1989. "Rural Society and Agricultural Change in 19th Century Britain." In George Grantham and Carol Leonard, eds., *Agrarian Organization in the Century of Industrialization: Europe Russia and North America* Greenwich, Conn.: JAI Press. 187–202.

Thornton, John. 1992. *Africa and Africans in the Making of the Atlantic World, 1400–1680*. Cambridge: Cambridge University Press.

Tilly, Charles. 1975. "Food Supply and Public Order in Modern Europe." In Charles Tilly, ed., *The Formation of National States in Western Europe*. Princeton: Princeton University Press. 380–455.

———. 1984. *Big Structures, Large Processes, Huge Comparisons*. New York: Russell Sage Foundation.

———. 1990. *Coercion, Capital and European States, AD 990–1990*. London: Basil Blackwell.

Totman, Conrad. 1989. *The Green Archipelago: Forestry in Preindustrial Japan*. Berkeley: University of California Press.

———. 1992. "Forest Products Trade in Pre-Industrial Japan." In John Dargavel and Richard Tucker, eds., *Changing Pacific Forests*. Durham, N.C.: Forest History Society. 19–24.

———. 1993. *Early Modern Japan*. Berkeley: University of California Press.

———. 1995. *The Lumber Industry in Early Modern Japan*. Honolulu: University of Hawaii Press.

Tracy, James. 1991. "Introduction." In James D. Tracy, ed., *The Political Economy of Merchant Empires*. Cambridge: Cambridge University Press. 1–21.

Tucker, Richard P., and J. F. Richards, eds. 1983. *Global Deforestation and the Nineteenth-Century World Economy*. Durham: Duke University Press.

Ukers, William. 1935. *All about Coffee*. New York: The Tea and Coffee Trade Journal Company.

Unschuld, Paul. 1986. *Medicine in China: A History of Pharmaceutics*. Berkeley: University of California Press.

Usher, Abbott Payson. 1913. *The History of the Grain Trade in France, 1400–1710*. Cambridge, Mass.: Harvard University Press.

Van der Wee, Herman. 1977. "Monetary, Credit, and Banking Systems." In E. E. Rich and C. H. Wilson, *The Cambridge Economic History of Europe*. Vol. 5. Cambridge: Cambridge University Press. 290–393.

Van Leur, J. C. 1955. *Indonesian Trade and Society: Essays in Asian Social and Economic History*. The Hague: W. Van Hoeve.

Van Schendel, Willem. 1991. *Three Deltas: Accumulation and Rural Poverty in Rural Burma, Bengal, and South India*. New Delhi: Sage Publications.

Vermeer, Eduard. 1990. "The Decline of Hsing-hua Prefecture in the Early Ch'ing." In Eduard Vermeer, ed., *Development and Decline of Fukien Province in the 17th and 18th Centuries*. Leiden: E. J. Brill. 101–63.

Vicziany, Marika. 1979. "The Deindustrialization of India in the 19th Century: A Methodological Critique of Amiya Kumar Bagchi." *Indian Economic and Social History Review* 16:2. 105–45.

Viraphol, Sarasin. 1977. *Tribute and Profit: Sino-Siamese Trade, 1652–1853*. Cambridge, Mass.: Harvard University Press.

Visaria, Leela, and Pravin Visaria. 1983. "Population." In Dharma Kumar, ed., *The Cambridge Economic History of India: Volume 2, 1757–1970*. Cambridge: Cambridge University Press. 463–532.

Von Glahn, Richard. 1996. *Fountain of Fortune: Money and Monetary Policy in China, 1000–1700*. Berkeley: University of California Press.

Von Tunzelmann, G. N. 1978. *Steam Power and British Industrialization to 1860*. Oxford: Oxford University Press.

Wadia, Ardeshir Ruttonji. 1955. *The Bombay Dockyard and the Wadia Master Builders*. Bombay: A. R. Wadia.

Wakefield, David. 1992. "Household Division in Qing and Republican China: Inheritance, Family Property, and Economic Development." Ph.D. diss., University of California, Los Angeles.

Waley-Cohen, Joanna. 1999. *The Sextants of Beijing: Global Currents in Chinese History*. New York: W. W. Norton.

Walker, Mack. 1971. *German Home Towns: Community, State, and General Estate, 1648–1871*. Ithaca: Cornell University Press.

Wallen, C. C., ed. 1970. *Climates of Northern and Western Europe*. Amsterdam: Elsevier Publishing Co.

Wallerstein, Immanuel. 1974. *Capitalist Agriculture and the Origins of the European World Economy*. New York: Academic Press.

———. 1989. *The Modern World-System III: 1730s-1840s*. New York: Academic Press.

Waltner, Ann. 1990. *Getting an Heir: Adoption and the Construction of Kinship in Late Imperial China*. Honolulu: University of Hawaii Press.

Wang Gungwu. 1990. "Merchants without Empire." In James Tracy, ed., *The Rise of Merchant Empires*. Cambridge: Cambridge University Press. 400–421.

Wang, Yeh-chien. 1973. *Land Taxation in Imperial China, 1750–1911*. Cambridge, Mass.: Harvard University Press.

———. 1989. "Food Supply and Grain Prices in the Yangtze Delta in the Eighteenth Century." In *The Second Conference on Modern Chinese History*. 3 vols. Taibei: Academia Sinica. 2:423–62.

———. 1986. "Food Supply in 18th Century Fukien." *Late Imperial China* 7:2 (December): 80–111.

———. 1992. "Secular Trends of Rice Prices in the Yangzi Delta, 1638–1935." In Thomas Rawski and Lillian Li, eds., *Chinese History in Economic Perspective*. Berkeley: University of California Press. 35–68.

Warden, Alexander J. 1967. *The Linen Trade*. London: Cass.

Warren, James. 1982. "The Sulu Sultanate." In Eduard de Jesus and Alfred McCoy, eds., *Philippine Social History: Global Trade and Local Transformation*. Quezon City: Ateneo de Manila University Press. 415–44.

Washbrook, D. A. 1988. "Progress and Problems: South Asian Economic and Social History, c. 1720–1860." *Modern Asian Economic and Social History* 22:1. 57–96.

Watson, Rubie. 1990. "Corporate Property and Local Leadership in the Pearl River Delta, 1898–1941." In Joseph Esherick and Mary Rankin, eds., *Chinese Local Elites and Patterns of Dominance*. Berkeley: University of California Press. 239–60.

Weatherill, Lorna. 1988. *Consumer Behavior and Material Culture in Britain, 1660–1760*. New York: Routledge.

Weber, Eugen. 1976. *Peasants into Frenchmen: The Modernization of Rural France, 1870–1914*. Stanford: Stanford University Press.

Weber, Max. 1992. *The Protestant Ethic and the Spirit of Capitalism*. London: Routledge.

Wei Qingyuan, Wu Qiyan, and Lu Su. 1982. *Qingdai Nubi Zhidu* (The bondservant system in the Qing Dynasty). Beijing: Zhongguo renmin daxue chubanshe.

Widmer, Ellen. 1996. "The Huanduzhai of Hangzhou and Suzhou: A Study in Seventeenth-Century Publishing." *Harvard Journal of Asiatic Studies* 56:1. 77–122.

Wigen, Karen, and Martin Lewis. 1997. *The Myth of Continents.* Berkeley: University of California Press.

Will, Pierre-Etienne. 1980. "Une cycle hydraulique en Chine: La province du Hubei du 16eme au 19e siècles" (A hydraulic cycle in China: The province of Hubei from the sixteenth through nineteenth centuries). *Bulletin de l'école française d'extreme orient* 68. 261–88.

———., and R. Bin Wong. 1991. *Nourish the People: The State Civilian Granary System in China, 1650–1850.* Ann Arbor: University of Michigan Press.

Williams, Eric. 1944. *Capitalism and Slavery.* New York: Russell and Russell.

Williams, Michael. 1990. "Forests." In B. L. Turner et al., *The Earth as Transformed by Human Action.* New York: Cambridge University Press. 179–202.

Williamson, Jeffrey. 1990. *Coping with City Growth during the British Industrial Revolution.* New York: Cambridge University Press.

———. 1994. "Leaving the Farm to Go to the City: Did They Leave Fast Enough?" In John James and Mark Thomas, eds., *Capitalism in Context: Essays on Economic Development and Culture in Honor of R. M. Hartwell.* Chicago: University of Chicago Press. 159–82.

Wills, John E., Jr. 1979. "Maritime China from Wang Chih to Shih Lang: Themes in Peripheral History." In Jonathan Spence and John Wills, eds., *From Ming to Ch'ing.* New Haven: Yale University Press. 201–38.

———. 1984. *Embassies and Illusions: Dutch and Portuguese Envoys to K'ang-hsi, 1666–1687.* Cambridge, Mass.: Harvard University Press.

———. 1993. "European Consumption and Asian Production in the Seventeenth and Eighteenth Centuries." In John Brewer and Roy Porter, eds., *Consumption and the World of Goods.* London: Routledge. 133–47.

———. 1994. *Mountain of Fame: Portraits in Chinese History.* Princeton: Princeton University Press.

———. 1995. "How We Got Obsessed with the 'Tribute System' and Why It's Time to Get Over It." Paper delivered at annual meeting of the Association for Asian Studies, Washington, D.C.

Wink, Andre. 1983. "Maratha Revenue Farming." *Modern Asian Studies* 17:4. 591–628.

Wittfogel, Karl. 1957. *Oriental Despotism: A Comparative Study of Total Power.* New Haven: Yale University Press.

Wolfe, Martin. 1972. *The Fiscal System of Renaissance France.* New Haven: Yale University Press.

Wong, R. Bin. 1997. *China Transformed: Historical Change and the Limits of European Experience.* Ithaca: Cornell University Press.

Wright, Mary C. 1962. *The Last Stand of Chinese Conservatism.* Stanford: Stanford University Press.

Wright, Tim. 1984. *Coal Mining in China's Economy and Society, 1895–1937.* Cambridge: Cambridge University Press.

Wrigley, E. Anthony. 1988. *Continuity, Chance, and Change: The Character of the Industrial Revolution in England.* Cambridge: Cambridge University Press.

———. 1990. "Brake or Accelerator? Urban Growth and Population Growth before the Industrial Revolution." In A. D. van der Woude, Akira Hayami, and Jan DeVries, eds., *Urbanization in History.* Oxford: Clarendon Press. 101–12.

Wrigley, E. Anthony. 1994. "The Classical Economists, the Stationary State, and the Industrial Revolution." In Graham Snookes, ed., *Was the Industrial Revolution Necessary?* London: Routledge. 27–42.

———, and Roger Schofield. 1981. *The Population History of England, 1540–1871.* Cambridge: Cambridge University Press.

Wu Chengming. 1983. *Zhongguo zibenzhuyi yu guonei shichang* (Chinese capitalism and the national market). Zhongguo shehui kexue chubanshe.

———, and Xu Dixin. 1985. *Zhongguo zibenzhuyi de mengya* (The sprouts of capitalism in China). Beijing: Renmin Chubanshe.

Wu Peiyi. 1992. "Women Pilgrims to Taishan." In Susan Naquin and Chun-fang Yu, eds., *Pilgrims and Sacred Sites in China.* Berkeley: University of California Press. 39–64.

Xiong Pingzhen. 1995. *Yuyu: Chuantong Zhongguo de qiangpao zhi dao* (Caring for the young: The newborn's way in traditional China). Taibei: Lianjing.

Xu Tan. 1986. "Ming Qing shiqi de Linqing shangye" (The commerce of Linqing in the Ming-Qing period). *Zhongguo jingji shi yanjiu* 2 (1986): 135–57.

———. 1995. "Ming Qing shiqi Shandong de liangshi liutong" (The circulation of grain in Ming-Qing era Shandong). *Lishi dangan* 57. 81–88.

Xu Xinwu, ed. 1992. *Jiangnan tubushi* (A history of Jiangnan native cloth). Shanghai: shehui kexueyuan chubanshe.

Xuxiu Licheng xianzhi (A further continuation of the gazetteer of Licheng county). 1968 (1924) Jinan. Taibei: Chengwen chubanshe. Reprint.

Yamamura, Kozo. 1974. *A Study of Samurai Income and Entrepreneurship: Quantitative Analysis of Economic and Social Aspects of the Samurai in Tokugawa and Meiji Japan.* Cambridge, Mass.: Harvard University Press.

Ye Xian'en. 1983. *Ming Qing Huizhou nongcun shehui yu dianpu zhi* (Rural village society in Ming-Qing Huizhou and the bondage system). Hefei: Anhui renmin chubanshe.

Yu Mingxia. 1991. *Xuzhou Meikuang shi* (A history of the Xuzhou coal mines). Nanjing: Jiangsu guji chubanshe.

Yu Yingshi. 1985. "Rujia sixiang yu jingji fazhan; Zhongguo jinshi zongjiao lunli yu shangren jingshen" (Confucian thought and economic development: Modern Chinese religious ethics and the merchant spirit). *The Chinese Intellectual* 6 (Winter): 3–45.

Zangheri, R. 1969. "The Historical Relationship between Agricultural and Economic Development in Italy." In E. L. Jones and S. J. Woolf, eds., *Agrarian Change and Economic Development.* London: Methuen. 23–40.

Zelin, Madeleine. 1986. "The Rights of Tenants in Mid-Qing Sichuan." *Journal of Asian Studies* 45:3 (May): 499–526.

———. 1988. "Capital Accumulation and Investment Strategies in Early Modern China: The Case of the Furong Salt Yards." *Late Imperial China* 9:1 (June): 79–122.

———. 1990. "The Fu-Rong Salt Yard Elite." In Joseph Esherick and Mary Rankin, eds., *Chinese Local Elites and Patterns of Dominance.* Berkeley: University of California Press. 82–112.

Zhang Gang. 1985. "Qingdai Zhili shangpin jingji fenxi" (An analysis of the commodity economy in Qing Dynasty Zhili). *Hebei shiyuan xuebao* #3. 9–104.

Zhang Xiaobo. 1995. "Merchant Associational Activism in Early Twentieth Century China: The Tianjin General Chamber of Commerce, 1904–1928." Ph.D. diss., Columbia University.

Zhang Zhongmin. 1988. *Shanghai cong kaifa dao kaifang, 1369–1843* (Shanghai from founding to opening). Kunming: Yunnan Renmin chubanshe.

Zhao Gang. 1983. "Zhongguo lishishang gongzi shuiping de bianqian" (Changes in the historic level of wages in China). *Zhonghua Wenhua fuxing yuekan* 16:9 (September): 52–57.

Zuo Dakang and Zhang Peiyuan. 1990. "The Huang-Huai-Hai Plain." In B. L. Turner et al., *The Earth as Transformed by Human Action*. New York: Cambridge University Press. 473–77.

INDEX

Abu-Lughod, J., 11n
accumulation. *See* capital, accumulation of
Adachi, K., 98n
"advantages of backwardness," 262–63, 283, 295
Africa: book's limited coverage of, 25; European trade with, 260–61; as source of slaves, 264–65. *See also* slavery
"agrarian individualism," 70, 76n
agriculture: in Asia, 45, 287; in Britain, 45; commercialization of, 164; demands on from industrialization, 286–87; in India, 293–95; in Japan, 164, 292; labor intensity in, 214, 216–17; market control of, 70–80; in the New World, 264–69; productivity of in Europe, 215–16; reallocation of labor in, 55; surplus labor in, 286; wages in, 92–93. *See also* ecology; labor; land
Allen, R., 51n
Ambrosoli, M., 216, 240
Amin, S., 3n
Anderson, E., 120n
Appadurai, A., 128, 129
Arasaratnam, S., 163
artisans: autonomy of in India and Southeast Asia, 163; consumption patterns of, 94, 135; effects of on technology, 64, 67; proletarianization of, 162–63; in Southeast Asia, 50, 163; and transmission of knowledge, 64, 66. *See also* handicrafts; proto-industrialization; textiles

Bairoch, P., 36, 53n
Batavia, Chinese merchants in, 202–3
Bayly, C. A., 133, 147, 148, 176–77, 282n, 293
birthrates: and accumulation, 40–41; in Japan and Southeast Asia, 41. *See also* fertility; population
Blaut, J., 27
Blayo, Y., 40
Bloch, M., 70, 76n
blockages, to industrialization, 3, 8, 9, 103–4. *See also* bottlenecks
books, production of, 44, 143
Boserup, E., 57

bottlenecks: ecological, 19, 22, 24, 211–63; and technological breakthroughs, 55. *See also* blockages; ecology
Braudel, F., 14, 15, 18–19, 39, 53, 77n, 86, 112, 118, 162, 166–67, 169, 170, 174, 179, 183, 185, 186, 199, 220, 221, 234, 235
Bray, F., 33n, 45n, 104n, 134
Brenner, R., 14–15, 49, 198n
Britain: agricultural productivity in, 216–19; agricultural stagnation in, 126; as beneficiary of the slave trade, 186–87; coal consumption in, 58n, 183; cotton production in, 138; early industrialization of, 6–7; ecology of, 274–79, 287; income distribution in, 137; liberalization in, 196–98; New World imports of, 274–79, 283–84; open fields in, 5–6n; resources in, 12; sugar consumption in, 118, 126; textile production in, 141–42. *See also* England
Britnell, R. H., 5n
Brook, T., 142
Buck, J. L., 122, 124, 144, 145
buildings: in Asia, 42–43, 134; in Europe, 31, 42–43; as signs of status, 129–30, 134; in Southeast Asia, 135. *See also* housing; living standards
business organizations, Asian, 170–72

Campbell, C., 37
capital:
—accumulation of, 3, 5, 10, 11, 16, 19, 24, 112–13, 166, 215; in Asia and Europe, 42–43; and birthrates, 41; from coercive trading, 186–88; in Europe, 69; and liberalization, 198–99; and monopolies, 200–201; and slavery, 186; and social institutions, 107
—in Asia, 32–36; costs of, and property rights, 170; in Europe, 31–32; and land, 19; and markets, 18; mobilization of, 4; movement of to the New World, 284; patient, 178, 198; separation of from owners, 169–71, 172; as spur to migration, 84; and state formation, 197; as substitute for land, 57; and transport, 183; widespread availability of, 179–80